Internal Self-determination and the Prevention of Secession in International Law

Developments in International Law

VOLUME 82

The titles published in this series are listed at *brill.com/diil*

Internal Self-determination and the Prevention of Secession in International Law

By

Sava Janković

BRILL | NIJHOFF

LEIDEN | BOSTON

This work was supported by National Science Centre, Poland/ Norwegian Financial Mechanism 2014–2020 (research project No. 2020/37/K/HS5/02762, *Methods of Prevention of Secession in International Law: The Problem of Internal Self-Determination* (starting year: 2021))

Library of Congress Cataloging-in-Publication Data

Names: Janković, Sava author
http://id.loc.gov/authorities/names/n2025017079
http://id.loc.gov/rwo/agents/n2025017079
Title: Internal self-determination and the prevention of secession in international law / edited by Sava Janković.
Description: Boston, Massachusetts : Brill, 2026. | Series: Developments in international law, 0924-5332 ; 82 | Includes bibliographical references and index.
Identifiers: LCCN 2025018750 (print) | LCCN 2025018751 (ebook) | ISBN 9789004722811 hardback | ISBN 9789004737501 ebook
Subjects: LCSH: Secession http://id.loc.gov/authorities/subjects/sh85119406 | State succession http://id.loc.gov/authorities/subjects/sh85127514 | Self-determination, National http://id.loc.gov/authorities/subjects/sh85119735 | Sovereignty http://id.loc.gov/authorities/subjects/sh85125696
Classification: LCC KZ4028 .J36 2026 (print) | LCC KZ4028 (ebook) | DDC 341.26–dc23/eng/20250416
LC record available at https://lccn.loc.gov/2025018750
LC ebook record available at https://lccn.loc.gov/2025018751

Typeface for the Latin, Greek, and Cyrillic scripts: "Brill". See and download: brill.com/brill-typeface.

ISSN 0924-5332
ISBN 978-90-04-72281-1 (hardback)
ISBN 978-90-04-73750-1 (e-book)
DOI 10.1163/9789004737501

This book is printed on acid-free paper and produced in a sustainable manner.

Contents

Acknowledgments

This academic endeavor consumed a wealth of time; hence, first and foremost, I wish to express my gratitude to those who showed understanding of my compromised engagement with them. Furthermore, I deeply appreciate their invaluable support during the completion of this oeuvre.

Striving not to omit anyone who deserves recognition in this regard, I must begin by acknowledging my closest family. Without their positive attitude, this work would not have taken the course it did, both through their emphasis on meticulous devotion and their insistence on the importance of taking breaks to maintain balance. I also wish to express special thanks to Dr. Jelena Vlajnić for her steadfast assistance throughout the project. Her diligence, insight and unwavering commitment greatly enriched the research and helped bring clarity to some of its most complex aspects.

I am equally indebted to Mr. Clayton, whose apartment in Saint-Jean-Cap-Ferrat greatly inspired me and became the place where my work progressed most significantly during the holiday season. Special appreciation is also due to the entire staff of the Dositej Obradović Library in Surdulica, who not only provided me with a private workspace but also treated me with snacks and engaged in stimulating and thoughtful conversations during coffee breaks.

Finally, I extend heartfelt thanks to those who contributed scientifically and organizationally to this monograph. This includes many experts in the field of international law, the individuals who participated in interviews during my field trips to European regions exhibiting varying degrees of separatist tendencies, the Institute of Law Studies of the Polish Academy of Sciences for their administrative support, and the anonymous reviewers and Brill for their kind cooperation throughout the publishing process.

In solidarity with the Palestinian people and their long-overdue realization of external self-determination, as well as their hindered pursuit of internal self-determination, this book is affectionately dedicated to them.

Abbreviations

ACHPR	African Commission on Human and Peoples' Rights
AJIL	American Journal of International Law
AKMO	Autonomous Kosovo-Metohija Oblast (Region)
ARSIWA	Articles on Responsibility of States for Internationally Wrongful Acts
ASEAN	Association of Southeast Asian Nations
ASSR	Autonomous Soviet Socialist Republic
BHV	Brussels-Halle-Vilvoorde
BYIL	British Yearbook of International Law
CERD	The Committee on the Elimination of Racial Discrimination
CESCR	Committee on Economic, Social and Cultural Rights
CHT	Chittagong Hill Tracts
CIL	Customary international law
CoE	Council of Europe
ECHR	European Convention on Human Rights
ECtHR	European Court of Human Rights
EJIL	European Journal of International Law
ESCOR	Official Records of the Economic and Social Council
ESD	External Self-determination
EULEX	European Union Rule of Law Mission in Kosovo
FRETILIN	Revolutionary Front for an Independent East Timor
FRY	Federal Republic of Yugoslavia
GAOR	General Assembly Official Records
HCNM	High Commissioner on National Minorities (OSCE)
HDZ	Croatian Democratic Union (Croatia)
HRC	Human Rights Council
HUP	Harvard University Press
IACHR	Inter-American Commission on Human Rights
IACtHR	Inter-American Court on Human Rights
ICCPR	International Covenant on Civil and Political Rights
ICERD	International Convention on the Elimination of All Forms of Racial Discrimination
ICESCR	International Covenant on Economic, Social and Cultural Rights
ICJ	International Court of Justice
IIFFMCG	Independent International Fact-Finding Mission on the Conflict in Georgia
ILA	International Law Association
ILC	International Law Commission

ILM	International Legal Materials
ILO	International Labour Organisation
ILR	International Law Reports
ISD	Internal Self-determination
KFOR	The Kosovo Force (NATO)
KPC	Katangese Peoples' Congress
LNTS	League of Nations Treaty Series
LTTE	Liberation Tigers of Tamil Eelam
NSGT	Non-Self-Governing Territories
OAS	Organization of American States
OAU	Organization of African Unity
OPT	Occupied Palestinian Territory
OSCE	Organization for Security and Co-operation
PACE	Parliamentary Assembly of the Council of Europe
RES	Resolution
RSD	Right to Self-determination
RSFSR	Russian Soviet Federative Socialist Republic
SAC	Statute of Autonomy of Catalonia
SAO	Serbian Autonomous Oblast
SDP	Serbian Democratic Party
SFRY	Socialist Federal Republic of Yugoslavia
SLR	Sri Lanka Law Reports
TRNC	Turkish Republic of Northern Cyprus
UDHR	Universal Declaration of Human Rights
UDI	Unilateral Declaration of Independence
UNDRIP	United Nations Declaration on the Rights of Indigenous People
UNGA	United Nations General Assembly
UNMIK	United Nations Mission in Kosovo
UNSC	United Nations Security Council
UNSG	United Nations Secretary-General
UNTAET	United Nations Transitional Administration in East Timor
USSR	Union of Soviet Socialist Republics
YILC	Yearbook of the International Law Commission
ZaöRV	Zeitschrift für ausländisches öffentliches Recht und Völkerrecht

CHAPTER 1

Introduction

> There is one thing stronger
> than all the armies in the world,
> and that is an Idea whose time has come.
>
> VICTOR HUGO

∴

1 Significance of the Topic

In 2008, Kosovo declared independence, which has since been recognized by the majority of UN Members (52%). In 2014, Crimeans orchestrated an independence referendum and soon after were incorporated into the Russian Federation, whereas in 2017, Catalonia conducted an independence referendum and promulgated independence. Furthermore, a number of secessionist claims have exacerbated in Europe and around the globe, with regions such as Gagauzia, Scotland, Kashmir, and Kurdistan likely to renew their aspirations for statehood in the foreseeable future. In light of these developments, two paramount questions have arisen: first, does international law confer an entitlement to claim statehood, and if so, under what conditions? Second, does international law provide mechanisms to prevent secession, and if so, what are those mechanisms?

The first question has been relatively well addressed in legal theory and state practice. The principle of self-determination, beyond 'agreed secession', disempowers the current administering authority in instances of decolonization (as in UN Non-Self-Governing Territories), occupation (e.g. Palestine), and arguably in extreme cases of prolonged oppression. In contrast, the second question remains less clearly resolved in peacetime. Apart from the prohibition on achieving statehood through foreign military intervention, against the will of the population concerned, or by means of forced population transfers and racial segregation – practices that violate the right to self-determination – it remains undetermined whether in the absence of these provisions, secession should be deemed legally prohibited.

 | DOI:10.1163/9789004737501_002

This legal ambiguity has motivated the author to undertake a comprehensive study of self-determination and secession in international law, with a particular emphasis on internal self-determination (ISD) and its counter-secession value. By examining the prohibitive limb of secession, as opposed to the more extensively explored permissive dimensions (as seen in primary and remedial secession theories), and proposing ISD as a mechanism to prevent secession, this work contributes to the legal regulation of secession and directly challenges the law's presumed neutrality on the matter. In so doing, the study transcends conventional, often formulaic references to the principles of sovereignty and territorial integrity, which are typically framed within an inter-state context and overlook the endogenous roots of secessionism.

The regulation of secession through legal frameworks offers substantial benefits. From a doctrinal perspective, it would enhance the coherence of international law as a discipline – by addressing the gaps haunting the law of statehood for a long time. Additionally, this work contributes to the elucidation and development of the concept of internal self-determination, particularly in light of its potential to counteract secessionist tendencies. This, in turn, advances both international law and international relations while opening avenues for further research.

From a practical outlook, this study is of considerable importance. Should an international norm emerge that prescribes governance standards which simultaneously meet legitimacy requirements and satisfy the needs of the population, while also preventing secession, it would represent a significant step toward strengthening global peace and stability. The proposition that internal self-determination could serve as a mechanism to prohibit secession is advantageous for both states, in preserving territorial integrity, and for populations, through the meaningful protection of human rights. As such, the hypothesis tested in this book proffers that ISD is not merely a rhetorical counterpoint to external self-determination (ESD), equating it with the principle of territorial integrity, but that its practical implementation constitutes a foundational mechanism for protecting territorial integrity.

Furthermore, this analytical endeavor gains additional significance in light of the dynamic nature of international relations and the likely emergence of new secessionist claims. By reviewing grassroots movements, analyzing the foundations of territorial claims, and examining the responses of states and international organizations, this research lays the groundwork for conceptualizing ISD in a manner that can accommodate contemporary needs by adapting to evolving trends in society and law. Ultimately, this research holds the potential to serve as a valuable resource for policymakers and other stakeholders in addressing secession in a pragmatic yet ethical manner.

2 Originality and the State of the Art in Legal Scholarship

The principle of self-determination has long stood as a cornerstone of international law, traditionally understood as granting peoples the right to freely determine their political status and to pursue their economic, social, and cultural development. Historically, this principle has been closely tied to the decolonization process and the formation of new states. However, recent advancements in international law, coupled with the growing complexity of secessionist movements worldwide, have prompted a reexamination of self-determination's role – not only in enabling the creation of states but also in sustaining the territorial integrity of existing ones.

This reconceptualization, marking an emerging and still highly underexplored frontier in legal scholarship, underpins this research, which focuses on internal self-determination – whereby the rights and aspirations of distinct groups within a state are accommodated through legal and political mechanisms that avert the need for secession.

ISD's uniqueness lies not only in its potential to address current territorial pretensions but also in its proactive nature, which can be utilized by states and international bodies to preempt secessionist tendencies. By enhancing internal self-determination, states can offer meaningful autonomy and cultural, social, and political rights to minority groups, thereby addressing grievances that often lead to secessionist claims. Self-determination, seen through this lens, departs from the orthodox view of it as a disruptive force, potentially threatening established states, and evolves, paradoxical as it may appear, into a state-preserving concept – arguably even more so than the principle of territorial integrity, which the ICJ in the *Kosovo* case deemed operative only in inter-state relations.

Accordingly, this research stands at the cutting edge of legal scholarship by proposing a framework in which self-determination is not merely a gateway to independence but a means to strengthen state cohesion. It challenges the prevailing view of secession as a legally neutral or inevitable outcome of self-determination struggles, instead positing that effective self-determination practices within states can mitigate the pressures that lead to secession.

This book differs from Senaratne's recent oeuvre *Internal Self-determination in International Law*, which is, in fact, the only comprehensive study on the matter.[1] However, the comprehensiveness of Senaratne's study pertains to

1 K. Senaratne, *Internal Self-determination in International Law History, Theory, and Practice* (CUP 2021) 2 (where the author carries out a literature review on the topic of internal self-determination).

various aspects of ISD, such as its historical development and the contrasting Western and Third World perspectives. While it occasionally touches on ISD's capacity to prevent secession, this theme is addressed only sporadically in chapters focused on its application to a state's population and minority rights. As Senaratne notes in the introductory part, his analysis unfolds along three main strands: historical (examining the development of the right), theoretical (defining the content of the right and identifying the rightsholders), and practical (exploring how internal self-determination is articulated, promoted, recognized, challenged, and rejected by different actors within states, with particular emphasis on his home country, Sri Lanka).[2]

Moreover, this book diverges from available articles, such as Fox's 'Self-determination in the Post-Cold War Era: A New Internal Focus?' which begins by questioning the contemporary relevance of self-determination and shifts toward a broader emphasis on its internal dimension, given the near completion of the decolonization process.[3] Fox primarily focuses on delineating and examining the subjects of internal self-determination – those exercising this right within the territorial framework of an existing state. To this end, he categorizes these subjects into self-defined groups, populations residing within existing administrative boundaries, and the entire populace within a state's territory.[4] Although Fox acknowledges the potential of internal self-determination to mitigate secessionist pressures, his analysis remains concise, with limited exploration of its legal foundations or its application in state and institutional practices.

Similarly, Rosas's article 'Internal Self-determination', featured in Tomuschat's edited collection *Modern Law of Self-determination*, highlights the distinction between internal and external aspects of self-determination, endorsing their differentiation.[5] Rosas focuses on uncovering the status and meaning of ISD in international law, beginning his academic inquiry by identifying traces of ISD in the works of international human rights bodies.[6] He highlights the trend in today's world to downplay state sovereignty in favour of popular sovereignty, human rights and democratic governance, but stops short of investigating the correlation between secession and internal self-determination.

2 *Ibid.* 5.

3 G. Fox, 'Self-determination in the Post-Cold War Era: A New Internal Focus?' 16(3) *Michigan Journal of International Law* (1995) 733.

4 *Ibid.* 739–756.

5 A. Rosas, 'Internal Self-determination' in C. Tomuschat (ed.) *Modern Law of Self-determination* (Martinus Nijhoff Publishers 1993) 228.

6 *Ibid.* 234–241.

As a result, the limited international legal scholarship on ISD often neglects its pivotal role in preventing secession. In contrast, scholars from related disciplines, particularly political science, more frequently propose strategies to address secession, including international diplomacy, constitutional reforms, economic coercion, and cultural assimilation. Jewkes, for example, examines the concept of multinational federalism, which advocates for significant devolved competences, enhanced central representation, and constitutional entrenchment.[7] While such approaches offer valuable insights, they do not seek to establish or substantiate a legal framework for ISD.

3 Methodology

This book navigates several methodological approaches to offer a comprehensive analysis of internal self-determination and its role in preventing secession. Anchored in the overarching aim of maintaining international peace and stability, the study integrates a doctrinal approach rooted in international legal positivism, emphasizing the identification and application of existing legal norms. The analysis encompasses both hard law – such as treaties and conventions – and soft law, including declarations and resolutions, to illuminate the legal contours of ISD. Key documents, such as the UN Friendly Relations Declaration (1970), the Vienna Declaration and Programme of Action (1993), and the UN Fiftieth Anniversary Declaration (1995) serve as pivotal points of reference. Although these declarations are formally non-binding, they provide critical insights into the relationship between ISD and territorial integrity, helping to clarify the legal and normative frameworks that underpin ISD and its application as a mechanism to prevent secession.

The consensus adoption of these declarations underscores states' shared conviction regarding the necessity of the so-called 'safeguard clause.' This pragmatic consensus is further supported by burgeoning international and domestic practices. The book explores states' positions taken in the *Kosovo* advisory proceedings, their domestic legislation and judicial decisions, including significant rulings by the Supreme Court of Sri Lanka in *Chandrasoma v. Senathirajah* (2017), the UK Supreme Court on the Scottish Referendum (2022) and the practice of international and regional bodies, like the African Commission on Human and Peoples' Rights in the case of *Katangese People's Congress v. Zaire* (1995).

In examining the evolution of the RSD, as evidenced by the diverse interpretations of ISD and its status as an emerging norm of customary international law, the book also draws on legal constructivism. This approach views

7 M. Jewkes, 'Self-determination without Secession' 28(2) *Public Affairs Quarterly* (2014) 147–167.

self-determination as a concept that is not static but is constructed and interpreted within specific legal and political contexts. ISD, as a right of peoples to participate in governance and pursue economic, social, and cultural development, is thus seen as a dynamic legal construct that adapts to changing political realities and interpretations.

Moreover, the rationale for ISD as both a political and legal method of preventing secession extends beyond the traditional realist approach, which emphasizes state behavior. The book argues that ISD must be understood from the perspective of grassroots movements and their needs. By incorporating these perspectives, the book demonstrates that the true constructivist nature of ISD lies in its responsiveness to the people it serves. This comprehensive approach also draws on socio-legal studies to enrich the analysis.

Chapter IV challenges the orthodox view of ISD, which posits that states can rely on internal self-determination to rule out secession without meaningfully realizing that right for their populations. Similarly, it interrogates the potential rigidity of ISD as a preventive rule, particularly in liberal democracies where historical contexts may influence the desire for independence. As such, this work navigates between doctrinal, critical, and socio-legal approaches, all guided by the overarching aim of safeguarding international peace and stability.

4 Chapters Outline

The following second chapter serves as a crucial introduction to the subject by elucidating the phenomenon of the right of a people to self-determination. It begins by briefly illustrating the significance of this right for peoples, highlighting its role in the creation of independent states, the enjoyment of other human rights, and the maintenance of international peace. Following this, the chapter addresses the inherent shortcomings of the right, particularly concerning its addressees, content, and continuity. These shortcomings impact its practical application, especially in the context of conflicts with the principle of territorial integrity. The chapter also explores the historical roots of the right to self-determination, beginning with its origins in the American and French revolutions. It then examines the influence of Lenin and Wilson on the development of the concept and concludes with the transformation of the principle into a recognized right in the 20th century. This evolution is corroborated by international documents and affirmed by the practices of international organizations and judicial bodies. By distinguishing between the two aspects of the right to self-determination and analyzing their respective content and addressees, this chapter lays the groundwork for a more in-depth discussion of the internal aspect in subsequent chapters.

The third chapter addresses the issue of secession in international law. It commences by exploring the legal, political, social, and economic motives that drive secession worldwide. The chapter then examines the regulation of secession from the perspective of international law, with the primary aim of determining whether a right to secession exists under positive international law and, if so, who the bearers of this right might be. The chapter argues that three distinct approaches to the relationship between secession and international law can currently be identified. The first approach, known as the negation theory, stipulates the prohibition of secession. The second approach allows for secession, with a distinction between whether this right is unconditional (primary theories) or conditional upon the violation of human rights (remedial rights theory). The third approach suggests that international law is ambivalent toward secession. As the chapter demonstrates, the third approach is the most prevalent. However, there are specific circumstances in which secession is considered permissible – particularly when gross human rights violations occur – or impermissible, such as when secession is linked to the breach of a peremptory norm of international law. Additionally, secession may be disallowed when internal self-determination is adequately respected. The latter aspect – the relationship between internal self-determination and the (il)legality of secession – will be the focus of the comprehensive analysis in the subsequent chapters of this monograph.

The fourth chapter explores the concept of internal self-determination as a method for preventing secession in international law. It begins by proposing various interpretations of ISD and linking these to discussions of ISD functioning more as a 'method' than a norm. Within this framework, two scenarios regarding ISD's potential to 'ban' secession are outlined: (a) Internal self-determination entirely excludes the possibility of external self-determination for groups within a state by virtue of its very meaning, and (b) Internal self-determination excludes the possibility of secession if ISD is meaningfully realized. This chapter also highlights several intuitive secession prevention mechanisms inherent in the ISD concept, such as democratic governance, federalism, and autonomism. It further examines how ISD interacts with core principles of international law that restrict secession, including the principles of territorial integrity, *uti possidetis juris*, and non-intervention, and, in addition, outlines non-legal secession prevention means like diplomatic efforts. The chapter also explores the potential obstacles to conceiving ISD as a legal counter-secession mechanism. A key concern is whether this concept contradicts the prevailing view that secession generally lies outside the scope of international law. Yet, this is not an insurmountable obstacle, as international law evolves and has occasionally addressed secession within legal frameworks. Another challenge is defining universally applicable ISD standards, given the diversity of national contexts. These standards could be tailored to local practices, with oversight by regional human rights bodies. A more intricate challenge would be the formal legal codification of ISD, which could conflict with the ethno-historical identities of statehood claimants, potentially undermining the principles of dignity and fairness. However, new norms have developed to address the emerging needs, and they are especially justified if they are going to serve a broader goal, which arguably is the case with ISD. In the final parts, the chapter assesses the overall benefits of utilizing ISD and reviews scholarly opinions on the hypothesis that ISD is a viable mechanism for preventing secession.

The fifth chapter aims to show how states and international organizations utilize and interpret internal self-determination as a means to prevent secession. To this end, it analyzes documents adopted in various international fora alongside state practice reflected in *travaux préparatoires* and subsequent references to these documents in submissions to international bodies. This analysis highlights reservations, shifts in policy, and independently developed arguments. The chapter also explores the practice of international organizations, including assemblies, commissions, councils, and committees, with a particular emphasis on the United Nations organs and agencies, where the issue of ISD has frequently been debated. Additionally, the chapter presents the perspectives of domestic and international judiciary bodies, analyzing relevant advisory opinions, judgments, dissenting opinions, notes, and reports. It illustrates how constitutional courts, from the Supreme Court of Canada in the *Quebec* case (1998) to the UK Supreme Court regarding the Scottish independence referendum (2022), frequently substantiate their decisions in internal self-determination. The chapter further investigates how ISD is invoked in contentious secession claims, examining how different institutions interpret ISD and whether a potential threshold for its application can be deduced from institutional practice. Finally, it assesses the quantitative and qualitative aspects of ISD as utilized by various institutions and states, providing valuable insights into its content and status as customary international law.

Chapter six not only addresses the *problematique* of internal self-determination in selected states but also showcases it from an anthropocentric perspective, meaning that the voices and argumentations of the grassroots movements, domestic organizations, and local collectives are presented. Given that one of the primary functions of ISD is to prevent secession, its essence and implementation are scrutinized in states with active secession movements or significant multiethnic compositions. The chapter employs a documentary analysis of the needs and concerns expressed by the populations of these regions, both historically and currently. It presents the viewpoints of local peoples and institutions regarding the central government's respect for ISD, contrasting these with the sometimes general perspectives of individual legal experts, some of whom are also residents of the studied regions. This comprehensive approach is methodologically sound as it allows for an exploration of the cultural, social, economic, and political factors that should inform the development and recognition of ISD as a binding legal norm. Furthermore, the directly articulated needs of the people may offer insights into the conditions necessary to effectively prevent secession. The applicability and value of ISD are examined through case studies of two federal states in Europe (Belgium and Germany), one unitary state (Finland), and the former state of Yugoslavia.

The final chapter summarizes the key findings and argues that the counter-secession hypothesis involving internal self-determination remains valid despite potential obstacles. It proposes a long-sought compromise between the principle of territorial integrity and the right of peoples to self-determination without directly contemplating 'the right to secession'. In essence, the solution is found within the self-determination norm itself, particularly in its internal variant. The chapter reiterates that the ideas presented in the book will contribute to maintaining international peace and stability, as desired by states, while also enhancing self-governance and respect for human rights, as sought by the people. By focusing on internal self-determination rather than the conflicting principles of territorial integrity and secession, the proposed norm aims to de-escalate ongoing conflicts and prevent new ones from emerging. This approach emphasizes placing a significant obligation on states to respect internal self-determination, rather than concentrating on whose (often irreconcilable) right takes precedence.

CHAPTER 2

The Right of Peoples to Self-determination

Ideals are like stars;
we may never reach them,
but they guide our path.
CARL SCHURZ

∵

1 The Meaning, Importance and Problems of the Right to Self-determination

The right of peoples to self-determination grants groups the power to choose their international political status and organize their affairs within a state without foreign interference. The right also enables them to freely pursue their economic, social, and cultural development.[1] The existence and significance of the right to self-determination (RSD) should neither be underestimated nor questioned. The International Court of Justice has notably recognized self-determination as 'one of the essential principles of contemporary international law'[2] and it is widely regarded as a *jus cogens* norm with an *erga omnes* character.[3]

1 International Covenant on Civil and Political Rights (16 Dec. 1966) 999 UNTS 171, Article 1; International Covenant on Economic, Social and Cultural Rights (16 Dec. 1966) 993 UNTS 3, Article 1 (hereinafter: the International Covenants on Human Rights).

2 ICJ, *Case Concerning East Timor (Portugal v. Australia)*, Judgment, ICJ Rep. 1995, para 29.

3 On *jus cogens* see UN Commission on Human Rights, Sub-Commission on Prevention of Discrimination and Protection of Minorities. Report Prepared by D. Ceausu (20 Sep. 1978) UN Doc. E/CN.4/1296, paras 163, 172; ILC, 'Fifth report on peremptory norms of general international law (*jus cogens*)' by Spec. Rapporteur D. Tladi (24 Jan. 2022) UN Doc. A/CN.4/747, Conclusion 23. See also HRC Res 49/28 (11 Apr. 2022). A more critical approach on that stance in 2.4.2. On *erga omnes* see ICJ, *Legal Consequences of the Construction of a Wall in the Occupied Palestinian Territory*, Advisory Opinion, ICJ Rep. 2004, paras 88, 156; ICJ, *Legal Consequences of the Separation of the Chagos Archipelago from Mauritius in 1965*, Advisory Opinion, ICJ Rep. 2019, para 180.

 | DOI:10.1163/9789004737501_003

Self-determination is often construed as a prerequisite for the realization of other human rights.[4] Its inclusion in the International Covenants on Human Rights, which have been ratified by over 170 parties, as well as in the Vienna Declaration and Programme of Action, adopted by consensus by more than 170 states, underscores the centrality of self-determination within the framework of human rights law and its universal applicability.[5] In General Comment No. 12, the UN Human Rights Committee emphasized the particular importance of the right to self-determination, stating that its implementation is essential for the observance, strengthening, and promotion of individual human rights.[6] The Committee further noted that it was for this reason that the right to self-determination was placed in Article 1 of the International Covenants on Human Rights, before all other rights. The Committee concluded with the statement that 'history has proved that the realization of and respect for the right of self-determination of peoples contributes to the establishment of friendly relations and cooperation between States and to strengthening international peace and understanding'.[7]

The right to self-determination has also been the foundation upon which new states have been formed. Since the creation of the United Nations, more than eighty former colonies, comprising approximately 750 million people, have gained independence.[8] The 20th century, often hailed as the 'century of self-determination', firmly established self-determination as one of the core principles of international law, while also associating it with the right to establish an independent state.[9] Former colonies exercised the right to

4 UNGA Res 637 (VII) (16 Dec. 1952) preamble; UN Commission on Human Rights, Sub-Commission on the Prevention of Discrimination and Protection of Minorities, 'The Right to Self-determination: Historical and Current Development on the Basis of United Nations Instruments'. Study Prepared by A. Cristescu (1981) UN Doc. E/CN.4/Sub.2/404/Rev.1, paras 30, 34, 228.

5 The World Conference on Human Right, Vienna Declaration and Programme of Action (12 Jul. 1993) UN Doc. A/CONF.157/23, Point 2 (hereinafter: the Vienna Declaration).

6 Human Rights Committee, General Comment No. 12: Article 1 (Right to Self-determination), The Right to Self-determination of Peoples (13 Mar. 1984) para 1. Šahović, the Yugoslav member of the UN Sixth Committee, argued that individuals could only benefit from the Covenants' rights within the 'framework of broad national communities formed through self-determination'. UN Doc. A/AC.125/SR.69 (4 Dec. 1967) 6.

7 *Ibid.* para 8.

8 The United Nations and Decolonization, <https://www.un.org/dppa/decolonization/en>.

9 P. Hilpold, 'Self-determination in the 21st Century – Modern Perspective for an Old Concept' 36 *Israel Yearbook on Human Rights* (2006) 247.

gain independence, and in this context, self-determination was primarily achieved in an external sense.[10]

With the almost completed decolonisation process, the right to self-determination has not lost its validity or importance.[11] Although many believed that the liberation of colonial territories fulfilled its purpose,[12] there is significant merit in extending the right's application in both time and scope, particularly since freedom can be compromised in contexts beyond traditional colonization. As Canada's Supreme Court noted in the *Reference re Secession of Quebec,* the right to independence arises 'where a people is subject to alien subjugation, domination or exploitation', not solely within a colonial framework.[13] Numerous instances demonstrate that the right to self-determination has been reinterpreted beyond its conventional meaning, reflecting a broader understanding that the right is continuous and not exhausted by a single application. In one of its statements UNESCO proclaimed that self-determination 'is not confined to a right to be enjoyed by formerly colonised peoples. It is not a right enjoyed once only and thereafter to be forever lost'.[14] Moreover, during the drafting of Article 1 of the 1966 Covenants, a spokesman emphasized that that placing temporal limits on this right would undermine its significance, particularly in its internal aspect, which safeguards from foreign interference.[15] Hence, both entities that gained their new political status in the wake of the

10 UNGA Res 1514 'Declaration on Granting Independence to Colonial Countries and Peoples' (14 Dec. 1960). See also UNGA Res 1541 'Principles which Should Guide Members in Determining whether or not an Obligation Exists to Transmit the Information Called for in Article 73[e] of the Charter of the United Nations' (15 Dec. 1960).

11 As of the present time, 17 territories are still classified by the United Nations as Non-Self-Governing Territories, pending the attainment of a full measure of self-government. For the list of Non-Self-Governing Territories see <https://www.un.org/dppa/decolonization/en/nsgt>.

12 For a discussion of the classic, colonial interpretation of the right to self-determination, see, among others, A. Heraclides, *The Self-determination of Minorities in International Politics* (Routledge 1991). See also L. S. Hanauer, 'The Irrelevance of Self-determination Law to Ethno-national Conflict: A New Look at the Western Sahara Case' 9 *Emory International Law Review* (1995) 132–133.

13 Supreme Court of Canada, *Reference re Secession of Quebec* (1998) 2 SCR 217, paras 131–133. Although the right to independence is generally construed to apply in cases of foreign occupation, Ali-Saab and Ahmed argue that the definition of 'domination' contained in Paragraph 2 of the Friendly Relations Declaration exceeds colonial and foreign occupation. See D. M. Ahmed, 'Domination as a Possible Instance for a Right to External Self-determination' in *Boundaries and Secession in Africa and International Law* (CUP 2015) 215–233; G. Abi-Saab, 'Wars of National Liberation in the Geneva Conventions and Protocols' 165 (IV) *Collected Courses of The Hague Academy of International Law* (1979) 394.

14 UNESCO statement to the Sub-Commission on the Prevention of Discrimination and the Protection of Minorities, UN Doc. E/CN.4/Sub.2/1992/6, para 3(d).

15 21 GAOR, 1966. Annexes. Vol. III, Agenda item 87, UN Doc. A/6230, para 480.

decolonization process, namely independence, as well as those which existed before and continue to do so have an obligation to promote and respect the said right within their states and in the international arena. New and existing states alike can freely determine their external political status, whether by merging with another state (e.g. the United Arab Republic), dissolving peacefully (e.g. Czechoslovakia) or joining an international organization with far-reaching competencies (e.g. the European Union).[16]

The continuous nature of self-determination is evident in several key international instruments, including the International Covenants on Human Rights, the Friendly Relations Declaration, the Helsinki Final Act, and the African Charter on Human and Peoples' Rights.[17] During the drafting of the Covenants, the original text of Article 1 contained the phrase 'all peoples and all nations shall have the right of self-determination', but the final version was revised to read: 'all peoples have the right of self-determination'.[18] It has been proffered that this change was made to emphasize the permanent character of the right.[19] The enduring nature of self-determination was further affirmed by the Human Rights Committee, which declared that Article 1(3) of the ICCPR is particularly important because it imposes specific obligations on the parties to the Covenant, not only in relation to their own populations but also in relation to all nations that have been unable, or have been deprived of the opportunity, to exercise their right to self-determination.[20] This obligation exists independently of whether a people entitled to self-determination depends on the party of the Covenant or not. The Friendly Relations Declaration is yet another confirmation that self-determination is not exhausted by the mere act of achieving independence. It is clear from the text that all states, not just former colonial powers, have an obligation to act in accordance with the right to self-determination.[21] Had the intention been to limit self-determination to colonial situations, the inclusion of this broad provision would have been unnecessary.

---

16 On the sovereignty of EU member states, see M. Muszyński, *Państwo w Prawie Międzynarodowym* (STO 2012) 66–67, 102–104, 114–117.

17 D. Raič, *Statehood and the Law of Self-determination* (Martinus Nijhoff Publishers 2002) 228.

18 See ESCOR, 1952, Suppl. No. 4, UN Doc. E/2256, para 91; 10 GAOR, 1955. Annexes, Agenda item 28–1, UN Doc. A/3077, para 57. 'Nations' and 'peoples' will hereafter be used interchangeably.

19 A. Cassese, *Self-determination of Peoples: A Legal Reappraisal* (CUP 1995) 54.

20 Human Rights Committee, General Comment No. 12 (n 6) para 6.

21 UNGA Res 2625(XXV) 'Declaration on Principles of International Law concerning Friendly Relations and Cooperation among States in accordance with the Charter of the United Nations' (24 Oct. 1970) (hereinafter: the Friendly Relations Declaration).

The temporal non-limitation of the right to self-determination by implication begs a troublesome question about its contemporary content and beneficiaries. Yet, post-colonial practice reveals certain patterns from which general conclusions could be drawn. Notably, self-determination retains its commonsense external meaning (a right to independence) with regard to entities legally entitled to it, like Non-Self-Governing Territories or Palestine, where the practical realization of this right has been very protracted.[22] Otherwise, various groups residing within established states – whether unitary or federal – generally do not possess the right to secede and form a sovereign state under international law. Thus, minorities or nations within Bangladesh or territories of former socialists blocks like Yugoslavia and the Soviet Union, who claimed this right, did not hold it, at least not on the international level.[23] The internal aspect of the RSD, on the other hand, is not subject to the same limitations. It is broader in scope and arguably constitutes the essence of the contemporary right to self-determination.[24] It encapsulates marginalized groups, indigenous populations and women, for whom this right is of particular importance.[25] Hence, the RSD has substantially evolved from a narrowly apprehended right of the externally oppressed and discriminated people to a more inclusive norm that protects the acquired status, both from external intervention and from the abuse of power by governments.[26]

The right to self-determination, as promulgated in the Covenants and subsequent instruments, is a multifaceted right, which in addition to internal and external political spectra consists of economic, social and cultural aspects. It is widely acknowledged that political sovereignty cannot be seen in the abstract:

---

22 See, *inter alia*, UNGA Res 2649 (XXV) (30 Nov. 1970); UNGA Res 3236 (XXIX) (22 Nov. 1974). Resolution 65/202 (11 Mar. 2011) reaffirmed 'the right of the Palestinian people to self-determination, including the right to their independent State of Palestine'.

23 P. Radan, 'Secessionist Self-determination: The Cases of Slovenia and Croatia' 48(2) *Australian Journal of International Affairs* (1994) 183–195. Pellet remarked: 'in its present state of development, international law does not make clear all the consequences which flow from this principle'. A. Pellet, 'The Opinions of the Badinter Arbitration Committee a Second Breath for the Self-determination of Peoples' 3 *EJIL* (1992) 179. See also J. Castellino, 'The Secession of Bangladesh in International Law: Setting New Standards?' 7 *Asian Yearbook of International Law* (1997) 84–85.

24 On ISD as the 'primary right' see M. Seymour, 'Internal Self-determination and Secession' in A. Pavković and P. Radan (eds.) *The Ashgate Research Companion to Secession* (Routledge 2011) 385–398. More on the addresses in section 2.6.

25 Generally, K. Knop, *Diversity and Self-determination in International Law* (CUP 2009); M. N. L. Zardo, 'Gender Equality and Indigenous Peoples' Right to Self-determination and Culture' 28(4) *American University International Law Review* (2013) 1053–1090 (cautioning against applying self-determination through a gender-neutral lens).

26 Raič (n 17) 234.

political independence is based on economic independence.[27] Economic self-determination manifests in two primary forms: as an economic postulate and as a legal right. While economic development is most effectively achieved during peacetime through independent institutions that allow for the free choice of economic systems and the respect for human rights, it is often compromised by the complex contemporary pressures exerted on poorer states, often geared toward exploiting their natural resources.[28] To secure the proper realization of the right to economic self-determination, states must maintain continuous and full control over their natural resources and apply national laws to all private industries, even in cases where previous laws authorised expropriation or nationalisation under just conditions.[29] Thus, economic self-determination is closely tied to the ownership and administration of land, though it does not necessarily presuppose exclusive control by the central government over land resources. The possession, *ergo*, near-complete rights to land by traditional tribal communities and indigenous peoples, was affirmed by the Inter-American Court on Human Rights,[30] which also referred to the close relationship between land possession and economic self-determination, as reflected in the work of the Committee on Economic, Social and Cultural Rights (CESCR).[31] In the *Awas Tingni* case, the Inter-American Court ruled that 'the close ties of indigenous people with the land must be recognized and understood as the fundamental basis of their cultures, their spiritual life, their integrity, and their economic survival',[32] while in *Saramaka People. v. Suriname* observed that

27 Study Prepared by A. Cristescu (n 4) para 44. For a thorough criticism of the Australian Counter-Memorial in the East Timor case, where Australia attempted to justify its exploitation of resources by arguing that 'a State can only breach the obligation to respect the right of people to self-determination if its conduct prevents or hinders the exercise by the people of a Non-Self-Governing Territory of their right freely to determine their political status' (para 375). See C. Drew, 'The East Timor Story: International Law on Trial' 12 *EJIL* (2001) 666.

28 On the prohibition of unfair exploitation of natural resources from both dependent territories and independent states, see UNGA Res 626 (VII) (21 Dec. 1952); 1803 (XVII) 'Permanent sovereignty over natural resources' (14 Dec. 1962). See also J. Oloka-Onyango, 'Heretical Reflections on the Right to Self-determination: Prospects and Problems for a Democratic Global Future in the New Millennium' 15 *American University International Law Review* (1999) 169 ff.

29 *See* UNGA Res 3281 (XXIX) 'The Charter of Economic Rights and Duties of States' (12 Dec. 1974); Study Prepared by A. Cristescu (n 4) paras 395–398.

30 D. L. Shelton, 'Self-determination in Regional Human Rights Law: From Kosovo to Cameroon' 105 *AJIL* (2011) 75.

31 CESCR, 'Consideration of Reports Submitted by States Parties Under Articles 16 and 17 of the Covenant. Concluding Observations: Russian Federation' (12 Dec. 2003) para 11.

32 IACtHR, *Mayagna (Sumo) Awas Tingni Cmty. v. Nicaragua* (ser. C) No. 79 (31 Aug. 2001) para 149.

indigenous peoples may 'freely dispose of their natural wealth and resources' so as not to be 'deprived of (their) own means of subsistence'.[33]

According to common Article 1 of the Covenants, peoples, on the basis of the right to self-determination, possess the right to pursue social development. Social development, broadly speaking, denotes the welfare and wellbeing of human beings as well as the advancement of societal institutions, whereby these 'institutions' should not only be understood in their literal sense as formal organisations but also as encompassing the values, behaviors, and motivations that shape collective life.[34] Social progress, in this context, is characterized as the continuous improvement of both the material and spiritual standards of societies and their members.[35]

Social development can be quantitatively assessed using the Index of Social Progress (IPS), which evaluates indicators such as education, health, the position of women, political participation, and cultural diversity, among others.[36] For minority groups, the indices of political participation and cultural diversity are of particular relevance. Political participation is measured by examining violations of civil and political freedoms, as well as the extent of human suffering, whereas cultural diversity refers to the variety of languages, religions and ethnicities present within a society.[37] Achieving social development thus connotes both a negative obligation to eliminate all forms of exploitation, war, (neo)colonialism and racism – factors that obstruct social progress – and a positive obligation to secure social justice for all, promote sustainable development, and ensure access to basic resources and services, with particular consideration of underdeveloped countries.[38]

Cultural self-determination is considered the right of nations and individuals within those nations, to determine, express, and develop their cultural identity.[39] During the drafting of the Covenants, this dimension of self-determination was initially less defined and developed later than its political and economic counterparts. However, from the outset, it was evident that the right to self-determination was not confined to the political realm but also

33 IACtHR, *Saramaka People. v. Suriname*, Preliminary Objections, Merits, Reparations, and Costs (ser. C) No. 172 (28 Nov. 2007) para 93.

34 U. Barten, *Minority Rights and Internal Self-determination* (Springer 2015) 209.

35 UNGA Res 5242(XXIV) 'Declaration of Social Progress and Development' (11 Dec. 1969).

36 R. J. Estes, 'Social Development Trends in Asia, 1970–1994: The Challenges of a New Century' 37 *Social Indicators Research* (1996) 121.

37 *Ibid.* 122–123.

38 See S. P. Subedi, 'Declaration on the Right to Development' *United Nations Audiovisual Library of International Law* (2021).

39 Cited after J. Summers, *Peoples and International Law* (Martinus Nijhoff 2014) 362, fn. 482.

encompassed social, and cultural dimensions.[40] Cultural self-determination is especially important for minority groups and indigenous peoples. The practice of the Human Rights Committee affirms that their cultural rights are protected under Article 27 of the International Covenant on Civil and Political Rights.[41] For instance, in the case of *Lansman v. Finland*, the Human Rights Committee found that minorities and indigenous peoples are entitled to safeguard their traditional activities, such as hunting, fishing or, as in this case, reindeer husbandry. It was determined that measures applied by states that could jeopardize these activities constitute a denial of their right to enjoy their minority culture.[42] Importantly, cultural self-determination, in view of the changing ethnic composition of states due to population movements, should not be read merely in terms of 'preservation' (as in ecological conservation) but rather as promoting democratic inclusiveness that respects the rights of 'foreign' individuals.[43]

Unfortunately, the right to self-determination is one of the rights most shrouded in controversy and ambiguity. Disputes surrounding this right frequently arise from its unilateral interpretation and the potential for misuse in nationalist agendas, which, in turn, emanate from the indeterminacy of the right's content and holders. Consequently, while the right is celebrated as a momentous achievement that 'gives hope to the people'[44] and 'contributes to the maintenance of international peace and stability',[45] it is also criticized as

---

40 UN Commission on Human Rights, 'Report of the 8th session' (14 April-14 June 1952) UN Doc. E/CN.4/669, paras 20–74.

41 See e.g. Human Rights Committee, *Äärelä and Näkkäläjärvi v. Finland*, Communication No. 779/1997 (24 Oct. 2001); *George Howard v. Canada*, Communication No. 879/1999 (26 Jul. 2005); *Ángela Poma Poma v. Peru*, Communication No. 1457/2006 (27 Mar. 2009).

42 Human Rights Committee, *Jouni E. Länsman et al. v. Finland*, Communication No. 671/1995 (30 Oct. 1996) para 10.3. In addition, these traditional activities of indigenous communities are threatened by the effects of climate change, which, in turn, endangers the very right to self-determination of the members of these groups. More in J. Vlajnić and Đ. Spasojević, 'Procedural Legitimation of Private Parties before the Court of Justice of the EU in the Light of Carvahlo Case' 3(4) *International Review* (2023) 241.

43 S. Salomon, 'Self-determination in the Case Law of the African Commission: Lessons for Europe' 50(3) *Verfassung und Recht in Übersee / Law and Politics in Africa, Asia and Latin America* (2017) 240–241.

44 G. Arangio-Ruiz, 'The Normative Role of the General Assembly of the United Nations and the Declaration of Principles of Friendly Relations' 137 *Collected Courses of The Hague Academy of International Law* (1972) chapter IV, section 4.

45 'The respect of that [self-determination] norm is a basis for the development of friendly relations, and is in effect, one of the appropriate measures to strengthen universal peace.' Special Rapporteur of the Sub-Commission on Prevention of Discrimination and Protection of Minorities (I/l/A) to Committee I/I (1 Jun. 1945) 703–704.

a principle that 'supports anachronistic nationalism and affects the integrity of states'.[46] As per Suzuki and Koskenniemi, self-determination is a double-edged concept that 'can act as a unifying as well as a disintegrative force',[47] and simultaneously 'supports and challenges statehood'.[48]

The unidimensional understanding of self-determination has contributed to the limited resolution of ethnic conflicts. Traditionally, self-determination has been perceived as an all-or-nothing solution.[49] As a result, the insistence on its overly simplistic application in its external form, particularly through secession, has sharpened conflicts rather than resolving them.[50] This book argues that self-determination is a multifaceted concept that should be apprehended more broadly and, contrary to conventional wisdom, can even prevent secession, especially in cases driven by purely democratic or nationalistic demands for secession, where a state respects the rights and specific needs of all its people (internal self-determination).[51]

The underlying problem that has spawned undesired ramifications in quests for statehood and continues to beset the RSD concerns its content and addressees. Leo Trotsky pertinently posed the question: 'the right of nations to self-determination is a right of whom to what'? Similarly, Tacik described the right to self-determination as an 'indefinable entitlement of an elusive subject to rather unspecified actions'.[52] Some states have sought to limit the circle of beneficiaries of this right, asserting that only colonial peoples have the right to self-determination.[53] Others have tried to restrict the scope of the right, stating

46 Z. Mustafa, 'The Principle of Self-determination in International Law' 5(3) *The International Lawyer* (1971) 483–484.

47 E. Suzuki, 'Review: Self-determination in International Law' 89(6) *The Yale Law Journal* (1980) 1247.

48 M. Koskenniemi, 'National Self-determination Today: Problems of Legal Theory and Practice' 43(2) *International and Comparative Law Quarterly* (1994) 249.

49 M. Weller, 'Settling Self-determination Conflicts: Recent Developments' 20(1) EJIL (2009) 112.

50 *Ibid.*

51 More in Chapter III, section 3.2.3 and chapter IV.

52 See P. Tacik, 'The Right of Peoples to Self-determination: A European Rebound of a Neglected Paradox' 19 *Problemy Współczesnego Prawa Międzynarodowego, Europejskiego i Porównawczego* (2021) 237.

53 See, in particular, India's declaration on the International Covenants on Human Rights 'With reference to Article 1 ... [of the Covenants] ... the Government of India declares that the words 'the right of self-determination' appearing in this article apply only to the people under foreign domination'. Centre for Human Rights, *Human Rights, Status of International Instruments* (United Nations 1987) 9.

that it is exhausted by the act of achieving independence.[54] It seems that the reason for such cautious treatment of the RSD lies in the fact that its external dimension comes into conflict with another fundamental principle of international law – the territorial integrity of states, a conflict that does not arise with internal self-determination.

Doubts and confusion as to the applicability of the RSD also stem from the contradictory positions taken by international organizations, such as the UN and OSCE, in their interpretation of the principle of territorial integrity and the RSD. The impression that the principle of territorial integrity limits, if not weakens, the right to self-determination is reinforced by some specific examples where the international community has shown restraint in responding to requests for secession, often prioritizing the preservation of state territorial integrity. The United Nations, for example, initially avoided taking a definitive stance on the secession of East Pakistan, condemned the secession of the Turkish Cypriots, and at the onset of the conflict in the former Yugoslavia stood for the preservation of its territorial integrity.

The mandated realization of the right to self-determination presents another significant challenge. Both internally and externally, it still leaves much to be desired, as evidenced by the hardships to complete the decolonization process (with 17 territories still awaiting decolonization) and to secure this right in long-standing conflict zones (e.g. Palestine), in authoritarian regimes (e.g. the Kurds in Iraq), and, to some extent, even in liberal democracies (e.g. Catalonia).

Owing to its inherent indeterminacy, varying interpretations, over-politicization, and flawed realization, the right to self-determination has rightly been labeled *lex imperfecta*.[55] Some critical voices go further, arguing that these shortcomings significantly undermine the viability of self-determination as a legal norm.[56] Nevertheless, despite these challenges, and given the enduring

54 Doudou Thiam, the Foreign Minister of Senegal, once stated: '1. No historical, geographical or ethnic considerations should justify one African state in claiming sovereignty over another African state or territory. 2. The frontiers drawn between the various African territories in the colonial era should be regarded as valid and should be maintained'. See also R. Emerson, *From Empire to Nation* (HUP 1960) 307–308. Cf. Castellino, 'The Secession of Bangladesh' (n 23) 87.

55 J. H. Verzijl, *International Law in Historical Perspective,* vol. I (A W Sijthoff 1968) 324–325. 'If an entity X may have right to self-determination, that does not mean that it may exercise its right to self-determination'. J. Klabbers 'The Right to Be Taken Seriously: Self-determination in International Law' 28(1) *Human Rights Quarterly* (2006) 188.

56 S. Tierney, 'The Search for a New Normativity: Thomas Franck, Post-modern Neo-tribalism and the Law of Self-determination' 13(4) *EJIL* (2002) 941. Earlier, G. Arangio-Ruiz, *The*

values and aspirations of legal scholarship, the right continues to oscillate between serving as an apology for past developments and a utopian vision for a fairer future.[57]

Be that as it may, self-determination does not operate in a legal vacuum but is closely intertwined with other principles of international law, most notably, territorial integrity, *uti possidetis* and the prohibition of the use of force, all of which share a demonstrably convoluted relationship.[58] Especially important is the tension between the right to (external) self-determination and the principles of territorial integrity and strict state sovereignty, because by their very nature, they are in fundamental contradiction.[59] While the principle of territorial integrity seeks to preserve the territorial *status quo*, self-determination, in its external form, often leads to a change of state borders. Requests for secession by groups invoking the right to external self-determination pose a direct challenge to the territorial integrity of states. This relationship is further complicated by the fact that the international community has not established legal principles managing secessionist situations, leaving outcomes largely dependent on the balance of power among the parties involved. What is clear, however, is that other states must not alone intervene in the domestic affairs of sovereign countries, whether by supporting or suppressing secessionist claims. Nevertheless, there exist divergent practices to this end, often justified through appeals to concepts such as 'humanitarian intervention' or by classifying certain groups within states as 'peoples' entitled to the right to self-determination.[60]

United Nations Declaration on Friendly Relations and the System of the Sources of International Law (Sijthoff & Noordhoof 1979) 132–134.

57 P. Hilpold, *Autonomy and Self-determination: Between Legal Assertions and Utopian Aspirations* (Elgar 2018) 9.

58 See J. Fisch, 'Adolf Hitler und das Selbstbestimmungsrecht der Völker' 290 *Historische Zeitschrift* (2010) 94; V. Epps, 'The New Dynamics of Self-determination' 3 *ILSA Journal of International and Comparative Law* (1997) 433–442.

59 Some authors argue that peoples are not the addressees of the norm protecting territorial integrity. If this is the case, the contradiction is not legal, but factual. Hilpold suggests that secession claims can sometimes strengthen state sovereignty by fulfilling these claims, and potentially in the long term as well, when the entity successfully secedes. See Hilpold, *Autonomy and Self-determination* (n 57) 49–53. Antonowicz observed that treating the people as sovereign, who can freely decide upon the internal system of the state and determine its external status, aligns with the concept of self-determination. L. Antonowicz, 'Samostanowienie Narodów Jako Zasada Prawa Międzynarodowego' 43 *Annales Universitatis Mariae Curie-Sklodowska* (1996) 77. That is why the emphasis in the text is placed on the phrase 'strict state sovereignty', denoting the authority of the state rather than that of the people.

60 In cases of colonialism and liberation movements, assistance was generally provided. For example, the support rendered by the People's Republic of Angola to the People's Repub-

The contemporary reluctance of states to support the application of the right to self-determination in its external form is rooted in the priority of maintaining the continuity of existing states. In the context of secessionist movements, it has been observed that 'international law is not a suicide club for states that would undermine its own security by allowing the right to secession'.[61] Post-World War II practice indeed indicates the international community has firmly stood on the side of the governments in cases of unilateral secessions, and no breakaway entity has been admitted to the United Nations.[62] Heed has been paid to the principle of territorial integrity, which, *nota bene,* is enshrined in almost all international instruments addressing self-determination. Nevertheless, some authors contend that territorial integrity and the right to self-determination are not mutually exclusive.[63] Those who assert that the RSD does not, in itself, jeopardise the principle of territorial integrity primarily refer to the internal form of self-determination, which is generally undisputed since it operates within the state's borders. With regard to the controversial external variant, proponents of the thesis that the principles of territorial integrity and self-determination can coexist suggest that external self-determination may prevail in instances where the internal right to self-determination is not upheld.[64]

The exercise of external self-determination by groups within a state is also constrained by the principle of *uti possidetis juris,* which seeks to align populations with a specific territory at the conclusion of belligerence, according to the current state of possession. The difference between the principles of territorial integrity and *uti possidetis* is that the former is continuous, while the latter is temporary. The principle of territorial integrity is applicable after the state is established in accordance with international law, whereas *uti possidetis* takes effect at the moment of sovereignty transfer, 'freezing' the territorial configuration as it exists at the time of independence. This principle thus defines

lic of Mozambique, and by the Republic of Zambia to the people of Zimbabwe in their 'just and legitimate struggle for the attainment of freedom and independence', was commended by the international community. See E. Chadwick, 'National Liberation in the Context of Post- and Non-Colonial Struggles for Self-determination' in M. Weller (ed.) *The Oxford Handbook of the Use of Force in International Law* (OUP 2015) 841–860. See also S. Yau, 'The Legality of the Use of Force for Self-determination' 21 *The Palestine Yearbook of International Law* (2020) 32–76.

61 J. Castellino, 'David Raic. Statehood and the Law of Self Determination' 16 *EJIL* (2005) 792.

62 J. Crawford, 'State Practice in International Law in Relation to Secession' 69 *BYIL* (1998) 92.

63 I. Cismas, 'Secession in Theory and Practice: The Case of Kosovo and Beyond' 2(2) *Goettingen Journal of International Law* (2010) 551.

64 J. Vlajnić, *The Right to Self-determination in International Law* (PhD thesis, University of Belgrade 2022) 126.

the territorial boundaries of the state to which the principle of territorial integrity will subsequently be applied.

Unsurprisingly, various groups in Africa have voiced opposition to this concept as conflicting with their right to self-determination. These groups were simply confined to colonial borders, but apparently, this was not questioned by the leaders of African states who were comfortable with the border lines established by Europeans at the time of regaining independence.[65] In the *Frontier Dispute* case, the ICJ observed that 'at first sight this principle [of *uti possidetis*] conflicts with another one, the right of peoples to self-determination',[66] but went on to point out that the African states agreed to preserve colonial borders for the sake of stability and international peace, and found that the same reasons encouraged them to 'take account of it [*uti possidetis*] in the interpretation of the principle of self-determination of people'.[67]

There is, therefore, no inherent tension between *uti possidetis* and the right to external self-determination in cases of decolonisation and where a geographical unit is entitled to exercise self-determination (territorial interpretation of the rightsholders), whereas such tension may appear in cases where minority-people claim the right (ethnic interpretation of the rightsholders).[68] It is in the latter instance that the concept raises legitimacy issues comparable to those associated with the territorial integrity principle. Yet, agreeing to an absolute, unlimited, application of self-determination is equally problematic.[69] Thus, the exercise of this right needs to be harmonised with other norms and principles of general international law. As stipulated in Article 5 of the ICCPR, the right must be applied in such a manner that respects individual human rights contained in the Covenant.[70] Besides, since *uti possidetis* is not *jus cogens* and is based on consent, nothing prevents entities from drawing a 'better' line between them. However, in reality, this is rarely achievable.

---

65 See 2nd Summit Conference of Heads of State or Government of the Non-Aligned Movement, Cairo Declaration (10 Oct. 1964) Doc. NAC-II/HEADS/5, 17.

66 ICJ, *Frontier Dispute (Burkina Faso/Republic of Mali)*, Judgment, ICJ Rep. 1986, 567.

67 *Ibid.*

68 Bursać opposed the political-democratic idea of the nation (people), hence *uti possidetis* should not be applicable to post-colonial situations, where the level of national-ethnic conscience is considerably higher. S. Bursać, 'Pravo na Samoopredeljenje Naroda' 62(2) *Međunarodni Problemi* (2010) 300–302. Cf. Badinter Commission, Opinion No. 2 (11 Jan. 1992), reprinted in 3 *EJIL* (1992) 183–184; A. Peters, 'The Principle of *Uti Possidetis Juris*: How Relevant it is for Issues of Secession' in C. Walter et al. (eds.) *Self-determination and Secession in International Law* (OUP 2014) chapter 6.

69 See R. Emerson, 'Self-determination' 60 *Proceedings of the American Society of International Law* (1966) 135–141.

70 Raič (n 17) 304.

2 History of the Right to Self-determination

Certain aspects of the principle of self-determination are as old as statehood or nation-states.[71] Traces of the idea of self-determination are also evident in the writings of 15th and 16th-century European philosophers and priests, such as Balthasar de Ayala, Bartolomé de Las Casas, Francisco de Vitoria, Francisco Suárez, and Erasmus of Rotterdam, who critically assessed the conquests of indigenous tribes, arguing that indigenous peoples were the rightful masters of their lands, capable of self-governance, and therefore, any form of external rule would require their consent.[72] Nevertheless, a significant part of the literature identifies the American and French Revolutions as the true inception of self-determination.[73] The genesis of the principle, and later the right to self-determination, can be delineated into four distinct phases. The first phase depicts self-determination as a political principle, galvanized by the American and French Revolutions as well as the nationalist movements of the 19th century. The second phase relates to the period of moulding the concept by Lenin and Wilson up to the outbreak of World War II. Self-determination eventually gains a legal foundation in the third phase, primarily during the decolonization period, channeled through the United Nations. The fourth and final phase sees self-determination as a peremptory norm (*jus cogens*) of positive international law, extending beyond decolonization to contemporary contexts of indigenous sovereignty and democratic legitimacy.[74]

---

71 See M. Batistich, 'The Right to Self-determination and International Law' 7(4) *Auckland University Law Review* (1995) 1013.

72 E. Rodrıguez-Santiago, 'The Evolution of Self-determination of Peoples in International Law' in F. Tesón (ed.) *The Theory of Self-determination* (CUP 2016) 202–204.

73 See J. Castellino, *International Law and Self-determination: The Interplay of the Politics of Territorial Possession with Formulations of Post-Colonial National Identity* (Brill 2000) 11; Raič (n 17) 172; Cassese, *Self-determination of Peoples* (n 19) 11.

74 Vučinić differentiates between the following phases: the anti-feudal or national-constitutive phase, the anti-imperial phase, the anti-colonial phase, and the anti-communist phase. N. Vučinić, 'Pravo Naroda na Samoopredeljenje' 3–4 *Prava Čoveka* (2002) 13–20. Ronen identifies five 'quests' for self-determinations: national self-determination (from the 1830s to the 1880s); class self-determination (advocated by Marxists in the mid-19th century); minority self-determination (especially advocated by Woodrow Wilson, between 1916 and the 1920s); racial self-determination (proclaimed by colonial nations, from 1945 to the 1960s); and ethnic self-determination (from the mid-1960s onwards, including Biafra, Scotland and Bangladesh). D. Ronen, *The Quest for Self-determination* (Yale University Press 1979) 9–12.

2.1 *Self-determination before WWII*

A significant step in the evolution of the concept of self-determination was the emergence of communities refusing to obey authorities they considered 'alien'.[75] This demand for self-governance found its expression in the American and French Revolutions. Both the U.S. Declaration of Independence and the French Declaration of the Rights of Man drew on the medieval notion of a right to resist unjust rule.[76] For European thinkers of the 17th and 18th centuries, such as Pufendorf, Grotius and Kant, it had already been natural to link the legitimacy of territorial transfers between rulers to the consent of entities entitled to (co)decide in political matters.[77] In the American and French Revolutions, however, these concepts merged with a new idea of popular sovereignty, signaling a radical transformation in political thought.[78]

The rebellion of the British colonies in North America represents the first instance in world history in which the right to national and democratic self-determination was explicitly mentioned.[79]

American colonists, influenced by John Locke's ideas on natural law, protested against overseas dominance and taxation without representation, asserting that political societies are founded on the consent of the governed, with individuals possessing natural rights to life, liberty, and property. A novel aspect in the conflicts that erupted between colonists and Britain revolved around the importance that settlers gave to popular sovereignty.[80] In this view, the ruler maintains sovereignty only as long as he takes care of the welfare of the people. This view was strengthened by the adoption of the U.S. Declaration of Independence by the Continental Congress in Philadelphia on 4 July 1776. The Declaration addressed key issues related to the modern doctrine of self-determination, asserting that all people are created equal and endowed with certain inalienable rights, and that governments derive their lawful powers from the consent of the governed. At the same time, it envisioned the right of the people to alter or abolish any form of government that becomes an obstacle to exercising their rights. However, this right should not be exercised for

---

75 Raič (n 17) 172–173.

76 S. Oeter, 'Self-determination' in B. Simma et al. (eds.) *The Charter of the United Nations: A Commentary* (OUP 2012) 317.

77 *Ibid.*

78 *Ibid.*

79 American Foreign Relations, 'Self-determination: The American Revolution' <https://www.americanforeignrelations.com/O-W/Self-determination-The-american-revolution.html>.

80 J. Fisch, *The Right of Self-determination of Peoples: The Domestication of an Illusion* (CUP 2015) 70.

trivial or transient reasons, but in response to 'a long train of abuses and usurpations, pursuing invariably the same Object evinces a design to reduce them under absolute Despotism'.[81] So, the Declaration suggests that peoples should not secede and form new governments at will, as the new governments may not be any better than the ones they replace. Instead, a more prudent solution could be governmental reform.[82]

The U.S. Declaration of Independence sought to portray two radical views: first, as noted, that 'governments are instituted among Men, deriving their just powers from the consent of the governed' and second, that by making governments accountable to the people, the new state entity gains 'a separate and equal station' in the community of states by showing 'respect to the opinions of mankind'.[83] This demonstrates that the right to self-determination, as pronounced in the U.S. Declaration, contains both an internal element (legitimate rule) and an external element (legitimacy within the community of sovereign states). Frank designates the first of these elements as 'democratic authority' and associates this concept of authority with the legitimacy of the government.[84]

The historical significance of the Declaration of Independence is beyond doubt. It marked the beginning of the decline of European colonial rule and represented the first broad implementation of the principle of national sovereignty. However, although the Declaration is a politically revolutionary document, its legal framework is quite traditional.[85] The independence the colonists aspired for was not based on a natural right to self-determination, but on the classical right to resistance that dates back to medieval European legal thought.[86] This right granted those who had been wronged the authority to rebel, to revolt, to overthrow rulers, and, in the view of many, even to oppose tyranny. Nowhere in the Declaration, implicitly or explicitly, is the request for self-determination mentioned. Yet, its adoption paved the way for the development of the concept of self-determination.[87]

---

81 Declaration of Independence: A Transcription (1776) <https://www.archives.gov/founding-docs/declaration-transcript>.

82 R. McGee, 'Secession and Emerging Democracies: The Kendall and Louw Solution' 2 *Journal of International Law & Practice* (1993) 327.

83 Castellino, *International Law and Self-determination* (n 73) 11.

84 T. M. Franck, 'The Emerging Right to Democratic Governance' 86(1) *AJIL* (1992) 46.

85 Fisch, *The Right of Self-determination of Peoples* (n 80) 71.

86 See Stanford Encyclopedia of Philosophy, 'Aquinas' Moral, Political, and Legal Philosophy' (2021) <https://plato.stanford.edu/ENTRIES/aquinas-moral-political/>.

87 Fisch, *The Right of Self-determination of Peoples* (n 80) 71–72.

Several years after the U.S. Declaration of Independence, revolutionary turmoil erupted on the European continent leading to the adoption of a document that would form a normative foundation for the later development of the principle of self-determination. The concept of self-determination took a new context during the French Revolution in 1789. Namely, in addition to denying the ruler's right to govern without the consent of the people, as highlighted during the American Revolution, the French Revolution emphasized the fundamental right of every people to freely organize their form of governance without interference from foreign powers.[88] France's Constitution of 3 September 1791 explicitly rejected the legitimacy of conquest wars, asserting that governance should be based on the will of the people, not on the authority of the king.[89]

Influenced by thinkers like John Locke, the revolution underscored the idea that states derive their legitimacy from the will of the people, not from monarchs or elites, positioning the nation as the source of political authority. The National Assembly's declaration of 1792 extended support to peoples striving for freedom, blending liberal principles of individual rights with political nationalism, wherein sovereignty inherently resides within the nation.

An important contribution of revolutionary political thought was the idea of government as an expression of the democratic will, in which the state is understood as sovereign in unity with the people. Prior to the emergence of these ideas, states rarely acted in response to the needs and wishes of their populations. Over time, however, societies began to reject authority they perceived as imposed or external. From this shift emerged the principle that the legitimacy of power rests on the will and acceptance of the people, rather than on the prerogative of monarchs, aristocrats, or privileged elites. In other words, nations are not merely subjects of the state; they possess the agency to constitute a state of their own.

While these revolutions significantly contributed to the concept of self-determination, their underlying ideology, rooted in liberalism and individualism, contrasts with the inherently collectivist nature of self-determination. Nevertheless, they laid the intellectual and political groundwork for its

---

88 B. Gavrilović, *Istorija Prava na Samoopredeljenje: (R)evolucija Prava na Samoopredeljenje* (Belgrade Centre for Human Rights 2013) 1–2.

89 Here we see how the young French Republic attempts to establish the foundation for the abolition of the monarchy and the survival of the republic through the concept of self-determination, which in 18th-century Europe was an unimaginable precedent given that the monarch's authority was legitimized by divine rather than popular will. If the monarch's power comes from a higher being, it is impossible to defy it. In such circumstances, the concept of self-determination could not develop. See Raič (n 17) 174.

development, particularly within the tradition of Western democratic political theory.

During the second half of the 18th century, theoretical and political thought began to emphasize the interconnected nature of the state as both a political organization and a socio-cultural entity.[90] The right of peoples to self-determination, particularly concerning political status, is closely tied to the doctrine of nationalism.[91] Central to nationalist theory is the premise that every nation is entitled to establish its own state. However, there is no universally accepted definition of a nation as a fundamental political unit, which renders the concept both indeterminate and flexible, yet also dynamic.[92] It can be argued that a nation consists of a territorially concentrated group of people who share certain common characteristics.

The principle of nationalism reached its zenith between 1848 and 1870, often manifesting through plebiscites.[93] As a way of direct expression of the will of the people, the plebiscites are closely related to the principle of self-determination. For instance, at an international congress held in Paris in 1856, it was decided to conduct a plebiscite under international supervision in Moldova and Wallachia to determine the future of these territories. Similarly, in the late 19th century, plebiscites were employed on the American continent to facilitate the transfer of power over three Danish West Indian islands among colonial powers and to resolve territorial disputes between Chile and Peru.[94]

Figures like Mazzini championed national self-determination, viewing it as vital for global peace,[95] though scholars like Cobban recognized its dual

---

90 *Ibid.* 176.

91 J. Summers, 'The Right of Self-determination and Nationalism in International Law' 12(4) *International Journal on Minority and Group Rights* (2005) 325.

92 *Ibid.* 326.

93 A. Cobban, *National Self Determination* (University of Chicago Press 1948) 6.

94 D. Heater, *National Self-determination: Woodrow Wilson and his Legacy* (St. Martin's Press 1994) 6. Broadly, S. Wambaugh, *A Monograph on Plebiscites, with a Collection of Official Documents* (Carnegie Endowment for International Peace 1920) (analysing popular consultations between 1791 and 1914); S. Wambaugh, *Plebiscites Since the World War* (Carnegie Endowment for International Peace 1933) (studying interwar period cases like Schleswig: 1920, Allenstein and Marienwerder: 1920, Teschen, Spisz and Orava: 1920, Upper Silesia: 1921, Sopron: 1921, the attempted plebiscites in Vilna: 1920–1921, Tacna and Arica: 1925–1926 and the Saar territory plebiscite of 1935).

95 *See* Heater, *National Self-determination* (n 94) 6; Fisch, *The Right of Self-determination of Peoples* (n 80) 106–107 (noting, however, that Mazzini was eager to limit fifty nationalities,

nature, encompassing both disintegration and unification.[96] The aftermath of World War I witnessed the rise of nation-states from the ruins of old European empires, with the principle of self-determination gaining prominence, though challenges in defining 'nationhood' persisted.[97] Self-determination's significance grew in tandem with the advent of the modern state, contrasting sharply with the feudal era's decentralized power structures. Notably, alongside the democratic ideals of the American and French Revolutions, nationalism's advocacy for objective national independence, especially against multinational empires, shaped Woodrow Wilson's articulation of self-determination in the post-war order.

The leader of the Bolshevik Revolution, Vladimir Ilyich Lenin, is credited with bringing the concept of self-determination to the forefront of international political discourse. Following the complete collapse of central authority in Russia in 1917, the Bolsheviks, addressing the national question within Russia and seeking to gain the support of non-Russian minority groups, foregrounded their theory of self-determination.[98] For Lenin, self-determination was the right of oppressed nations to secede from their oppressors and create new, independent states.[99] His interpretation of self-determination explicitly included the right to secession. According to Lenin, there should be no hesitation stemming from fears of state disintegration, on the contrary, he asserted that 'from the viewpoint of democracy in general, the very opposite is the case: recognition of the right to secession reduces the danger of the 'disintegration of the state'.[100]

However, Lenin advocated the differentiation between the *right to secession* and the *actual invocation of secession*. He argued that secession should be invoked

> only when national oppression and national friction make joint life absolutely intolerable and hinder any and all economic intercourse. In that

---

and therefore states, to thirteen or fourteen of equal size to reduce dominance, which was, ultimately contrary to the idea of national self-determination).

96 Cobban (n 93) 6.

97 J. Summers, *The Idea of the People: The Right of Self-determination, Nationalism and the Legitimacy of International Law* (Doctoral Dissertation, University of Helsinki 2004) 76.

98 Raič (n 17) 184.

99 V. I. Lenin, 'The Socialist Revolution and the Right of Nations to Self-determination (Theses)' 3 (The Meaning of the Right to Self-determination and its Relation to Federation) <https://www.marxists.org/archive/lenin/works/1916/jan/x01.htm>.

100 V. I. Lenin, 'The Right of Nations to Self Determination' *Marxists Internet Archive* <https://www.marxists.org/archive/lenin/works/1914/self-det/ch05.htm>.

> case, the interests of capitalist development and of the freedom of the class struggle will be best served by secession.[101]

Lenin, therefore, saw secession as a measure of last resort, a perspective that aligns with the principles of the remedial theory of secession, which will be discussed later. As the second quoted sentence illustrates, Lenin's conception of self-determination does not primarily function to protect the collective identity or interests of a nation.[102] Instead, Lenin perceived self-determination, particularly in the form of the right to secession, as a strategic instrument to achieve the ultimate goal of integrating all nations into a universal socialist community.

Cassese identified three different components in Lenin's formulation of the right to self-determination.[103] For one thing, self-determination served as an instrument for ethnic and national groups to determine their fate. Such a goal could be achieved with greater autonomy within the framework of an existing state or through outright secession. In its second meaning, self-determination was intended to function as a guiding principle in the post-war territorial reconfiguration between sovereign states, prohibiting territorial annexation against the will of the people concerned. Third, colonial nations could invoke the right to self-determination in their struggle for independence against imperialist powers. This last component should not be underestimated, since the Soviet Union's advocacy for the liberation of oppressed peoples played a significant role in advancing decolonization within the UN.[104] Cassese notes that the second component, which prohibits territorial annexation against the will of the people echoes the principle of self-determination proclaimed by the French revolutionaries at the end of the 18th century. In contrast, the first and third components are largely innovative.[105]

The contemporary concept of self-determination is inextricably linked to U.S. President Woodrow Wilson, who likewise played a pivotal role in bringing it to the international stage. Indeed, without Wilson's espousal of self-determination, the subsequent institutionalization of the concept and its codification in the 1945 UN Charter would have been unlikely.[106] In fact, Wilson

101 *Ibid.*

102 Raič (n 17) 186.

103 Cassese, *Self-determination of Peoples* (n 19) 32.

104 *Ibid.* 36.

105 *Ibid.* 34.

106 R. Knudsen, *Moments of Self-determination: The Concept of 'Self-determination' and The Idea of Freedom in 20th- and 21st Century International Discourse* (PhD thesis, The London School of Economics and Political Science 2013) 91.

was considered so central to the principle of self-determination that some of his political activities and ideas were retrospectively associated with the concept, even when this was not explicitly the case.[107] An obvious example is his famous address to the U.S. Congress known as the 'Fourteen Points'. Despite the absence of any direct mention of self-determination in this speech, it has nonetheless become a key reference point for the concept.[108]

Unlike Lenin, who grounded self-determination in social-political philosophy, Wilson conceptualized it within the framework of American democratic ideals, emphasizing the consent of the governed and the accountability of governments.[109] Wilson's wartime rhetoric was centered on principles specifically addressing oppressed nations. He often emphasized the principle of the 'equality of nations' – the idea that small, weak nations have the same rights in the international community as great powers.[110] A related principle was that international disputes should be resolved through peaceful means, such as arbitration or institutional arrangements – eventually embodied in the goals of the League of Nations – rather than through armed conflict.[111] Wilson's third, and perhaps most famous principle, is 'the consent of those governed', which refers to the rejection of any international arrangement that would not obtain the approval of the people concerned. This principle was used by Wilson as a synonym for the people's right to self-determination.[112]

Despite opposition from his Secretary of State, Robert Lansing, who considered the concept dangerous and impractical,[113] Wilson persisted in promoting self-determination internationally, albeit with certain limitations concerning colonial territories. A close analysis of the 'Fourteen Points', as well as the Four Principles he later formulated, reveals that Wilson's conception of

---

107 E. Manela, *The Wilsonian Moment: Self-determination and the International Origins of Anticolonial Nationalism* (OUP 2007); T. Thronveit, 'The Fable of the Fourteen Points: Woodrow Wilson and National Self-determination' 35(3) *Diplomatic History* (2011).

108 Manela (n 107) 47–51; Thronveit (n 107) 445.

109 G. Anderson, 'A Post-Millennial Inquiry into the United Nations Law of Self-determination: A Right to Unilateral Non-Colonial Secession?' 49(4) *Vanderbilt Journal of Transnational Law* (2016) 1199.

110 Manela (n 107) 22.

111 Covenant of the League of Nations (28 Apr. 1919) 108 LNTS 188, Preamble.

112 Manela (n 107) 22.

113 Secretary Lansing, a lawyer by profession, regarded President Wilson's advocacy for the right to self-determination as delusional and strongly opposed the concept. He argued that the absence of a clearly defined holder of the right to self-determination rendered the concept not only 'pointless but also dangerous'. Lansing's assertion that self-determination was 'loaded with dynamite' has since become famous. See R. Lansing, *The Peace Negotiations: A Personal Narrative* (Houghton Mifflin Co. 1921) 97.

self-determination was shaped not only by democratic political thought but also by the ideology of nationalism.[114] Wilson regarded self-determination as a strategic tool for the reconfiguration of post-war Europe. In this regard, he incorporated elements of nationalist ideology, specifically the notion that large, artificial multinational empires – products of conquest or dynastic unification – ought to be dismantled into smaller, more natural entities termed 'nationalities' or 'nations.[115] This approach was underpinned by the belief that such artificial empires were inherently unnatural and, thus, illegitimate political entities. As such, Wilson expanded the concept of 'the governed' to encompass not only internal governance but also external relations.

Nevertheless, Wilson is often criticized for several significant missteps in articulating his ideas. First, he presented self-determination in a fairly general and universal sense, thus 'raising hopes which can never be realized'.[116] Second, his idealistic belief that rightful claimants of self-determination would be clear and straightforward to identify proved problematic. This assumption formed the basis of his view of self-determination as a universal principle for ensuring peace and redrawing borders in Europe. In practice, however, neither the post-World War I settlements nor the Covenant of the League of Nations fully embraced Wilson's ideas. Where they were adopted, they were largely limited to peripheral regions.

Despite these shortcomings, Wilson's efforts laid the foundation for minority protection and the mandate system within the League of Nations, though he did not succeed in establishing self-determination as a concrete international legal norm. Today, Wilson is sometimes labelled the 'father' of self-determination.[117] He irrefutably contributed to the internationalisation of this concept, and his ideas and arguments were referenced in later discussions of this right. However, while Wilson's theory of self-determination is reflected in subsequent discourse, Lenin's role in introducing the concept at the international level should not be overlooked. As Pomerance aptly notes, Wilson might

114 Raič (n 17) 180.

115 *Ibid.* 181.

116 See in B. Neuberger, 'National Self-determination: A Theoretical Discussion' 29(3) *Nationalities Papers* (2001) 391.

117 D. Whitehall, 'A Rival History of Self-determination' 27(3) EJIL (2016) 740 (calling Wilson as the champion of liberal internationalism and Lenin as the 'champion' of its alternative). Whitehall acknowledges Rosa Luxemburg's marginal yet significant contribution to the discourse on self-determination, noting that during that period, the concept 'was still a coin in the air waiting to fall into one side's hand, a question that was equally Wilson's, Lenin's or Luxemburg's as much as it represented the claim for independence of Europe's minorities or of other peoples oppressed by imperial rule', 742.

be more accurately described as the 'foster father' of self-determination.[118] Both Lenin's and Wilson's theories significantly influenced the international understanding and evolution of this right.

In a related development, it is important to revisit the case of the Åland Islands, which paved the way for the inclusion of the concept of self-determination in the UN Charter. The Åland Islands are an autonomous, demilitarised and monolingual Swedish province of Finland. This archipelago is located at the entrance to the Gulf of Bothnia in the Baltic Sea, tentatively half the sea route between Finland and Sweden.[119]

At the end of World War I, the Åland Islands remained under Finland's sovereignty, despite the aspirations of the Swedish-speaking population to join Sweden. In 1917, the islanders petitioned the Swedish monarch to propose unification with Sweden and sought to raise the issue at the 1919 Paris Peace Conference. However, their plea was deferred. Soon after, the case was brought to the international stage, when Britain, in June 1920, requested the League of Nations to resolve the Åland Islands' situation. Britain cited Article 11 of the Covenant of the League of Nations, which states that each member has a 'friendly right' to 'bring to the attention of the Assembly or of the Council any circumstance whatever affecting international relations which threatens to disturb international peace or the good understanding between nations upon which peace depends'.[120] Other appeals to the League of Nations followed, emphasizing the importance of international peace and security, and, at times, referencing 'self-determination of peoples'.[121] Representatives of the Åland Islands stated, among other things, that they could suffer assimilation if they remained under Finnish sovereignty, which implied that the Islands might not remain peaceful. Swedish submissions to the League of Nations framed the Ålanders' right to self-determination as a matter of international importance, believing that unification with Sweden was a legitimate expression of that right.

118 M. Pomerance, 'The United States and Self Determination: Perspectives on the Wilsonian Conception' 70(1) *AJIL* (1976) 1.

119 Because of its important strategic position, the islands suffered several invasions during the 1853–1856 Crimean War. Britain, Russia, France, Germany and Finland participated, thus shaping the archipelago's fate. See B. Krivokapić, 'Alandska Ostrva–Osam Decenija Široke Autonomije' in B. Krivokapić et al. (eds.) *Alandska Ostrva–Primer Uspešne Autonomije* (Institut za Uporedno Pravo, Forum za Etničke Odnose 2001) 7; Knudsen (n 106) 135.

120 Covenant of the League of Nations (n 111) Article 11.

121 P. M. Brown, 'The Aaland Islands Question' 15(2) *AJIL* (1921) 269–270.

However, the Finnish government argued that internationalizing the Åland Islands case and permitting secession would set a dangerous precedent, one that could jeopardize the stability of League of Nations members and global order more broadly. Finland's position anticipated a common argument against the broad application of self-determination – a cautionary view that would persist for decades. Nearly a century later, Serbia echoed this argument before the International Court of Justice (ICJ) in opposition to Kosovo's unilateral declaration of independence.

In July 1920, the League of Nations established a Committee of Jurists to determine whether sovereignty over Åland fell within the League's jurisdiction.[122] The Committee submitted its report to the League in September 1920, in which it concluded that the League had jurisdiction and articulated its view of self-determination as follows:

> Although the principle of self-determination of peoples plays an important part in modern political thought, especially since the Great War, it must be pointed out that there is no mention of it in the Covenant of the League of Nations. The recognition of this principle in a certain number of international treaties cannot be considered as sufficient to put it upon the same footing as a positive rule of the Law of Nations.[123]

The Committee further concluded that national groups were not entitled to secession 'by simply expressing their wish'. According to the Committee, deciding on separatist demands fell within the internal jurisdiction of states, because

> Positive International Law does not recognise the right of national groups, as such, to separate themselves from the State of which they form part by the simple expression of a wish, any more than it recognises the right of other States to claim such a separation. Generally speaking, the grant or refusal of the right to a portion of its population of determining its own political fate by plebiscite or by some other method, is, exclusively, an attribute of the sovereignty of every State which is definitively

---

122 I. Janson, 'The Implementation of an International Decision at the Local Level: The League of Nations and the Åland Islands 1920–1951' 4(1) *Journal of Autonomy and Security Studies* (2020) 38.

123 'Report of the International Committee of Jurists Entrusted by the Council of the League of Nations with the Task of Giving an Advisory Opinion upon the Legal Aspects of the Aaland Islands Question' *League of Nations Official Journal*, 3 Special Supplement (1920) 5.

> constituted. A dispute between two States concerning such a question, under normal conditions therefore, bears upon a question which International Law leaves entirely to the domestic jurisdiction of one of the States concerned.[124]

The League of Nations remained seized of the matter and, on 20 September 1920, established the Commission of Rapporteurs. This body was tasked with touring the islands, investigating the case, and recommending further proceedings. The Commission submitted its findings to the League in the form of a report in April 1921.

In its report, the Commission of Rapporteurs determined that the principle of self-determination was not, strictly speaking, a binding rule of international law. It characterized the principle as articulated through an indefinite and general formula, which led to various interpretations and divergent opinions.[125] Consequently, the Commission concluded:

> To concede to minorities, either of language or religion, or to any fractions of a population the right of withdrawing from the community to which they belong, because it is their wish or their good pleasure, would be to destroy order and stability within States and to inaugurate anarchy in international life; it would be to uphold a theory incompatible with the very idea of the State as a territorial and political unity.[126]

The Commission of Rapporteurs, echoing the earlier findings of the Committee of Jurists, emphasized that while self-determination exists as a principle, it does not constitute a part of positive international law, as it is not enshrined in the Covenant of the League of Nations. The Commission further clarified that self-determination, when understood as the right of a minority to determine its political fate by seceding from its home state, cannot be regarded as an absolute right that members of a minority group can exercise independently of external circumstances or merely by expressing their will. Nevertheless, this does not imply that the Commission entirely dismisses the right of minorities to secede, as it goes on to assert the following:

124 *Ibid.* 4.

125 Report Submitted to the Council of the League of Nations by the Commission of Rapporteurs (1921) League of Nations Doc. B7 [C] 21/68/106, 27.

126 *Ibid.* 28.

> The separation of a minority from the State of which it forms a part and its incorporation in another State can only be considered as an altogether exceptional solution, a last resort when the State lacks either the will or the power to enact and apply just and effective guarantees.[127]

This statement from the Commission of Reporters reveals the early foundations of what would later be recognized in international law as the right to remedial self-determination. Specifically, the notion of secession by minorities is framed as a last resort, applicable in situations where the state is either unable or unwilling to safeguard their rights – a central tenet of the theory of remedial self-determination. On the other hand, this statement can also be viewed as a foundational principle for internal self-determination, positioning it as a political and legal mechanism to prevent secession.[128]

The Åland Islands case represents the first instance of institutional engagement with the issue of self-determination, marking an effort by a major international body to elucidate the concept and assess its political implications. However, the resolution of the case did not yield new insights into the legal treatment of self-determination. Ultimately, despite the case's significance, the issue of self-determination remained outside the formal scope of international law.

The significance of self-determination during the interwar period is underscored by its appropriation by various actors, including those with ignoble intentions. Notably, the Nazi regime's use of the term 'self-determination' in the 1930s was particularly consequential. The Nazis argued that freedom would be violated if the natural development of a people were hindered by foreign powers. In practice, the Nazi regime invoked self-determination to justify its expansionist ambitions, specifically by claiming the right to annex territories inhabited by ethnic Germans living outside Germany's borders.[129]

---

127 *Ibid.*

128 L. Hannikainen, 'The International Legal Basis of the Autonomy and Swedish Character of the Aland Islands' in M. Suksi (ed.) *Autonomy: Applications and Implications* (Brill 1998) 74–78.

129 S. S. Bates, *The Prostitution of Self-determination by Hitler in Austria* (M.A. Thesis, North Texas State College 1955) 1; J. Mason, 'National Self-determination and the Failure of International Institutions to Uphold Human Rights in the Twentieth Century' 6 *Off Campus: Seggau School of Thought* (2020) 69–72 (illustrates also the abuse of the right by Italian fascists, explores the ramifications of France's denial of the existence of national minorities, such as in Alsace-Lorraine, and generally condemns the policies of homogenization that national self-determination provoked). See also H. Arendt, *The Origins of Totalitarianism* (Harcourt 1951) 268.

Although the Nazi interpretation of self-determination garnered some attention, particularly in Western circles, it did not result in any shift in the international understanding of the concept. There was no substantial international discourse on the meaning of self-determination, nor was the language of self-determination incorporated into international treaties during that period.[130] However, the post-war era saw significant developments in the field of individual human rights, and it was in this context that the concept of self-determination re-emerged on the international stage.

2.2 *United Nations Era*

During World War II, self-determination gained renewed prominence and was notably reflected in the 1941 Atlantic Charter, which advocated for the freely expressed will of peoples and their right to choose their form of government. This principle was reiterated in subsequent declarations and agreements, such as the UN Declaration of 1942 and the Moscow Declaration of 1943.[131] The inclusion of self-determination in the UN Charter at the 1945 San Francisco Conference, however, proved contentious. Drafters employed intentionally vague language to reconcile conflicting views – a compromise that invited divergent interpretations but ultimately secured its codification in Article 1(2), affirming the 'equal rights and self-determination of peoples'.[132] This formulation significantly influenced the treatment of Trust and Non-Self-Governing Territories. Article 76(b) outlines that the international trusteeship system aims to advance the political, economic, social, and educational development of trust territories, guiding them progressively toward self-government or independence, according to their specific circumstances and the wishes of their people.[133] Therefore, independence was recognized as a possible outcome, but only after the gradual development of the inhabitants of trust territories had been achieved.

---

130 E. Hula, 'National Self-determination Reconsidered' 10 *Social Research* (1943) 1–3, (theorizing the future of national self-determination before the end of World War II, observed that the concept, as it was understood prior to World War II, had not progressed. This stagnation was particularly evident given the constraints imposed by Article 2 of the Atlantic Charter, which stipulated that no territorial changes would occur without the consent of the people concerned, and by Article 3, which prioritized the restoration of sovereignty to conquered states).

131 Study Prepared by A. Cristescu (n 4) para 93.

132 Charter of the United Nations (24 Oct. 1945) XV UNCIO 335, amendments in 557 UNTS 143, 638 UNTS 308 and 892 UNTS 119, Article 1.

133 *Ibid.* Article 76(b).

While the UN Charter codified the principle of self-determination, it left significant questions unanswered, such as who qualifies as a 'people' and whether the principle extends beyond anti-colonial efforts to include groups with secessionist aspirations.[134] Despite this ambiguity, the Charter represented a critical milestone by establishing self-determination as a key objective of the United Nations, serving as a foundation for the development of friendly relations among nations.

In the subsequent decades, the norm of self-determination was further clarified through General Assembly resolutions, particularly in the context of decolonization. Among these, Resolution 1514, entitled 'Declaration on the Granting of Independence to Colonial Countries and Peoples' played a pivotal role in dismantling colonialism and advancing self-determination. The Declaration affirms that the imposition of foreign domination, subjugation, or exploitation upon peoples constitutes a breach of fundamental human rights, contravenes the UN Charter, and obstructs global peace and cooperation. By explicitly invoking the notion of a 'right' in paragraph 2, the Declaration effectively elevated self-determination from a guiding principle to a legally recognized entitlement.[135] Paragraph 5 envisions immediate steps in Non-Self-Governing Territories and Trust Territories – indeed in all territories yet to achieve independence – to transfer power to the people of those territories. Such a transfer must be unconditional, in accordance with the freely expressed desires and needs of the people, and free from discrimination based on race, religion or colour.

A day later, the General Assembly adopted Resolution 1541, which further elaborated the practical implementation of self-determination. Principle VI delineates that a Non-Self-Governing Territory achieves full self-government through either: (a) becoming a sovereign independent State, (b) freely associating with an independent State, or (c) integrating with an independent State.[136] This articulation of external self-determination focuses on the international legal status of territories and their peoples. The ordering of the three options, with independence listed first, may suggest a normative preference

134 C. Eagleton, 'Self-determination in the United Nations' 47(1) *AJIL:* Editorial Comment (1953) 88–93 (where he observed that similar indeterminacy pertains to Article 76(b) – who will decide when the NSGT is 'ready to go'? The Comment also provides insights for varying interpretations of the concept of self-determination, which associated it with non-aggression, non-intervention, conceptualized it as the right of individuals or 'all' people, but also as an excuse for nationalization).

135 UNGA Res 1514 (n 10), para 2 (All peoples have the *right to self-determination; by virtue of that right* ...).

136 UNGA Res 1541 (n 10) Principle VI.

for this pathway, especially within the decolonization context.[137] Principles VII and IX reinforce that both free association and integration must result from the freely expressed and voluntary choice of the people concerned, implying the centrality of impartial democratic processes.

The adoption of such resolutions in the General Assembly, rather than the Security Council, was a tactical decision to bypass potential vetoes from colonial powers. Likewise, the use of soft law instruments reflected a deliberate strategy to secure widespread support while minimizing resistance.

Collectively, the revolutionary Declaration on Decolonization (Resolution 1514), the framework of Resolution 1541, and later the authoritative Declaration on Friendly Relations contributed significantly to the progressive development of the right to self-determination under international law.

In the decolonization era, the emphasis was primarily on the external aspect of the right to self-determination, focusing on the right of oppressed, colonized peoples to establish their own states. In recent decades, however, state practice, along with legal and political documents, has increasingly underscored the importance of the internal dimension of the right to self-determination, particularly concerning the relationship between a people and its government.

On the day of the adoption of the Universal Declaration of Human Rights (UDHR) in 1948, the UN General Assembly requested that the Commission on Human Rights 'continue to give priority in its work to the preparation of a draft Covenant on Human Rights and draft measures of implementation'.[138] Following an extended drafting process, the General Assembly unanimously adopted the International Covenant on Economic, Social and Cultural Rights and the International Covenant on Civil and Political Rights in December 1966. These Covenants serve as foundational instruments for internal self-determination, affirming the rights to political participation, internal autonomy, and representative governance. Both treaties amplified the influence of the UDHR, and sought to establish political, economic, social and cultural rights as peremptory norms of international law.[139]

The right to self-determination is enshrined in Article 1(1), which is common to both Covenants and reads: 'All peoples have the right of self-determination. By virtue of that right they freely determine their political status and freely

---

137 See R. McCorquodale, 'Self-determination: A Human Rights Approach' 43(4) *International and Comparative Law Quarterly* (1994) 863–864; Raič (n 17) 289; D. Thürer and T. Burri, 'Secession' *Max Planck Encyclopedias of Public International Law* (2009) para 24.

138 Cited after H. Hannum, 'Rethinking Self Determination' 34(1) *Virginia Journal of International Law* (1993) 17–18.

139 Anderson (n 109) 1212.

pursue their economic, social and cultural development.' While the provision does not clearly delineate the scope or specific contexts in which the right applies, it is frequently cited as evidence of the universality of the right to self-determination, as it unequivocally affirms that 'all peoples' are entitled to this right.[140] The phrase 'all peoples', combined with the fact that these are human rights instruments intended for universal application, strongly suggests that the right to self-determination extends beyond the context of decolonization.[141]

Of equal significance is the second paragraph of Article 1, which accentuates the people's entitlement to manage their natural resources. It states that all peoples have the liberty to utilize their natural wealth and resources for their own purposes, with due consideration to international economic cooperation obligations, premised on mutual benefit and compliance with international law. Importantly, no people should ever be denied access to their essential means of subsistence. The principle of equal rights would be undermined if only certain categories of people had the right to freely manage their natural resources.[142]

The third paragraph of the common Article 1 also supports this interpretation, as it states that the parties of this Covenant, including those responsible for managing Non-Self-Governing Territories and Trust Territories, are obliged to facilitate the realization of the people's right to self-determination and to respect this right pursuant to the provisions of the UN Charter. A distinct emphasis laid on the obligation to foster the right to self-determination also by those states responsible for managing Non-Self-Governing and Trust Territories suggests that self-determination is not only related to colonial situations. This view has been reinforced by the Human Rights Committee in the already mentioned General Comment No. 12.[143]

During the drafting of the Covenants, various proposals were submitted regarding the definition of a 'people' for the purposes of self-determination. Ultimately, it was suggested that the term should be understood in its broadest

140 R. Emerson, 'Self-determination' 65 *AJIL* (1971) 463; T. Gadkowski, 'The Principle of Self-determination in the Context of Human Rights' 7 *Adam Mickiewicz University Law Review* (2017) 28–29.

141 Raič (n 17) 228; Hannum, 'Rethinking Self Determination' (n 138) 18; R. Rosenstock, 'The Declaration of Principles of International Law Concerning Friendly Relations: A Survey' 65(5) *AJIL* (1971) 731; A. Rosas, 'Internal Self-determination' in C. Tomuschat (ed.) *Modern Law and Self Determination* (Martinus Nijhoff Publishers 1993) 225–283.

142 H. Quane, 'The United Nations and the Evolving Right to Self Determination' 3 *International and Comparative Law Quarterly* (1998) 559.

143 Human Rights Committee, General Comment No. 12 (n 6) para 6 (note the phrase 'vis-à-vis all peoples').

sense, and that a precise definition might not be necessary for the principle to achieve its objectives.[144]

This raises the question of whether the formulation of self-determination in the International Covenants on Human Rights has formed a new legal construct consistent with general international law, or whether it is a particular institute related to the field of human rights. This dilemma chiefly centres on the understanding of the element of free political self-determination.[145] Specifically, it examines whether the right to self-determination, as articulated in the Covenants, is limited to internal political organization (i.e. the right to decide within which state the people wish to live, or political self-determination), or whether it also encompasses the right to establish a new independent and sovereign entity (i.e. territorial self-determination).[146] The drafting history of the Covenants suggests that internal self-determination was intended to be a standard and integral component of the right. In contrast, the application of external self-determination, which involves establishing a new state, is treated as an exceptional circumstance, to be assessed in conjunction with other legal principles.[147]

One of the key milestones in advancing the modern concept of the people's right to self-determination was the adoption of the Friendly Relations Declaration on 24 October 1970. The General Assembly adopted the Declaration almost unanimously as Resolution 2625 (XXV). Despite its legally non-binding nature, the Friendly Relations Declaration is now generally seen as the most authoritative expression of the scope and meaning of the basic principles of the international legal order. Its significance is further underscored by the fact that it was adopted by acclamation (without a vote), and therefore it can be said to reflect the *opinio juris* of states. Moreover, this Declaration is often cited as a rare example of so-called 'instant custom', i.e. a custom that forms in a relatively short time. It is maintained that that the unanimous expression of *opinio juris* by the international community regarding a number of core principles of international law was sufficient to generate customary norms, even in

---

144 Study Prepared by A. Cristescu (n 4) paras 44, 274, 278.

145 T. Šurlan, 'Savremena Primena i Tumačenje Pravnih Instituta: Samoopredeljenje i Secesija sa Stanovišta Međunarodnog Javnog Prava' in Z. Knežević and K. Čavoški (eds.) *Secesija sa Stanovišta Unutrašnjeg i Međunarodnog Prava i Njene Političke Posledice* (Serbian Academy of Sciences and Arts 2020) 112.

146 A. Cassese, 'Political Self-determination – Old Concepts and New Developments' in A. Cassese (ed.) *UN Law-Fundamental Rights: Two Topics in International Law* (Sijthoff & Noordhoff 1979) 141–143.

147 Raič (n 17) 234.

the absence of corresponding state practice.[148] The right to self-determination is articulated in Principle v of the Declaration as follows

> By virtue of the principle of equal rights and self-determination of peoples enshrined in the Charter of the United Nations, all peoples have the right freely to determine, without external interference, their political status and to pursue their economic, social and cultural development, and every State has the duty to respect this right in accordance with the provisions of the Charter.[149]

The Declaration recognizes the right to self-determination for *all* peoples, implying that the principle is universally applicable. This interpretation is supported by the fact that the principle is included in a declaration intended to govern relations among all states. Further confirmation of this claim is found in the preparatory work on the Declaration, where the drafting committee concluded that the Declaration should reflect the universal applicability of its principles. Several states explicitly emphasized the universal applicability of the right to self-determination during these deliberations. Accordingly, taking into account the text of the Declaration, its normative context, and the drafting history, it can be concluded that the right to self-determination is intended to apply to all peoples.[150]

In addition to the fact that self-determination applies to all nations, it also represents a continued obligation for existing states. Paragraph 7 of Principle v points out:

> Nothing in the foregoing paragraphs shall be construed as authorizing or encouraging any action which would dismember or impair, totally or in part, the territorial integrity or political unity of sovereign and independent States conducting themselves in compliance with the principle of equal rights and self-determination of peoples as described above and thus possessed of a government representing the whole people belonging to the territory without distinction as to race, creed or colour.[151]

---

148 Statement of Principles Applicable to the Formation of General Customary International Law' by the Committee on Formation of Customary (General) International Law of the International Law Association (London Conference 2000) 40; ICJ, *Military and Paramilitary Activities in and against Nicaragua* (*Nicaragua v. United States of America*), Judgment, ICJ Rep. 1986, para 188.

149 UNGA Res 2625 (n 21) Principle v, paragraph 1.

150 Quane, 'The United Nations' (n 142) 562–563.

151 UNGA Res 2625 (n 21) Principle v, paragraph 7.

This is the so-called 'safeguard clause', which will be dealt with more thoroughly when considering the existence of the 'right' to remedial secession. Principle v makes it clear that the right to self-determination does not cease upon the attainment of independence, as it links self-determination to the internal commitment of 'a government representing the whole people belonging to the territory without distinction as to race, creed or colour'.[152] The inclusion of this phrase was directly related to the international community's concerns at the time of the drafting of the Declaration, particularly regarding the apartheid regime in South Africa and the rule of the white minority in South Rhodesia (now Zimbabwe), where non-white majority populations were denied the right to representative government. Taking into account the aforementioned phrase and the preparatory work on the Declaration, it is evident that, like the 1966 Covenants, the Declaration was intended for universal application, extending beyond colonial contexts. Some states expressed fears that the inclusion of Principle v in the Declaration would encourage the progressive development of a right to self-determination that could encompass secession.[153] Consequently, the Declaration stressed the importance of the principles of territorial integrity and political unity of sovereign and independent states. However, secession was not explicitly excluded either. This prompted a significant number of authors to conclude that the Friendly Relations Declaration actually have opened the door to the possibility of unilateral secession.

The Declaration distinguishes between the external and internal forms of the right to self-determination. The existence of a representative government is key to the realization of the right to internal self-determination. Principle v outlines the ways in which the right of peoples to self-determination can be achieved, including:

1. The establishment of a sovereign and independent State,
2. The free association or integration with an independent State; or
3. The emergence into any other political status freely determined by a people.[154]

This represents an external dimension of the right to self-determination, though it can also be interpreted more broadly to suggest that the political order, as determined by the will of the people, may include forms of self-government or autonomy as expressions of internal self-determination.

---

152 See Raič (n 17) 230.

153 Quane, 'The United Nations' (n 142) 564; Cassese, *Self-determination of Peoples* (n 19) 288–289.

154 UNGA Res 2625 (n 21) Principle v, paragraph 4.

The physiognomy of the right to self-determination adopted in the 1970 Friendly Relations Declaration was reaffirmed by the Helsinki Final Act of 1975.[155] The Helsinki Final Act clearly distinguishes between internal and external variants of self-determination, serving as a compromise between the socialist states and the Western bloc. The socialist states advocated for the inclusion of the RSD in the document, interpreting it as both a colonial right and a principle of non-intervention. In contrast, the Western states supported a broader conception of self-determination, emphasizing the democratization of states.[156] Principle VIII by providing that 'all peoples always have the right, in full freedom, to determine' underlines its universality and continuity. At the same time, it introduces the idea of 'internal' freedom allowing for the adaptation of existing social and political structures to meet new demands.[157]

Equally significant is the Vienna Declaration and Programme of Action, adopted at the 1993 World Conference on Human Rights. The Vienna Declaration addresses self-determination in Article 2, reiterating the language of the Friendly Relations Declaration.[158] When viewed through the lens of this article, one might conclude that it endorses a comprehensive right to self-determination, applicable in both internal and external contexts.[159] However, subsequent provisions reflect a more traditional approach, addressing the situation of peoples under colonial or foreign domination, and underscore the importance of preventing violations of territorial integrity. Paragraph 2 acknowledges that in specific circumstances involving peoples living under colonial or other forms of foreign domination or occupation, the World Conference on Human Rights recognizes their right to pursue legitimate actions, in accordance with the United Nations Charter, to achieve their inherent right to self-determination. The Conference further asserts that the denial of the right to self-determination constitutes a violation of human rights and emphasizes the critical importance of ensuring the effective realization of this right. While the Declaration stresses the situation of colonial peoples and those under foreign domination, it does not imply that the right to self-determination is limited to these contexts – it applies universally to all peoples within states. The

155 A. Cassese, 'The Helsinki Declaration and Self-determination' in T. Buergenthal (ed.) *Human Rights, International Law and the Helsinki Accord* (Montclair, N.J. Allanheld, Osmun & Co 1977).

156 A. Cassese, 'The Approach of the Helsinki Declaration to Human Rights' 13(2) *Vanderbilt Journal of Transnational Law* (1980) 284.

157 Conference on Security and Co-operation in Europe (CSCE): Final Act of Helsinki (1 Aug. 1975) reprinted in 14 *ILM* (1975) 1293–1325, Principle VIII.

158 Vienna Declaration (n 5), Article 2.

159 Hilpold, 'Self Determination in the 21st Century' (n 9) 273.

Declaration, by stating that 'the denial of the right of self-determination is a violation of human rights', affirms that human rights extend beyond colonial peoples alone.

Finally, a mention should be made to a significant auxiliary source of the RSD – the jurisprudence of the International Court of Justice, which has greatly contributed to the crystallization of the right, but also its positioning within the corpus of norms with *erga omnes* effect.[160] This review of the normative framework underscores the enduring relevance of the right to self-determination, applicable to all peoples, not solely those that were colonized or oppressed in the context of historical imperialism. Moreover, the legal framework explicitly distinguishes between the internal and external dimensions of this right, a distinction that will be explored in greater detail below.

3 Two Main Aspects of the Right to Self-determination

It is largely indisputable that the right to self-determination has two aspects: the internal and the external. The internal aspect can be summarized as the right of a people to govern themselves without external interference, while the external aspect refers to the right of a people to determine their own political status on the international stage. So, if we are talking about internal self-determination, it is about achieving self-determination within the borders of the existing state. In the case of external self-determination, however, we are talking about achieving self-determination in relation to other peoples and states.[161] Or, as Mustafa put it, the internal aspect denotes the right of a people of an already recognized state to choose their government, whereas the external aspect implies the right to determine their nationality or statehood.[162] However, it should be noted that this division does not mean that there are two different rights to self-determination. It is just about different forms of achieving the same right. Šurlan correctly remarked that both aspects of the right to self-determination – internal and external – enable the expression of the peoples' will, both domestically and internationally. Domestically, this entails

160 *East Timor* (n 2) para 29; *Construction of a Wall* (n 3) paras 155–156; *Chagos Archipelago* (n 3) para 180.

161 P. Thornberry, 'The Democratic or Internal Aspect of Self-determination with Some Remarks on Federalism' in C. Tomuschat (ed.) *Modern Law of Self-determination* (Martinus Nijhoff 1993) 101.

162 Mustafa (n 46) 479.

determining *what* kind of state they wish to live in, whereas internationally, it pertains to *which* state they wish to belong to.[163]

The report from the UNESCO International Conference of Experts, titled 'The Implementation of the Right to Self-determination as a Contribution to Conflict Prevention' defines the two aspects of the right to self-determination in the following way:

> By internal self-determination is meant participatory democracy: the right to decide the form of government and the identity of rulers by the whole population of a state and the right of a population group within the state to participate in decision making at the state level. Internal self-determination can also mean the right to exercise cultural, linguistic, religious or (territorial) political autonomy within the boundaries of the existing state.
>
> By external self-determination (described by some as "full" self-determination) is meant the right to decide on the political status of a people and its place in the international community in relation to other states, including the right to separate from the existing state of which the group concerned is a part, and to set up a new independent state.[164]

The Committee for the Elimination of Racial Discrimination, when considering the right to self-determination in the context of racial discrimination, also highlighted two aspects of this right:

> In respect of the self-determination of peoples two aspects have to be distinguished. The right to self-determination of peoples has an internal aspect, i.e. the rights of all peoples to pursue freely their economic, social and cultural development without outside interference. In that respect there exists a link with the right of every citizen to take part in the conduct of public affairs at any level as referred to in article 5(c) of the International Convention on the Elimination of All Forms of Racial Discrimination. In consequence, governments are to represent the whole population without distinction as to race, colour, decent, national, or ethnic origins. The external aspect of self-determination implies that all

163 Šurlan (n 145) 105–133.

164 UNESCO, 'The Implementation of the Right to Self Determination as a Contribution to Conflict Prevention; report of the International conference of experts held in Barcelona from 21 to 27 November 1998' (1999).

> peoples have the right to determine freely their political status and their place in the international community based upon the principle of equal rights and exemplified by the liberation of peoples from colonialism and by the prohibition to subject peoples to alien subjugation, domination, and exploitation.[165]

The accentuation of the two forms of the right to self-determination has mostly been employed to illustrate the political content of the right in various contexts and to rebuff the claim of linking self-determination solely with colonial independence.[166] Internal self-determination in normative terms rests on the UN Charter and International Covenants on Human Rights, while external self-determination is based on the UN Charter and the 1970 Friendly Relations Declaration. The political entitlements of both aspects of the right to self-determination are different and it is necessary to consider them also in view of determining the positive law status of the norm.[167]

3.1 *External Self-determination*

External self-determination (ESD) is conventionally associated with colonial independence. Indeed, it is where international law indisputably grants people the right to liberation from domination.[168] The position of colonies and other Non-Self-Governing Territories (NSGT), as well as the decolonization process in general, is outlined in Chapter XI of the UN Charter, titled 'The Declaration regarding Non-Self-Governing Territories', Chapter XII, titled 'International Trusteeship System', and Chapter XIII, titled 'the Trusteeship Council'. Unlike the softer and somewhat vague language in Article 1(2) of the Charter, Article 76 clearly indicates that one of the goals of the trusteeship system is to promote 'progressive development towards self-government or independence' for the populations of territories under trusteeship.

The 1960 Declaration on the Granting of Independence to Colonial Countries and Peoples established the basis for the self-determination of peoples under colonial domination. Here, the right to self-determination implies the right of these people to free themselves from foreign dominance and to gain independence, if necessary, through the use of force. States, on the other hand,

165 Committee on the Elimination of Racial Discrimination, 'General Recommendation 21, The right to self-determination' (8 Mar. 1996) para 4.

166 The ICJ in the *Chagos* AO asserted that it 'is conscious that the right to self-determination, as a fundamental human right, has a broad scope of application'. *Chagos Archipelago* (n 3) para 144.

167 More on the content of the right to self-determination in section 2.5.1.

168 B. Rakić, *Srbija Pred Svetskim Sudom* (Pravni Fakultet, Sluzbeni Glasnik 2009) 57.

have the obligation not to suppress such independence movements.[169] This entitlement, including the legitimacy of using force, is further supported by cyclic General Assembly resolutions titled 'Importance of the universal realization of the right of peoples to self-determination and of the speedy granting of independence to colonial countries and peoples for the effective guarantee and observance of human rights'.[170] In paragraph 2 of these resolutions, the General Assembly affirms 'the legitimacy of the people's struggle for independence, territorial integrity, national unity and liberation from colonial domination, apartheid and foreign occupation, by all available means, including armed struggle'.[171]

It should be noted that the exercise of the right to self-determination by colonial peoples and other Non-Self-Governing Territories, through their acquisition of independence, does not violate the territorial integrity of the administering states.[172] The Friendly Relations Declaration clearly stipulates that the territory of a colony or other Non-Self-Governing Territory, in accordance with the Charter, holds a separate and distinct status from the state that governs it. This separate status remains 'until the people of the colony or Non-Self-Governing Territory have exercised their right of self-determination in accordance with the Charter, and particularly its purposes and principles'. Also, Article 74 of Chapter XI of the UN Charter indicates that Non-Self-Governing Territories and the territories of their metropolis are treated as separate entities. Therefore, in this context, independence is not synonymous with the violation of territorial integrity. Instead, it signifies the cessation of the administering state's control, not the forfeiture of ownership, as legal ownership never existed.

The legal entitlement and legitimacy of independence is not confined to colonial peoples and those inhabiting NSGT, but extends to all peoples who find themselves in a state of 'alien subjugation, domination and exploitation'.[173] This form of achieving external self-determination is

---

169 The practice of using mercenaries against national liberation movements in the colonial Territories was termed as 'a criminal act' by the General Assembly. UNGA Res 3103 (XXVIII) (12 Dec. 1973).

170 See e.g. resolutions 3070 (XXVIII) (30 Nov. 1973), 3246 (XXIX) (29 Nov. 1974), 45/130 (14 Dec. 1990).

171 *Ibid.* See also UNGA Res 3103(XXVIII) 'Basic principles of the legal status of the combatants struggling against colonial and alien domination and racist regimes' (12 Dec. 1973).

172 Rakić (n 168) 59.

173 J. Klabbers and R. Lefeber, 'Africa: Lost between Self-determination and Uti Possidetis' in C. Brölmann, R. Lefeber and M. Zieck (eds.) *Peoples and Minorities in International Law* (Martinus Nijhoff Publishers 1993) 41. See also *Reference re Secession of Quebec* (n 13) para 133.

mentioned in the Decolonization Declaration (1960), the Friendly Relations Declaration (1970) and the Declaration on the Occasion of the 50th Anniversary of the United Nations (1995).[174] Nevertheless, legal practice has constantly interpreted the 'alien subjugation, domination and exploitation' tripartite formula primarily in connection with the era of colonialism, with the notable exception of foreign military occupation. For example, in the *Kosovo* Advisory Opinion, the ICJ stated that it remains contentious

> whether outside the context of non-self-governing territories and peoples subject to alien subjugation, domination and exploitation, the international law of self-determination confers upon part of the population of an existing State a right to separate from that State.[175]

This statement exemplifies the contemporary reluctance to apply the tripartite formulation to cases involving oppressed minorities.[176] Authors who are inclined towards a broader application of the phrase have been cautious in pronouncing a separate legal entitlement, typically referring to either racist regimes or 'colonial-style' domination.[177] While there is ongoing debate about whether internal oppression of sub-groups can justify external self-determination (with the prevailing view being that oppression of a state's 'own' citizens does not), it is clear that the right to independence remains unequivocal in situations of total (e.g. Kuwait in 1990) or partial (e.g. Ukraine in 2022) annexation.[178] In such cases, independence and the right to external self-determination may be defended and reasserted by all available means, including armed struggle. Therefore, as in cases of emancipation from colonial domination, the exercise of self-determination in the context of foreign occupation does not conflict with the principle of preserving territorial integrity, as

174 See also Article 1, Paragraph 4 of Protocol Additional to the Geneva Conventions of 12 August 1949 and relating to the Protection of Victims of International Armed Conflicts (Protocol I) (8 Jun. 1977).

175 ICJ, *Accordance with International Law of the Unilateral Declaration of Independence in Respect of Kosovo,* Advisory Opinion, ICJ Rep. 2010, para 82.

176 Cf. Separate Opinions of Judge Yusuf, paras 7, 11–12; Judge Cancado Trinidade, para 208.

177 Ahmed (n 13) 227–230; H. Gros-Espiell, *The Right to Self-determination: Implementation of United Nations Resolutions: Study* (United Nations 1980) 10, 14; M. Shaw, 'Peoples, Territorialism and Boundaries' 8(3) *EJIL* (1997) 478, 512.

178 'Annexation is nothing less than the negation of the new law of self-determination'. ICJ, *Legal Consequences for States of the Continued Presence of South Africa in Namibia (South West Africa) Notwithstanding Security Council Resolution 276 (1970)*, Advisory Opinion, ICJ Rep. 1971 (Judge Ammoun, concurring) 91.

legally, the occupied territory is not considered an integral part of the occupying power's territory.[179]

Independence is the most illustrious and preferred way of achieving external self-determination, however, other political status options remain available to the inhabitants.[180] As the Friendly Relations Declaration notes, self-determination may be implemented by 'the establishment of a sovereign and independent State, the free association or integration with an independent State or the emergence into any other political status freely determined by a people'. Still, it is highly doubtful whether, in any scenario other than a sovereign state, people can determine on an equal footing with other states and, most importantly, whether they can 'determine' unchaperoned. If, however, the essence of the right lies solely in the *opportunity* to choose a political status different from the existing one, then it becomes irrelevant whether the people concerned co-determine with others in the case of a union or merger, or self-determine internally if they choose that option. A mere choice, therefore, does not necessarily yield the benefits of a total cut-off from the previous umbilical cord and may result in the people concerned remaining in a similar position. This is why independence has been the most advanced scenario in the decolonization process.[181]

It is otherwise uncontroversial that colonial peoples, as well as the populations of independent states, retain the right to alter their existing political and territorial status, while the same cannot be said for sub-groups within a state, who, instead, enjoy internal self-determination.[182]

3.2 *Internal Self-determination*

The idea of the right of a people to internal self-determination is hailed as a post-WWII occurrence, which has gained particular momentum in recent

---

179 Rakić (n 168) 62.

180 Note that the primary responsibility of implementing decolonization, apart from the administering Powers, is vested institutionally in the C-24 Committee, officially known as the Special Committee on the Situation with Regard to the Implementation of the Granting of the Independence to Colonial Countries and Peoples. The name of the Committee is intuitive. See UNGA Res 1654 (XVI) (27 Nov. 1961).

181 In resolution 45/130, General Assembly 'welcomed the independence of Namibia'. In its annual resolution 'Universal realization of the right of peoples to self-determination' General Assembly in the second paragraph welcomes 'the progressive exercise of the right to self-determination by peoples under colonial, foreign or alien occupation and their emergence into *sovereign statehood and independence*' (emphasis added). See UNGA Res 76/152 (16 Dec. 2021) and all previous ones.

182 UNESCO, International Meeting of Experts 'Further Study of the Concept of the Rights of Peoples' Final Report and Recommendations (22 Feb. 1990) UNESCO Doc SHS-89/CONF.602/7, para 5.

years.[183] Arguably, its main rationale is to counterbalance the perceived danger of associating self-determination exclusively with bestowing independence upon a vast number of recipients.[184] Nonetheless, some scholars have doubted the existence of ISD or even opposed it.[185] In 1988, Hannikainen argued that 'the international community of states has not really required the realization of internal self-determination within existing states'.[186] Similarly, Tomuschat expressed scepticism about whether understanding self-determination as internal self-determination has achieved widespread acceptance.[187] Perkowski suggested that internal self-determination might either be subsumed under the notion of state sovereignty or viewed as a tool for the 'creation' of a sovereign and democratic state, particularly in multi-ethnic contexts.[188] Despite these critiques, the practice of states and prevailing legal doctrine largely support the separate existence of internal self-determination, which, as noted, aligns with the modern trend of curtailing state sovereignty in favour of protecting human rights, and serves a counterbalance to secessionist claims.[189]

It is reasonable to assert that the International Court of Justice encapsulated the essence of the RSD in its advisory opinion on *Western Sahara*, where it stressed 'the need to pay regard to the freely expressed will' of the people.[190]

---

183 Summers associates internal self-determination with Indonesia's independence in 1949 but notes its earlier presence in the 1920 advisory opinion of the International Committee of Jurists on the Åland Islands question. J. Summers, 'The Internal and External Aspects of Self-determination Reconsidered' in D. French (ed.) *Statehood and Self-determination Reconciling Tradition and Modernity in International Law* (CUP 2013) 230.

184 G. Fox, 'Self-determination in the Post-Cold War Era: A New Internal Focus?' 16(3) *Michigan Journal of International Law* (1995) 754.

185 Rosas, 'Internal Self-determination' (n 141) 228.

186 L. Hannikainen, *Peremptory Norms (Jus Cogens) in International Law: Historical Development, Criteria, Present Status* (Finnish Lawyers' Publishing Company 1988) 357.

187 C. Tomuschat, 'Democratic Pluralism. The Right to Political Opposition' in A. Rosas and J. Helgesen (eds.) *The Strength of Diversity: Human Rights and Pluralist Democracy* (Kluwer Law International 1992) 39.

188 M. Perkowski, *Samostanowienie Narodów w Prawie Międzynarodowym* (PWN 2001) 73. See also J. Tyranowski, *Integralność Terytorialna, Nienaruszalność Granic i Samostanowienie w Prawie Międzynarodowym* (PWN 1990) 283.

189 See, among others, H. Johnson, *Self-determination within the Community of Nations* (A. W. Sijthoff 1967) 28; Cassese, *Self-determination of Peoples* (n 19) 5 ff; Raič (n 17) 226–307; M. Pomerance, *Self-determination in Law and Practice: The New Doctrine of the United Nations* (Martinus Nijhoff 1982) 37–42; McCorquodale, 'Self-determination (n 137) 863–865; U. O. Umozurike, *Self-determination in International Law* (Archon Books 1972) 1; K. Henrard, *Devising an Adequate System of Minority Protection: Individual Human Rights, Minority Rights and the Right to Self-determination* (Martinus Nijhoff 2000) 281, 299–301.

190 ICJ, *Western Sahara*, Advisory Opinion, ICJ Rep. 1975, para 59. It must though be noted that this remark of the Court refers to dependent territories. See also Cassese, *Self-*

This implies that any decision impacting the inhabitants of a specific territory must be made in accordance with 'the free and genuine expression of the will of the people concerned'.[191] Stated differently, the will of the people should remain unconstrained, both by internal and external forces, whether during their pursuit of an external status or within already established states. Relatedly, the UN Declaration on the Rights of Indigenous People underscores the principle of 'free, prior and informed consent', which features in Articles 10–11, 19, 28–29 and 32, and relates to all crucial aspects of indigenous peoples' lives.[192] Consequently, freedom and non-intervention are essential prerequisites of internal self-determination (ISD).[193] It is obvious that fomenting internal strikes or trying to direct or impose specific ways of behaviour, especially by utilizing threats, force or other coercive measures, would stand in clear contradiction with the 'free will' underpinning internal self-determination.[194] For example, the Soviet interventions in Hungary in 1956 and Czechoslovakia in 1968, or more recently the Russian intervention in Ukraine, represent outright violations of the principle of non-intervention in domestic affairs, thereby breaching the right to internal self-determination.[195] Moscow has not denied its commitment to self-determination but seemed to treat it 'with gradation'. Put plainly, during the Cold War, if the socialist system was undermined or its national security threatened – as was allegedly the case with Ukraine more recently – these considerations took precedence over internal

determination of Peoples (n 19) 89, 128; Rosas, 'Internal Self-determination' (n 141) 232–236; S. F. Van den Driest, *Remedial Secession: A Right to External Self-determination as a Remedy to Serious Injustice* (Intersentia 2013) 50.

191 *Western Sahara* (n 190) para 55. Consult UNSC Res 2703 (30 Oct. 2023) speaking of a 'mutually acceptable political solution, based on compromise, which will provide for the self-determination of the people of Western Sahara in the context of arrangements consistent with the principles and purposes of the Charter of the United Nations'.

192 UNGA Res 61/295 'United Nations Declaration on the Rights of Indigenous Peoples' (13 Sep. 2007). See also HRC, Study of the Expert Mechanism on the Rights of Indigenous Peoples 'Free, prior and informed consent: a human rights-based approach' (10 Aug. 2018) UN Doc. A/HRC/39/62, para 14.

193 Senese contends that internal self-determination can only be exercised in independent states. S. Senese, 'External and Internal Self-determination' 16(1) *Social Justice* (1989) 19.

194 UN Secretary-General considered the use of private security contractors to limit and prohibit people's right to liberty and free movement through deprivation of liberty as a means of deliberately undermining a people's right to self-determination. See 'Report of the Working Group on the use of mercenaries as a means of violating human rights and impeding the exercise of the right of peoples to self-determination' (17 Oct. 2023) UN Doc. A/78/535.

195 S. Janković and V. Roeben, 'The Threat of Russia's Force in Ukraine' 11 *Journal on the Use of Force and International Law* (2024) 87–107.

self-determination. The United States, in a similar manner, has attempted to exert influence on foreign populations and introduce systems favorable to its interests. One such example is President Johnson's declaration during the crisis in the Dominican Republic: 'the American nations cannot, must not, and will not permit the establishment of another Communist government in the Western Hemisphere'.[196] Such arguments are legally indefensible as they contradict the principles of sovereignty and equality of states and the supposed freedom derived from them. A corollary of the non-intervention principle is the right to freely express domestic intentions and interests in the international arena. In this regard, states, as representatives of their people, should be able to freely conclude treaties, join international organizations, and nominate their representatives to other countries and institutions.[197]

There exists, however, a second, equally meaningful apprehension of internal self-determination, which is grounded in the relationship between the people and the state or, more precisely, its government. Within this understanding of ISD, the government must ensure that all people under its authority have impartial chances to develop politically, socially, culturally and economically – an aspect that is particularly relevant for minorities. According to Brownlie, the essence of internal self-determination lies in the right of a community with a distinct character 'to have this character reflected in the institutions of government under which it lives'.[198] Power-sharing, equality, solidarity and non-discrimination thus form the another linchpin of ISD.[199] In *Diergaardt et al. v. Namibia,* the Human Rights Committee explicitly linked the right to self-determination with Articles 26 and 27 of the ICCPR treating about the equality before the law of all persons, irrespective of their race, political or other opinion, national or social origin, property, birth, or other status, and imposing an obligation on states to respect religious, cultural and linguistic rights

---

196 U.S. General Services Administration, 'Public Papers of the President: Lyndon Baines Johnson, 1965' (Washington, DC: Government Printing Office 1966) 469- 474.

197 Article 52 of the VCLT gives no effect to treaties concluded under coercion. Consult T. Christiano, 'Self-determination and the Human Right to Democracy' in R. Cruft, M. Liao and M. Renzo (eds.) *Philosophical Foundations of Human Rights* (OUP 2015) 468 ff.

198 I. Brownlie, 'The Rights of Peoples in Modern International Law' in J. Crawford (ed.) *The Rights of Peoples* (Bulletin of the Australian Society of Legal Philosophy 1985) 107–108. Higgins advocated a majoritarian aspect: the right of self-determination should be defined as 'the right of a majority … to the exercise of power'. R. Higgins, *The Development of International Law Through the Political Organs of the United Nations* (OUP 1963) 104–105.

199 See OHCHR, 'Protecting Minority Rights – A Practical Guide to Developing Comprehensive Anti-Discrimination Legislation' (6 Dec. 2022) 122–200.

of minorities.[200] The European Court of Human Rights, on its part, found the constitutional framework of Bosnia and Herzegovina discriminatory, because it stipulated that only 'constituent people' – Croats, Serbs and Bosniaks – could run for election to certain governmental bodies, including the Presidency, while other citizens could not.[201] In this latter case, individual human rights might be said to limit the right to self-determination.

When considering relevant human rights instruments, one can get an impression that the recognition of the right to internal self-determination would require the establishment of a Western-style democratic system of government. That appears to be the view of the Human Rights Committee, which identifies peoples of the existing states as the beneficiaries of this right.[202] The Committee stressed that the individual rights to political participation provided by Article 25 of the ICCPR are related to the right to self-determination of the people (albeit different from it).[203] Admittedly, if the rights to direct and indirect participation in the conduct of public affairs are not secured, free choice is not possible, and there cannot be actual application of internal self-determination. Yet, democratic processes, and by extension, internal self-determination, not only presuppose the voting rights but also imply concomitant entitlements, such as the right to freedom of thought (Article 18 of the ICCPR), the right to peaceful assembly (Article 21 of the ICCPR), the right to freedom of association (Article 22 of the ICCPR) and the right to freedom of expression (Article 19 of the ICCPR). Without them real political participation is inconceivable.[204]

Hence, one author reasoned that the right to internal self-determination may call for the establishment of a democratic form of government – specifically, one in which political power rests on the will of the people, providing all citizens equal opportunity to participate in political life.[205] This view

200 Human Rights Committee, *J. G. A. Diergaardt et al. v. Namibia*, Communication No. 760/1997 (25 Jul. 2000) para 10.3.

201 ECtHR, *Sejdić and Finci v. Bosnia and Herzegovina*, Applications Nos. 27996/06 and 34836/06, Judgment (22 Dec. 2009) para 56.

202 J. Crawford, 'Democracy and the Body of International Law' in G. Fox and B. Roth (eds.) *Democratic Governance and International Law* (CUP 2000) 94–95.

203 Human Rights Committee, General Comment No. 25: The right to participate in public affairs, voting rights and the right of equal access to public service (12 Jul. 1996) para 25.

204 On political participation as a cornerstone of democratic governance see UNMIT, 'Democratic Governance' <https://unmit.unmissions.org/democratic-governance>. See also UNESCO, 'Further Study of the Concept of the Rights of Peoples' (n 182) para 27(a).

205 S. Wheatley, 'Democracy in International Law: A European Perspective' 51(2) *International and Comparative Law Quarterly* (2002) 232. Similarly, J. Crawford, *Democracy in International Law* (1994) 4. See also periodic state reports to the Human Rights Commit-

suggests that a system of democratic governance aligns with internal self-determination by enabling broad representation and participation. However, democracy should not be seen solely as the rule of the majority. Hilpold contends that in a genuine democracy that respects internal self-determination, safeguards must be in place to ensure that minority interests are considered with equal importance as those of the majority.[206] Jankov and Ćorić further observe that state practice frequently equates internal self-determination with democratic governance,[207] while Dimitrijević and Paunović similarly associate it with the democratization of the state and representative government.[208] For Perkowski, the fact of the equation of democratic standards with internal self-determination may, at first glance, seem at odds with the very essence of the right to self-determination but that presumption, he maintains, is illusory, as a democratic system is the only framework that contains mechanisms for genuine and free determination by the 'nation' of a broadly understood system of its country.[209]

While the argument for democratic governance as a pathway to internal self-determination is cogent, it does not imply that this governance model must mirror a Western-style democracy, particularly one based on periodic elections.[210] Imposing a specific political structure on a population contradicts the core of self-determination: the people's free choice. In this context, it is important to recognize that there is no particular generally accepted model of democracy.[211] As former UN Secretary-General Kofi Annan stated, democracy 'is not a model to be copied but a goal to be attained'.[212] Democracies indeed take different forms, encompassing various – more or less established – formats

tee, *inter alia* of the Republic of Korea (1 Nov. 1999) UN Doc. CCPR/C/114/Add 1, para 18 or Lesotho (7 Apr. 1999) UN Doc. CCPR/C/81/Add 14, paras 4–8.

206 Hilpold, *Autonomy and Self-determination* (n 57) 43.

207 F. Jankov and V. Ćorić, 'Uti Possidetis i Pravo na Samoopredeljenje' 13 *Pravni Život* (2007) 974.

208 V. Dimitrijević and M. Paunović, *Ljudska Prava – Udžbenik* (Beograd 1997) 397.

209 M. Perkowski, 'Forsowanie Samostanowienia We Współczesnej Europie. Uwagi Na Tle Przypadków Krymu i Katalonii' in M. Perkowski, J. Szymański and M. Zdanowicz (eds.) *Człowiek i Prawo Międzynarodowe. Księga dedykowana Profesorowi Bogdanowi Wierzbickiemu* (Temida 2014) 390.

210 See UNGA Res 54/168 'Respect for the principles of national sovereignty and non-interference in the internal affairs of States in their electoral processes' (17 Dec. 1999).

211 The UN Commission on Human Rights has recognised the 'rich and diverse nature of the community of the world's democracies'. UN Commission on Human Rights, 'Promotion of the right to democracy' (27 Apr. 1999).

212 UN Secretary-General, 'Support by the United Nations System of the Efforts of Governments to Promote and Consolidate New or Restored Democracies' (21 Oct. 1997) UN Doc. A/52/513, para 27.

of political participation and representation. Many regimes in the world are not similar to Western parliamentarianism, yet can be considered fairly representative of their people, conforming to their own social and historical traditions.[213] Apart from the fact that it is possible to collectively self-determine non-democratically if a group wishes so, it should be underlined that political representation depends on epistemological approaches to governance, and is present only where there exists irreducibly collective moral aspiration to political self-determination.[214] At times, passive citizenship may prove more beneficial than active participation. In any case, the concept of participation within the framework of self-determination should not be strictly looked at from the political angle, but rather understood in a broader societal context. This broader context also encompasses, for example, the right to development, as recognized in the 1986 Declaration on the Right to Development and the 1993 Vienna Declaration and Programme of Action.[215] Consequently, full respect for the political rights envisaged by the ICCPR should be seen as one *possible* way of realizing the internal dimension of the right to self-determination. Yet, the notion of democracy does not only boil down to the Western concept of multiparty political system. As long as the people are allowed to freely express their will and there are representative institutions that reflect that will, it can be said that ISD is respected and upheld.[216]

4 The Position of the Right to Self-determination in International Law

4.1 *Erga Omnes Character*

In the *Barcelona Traction* case, the ICJ established a firm distinction between the two sets of legal obligations.[217] *Erga omnes* obligations are those owed by a state to the international community as a whole. These obligations must be

---

213 J. Salmon, 'Internal Aspects of the Right to Self-determination: Towards a Democratic Legitimacy Principle?' in C. Tomuschat (ed.) *Modern Law of Self-determination* (Martinus Nijhoff 1993) 280.

214 A. Altman and C. Wellman, 'Self-Determination and Democracy' in *A Liberal Theory of International Justice* (OUP 2009) 17.

215 See A. Rosas, 'The Right to Development' in A. Eide, C. Krause and A. Rosas (eds.) *Economic, Social and Cultural Rights* (Brill 2001) 127–129.

216 J. Vidmar, *Democratic Statehood in International Law: The Emergence of New States in Post-Cold War Practice* (Hart 2013) 21, 141–151.

217 ICJ, *Barcelona Traction, Light and Power Company, Limited (Belgium v. Spain)*, Judgment, ICJ Rep. 1970.

fulfilled regardless of the conduct of other states in the same area. This contrasts with obligations that occur only in relations between individual states, which in nature are reciprocal or compulsory (bilateral obligations), meaning that their fulfilment by one state is conditional upon their fulfilment by another state.[218]

Today, it is generally accepted that the right to self-determination applies beyond the context of decolonization. Following the ICJ's advisory opinion in the *East Timor* dispute, the right to self-determination was recognized as undoubtedly possessing an *erga omnes* character. Both within and outside the United Nations, there is broad consensus that all states must respect self-determination – whether they are occupying powers, colonial authorities, or regimes denying racial groups equal political participation. Moreover, this respect for self-determination is required independently of whether other states, if found in a similar situation, would comply with the self-determination norm.

4.2 *Jus Cogens*

Experts continue to debate whether the norm of self-determination has attained *jus cogens* status, as opinions on this issue remain divided.[219] One group of scholars believes that the right to self-determination possesses *jus cogens* character in its entirety.[220] On the other hand, there exists a viewpoint that the RSD qualifies as a *jus cogens* norm, albeit in a limited sense. An example of the latter view is reflected in the study 'The Right to Self-determination: Implementation of United Nations Resolutions', prepared by the Special Rapporteur of the Subcommission for the Prevention of Discrimination and Protection of Minorities, Héctor Gross-Espiell, in 1980.[221] This study recognized the *jus cogens* nature of the right to self-determination norm, but solely

218 *Ibid.* para 33. The Court contrasted here bilateral obligations stemming from diplomatic protection with those that originate from 'outlawing of acts of aggression, and of genocide, as also from the principles and rules concerning the basic rights of the human person, including protection from slavery and racial discrimination', para 34. See ICJ, *Reservations to the Convention on the Prevention and Punishment of the Crime of Genocide*, Advisory Opinion, ICJ Rep. 1951, 23.

219 M. Saul, 'The Normative Status of Self-determination in International Law: A Formula for Uncertainty in the Scope and Content of the Right? '11(4) *Human Rights Law Review* (2011) 610.

220 Castellino, *International Law and Self-determination* (n 73) 99, 101, 123; Raič (n 17) 289 fn. 254; A. Clapham, 'Secession, Terrorism and the Right of Self-determination' in M. Kohen (ed.) *Secession: International Law Perspectives* (CUP 2006) 58. See also ILC, 'Fourth report on peremptory norms of general international law (*jus cogens*)' by Spec. Rapporteur D. Tladi (31 Jan. 2019) UN Doc. A/CN.4/727, 48–52.

221 Gros-Espiell, *The Right to Self-determination* (n 17) paras 21, 70–75.

in cases of colonial or foreign domination. Such a perception was largely determined by the mandate of the Special Rapporteur, which was confined to colonial situations. Hannikainen in his study also considered the right to self-determination as a conditional *jus cogens* norm, though for different reasons. He argued that although 'many international instruments speak of the right to self-determination of all peoples (...) the international community of States has not really required the realisation of internal self-determination within existing states',[222] which led him to affirm the peremptory status only for the right's external dimension. Thus, both Gross-Espiell and Hannikainen ultimately confined the *jus cogens* recognition of self-determination to colonial or foreign domination – Gross-Espiell due to the scope of his mandate, and Hannikainen based on his assessment of state practice.[223]

Finally, there is a third view that, unlike previous ones, does not provide a definitive answer to the question of the status of the right to self-determination. According to this perspective, there merely exists a possibility that the RSD has attained *jus cogens* standing, either in its entirety[224] or in specific aspects.[225] Authors representing this stance generally provide no explanation as to why they hesitate to acknowledge that the norm of self-determination, whether in whole or in part, holds *jus cogens* status.[226] This ambiguity may partly stem from the ILC's observation that there is no simple test to identify whether a norm qualifies as *jus cogens*,[227] despite the two-step approach provided in Article 53 of the Vienna Convention on the Law of Treaties (VCLT). This framework

222 Hannikainen (n 186) 357.

223 See Saul, 'The Normative Status of Self-determination' (n 219) 637–638 (critique of Hannikainen's methodology).

224 For instance, A. Conte et al., *Defining Civil and Political Rights: The Jurisprudence of the United Nations* (Ashgate Publishing 2004) 14.

225 See R. McCorquodale, 'Rights of Peoples and Minorities' in D. Moeckli et al. (eds.) *International Human Rights Law* (OUP 2010) 372–373; M. Shaw, *Title to Territory in Africa: International Legal Issues* (OUP 1986) 91; M. Craven, 'The European Community Arbitration Commission on Yugoslavia' 66(1) *BYIL* (1996) 382–383.

226 Consult S. Matsumoto, 'Jus Cogens and the Right to Self-determination- Falsifiability of Tests' 12 *Policy Center for the New South* (2020) 13 (who argues that 'when the proper tests for identifying a norm as jus cogens are considered, falsifiability should not be missed' (...) Only if it is possible to establish that a hypothesis is unambiguously false, a proposition may be scientific. Though it is not a sufficient condition, falsifiability is one of the necessary conditions for a scientific proposition).

227 See ILC, 'Second report on jus cogens' by Spec. Rapporteur D. Tladi (24 Mar. 2017) UN Doc. A/CN.4/706, para 32; ILC, 'Fifth report on peremptory norms' (n 3) para 216 ('The Commission decided that to prepare a list of its own [peremptory norms] was not practical. It was understood that to prepare a list on the basis of the methodology adopted in the draft conclusion would take decades').

requires (a) the existence of a general international law norm, and (b) its acceptance and recognition by the international community of States as a whole as a norm from which no derogation is permitted and which can be modified only by a subsequent norm of general international law having the same character.[228]

From the foregoing, it is evident that there is disagreement among the commentators regarding the *jus cogens* quality of the right to self-determination. In order to determine whether the RSD enjoys peremptory status outside colonial situations, it is necessary to investigate more closely the practice of states. However, states have rarely made explicit pronouncements concerning the normative hierarchy of self-determination. Proponents of the *jus cogens* status of self-determination regularly cite the example of the six states proposing such recognition at the UN Conference on the Law of Treaties (1968–1969).[229] Yet, less attention is paid to the fact that during the preparation of the Friendly Relations Declaration, the Netherlands and the U.S. voted against Iraq's proposal to consider the core principles contained in the Declaration as *jus cogens*.[230] In another instance, forty-one state delegates voted for, six abstained, and one was against the resolution of the Commission on Human Rights, entitled 'Situation in occupied Palestine' which, among other things, affirmed the *jus cogens* character of the right to self-determination.[231] Still, one can justly wonder whether this context-specific mention can be taken as an expression of universal validity beyond the contexts of decolonization and occupation. The reluctance of states to affirm the (universal) *jus cogens* standing of the right to self-determination continued in the ICJ's advisory proceedings on *Kosovo*. While many states addressed the content and meaning of self-determination in their submissions, relatively few directly engaged with the question of its alleged peremptory status.

A slight shift can, however, be observed in the ICJ's advisory opinions on *Chagos Archipelago* and *Policies and Practices of Israel in the Occupied Palestinian Territory* (OPT), the latest significant instances where the Court dealt

228 Vienna Convention on the Law of Treaties (23 May 1969) 1155 UNTS 331, Article 53; ILC, 'Second report on jus cogens' (n 227) paras 40–89.

229 Saul, 'The Normative Status of Self-determination' (n 219) 642.

230 *Ibid.*

231 UN Commission on Human Rights, Res 2004/4 'Situation in occupied Palestine' (7 Apr. 2000) UN Doc. E/CN.4/RES/2000/4. To the same effect, HRC Res 16/30 'Right of the Palestinian people to self-determination' (13 Apr. 2011) (adopted by a recorded vote of 45 to 1-the U.S.-, with no abstentions). Most recently, HRC Res 49/28 (1 Apr. 2022) (adopted by a recorded vote of 41 to 3, with 3 abstentions).

with the issue of self-determination and its character. In *Chagos Archipelago*, the Court underlined that 'the right to self-determination is an obligation *erga omnes*' (not an *erga omnes* right) and all states have a legal interest in protecting that right.[232] Although more states characterized the right to self-determination as a *jus cogens* norm in the proceedings, the Court itself did not follow suit in its ruling.[233] Some authors have nevertheless inferred that the Court did so implicitly by conflating the obligation to cooperate with the UN to end the decolonization of Mauritius with the consequences of a serious violation of a peremptory norm under Articles 40–41 of the Articles on Responsibility of States for Internationally Wrongful Acts (ARSIWA).[234] Eggett and Thin argue, however, that deducing *jus cogens* character from the existence of an *erga omnes* obligation constitutes an unwarranted shortcut.[235] In *Policies and Practices of Israel in the OPT*, the Court found that among the *erga omnes* obligations violated by Israel are the obligation to respect the right to self-determination, the prohibition against acquiring territory by force, and specific obligations under international humanitarian law and international human rights law but also recognized that 'in cases of foreign occupation such as the present case, the right to self-determination constitutes a peremptory norm of international law'.[236] The latter pronouncement may be treated as *obiter dictum*, but as judge Taldi remarks, its qualifying phrase introduces ambiguity – is self-determination a peremptory norm in other settings than military occupation? Taldi also criticizes the obligations established by the court for third states, namely, to cooperate with the UN to end Israel's presence in the OPT and not to enter into any relations with Israel that concern the OPT,

---

232 *Chagos Archipelago* (n 3) para 180. Cf. *East Timor* (*Portugal v. Australia*) where the Court underlined the *erga omnes right*'s character of the RSD, para 29.

233 While the Court does not explicitly use the terms peremptory norms or *jus cogens*, several judges do (Judges Cançado Trindade, Sebutinde, and Robinson), and no judge challenged this assumption. Moreover, during the proceedings, several states also referred to the peremptory status of self-determination (Belize, Cyprus, the Netherlands, Brazil, South Africa, Mauritius, Kenya, Nicaragua, Serbia and representing 55 States, the African Union) with no State challenging this view.

234 M. Milanović, 'ICJ Delivers Chagos Advisory Opinion, UK Loses Badly' *EJIL:Talk!* (25 Feb. 2019). See also a comment of Dire Tladi on Craig Eggett and Sarah Thin's, 'Clarification and Conflation: Obligations Erga Omnes in the Chagos Opinion' *EJIL:Talk!* (21 May 2019).

235 'It is generally recognised that while all peremptory norms entail obligations *erga omnes*, not all obligations *erga omnes* arise from peremptory norms'. Eggett and Thin, 'Clarification and Conflation' (n 234).

236 ICJ, *Legal Consequences arising from the Policies and Practices of Israel in the Occupied Palestinian Territory, including East Jerusalem*, Advisory Opinion, ICJ Rep. 2024, paras 233, 274.

which appear to flow from the *erga omes* precept rather than from a breach of a peremptory norm.[237]

It seems that the Court was partially inclined to lend weight to around half of the states that recognized the *jus cogens* value of the right to self-determination in their submissions.[238] However, as Judge Robledo remarks in his separate opinion, it is 'regrettable that the Court has not directly established the link between the finding that the right to self-determination has the status of a peremptory norm and the consequences of its violation'.[239]

The nonunanimous practice of states, coupled with conflicting views of legal experts, leads to the conclusion that the (general) peremptory status of the right to self-determination has yet to be conclusively established.

5 Content

The UNESCO conference held in Budapest in 1991 observed that while the existence of right of peoples to self-determination cannot be seriously questioned, legitimate doubts remain regarding the precise meaning of self-determination.[240] Indeed, since its first promulgation in the UN Charter, this right has undergone significant development in terms of content and has been

237 *Ibid.* Declaration of Judge Taldi, paras 14–15, 28. Even though, the Judge is generally persuaded as to the peremptory character of the right to self-determination, paras 18–23.

238 See Written Statement of the Hashemite Kingdom of Jordan (25 Jul. 2023) para 4.18; Written Statement of the Republic of Chile (23 Jul. 2023) para 110; Written Statement of the People's Republic of Bangladesh (24 Jul. 2023) paras 26, 29; Written Comments of the Principality of Liechtenstein (17 Jul. 2023) para 4; Written Statement of Lebanon (24 Jul. 2023) paras 18–19; Written Statement of the Government of the People's Democratic Republic of Algeria (24 Jul. 2023) para 5.2; Written Statement of the Arab Republic of Egypt (25 Jul. 2023) para 326; Written Statement by the Cooperative Republic of Guyana (25 Jul. 2023) para 26; Written Statement of the Kingdom of Saudi Arabia (25 Jul. 2023) para 31; Written Statement of the State of Qatar (25 Jul. 2023) para 4.3; Written Statement Submitted by the Government of the Republic of South Africa (25 Jul. 2023) para 9.

239 Separate Opinion of Judge Gómez Robledo, para 22.

240 UNESCO, International Meeting of Experts 'Peoples' Rights and Self-determination' (Budapest, 25–29 Sep. 1991). See M. Kirby, 'People's Rights and Self-determination' 61 *Bulletin of the Australian Society of Legal Philosophy* (1993) 33–34. Earlier, International Experts in their report 'Further Study of the Concept of the Rights of Peoples similarly concluded that 'the debate among experts is no longer whether peoples' rights are recognised (...) but about their content' (n 182) para 19.

gradually expanded to encompass the various political, economic, social, and cultural aspects of the lives of peoples.[241]

5.1 *Entitlements Contained in External Self-determination*

In its external fashion, the core tripartite right's content is well-known: independence, association or integration with an independent state, and the pursuit of any other freely chosen political status. Though, it has been noted that various phases of the realisation of the RSD connote concomitant transitional entitlements. Hence, prior to statehood, the right to self-determination may manifest as a claim to autonomy, whereas after statehood is achieved, it may take the form of the right to preserve it. Similarly, before unification with a sovereign state, it may imply the right to association, and following unification, the right to maintain the integrity of that union.[242] In cases of prolonged occupation, such as that of Palestine, the law of occupation underpins the Palestinians' self-determination right before the ultimate acquisition of independence. The Forth Geneva Convention specifies that the occupying power must consider labour conditions (Article 51) and avoid creating unemployment (Article 52). Additionally, the occupied population should have meaningful influence over how the administration is conducted in aspects such as children's education (Article 50) and the supply of foodstuffs and medical resources to civilians (Article 55).[243] Accordingly, as long as political negotiations regarding Palestine continue, Israel is obliged to respect the Palestinians' internal self-determination in line with the 'conservationist principle', ensuring that the choices available to the Palestinian people at the conclusion of the occupation are not preempted or distorted.[244] Strictly viewed, ESD resembles less a classical human right and is more bound up with the notions of sovereignty and the title to territory. However, the transitional stages leading to the realization of any of the possible statuses significantly 'humanize' the concept. Each intermediate stage encompasses the right to economic, social, and cultural development.

During the decolonization period, the 'territorial' entitlement originating from the right to self-determination was said to encapsulate '(a) the right to

241 Study Prepared by A. Cristescu (n 4) para 299.

242 Perkowski, *Samostanowienie Narodów* (n 188) 137.

243 Geneva Convention Relative to the Protection of Civilian Persons in Time of War (Fourth Geneva Convention) (12 Aug. 1949) 75 UNTS 287.

244 M. Saul, 'The Right to Self-determination and the Prolonged Occupation of Palestinian Territory' in G. Zyberi (ed.) *Protecting Community Interests through International Law* (Intersentia 2021) 217–227.

exist demographically and territorially as a people; (b) the right to territorial integrity; (c) the right to permanent sovereignty over natural resources; (d) the right to cultural integrity and development; and (e) the right to economic and social development'.[245] However, in addition to the *substantive* content of the right, there must exist a *procedural* one. How else can the future territorial and political organization be decided? The foundation of the procedural aspect is indisputably the freely expressed will of the people.[246] Arguably, such a will is best expressed in a democratically organized referendum or plebiscite, which offers a reasonable choice of options.[247] Unfortunately, during the decolonization era, the procedural aspect was often reduced to the 'independence' option (the territorial notion of people), thereby neglecting the broader groups' right to self-determination.[248]

The Friendly Relations Declaration outlines the modes of application of the right to self-determination. Initially, it affirms the right of 'all' peoples to freely determine their political status and pursue their development. It then specifies that this right can be exercised through 'the establishment of a sovereign and independent state, free association or integration with an independent state, or the creation of any other political order freely determined by the people'. This framework envisions the possibility of altering existing territorial and governmental structures. It also includes the re-establishment of *de facto* independence for peoples who find themselves under foreign occupation in violation of international law.[249] A pertinent example is the 1990 annexation of Kuwait by Iraq, where the Kuwaiti people had the right, under international law, to reclaim their sovereignty with the assistance of the international community.[250]

Dissolution refers to the creation of a new independent state by separating one or more integral parts of the territory from an existing state, resulting in the discontinuation of the legal personality of the previous sovereign.[251] Dis-

245 Drew (n 27) 663. Sands, acting as counsel for Palestine, argued before the ICJ that Israel's demographic manipulations, occupation of land, exploitation of resources, curtailment of political freedoms, and assaults on cultural institutions violate all five freedoms. *Legal Consequences arising from the Policies and Practices of Israel in the Occupied Palestinian Territory, including East Jerusalem*, CR 2024/4 (19 Feb. 2024) 89–96.

246 *Western Sahara* (n 190) paras 55, 59, 70.

247 *Ibid.* Separate Opinion of Judge Dillard, 122–123.

248 *Ibid.* 'it is for the people to determine the destiny of the territory and not the territory the destiny of the people'.

249 Raič (n 17) 289.

250 *Ibid.* 292.

251 M. Weller, *Escaping the Self-determination Trap* (Martinus Nijhoff Publishers 2009) 20–22.

solution usually occurs in the context of federal-type territorial units, and the possibility of dissolution is often provided for in the constitution recognizing the right to self-determination of constituent units.[252] The disintegration of the SFRY and the USSR are commonly cited as examples of this process.

External self-determination can also be achieved through free association, where two or more states consolidate to form a new sovereign state, regardless of whether they previously existed as one entity or as separate states. Such instances are rare, with the reunification of West and East Germany in 1990, following the fall of the Berlin Wall, being one of the most notable examples.[253] Another instance worth mentioning is the establishment of the United Arab Republic by the sovereign states of Egypt and Syria in 1958.[254]

A further method sometimes discussed in the context of external self-determination is secession.[255] Secession involves the establishment of a new independent state by withdrawing an integral part of the territory from an existing state, typically carried out by the population of that territory. This process can occur with or without the consent of the parent state or its internal constitutional authority.[256] If secession occurs without the consent of the parent state or constitutional provision, it is usually referred to as unilateral secession.

5.2 *Entitlements Contained in Internal Self-determination*

Irrefutably, most uncertainties surrounding self-determination pertain to its internal aspect, and the doctrine remains divided on the scope of entitlements that a people should enjoy within the state.[257] Summers wonders whether ISD translates to something more than 'an expression of state's constitutional provisions or its international human rights obligations'.[258] On the other hand, Cassese submitted that the right to internal self-determination presupposes that all peoples 'must be enabled freely to express their wishes in matters

252 *Ibid.*
253 J. Crawford, *The Creation of States in International Law* (OUP 2006) 452–466.
254 *Ibid.* 489.
255 For a discussion on whether secession has a basis in the right to self-determination, see section 3.2.2.
256 Van den Driest (n 190) 6. More in 3.2.1.
257 Mr. Mavrommatis, member of the Human Rights Committee, stated that 'it was not certain that everyone meant the same thing by internal aspect of self-determination' 43–45 HRCOR (1991–2) I, SR.1092, para 47. See also H. Knop, *Diversity and Self-determination in International Law* (CUP 2002) 18; Saul (n 219) 614.
258 Summers, 'The Internal and External Aspects' (n 183) 237.

concerning their condition'.[259] In this vein, ISD is closely correlated with various human rights, principles of non-discrimination, democratic governance and autonomy.[260] Additionally, the ability to control one's own destiny inherently implies the absence of foreign interference (a defensive aspect).[261]

People's participation in the political decision-making process of a state has long been considered essential to the realization of internal self-determination, a view emphasized by various experts, international organizations and judicial bodies. In alignment with the aim of self-determination, the right to participate should include issues directly or indirectly related to the protection, preservation, strengthening or development of a nation's cultural, ethical and/or historical identity.

The level of participation in the decision-making process does not always have to be the same, but varies depending on the circumstances of each case. For instance, the Australian Government believes that it is vital to include Aboriginal and Torres Strait Islander peoples in the processes of democratic governance and allow them to exercise meaningful control over their own affairs. To this end, the National Congress of Australia's First Peoples was established in 2009, alas functioned only until 2019.[262] The scope of matters upon which a given community can decide is not all-encompassing and can be limited by legal or political considerations. Thus, while the Scottish National Party (SNP) regarded another independence referendum as 'vital', the Conservative Government expressed reluctance to authorize it in 2020.[263] In 2022, the Supreme Court of the United Kingdom unanimously ruled that the Scottish Parliament lacks the authority to legislate for an independence referendum,[264] finding that the principle of self-determination – particularly as a ground for secession – was 'not in play' in this context, as the Scottish people's right to internal self-determination was adequately respected within the existing constitutional framework.[265]

---

259 Cassese, *Self-determination of Peoples* (n 19) 128.

260 See section 2.3.2. See also Articles 2 and 5 of CERD.

261 See the submission of Azerbaijan in the *Kosovo* case. 27th Public Sitting (3 Dec. 2009) CR 2009/27, 21, para 30. ISD various meanings are elaborated in more detail in 4.2.

262 For more examples of advisory structures, including Prime Minister's Indigenous Advisory Council or Torres Strait Regional Authority see Parliament of the Commonwealth of Australia, Joint Select Committee on Constitutional Recognition relating to Aboriginal and Torres Strait Islander Peoples, 'Interim Report (2018) 67–84.

263 On the transfer of powers necessary to hold a second referendum consult Section 30 of the 1998 Scotland Act.

264 [2022] UKSC 31, para 92.

265 *Ibid.* paras 88, 89.

The right to participation is inseparable from the formation and evolution of a state's political system.[266] Because the right to self-determination is inalienable, it implies that the people retain the ability to change their political institutions over time. As such, the right of participation would stretch to amending the constitution; indeed, even to resisting tyranny and oppression. However, the right to participation should not be reduced only to these areas, because self-determination encompasses not only the determination of the political position but also the entitlement of a people to pursue economic, cultural and social development. Thus, the right to participation extends to the broader decision-making processes within the state.

Several institutional models can give effect to internal self-determination within a state, including federalism and a spectrum of political autonomy arrangements. Tomuschat contended that the core of internal self-determination lies in political autonomy, and spoke of the need for the so-called 'federal right to self-determination', thanks to which minority groups would achieve a 'qualitative progress'.[267] 'Multinational federalism' based on devolved competences, enhanced central representation and constitutional entrenchment, is arguably the best form of autonomy for realizing internal self-determination by sub-groups.[268] In this vein, Jovanović noted that the most far-reaching solution is to institutionalise the collective right to self-government by federalising the country along the demarcation lines of ethnocultural communities.[269] Of course, such arrangements are not easy to achieve, and the risk of secession always looms, especially in multiethnic societies.

266 Thus, President Prado of Peru has declared it 'indispensable' for the principle of self-determination 'that the will of the people must be able to express itself through free elections periodically held'. Cited from V. Van Dyke, 'Self-determination and Minority Rights' 13(3) *International Studies Quarterly* (1969) 228. In 1962, the Inter-American Peace Committee reported to the American Ministers of Foreign Affairs that Castro's government in Cuba impedes the exercise of the right of self-determination, as it is conceived in the inter-American system, that is, as the right of each and all of the citizens to contribute with his vote, given in free elections, to the formation of the government that they may prefer to give themselves. OAS, Inter-American Peace Committee, Report to the Eighth Meeting of Consultation of Ministers of Foreign Affairs (1962) Doc. OEA/Ser.l/III. CIP/1/62, 3 (Pan American Union 1962) 46.

267 C. Tomuschat, 'Self-determination in a Post-Colonial World' in C. Tomuschat (ed.) *Modern Law and Self-determination* (Martinus Nijhoff Publishers 1993) 13–14.

268 M. Jewkes, 'Self-determination without Secession' 28(2) *Public Affairs Quarterly* (2014) 147–167.

269 M. Jovanović, *Kolektivna Prava u Multikulturnim Zajednicama* (Službeni Glasnik 2004) 221. At the same time, a distinction should be made between classic federations, such as the American one, which are not an expression of recognition of the right of minority communities to self-governance, and the so-called multinational federations where deci-

Nevertheless, Jovanović added that no form of federal political system, which implies territorial autonomy, i.e. self-government of different ethnocultural groups, can serve to remove social conflicts, but to govern them, because 'true' autonomy prevents, not promotes secession.[270]

Thornberry, by contrast, located the essence of ISD not so much in territorial autonomy but in the right of minority communities to actively take part and be represented in the political life.[271] This emphasis does not suggest, however, an antithesis between autonomy and participation; rather it implies that individuals and groups should identify levels of organization that enable effective participation at both national and international levels.[272] While self-determination traditionally includes a right to national participation, its application at the international level has not been fully explored. Nevertheless, the development of self-determination law points toward a collective right of peoples to participate in international law-making. Indigenous people have regularly partaken in diverse UN fora, including the World Intellectual Property Organization (WIPO) or the Food and Agriculture Organization (FAO).[273] Some of the organizations assembling indigenous peoples also achieved consultative status with the Economic and Social Council (ECOSOC).[274] This phenomenon has been termed the 'rise of the affectedness paradigm', reflecting a response to the legitimacy crisis facing key international organizations for being overly state-centric.[275] Consequently, it is of vital importance that the modes of self-government provided to sub-groups are not only theoretically present but also operative in practice, with sufficient scope and depth of devolved competences that shall remain subject to continuous reform.[276]

---

sions on boundaries and powers must consciously express the needs and aspirations of minority groups.

270 *Ibid.* 223.

271 Thornberry (n 161) 134.

272 *Ibid.*

273 See N. Jones, 'Self-determination and the Right of Peoples to Participate in International Law-Making' 90 *BYIL* (2021) 3–5.

274 Indigenous peoples argue that their organizations differ from NGOs and struggle to meet the criteria for consultative status, making NGO observer accreditation unsuitable. See UNGA Res 71/321 'Enhancing the Participation of Indigenous Peoples' Representatives and Institutions in Meetings of Relevant United Nations Bodies on Issues Affecting Them' (8 Sep. 2017); HRC Res 45/12 'Human rights and indigenous peoples' (6 Oct. 2020) paras 13–14.

275 Jones (n 273) 3. Generally, J. Sändig, J. von Bernstorff and A. Hasenclever (eds.) *Affectedness and Participation in International Institutions* (Routledge 2020).

276 Jewkes (n 268) 150–151.

An essential feature of ISD is that its implementation does not alter a state's external (international) borders, unlike external self-determination. Nevertheless, it is imperative to note that the application of self-determination within the state cannot be separated from the principle of equal rights and the associated principles of non-discrimination and non-domination of any group.

Finally, it is also sometimes argued that since the interests of relevant groups in the state can be protected by individual human rights, there is no need for an internal form of self-determination, and, as a result, its existence as a right of the collectives should be called in question.[277] This thinking doesn't seem right for several reasons. First, the identity of the group as such differs from the sum of identities of the group members.[278] Group identity represents a collective good, while the well-being of the members of the group largely depends on respect accorded to the group's identity. Although necessary, individual human rights are not always sufficient for protecting, developing and strengthening the group's identity. For instance, the right to participate in a democratic political system through voting, assembly or expression of opinion may not fully address the demands of self-determination envisioned for collectives. These rights can likewise be of limited value in situations where a democratically elected majority oppresses or disregards the interests of a minority, particularly when the collective identity or interests of the group are in peril.[279] Guaranteeing individual rights based solely on equality among individuals, without taking into account the collective interests of distinct groups, could ultimately result in the erosion or destruction of the subgroup's distinct identity.[280]

6 Addressees

Although it is well-established that only 'peoples' are bearers of the right to self-determination, the inability to ascertain who exactly the proverbial

277 Human Rights Committee has consistently made it clear that under First Optional Protocol no claims can be brought with regard to self-determination as the Protocol applies only to individuals. Human Rights Committee, General Comment No. 23: Article 27 (Rights of Minorities) (8 Apr. 1994).

278 On the protection of a 'group identity' see Badinter Opinion No. 2, which stated that 'where there are one or more groups within a State constituting one or more ethnic, religious or language communities, they have the right to recognition of their identity under international law'. Opinion No. 2 (n 68) para 2.

279 Hannum, 'Rethinking Self Determination' (n 138) 60–61.

280 Raič (n 17) 240.

'peoples' are, accounts for the right's major detracting force. The instances of denying certain groups the status of 'peoples', despite the continuous insistence on the 'all peoples' entitlement formula, seem both hypocritical and humiliating.[281] Holder once wondered why it is necessary to analyze who constitutes 'peoples' in order to enjoy the human rights of peoples, when the same analysis is not required for a 'person' as the holder of individual human rights.[282] Although certain authors advocate for dispensing with the definition of the rightsholder and focusing on the content, the disgust over the rejection or selective acceptance of the self-determination claims inevitably remains.[283] It is thus suggested that international law should finally delineate the rightsholders of self-determination in its external sense by applying criteria such as temporality or special circumstances (colonialism, illegal occupation or alien subjugation) and confirm the pertinence of internal self-determination for 'all peoples' under the jurisdiction of a state. This would limit the unsubstantiated claims[284] and circumvent the asymmetry in the treatment of a plethora of the right claimants and the cumbrance of defining their independence struggles as illegal (Crimea), ineffective (Catalonia) or *sui generis* (Kosovo).[285] The perpetuation of the 'universality of independence' thesis is simply incongruent with state practice, which primarily interprets 'peoples' territorially rather than ethnically. State practice emphasizes that inter-communal conflicts are best addressed within a human rights framework that provides sufficient

281 See ICJ once noted: 'Those instances were based either on the consideration that a certain population did not constitute a 'people' entitled to self-determination (…)'. *Chagos Archipelago* (n 3) para 158.

282 C. Holder, 'Self-determination as a Universal Human Right' 7 *Human Rights Review* (2006) 6.

283 See A. Watts, 'The Liechtenstein Draft Convention on Self-determination Through Self-Administration' in A. Watts and W. Danspeckgruber (eds.) *Self-determination and Self-Administration* (Lynne Rienner Publishers 1997) 24. On rejecting claims from national minorities, like Scots or Catalans see more in W. Żbikowski, 'Samostanowienie Narodów w Prawie Międzynarodowym' *Zeszyt Studencki Kół Naukowych Wydziału Prawa i Administracji UAM* (2015) 245.

284 'If every self-defined group in a society constitutes a 'people' with a separate right to self-determination, then 'self-determination' becomes an incoherent and ultimately unrealizable ambition.' See M. Sellers, 'Republican Principles in International Law' 11 *Connecticut Journal of International Law* (1996) 403, 423.

285 *Kosovo Advisory Opinion* (n 175) Separate Opinion of Judge Yusuf, 620-622, paras 4, 9–11. See also Quane, 'The United Nations' (n 142) 572; Perkowski, 'Forsowanie Samostanowienia' (n 209) 400; S. Oeter, 'The Kosovo Case – An Unfortunate Precedent' 75 *ZaöRV* (2015) 51–74.

guarantees for minorities rather than a separation entitlement, perhaps with the exclusion of the most severe cases.[286]

A people-based interpretation of rights, as opposed to a territorial-based one, may be more morally appealing but is also fraught with controversies in the context of internal self-determination. First, some states might not recognize certain groups as entitled to the privileges associated with ISD, such as autonomy or special minority rights. Second, even if such rights are granted to a specific group (e.g. a minority) rather than to a territorial population, practical issues arise: What about members of the group who are dispersed or reside in neighboring states or form part of a global diaspora? Which entitlements of ISD would then apply to them?[287]

Another intriguing question concerns the deconstruction of the notion of 'totality of the population' under a state's jurisdiction – a topic often overlooked in doctrinal analysis, which tends to focus on a binary distinction between the minority and the majority. Are foreign students or irregular migrants also entitled to the right to self-determination? To what extent do their connection to the state and the longevity of their stay determine their right-holding status? It seems that these components of the population would primarily be beneficiaries of internal self-determination, especially within the human rights framework.[288] However, their role in other areas, such as the ability to shape state policies or their interest in being free from foreign domination, appears somewhat irrelevant. This irrelevance also diminishes their ability to claim ESD in the event of the non-respect of ISD.

6.1 *Rightsholders of External Self-determination*

The addresses of the principle, and later the right, to self-determination in its external, common-sense fashion can, broadly speaking, be allocated into three centuries: the 19th, 20th, and 21st.[289] In the mid-19th century, when self-determination entered common usage, its beneficiaries were typically groups who spoke the same language, such as Italians or Germans. On that,

286 See *Kosovo Advisory Opinion* (n 175) written comments of Bolivia (17 Jul. 2009) para 12; written statement of Iran (17 Apr. 2009) para 4.1; written statement of Egypt (16 Apr. 2009) paras 63–74. On the ethnic interpretation of 'a people' see UNESCO, 'Further Study of the Concept of the Rights of Peoples' (n 182) paras 22, 30, 45. Consult ACHPR, *Kevin Mgwanga Gunme et al. v. Cameroon*, 266/03, 2009, paras 168–169, 176.

287 Summers, 'The Internal and External Aspects' (n 183) 235.

288 See L. Slingenberg, 'Evaluating 'Life Steeped in Power': Non-Domination, the Rule of Law and Spatial Restrictions for Irregular Migrants' 12 *Hague Journal on the Rule of Law* (2020) 399–420.

289 Hannum, 'Rethinking Self Determination' (n 138) 2–29.

and other ethnic bases, they were allowed (sometimes forcefully) to unite and form a state. In a similar vein, at the turn of the 19th and 20th centuries, a number of nation-states were 'approved' to emerge from large empires like the Russian, Ottoman and Austro-Hungarian Empires.[290] However, it should be noted that only politically and militarily viable ethnic organizations were able to attain statehood. This period could be labelled as 'nationalistic self-determination'.

The second period, which can be characterized as 'institutional self-determination', unfolded within the framework of the United Nations. It is in this period that self-determination evolved from a principle to a recognized right, as reflected in UN General Assembly Resolution 2200A, which introduced the International Covenants on Human Rights and affirmed the *right* to self-determination. The primary beneficiaries were colonies, regardless of their ethnic composition.[291] Unlike the preceding ethnic-based notion, this version was predominantly territorial, where previously demarcated territories, rather than language, ethnicity, or culture, determined statehood status.[292]

The third period, beginning in the 21st century, represents a complex and multifaceted approach to self-determination, characterized by five verticals in which the concept currently operates. These verticals persist due to ongoing advocacy for the continuity of the right to self-determination and efforts by scholars and legal frameworks to adapt it to contemporary needs.

The *first* vertical of self-determination in the 21st century is the most straightforward and applies to entire populations of existing states, which can decide to change their political status, whether by extending, limiting, or even losing their independence. This effectively means that states can merge with other states or join federal-like organizations.

The *second* vertical is linked to the 20th-century institutional self-determination and concentrates on the accomplishment of the decolonization

---

290 On 3 March 1878, the Treaty of San Stefano between the Russian and Ottoman Empires provided for the independence of the Balkan countries (Serbia, Bulgaria, Romania and Montenegro). On 3 March 1918 – Soviet Russia, under the Treaty of Brest-Litovsk, defaulted on all of Imperial Russia's commitments to the Allies and recognized the independence of eleven nations in Eastern Europe and Western Asia.

291 E. Riedel, 'Human Rights Protection as a Principle' in J. E. Viñuales (ed.) *The UN Friendly Relations Declaration at 50* (CUP 2020) 250.

292 BADIL Resource Center for Palestinian Residency and Refugee Rights, 'Palestinian Self-determination: Land, People, and Practicality' 28 *Working Paper* (2021) 6-8. (The paper considered the possibility of re-bestowing Palestine with the 'Non-Self-Governing Territory' title). Cf. S. Sakran, 'Revisiting the 'Recognition' of the Palestinians' Right to Self-determination: Peoples as Territories' 7(2) *Groningen Journal of International Law* (2020) 243–248.

process for the remaining 17 Non-Self-Governing Territories, whose RSD is well established and unquestionable.[293] Sometimes, however, the realization of the right can be hindered, as seen in the case of Western Sahara, where conflicts over voter eligibility prevent the staging of a status referendum.[294] Generally, the territorial criterion is a rule, denoting that ethnic groups within a NSGT do not, and will not, have the right to secede – there is no secession from 'secession'.[295] A question may also arise about who, in the context of ongoing decolonization, has the right to exercise self-determination on behalf of the people fighting for liberation. For the realization of ESD, international customary law requires the existence of a 'liberation movement or some other body representing the entire people'.[296]

The *third* vertical of 21st-century self-determination partially overlaps with the institutional phase, particularly through acts stemming from international bodies such as UN Security Council resolutions. This vertical concerns peoples in territories unable to realize their right to self-determination due to unsettled territorial disputes. The protracted right of the Palestinian people to self-determination is the best evidence thereof.[297] Israeli control over Palestinian territories since 1967 has prevented Palestine from being treated as a state, but diplomatic efforts and pressure are carried out to effectuate Palestine's self-determination, based on a two-state solution.[298] The third vertical arguably also befits the instances of international territorial administration, such as those in Kosovo or East Timor, where UN missions (UNMIK and UNAMET/UNTAET respectively) were installed to facilitate the arrangements leading to the determination of a future status and to secure peace, rule of law and human rights.[299] Yet, granting or facilitating external status for entities belonging to a

293 United Nations, The United Nations and Decolonization <https://www.un.org/dppa/decolonization/nsgt>.

294 UNSC Res 658 (29 Apr. 1990) and 690 (29 Apr. 1991). See further, Report of the Secretary-General concerning the situation in Western Sahara, UN Doc. S/2003/565 ('Baker Plan II').

295 See G. Simpson, 'The Diffusion of Sovereignty: Self-determination in the Post-Colonial Age' 32(2) *Stanford Journal of International Law* (1996) 273. As will be illustrated, achieving decolonization can hardly be termed as 'secession' in the proper sense. See 3.2.

296 M. Jovanović, *Collective Rights. A Legal Theory* (CUP 2012) 137.

297 H. Hannum, 'The Right of Self-determination in the Twenty-First Century' 55 *Washington and Lee Law Review* (1998) 775–776.

298 Consult: Madrid terms of reference, including the principle of land for peace, the Arab Peace Initiative and the Quartet Roadmap. See also UNSC Res 2334 (23 Dec. 2016).

299 See UNSC Res 1244 (10 Jun. 1999) (Kosovo); UNSC Res 1246 (11 Jun. 1999) and 1272 (25 Oct. 1999) (East Timor).

sovereign state under international administration would be *ultra vires,* with the outcome ultimately depending on international recognition.[300]

The *fourth* spectrum of modern self-determination is linked to the rule of non-intervention, embracing especially military occupation, and is unconditionally valid. The right of the Ukrainian people to self-determination was clearly breached by Russia's military invasion in early 2022, as would be any purported imposition of a favorable, amenable government.[301] In the same manner, the unlawful administration of the Chagos Archipelago by the United Kingdom was pronounced by the ICJ in 2019 as a violation of Mauritius's right to self-determination.[302] The fourth spectrum thus pertains to established countries and territorial entities legally endowed with substantial sovereign powers, which have suffered violations of their sovereign rights, including economic rights.

The *fifth* and final strand pertains to subgroups residing within established states and includes, among others, national minorities, indigenous peoples, and nations within larger multiethnic states that possess separate territorial arrangements. The separation entitlement in this strand is largely entrenched in moral philosophy, contract theory and justice understood as multinational fairness. It also finds legal support in paragraph 7 of the Friendly Relations Declaration (the safeguard clause) and certain practices observed during the dismemberment of socialist blocks (Czechoslovakia, SFRY and the Soviet Union).[303] This strand is most closely linked to the 19th-century vision of self-determination, as it usually predicates on an ethnic basis. However, it is generally agreed that subgroups do not constitute the proverbial 'people' within the meaning of ESD in peacetime. The dismemberments of the early 1990s in Europe and the inverted reading of paragraph 7 remain incidental and as such do not change of the mainstream international law standpoint (*de lege*

300 The United Nations Special Envoy for Kosovo, Martti Ahtisaari, drafted a Comprehensive Proposal for the Kosovo Status Settlement, which was effectively tantamount to Kosovo's independence. However, Russia indicated that it would block the proposal if it were brought to a vote in the UN Security Council. See Letter dated 26 March 2007 from the Secretary-General addressed to the President of the Security Council, UN Doc. S/2007/16.

301 Janković and Roeben, 'The Threat of Russia's Force in Ukraine' (n 195) 95.

302 P. Hilpold, 'Humanizing' the Law of Self-determination – the Chagos Island Case' 91(2) *Nordic Journal of International Law* (2022) 189–215.

303 See, generally, P. Bossacoma Busquets, *Morality and Legality of Secession A Theory of National Self-determination* (Palgrave 2020). See also H. Quane, 'A Right to Self-determination for the Kosovo Albanians?' 13 *Leiden Journal of International Law* (2000) 223; Perkowski, 'Forsowanie Samostanowienia' (n 209) 388.

lata).[304] The same holds true for potential new social groups, such as those organized around ecological or ideological trends, who might hypothetically seek new forms of territorial arrangements in the future, including those that would separate them from a government unable to meet their expectations. Nonetheless, if there is consent from the parent state, ideally expressed through a constitutional provision, then subgroups within a state can exercise external self-determination. This refers to cases of so-called consensual secession.

6.2 *Rightsholders of Internal Self-determination*

Internal self-determination is increasingly gaining prominence and is set to be the most discussed, reformed, and applied aspect of the RSD, as evidenced by continuous state practice and growing scholarly attention.[305] When it comes to ISD's bearers, it frequently happens that there is an overlap in categories, meaning that those who possess the external right to self-determination enjoy the internal right at the same time. Nowadays, indisputably to this hybrid category belong the total populations of existing states and the populations of the Non-Self-Governing Territories.[306] This understanding is typical among those who conceptualize ESD as the right to freedom from a (former) colonial power, and ISD as the independence of an *entire* state's population from foreign intervention or influence.[307]

That the NSGT enjoy internal self-determination testifies, for instance, the UK Overseas Territories Association (UKOTA) statement, in which the UK pledged to respect any decision made by the Overseas Territories (such as the Falkland Islands and Gibraltar) with regard to their political and constitutional development, including granting a maximum level of self-government. The UK also accepted the revocation of its 'reserved powers' in the international context should the OT choose the independence path through the freely

---

304 Quane, 'The United Nations' (n 142) 572. When disintegration becomes a reality, international law tends to accommodate new entities within preexisting frameworks, often relying on constitutional law settings, as seen in the cases of Yugoslavia and the USSR. Kohen argues that constitutional provisions on self-determination may confer a right to external self-determination, but it is doubtful whether this can be equated with an entitlement under international law. See M. Kohen, 'Self-determination' in J. E. Viñuales (ed.) *The Principles of the Friendly Relations Declaration* (CUP 2020) 160.

305 See Hilpold, *Autonomy and Self-determination* (n 57) 7–55; B. Roth, 'Self-determination Short of Secession' in J. Vidmar (ed.) *Research Handbook on Secession* (Elgar 2022) 59–74.

306 Note that although independent states cannot become 'independent' again they still possess a right to amend their external political status.

307 H. Hannum, *Autonomy, Sovereignty, and Self-determination; The Accommodation of Conflicting Rights* (University of Pennsylvania Press 1990) 49.

expressed will of their populations.[308] A parallel case is Morocco's proposal to the Security Council for autonomy for the Sahara region, providing that the Sahrawi people would govern themselves as long as they remain under Moroccan rule.[309] However, in such cases, one might doubt whether internal self-determination is not, in fact, tantamount to *state-determination,* where any rights are granted at the state's mercy and where that state endowers to uphold dominance and control.[310] For some, therefore, internal self-determination can only be achieved upon independence.[311]

To a bit more problematic category belong entities placed under international territorial administration, where the possibility of choosing an external status remains highly controversial in established states, whereas securing internal self-determination is usually the pivotal aim.[312]

The most contentious yet important addressees today, particularly in light of the continued validity of internal self-determination, are subgroups within the state. To say that the German or American people collectively exercise the RSD carries symbolic weight given that such claims primarily serve to reinforce state sovereignty – a status which is already safeguarded by numerous overlapping legal frameworks.[313] Although the external aspect is still a way more controversial issue, there exists no universal agreement on whether and which subgroups are the bearers of internal self-determination, especially given the absence of explicit legal provisions in key documents or a recognized linkage between subgroups and the concept of a 'people', with the notable exception of indigenous peoples.[314]

308 UKOTA Statement: UK Overseas Territories Self-determination <https://ukota.org/manage/wp-content/uploads/UKOTA-statement-self-determination_F_logo-1.pdf>.

309 See Letter dated 11 April 2007 from the Permanent Representative of Morocco to the UN addressed to the President of the Security Council, UN Doc. S/2007/210.

310 Oloka-Onyango (n 28) 168; Senese (n 193) 19.

311 I. Diaconu, 'Minorities in International Law' 7(3–4) *Romanian Journal of International Affairs* (2001) 172–173; Bursać (n 68) 287.

312 S. Janković, 'Prawo Międzynarodowe A Zmiany Terytorialne. Kazus Krymu' 14 *Problemy Współczesnego Prawa Międzynarodowego, Europejskiego i Porównawczego* (2016) 85.

313 J. R. Morss, '"Mars for the Martians"? On the Obsolescence of Self-determination' in F. Tesón (ed.) *The Theory of Self-determination* (CUP 2016) 186. Note the overlap, for instance, with the right of a sovereign state to 'freely choose and develop its political, social, economic and cultural systems 'enshrined in the Friendly Relations Declaration. This overlap supports the idea of popular sovereignty. See B. Roth, *Sovereign Equality and Moral Disagreement: Premises of a Pluralist International Legal Order* (OUP 2011) 81.

314 UN documents, beginning with the most relevant Article 27 of the 1966 ICCPR, and most notably the UN Declaration on the Rights of Persons Belonging to National, Ethnic, Religious, and Linguistic Minorities, adopted by the UN General Assembly (UNGA Res 47/137,

Nevertheless, various subgroups make up the population of the entire state and, in this sense, they are certainly the bearers of the right, albeit only within the framework of recognized entitlements for the whole population, such as civil and political rights.[315] This situation raises the question of whether formal equality effectively leads to the assimilation of minority groups into the dominant population, *a fortiori*, to the erosion of their distinct identity and of internal self-determination in the proper sense.[316] Addressing this issue requires the adoption positive measures, such as the introduction of autonomy arrangements, extensive consultations with, and participation of, minorities in decisions affecting them, as well as the faithful implementation of specific conventions concerning cultural and educational rights.[317]

Still, setting off from the logical assumption that the very purpose of the RSD is to protect the collective identity of a people as a larger group, then excluding ethnic, religious, linguistic, or other cohesive groups from its scope becomes logically untenable. Also, if documents, as well as the practices of certain bodies, stipulate that the right to self-determination must be interpreted in accordance with the principle of territorial integrity of states – implying that the exercise of this right is constrained by the territorial boundaries of the state – this leads to the conclusion that substate groups must qualify as legitimate bearers of the RSD.[318] To argue otherwise would render the insistence on territorial integrity superfluous.[319] The Liechtenstein Draft Convention on Self-determination by Self-Government, not only acknowledges the relationship between self-determination and territorial integrity but also explicitly mentions 'communities' as the holders of the right to self-determination.

---

18 Dec. 1992), as well as regional documents from European organizations, do not mention the right of self-determination for minorities.

315 S. Trifunovska 'One Theme in Two Variations – Self Determination for Minorities and Indigenous Peoples' 5(2) *International Journal on Minority and Group Rights* (1997) 186.

316 K. Senaratne, *Internal Self-determination in International Law* (CUP 2021) 83–84.

317 See J. Mowbray, 'Language Rights and Linguistic Justice in International Law: Lost in Translation?' in C. D. Mellinger and E. Monzó-Nebot (eds.) *Language Policies for Social Justice* (Special issue, 'Just'. Journal of Language Rights & Minorities 2022) 37–68 (considering flawed assumptions about translation embedded in international legal discourse).

318 In the *Kosovo Advisory Opinion* (n 175), the Court declared that territorial integrity principle applies only between states, para 80.

319 *Reference re Secession of Quebec* (n 13) para 124; UN Commission on Human Rights, Sub-Commission on Prevention of Discrimination and Protection of Minorities, Working Group on Indigenous Populations, Standard-Setting Activities: Evolution of Standards Concerning the Rights of Indigenous Peoples. Working Paper by the Chairperson-Rapporteur, Mrs. Erica-Irene A. Daes, on the concept of "indigenous people", UN Doc. E/CN.4/Sub.2-AC.4/1996/2.

According to Article 1, such a 'community' must be (a) a 'distinct group'; (b) inhabiting 'a limited area within a state'; and (c) having a 'sufficient degree of organization'.[320]

The most archetypal example of an international document referring to minorities, and indeed endowing such minorities with the right to self-determination, is the UN Declaration on the Rights of Indigenous Peoples.[321] Article 3 of the Declaration enshrines the right of indigenous peoples to self-determination, enabling them to freely determine their political status and pursue their economic, social, and cultural development. As indigenous peoples represent a subgroup within the state in which they live, their entitlement to internal self-determination indicates that the RSD extends not only to the entire population but also to subgroups. The overwhelming adoption of the Declaration by states reflects emerging *opinio juris* that expands the conventional interpretation of 'peoples' in international law.[322]

As a counterargument to this conclusion, it has been submitted that *opinio juris* generated by the UNDRIP applies only to indigenous peoples, not to other subgroups.[323] However, there are several reasons why this counterargument is not valid. First, foundational international documents frame the right to self-determination as belonging to 'all peoples', not a singular category. The consistent pairing of 'peoples' with 'nations' and 'states' in these texts indicates an inclusive interpretation beyond indigenous contexts.[324] Moreover, limiting the recognition of the right to self-determination solely to indigenous peoples as a subgroup would likely be inconsistent with the concept of representative government.[325]

The application of the right to self-determination to different subgroups within the state has also been affirmed by judicial bodies. The African Commission on Human and Peoples' Rights in the case of *Katangese People's Congress*

320 Watts (n 283) 38.

321 UNGA Res 61/295 (n 192).

322 R. Coulter, 'The Law of Self-determination and the United Nations Declaration on the Rights of Indigenous Peoples' 15(1) *UCLA Journal of International Law and Foreign Affairs* (2010) 11, 19.

323 H. Quane, 'Self-determination and Minority Protection After Kosovo' in J. Summers (ed.) *Kosovo: A Precedent?* (Brill Nijhoff 2011) 192.

324 UN Commission on Human Rights, 'Summary Record of 256th meeting' (1 May 1952) UN Doc. E/CN.4/SR.256, 7 (Yugoslavia), 9 (Belgium). More broadly, ESCOR, 1952, Suppl. No. 4, 'Report to the Economic and Social Council on the eighth session of the Commission, held in New York, from 14 April to 14 June 1952' (n 18) paras 20–91.

325 On the necessity for states to enhance the implementation of internal self-determination of indigenous peoples consult ILA Res 5/2012 'Rights of Indigenous Peoples' (26–30 Aug. 2012).

v. Zaire found that the Katangese, a distinct group within Zaire, can be considered a 'people' entitled to internal self-determination.[326] Similarly, in the case of *Kevin Mgwanga Gunme et al. v. Cameroon*, the Commission determined that Southern Cameroonians – although part of Cameroon's population – constituted a self-determination unit.[327] This approach was also endorsed by the Supreme Court of Canada in its decision concerning Quebec's secession, where the Court held that it is beyond doubt that the term 'people' also embraces a 'portion of the population of an existing state'.[328]

From all the above, it could be concluded that, in addition to the entire population of a state's territory, subgroups within the state are entitled to internal self-determination. Crucially, such groups are not restricted to racial or religious minorities but also include ethnic and national minorities with distinct collective identities.[329]

Authors and institutions that negated the existence of self-determination for subgroups, often did so due to the then-entrenched opinion of equating self-determination with independence or possibly leading to this outcome. The univectorial understanding was evident in several key decisions. For instance, in 1991, the French Constitutional Court withheld from Corsicans the designation of a 'people',[330] the Badinter Commission in its Opinion No. 2 from 1992 classified Bosnian Serbs as a national minority, who do not possess the right to self-determination,[331] and, consequently, Dame Higgins in her widely acclaimed 1995 book rejected the applicability of self-determination to minorities.[332] Yet, in all these instances it was submitted that national minorities enjoy specific rights under the human rights law, which could be seen an

---

326 ACHPR, *Katangese Peoples' Congress v. Zaire*, Communication No. 75/92 (1995) para 3.

327 *Kevin Mgwanga Gunme* (n 286).

328 *Reference re Secession of Quebec* (n 13) para 124.

329 Brownlie (n 198) 104–119; L. C. Buchheit, *Secession: The Legitimacy of Self-determination* (Yale University Press 1978) 9–11; Crawford, 'State Practice' (n 62) 114; O. Kimminich, 'A Federal Right of Self-determination' in C. Tomuschat (ed.) *Modern law and Self Determination* (Martinus Nijhoff Publisher 1993) 92; U. O. Umozurike, *Self-determination in International Law* (Archon Books 1972) 192. The United Kingdom ratified the Framework Convention for the Protection of National Minorities on the understanding that it would apply to 'racial groups' within the meaning of Section 3(1) of the Race Relations Act 1976, which excluded the Cornish people. This led to pleas to recognise the Cornish as a national minority, which happened in 2014 and gave them the right to 'express, preserve, share, and develop their distinct culture and identity' <https://www.cornwall.gov.uk/people-and-communities/equality-and-diversity/cornish-national-minority/>.

330 Cour Constitutionnel, Décision 91–290 DC (9 May 1991) *Revue du Droit Public* (1991) 971.

331 Badinter Commission, Opinion No. 2 (n 68).

332 R. Higgins, *Problems and Process: International Law and how We Use it* (OUP 1995) 124.

implicit recognition of internal self-determination (albeit not clearly stated due to the prevailing unipolar apprehension).[333]

The expansion of the right to self-determination to substate groups raises a critical challenge: how to identify legitimate claimants when such groups assert specific internal self-determination rights distinct from those of the general population.[334] This inevitably prompts the question: what criteria must a group satisfy to justify its claim to ISD? A widely proposed standard is 'collective distinctiveness' – the idea that not every social or political faction qualifies as a 'people' under international law.[335] This concept typically requires that the group share identifiable traits setting it apart from others. Specifically, these characteristics include 1) territorial connection (historical or current) where the group represents a majority; 2) common language; 3) shared historical narrative; 4) ethnic or ancestral ties; 5) distinct cultural practices; and 6) common religion or ideology.[336] These characteristics, while commonly cited in the literature, are not exhaustive.[337] Nor does their invocation imply that they are entirely accurate, immutable over time, or independent of the subgroup's own self-identification and evolving perceptions. Rather, they are objectively visible to external observers and are often associated with particular ethnic groups.[338] Even though territorial connectivity is generally regarded as a necessary condition for the existence of 'collective individuality' or 'peoplehood',[339] it is not sufficient for establishing collective distinctiveness,[340] and must be

333 According to Diaconu, minorities do not possess an independent right to self-determination; rather, they may 'join' the majority in the exercise of this right. Diaconu (n 311) 184.

334 More about various meanings and entitlements of ISD in 4.2.

335 Van den Driest (n 190) 68; Hannum, 'Rethinking Self-determination' (n 138) 35–36.

336 Raič (n 17) 262.

337 Study Prepared by A. Cristescu (n 4) para 279; UNESCO, 'Further Study of the Concept of the Rights of Peoples' (n 182) 7–8; D. Murswiek, 'The Issue of a Right of Secession – Reconsidered' in C. Tomuschat (ed.) *Modern Law of Self-determination* (Martinus Nijhoff Publishers 1993) 37.

338 For instance, Americans can hardly be identified in ethnic terms, while a plethora of languages and dialects within the same state – e.g. India, Belgium, Caucasus region – makes the definition of a group contingent upon an external judgment in the end. See E. J. Ruíz Vieytez, 'Art. 1. Definitions' in A. Nogueira López et al. (eds.) *Shaping Language Rights: Commentary on the European Charter for Regional or Minority Languages in Light of the Committee of Experts' Evaluation* (Council of Europe 2012) 35, 45.

339 Castellino rejects the right to internal self-determination to minorities who do not live on 'contiguous territories'. J. Castellino, 'International Law and Self-Determination: Peoples, Indigenous Peoples, and Minorities' in C. Walter et al. (eds.) *Self-determination and Secession in International Law* (OUP 2014) 38.

340 Murswiek (n 337) 37; Brownlie (n 198) 107.

complemented by a subjective criterion, which Raič describes as 'the belief of being a distinct people distinguishable from any other people inhabiting the globe, and the wish to be recognized as such, as well as the wish to maintain, strengthen and develop the group's identity'.[341] This subjective element was previously employed by UN experts Francesco Capotorti and Jules Deschenes in their studies on minorities, where they termed it as a sense of solidarity, motivated by a collective will to survive and preserve the group's identity.[342]

Therefore, the 'peoplehood' of the group is determined by a combination of objective and subjective characteristics. Yet, even when these criteria are applied, it remains challenging to identify a subgroup that can rightfully claim the status of a 'people' entitled to the internal self-determination. This difficulty is particularly pronounced when assessing the existence of the subjective element, which hinges on the group's internal self-perception. Notwithstanding these complexities, the subjective criterion is often considered as the most crucial. Objective characteristics (such as shared language, culture, or territory) can be preserved as long as the members of the group genuinely desire to maintain these distinguishing traits. Moreover, external recognition of a group's collective identity typically follows the expression of this subjective element through political organization and action. This dynamic suggests that 'peoplehood' is ultimately constituted not through passive ethnographic characteristics or 'naturalist' attributes, but rather through the active exercise of collective political will. The capacity to organize and articulate demands for self-determination thus becomes the defining feature of a 'people' in international legal terms.[343]

7 Self-determination as Both a Collective and an Individual Right

A literal interpretation of the right to self-determination suggests it applies to collective entities ('peoples') rather than individuals. However, since peoples are ultimately composed of individuals, the right implicitly extends to persons as constituent members. The phrase 'all peoples' encompasses diverse collectives – from nations (e.g., Jewish people, Americans) to smaller groups like the

341 Raič (n 17) 262–263.

342 F. Capotorti, 'Study on the Rights of Persons Belonging to Ethnic, Religious and Linguistic Minorities' (1979) UN Doc. E/CN.4/Sub.2/384/Rev.1, para 568; J. Deschenes, 'Proposal Concerning a Definition of the Term 'Minority'' (23 Jul. 1985) UN Doc. E/CN.4/Sub.2/1985/31, paras 105, 109.

343 U. Saxer, *Die Internationale Steuerung der Selbstbestimmung und der Staatsentstehung* (Springer 2010) 217; Oeter, 'The Kosovo Case' (n 285) 57–58.

Yanomami tribe in the Amazon or the Algonquin indigenous community in Canada. Crucially, the concept of 'peoples' is ontologically grounded in the indivisible dignity of the human person, meaning every individual, irrespective of faith, ethnicity, or gender, manifests this collective dimension of identity.

The broad conceptualization of the RSD's addressees is evident in the work of the African Commission on Human and Peoples' Rights. In *Katanga* and *Casamance* cases, the Commission dealt with the right to self-determination of distinct ethnic groups.[344] In *Democratic Republic of the Congo* (*DRC*) *v. Burundi, Rwanda and Uganda*, the Commission by referring to 'Congolese peoples' rights' equated 'peoples' with the territorial demarcation of the State,[345] while in *Legal Resources Foundations v. Zambia*, it interpreted the term 'peoples' to mean groups of individuals sharing distinctive characteristics.[346] The neat relationship between individuals, collectives and 'peoples' within the scope of the right to self-determination was once explained by the Special Rapporteur in the following way:

> The right to self-determination is a collective right (…) the beneficiaries of which are peoples – whether or not constituted as independent States – nations and States. Individuals participate, both directly and through the realization of other human rights, in the exercise of this right.[347]

This statement, from the outset, suggests that not every individual or group has the right to self-determination, at least not an equal right. It is somewhat misleading and even contradictory to state that an individual has the right to self-determination if he or she 'self-determines' within a colony or an established state, yet he or she does not have the same right if he or she wishes to self-determine externally on a lower level, for example, within a state' sub-group.

Another conclusion that flows from this statement is that individuals have only an instrumental role in the traditional self-determination process and a peripheral role in its subsequent utilization. They are directly needed for the effectuation of the RSD but do not directly benefit from it. By way of example, a 'collection' of individuals is required to express an opinion on separation,

---

344 See Report on Mission of Good Offices to Senegal of the African Commission on Human and Peoples' Rights (1–7 Jun. 1996) in *Tenth Annual Activity Report of the African Commission on Human and Peoples' Rights* (*1996–1997*) Doc. ACHPR/RPT/10th, Annex VIII (1997).

345 ACHPR, *DRC v. Burundi, Rwanda and Uganda*, Communication No. 227/1999 (2003) paras 68, 77.

346 ACHPR, *Legal Resources Foundation v. Zambia*, Communication No. 211/98 (2001) para 73.

347 UN Commission on Human Rights, 'The Right to Self-determination: Historical and Current Development' (n 4) para 691.

with individual votes being counted in an independence referendum, whereas an individual alone cannot 'secede' from a state, and in the case of a lost referendum even a large portion of individuals does not have a remedy.[348] Moreover, even following a successful referendum, an average individual derives no direct advantage from independence, such as a personal entitlement to natural resources or a right to represent the state externally. These are 'collective' goods owned by a state and administered by its government. Consequently, even if individuals partake in the exercise of self-determination as members of a broader collective – whether defined by ethnicity, citizenship, or a territorially demarcated political entity such as a NSGT or an established state – their rights cannot be equated with those of the collective itself. The violation of an individual's human rights alone is insufficient to justify a change in government or secession, whereas widespread violations affecting many individuals may potentially ground such claims. In addition, individuals will need to represent a qualified self-determination subject in order to claim particular privileges and rights. Thus, while the breach of women's rights, regardless of its scale, may not permit secession, it might lead to a change in government. It should also be noted that in collective self-determination, the will of the individual always succumbs to the will of the group, which is why it is hard to say that an individual in reality 'self-determines'.[349] On the other hand, it is not excluded that an influential persona, such as a spiritual leader or a well-known canny politician, might exert an impact on a larger group.

Finally, this statement highlights the fact that self-determination is not an individual human right *per se*. This runs contrary to the positioning of the RSD within the ICCPR and the ICESCR, thoroughly individualistic human rights frameworks.[350] It is true, that the Human Rights Committee continues to refuse complaints from individuals regarding the RSD,[351] yet states still have

348 R. Howse and K. Knop, 'Federalism, Secession, and the Limits of Ethnic Accommodation' 1 *New Europe Law Review* (1992–1993) 304. See also A. Buchanan, 'Democracy and Secession' in M. Moore (ed.) *National Self-determination and Secession* (OUP 1998) 14, 25.

349 A person can naturally self-determine with regard to himself or herself, which refers to autonomous decision-making over his or her own body and life, the right to independently decide in matters like medical treatment, family life, (anti-)conception, reproduction, marriage, or life and death. Yet, this freedom has to be distinguished from the elaborated right to self-determination in international law.

350 P. Tacik, *Deconstructing Self-determination in International Law* (Brill 2023) 425.

351 Human Rights Committee, *Chief Bernard Ominayak and Lubicon Lake Band v. Canada*, Communication No. 167/1984 (26 Mar. 1990) para 13.3. On the other hand, the African Commission has heard the cases brought by minorities and indigenous peoples. See ACHPR, *The Social and Economic Rights Action Centre for Economic and Social Rights v. Nigeria*, Communication No. 155/96 (2001).

an obligation under Article 40 of the ICCPR to report on Article 1.[352] It appears that both the Committee and states tend nowadays to see the RSD as ISD, which departs from the notion of collectiveness needed to effectuate the territorial status and embraces to a significant extent individual rights, such as the right to democratic participation, including the right to stand for elected office and to participate in election – individual rights contained in the UDHR and the ICCPR. Weller has argued that the RSD is 'an inherent right of peoples' and that it applies to four subjects: individuals, groups, minorities and indigenous peoples, each of which benefit differently from the right.[353]

Additionally, it is worth highlighting the philosophical underpinnings of the right to self-determination, both on the individualist and collectivist planes, particularly in relation to the notion of freedom. According to Fisch, self-determination is freedom understood in the broadest sense.[354] Fisch noted that someone who self-determines has the freedom to do something, but also the freedom to refrain from doing something. Only when someone's freedom is to collide with someone else's, then it is restricted. In this vein, he posits that the real meaning of self-determination lies precisely in the identity of the subject that determines (in the normative sense) and the object to be determined, irrespective of whether the subject is an individual or a group. If that sameness is missing; if one entity determines for another, then it is not about self-determination, but about foreign determination (*alien determination*). Hence, the idea of freedom applies both to individuals and groups, and we can say that 'a self-determined individual is a free individual, just as a self-determined people are a free people'.[355] Self-determination, *ergo* reflexive determination and alien determination, *ergo* non-reflexive determination or domination, are human-induced actions, which can be affected by external forces. In that case, the zero-sum logic retains validity: if the political dominance of one person over another is disturbed by external forces, the

352 J. Wright, 'Minority Groups, Autonomy, and Self-determination' 19(4) *Oxford Journal of Legal Studies* (1999) 624.

353 For groups, self-determination involves the right to collective representation of their interests. These groups are typically formed based on common characteristics among their members, such as religion, sexual orientation, or other shared attributes. For ethnic minorities, self-determination manifests in a broad range of minority rights. In the case of indigenous groups, self-determination includes specific rights related to land and resources, as well as elements of cultural and territorial autonomy. See M. Weller, 'Self-determination and Peace-Making' in M. Weller et al. (eds.) *International Law and Peace Settlements* (CUP 2021) 401–402.

354 Fisch, *The Right of Self-determination of Peoples* (n 80) 19.

355 *Ibid.*

freedom of the affected person or group rises commensurately.[356] The exploration of external forces, sometimes termed 'technical', is certainly an interesting undertaking, both in terms of their substance and evolution. How have factors such as religion, natural catastrophes, or human incapacities – such as mental illness or age – impacted the ability to 'self-determine'? The capacity for self-determination may also be hampered by international processes, as illustrated by the situations in Palestine and Western Sahara. However, these examples primarily concern the non-recognition of a collective will rather than its active suppression.[357]

With regard to the freedom or capacity of a group to self-determine, it substantially diverges from that of an individual. A collective does not have *a priori*-formed capacity to act, as it represents an amalgam of both qualified and unqualified participants (whether due to mental capacity, age, or other factors). Nor is the size of a self-determining group established beforehand. Furthermore, the very existence of a collective will is highly problematic. Thus, for a collective to self-determine freely in terms of its desires and the effects of its actions, a high degree of symbiosis and coordination is essential. In practice, collective self-determination can never achieve the same degree of autonomy as individual self-determination.[358]

Relatedly, a further question surfaces: can collectives at all be subjects of law? Do they possess the necessary properties to qualify as rightsholders? Jovanović notes that approaches based solely on the description, rather than evaluation, of rights cannot provide an adequate answer to this question.[359]

The terms 'collective' or 'group', in the context of 'collective' or 'group' rights, describe rights held by the group as a singular entity rather than separately by its individual members.[360] The basic normative assumption underlying every account of collective rights, Jovanović says, concerns the recognition of a group's irreducible particularity – a qualitative uniqueness that resists absorption into universalizing notions of identity. Hence, in order to conceptualize the titular of collective rights, it is essential to understand the legal construction of a group's diversity. To that end, Heinze

356 *Ibid.* 20–21.

357 Cassese, *Self-determination of Peoples* (n 19) 142.

358 Fisch, *The Right of Self-determination of Peoples* (n 80) 26.

359 M. Jovanović, 'Društveni Identitet i Pravni Subjektivitet – Kolektiviteti kao Subjekti Prava?' 3 *Etnoantropološki Problemi* (2009) 225–226.

360 Cf. 'To assert that self-determination constitutes a collective right of peoples does not mean that an individual right, to which all human beings are entitled, cannot exist at the same time'. Gros-Espiell, *The Right to Self-determination* (n 177) para 57.

offered a three-step 'construction of difference' scheme.[361] The first of them is 'the recognition of other people or groups as such – as different from one's own', based on, say, origin, geography, anatomy, language, religion or custom. The second step consists of 'naming the difference', while the third refers to the 'evaluation of that difference through attribution of normative significance to it'.[362] By following this scheme, it is possible to classify nations and ethnic minorities as legitimate holders of collective rights.

---

361 E. Heinze, 'The Construction and Contingency of the Minority Concept' in D. Fottrell and B. Bowring (eds.) *Minority and Group Rights in the New Millennium* (Martinus Nijhoff Publishers 1999) 34.

362 *Ibid.* 34–37.

CHAPTER 3

The Right to Secession in International Law

> There exists no law that forbids, nor one that commands,
> whether a family may or may not move into the house of the deceased.
> And since no written statute governs such a case,
> the matter must be left to the guidance of natural law -
> that higher law which grants the family the right
> to care for the property left behind by their departed kin .
>
> BRANISLAV NUŠIĆ

∵

1 Motives for Secession

Secession, or the act of a region or group within a country breaking away to form a new independent state, can occur for a variety of reasons. These reasons are often complex and multifaceted, involving political, social, economic, cultural, and historical factors.

1.1 *Economic Reasons for Secession*

Economic reasons are often identified as a complimentary trigger for secession, however, a conviction that independent micro and macroeconomic policy would bring better off is generally present in all secessionist movements. To the most common motives for secession belong: economic disparities, the desire to control resources, the thrust for fiscal autonomy, and diverging views toward the general economic strategy.[1]

Regions seeking secession may feel economically marginalized within the existing state, experiencing disparities in wealth distribution, access to resources, investment, infrastructure, and economic development opportunities compared to other regions. These disparities can create grievances and fuel aspirations for independence to gain greater control over economic resources and decision-making.

1 M. Stermšek and A. Rodríguez-Pose, 'The Economics of Secession: Case of the Former Yugoslavia' *CEPR* (2014).

 | DOI:10.1163/9789004737501_004

Secessionist movements may also emerge in in resource-rich regions possessing valuable endowments of hydrocarbons, mineral deposits, or arable land. When local populations perceive that central authorities are either extracting disproportionate benefits or mismanaging these resources, demands for resource sovereignty often intensify, potentially escalating into full-fledged independence movements. This dynamic reflects what scholars have termed the 'resource curse of federalism', where subnational units with concentrated natural wealth challenge centralized resource governance models.

A parallel economic driver involves fiscal autonomy aspirations. Regions frequently seek independent taxation authority, discretionary budget allocation powers, and control over revenue generation mechanisms. Such demands typically stem from perceptions of fiscal exploitation – whether through inequitable redistribution schemes, extractive transfer systems, or constrained subnational fiscal policymaking.

On the other hand, regions with distinct economic structures, industries, or economic policy preferences may seek independence to pursue their own economic agendas tailored to their specific needs and priorities. Economic policy divergence from the central government, such as differences in trade policies, taxation, regulations, or economic ideology, can contribute to calls for secession. Secessionist movements may likewise argue that independence offers the opportunity to pursue economic policies better suited to promoting stability, growth, and prosperity. Proponents of secession may envision more efficient and responsive governance structures, better suited to address local economic challenges and opportunities.

The examples of past and contemporary secessionist movements driven, at least in part, by economic motives include the Southern United States, Menton in Monaco, Catalonia in Spain, Veneto in Italy, Scotland in the UK, and Quebec in Canada.

At the outbreak of the American Civil War (1861–1865), sharp economic disparities divided the industrialized, urban North and the agrarian South, which depended on slave labour to produce key export crops like cotton, tobacco, rice, and sugar. Southern plantation owners, whose prosperity relied on slavery, increasingly clashed with the North's growing anti-slavery sentiment.[2] The South also favored low tariffs to maintain trade with Europe, while economic competition and disputes over land, labor, and markets fueled the drive toward secession.[3] In 1848, Menton and its neighbouring

2 M. L. Chacón and J. L. Jensen, 'The Political and Economic Geography of Southern Secession' 80(2) *The Journal of Economic History* (2020) 386.

3 See Z. Liscow, 'Why Fight Secession? Evidence of Economic Motivations from the American Civil War' 153 *Public Choice* (2012) 37–54 (claiming that the economic interests of manufac-

town Roquebrune seceded from Monaco, partly due to a tax imposed on lemon exports, and declared themselves the Free Cities of Menton and Roquebrune.[4] In Spain, Catalonia has a long history of seeking greater fiscal autonomy and control over its finances.[5] Economic grievances, including disparities in taxation and revenue redistribution, have fuelled calls for independence.[6] One of the richest regions in Italy, Veneto, is likewise discontent with Rome's administration of funds and the fact that they have to finance the poorer south getting in return incommensurably less in benefits. The independence campaigners have shown frustration at the corruption and endemic tax evasion in other parts of the country, as well as the influence of organized crime.[7] In Scotland, the independence movement has cited economic reasons, such as the desire to control North Sea oil revenues, manage fiscal policy independently, and pursue economic policies aligned with Scotland's interests.[8] The Quebec sovereignty movement in Canada has been driven in part by economic concerns, including the desire to protect the French language and culture, promote economic development, and gain control over taxation and social policies.[9]

These examples illustrate how economic factors can intersect with political, social, cultural, and historical dynamics to shape secessionist movements and aspirations for independence. However, it is essential to recognize that secessionist movements are often complex and multifaceted, and economic motives are just one aspect of broader grievances and aspirations for self-determination.

1.2 *Legal-Political Reasons for Secession*

Legal-political reasons for secession involve afflictions related to constitutional, legal, or political arrangements within a state, as well as disputes over

turing were decisive for the North to fight secession).

4 Gouvernement Princier de Monaco, 'Secession of Menton and Roquebrune' <https://en.gouv.mc/Government-Institutions/History-and-Heritage/Periods/Times-of-trouble-1793-1861/Secession-of-Menton-and-Roquebrune>.

5 X. Cuadras-Morató, 'The Economic Debate' in X. Cuadras-Morató (ed.) *Catalonia: A New Independent State in Europe?* (Routledge 2016) 151–157.

6 Pau Bossacoma Busquets, 'Self-determination and Coercion in Spain. The Case of Catalonia' 34 *Revista d'Estudis Autonomics i Federals* (2021) 305–306.

7 E. J. Lyman, 'Venice Wants Out of Italy' *USA Today* (2014) <https://eu.usatoday.com/story/news/world/2014/04/19/venice-italy-seccession/7563295/>.

8 The Scottish Government, 'Scotland's Future: Your Guide to an Independent Scotland' (Nov. 2013) Chapter 3. See also Statement to Parliament by First Minister Nicola Sturgeon on 28 June 2022. Note the moves to recast the constitutional status of Orkney, Shetland and the Western Isles to get a greater share of the oil revenues.

9 See Manifesto of the Alliance Laurentienne 104 *Laurentie* (1958); M. Rioux, 'The FLQ Manifesto' in *Quebec in Question* (James Lewis & Samuel 1971).

the legitimacy of governance structures and decision-making processes. These reasons often revolve around issues of representation, democracy, rule of law, and the exercise of political power.[10]

As such, secessionist movements may emerge in response to perceived deficiencies in democratic representation, such as unfair electoral systems, gerrymandering, or the marginalization of certain regions or groups within the political process. Groups may seek greater autonomy or independence in order to establish more inclusive and representative governance structures.

Another reason concerns the violations of constitutional rights. Groups may assert that the central government has overstepped its constitutional authority, infringed upon fundamental rights and freedoms, or failed to uphold the principles of constitutional governance. Secession here may be seen as a means of protecting constitutional rights and restoring the rule of law.

Furthermore, secessionist movements may arise in response to perceived centralization of power and authority within the central government, particularly if this leads to the marginalization or disenfranchisement of regions or groups. As a result, groups may seek greater autonomy or independence in order to decentralize political power and decision-making processes, thereby ensuring greater local control and accountability.

Finally, and most importantly, discrimination based on ethnicity, religion, or other identity markers can be a catalyst for secessionist movements, particularly if minority groups face systematic oppression, persecution, or exclusion from political power. Accordingly, groups may seek independence as a means of escaping discrimination and establishing governance structures that respect and protect their rights and identity.

Scotland, Catalonia and Quebec could be again used as examples of secessionist movements driven by legal-political reasons. The concerns there relate to the perceived violations of democratic rights, lack of autonomy, and centralization of power by the Spanish government (Catalonia), democratic representation, political autonomy, and the centralization of power in Westminster (Scotland) and grievances related to cultural and linguistic identity, lack of recognition of Quebec's distinctiveness, and perceived violations of provincial autonomy by the federal government (Quebec). However, one could also furnish the example of South Sudan, where its secession from Sudan in 2011 was driven by longstanding resentment related to political marginalization, economic disparities, and violations of human rights by the central government

10 Consult D. Muro, 'The Causes of Secession' in R. D. Griffiths, A. Pavković and P. Radan (eds.) *The Routledge Handbook of Self-determination and Secession* (Routledge 2023) 133–146.

in Khartoum, and that of East Timor, which gained independence from Indonesia in 2002 after decades of resistance against occupation and repression. Bangladesh's independence from Pakistan was similarly rooted in political and economic exclusion, compounded by deep cultural and linguistic divides between East and West Pakistan.[11]

1.3 *Socio-Cultural Reasons for Secession*

Socio-cultural reasons for secession include cultural identity and autonomy, language and linguistic rights, religion and religious freedom, historical grievances and identity narratives as well as ethnic solidarity and kinship ties. Secessionist movements may thus arise from efforts to preserve and promote distinct cultural identities, traditions, and customs that are perceived to be under threat within the existing state. Minority groups may seek greater autonomy (the Basque Country, Flanders, and South Tyrol) or independence (Catalonia, Scotland) in order to safeguard their cultural heritage and exercise control over cultural, educational, and linguistic policies. Moreover, language can be a powerful marker of identity and belonging, and rancour related to language rights can fuel secessionist sentiments.[12] Minority linguistic groups may seek independence in order to protect their language from assimilation, promote its use in education and public life, and ensure linguistic equality and recognition within the state.[13]

Next, religious differences and tensions can contribute to secessionist movements, particularly in countries where religion plays a significant role in shaping social and political identity, like in the former Yugoslavia.[14]

---

11 Consult J. Ker-Lindsay and M. Fabry, *Secession and State Creation: What Everyone Needs to Know* (OUP 2023) 21–23.

12 In May 2024, Poland's President Andrzej Duda vetoed legislation that would have recognized Silesian as a regional language - a status equivalent to that of Kashubian. In justifying his decision, President Duda argued that Silesian constitutes a dialect no distinct from those spoken in the Masovian or Lesser Poland voivodeships.

13 The enactment of a law recognizing Silesian as regional language would, among other things, denote the possibility of introducing voluntary classes in the Silesian language in schools, installing bilingual signs with the names of localities where more than 20% of inhabitants declare the use of the Silesian language, funding activities related to the preservation of the Silesian language, and including two representatives of Silesian speakers to the Joint Government and National and Ethnic Minorities Committee.

14 Religion is one of the factors that needs to be considered in order to understand the Yugoslav wars of the 1990s. Some of the key leaders involved in the conflict referred to religion in their rhetoric and had the support of religious organizations. See N. Mirilović, 'War and Religion: The Yugoslav Wars of the 1990s' *Oxford Research Encyclopedia of Politics* (2019).

Historical grievances, such as past injustices, colonialism, or conflicts, can likewise fuel secessionist sentiments by fostering collective identity narratives and perceptions of victimization or injustice. Groups may seek independence as a means of rectifying historical wrongs, reclaiming ancestral lands, or asserting their right to self-determination based on historical claims. Yet, these demands are frequently coupled with aspirational visions for a better future. Elias and Franco-Guillén note that Catalan secessionist discourse combines grievances against the Spanish state with a forward-looking vision of a future Catalan Republic.[15]

Lastly, ethnic solidarity and kinship ties can play a significant role in secessionist movements, particularly in regions where ethnic communities share strong bonds of identity, history, and kinship, as evidenced in the Caucasus. Ethnic groups may seek independence in order to establish governance structures that reflect and protect their ethnic identity, promote social cohesion, and foster solidarity among community members.

More examples of secessionist movements driven by socio-cultural reasons include (a) the Basque Country in Spain, where concerns over cultural identity, language rights, and historical autonomy have incited demands for independence; (b) the Tamil Tigers in Sri Lanka, who waged a decades-long separatist insurgency in pursuit of Tamil self-determination and protection of Tamil language and culture, (c) the Aceh region in Indonesia, where the Free Aceh Movement (GAM) sought independence in order to preserve Acehnese culture, religion, and autonomy, and (d) the Chechen Republic in Russia, where separatist movements have been driven by sentiments related to religion, cultural identity, and a legacy of contested autonomy.[16]

---

15 A. Elias and N. Franco-Guillén, 'Justifying Secession in Catalonia: Resolving Grievances or a Means to a Better Future?' (2021) 9(4) *Politics and Governance* 460. Similarly, the Parti Québécois (PQ) during the 1980 referendum campaign advocated that sovereign Quebec could fully emancipate francophone residents and best protect and enhance their socio-economic, cultural, and linguistic interests. Additionally, the PQ argued that independence could contribute to the creation of a fairer, more egalitarian society, where the state could bridge the gap between the rich and the poor. A. Lecours, 'The Two Quebec Independence Referendums: Political Strategies and International Relations' in R. D. Griffiths and D. Muro (eds.) *Strategies of Secession and Counter-Secession* (ECPR Press 2020) 64.

16 See M. Sornarajah, 'Eelam and the Right to Secession', Speech to the International Tamil Foundation at London (25 Jun. 2000) <https://tamilnation.org/selfdetermination/tamileelam/0006sornarajah>; A. Dufseth, 'Indonesia's 1999 Political Laws: The Right of Association in Aceh and Papua' 11 *Pacific Rim Law & Policy Journal* (2002) 620; C. Ahrens, 'Chechnya and the Right of Self-determination' 42 *Columbia Journal of Transnational Law* (2004) 575–615.

2 Secession: Notions, Position in International Law and Theoretical Perspectives

2.1 *Definitional Attempts*

The development of international legal doctrine on state secession has evolved in parallel with shifting conceptions of state sovereignty. This symmetry has been permeated by philosophical premises stemming from epistemological standpoints on the idea of the state, and law in general.[17] Given that contemporary state theory supersedes the earlier conceptual approaches, which brought secession down to a meta-legal problem, any scientifically grounded discourse must integrate legal doctrine with practical considerations. All the more so, since the process of secession instigates a plethora of legal questions of substantial importance for the existence of a state, whose resolution demands a broader debate. In international legal doctrine exists no consensus on the determination of the term 'secession', which has resulted in the surfacing of more restrictive meanings at one point and more extensive at another, depending on different ideological directions to which theorists incline.[18] Irrespective of whether these divergences arise out of metaphysical teachings of natural law or empirical findings of legal positivism, the commonly posed questions in the doctrine of international law relate to the phenomenology of this social occurrence. The questions include legal and political motives due to which the secession arises, methods and means in which secession is conducted as well as consequences which secession produces, and which coincide with the creation of new states or the enlargement of the existing ones. To provide an adequate answer to the mentioned questions, an evolutionary development of secession needs to be addressed wherefrom also its contemporary meaning arises.[19]

There are various theoretical standpoints on the notion of secession espoused by public law experts, political scientists and philosophers. These viewpoints, however, in their criticality, theoretical and practical differentiality do not pay enough attention to all genuine reasons for the emergence of this phenomenon, which arises from the facticity of social relations, and whose variables direct ways of the development of international legal practice.

---

17 D. Dimitrijević, 'Secesija Država u Doktrini i Praksi Međunarodnog Prava' in Z. Knežević and K. Čavoški (eds.) *Secesija sa Stanovišta Unutrašnjeg i Međunarodnog Prava i Njene Političke Posledice* (Serbian Academy of Sciences and Arts 2020) 53.

18 *Ibid.*

19 *See* J. Crawford, *The Creation of States in International Law* (OUP 2006) 374–448.

In international legal doctrine, secession predominantly refers to the separation of a part (or parts) of a territory with the aim of the emergence of a new independent state. Similarly, secession covers the cases of separation or detachment of a portion of state territory for the sake of enlargement of territories of other states through incorporation, that is, annexation or integration. In this second sense, secession is often compared to irredentism, in *sensu politico*, since it presupposes a political ideology aimed at achieving ethnic homogeneity through the alteration of state borders by separating a portion of a territory where ethnic and national minorities live and their inclusion into a neighbouring state(s). The detachment of part of a territory is not carried out for the sake of gaining independence, *ergo* forming a new state, but for the liberation from an alien governor and unification in a unitary state where it is possible to achieve national and territorial unity.

Purposefulness is not, however, as divisive or legally significant as the modalities through which secession is executed and the scope it encompasses. Crawford, for instance, initially believed that secession means 'the creation of a state by the use or threat of force without the consent of the former sovereign'.[20] This approach excludes all cases of secession that do not imply the use or threat of use of force and a continuator state, like the dissolution of the Soviet Union or Czechoslovakia, sometimes termed as 'negotiated independence', but could include colonial territories.[21] Kohen, on the other hand, sees secession as 'the creation of a new independent entity through the separation of part of the territory and population of an existing State, without the consent of the latter'.[22] The element common to both definitions is the absence of the consent of the former state, i.e. the state from which a particular entity is seceding. Crawford's definition insisting on the threat or use of force by an entity that undertakes secession together with the opposition of the parent state evidences a double restrictive element. Thus, Crawford's and Kohen's definitions of secession presuppose only unilateral separation, while the secession that takes place with the consent of the parent state, *ergo* consensual secession, according to their interpretation, would not qualify as secession at all. This is thought to be so because secession that takes place with the consent of the parent state is not problematic from the international law point of view and practice, and

20 *Ibid.* 375.

21 P. Radan, 'The Meaning of Secession' in R. D. Griffiths, A. Pavković and P. Radan (eds.) *The Routledge Handbook of Self-determination and Secession* (Routledge 2023) 32–35.

22 M. Kohen, 'Introduction' in M. Kohen (ed.) *Secession: International Law Perspectives* (CUP 2006) 3.

as such, the process could hardly be labelled 'secessionist'.[23] If a state's domestic legal framework grants a right of separation to part of its population, this would be considered a national internal right, and the same pertains to any *ad hoc* political devolution agreement.[24]

Nevertheless, Crawford substantially revised his viewpoint in the co-authored expert opinion on the Scottish independence referendum, where he and Boyle contended that secession is essentially a unilateral 'process by which a group seeks to separate itself from a state to which it belongs and to create a new state on part of that state's territory'.[25] This definition is less narrow as it does not condition secession on the use or threat of force or on opposition from the parent state. However, by emphasizing the notion of (legal) belonging, it might exclude colonial situations. The phrase 'on part of' indicates the continued existence of the host state. In this sense, the secessions of Eritrea or South Sudan would fit this definition, whereas Yugoslavia, which ceased to exist, would not.[26] Similarly, according to legal theorists Thürer and Burri, secession may involve the withdrawal of a constituent part of a state with territory and population, in order to form a new state regardless of whether the withdrawal occurs with or without the consent of the parent state.[27] This approach falls within a group of extensive definitions of secession. Pavković and Radan build on Thürer and Burri's approach and put forward a more concise formulation: 'Secession is the creation of a new state by the withdrawal of a territory and its population where that territory was previously part of an existing state'.[28] This definitional attempt, containing the word 'previously', would not necessarily demand the continuation of the host state.

23 Košutić opined that secession with consent would be tantamount to devolution. B. Košutić, 'Secesija, Disolucija, Devolucija' in Z. Knežević and K. Čavoški (eds.) *Secesija sa Stanovišta Unutrašnjeg i Međunarodnog Prava i Njene Političke Posledice* (Serbian Academy of Sciences and Arts 2020) 27.

24 H. T. Mateu, 'Self-determination and Access to Independence under Current International Law: From Language to Concept' 23 *Spanish Yearbook of International Law* (2023) 42–43.

25 J. Crawford and A. Boyle, 'Annex A Opinion: Referendum on the Independence of Scotland – International Law Aspects' (2012) para 22.1 <https://assets.publishing.service.gov.uk/government/uploads/system/uploads/attachment_data/file/79408/Annex_A.pdf>.

26 Badinter Commission, Opinion No. 1 (29 Nov. 1991) noting that Yugoslavia is 'in the process of dissolution', reprinted in 3 *EJIL* (1992) 184. See also UNSC Res 757 (30 May 1992) rejecting the FRY's claim to be considered a successor of the SFRY.

27 D. Thürer and T. Burri, 'Secession' *Max Planck Encyclopedias of International Law* (2009) para 4.

28 A. Pavković and P. Radan, *Creating New States: Theory and Practice of Secession* (Routledge 2016) 5. See also J. Vidmar, S. McGibbon and L. Raible, 'Introduction' in *Research Handbook on Secession* (Elgar 2022) 1.

The question of how broadly the concept of secession should be understood in international law remains a subject of intriguing debate. Besides the already mentioned consensual separation, scholars discuss whether the recovery of occupied territory and the decolonization process could be subsumed under the notion of secession. Regarding occupied territory, Kolb and Christakis claim that the right to secede undoubtedly arises in this context, yet they describe the situation in slightly different terms. Kolb refers to 'a foreign occupation and domination', whereas Christakis mentions 'military occupation'.[29] However, it is doubtful whether this situation concerns the right to secession or the re-establishment of independence through various means. Even if the territory would be characterized as 'annexed' rather than occupied (which is more reflective of territorial detachment), the legal title is not automatically transferred to the occupant.[30] Similar complexities arise in the context of decolonization. Coggins and Anderson argue for colonial secession, suggesting that colonial territories cannot be considered states prior to independence. In contrast, Kohen and Dahlitz are hesitant to classify colonies as territorial possessions of their administrators, as they were never legally integrated into their governing states.[31] Crawford and Anderson allude to the 'dissolution' of Yugoslavia, steered by the fact that there was no clear successor left from the process (in comparison to the USSR). Conversely, Dugard and Radan assert that Slovenia, Croatia, and Macedonia simply seceded from Yugoslavia, disputing the dissolution narrative.[32] Secession, therefore, in a broader outlook may

---

29 R. Kolb, 'Autodétermination et «sécession-remède» en droit international public' in M. Bassiouni et al. (eds.) *Global Community Yearbook: Global Trends: Law, Policy & Justice Essays in Honour of Professor Giuliana Ziccardi Capaldo* (OUP 2013) 69. T. Christakis, 'L'État en tant que «fait primaire»: Réflexions sur la portée du principe d'effectivité' in M. Kohen (ed.) *Secession: Contemporary International Law Perspectives* (CUP 2006) 142.

30 Under contemporary international law the territory is considered occupied when it is actually placed under the authority of the hostile army. See Convention Respecting the Laws and Customs of War on Land (18 Oct. 1907) 205 CTS 227, Article 42.

31 See B. Coggins, 'The History of Secession: An Overview' in A. Pavković and P. Radan (eds.) *The Ashgate Research Companion to Secession* (Routledge 2011) 26; G. Anderson, 'Secession in International Law and Relations: What Are We Talking About?' 35(3) *Loyola of Los Angeles International and Comparative Law Review* (2013) 376–379. Cf. J. Dahlitz. 'Introduction' in J. Dahlitz (ed.) *Secession and International Law Conflict Avoidance – Regional Appraisals* (TMC Asser Press 2003) 6–7; Kohen, 'Introduction' (n 22) 14.

32 Crawford and Boyle (n 25) paras 79–92; Anderson (n 31) 384. Cf. Radan, 'The Meaning of Secession' (n 21) 34–36. J. Dugard, 'A Legal Basis for Secession – Relevant Principles and Rules' in J. Dahlitz (ed.) *Secession and International Law Conflict Avoidance – Regional Appraisals* (TMC Asser Press 2003) 94.

encompass phenomena, like state succession, which deals with the identity and continuity of states.[33]

Secession, often a protracted process, can be categorized based on its outcome: successful, resulting in the creation of a recognized new state, or unsuccessful, typically due to a lack of international recognition of the new state.[34] However, linking the success of secession solely to the recognition of the new state does not align with the dominant declarative theory of state recognition. According to this theory, recognition is not a constitutive element of statehood. Secession primarily involves territorial change or the loss of part of a state's territory and does not always hinge on the consent or recognition of other states.[35]

2.2 *Secession and the Right to Self-determination*

Conceptualizing and discussing self-determination and secession in parallel is occasionally observed in legal doctrine. Yet, these two terms have never been formally redacted together.[36] There is even some doubt as to whether secession can truly be considered an established institution of international law.[37] Nonetheless, theorists often synthesize the two concepts, explaining them in terms of graduality. According to this view, the fundamental right is the right to internal self-determination, while when it is not possible to consume (realize) it, then the right to external self-determination comes into play. External self-determination represents an extreme dimension of the RSD, manifested through the emergence of a new state, and is tantamount to secession. This is how secession has entered the terminological sphere of self-determination. Earlier, lapidary conceptions of these two terms, that is, institutes, differed. Self-determination was conceived as a legal right and an acceptable concept,

---

33 See ILC, 'First report on succession of States in respect of State responsibility' by Spec. Rapporteur P. Šturma (31 May 2017) UN Doc. A/CN.4/708. Some have suggested the *secessio plebis* (withdrawal of the commoners, or secession of the plebs) in Ancient Rome, which resulted in concessions from the patricians, as an example of an extensive perception of secession. B. Krivokapić, *Enciklopedijski Rečnik Međunarodnog Prava i Međunarodnih Odnosa* (Službeni Glasnik 2010) 968.

34 Pavković and Radan (n 28) 6.

35 Cf. S. Janković, *The Importance of Recognition for a State: A Critical Appraisal of the Declaratory Theory of Recognition and the Concept of Statehood* (PhD thesis, University of Dundee 2020).

36 T. Šurlan, 'Savremena Primena i Tumačenje Pravnih Instituta – Samoopredeljenje i Secesija Sa Stanovišta Međunarodnog Javnog Prava' in Z. Knežević and K. Čavoški (eds.) *Secesija Sa Stanovišta Unutrašnjeg i Međunarodnog Prava i Njene Političke Posledice* (Serbian Academy of Sciences and Arts 2020) 132.

37 Cf. D. Ahmed, *Boundaries and Secession in Africa and International Law* (CUP 2015) 215.

while secession was seen as a para-legal concept, that is, an impermissible act not regulated by law. Acts of secession were thus considered *contra legem*.[38]

Chronologically, self-determination was first articulated in international legal terms in the UN Charter, marking a significant achievement given its absence in the Covenant of the League of Nations. Thereafter, it was included in the 1966 Covenants on Human Rights and the 1970 UN Friendly Relations Declaration.[39] Thus, self-determination has a clear legal genesis, something that cannot be said of secession. Secession is not enshrined in any international legal framework. To decrease the scale of this obvious shortcoming, some have tried to argue, by way of interpretative methods, that 'what is not forbidden is allowed'. Yet, there is another ideological stance which states that only what is explicitly permitted is lawful. There is also a neutral position, which suggests that the approach should depend on the specifics of each case.

The most notable example of secession entering the legal sphere (excluding decolonization and liberation entitlements)[40] is the concept of remedial secession, first patently applied in the case of Kosovo.[41] Remedial secession allegedly possesses a legal foundation in the 1970 Friendly Relations Declaration, whose *a contrario* interpretation indicates that unrepresented and discriminated peoples have the right to seek a separate political status.[42] However, the practical application of remedial secession raises a significant issue: who determines whether there has been a lack of democratic governance or evidence of systemic human rights abuses? In the absence of a central adjudicatory mechanism with binding authority in the otherwise decentralized international system, it appears that powerful states often assume this role.

38 See M. Nawaz, 'The Meaning and Range of the Principle of Self-determination' 1965 *Duke Law Journal* (1965) 82–101; D. Bowett, 'Self-determination and Political Rights in The Developing Countries' 60 *Proceedings of the American Society of International Law* (1966) 129–135; O. S. Kamanu, 'Secession and the Right of Self-determination: An O.A.U. Dilemma' 12(3) *The Journal of Modern African Studies* (1974) 355–376.

39 Consult chapter 2 on the history of the right to self-determination.

40 Decolonization, the most important means of creation of new States during the second half of the twentieth century, was not viewed by the international legal order as an act of secession. One of the reasons for this is summarised in the Friendly Relations Declaration stating: 'the territory of a colony or other non-self-governing territory has, under the Charter, a status separate and distinct from the territory of the State administering it'. UN Doc. A/RES/25/2625 (24 Oct. 1970).

41 See 5.2.4. and 5.3.1.7.

42 D. Dimitrijević, 'Međunarodnopravni Tokovi Secesije Država' in J. Perović Vujačić (ed.) *Unification of Law and Legal Certainty* (Proceedings of the 33rd Meeting of Kopaonik School of Natural Law 2020) 367–368.

Consequently, remedial secession risks being 'delegalized', as its application depends more on geopolitical power than on objective legal principles.

2.3 *Theories of Secession (Introductory Remarks)*

The question of whether there is, or should be, a right to secession in international law has elicited diverse perspectives within legal and philosophical doctrine. One prominent viewpoint holds that positive international law prohibits all forms of secession outside the context of decolonization or foreign occupation – assuming, indeed, that such instances can even be properly classified as secession.[43] This approach, often referred to as the negation theory, rests on two key assumptions: the methods by which secession is pursued and the concept of a protected legal interest (object). In terms of methods of achieving secession, the negation theory generally denies such possibility, be it consensual and peaceful or unilateral and forceful. From the perspective of a protected object, the negation theory argues that secession in itself represents a violation of sovereignty, territorial integrity and political independence of a state.[44] Since (counter)secession is considered an 'internal matter' of the state, foreign interference to effectuate secession is not allowed.[45] Such interference, if carried out under the aegis of the UN outside the framework of Chapter VII, would contravene Article 2(7) of the UN Charter which prohibits the organization from intervening in matters essentially within the domestic jurisdiction of states. Similarly, external armed intervention to support secessionist movements would violate the prohibition on the use of force under Article 2(4) of the Charter. Yet, to the contrary, foreign intervention by invitation of a government to suppress aggressive secessionist attempts would be permitted.[46] Under this 'conservative' approach, self-determination does not grant a right to unilateral secession and, *a fortiori*, explicitly forbids it. At first blush, the negation theory appears persuasive, but when the practical consequences of its application are weighted, a laxer approach seems more opportune. According to Rakić, the conservative apprehension of secession is more frequently and directly endorsed by the organs and officers of international organisations in relation to the international documents enacted by them, than in theoretical

---

43 X. Raflos, 'Secession in International Law' (25 May 2022) <http://idpbarcelona.net/docs/blog/secession.pdf>.

44 Dimitrijević, 'Secesija Država u Doktrini i Praksi Međunarodnog Prava' (n 17) 58.

45 M. Bartos, *Medjunarodno Javno Pravo*, (Kultura 1954) 272. See also Declaration on the Inadmissibility of Intervention, UN Doc. A/RES/36/103 (9 Dec. 1981) Annex, para f.

46 G. Nolte, 'Secession and External Intervention' in M. Kohen (ed.) *Secession: International Law Perspectives* (CUP 2006) 79–86.

works of legal experts, who often subscribe to different strands, notably remedial and abstinence (agnostic) theories.[47]

The abstinence theories are based on the assumption that secession is neither a legal nor an illegal act. Instead, it is a political, legally neutral act. Consequently, the emergence and disappearance of states is a factual rather than a legal issue. This neutrality arises from the absence of specific international legal rules governing secession; international law neither prohibits nor permits it. Secession is thus regarded as a factual event that creates a new reality.[48] Once this new state of affairs consolidates, international law addresses its consequences by defining and regulating the situation. International law in such situations contributes to answering such questions as whether the entity established by secession qualifies as a state in the sense of international law and whether other states should receive that entity as an equal member of the international community. The role of international law in that sense is not confined only to the regulation of the consequences of secession, but also to monitoring the implementation of international rules on international recognition and succession of states.[49]

Theories advocating the existence of the right to secession can be divided into two groups: *Primary Right Theories* and *Remedial Right Theories*. According to the latter, the right to secession exists as a remedy for the infringement of fundamental rights (freedom from). According to primary right theories, however, the right to unilateral secession exists regardless of any prior violations of rights (freedom to).[50]

Primary rights theories are further divided into two kinds: nationalist and democratic. Nationalist theories of secession are based on the premise that there exists inherent moral value in the nation, i.e. a sense of affinity for the 'culturally homogeneous' community. In that sense, they are 'ascriptive' because membership in a group (usually a nation) is predestined in advance and predicates simply on the existence of a nationally-focused linkage. The legitimacy of secession under this model hinges on two requirements: the existence of a 'nation', underpinned by the identity argument, and the presence

---

47 A. Rakić, *Srbija Pred Svetskim Sudom* (Pravni Fakultet Univerziteta u Beogradu 2009) 66–67.

48 H. Hannum, *Autonomy, Sovereignty and Self-determination: The Accommodation of Conflicting Rights* (University of Pennsylvania Press 1990) 27 ff.

49 Thürer and Burri (n 27) para 42.

50 S. Mancini, 'Secession and Self Determination' in M. Rosenfeld and A. Sajó (eds.) *The Oxford Handbook of Comparative Constitutional Law* (OUP 2012) 483.

of a bond between the nation and the given territory.[51] This triggers practical problems, because there may be several different groups that have equally legitimate claims over the same territory. Furthermore, even if all nations are, in principle, entitled to their own state, in practice, fulfilling the aspirations of some nations would inevitably mean leaving the aspirations of others unmet. Within a certain secessionist sub-unit (a territory that has seceded on the basis of national self-determination) minorities may also seek to to invoke the same right, creating a vicious cycle. Ultimately, this model legitimizes secession only if it results in the creation of ethnically homogeneous rather than multinational states, thereby disregarding the reality of the predominantly multiethnic composition of most states in the contemporary international system.

The other kind of primary right secession theories can be termed democratic or choice theories.[52] These theories also posit an unlimited, unconditional right to secession. However, their focus is not on 'the collective autonomy of nations, but rather on the individual autonomy of the group's members'.[53] Choice theories are essentially based on the same sort of legitimacy as democracy itself, and according to them, it doesn't matter if the group represents the nation or whether there has been an infringement of rights – any majoritarian group within a given territory of the existing state favouring secession is authorized to use that right.[54] Therefore, there is no 'national', but 'political-territorial' right to secession legitimized by combined individual choices.[55] These theories argue that guaranteeing the right to secession solely to nations would not only undermine democratic principles, but would also cause uncertainty, given the difficulty of determining whether a particular group represents one or more nations. However, choice theories are typically effectuated by referendum or plebiscite,[56] which seems to replicate similar problems to

51 *Ibid.* 484; A. Buchanan, *Justice, Legitimacy, and Self-determination: Moral Foundations for International Law*, (OUP 2003) 373, 379. Beran adds a sufficient size of a community as a prerequisite for liberal secession. H. Beran, 'Self-determination: A Philosophical Perspective' in W. Macartney (ed.) *Self-determination in the Commonwealth* (Aberdeen University Press 1988) 28. See also W. Kymlicka, *Multicultural Citizenship* (OUP 1995) 107–115.

52 Mancini (n 50) 484.

53 *Ibid.*

54 D. Philpott, 'Self-determination in Practice' in M. Moore (ed.) *National Self-determination and Secession* (OUP 2003) 80.

55 In this vein, any salt water or proximity doctrines confining peoples' political choices are illegitimate. D. Bowett, 'Self-determination and Political Rights in the Developing Countries' 60 *Proceedings of the American Society of International Law* (1966) 131–132.

56 H. Beran, 'In Defense of the Consent Theory of Political Obligation and Authority' 87(3) *Ethics* (1977) 265; D. Philpott, 'In Defense of Self-determination' 105(2) *Ethics* (1995) 352–385.

those connected with nationalist theories, particularly regarding the proper delineation of the voting territory and electorate. If the constituency is defined along national lines, the choice theory effectively aligns with the nationalist theory. If it includes a broader population, however, the voting results will likely differ, creating a problem of majority rule in a newly formed state. A case in point is the 2006 independence referendum in Montenegro, where 55% of people decided to leave the State Union of Serbia and Montenegro, making the majority of Serbs voting against independence live in a new state – Montenegro. This is not to say that all Serbs voted against independence, or that all Montenegrins voted for it, in like manner as not all Scots wanted to leave the UK in 2014. Rather, such cases expose the fragile democratic legitimacy underlying the choice theory. However, the choice theory is not in itself restricted, hence the initial illegitimacy can be rectified in subsequent votes by an unsatisfied new minority, but this is only feasible in enclaves, not in places where the population is dispersed.[57] What also speaks against the ostensible benefits of the 'selves' right to determine their political destiny, including the withdrawal of consent to be governed, is the lack or indeterminacy of 'territorial temporariness', meaning that a group of migrants who settled relatively recently could seek statehood.[58] In this vein, one can indeed wonder whether the choice theory, based on individual rights to democracy and autonomy, is compatible with the common good of a cohesive collective.[59] One should thus seriously think about whether and in what way both nationalist and choice theories should be modified and applied in practice.[60]

As a consequence, although both nationalist and choice theories are tempting for secessionist movements, they have not found many supporters in legal philosophy and international law,[61] both because of the above-mentioned deficiencies and because they come into direct conflict with the principle of

---

57 See T. W. Waters, *Boxing Pandora: Rethinking Borders, States, and Secession in a Democratic World* (Yale University Press 2020) 128–132 (proposing the requirement of a supermajority, as it reflects legitimacy by including as many citizens in favour of secession as possible, while minimizing the number of residents compelled to secede against their will; and holding cascading plebiscites to account for the desires of citizens who oppose secession).

58 H. Hannum, 'Rethinking Self Determination' 34(1) *Virginia Journal of International Law* (1993) 43; Mancini (n 50) 485.

59 D. Raič, *Statehood and the Law of Self-determination* (Martinus Nijhoff Publishers 2002) 310.

60 Political stability, territorial contiguity, and the overall practicability should thus be primarily considered. See C. H. Wellman, *A Theory of Secession: The Case for Political Self-determination* (CUP 2005) 34 ff.

61 *Ibid.*

territorial integrity. On the other hand, theories of a conditional, qualified right to secession have garnered more support.[62]

Remedial theories of secession assert that the right to secede, if it exists or should be recognized, is not inherent but rather conditional, arising only in response to serious and enduring violations of rights inflicted by the parent state.[63] Unlike nationalist or choice theories, which frame secession as a primary right based on self-determination or political preference, remedial theories regard it as a remedial measure that applies only in specific circumstances, when particular conditions are met. The right to separate is grounded in the experience of injustice, but a forthcoming political entity has to be viable in terms of not repeating the mistakes of its predecessor in order to secure recognition. Consequently, there is no (general) right to secede from a just state.[64]

As Buchanan pointed out, the idea of the qualified right to secession has roots in early natural law theory.[65] Although the approach of natural law is not aimed at collective rights as such, the development of a 'federalist' theory of social structure in the 16th century resulted in collectives gaining a place under natural law. Such collectives were considered to be entitled to secession, but only if the application of this right was necessary for the group's continued existence. Similarly, Grotius acknowledged minorities' right to secession under exceptional circumstances. According to Grotius, part of the population cannot unilaterally secede from the state 'unless it is obvious that it cannot be saved in any other way'.[66] Elements of this perspective can also be found in Locke's work. Although Locke did not directly address the right to secession, he applied a similar logic to the conditions under which the right to resist could be invoked. For Locke, this resistance was justified when the legislative or executive authority became tyrannical.[67]

62 P. Bossacoma Busquets, *Morality and Legality of Secession A Theory of National Self-determination* (Palgrave 2020) XI.

63 A. Buchanan, *Secession: The Morality of Political Divorce from Fort Sumter to Lithuania and Quebec* (Westview Press 1991) 152–153.

64 A. Buchanan, 'Theories of Secession' 26 *Philosophy & Public Affairs* (1997) 37.

65 Buchanan, *Justice, Legitimacy, and Self-determination* (n 51) 21–25, 440 ff.

66 H. Grotius, *De Jure Belli ac Pacis Libri Tres* (1646) (Clarendon Press 1925) para 4 <https://archive.org/stream/hugonisgrottiideoogrotuoft/hugonisgrottiideoogrotuoft_djvu.tx>. According to Grotius, self-preservation occurred if there was an imminent threat of death for the people and, even then, the people had the right to resist their sovereign, but not to use violence against him. H. Grotius, *Le droit de la guerre et de la paix* (J. Barbeyrac trans. Pierre de Coup, Amsterdam 1724) 181–182, 185.

67 J. Locke, *Two Treaties on Government* (1764) 334–335, para 168 <https://archive.org/details/twotreatisesofgoolockuoft/page/184/mode/2up>. See also E. de Vattel, *La droit des gens ou principes de la loi naturelle*, vol. I (J. P. Aillaud, Paris 1835) 264 (on the right to separation

Remedial theories also raise a number of thorny questions. The first indeterminacy lies in identifying the subject entitled to secession – is it the whole population or a certain group? Should the same identification rule apply as in the case of a 'people' as holders of the right to self-determination? Secondly, what should form the basis for secession? If it is violations of human rights and internal self-determination, which is the argument most commonly alluded to, then what specific violations should trigger the right to secede, and what threshold must be met? Scholars like Cassese argue for a high threshold, demanding gross breaches of fundamental human rights coupled with no prospects of realizing internal self-determination.[68] This suggests that not every form of discrimination justifies secession. Factors such as the 'quality and quantity' of discrimination, whether the state is willing to end the violence, and whether effective legal remedies exist within domestic institutions should all be taken into account.[69] In terms of specific human rights violations, Oeter has proposed that secession might be triggered if

> the discriminated minority is exposed to actions of a sovereign state that involve obvious and brutal violation of the fundamental human rights e.g. through killing or indefinite detention without legal protection, destruction of family ties, expropriation without taking into account the necessary means for life, through special prohibitions directed against a certain religious community or the use of one's own language and finally through the enforcement of these prohibitions by brutal means and measures.[70]

This is, of course, an indicative, non-exhaustive list. Finally, it has been debated whether the right to secede would continue to exist, once the oppression has ended.[71]

Another problem, of a deeper nature, concerns seeing secession from a historical angle, where it serves as a remedy to injustices done in the past, particularly those involving territorial dispossession.[72] According to this version

---

in case of the 'abandonment', that is, the refusal of the sovereign to provide security to the people).

68 A. Cassese, *Self-determination of Peoples* (CUP 1995) 119–120.

69 V. Dimitrijević, *Savremeno Shvatanje Prava Naroda Na Samoopredeljenje* (Belgrade Centre for Human Rights 2011) 36.

70 S. Oeter, 'Self-determination' in B. Simma (ed.) *The Charter of the United Nations: A Commentary* (OUP 1995) 58.

71 Thürer and Burri (n 27) para 19.

72 Mancini (n 50) 486–487.

of remedial theory of secession, which Brilmayer labels a 'territorial interpretation', secession should not depend on ethnic characteristics that distinguish a group from most of the state's population. Instead, secessionists must demonstrate that their claim for territorial rights is reasonable and rooted in historical titles. As she claims,

> What matters is not that it is "a people" who are seeking to be free. What matters is that this group – whether a homogeneous "people" or not – has a right to a particular parcel of land, a right that was wrongfully taken from them by a powerful neighbor.[73]

Yet, this interpretation is problematic for multiple reasons. From a moral standpoint, it is not clear why a historically based demand for self-determination should prevail over one based on ethnicity,[74] and why peoples could simply not 'earn' sovereignty over land.[75] Indeed, current state boundaries are neither natural nor just, but the same could be said of previous boundaries. Also, a territorial request can be fair to most members of a particular group, yet unfair to minorities. Furthermore, the similarity between 'the people at the moment of lost independence' and 'the present people' may have eroded over time.

As it stands, international law has not developed a clear-cut standpoint towards secession, and it is very difficult to conclusively state which theoretical approach to secession is most plausible, as all are in great measure clothed in uncertainties. Any secession entitlement (or its denial) should be carefully assessed by taking into consideration other principles of international law, the interests of the concerned parties and, most importantly, international peace and stability. This makes the law of secession context-dependent and, by and large, subscribes to the thesis of preserving territorial integrity when internal self-determination is granted.

73 L. Brilmayer, 'Commentaries on Lea Brilmayer, Secession and Self-determination: A Territorial Interpretation: One Decade Later' 25 *The Yale Journal of International Law* (2000) 284.

74 Mancini (n 50) 487.

75 See P. R. Williams, M. P. Scharf and J. R. Hooper, 'Resolving Sovereignty-based Conflicts: The Emerging Approach of Earned Sovereignty' 31 *Denver Journal of International Law & Policy* (2003) 349–387; P. R. Williams and F. J. Pecci, 'Earned Sovereignty: Bridging the Gap Between Sovereignty and Self-determination' 40(2) *Stanford Journal of International Law* (2004) 347–387.

3 Threefold Understanding of the Relationship between International Law and Secession

3.1 *Secession as a Legally Irrelevant Fact: A Critical Analysis of the General Claim*

The argument that secession is not regulated by international law dominates contemporary legal discourse.[76] This, as noted, results from the non-existence of a general international law norm governing secession. On the one hand, it is convenient for international lawyers to defer to domestic (constitutional) law or political discretion, thereby avoiding doctrinal engagement with the profound ramifications that this 'hot potato' entails. On the other hand, by sidestepping a definite stance on secession, these same lawyers impoverish the science of international law at its very base, leaving the question of the determination of the main subjects of the international legal order unresolved. Yet, as will be demonstrated, lawyers tend to adopt the general ambivalence thesis more formulaically, often applying specific caveats. Before delving into these nuances, however, it is necessary to first exemplify the problematic implications of the view that unilateral secession falls entirely outside the purview of international law.

First and foremost, this perspective assumes a distancing – or even a complete detachment – of secession from the right to self-determination. It thereby implies that the rules established within the self-determination framework, such as the permissibility of independence in cases of incomplete decolonization or the exclusion of minorities from external self-determination, are not extended to the realm of unilateral secession.

Secondly, the marked legal indifference toward unilateral secession necessitates a reimagining of the principle of territorial integrity. In essence, if secession is not prohibited under international law, the principle of territorial integrity becomes, in practice, subordinate to unilateral secession. Some have argued that territorial integrity binds only other states but does not shield a state from internal attempts at separation, a view affirmed by the ICJ in *Kosovo* Advisory Opinion.[77] Conversely, others contend that the Court implicitly excluded minorities from the scope of secession by asserting that

---

76 See in T. Christakis, *Le droit à l'autodétermination est-il moribond en dehors des situations de décolonisation* (1999) 74; 'Secession' in J. Salmon (ed.) *Dictionnaire de droit international public* (Bruylant 2001) 1022.

77 T. Franck, R. Higgins, A. Pellet, M. Shaw and C. Tomuschat, 'The Territorial Integrity of Québec in the Event of the Attainment of Sovereignty' Expert opinion prepared in 1992 for Québec Ministère des Relations internationals, para 3.15; ICJ, *Accordance with Inter-*

> during the second half of the twentieth century, the international law of self-determination developed in such a way as to create a right to independence for the peoples of non-self-governing territories and peoples subject to alien subjugation, domination and exploitation.[78]

In any case, the inter-state outlook appears oversimplistic, as territorial integrity is a broad concept, envisaged as a protection from all sorts of dangers, including internal ones.[79] Thinking otherwise would indicate a cohabitation between two openly contrasting terms: secession and territorial integrity,[80] and substantially relativise the very notion of 'integrity', reducing it to a principle actionable only in cases of external aggression or occupation.

Limiting the principle of territorial integrity exclusively to external intervention is both anachronistic and detrimental to the coherence of international law. Contemporary perils to territorial unity predominantly stem from internal strifes, which have become far more prevalent than cross-border invasions. Rejecting protection against internal disruptive movements is inconsistent with the progressive practice of endowing non-state actors with rights and obligations.[81] Furthermore, this rejection by a ricochet undermines the principle of non-intervention in internal affairs. Paradoxically, such a legal lacuna could incentivize 'legitimate insurgents' to appeal for more assistance for their causes, while some states may exploit these ambiguities to conduct hybrid warfare through domestic proxies.

---

national Law of the Unilateral Declaration of Independence in Respect of Kosovo, Advisory Opinion, ICJ Rep. 2010, para 80.

78 *Kosovo Advisory Opinion* (n 77) para 79. In its 2016 judgment, the ECJ (Grand Chamber) held that the principle of self-determination is 'applicable to all non-self-governing territories and to all peoples who have not achieved independence yet'. *Council v Front Polisario*, C-104/16, EU:C:2016:973, para 88. See R. Kolb and T. Gazzini, 'The Autonomous Community of Catalonia and International Law' 31 *Swiss Review of International and European Law* (2021) 11.

79 C. Marxsen, 'Territorial Integrity in International Law – Its Concept and Implications for Crimea' 75 *ZaöRV* (2015) 12–14. Also, the Independent International Fact-Finding Mission on the Conflict in Georgia (IIFFMCG), The Report, vol. II (2009) 137.

80 A. Orakhelashvili, 'Statehood, Recognition and the United Nations System: A Unilateral Declaration of Independence in Kosovo' 12 *Max Planck Yearbook of United Nations Law* (2009) 13.

81 For instance, Article 8 c of the 1998 Rome Statute posits that non-international armed conflicts shall not undermine a government's responsibility to defend the unity and territorial integrity of the state, while Article 46 of the 2007 UN Declaration on the Rights of Indigenous Peoples provides that 'any State, people, group or person' is obliged to respect the territorial integrity and unity of a state.

The emphasis on protecting states' territory 'from outside' assumes that states cannot resort to armed force in their relations.[82] Yet, this assumption inevitably instigates new speculations such as, since when does territorial integrity protect the seceding state? Under what circumstances, and at what point, can other states act in collective self-defense of a new state? And could external parties intervene earlier to prevent potential atrocities during a secession process?[83] Among these considerations, the timing of recognition – viewed as a particular form of intervention – is especially relevant, as it both acknowledges a new reality and influences its future trajectory.[84] Thus, applying the principle of territorial integrity in an 'inter-state' format during secession is very troublesome as it is not clear when a breach of the principle occurs and when it evokes international responsibility. In this sense, the alleged protection 'from outside' oddly both favours and disadvantages secessionist claims. Therefore, dividing the protection of state borders into external and internal should be contested as these two aspects are consequentially interlinked.

Thirdly, propagating the utterly abstentionist view on secession presupposes not only that it is a *process*, which is unregulated *ab initio* – with declarations of independence deemed political acts beyond legal regulation[85] – but also that its resulting *substance* is placed aside from legal considerations. This view corresponds to the basic version of the declaratory theory of recognition propounding the emergence of a state upon meeting criteria adumbrated in Article 1 of the Montevideo Convention (a permanent population, a defined

82 O. Corten, 'Territorial Integrity Narrowly Interpreted: Reasserting the Classical Inter-State Paradigm of International Law' 24 *Leiden Journal of International Law* (2011) 90–91. See also ICJ, *Legal Consequences of the Construction of a Wall in the Occupied Territories*, Advisory Opinion, ICJ Rep. 2004, para 139.

83 Frowein proposed a 'pacified international position' as an indicator for determining when international rules start to apply. J. Frowein, *Das de facto-Regime im Völkerrecht* (Hermann Mosler 1968) 69. Fox suggested that general recognition of a liberation movement provides it with corresponding statehood rights. G. Fox, 'Self-determination in the Post-Cold War Era: A New Internal Focus?' 16 *Michigan Journal of International Law* (1995) 742.

84 Hersch Lauterpacht proposed a duty of recognition. See E. Lauterpacht, *The Life of Hersch Lauterpacht* (CUP 2010) 299–300, 332–338. See also C. Hillgruber, 'The Admission of New States to the International Community' 9(3) *EJIL* (1998) 495 ff.

85 'A declaration of independence (...) constitutes a purely internal legal act and not an international legal act.' ICJ, *Kosovo Advisory Opinion* (n 77) Public sitting (4 Dec. 2009) CR 2009/28, 27, 31 (argument of Jean d'Aspremont on behalf of Burundi, emphasis in original); 'A declaration [of independence] issued by persons within a State is a collection of words writ in water (...). What matters is what is done subsequently, especially the reaction of the international community.' ICJ, *Kosovo Advisory Opinion* (n 77) Public sitting (10 Dec. 2009) CR 2009/32, 47, para 6 (argument of James Crawford on behalf of the United Kingdom).

territory, government, and the capacity to enter into relations with the other states).[86] It is also in line with the facticist version of statehood (*ex factis jus oritur*). This reasoning is however not compliant with state practice, which imposes stringent rules on the secessionist entities, placing a huge emphasis on their independence and effectiveness,[87] as well as with the development of international law and the interrelatedness of international norms.

It is now well established that states cannot be created in the wake of foreign military intervention or in breach of the self-determination norm. Accordingly, declarations of independence by entities formed through such means are considered invalid from the beginning.[88] Earlier, the UN Security Council condemned the unilateral secession of Katanga from Congo,[89] which was facilitated by foreign mercenaries and aid from Belgium. The Council condemned not only the external assistance as unlawful but also the very act of secession itself, deeming it illegal and illegitimate. Similarly, in Resolution 541, the UN Security Council censured the establishment of the Turkish Republic of Northern Cyprus in 1983 accomplished thanks to Turkish armed intervention, yet it also recalled two treaties: the 1960 Treaty Concerning the Establishment of the Republic of Cyprus and the 1960 Treaty of Guarantee.[90] This testifies that both contractual law and acts of international organisations, which implicitly or explicitly prohibit secession, are ignored by the supporters of the strict abstentionist view.

Finally, the legal indifference towards unilateral secession conducted within a state, which constitutes a 'purely internal matter' (sic), applies equally to both established and newly created states. This perspective implies a lack of protection for the territorial integrity of new states, which conflicts with the principle of *uti possidetis*, applicable in the context of decolonization[91] and arguably beyond.[92] Such an approach risks fostering chaos and anarchy.

86 Montevideo Convention on the Rights and Duties of States (1933) 165 LNTS 19, Article 1.

87 For the 'ultimate success' doctrine in Southern Rhodesia, see Privy Council *Madzimbamuto v. Lardner Burke*, Appeal Cases, 1969, 645. In the case of the Turkish Republic of Northern Cyprus, see the US Court of Appeals in *Autocephalous Greek-Orthodox Church of Cyprus and the Republic of Cyprus v. Goldberg and Feldman Fine Arts, Inc.* (1990) 917 F.2d (7th Circuit 1990) 278.

88 *Kosovo Advisory Opinion* (n 77) para 81.

89 UNSC Res 143/1960 (14 Jul. 1960), 145/1960 (22 Jul. 1960), 161/1961 (21 Feb. 1961), 169/1961 (24 Nov. 1961).

90 UNSC Res 541/1983 (18 Nov. 1983).

91 ICJ, *Frontier Dispute (Burkina Faso/Republic of Mali)*, Judgment, ICJ Rep. 1986, 565.

92 Badinter Commission, Opinion No. 3 (11 Jan. 1992), reprinted in 3 *EJIL* (1992) 184–185.

As mentioned, the challenges associated with the pure ambivalence stance have prompted both theorists and practitioners to adopt a more nuanced and flexible perspective, which Sachs and Rakić describe as a 'curiously agnostic approach'.[93]

For instance, Higgins, former president of the ICJ, contended that minorities do not have the right to self-determination and that 'peoples', as titleholders, should be understood as the total population of a state.[94] Under this view, secession would be inadmissible, as it is unrealistic to expect an entire state population to secede (except under an alternative conceptualization of secession, self-determination, and statehood, like secession from colonies etc). Nevertheless, Higgins later argued that

> there is nothing in international law that prohibits secession or the formation of new states. The principle *uti possidetis* provides that states accept their inherited colonial boundaries. It places no obligation upon minority groups to stay a part of a unit that maltreats them or in which they feel unrepresented.[95]

Further, she added that 'if they do in fact establish an independent state, or join with an existing state, then that new reality is one which, when its permanence can be shown, will in due course be recognized by the international community'.[96] Franck, Pellet, Higgins, Tomuschat and Shaw in their expertise for Quebec's Ministry of International Relations drew similar conclusions:

1. international law does not provide for the right to secede and, more particularly, one would search in vain "for a text or practice in positive law enabling us to deduce a right to secede from the right to self-determination";

---

93 S. Sachs, 'Self-determination and Disorder' *International Relations,* Merton College, Oxford, Michaelmas Term, 2003 <https://www.stevesachs.com/papers/paper_selfd.html>; Rakić (n 47) 77. On 'doctrinal attempts refuting the [neutrality] paradigm' see also A. Tancredi, 'A Normative 'Due Process' in the Creation of States Through Secession' in M. Kohen (ed.) *Secession: International Law Perspectives* (CUP 2006) 175 ff.

94 The 1937 Constitution of Ireland in Article 1 provides 'The Irish *nation* hereby affirms its inalienable, indefeasible, and sovereign right to choose its own form of Government, to determine its relations with other nations, and to develop its life, political, economic and cultural, in accordance with its own genius and traditions.' Article 2 sets forth that 'It is the entitlement and birthright of every person born in the island of Ireland, which includes its islands and seas, *to be part of the Irish Nation'* (emphasis added).

95 R. Higgins, *Problems and Process: International Law and How We Use It* (Clarendon Press 1994) 125.

96 *Ibid.*

2. when faced with secessionist attempts, third-party States generally manifest great reservations (except when they are particularly interested in the successful outcome of the attempt);
3. however, there is no legal rule precluding secession; the principle of territorial integrity appears to be strictly an inter-State rule whose effect is partially confused with the principle of non-intervention;
4. once secession has succeeded, the effective exercise of State powers by the new authorities is sufficient to establish the existence of the new State; secession also appears to be "a political fact from which international law is content to draw conclusions when it leads to the establishment of effective and stable State authorities";
5. however, third-party States reserve a right of control by affording the new State recognition, or withholding recognition where its existence is doubtful or brought about by armed force, especially where such force stems too obviously from outside assistance.[97]

Finally, Cerone, in his article in the Belgrade Law Review regarding Kosovo's independence, argued that stating something is not allowed by international law is not the same as saying that it is forbidden. Similarly, asserting that something is not forbidden by international law does not equate to saying it is allowed. Cerone noted that the ICJ, in its advisory opinion on the *Legality of the Threat or Use of Nuclear Weapons*, recognized that certain matters are *non liquet*. But, he suggested that one should adhere to the traditional understanding espoused in the SS *Lotus* case, that what is allowed is simply what is not forbidden.[98] Building on this foundation, Cerone maintained that secession falls outside the scope of international law's direct concern. Moreover, he argued, international law prohibits external interference in a state's secession process. Once secession is completed without external factors, international law then assesses the resulting entity according to the Montevideo Convention's statehood criteria.[99] Lastly, Cerone added, albeit in a footnote, that secession might in certain situations be opposed by the UN Security Council, yet he refrained from asserting the legal effect of such opposition on the existence of the newly formed entity.

Consequently, the authors' stance may broadly be summarized as follows. Firstly, secession and self-determination are distinct concepts, as no right to

---

97 Franck, Higgins, Pellet, Shaw and Tomuschat (n 77) para 3.14.

98 J. Cerone, 'The Legality and Legal Effect of Kosovo's Purported Secession and Ensuing Acts of Recognition' 56(3) *Annals of the Faculty of Law in Belgrade* (2008) 62–63.

99 *Ibid.* 64.

secession can be extrapolated from the right to self-determination.[100] Secondly, secession constitutes a legally neutral act, being a domestic matter over which international law has no competence. In this vein, the territorial integrity principle does not operate.[101] Similarly, there exists no prohibition on the use of force, either by the parent state or by the secessionist entity.[102] Hence, it is possible to submit as well that secession only in legal theory trumps territorial integrity, as it is usually the parent state that disposes of a mighty arsenal capable of quashing revolutionary upheavals.[103] Thirdly, other parties should refrain from intervening in secession processes, as such interference would clearly contravene the principles outlined in Article 2 of the UN Charter. It is in this regard that the authors are inclined to deviate from the neutrality axiom and see secession (and its results) as prohibited in line with the maxim *ex injuria jus non oritur*. Although somewhat reluctantly, the authors also acknowledge that secession processes and their outcomes may be subject to determination by the UN Security Council, which has addressed the legal effects of such secessions. Such a pronouncement is vital for legal analysis, as it transcends the issue of effectiveness and affirms the right to reassert territory without violating other principles, particularly the territorial integrity of an inadequately formed 'state'. Otherwise, most authors agree that international law becomes relevant only when evaluating the statehood conditions of

100 More in N. Dinh, P. Daillier and A. Pellet, *Droit International Public* (Librairie Générale de Droit et de Jurisprudence 1987) 467. Cf. M. Weller, 'Remedial Self-determination' in M. Weller (ed.) *Escaping the Self-determination Trap* (Martinus Nijhoff Publishers 2009) 59–69.

101 More in Report by James Crawford: 'Response to Experts Reports of the *Amicus Curiae*' in A. Bayefsky (ed.) *Self-determination in International Law: Quebec and Lessons Learned: Legal Opinions* (Kluwer Law International 2000) 157. See also G. Abi-Saab, 'The Effectivity Required of an Entity that Declares its Independence in Order for it to be Considered a State in International Law' in *Ibid.* 72–73; B. S. Diallo, 'The Issues of Secession in the Process of the Rise and Fall of States in the Light of International Law' 8 *Adam Mickiewicz University Law Review* (2018) 138.

102 More in T. Musgrave, *Self-determination and National Minorities* (OUP 1997) 193. See also J. Salmon, 'Internal Aspects of the Right to Self-determination: Towards a Democratic Legitimacy Principle?' in C. Tomuschat (ed.) *Modern Law of Self-determination* (Martinus Nijhoff 1993) 256 (who argues that peoples fighting to overthrow the government or to form a new state are *de facto* excluded from the ambit of rights associated with external self-determination. However, even though international law does not confer legitimacy on the use of force in these instances, it does not prohibit it. There is 'a situation of legal neutrality or, if preferred, a situation of *legal lacuna*').

103 Vidmar, Raible and McGibbon claim that apparent legal neutrality does in fact favour the territorial integrity principle. J. Vidmar, L. Raible and S. McGibbon (eds.) *Research Handbook on Secession* (Elgar 2022) 2.

a given entity – provided the process is purely internal – and that such entities merit international recognition.

3.2 *Secession is Prohibited: International and Domestic Practice*

Opponents of the right to secession continue to emphasize the supreme importance of protecting territorial integrity, state sovereignty, and the principle of *uti possidetis juris*.[104] For some, the purported existence of the right to secession signals a serious systemic inconsistency – international law cannot guarantee territorial integrity without prohibiting secession.[105] For others, secession encroaches upon sovereignty and may even threaten the very survival of a state.[106] In the opponents' view, the prohibition of secession can be derived from international instruments, state practice, and judicial rulings. Although the argument for the absolute supremacy of territorial integrity over the right to secede and form a new state is not universally accepted, there are three instances in which secession is generally deemed prohibited, with broad consensus on these points. The first is the well-known rule prohibiting the acquisition of territory by force. This rule has been extended to the context of secession, meaning that any external military assistance to secessionist movements will be deemed a breach of the peremptory norm on the non-use of force, thereby invalidating secession.[107] The second is that secession cannot be imposed by a governing authority against the will of the majority of the population concerned. Consequently, any non-consensual secession will be considered a breach of the right to self-determination, deemed illegal, and will not be recognized by the international community.[108] Interestingly, forced population transfers or similar policies have not yet been categorically recognized

104 Like in the previous section, the views are presented literally, in their general meaning, while the advanced possible exceptions e.g. permissibility of secession as a remedy, but prohibition in other circumstances are outlined in individual authors' opinions.

105 Orakhelashvili (n 80) 13–14.

106 J. Summers, 'The Principle of Territorial Integrity' in J. Vidmar, S. McGibbon and L. Raible (eds.) *Research Handbook on Secession* (Elgar 2022) 42.

107 A. Tancredi, 'Secession and Use of Force' in C. Walter, A. von Ungern- Sternberg and K. Abushov (eds.) *Self-determination and Secession in International Law* (OUP 2014) 89–91.

108 This, in part, stems from the right to a sovereign and democratic state, which, like autonomy cannot be taken away. Obviously, then, non-consensual secession cannot be equated with a lost referendum in a democratic state, regardless of the result. Consult M. Perkowski, 'Forsowanie Samostanowienia We Współczesnej Europie. Uwagi Na Tle Przypadków Krymu i Katalonii' in M. Perkowski, J. Szymański and M. Zdanowicz (eds.) *Człowiek i Prawo Międzynarodowe. Księga dedykowana Profesorowi Bogdanowi Wierzbickiemu* (Temida 2014) 389.

as obstacles to secession.[109] The third argument, less prominent than the first two, concerns the limits of the right to self-determination. It posits that if internal self-determination is adequately respected, a population does not have the right to secede. As such, the prohibition of secession is grounded in or contingent upon the respect for other core principles of international law.

3.2.1 The Cultivation of Territorial Integrity: International Practice

3.2.1.1 *League of Nations*

The League of Nations had the opportunity to consider the application of self-determination and the possibility of secession in the case of the Åland Islands. On that occasion, a Committee of Jurists and a Commission of Rapporteurs were formed with the task of investigating the case and submitting reports to the Council of the League of Nations. The Committee concluded in its report that national groups do not have the right to secede merely by expressing their will. According to the Committee, deciding on separatist claims falls within the internal jurisdiction of states. Namely,

> Positive International Law does not recognise the right of national groups, as such, to separate themselves from the State of which they form part by the simple expression of a wish, any more than it recognises the right of other States to claim such a separation.[110]

The Commission of Rapporteurs affirmed that Finland, including the Åland Islands, became a fully independent state following its declaration of independence from Russia in 1917. Although the Commission acknowledged that the majority of the Åland population would likely vote for union with Sweden in a referendum, it arrived at a similar conclusion regarding the scope of self-determination. Therefore, it is not possible

---

109 The IIFFMCG considered Abkhazia as a 'state-like entity' and only questioned its legitimacy on the basis of the expulsion of the Georgians. (n 79) 134. Consult M. Lister, 'Self-determination, Dissent, and the Problem of Population Transfers' in F. R. Tesón (ed.) *The Theory of Self-determination* (CUP 2016) 145–147. The change in demographic composition of Occupied East Jerusalem by the construction of a wall was considered contrary to the Fourth Geneva Convention and the right of Palestinians to self-determination. *Construction of a Wall* (n 82) paras 115, 120, 134.

110 'Report of the International Committee of Jurists Entrusted by the Council of the League of Nations with the Task of Giving an Advisory Opinion upon the Legal Aspects of the Aaland Islands Question' *League of Nations Official Journal,* 3 Special Supplement (1920) 5.

> to concede to minorities, either of language or religion, or to any fractions of a population the right of withdrawing from the community to which they belong, because it is their wish or their good pleasure, would be to destroy order and stability within States and to inaugurate anarchy in international life; it would be to uphold a theory *incompatible with the very idea of the State as a territorial and political unity.*[111]

Consequently, self-determination, as a right for a minority to secede from the parent state, based solely on their will, was dismissed as an absolute right. However, this does not imply a complete rejection of the right of minorities to secede. The Commission also stated:

> The separation of a minority from the State of which it forms a part and its incorporation in another State can only be considered as an altogether exceptional solution, a last resort when the State lacks either the will or the power to enact and apply just and effective guarantees.[112]

In this statement of the Commission of Rapporteurs, the roots of what would later be designated in international law as remedial secession can be discerned. Specifically, secession is framed as a last resort, to be pursued only when a state is either unable or unwilling to protect the rights of a minority. Consequently, the Åland Islands case cannot be regarded as an outright prohibition of secession, and thus only partially supports the argument against it.

3.2.1.2 *United Nations*

3.2.1.2.1 UN Charter

The UN Charter, in Articles 1 and 55, recognizes the right to self-determination. However, the Charter's treatment of self-determination is phrased in general terms, from which neither a clear prohibition nor entitlement to secession can be inferred.[113] Indeed, it would be historically false to claim that the UN Charter 'provided for and required self-determination in the form in which it

111 Report Submitted to the Council of the League of Nations by the Commission of Rapporteurs (1921), League of Nations Doc. B7 [C] 21/68/106, 28. (emphasis added).

112 *Ibid.*

113 S. F. Van den Driest, *Remedial Secession: A Right to External Self-determination as a Remedy to Serious Injustice* (Intersentia 2013) 100. See also UN Doc. A/C.3/SR.447 (18 Nov. 1952) (Netherlands) para 8.

evolved'.[114] Still, the reading of the relevant Charter's provisions should not be done in the abstract, but rather in connection with their drafting history, other related clauses present in the document and the overall political context. And this is (only) where the inclination of the UN Charter towards the prohibition of secession can be found.

During the preparatory work on the drafting of the UN Charter, considerable debates were devoted to the relationship between self-determination and secession. The Columbian delegate emphatically pronounced that they had no objection to including a self-determination clause so long as it meant self-government. But,

> if it were to be interpreted, on the other hand, as connoting a withdrawal, the right of withdrawal or secession, then we should regard that as tantamount to international anarchy, and we should not desire that it be included in the text of the Charter.[115]

Very similar remarks were voiced by the British and French delegates.[116] Ultimately, the UN Sixth Committee in its final report concluded that the principle of self-determination is in accordance with the goals of the Charter 'only insofar as it implied the right of self-government of peoples and not the right of secession'.[117] This led some authors to conclude that there was no intention to include the right to unilateral secession in the Charter,[118] while others believe

114 R. Higgins, *Themes and Theories: Selected Essays, Speeches, and Writings in International Law* (OUP 2009) 828.

115 Cited after Cassese (n 68) 39–40.

116 '[Britain does] not believe that the principle of self-determination [is] intended to form a basis upon which provinces or other parts of independent states [can] claim a right to secession'. Cited after G. Anderson, 'A Post-Millennial Inquiry into the United Nations Law of Self-determination: A Right to Unilateral Non-Colonial Secession?' 49(5) *Vanderbilt Journal of Transnational Law* (2016) 1207.

117 Final Report of the Sixth Committee, San Francisco 1945, UNCIO Doc. 343, I/1/16, vol. 6 (1945) 296.

118 D. Murswiek, 'The Issue of a Right of Secession – Reconsidered' in C. Tomuschat (ed.) *Modern Law of Self-determination* (Martinus Nijhoff Publishers 1993) 34–35; G. Lauwers and S. Smis, 'New Dimensions of the Right to Self-determination: A Study of the International Response to the Kosovo Crisis' 6 *Nationalism and Ethnic Politics* (2000) 62; T. F. Musayev and R. Sadigbayli, 'The Purposes and Principles of the UN Charter Origins, Subsequent Developments in Law and Practice and (Mis)interpretation in the Context of Unilateral Secession Claims in the OSCE Area' 28 *Security and Human Rights* (2017) 211–213; M. Kohen, 'Self-determination' in J. E. Viñuales (ed.) *The UN Friendly Relations Declaration at 50: An Assessment of the Fundamental Principles of International Law* (CUP 2020) 140.

that a definitive answer cannot be given and that the drafters of the Charter remained neutral on the issue of unilateral secession.[119] According to one commentator, who subscribes to the view that the Charter countervails secession,

> the reference to self-determination encompasses the principle of self-government, but does not justify secession. Finally, the principle of self-determination was formulated as a basis for friendly relations among nations. Thus, according to the drafters of the Charter, a hierarchy of principles existed in that the right of self-determination should be pursued so long as it does not disturb friendly relations among nations.[120]

Accordingly, it is submitted that the right to self-determination enshrined in the Charter refers to peoples organised as states and to the inhabitants of Non-Self-Governing Territories and Trust Territories (*implicitly* under Articles 73 and 76b). However, while peoples organized as states inherently possess the right to independence, the latter category of peoples – understood territorially – are specifically entitled to self-government or independence under the Charter.[121]

Despite the fact that the Charter does not explicitly address the issue of secession, some inferences can be drawn from its broader principles. Notably, the prohibition of secession can be indirectly derived from key provisions such as Article 2(4), which prohibits the use of force, and Article 2(7), which enshrines the principle of non-intervention – particularly with regard to supporting or instigating disruptive internal movements.

In conclusion, the UN Charter does not, in itself, provide sufficient support for the secession prohibition thesis, at least not in the literal sense.

3.2.1.2.2 UN Covenants on Human Rights

What has been established with regard to the UN Charter can easily be repeated with reference to the 1966 Covenants on Human Rights – the text itself, as well as the preparatory work on their drafting are not enough to draw a definite conclusion on the legal qualification of secession. Essentially, common Article 1 of the Covenants does not explicitly mention a right to secession, but it is

---

119 Musgrave (n 102) 181–182; L. C. Buchheit, *Secession: The Legitimacy of Self-determination* (Yale University Press 1978) 73.

120 R. Wolfrum, 'Article 1' in B. Simma et al. (eds.) *The Charter of the United Nations: A Commentary* (OUP 2012) 114.

121 'When the principle applied to States it meant sovereign equality and it was possible to speak of a legal right to self-determination'. See H. Quane, 'The United Nations and the Evolving Right to Self-determination' 47(3) *International and Comparative Law Quarterly* (1998) 547.

worth noting that the provision refers to a 'right', unlike the UN Charter's reference to a 'principle'. This distinction might suggest the existence of remedies in cases of infringement, potentially including unilateral secession. Nevertheless, a closer insight into the full text, opinions of states, and subsequent practice of the established supervisory bodies brings one nearer to the conclusion that the Covenants do not endorse a right to secession.

For instance, even though Article 1(1) of the Covenants uses the phrase 'all peoples', which should be interpreted in 'its most general sense',[122] denoting *de facto* universal applicability of the right,[123] states refrained from specifying the modalities for exercising this right.[124] Moreover, they rejected proposals explicitly referencing the right to secession during thorough debates in the Commission on Human Rights. Notably, Yugoslavia proposed an amendment asserting that self-determination includes 'the right to secede and to establish a politically and economically independent state'.[125] This proposal, however, was not adopted.[126] In addition, state reports submitted to the Human Rights Committee rarely mention the right to secession. When they do, it is typically in the context of constitutional secession rather than as an inherent or universally applicable right.[127]

In the context of a holistic reading of the Covenants, it is important to highlight Article 27 of the International Covenant on Civil and Political Rights. This article guarantees minorities the right to enjoy their cultural life, profess their religion and use their language. As these are expressly recognized as justiciable rights – implying available legal remedies for violations – most authorities agree they cannot serve as legal grounds for unilateral secession.[128] It is widely agreed that minorities, as opposed to peoples,

---

122 Cited in M. Bossuyt, *Guide to the "Travaux Préparatoires" of the International Covenant on Civil and Political Rights* (Martinus Nijhoff Publishers 1987) 32.

123 The first document to use the 'all peoples' formula was General Assembly Resolution 1514 (XV) but its title 'The Declaration on the Granting of Independence to Colonial Countries and Peoples' effectively limited the rightbearers.

124 Van den Driest (n 113) 42.

125 UN Commission on Human Rights Draft Res 'Recommendations concerning international respect for the self-determination of peoples: Yugoslavia' (15 Apr. 1952) UN Doc. E/CN.4/L.22.

126 See also UN Doc. A/C.3/SR.444 (13 Nov. 1952) (Haiti) para 41; UN Doc. A/C.3/SR.447 (18 Nov. 1952) (Netherlands) para 8; UN Doc. A/C.3/SR.454 (24 Nov. 1952) (Ecuador) para 6; UN Doc. A/C.3/SR.458 (28 Nov. 1952) (Venezuela) para 60.

127 Van den Driest (n 113) 101.

128 T. M. Franck, 'The Emerging Right to Democratic Governance' 86(1) *AJIL* (1992) 58; Buchheit (n 119) 84–85.

do not have the right to (external) self-determination.[129] Moreover, Article 27 applies exclusively to individuals, and is not considered as a collective right in the same sense as the right of peoples to self-determination.[130] This interpretation is supported by jurisprudence before the Human Rights Committee under the Optional Protocol, including cases such as *Kitok v. Sweden*,[131] *Lansmann v. Finland*,[132] and *Chief Ominayak and the Lubicon Lake Band v. Canada*.[133] Additionally, the Human Rights Committee's General Comment on Article 27, specifically in point 3.1, clarifies that while the right to self-determination belongs to peoples, Article 27 instead 'relates to rights conferred on individuals'.[134] In this vein, neither Covenant provides a basis for recognizing a right to unilateral (remedial) secession.

3.2.1.2.3 UN Secretary-General

A much more articulated stance on secession was taken in 1970 by UN Secretary-General U Thant, who, referring to the separation attempt of the so-called 'Biafra Republic' from Nigeria, emphasised that

> as far as the question of secession of a particular section of a Member State is concerned, the United Nations' attitude is unequivocal. As an international organization, the United Nations has never accepted and

129 See section 2.5.2. Nonetheless, some authors critique the distinction between peoples and minorities as holders of the right to (external) self-determination. See A. Whelan, 'Self-determination and Decolonisation: Foundations for the Future' 3(4) *Irish Studies in International Affairs* (1992) 47. Makinson treats it as a mere 'semantic blockage' aimed for limiting the rightsholders. D. Makinson, 'The Rights of Peoples: A Logician's View' in J. Crawford (ed.) *The Rights of Peoples* (OUP 1988) 77.

130 Norway's Supreme Court remarked that the ICCPR's Article 27 protects individuals, but 'has a certain collective character'. *Statnett SF et al. v. Sør-Fosen sijte et al.* HR-2021-1975-S (2021) para 106. In the *Sara* judgment, the Court noted that it must be possible for the culture to be practiced jointly with other members of the group. HR-2017-2428-A (2017) para 55.

131 Human Rights Committee, *Ivan Kitok v. Sweden*, Communication No. 197/1985 (27 Jul. 1988) para 6.3.

132 Human Rights Committee, *Lansman et al. v. Finland*, Communication No. 511/1992 (26 Oct. 1994) para 9.2.

133 Human Rights Committee, *Chief Bernard Ominayak and Lubicon Lake Band v. Canada*, Communication No. 167/1984 (26 Mar. 1990) para 13.3.

134 Human Rights Committee, General Comment No. 23: Article 27 (Rights of Minorities) (8 Apr. 1994).

> does not accept and I do not believe it will ever accept the principle of secession of a part of its Member State.[135]

This stance is clearly supported by non-membership in the UN of entities created by unilateral secession against the declared will of the government of the predecessor State.[136] An analysis of relevant UN practice, either explicitly or implicitly, confirms this policy with regard to secession. Thus, for instance, in 2002 the Special Representative of the Secretary-General declared null and void the 'Resolution on the protection of the territorial integrity of Kosovo' adopted by the Assembly of Kosovo, which envisaged to challenge the legality of the border agreement between Macedonia and the FRY in 2001.[137]

In the absence of compelling reasons to invalidate secession – such as external intervention or denial of internal self-determination – the two most significant organs of the United Nations, the Security Council and the General Assembly, have consistently invoked the principle of territorial integrity of states as their main legal argument. This principle aligns closely with the doctrine of state continuity and supports the broader goal of maintaining international stability, particularly with regard to borders.

3.2.1.2.4 UN Security Council

The UN Security Council has repeatedly and unequivocally prioritized the principle of territorial integrity over attempts at secession occurring within existing states. While urging parties to resolve disputes through dialogue, the Council has often emphasized the territorial integrity of states, thereby condemning unilateral actions by separatist movements. For instance, in operative paragraph 1 of Resolution 752 (1992) concerning Bosnia and Herzegovina, the Council demanded:

> that all parties and others concerned in Bosnia Herzegovina stop the fighting immediately, respect immediately and fully the cease-fire signed on 12 April 1992, and cooperate with the efforts of the European Community

135 UN Secretary-General U Thant, 'Press Conference held in Dakar, Senegal' (4 Jan. 1970) 7(2) *United Nations Monthly Chronicle* 34–38.

136 Crawford (n 19) 390. More in J. Dugard, *Recognition and the United Nations* (Grotius 1987) 86–111.

137 See UNMIK/PR/740 (23 May 2002). See Agreement for the delineation of the borderline between the Republic of Macedonia and the Federal Republic of Yugoslavia (23 Feb. 2001) 2174 UNTS 4.

> to bring about urgently a negotiated political solution *respecting the principle that any change of borders by force is not acceptable.*[138]

Similarly, in Resolution 787 (1992), the Council expressed its deep concern over 'the threats to the territorial integrity of the Republic of Bosnia and Herzegovina'. In particular, in operative paragraph 3, the Council

> strongly reaffirms its call on all parties and others concerned to *respect strictly the territorial integrity of the Republic of Bosnia and Herzegovina*, and affirms that any entities unilaterally declared or arrangements imposed in contravention thereof will not be accepted.[139]

In Resolution 982 (1995), the Council further affirmed

> its commitment to the search for an overall negotiated settlement of the conflicts in the former Yugoslavia, *ensuring the sovereignty and territorial integrity of all the States* there within their internationally recognized borders, and stressing the importance it attaches to the mutual recognition thereof.[140]

In the case of Georgia, the Security Council in Resolution 1808 (2008) noted that the United Nations will 'continue to support the process of conflict resolution between the Georgian and Abkhaz sides' but also reaffirmed the territorial integrity of Georgia and praised all efforts by the United Nations and the Group of Friends of the Secretary-General to settle the Georgian-Abkhaz dispute 'by peaceful means and within the framework of the Security Council resolutions'.[141]

Another illustration of the Security Council's commitment to the principle of territorial integrity is its response to the civil war in Sudan. Prior to South Sudan's independence and its admission to the United Nations in 2011, following a referendum under the Comprehensive Peace Agreement,[142] the Secu-

138 UN Doc. S/RES/752 (15 May 1992) (emphasis added).

139 UN Doc. S/RES/787 (16 Nov. 1992) (emphasis added). See also UNSC Res 836 (4 Jun. 1993); 847 (30 Jun. 1993); and 859 (24 Aug. 1993).

140 UN Doc. S/RES/982 (31 Mar. 1995) (emphasis added). See also UN Res 990 (28 Apr. 1995); 994 (17 May 1995) and 1009 (10 Aug. 1995).

141 UN Doc. S/RES/1808 (15 Apr. 2008). See also the Council's Presidential Statement of 8 April 1994, UN Doc. S/PRST /1994/78 (2 Dec. 1994).

142 98.83% of those who took part in the referendum voted for separation or independence. See Comprehensive Peace Agreement between the Government of Sudan and the

rity Council constantly stood on the side of the indivisibility of the country, opposing unilateral actions leading to secession. For instance, in its Resolution 1556 (2004), the Council endorsed the 'deployment of international monitors, including the protection force envisioned by the African Union, to the Darfur region', while reaffirming its 'commitment to the sovereignty, unity, territorial integrity, and independence of Sudan'.[143] Similarly, in Resolution 1769 (2007), the Council reiterated its 'strong commitment to the sovereignty, unity, independence and territorial integrity of Sudan'.[144]

Heed was likewise paid by the Security Council to territorial integrity in Somalia, particularly in response to secessionist pressures from Somaliland and Puntland. The Security Council, in its Resolution 1766 (2007), restated 'the importance of the sovereignty, territorial integrity, political independence and unity of Somalia', while extending the mandate of the Monitoring Group referred to in paragraph 3 of resolution 1558 (2004) regarding the arms embargo, and emphasized the need for the Transitional Federal Institutions to continue 'working towards establishing effective national governance in Somalia'.[145] After the establishment of the Federal Government of Somalia in 2012, which gained international recognition, the Security Council consistently commended efforts to promote peace and security, notably through the African Union Transition Mission in Somalia (ATMIS). It also acknowledged the right of Somalia's government to seek international assistance in combatting radical Islamist groups (Al-Shabaab) that could endanger the stability and territorial integrity of the state.[146] These efforts are comparable to measures taken against ISIL/Da'esh in Iraq and Syria.

Thus, it is beyond doubt that the UN Security Council has consistently reaffirmed the territorial integrity of existing states, particularly in cases of internal conflicts or disputes that could jeopardize sovereignty, political independence, and, above all, territorial unity.[147] It remains so even where there was

---

SPLM/SPLA (with Annexes) <https://peacemaker.un.org/sites/default/files/document/files/2024/05/sd060000the20comprehensive20peace20agreement.pdf>.

143 UN Doc. S/RES/1556 (30 Jul. 2004).

144 UN Doc. S/RES/1769 (31 Jul. 2007) preambular para 2.

145 UNSC Res 1766 (23 Jul. 2007). See also UNSC Res 733 (23 Jan. 1992); 1519 (16 Dec. 2003); 1558 (17 Aug. 2004); 1587 (15 Mar. 2005) and 1744 (21 Feb. 2007).

146 UNSC Res 2687 (27 Jun. 2023). See also UNSC Res 2551 (12 Nov. 2020) and 2628 (31 Mar. 2022).

147 See also Security Council resolutions 1780 (2007) and 1840 (2008) with regard to Haiti; resolution 1796 (2008) with regard to Nepal; resolutions 1782 (2007), 1765 (2007), 1795 (2008) and 1826 (2008) with regard to Côte d'Ivoire; resolutions 1719 (2006) and 1791 (2007) with regard to Burundi; resolutions 1386 (2001), 1510 (2003), 1707 (2006), 1746 (2007) and 1776 (2007) with regard to Afghanistan; resolution 1701 (2006) with regard to Lebanon; resolu-

a lack of real control over contested territory or where a government was not internationally recognized (e.g. Somalia).[148] The conclusion to be drawn from this stance is that the Security Council understands the principle of territorial integrity broadly, applying it not only to relations between states, especially neighboring ones, but also to groups within a state seeking non-consensual secession.[149]

3.2.1.2.5 UN General Assembly

The presumption against secession is also visible in the work of the UN General Assembly. This most representative organ of the international community either directly renounced and condemned separatism, including in instances where the Security Council action was blocked by the veto, or produced acts which obstruct the deduction of any secession entitlement due to insistence on territorial integrity in these same acts.

With reference to Comoros, which achieved independence in 1974, the UN General Assembly has systematically defended territorial unity of this African archipelago, which consists of four islands, including Mayotte. On the other hand, France, argues that Mayotte voted against its independence from France in 1974, and therefore considers the island as its overseas department.[150] But, as noted once by the Secretary-General, this position contradicts France's pre-independence commitments not to divide the archipelago and directly violates paragraph 6 of Resolution 1514 (XV) stating that 'any attempt aimed at the partial or total disruption of the national unity and the territorial integrity of a country is incompatible with the purposes and principles of the Charter of the United Nations'.[151] Accordingly, in Resolution 46/9 (1991) – after France vetoed Security Council resolutions[152] – the General Assembly underlined 'the necessity of respecting the unity and territorial integrity of the Comoro Archipelago, composed of islands Anjouan, Grande-Comore, Mayotte and Moheli'

---

tion 1306 (2000) with regard to Sierra Leone; resolution 1268 (1999) with regard to Angola; Security Council Presidential statement of 20 July 1993, UN Doc. S/26118 with regard to Ukraine.

148 Effective governmental control is a key precondition for statehood, but its interpretation is less stringent in the case of existing states due to the doctrine of state continuity. Consult Y. Rim, 'State Continuity in the Absence of Government: The Underlying Rationale in International Law' 32(2) *EJIL* (2021) 485–506.

149 Written Statement of Serbia in the Kosovo case (15 Apr. 2009) para 476.

150 Mayotte became an overseas department and a region of France in 2011 following a referendum which was passed overwhelmingly.

151 Report of the Secretary-General, 'Question of the Comorian Island of Mayotte', UN Doc. A/49/584 (28 Oct. 1994) part III.

152 See draft resolution S/11967 (5 Feb. 1976).

and expressed hope for finding a just and lasting solution of the question of Mayotte based territorial unity and territorial integrity of the Comorian archipelago.[153] Similarly, in Resolution 49/18 (1994), the Assembly reminded that the UN and its members had agreed to respect Comoros' sovereignty and territorial integrity by dint of a resolution on its admission to the United Nations in 1975. It also noted agreements signed between France and Comoros in 1973 which committed both parties to respect the results of the 1974 referendum and treat the archipelago's independence 'on a global basis not island by island'.[154] Consequently, the General Assembly in this case clearly spoke against internal separatism and reinforced the unity of former colonial territories.

In 2008, the General Assembly expressed its support for territorial integrity of Azerbaijan. In Resolution 62/243 (2008), the Assembly reaffirmed its 'continued respect and support for the sovereignty and territorial integrity of the Republic of Azerbaijan within its internationally recognized borders' but at the same time recognized 'the necessity of providing normal, secure and equal conditions of life for Armenian and Azerbaijani communities in the Nagorno Karabakh region of the Republic of Azerbaijan'.[155] Consequently, the Assembly opposed the dismemberment of Azerbaijan and, by extension, the *de facto* existence of the Nagorno-Karabakh Republic since 1991, advocating instead for internal self-determination.[156] Similarly, through Resolution 68/262 (2014), the Assembly swiftly reacted to secessionist activities in Crimea.[157] It not only upheld its commitment to Ukraine's territorial integrity but also declared that the referendum aimed at altering the status of the Autonomous Republic of Crimea was invalid and called upon states not to recognize any consequences stemming from it. In both cases, the General Assembly noted external interference – by Armenia and Russia, respectively – which could be interpreted as a factor prohibiting secession. However, since the international reaction was not as vociferous, considerable and firm as in the cases of Northern Cyprus or Donbas, where military involvement and subsequent recognition by Turkey and Russia occurred, it is plausible to contend

153 UN Doc. A/RES/46/9 (16 Oct. 1991).

154 UN Doc. A/RES/49/18 (28 Nov. 1994).

155 UN Doc. A/RES/62/243 (14 Mar. 2008).

156 On September 2, 1991, the NKR declared independence. On December 10, 1991, the results of the independence referendum were announced and 99,89% of those taking part voted in favour.

157 UN Doc. A/RES/68/262 (27 Mar. 2014).

that in these cases the principle of territorial integrity was more used to hamper ethnohistorical grassroots attempts at secession.[158]

Yet, the insistence on the principle of territorial integrity is not a recent phenomenon that applies only to existing, independent states. The General Assembly stressed this principle with regard to dependent territories already in the decolonization era, as indicated above when considering the situation of Mayotte.[159] The threat of the secession of Katanga from Congo and West Irian from Indonesia, which coincided with the debates on the 'decolonization resolution' (Resolution 1514), undoubtedly influenced the inclusion of paragraph 6, which considered the fragmentation of a country as a violation of the UN Charter.[160] According to some delegates, attempts to carve up colonies that were in the process of achieving independence, formed part of a 'divide and rule' strategy with the 'white man's burden' invoked as a pretext for perpetuating colonial domination.[161]

The use of the term 'country' in paragraph 6 should be interpreted to encompass both colonial territories (including present-day NSGT), which should preserve their territorial integrity during the process of gaining independence and afterward[162] as well as already independent states, where unilateral secession is prohibited.[163] During the drafting of the 'decolonization resolution', representatives of states were careful to preclude any basis for calling for unilateral

158 In Security Council resolutions 822 (1993); 853 (1993); 874 (1993) and 884 (1993) foreign (Armenian) forces were limited to the territories surrounding Nagorno-Karabakh. In Nagorno-Karabakh there were 'local' forces. The text was supposedly influenced by France in the Security Council. See more in S. Janković and V. Roeben, 'Validity of Contested Title to Territory in Frozen Conflict Zones: The Case of Nagorno Karabakh with Particular Reference to the 2020 War' 39 *Chinese (Taiwan) Yearbook of International Law and Affairs* (2022) 100. On the other hand, Resolution 68/262 garnered only 100 votes in favour (11 state delegations voted against, 58 abstained, while 24 were absent). Consult S. Janković and V. Roeben, 'Russia's Recognition of the DPR and LPR: The Revival of the Constitutive Theory of Recognition? *Opinio Juris* (12 Mar. 2022).

159 UNGA Res 1514 (XV) (14 Dec. 1960).

160 J. Trinidad, 'Territorial Integrity and the Limits of Self-determination: Paragraph 6 of the Colonial Declaration' in *Self-determination in Disputed Colonial Territories* (CUP 2018) 21–38.

161 See e.g. comments of Indonesian delegate, UN Doc. A/PV.936 (5 Dec. 1960) 1153, paras 53–55; Moroccan delegate's comments, UN Doc. A/PV.947 (14 Dec. 1960) 1284, paras 158–161.

162 This principle was found to interdict Britain to separate Chagos Islands from Mauricius before it became independent. ICJ, *Legal Consequences of the Separation of the Chagos Archipelago from Mauritius in 1965*, Advisory Opinion, ICJ Rep. 2019, paras 136–137, 170–174.

163 Anderson (n 116) 1209.

secession. For example, Guatemala and Sweden emphasized the primacy of state sovereignty and territorial integrity, with Sweden even proposing an amendment to the draft that would prohibit the possibility of a 'segment of a population or region of a state' to pursue unilateral secession.[164] In addition to the obvious preference to protect the existing state-centric order, two other significant reasons could be brought forward as to why the 'decolonization resolution' prohibited unilateral secession: first, the desire to prevent conflicts between feuding indigenous tribes, especially in Africa; and second, the concern that such conflicts would hinder the decolonization process.

Another document where the ascendency of territorial integrity over secession is perceptible is the 1970 Declaration on Principles of International Law concerning Friendly Relations and Co-operation among States in accordance with the Charter of the United Nations.[165] First, in paragraph 7 of the principle of equal rights and self-determination of peoples, often referred to as the 'safeguard clause' and second, in the following paragraph providing that 'every State shall refrain from any action aimed at the partial or total disruption of the national unity and territorial integrity of any other State or country'.

Although some authors actually deduce the secession entitlement from the 'safeguard clause', it should be remarked that this is an exception to the rule, not the rule *per se* – an interpretation that could, at best, be regarded as *de lege ferenda*.[166] For this reason, it is appropriate to align with the view of Espiell, Special Rapporteur on the on the Implementation of UN Resolutions relating to the Right of Peoples under Colonial and Alien Domination to Self-determination, who concluded in his report that:

> Where the territorial integrity of the state is involved, the right to self-determination does not in principle apply. The express acceptance in these instruments (Resolutions 1514 (XV) and 2625 (XXV)) of the principles of the national unity and the territorial integrity of the state implies non-recognition of the right to secession.[167]

---

164 See 15 GAOR, Plen., 946 mtg. (14 Dec. 1960) UN Doc. A/15/PV.946, 1266 (referring to Leopoldville); 15 GAOR, Plen., 947 mtg. (14 Dec. 1960) UN Doc. A/15/PV.947, 1271 (the representative of Guatemala stated that Guatemala would like the concept of territorial integrity to be more clearly expressed). Guatemala also attempted unsuccessfully to insert a paragraph into the Declaration recognising the right of states to recover national territory. UN Doc. A/L.325, Annexes.

165 UN Doc. A/RES/2625 (XXV) (24 Oct. 1970).

166 See section 3.3.3.2.

167 Sub-Commission for Prevention of Discrimination and Protection of Minorities, 'Implementation of United Nations Resolutions Relating to the Right of People under Colonial

3.2.1.2.6 International Court of Justice

The International Court of Justice, the principal judicial organ of the United Nations has on numerous occasions emphasized the paramount importance of the principle of territorial integrity. In the *Corfu Channel* case, the Court underlined that 'between independent States, respect for territorial sovereignty is an essential foundation of international relations',[168] while in *Nicaragua*, it reaffirmed 'the duty of every State to respect the territorial sovereignty of others'.[169] In the *Kosovo* Advisory Opinion, the Court recalled that 'the principle of territorial integrity is an important part of the international legal order' and against the bedrock of the Friendly Relations Declaration and the Helsinki Final Act, it concluded that the scope of the territorial integrity principle is 'confined to the sphere of relations between States'.[170]

Although, unquestionably, states must respect each other's territorial integrity, a question appears what does this obligation in reality connote. In its most basic sense, the principle denotes territorial inviolability and political independence, safeguarding states not only from external armed aggression but also from other destabilizing activities, such as financial, logistical, or military support for separatist movements – although adherence to this standard is not universal.[171] Importantly, the non-intervention rule, as an extension of this principle, serves as an indirect mechanism to prevent secession by prohibiting external interference but does not regulate how a state manages entities within its own territory.

The ICJ has not yet issued a definitive ruling on the relationship between territorial integrity and secession in non-colonial contexts, yet its dicta have established important guiding principles.[172] In the *Burkina Faso/Mali* case, the Court linked external self-determination with territorial integrity in the

---

and Alien Domination to Self-determination'. Report prepared by Spec. Rapporteur H. G. Espiell (1977) UN Doc. E/CN.4/Sub.2/390, paras 73–74.

168 ICJ, *The Corfu Channel Case (United Kingdom of Great Britain and Northern Ireland v. Albania)*, Judgment, ICJ Rep. 1949, 35.

169 ICJ, *Military and Paramilitary Activities in and against Nicaragua (Nicaragua v. United States of America)*, Judgment, ICJ Rep. 1986, paras 213, 251–252.

170 *Kosovo Advisory Opinion* (n 77) para 80.

171 ICJ, *Armed Activities on the Territory of the Congo (Democratic Republic of the Congo v. Uganda)*, Judgment, ICJ Rep. 2005, paras 163–165. As noted, restricting the applicability of the territorial integrity principle to inter-state relations may, in fact, undermine the non-intervention rule. S. Blay, 'Territorial Integrity and Political Independence' *Max Planck Encyclopedias of Public International Law* (2010) paras 6–7, 14–16.

172 M. Shaw, 'The International Court of Justice and the Law of Territory' in C. Tams and J. Sloan (eds.) *The Development of International Law by the International Court of Justice* (OUP 2013) 173.

context of former colonies.[173] More broadly, in the *Temple of Preah Vihear* judgment, the Court articulated a positive obligation on states under the principle of territorial integrity: 'once a dispute regarding territorial sovereignty has been resolved and uncertainty removed, each party must fulfil in good faith the obligation which all States have to respect the territorial integrity of all other States'.[174]

This obligation implies that states are required to address separatist challenges within existing states through viable solutions, employing mechanisms such as dialogue, mediation, and good offices. Other states are expected to assist, insofar as possible, in implementing those solutions in a manner consistent with territorial integrity.

3.2.1.3 *African Union*

It is also relevant to consider the African Charter as the most significant regional instrument encompassing the right to self-determination alongside other rights of peoples. Article 20, paragraph 1, of the Charter enshrines the right to self-determination as follows:

> All peoples shall have the right to existence. They shall have the unquestionable and inalienable right to self – determination. They shall freely determine their political status and shall pursue their economic and social development according to the policy they have freely chosen.[175]

The first paragraph of Article 20 is similar to the common Article 1 of the International Covenants on Human Rights, guaranteeing the right to self-determination to all peoples as the ability to choose their political status and to pursue economic, social and cultural development. However, the second and third paragraphs expand this guarantee to include external self-determination in certain circumstances. Paragraph 2 recognizes the right of colonized or *oppressed* peoples to free themselves from domination through means acknowledged by the international community, while paragraph 3 stipulates that all peoples have the right to receive assistance from the State Parties to the Charter in their liberation struggles against foreign political, economic, or cultural domination. Nevertheless, the African Commission on Human and Peoples' Rights has set a limit on such an extensive interpretation

---

173 *Frontier Dispute* (n 91) paras 18–22.

174 ICJ, *Request for Interpretation of the Judgment of 15 June 1962 in the Case concerning the Temple of Preah Vihear (Cambodia v. Thailand)*, Judgment, ICJ Rep. 2013, para 105.

175 Organization of African Unity (OAU), African Charter on Human and Peoples' Rights (Banjul Charter) (27 Jun. 1981), reprinted in 21 *ILM* (1982) 58.

of the right to self-determination in the case of *Katangese Peoples' Congress v. Zaire*. Namely, on that occasion, it was emphasized that the right to self-determination enshrined in Article 20 should be applied in any form that is in accordance with the wishes of the people, but in strict observance of the principles of sovereignty and territorial integrity, despite the silence of the Charter on this issue.[176] This rationale was upheld in the later verdict in *Kevin Mgwanga Gunme et al. v. Cameroon*.[177] As Hannum notes, the African states were among the forerunners of the development of the concept of self-determination during decolonization, but in the postcolonial context, they adopted a very narrow interpretation of the right to self-determination.[178] Priority has been given to the principles of territorial integrity and national unity, largely due to the ethnic heterogeneity of most African states and the associated difficulties in fostering a unified national identity.[179] In light of the foregoing, it can be concluded that the right to self-determination as articulated in the African Charter is primarily understood as internal self-determination. The Commission's emphasis on territorial integrity effectively limits the exercise of external self-determination, ruling out secession as a legitimate expression of this right under normal circumstances.[180]

To summarize, it is indicative that relevant instruments addressing the right to self-determination either explicitly link this right to the principle of territorial integrity or establish such a connection through the practice of states and international bodies. This linkage serves to prohibit the full or partial dismemberment of sovereign states, particularly when those states uphold the principle of equal rights and (internal) self-determination of peoples.

3.2.1.4 *Bilateral and Multilateral Relations (International Recognition)*

States, concerned about secession within their own borders, consistently oppose it on the international level. Governments attempting to suppress secessionist movements tend to receive more international support than the secessionist movements themselves.[181] Although intrastate entities may occasionally

---

176 ACHPR, *Katangese Peoples' Congress v. Zaïre*, Communication No. 75/92 (1995) para 4.

177 ACHPR, *Kevin Ngwanga Gumne et al. v. Cameroon*, Communication No. 266/2003 (2009) paras 163, 191.

178 Hannum, 'Rethinking Self Determination' (n 58) 30.

179 *Ibid.*

180 However, it should be noted that the Commission has scrutinized whether violations of the right to representative government have occurred, thereby implying that remedial secession could potentially arise as an exceptional measure. See 3.3.3.2.

181 See A. Heraclides, 'Secession, Self-determination and Nonintervention: in Quest of a Normative Symbiosis' 45(2) *Journal of International Affairs* (1992) 399–420.

garner moral or logistical backing, this rarely translates into formal recognition of the territories they claim. Thus, Kurds in Iraq have been given considerable military and humanitarian assistance, yet discussions of their independence have been studiously avoided. India for a time aided Tamil separatists in Sri Lanka, but with the 1987 Indo-Sri Lanka Accord, signaled it would not support a separate Tamil state.[182] To date, no state has accorded recognition to the Chechen Republic, despite widespread condemnation of Russia's actions in suppressing the rebellion, and the Tibetan and Taiwanese bids for independence have elicited little beyond rhetorical backing. Even Saudi Arabia, which supported the unsuccessful secession attempt by southern Yemenis from the newly unified nation, stopped short of formal recognition.[183]

One can, however, wonder whether international recognition is indeed a practical gauge of secession denial, especially when considering contacts with formally non-recognized states, such as Russia's dealings with Transnistria and Nagorno Karabakh, the U.S. partnership with Taiwan, and the EU's informal relations with Abkhazia. These examples demonstrate that territorial integrity can be undermined through indirect means, suggesting that the suppression of effective entities is the most significant indicator in state practice.

3.2.2 The Cultivation of Territorial Integrity: Domestic Practice

3.2.2.1 *Constitutional Provisions*

A great majority of states' constitutions – either directly (around 60) or through broader references (around 204) – forbid secession.[184] Examples of the former include Ecuador's Constitution, which in Article 238 states quite clearly that 'under no circumstances shall the exercise of autonomy allow for secession from the national territory',[185] or Myanmar's Constitution, which in Article 10 explicitly forbids secession by stating 'no part of the territory constituted in the Union such as Regions, States, Union Territories and Self-Administered Areas shall ever secede from the Union'.[186]

---

182 S. W. R. de A. Samarasinghe, 'The Dynamics of Separatism: The Case of Sri Lanka' in R. R. Premdas et al. (eds.) *Secessionist Movements in Comparative Perspective* (1990) 48, 60–63.

183 Fox (n 83) 741.

184 T. Ginsburg, 'Constitution Brief: Secession' Institute for Democracy and Electoral Assistance (2018) <https://www.idea.int/sites/default/files/publications/constitution-brief-secession.pdf>.

185 Constitution of Ecuador (2008) <https://pdba.georgetown.edu/Constitutions/Ecuador/english08.html>.

186 Constitution of the Republic of the Union of Myanmar (2008), MMR-2008-C-79572.

The 'broader' constitutional references typically navigate around the notion of territorial integrity and are reflected in various semantic forms, ranging from 'the indivisibility of the state' to the concept of 'state unity or national unity'. By protecting territorial integrity, these constitutions practically bar secession.[187] For instance, Article 2 of the Spanish Constitution stipulates that 'the Constitution is based on the indissoluble unity of the Spanish nation, the common and indivisible country of all Spaniards'.[188] Article 5 of the Italian Constitution prescribes that 'the Republic, which is one and indivisible, recognises and promotes local autonomy'.[189] Article 8 of the Serbian Constitution states 'the territory of the Republic of Serbia is inseparable and indivisible'.[190]

It is clear that provisions allowing for amendments or exceptions to the general rule of territorial integrity can only be sought within the same constitutional framework, due to the prime position of constitutions in the hierarchy of domestic legal acts.[191] This constitutional primacy mirrors the Vienna Convention's requirement that territorial dispositions satisfy the highest domestic legal thresholds (Article 46), reflecting international law's preference for orderly, rule-bound territorial transitions. Accordingly, the Serbian Constitution sets forth that 'the border of the Republic of Serbia is inviolable and may be altered in a procedure applied to amend the Constitution'.[192] Uzbekistan's Constitution is more specific: Article 74(1) asserts that the Republic of Karakalpakstan 'shall have the right to secede from the Republic of Uzbekistan on the basis of a nation-wide referendum held by the people of Karakalpakstan'.[193] Article 4 of Liechtenstein's Constitution permits secession of individual communes, provided that a majority of their voting-eligible citizens initiates the process, and that 'secession shall be regulated by a law or, as the case may be, a treaty'.[194] The various modes for implementing secession entitlements are thus stipulated in constitutions and the validity of any secession must be judged through the prism of these constitutional provisions. Consequently, secession is not a

---

187 Venice Commission, 'Self-determination and Secession in Constitutional Law', Doc. CDL-INF (2000) 2.

188 Constitution of Spain (1978) <https://www.senado.es/web/conocersenado/normas/constitucion/detalleconstitucioncompleta/index.html?lang=en>.

189 Constitution of the Italian Republic (1947) GU Serie Generale n.298 del 27-12-1947.

190 Constitution of the Republic of Serbia (2006) Official Gazette of the RS No. 98/2006.

191 Note that in *Sentenca 1146* of 1988, the Italian Constitutional Court ruled that 'the unity of the Republic' is removed even from the power of constitutional revision.

192 Constitution of the Republic of Serbia (n 190) Article 8.

193 Constitution of the Republic of Uzbekistan (1992) <https://www.constituteproject.org/constitution/Uzbekistan_2011.pdf?lang=en>.

194 Constitution of the Principality of Liechtenstein (1921) <https://www.constituteproject.org/constitution/Liechtenstein_2011?lang=en>.

universal right of peoples but is limited to constitutionally defined entities in certain states. Constitutional secession has been advanced in the *Quebec Reference*, where the Court observed that the 'legality of unilateral secession must be evaluated, at least in the first instance, from the perspective of the domestic legal order of the state from which the unit seeks to withdraw'.[195] Scholars tend to endorse this view, with some extending it beyond 'express constitutional self-determination/secession' to include peace settlements (as in South Sudan),[196] dissolution of federal-type states (like Yugoslavia) and even 'implied constitutional self-determination' (which could apply to Quebec, Faroe Islands and Scotland).[197]

3.2.2.2 *Judicial Practice*

Domestic judicial practice not only confirms the applicability of rules prohibiting secession but also reveals the stance taken by courts when such rules are not explicitly enshrined in the constitution, as was the case in Canada.

In the second half of the 20th century, the population of Quebec demanded greater autonomy within Canada.[198] These demands culminated in a 1995 referendum, in which Quebecers had the opportunity to express their opinion on secession and the creation of an independent state of Quebec. By a narrow margin, the voters decided to remain part of Canada. This outcome prompted Quebec's leaders to consider holding another referendum, while Canada's Governor in Council referred the issue of the legality of unilateral secession by a Canadian province to the Supreme Court.

Faced with this question, the Supreme Court of Canada took a cautious approach towards Quebec's secession, stating that the 'underlying principles that animate' the Canadian Constitution preclude secession, in spite of no specific textual provision prohibiting the dismantling of the Canadian state.[199]

---

195 *Reference re Secession of Quebec* (1998) 2 SCR 217, para 83.

196 The 2002 Machakos Protocol in part A, Art. 1(3) guaranteed a referendum on secession to South Sudan, after an interim period of six years. Similarly, the 2001 Kokopo Agreement in Art. 1–4 foresaw an independence referendum for Bougainville within 15 years of its conclusion.

197 M. Weller, 'The UK Supreme Court Reference on a Referendum for Scotland and the Right to Constitutional Self-determination: Part II' *EJIL:Talk!* (13 Dec. 2022). The court in the *Quebec Reference* seemed to support that by stating: 'the clear repudiation by the people of Quebec of the existing constitutional order would confer legitimacy on demands for secession' (n 195) para 88.

198 B. H. Oxman and S. J. Toope, 'Self-determination – Canada – Quebec – Right to Secede Under Constitutional Law and Public International Law – Role of International Law in Canadian Courts' 93(2) *AJIL* (1999) 519–525.

199 *Ibid.*

Nevertheless, if Quebecers were to approve secession in voting by 'a clear majority on a clear question', democratic legitimacy would be bestowed upon the secessionist project and a constitutional duty to negotiate would emerge, binding the other provinces and the federal authority.[200] The Supreme Court also made a distinction between internal and external self-determination. It defined internal self-determination as 'a people's pursuit of its political, economic, social and cultural development within the framework of an existing state', while external self-determination was recognized as arising 'only in the most extreme of cases', potentially taking the form of unilateral secession.[201] According to the Court, if a people's right to self-determination is 'totally frustrated', they would be empowered to exercise external self-determination through remedial secession.[202] The ruling of the Canadian court is thus in conformity with the general superiority of the territorial integrity principle, since it only allows secession in *extreme* (extraordinary) situations.[203]

In truth, constitutional courts have mainly referred to constitutional provisions protecting territorial integrity in cases of attempted secessionism. Thus, when the Veneto's pro-independence party (*Indipendenza Veneta*) campaigned for the organization of an independence referendum in 2012, and when the Veneto Regional Council passed two laws in 2014 on the organization of two consultative referendums on autonomy and independence, the Italian Constitutional Court intervened.[204] In its judgment 115/2008, the Italian Constitutional Court ruled that a

> a referendum initiative, as also that under examination, at odds with the unity of the Republic could never involve the legitimate exercise of power by regional institutions and is therefore *extra ordinem*.[205]

The illegality also stemmed from the fact that the referendum in itself 'suggested the subversion of the institutions in a manner that is inherently incompatible with the founding principles of the unity and indivisibility of the Republic laid down in Article 5 of the Constitution'.[206]

---

200 *Reference re Secession of Quebec* (n 195) paras 151–153.

201 *Ibid.* para 126.

202 *Ibid.* para 135.

203 *Ibid.* paras 131, 154.

204 The laws of the Veneto Region 19 June 2014, N. 15 (Consultative Referendum on the autonomy of the Veneto), and 19 June 2014, N. 16 (Calling of the consultative referendum on the independence of the Veneto).

205 *Sentenca* No. 118/2015, para 7.2.

206 *Ibid.*

The German Federal Constitutional Court (*Bundesverfassungsgericht*) in 2016 rendered a decision regarding the potential independence of Bavaria, a federal state of Germany.[207] The decision is short, with only three sentences. As first, the Court noted that Germany rests upon the constituent power of the German people as a whole. This implies that federal units (*Länder*) are not 'masters the Constitution', i.e. Basic Law (*Grundgesetz*). There is, therefore, no room under the Basic Law for *Länder* to seek secession.[208] The Court, obviously, took a straightforward approach grounded solely in domestic law, making no references to international law. Its reasoning echoed that of the Spanish Constitutional Tribunal, which has consistently rejected any right of the Catalan people to self-determination, relying instead on a conception of mononational and unitary sovereignty.[209]

The Iraqi Supreme Federal Court initially ordered the suspension of the Kurdish regional government's independence referendum scheduled for 25 September 2017, and subsequently declared it unconstitutional, ruling that all results and effects of the referendum were null and void.[210] Constitutional courts, however, do not restrict themselves to merely invalidating unconstitutional acts, but also underline that attempts at territorial dismemberment are punishable under the law. In Turkey, for instance, the Constitutional Court has dissolved several political parties thought to be promoting the fragmentation of the state, including the Freedom and Democracy Party (ÖZDEP), the People's Labour Party (HEP), and the Democratic Party (DEP).[211] Dividing the Turkish nation into two groups, 'Turks' and 'Kurds', advocating for their self-determination, or even opting for a federal system was pronounced unconstitutional.[212]

Moreover, domestic courts may align with a state's official foreign policy and refer to the legal status of other separatist entities in their rulings, as was the case with the German Higher Administrative Court of Rhineland-Palatinate

207 Federal Constitutional Court of Germany (*Bundesverfassungsgericht*), Decision of the Second Chamber of the Second Senate (16 Dec. 2016) 2 BvR 349/16.

208 Supporters of the implicit right to secession argue that the Constitution also does not prohibit secession and point out that, just *as Grundgesetz* accession through free will was based on Article 178 of the Bavarian Constitution of 1946, so too could secession be justified in a similar manner. See K. J. Nagel, 'Bavaria. A Right to self-determination and secession?' in D. Turp and M. Sanjaume–Calvet (eds.) *The Emergence of a Democratic Right to Self-determination in Europe* (Centre Maurits Coppieters 2016) 40.

209 See 5.2.7.2. and 5.2.7.5.

210 Judgement of the Federal Supreme Court of the Republic of Iraq, Ref. 89 & 91 & 92 & 93/ federal/2017 (20 Nov. 2017).

211 Bulletin on Constitutional Case-Law, TUR-1993-3-002; TUR-1994-1-001; TUR-1994-2-003.

212 Bulletin on Constitutional Case-Law, TUR-1993-3-002; TUR-1994-1-001.

and the Bavarian Administrative Court, both of which in 2016 ruled that Nagorno-Karabakh is not an independent state, but is part of the territory of Azerbaijan.[213]

3.2.3 Cases of Invasion and Violations of the Right to Self-determination

As argued earlier, the traditional view that secession is a purely factual issue can lead to the erroneous conclusion that there is complete 'legal neutrality' regarding the process of secession and its outcome. However, secession does not take place in a legal vacuum. If a secessionist entity violates a peremptory norm or other fundamental principles of international law during the secession process, that entity is denied the status of a state under international law. Consequently, all acts and processes leading to this status, such as referendums, parliamentary resolutions etc. are likewise deemed invalid.[214] Post-WWII state practice confirms that entities established in violation of peremptory norms are routinely denied recognition by the international community. This principle is exemplified by three key cases. First, Rhodesia's 1965 Unilateral Declaration of Independence (UDI) by a white minority regime – which sought to perpetuate racial oppression – was universally condemned as illegal. Second, the Turkish Republic of Northern Cyprus, declared in 1983 following Turkey's military intervention, violated Cyprus's territorial integrity and the prohibition on the use of force. Conversely, East Timor's 1999 independence struggle, though initially met with Indonesian repression, gained global support precisely because it aligned with *jus cogens* norms: Indonesia's occupation (1975–1999) had violated the Timorese people's right to self-determination, and their eventual sovereignty was achieved through a UN-backed referendum. These cases collectively demonstrate that recognition hinges on adherence to fundamental norms: territorial integrity, the prohibition of force, and the right to self-determination exercised free from coercion or discrimination.

3.2.3.1 *Rhodesia*

In the 19th century, Britain established a sphere of influence over what would become Southern Rhodesia, centered on the extraction of mineral resources. It is noted in the literature that the origins of the crisis that broke out in 1965

213 Decision BayVGH (10 Aug. 2006) 9 B 03.30076, RN 34; Decision of the OVG Rheinland-Pfalz (28 Aug. 2006) 6 A 10813/06, RN 4 f.; in this spirit also BayVGH (18. Aug. 2006) 9 B 04.30794, RN 20.

214 Consult A. Peters, 'Sense and Nonsense of Territorial Referendums in Ukraine, and Why the 16 March Referendum in Crimea Does Not Justify Crimea's Alteration of Territorial Status under International Law' *EJIL:Talk!* (16 Apr. 2014).

can be traced to Britain's initial policy of entrusting local administration to chartered companies (company rule) and the gradual delegation of authority to European settlers. This approach ultimately resulted in a minority group gaining a significant degree of internal self-government.[215]

On June 12, 1962, the UN General Assembly adopted Resolution 1747,[216] which designated Southern Rhodesia as a Non-Self-Governing Territory under Chapter XI of the UN Charter. The resolution also reaffirmed the United Kingdom's obligation under paragraph 5 of Resolution 1514 to 'transfer all powers to the people of Southern Rhodesia'. In addition, the United Kingdom, as the administering authority, was urged to grant equal political rights and freedoms to the Black majority population and to propose a non-discriminatory constitution, specifically ensuring that the majority would have equal voting rights under the proviso 'one man, one vote'.[217]

On the eve of the Rhodesian elections scheduled for May 7, 1965, and amid preparations for a unilateral declaration of independence, the UN Security Council adopted Resolution 202, which appealed to the United Kingdom and all member states of the United Nations not to recognize any unilateral declaration of independence by the minority government of Southern Rhodesia. It further urged the UK

> not to transfer under any circumstances to its colony of Southern Rhodesia, as at present governed, any powers or attributes of sovereignty, but to promote the country's attainment of independence by a democratic system of government in accordance with the aspirations of the majority of the population.[218]

The Rhodesian Front, a political party representing the white settler population, won the elections. Shortly thereafter, Prime Minister Ian Smith demanded immediate independence from Britain. This request was rejected, and in response, Britain set out five conditions that must be met before granting independence, including demonstrable progress in eliminating racial discrimination and the stipulation that any proposal for independence must be acceptable to the entire population of Rhodesia.[219] The latter negotiations between

215 V. Gowlland-Debbas, 'Collective Responses to the Unilateral Declarations of Independence of Southern Rhodesia and Palestine: An Application of the Legitimizing Function of The United Nations' 61 *British Yearbook of International Law* (1991) 137.

216 UNGA Res 1747(XVI) 'The Question of Southern Rhodesia' (12 Jun. 1962).

217 *Ibid.* point 2.

218 UNSC Res 202 (6 May 1965).

219 Raič (n 59) 128.

British and Southern Rhodesian authorities did not bear fruit, and Southern Rhodesia was unilaterally declared an independent state by the regime of Ian Smith on November 11, 1965. The very next day, the UN Security Council passed a resolution condemning the UDI, denouncing the racist minority regime in Southern Rhodesia, and urging all states to withhold recognition and any form of assistance to the illegitimate regime.[220]

In an attempt to secure legitimacy, the minority regime planned to hold elections in April 1979, but the Security Council thwarted such an attempt, stating that it:

> declares any elections held under the auspices of the illegal racist régime and the results thereof null and void and that no recognition will be accorded either by the United Nations or any Member State to any representatives or organ established by that process.[221]

Southern Rhodesia remained an unrecognized entity until 1979, when, following a conference in London, the British resumed administration. This led to the territory's independence in 1980, and it was subsequently renamed Zimbabwe.

It can be unequivocally concluded that the non-recognition of the regime and the unilateral declaration of independence by Southern Rhodesia stemmed from the violation of the right to self-determination of its people. The right to self-determination of the people of Southern Rhodesia was affirmed by numerous resolutions of the UN General Assembly and the Security Council. Furthermore, the International Court of Justice clarified the status of Non-Self-Governing Territories when it established the following:

> the subsequent development of international law in regard to non-self-governing territories, as enshrined in the Charter of the United Nations, made the principle of self-determination applicable to all of them.[222]

As established in earlier discussions on the decolonization-era conception of self-determination, the 'people' entitled to this right were understood in territorial – not ethnic – terms. This interpretation necessarily applied the principle to the entire population of a given Non-Self-Governing Territory.

---

220 UNSC Res 216 (12 Nov. 1965).

221 UNSC Res 445 (8 Mar. 1979).

222 ICJ, *Legal Consequences for States of the Continued Presence of South Africa in Namibia (South West Africa) notwithstanding Security Council Resolution 276* (1970), Advisory Opinion, ICJ Rep. 1971, para 52.

Consequently, the people of Southern Rhodesia, as a whole, held the right to self-determination and the unilateral declaration of independence by Ian Smith's minority racist regime constituted a violation of this right.[223] A regime that denies political participation to the majority population in its territory on a racially discriminatory basis cannot be qualified as representative. This conclusion is substantiated by the circumstances under which the declaration was made, as well as the consistent position of the United Nations on the matter.

Interestingly, Rhodesia fulfilled all other criteria of statehood under international law, making the basis for its non-recognition a critical point of analysis. Namely, it indisputably had established borders, a permanent population, and, under Smith's regime, effective control over state institutions. The regime also demonstrated administrative capacity by issuing passports and maintaining power for over fourteen years despite significant external pressures.[224] However, despite fulfilling these criteria, Rhodesia was not recognized by the international community, creating an apparent inconsistency with the declarative theory of state recognition.

This inconsistency can be resolved by acknowledging that the non-recognition and diplomatic isolation of Rhodesia's European minority regime were rooted in its violation of the right to self-determination of the people of Southern Rhodesia. This right took precedence over the otherwise prevailing criterion of effectiveness in assessing statehood.[225] A comparable situation arose in South Africa, where the white minority regime implemented apartheid policies and created four so-called 'Bantustans' (Transkei, Bophuthatswana, Venda and Ciskei) as nominally independent black homelands. These entities were universally deemed incompatible with genuine independence, national unity, and sovereignty.[226] Consequently, they were subject to widespread international condemnation and failed to achieve recognition or long-term viability.[227]

223 In another case, the ICJ stressed that the determination of a political status can only be achieved by an 'own freely expressed will'. ICJ, *Western Sahara,* Advisory Opinion, ICJ Rep. 1975, paras 59, 70.

224 Gowlland-Debbas (n 215) 139.

225 Crawford, describing the status of Southern Rhodesia, noted that 'the principle of self-determination in this situation prevents an otherwise effective entity from being regarded as a State', so that '[i]t appears then a new rule has come into existence, prohibiting entities from claiming statehood if their creation is in violation of an applicable right to self-determination'. Crawford, *The Creation of States* (n 19) 77–78, 83–84 and 103–106.

226 UNGA Res 37/43 (3 Dec. 1982).

227 UNSC Res 216 (12 Nov. 1965); 217 (20 Nov. 1965); 283 (29 Jul. 1970); 402 (22 Dec. 1976); 407 (25 May 1977); J. Dugard, 'Collective Non-recognition: The Failure of South Africa's Bantustan States' in B. Boutros-Ghali (ed.) *Amicorum Discipulorumque Liber* (Bruylant 1998) 383–403.

3.2.3.2 *Northern Cyprus*

The Turkish Republic of Northern Cyprus (TRNC) is a *de facto* state that occupies the northern part of the island of Cyprus, recognized only by the Republic of Türkiye. The vast majority of Cyprus residents are Greek Cypriots, constituting approximately 70–75 percent of the population, while Turkish Cypriots account for around 20–24 percent. The presence of Turkish Cypriots on the island can be traced back to the Ottoman period, during which Cyprus was part of the Ottoman Empire. After the Congress of Berlin, the Ottoman Empire, in exchange for political and military support, handed over Cyprus to British administration, thereby establishing the island as a British protectorate.[228]

Tensions between the Greek and Turkish Cypriot communities escalated during the anti-colonial struggle for Cypriot independence from the United Kingdom, ultimately achieved on August 16, 1960, through the signing of the Treaties of Establishment, Guarantee, and Alliance – documents previously negotiated in London and Zurich.[229] Then the governments of the Great Britain, Turkey, and Greece renounced their claims to the island and an independent Cyprus was declared, with Archbishop Makarios serving as its first president. In 1963, armed conflicts erupted between the Greek and Turkish Cypriot communities, culminating in the island's division into Greek-controlled and Turkish-controlled zones. The situation deteriorated further in July 1974 when the Greek military junta and the National Guard of Cyprus supported a coup led by Greek Cypriots, declaring the so-called 'Hellenic Republic of Cyprus'. Turkey invoked the 1960 Treaty of Guarantee, arguing that the coup constituted grounds for military intervention to protect the Turkish Cypriot population. On July 20, 1974, Turkey launched an invasion of Cyprus, asserting that its goal was to 'bring peace not only to the Turks but also to the Greeks'.[230] Despite calls from the United Nations for a ceasefire, a second Turkish military offensive occurred in August 1974.[231] Citing Article 4 of the Treaty of Guarantee, Turkish forces expanded their control over Cypriot territory, solidifying

228 A. Yfantidis, 'The Limits of Self-determination and the Cases of Forced Separatism: The Example of Northern Cyprus' 6 *Open Journal of Political Science* (2016) 162.

229 *Ibid.* 163. More on the Zurich and London Agreements preceding the creation of the Republic Cyprus and the history of political tensions in Ž. Simić and A. Janković, *Cipar – Povijest Ujedinjenja* (Alberta 2015) 25–45.

230 *Ibid.* 164. The second paragraph of Article 4 sets forth 'In so far as common or concerted action may not prove possible, each of the three guaranteeing Powers reserves the right to take action with the sole aim of re-establishing the state of affairs created by the present Treaty'. Treaty of Guarantee signed at Nicosia (16 Aug. 1960) 385 UNTS 5475.

231 C. Akgün, 'The Case of TRNC in the Context of Recognition of States under International Law' *Ankara Bar Review* (2010) 10.

the island's division into northern and southern zones – a division that persists today.[232] In 1983, the Turkish Cypriot parliament unilaterally declared the establishment of the Turkish Republic of Northern Cyprus.

The Security Council condemned the Turkish invasion as a violation of the sovereignty of the Republic of Cyprus[233] and an illegal attempt to create a new state.[234] In 1987, Turkey highlighted the general similarity between the case of Northern Cyprus and the intervention of Indian troops in Sri Lanka, drawing attention to the differing reactions of the international community. While the unilaterally declared independence of Northern Cyprus was condemned and the entity was not recognized, India's intervention in Sri Lanka was largely accepted.[235] India and Sri Lanka, on the other hand, pointed to a key difference that lies in the fact that Indian troops intervened at the invitation of the Sri Lankan government.[236] The principal reasons cited for the non-recognition of the Turkish Republic of Northern Cyprus include Turkey's illegal use of force against Cyprus in 1974 and its violation of the 1960 Treaty of Guarantee, signed by Cyprus, Greece, Turkey, and the United Kingdom. This treaty guarantees the territorial integrity of Cyprus and prohibits the division of the island.[237]

From the perspective of the Turkish Cypriots, the Turkish intervention in 1974 was not unlawful, as it was based on Article 4 of the Treaty of Guarantee, according to which Turkey, as a guarantor power, claimed the right and obligation to intervene in order to restore the constitutional status quo and to protect the Turkish Cypriot community.[238] Turkey also sought to justify its intervention on account of the successful *coup d'état* orchestrated by the Greek Cypriot National Guard, which pursued the policy of *Enosis* (political union of Greece).[239] In this respect, the Greek Cypriots leadership was alleged to have violated Article 1 of the Treaty of Guarantee, which required the maintenance of Cyprus's independence, territorial integrity, and constitutional order. Turkey submitted that the new government formed after the coup not only

232 *Ibid.*

233 UNSC Res 353 (20 Jul. 1974).

234 UNSC Res 541 (18 Nov. 1983). On May 11, 1984, the Security Council adopted Resolution 550, which reinforced its stance by condemning all secessionist actions, including the purported exchange of ambassadors between Turkey and the Turkish Cypriot leadership, declaring them illegal and invalid, and calling for their immediate withdrawal.

235 Nolte (n 46) 77.

236 Letter dated 17 December 1987 from the Permanent Representative of India to the United Nations addressed to the President of the Security Council, UN Doc. S/19354.

237 J. Dugard and D. Raič, 'The Role of Recognition in The Law and Practice of Secession' in M. Kohen (ed.) *Secession: International Law Perspectives* (CUP 2006) 133.

238 Akgün (n 231) 16.

239 Simić and Janković (n 229) 15–24.

ignored these provisions but was also likely to continue doing so.[240] Furthermore, Turkish authorities contended that the TRNC did not result directly from the Turkish intervention, but was established some nine years later, in 1983, as an expression of the Turkish Cypriots' right to self-determination.[241] Finally, the Turkish side also used the argument of remedial secession, pointing out that the principle of territorial integrity, as contained in the Friendly Relations Declaration, is contingent upon the existence of a representative government. This condition, Turkey argued, had not been fulfilled in Cyprus given the exclusion of Turkish Cypriots from governance.[242]

On the other hand, the Greek Cypriots contest the validity of these arguments. According to them, Article 4 of the aforementioned agreement does not give Turkey the right to carry out an 'armed intervention', and even if that was the case, the prohibition of the use of force enshrined in Article 2(4) of the UN Charter would supersede any conflicting contractual provisions by virtue of Article 103 of the Charter.[243] The Treaty only provides for the re-establishment of the *status quo ante*, which was arguably achieved by the first intervention of the Turkish army, whereas the second intervention has created a new situation that cannot be regarded legal under international law. Consequently, it is the disproportionate nature of the response and its enduring effect – resulting in the effective partition of the island – that contravenes the Treaty of Guarantee.[244]

From the beginning of the conflict between Turkish and Greek Cypriots, the international community has opposed any division of the island and supported the preservation of territorial integrity of Cyprus. Notably, in 1965, the UN General Assembly urged all states to respect 'the sovereignty, unity, independence and territorial integrity of the Republic of Cyprus'.[245] The UN Security Council in its 1999 resolution on the extension of the mandate of the UN Peacekeeping Force in Cyprus (UNFICYP) reiterated that a Cyprus settlement

240 Article 1 reads: 'The Republic of Cyprus undertakes to ensure the maintenance of its independence, territorial integrity and security, as well as respect for its Constitution'.

241 Akgün (n 231) 16.

242 *Ibid.*

243 L. Hargrove et al., 'Cyprus: International Law and the Prospects for Settlement' 78 *Proceedings of the American Society of International Law* (1984) 117.

244 As Kelsen stated in his 1959 Legal Opinion commissioned by the UN, 'the right to take action' does not mean 'an unqualified right to intervene by the use of armed force'. The opinion is reproduced in S. Soulioti (ed.) *Fettered Independence: Cyprus 1878–1964, The Documents,* vol. II (Minnesota Mediterranean and East Monographs 2006) 253–260. See also S. K. N. Blay, 'Self-determination in Cyprus: The New Dimensions of an Old Conflict' 68 *Australian Year Book of International Law* (1981–1983) 67, 82.

245 UNGA Res 2077 (18 Dec. 1965).

> must be based on a State of Cyprus with a single sovereignty and international personality and a single citizenship, with its independence and territorial integrity safeguarded, and comprising two politically equal communities as described in the relevant Security Council resolutions.[246]

Nevertheless, Northern Cyprus can be described as functioning *de facto* as a puppet state. In the landmark judgment *Loizidou v. Turkey*, the European Court of Human Rights (ECtHR) held Turkey accountable for violations of property rights in the northern part of Cyprus, attributing this responsibility to Turkey's effective military control over the territory.[247] Beyond the illegality of its creation through Turkey's 1974 military intervention, the TRNC's enduring dependence on Turkish military, economic, and political support fundamentally negates its claim to genuine independence.[248] This position was further solidified in *Cyprus v. Turkey*, where the Court unequivocally denied the TRNC any legal standing, stating:

> it was evident from international practice and the various strongly worded resolutions referred to above that the international community did not regard the TRNC as a State under international law.[249]

The Court reiterated the conclusion reached in its *Loizidou* judgment that 'the Republic of Cyprus has remained the sole legitimate government of Cyprus'.[250]

Thus, although Northern Cyprus exhibits many characteristics of a *de facto* state, the international community has steadfastly refused to recognize it as an independent state, viewing Turkey's contravention of international law as grounds for non-recognition, in accordance with the maxim *ex injuria jus non oritur.* Consequently, any secession effectuated by foreign military intervention is inherently deprived of legal effect under international law.[251]

---

246 UNSC Res 1251 (29 Jun. 1999).

247 ECtHR, *Loizidou v. Turkey*, Application No. 15318/89, Judgment (Merits) (18 Dec. 1996) paras 56, 62.

248 A. Kaczorowska-Ireland, *Public International Law* (Routledge 2015) 178.

249 ECtHR, *Cyprus v. Turkey*, Application No. 25781/94, Judgment (Merits) (10 May 2001) para 61.

250 *Ibid.*

251 S. Talmon, *Kollektive Nichtanerkennung illegaler Staaten: Grundlagen und Rechtsfolgen einer international koordinierten Sanktion, dargestellt am Beispiel der Türkischen Republik Nord-Zypern* (*Mohr Siebeck 2006*) *32–48;* Crawford, *The Creation of States* (n 19) 145–146.

3.2.3.3 *East Timor*

The island of Timor was once colonized by two European powers: Portugal and the Netherlands. West Timor, which was under Dutch colonial rule, gained independence in 1949 and became part of Indonesia, where it remains today as a province. In contrast, East Timor was a Portuguese colony from the 16th century until 1975, though prior to colonization, the island was divided into small tribal states. Portugal's engagement with East Timor was relatively limited, especially when compared to its other colonies, and the island was often neglected in terms of economic development and attention.[252] At the dawn of the 20th century, however, Portugal's declining economy compelled it to focus more heavily on exploiting its island colonies, including East Timor. This shift in policy met with resistance from the indigenous population, resulting in a prolonged cycle of exploitation and repression. During World War II, East Timor was occupied by Japan, but following the end of the war, Portugal regained control of the island. The situation in East Timor changed dramatically after the Carnation Revolution of 1974, which resulted in the fall of Portugal's authoritarian Salazar regime, the last in Europe to embrace decolonization. Amid the political upheaval, both the East Timorese, who had long struggled for independence, and Indonesia, which had long sought to expand its territorial claims, saw an opportunity. Upon Portugal's withdrawal from East Timor in 1975, Indonesia, which had claimed East Timor since its own independence, annexed the territory. To justify this act, Indonesia coerced certain East Timorese political leaders into signing the Balibo Declaration, a document that purported to support annexation, despite overwhelming opposition from the population.[253] This annexation also took on a religious dimension, as Indonesia, a majority-Muslim country, occupied East Timor, a region predominantly inhabited by Catholics. This disparity fueled tensions, and a bloody civil war broke out. Indonesia's occupation of East Timor lasted 24 years and was marked by widespread human rights abuses and significant loss of life.

Both the General Assembly and the Security Council adopted numerous resolutions condemning the annexation and affirming the East Timorese people's right to independence and self-determination.[254] In fact, between 1960 and 2002, East Timor was regarded by the UN as a Non-Self-Governing Territory

252 M. Sterio, *The Right to Self-determination under International Law: "Selfistans", Secession, and the Rule of Great Powers* (Routledge 2013) 103–107.

253 Reliefweb, 'Chega! The Report of the Commission for Reception, Truth, and Reconciliation Timor-Leste' (2005) <https://reliefweb.int/report/timor-leste/chega-report-commission-reception-truth-and-reconciliation-timor-leste>.

254 UNGA Res 3485(XXX) (12 Dec. 1975); UNSC Res 384 (22 Dec. 1975) and 389 (22 Apr. 1976).

administered by Portugal.[255] Thus, Portugal was designated as the *de jure* continuous administrator, even though it was *de facto* ruled by Indonesia from 1975 to 1999.

However, the international community remained virtually on the sidelines during Indonesia's occupation. The General Assembly and the Security Council did condemn the Indonesian occupation, but that was more or less all that could be done within the UN. The Security Council could not act on the basis of Chapter VII of the Charter, that is, to approve military intervention in East Timor, because such an attempt would have been thwarted by the adoption of a veto by permanent members, specifically the U.S. and the United Kingdom, both of which maintained strong ties with the Indonesian regime.[256] Meanwhile, the FRETILIN guerrillas continued their struggle for independence, and the situation in East Timor attracted renewed global attention following the tragic events of 1991, when Indonesian forces opened fire on a memorial procession in the capital, Dili, resulting in the deaths of over 270 people.[257] While this massacre highlighted the severity of the Indonesian occupation, it was not until 1996 that the international community began to engage with the issue more critically. That year, the Nobel Peace Prize was awarded to Bishop Carlos Belo and FRETILIN leader José Ramos-Horta in tribute to their struggle for a peaceful resolution of the conflict in East Timor. The turning point came in 1998, when Indonesia faced an economic crisis and the long-time dictator Suharto was forced to resign, leaving the presidency to his vice president, B. J. Habibie. As part of Indonesia's broader political opening, Habibie offered East Timor 'special status' within Indonesia, but this proposal was rejected by the East Timorese population, which continued to demand full independence.

In May 1999, a tripartite agreement was signed in New York between the UN, Portugal, and Indonesia, which provided for the holding of a referendum for the residents of East Timor, offering the options of autonomy within Indonesia or independence.[258] To facilitate the organization and conduct of the popular consultation, the UN established the Transitional Administration in East

---

255 UNGA Res 1699 'Non-compliance of the Government of Portugal with Chapter XI of the Charter of the United Nations and with General Assembly resolution 1542 (XV)' (19 Dec. 1961). See also UNGA Res 56/282 (1 May 2002) (removing East Timor from the list of UN Non-Self-Governing Territories).

256 Sterio (n 252) 2013, 105.

257 M. Benzing, 'Midwifing a New State: The United Nations in East Timor' 9 *Max Planck Yearbook of United Nations Law* (2005) 303.

258 Question of East Timor: Report of the Secretary-General to the Security Council, UN Doc. A/53/951-S/1999/513, Annex 1 (1999).

Timor (UNTAET) through a Security Council resolution.[259] More than 98% of those who had the right to vote participated in the referendum, and 78.5% rejected the autonomy proposal. The international community interpreted this result as a clear expression of the desire of the people of East Timor to 'secede' from Indonesia.[260]

Dissatisfied with the outcome, Indonesia launched a violent military campaign in retaliation. In response, the UN established a peace and security restoration mission in September 1999.[261] This mission was tasked with providing administrative support to East Timor during its transition to independence, drafting a new constitution, conducting elections, and rebuilding infrastructure. East Timor gained independence on May 20, 2002, and Xanana Gusmão was elected as its first president. In September of the same year, East Timor become a member of the United Nations.

The East Timor saga evidences a profound failure of the international system to enforce the right to self-determination. Unlike the Security Council's swift response to Iraq's 1990 annexation of Kuwait, Indonesia's 1975 annexation of East Timor provoked little meaningful action.[262] This inaction persisted despite Indonesia's brutality, which led to the deaths of between 100,000 and 200,000 East Timorese – a scale of violence that should have warranted a tougher response. The path to independence remained obstructed, even as legal scholars argued that remedial secession might apply in this non-colonial context.[263] Arguably, as some observers pointed out, the tepid international reaction reflected a 'lethal encounter of international law and geopolitics'.[264] Even the International Court of Justice did not live up to expectations in condemning Indonesian wrongdoing. In the *Case Concerning East Timor (Portugal v. Australia)*, it implicitly hid behind the *Monetary Gold* principle, *ergo*, rejected to rule against a non-consenting absent party (Indonesia).[265] The Court only reiterated the substance of the right to self-determination, declaring that East Timor possessed this right as a Non-Self-Governing

259 UNSC Res 1246 (11 Jun. 1999).

260 H. Fan, 'The Missing Link between Self-determination and Democracy' 6 *Northwestern Journal of International Human Rights* (2007) 179.

261 UNSC Res 1272 (25 Oct. 1999).

262 Cf. F. Malekian, *Condemning the Use of Force in the Gulf Crisis* (Almqvist & Wiksell International 1992). See UNSC Res 660 (2 Aug. 1990).

263 C. Drew, 'The East Timor Story: International Law on Trial' 12 *EJIL* (2001) 656–657.

264 R. Falk, 'The East Timor Ordeal: International Law and Its Limits' 32(1/2) *Bulletin of Concerned Asian Scholars* (2000) 49–54.

265 I. Scobbie and C. Drew, 'Self-determination Undetermined: The Case of East Timor' 9(1) *Leiden Journal of International Law* (1996) 189–190.

Territory, and introduced the juridical novelty – that the right to self-determination is an *erga omnes* right.[266] However, the Court refused to adjudicate the lawfulness of the conduct of another state – Indonesia – in the absence of its consent. As a result, the legal status of East Timor's annexation, the validity of the treaty between Indonesia and Australia regarding hydrocarbon resources, and the question of states' obligations not to recognize the annexation, remained unresolved.[267] What is more, the Court appeared to downplay the relevance of resolutions issued by UN political bodies, particularly the Security Council, arguing that these resolutions did not provide a sufficient basis for rejecting Indonesia's authority over the territory or for obliging states to deal exclusively with Portugal.[268] Insofar as one can agree with the latter point, it is hard to concur with the former. As Grant remarked, the Court may have been influenced by the relatively inconspicuous rule of non-recognition, which could be opposable to third parties.[269]

The mundane stipulation of the self-determination substance, highly relativized by the ICJ, which failed, *inter alia*, to clearly pronounce East Timor's sovereignty over natural resources, does not exhaust the shortcomings of the international community.[270] In particular, the *procedural* aspect of the right was long overdue. Only in 1999, the UN decided to assist in the organisation of a referendum, where the free will of the East Timorese people could be expressed. Before, it restricted itself to good offices and calls for de-escalation.[271]

Be that as it may, the implications of this case for secession should be clear. Indonesia occupied by force the territory of East Timor in 1975, which

266 ICJ, *Case Concerning East Timor (Portugal v. Australia)*, Judgment, ICJ Rep. 1995, paras 29, 31.

267 *Ibid.* Concurring opinion of Judge Skubiszewski, 262–264.

268 *Case Concerning East Timor* (n 266) paras 30–31.

269 T. Grant, 'East Timor, the U.N. System, and Enforcing Non-Recognition in International Law' 33 *Vanderbilt Law Review* (2021) 273, 300–310. See also ILC, Responsibility of States for Internationally Wrongful Acts 'ARSIWA' in 'Report of the International Law Commission on the work of its fifty-third session, 23 April 1 June and 2 July – 10 August 2001', UN Doc. A/56/10 II (2) YILC, Article 40.

270 In the *Chagos Archipelago* Advisory Opinion (2019), the ICJ not only spelled out the UK's obligation to bring an end to its administration of the Chagos Archipelago but also stated that such an administration constitutes a wrongful act entailing the international responsibility of the UK (paras 177–178). The Court underlined that the right to self-determination creates an obligation *erga omnes* and all States have to cooperate with each other and comply with the General Assembly's proposals to complete the decolonization of Mauritius, which includes the resettlement of previously expelled Chagossians (paras 180–181). See S. Janković and V. Roeben, 'Unpacking Sovereignty and Self-determination in ITLOS and the ICC: A Bundle of Rights?' *EJIL:Talk!* (4 Mar. 2011).

271 See, for example, UNGA Res 37/30 (23 Nov. 1982).

amounted to an act of aggression and by no means should be recognized. According to the 1970 Friendly Relations Declaration, 'the territory of a State shall not be the object of acquisition by another State resulting from the threat or use of force. No territorial acquisition resulting from the threat or use of force shall be recognized as legal'.[272] The 1974 UN General Assembly Resolution 3314 'Definition of Aggression' affirms the same principle, asserting that 'no territorial acquisition or special advantage resulting from aggression is or shall be recognized as lawful'.[273] Accordingly, both Indonesia's occupation and Australia's agreements with Indonesia regarding East Timor are contrary to international law.[274]

3.2.4 Instances of Realized Internal Self-determination (Generally)

This is the central argument advanced in this book and will be elaborated on in detail in subsequent sections. For now, it suffices to indicate that the fulfillment of internal self-determination constitutes a significant impediment to secession. Unlike previous instances, where secession was considered invalid on the strength of a violation of *other* norms, such as the prohibition of the use of force, the determination of the fate of a people by others, or territorial integrity, here the prohibition of secession can be extrapolated directly from the very concept of self-determination. Ironically, self-determination emerges then as a norm which both enables secession and disallows it. Namely, while external self-determination may lead to independence as a viable outcome, internal self-determination precludes this possibility, provided its core principles are upheld. The idea of using internal self-determination as a barrier to secession was globally coined in the safeguard clause of the 1970 Friendly Relations Declaration, which provides that

> Nothing in the foregoing paragraphs shall be construed as authorizing or encouraging any action which would dismember or impair, totally or in part, the territorial integrity or political unity of sovereign and independent States conducting themselves in compliance with the principle of equal rights and self-determination of peoples as described above and

272 UNGA Res 2625(XXV) (24 Oct. 1970) Principle 1.

273 See UNGA Res 3314 (14 Dec. 1974) Article 5(3).

274 Consult S. Clark, 'Timor Gap: The Legality of the Treaty on the Zone of Cooperation in an Area Between the Indonesian Province of East Timor and Northern Australia' 4 *Pace Yearbook of International Law* (1992) 76–92.

> thus possessed of a government representing the whole people belonging to the territory without distinction as to race, creed or colour.[275]

A similar phrasing determining the relationship between secession and the right to self-determination is found in the 1933 Vienna Declaration and Programme of Action. According to point 2, the right of all peoples to self-determination

> shall not be construed as authorizing or encouraging any action which would dismember or impair, totally or in part, the territorial integrity or political unity of sovereign and independent States conducting themselves in compliance with the principle of equal rights and self-determination of peoples and thus possessed of a Government representing the whole people belonging to the territory without distinction of any kind.[276]

This nuanced understanding of the interplay between secession and self-determination is often implicit and remains underexposed in academic literature. However, it becomes prominent in specific contexts, where it is both clearly articulated and valued as pragmatic. For example, this interpretation features prominently in state, institutional, and scholarly analyses of the Kosovo question. Submissions by states to the Human Rights Committee are reflective of the significance of internal self-determination, a principle that also informs the reasoning of domestic courts faced with secessionist issues, as exemplified by the Supreme Court of Canada's ruling in the *Quebec Secession Reference*. Finally, the growing relevance of this approach is evidenced by its inclusion in the Declaration on the Occasion of the Fiftieth Anniversary of the United Nations.[277]

3.3 *Secession is Permitted (Remedial Theory and Moral Justifications)*

In opposition to legal theorists who advocate for an unrestricted right to unilateral secession – a minority perspective that will not be addressed here – proponents of remedial secession acknowledge the general primacy of the principle of territorial integrity over the right of peoples to self-determination.[278] Accord-

---

275 UNGA Res 2625(XXV) (n 272).

276 The World Conference on Human Right, Vienna Declaration and Programme of Action (12 Jul. 1993) UN Doc. A/CONF.157/23.

277 UNGA Res 50/6 'Declaration on the Occasion of the Fiftieth Anniversary of the United Nations' (9 Nov. 1995). See chapter 5.

278 A. Szpak, 'Secesja Państwa w Świetle Prawa Międzynarodowego' 38 *Państwo i Prawo* (2014) 43; A. Muś, *Rewizja Stosowania Prawa do Samostanowienia w XXI Wieku. Nowe Wyzwania*

ingly, the standard application of the right to self-determination pertains to its internal aspect, which does not infringe upon existing state borders. However, unlike supporters of negation theories, adherents of remedial secession reject the notion that the principle of territorial integrity is inviolable or absolute. They argue that, under specific remedial circumstances, it should yield to the application of external self-determination in the form of secession.[279] Remedial circumstances most often mentioned in the literature include severe and systematic violations of basic human rights as well as the denial of internal self-determination. Thus, the invocation of secession can take place when a state fails to uphold or actively violates internal self-determination. Similarly, ongoing and pervasive breaches of fundamental human rights may also trigger the right to secession. However, it is uncertain whether past injustices (not occurring now) warrant the same entitlement.[280] The prevailing view holds that external self-determination, i.e. secession, is a measure of last resort, achieved only if all other possible solutions have been exhausted, and the state continues, or is likely to continue, to expose the people to serious grievances. Secession is, therefore, envisaged as a mechanism to place victims beyond the reach of an oppressive state.[281]

3.3.1 Gross and Systematic Violations of Human Rights

'Gross and systematic violations' of human rights is a phrase conventionally associated with a problem of a graver nature than the denial of internal self-determination. Consequently, it emerges as a more compelling justification for effectuating secession.

From a linguistic standpoint, 'gross and systematic violations' of human rights can encompass the denial or infringement of ISD, given that such deprivations may similarly be described as 'grave' or 'flagrant' and are often equally traumatic, stripping communities of dignity. However, the expression 'gross and systematic violations' is a term of art, generally separated in the doctrine from ISD violations, despite substantive overlaps. For instance, racial and

---

Dla Prawa Międzynarodowego (Wydawnictwo Uniwersytetu Śląskiego 2019) 72.

279 S. Oeter, 'Selbstbestimmungsrecht im Wandel. Überlegungen zur Debatte um Selbstbestimmung, Sezessionsrecht und "vorzeitige" Anerkennung' 52 *ZaöRV* (1992) 753 ff; T. Marauhn, 'Anspruch auf Sezession?' in H. J. Heintze (ed.) *Selbstbestimmungsrecht der Völker – Herausforderung der Staatenwelt?* (Dietz 1997) 107 ff.

280 Busquets (n 62) 130, 176.

281 Dimitrijević, *Savremeno Shvatanje Prava Naroda Na Samoopredeljenje* (n 69) 35.

religious discrimination may constitute breaches of both categories, whereas the abolition of autonomy is specific to ISD.[282]

Although international practice has not yet developed an exhaustive catalogue of 'gross and systematic violations' of human rights, it is agreed that this category includes genocide, summary or arbitrary execution, enforced disappearances, slavery, prolonged and arbitrary detention, torture or cruel, inhuman, or degrading treatment or punishment, crimes against humanity, apartheid and systematic racial and religious discrimination.[283]

When classifying violations as gross and systematic, four fundamental elements should be considered: quality, quantity, duration, and premeditation.[284] First, such violations should possess a certain quality. This necessitates assessing which rights are affected, the nature of the violation, and the status of the victim.[285] Arguably, to satisfy the quality element, a violated human right should be classified as *jus cogens,* whose observance by the authority must be strict and permit no derogation, even during the war.[286] The International Covenant on Civil and Political Rights in Article 4(2), the Convention for the Protection of Human Rights and Fundamental Freedoms in Article 15(2) and the American Convention on Human Rights in Article 27(2), for instance, consider the following rights as non-derogable: the right to life, freedom from slavery or servitude, freedom from torture or inhuman and degrading treatment, and the principle of non-retroactivity of penal laws.[287] The jurisprudence of international courts and reports of international bodies indicate however that certain rights, in addition to non-derogable ones, might befit the 'gross violation' scheme. For example, in *Armed Activities in the Territory of the Congo*, the

282 L. F. Damrosch, 'Gross and Systematic Human Rights Violations' *Max Planck Encyclopedias of International Law* (2011) para 12.

283 *Ibid.*; T. Buergenthal, 'Codification and Implementation of International Human Rights' in A. Henkin (ed.) *Human Dignity: The Internationalization of Human Rights* (Aspen Institute for Humanistic Studies 1979) 17; R. Liwanga, 'The Meaning of Gross Violation of Human Rights: A Focus on International Tribunals: A Focus on International Tribunals Decisions over the DRC Conflicts' 44 *Denver Journal of International Law & Policy* (2015) 72. See Vienna Declaration (n 276) para 30.

284 Liwanga (n 283) 73–80.

285 C. M. Quiroga, *The Battle of Human Rights: Gross, Systematic Violations and the Inter-American System* (Martinus Nijhoff Publishers 1988) 12–15.

286 K. Teraya, 'Emerging Hierarchy in International Human Rights and Beyond: From the Perspective of Non-derogable Rights' 12 *EJIL* (2001) 918–920.

287 International Covenant on Civil and Political Rights (16 Dec. 1966) 999 UNTS 171, Article 4(2); Convention for the Protection of Human Rights and Fundamental Freedoms (4 Nov. 1950) 213 UNTS 221, Article 15(2); American Convention on Human Rights (22 Nov. 1969) 1144 UNTS 123, Article 27(2).

ICJ, apart from torture, included the destruction of civilian houses under the heading of massive human rights violations.[288] In its 2015 report, the UN Commission of Inquiry on Human Rights in Eritrea concluded that gross and systematic human rights violations persist in Eritrea and that under the authority of the Government in Eritrea, such atrocities as 'extrajudicial executions, torture, violations in the areas of national service and forced labour' have been and are being committed and that they may constitute crimes against humanity.[289] The African Commission, on some occasions, has categorized infringements of rights such as education, property, housing, and healthcare services as 'serious violations'. However, it is more challenging to consider these rights as grounds for secession, especially given the socioeconomic underdevelopment of the African continent, unless such violations are deliberate.[290]

The quantitative element is a second critical precondition. This involves assessing both the number of rights violated and the number of victims affected. Although no clear consensus exists on this aspect, a single violation of an individual's right is indisputably insufficient for remedial secession, which is inherently a collective right exercised by the affected community.[291] Therefore, the term 'massive' is often invoked in cases where organizations provide numerical evidence or reference multiple instances of rights violations.[292] For instance, the complainant before the African Commission in *Sudan Human Rights Organization and Centre on Housing Rights and Evictions v. Sudan* noted that in the Darfur region 'thousands' of individuals were killed, forcibly evicted, and had their properties destroyed.[293] Similarly, the Special Rapporteur on the situation of human rights in Belarus in her 2021 report cited information regarding 'massive police violence against protesters, cases of enforced

288 ICJ, *Armed Activities on the Territory of the Congo* (n 171) 206–207.

289 HRC, 'Report of the Commission of Inquiry on Human Rights in Eritrea' (29 Oct. 2015) UN Doc. A/HRC/29/CRP.1.

290 See ACHPR, *World Organization against Torture v. Zaire*, Communication Nos. 25/89, 47/90, 56/91, 100/93 (1996) para 40.

291 The definition of 'crime against humanity' in Article 7 of the Statute of the International Criminal Court requires that the acts be committed 'as part of a widespread or systematic attack directed against any civilian population'.

292 See ECtHR, *Georgia v. Russia* (I), Application No. 13255/07, Judgment (Merits) (3 Jul. 2014) para 159; *Chiragov et al. v. Armenia*, Application No. 13216/05, Judgment (Just satisfaction) (12 Dec. 2017) para 46; *Sargsyan v. Azerbaijan*, Application No. 40167/06, Judgment (Just satisfaction) (12 Dec. 2017) para 28.

293 ACHPR, *Sudan Human Rights Organization and Centre on Housing Rights and Evictions / Sudan*, Communication Nos. 279/03 – 296/05 (2009) paras 113–114.

disappearance, allegations of torture and ill-treatment and the continuous intimidation and harassment of civil society actors'.[294]

The temporal element is another crucial prerequisite, reflected in the notions of 'systematic' or 'consistent' violations of human rights. For remedial secession to be initiated, there must be a repetitive pattern or practice of rights violations over a sustained period.[295] The European Court of Human Rights clarified the meaning of a 'consistent pattern' in *Ireland v. United Kingdom*, wherein it held that:

> a practice incompatible with the Convention consists of an accumulation of identical or analogous breaches which are sufficiently numerous and inter-connected to amount not merely to isolated incidents or exceptions but to a pattern or system; a practice does not of itself constitute a violation separate from such breaches.[296]

It follows from the ruling that repercussions cannot be triggered by a single violation or very sporadic practice. Indeed, secession, as a last-resort remedy, should not be a response to short-lived practices. A more contentious issue is whether past, long-standing practices can justify entitlement to separation.

Finally, there is an element of planning, implicit in the concept of a 'consistent pattern', as the sustained execution of oppressive operations typically entails deliberate orchestration. The International Criminal Tribunal for the former Yugoslavia (ICTY) referenced this correlation in the *Blaksić* case, ruling that the term 'systematic' implies

> the existence of a political objective, a plan pursuant to which the attack is perpetrated or an ideology, in the broad sense of the word, that is, to destroy, persecute or weaken a community.[297]

---

294 HRC, 'Report of the Special Rapporteur on the situation of human rights in Belarus' (4 May 2021) UN Doc. A/HRC/47/49, para 4.

295 Liwanga (n 283) 78; T. Karimova, 'What Amounts To 'A Serious Violation of International Human Rights Law?: An Analysis of Practice and Expert Opinion for the Purpose of the 2013 Arms Trade Treaty' 6 *Academy Briefing* of *the Geneva Academy of International Humanitarian Law and Human Rights* (2014) 15.

296 ECtHR, *Ireland v. United Kingdom*, Application No. 5310/71, Judgment (Merits) (18 Jan. 1978) para 159.

297 ICTY, *Prosecutor v. Blaksic*, IT-95-14-T, Judgment (3 Mar. 2000) 203.

Therefore, 'gross and systematic violations' of human rights, such as genocide often necessitate an underlying plan and intent. Not all violations must be planned, but those planned are usually 'gross and systematic'.[298]

Gross and systematic violations of human rights have been established as a requirement for triggering jurisdiction and consequences, including remedies. For instance, the Economic and Social Council set a jurisdictional threshold for the UN Sub-Commission on Prevention of Discrimination and Protection of Minorities, allowing it to accept communications that disclose 'gross and reliably attested violations of human rights and fundamental freedoms'.[299] Similarly, according to the Commentary on Article 40 of the ILC Articles on State Responsibility, breaches of obligations arising under peremptory norms lead to consequences for third states to the extent that they are serious. In turn, they are serious (a) when they are carried out in an organized and deliberate way (systematic) and (b) if they amount to a direct and outright assault on the values protected by the rule (gross).[300]

A pertinent question thus arises: can secession be justified in cases of 'gross and systematic violations' of human rights? Although international law has not explicitly regulated statehood on such grounds, principles of justice and moral logic suggest that such egregious abuses demand viable remedies. Immediate responses should include the cessation of wrongdoing, the provision of security guarantees, and the initiation of constructive dialogue. Subsequent measures should encompass compensation, official apologies, the disclosure of misdeeds, the return of fugitives, prosecution of those responsible, and the rehabilitation of victims.[301]

As such, 'gross and systematic violations' of human rights may not automatically necessitate the reconfiguration of external borders of existing states. Rather, the adoption of such drastic measures could hinge on the failure of other remedies, including the implementation of security guarantees and meaningful dialogue. In this context, proposals for enhanced territorial status – such as increased autonomy – could be explored.[302] This approach aligns

---

298 See ICTY, *Prosecutor v. Goran Jelisić*, IT-95-10-A, Judgement (5 Jul. 2001) 47–48.

299 ECOSOC Res 1503 (XLVIII) 'Procedure for dealing with communications relating to violations of human rights and fundamental freedoms' (27 May 1970).

300 ILC, ARSIWA (n 269) 113, paras 7–8.

301 Consult ILC, 'Fourth Report on the obligation to extradite or prosecute (*aut dedere aut judicare*)' by Spec. Rapporteur Z. Galicki (31 May 2011) UN Doc. A/66/10, paras 294–332. See also ICJ, *Arrest Warrant of 11 April 2000 (Democratic Republic of the Congo v. Belgium)*, Judgment, ICJ Rep. 2002, paras 11–12.

302 C. Tomuschat, 'Secession and Self-determination' in M. Kohen (ed.) *Secession: International Law Perspectives* (CUP 2006) 38–39.

with seeing secession as the *ultima ratio*. That said, retaining a minority within a state where it faces severe violations of basic human rights, particularly to the extent that the group's physical existence is threatened, undermines the very essence of the right to self-determination. At its core, this right entails liberation from subjugation, intimidation and exploitation. Quite a number of scholars concur with this view. Umozurike, for instance, notes:

> if a majority or a minority insists on committing an international crime such as genocide or enforces a wholesale denial of human rights as a deliberate policy against the other part, the oppressed party may have recourse to the right of self-determination up to the point of secession.[303]

Busquets shares a similar opinion but does not strictly limit remedial secession to the breach of most egregious crimes against humanity or non-derogable norms. Instead, he speaks of the violation of 'fundamental rights' – a broader, yet still principled, threshold.[304] He astutely remarks that secession is primarily applicable to ethnic groups and minorities within a state, as it would be ludicrous to suggest that a government engaging in indiscriminate repression of the entire population would be liable to territorial disintegration.[305] In such cases, the government would instead be susceptible to overthrow. However, if there is a selective violation of the 'liberties' of a minority within a state, such a minority, according to Rawls's principle of justice, would be entitled to revolt.[306] Busquets's argumentation is grounded in the equality principle, as applied in the *Åland* case, where the Court leaned towards allowing the separation of a minority, but only if the central government was unwilling or unable to 'apply just and effective guarantees'.[307] Accordingly, for Busquets, differential treatment from other citizens, without objective and reasonable justification, constitutes a sufficient reason for secession. However, he adds that such differential treatment must be severe and enduring.[308]

It can be concluded that, from a moral point of view, the theory of remedial secession is justified and well-grounded, especially in cases where a people are

---

303 U. Umozurike, *Self-determination in International Law* (Archon Books 1972) 199.

304 Busquets (n 62) 129.

305 *Ibid.*

306 According to Rawls 'Each person is to have an equal right to the most extensive scheme of equal basic liberties compatible with a similar scheme of liberties for others'. J. Rawls, *A Theory of Justice* (Belknap Press 1999) 53.

307 Report Submitted to the Council of the League of Nations by the Commission of Rapporteurs (1921) League of Nations Doc. B7 [C] 21/68/106, 21, 28.

308 Busquets (n 62) 129.

subjected to extreme and unremitting persecution coupled with a lack of any reasonable prospect for a peaceful challenge. This is particularly true when the very survival of the people is at stake.[309]

3.3.2 Denial of Internal Self-determination (Safeguard Clause)

The denial of internal self-determination as an avenue for secession has garnered much sympathy among legal scholars and occupies a prominent place in key legal documents. For instance, the infamous 'safeguard clause' from the 1970 Friendly Relations Declaration stipulates that a state must have a representative government that does not distinguish among a people on the basis of race, creed, or color to avoid secession and maintain territorial continuity. The 1993 Vienna Declaration places a similar condition, yet prohibits 'any kind' of discrimination. The UN Committee on the Elimination of Racial Discrimination (CERD), in its General Recommendation 21 from 1996, reiterated the Friendly Relations Declaration's formulation, asserting that there currently is no *general* right to secession.[310] This principle has also been supported in case law. In *Katangese Peoples' Congress v. Zaire*, the African Commission found that Katangese peoples might invoke independence if they were denied the right to participate in the government.[311] Similarly, the Supreme Court of Canada in its ruling on *Quebec* stated that Quebecers could potentially secede from Canada if they were 'blocked from the meaningful exercise of [their] right to self-determination internally'. Secession as a remedy is thus a conditional or, as some have termed it, a 'dormant' right, which becomes actionable only upon the violation of internal self-determination, *ergo*, the failure of governmental representativeness and the absence of relevant protective measures.[312] But what constitutes a representative government within the framework of internal self-determination? Moreover, to what extent must a group's under-representation or misrepresentation rise in severity to justify secession? These questions remain pivotal in debates surrounding self-determination and its practical limits.

In general, a government fulfils the criterion of representativeness if it adheres to the will of the entire population while also granting self-rule powers to minorities and implementing mechanisms for shared governance. In

309 C. Griffioen, *Self Determination as a Human Right* (Science Shop of Law, Economics and Governance, Utrecht University 2010) 97; Blay, 'Territorial Integrity and Political Independence' (n 171) para 37.

310 CERD, General Recommendation XXI(48) (8 Mar. 1996) para 6.

311 *Katangese Peoples' Congress v. Zaire* (n 176) para 6.

312 Thürer and Burri (n 27) para 17. See 4.2.

this vein, minorities should, for example, have the right to influence the form of government, participate in constitutional amendment processes, engage in state-level decision-making, and possess exclusive competencies over matters concerning their own communities.[313] Additionally, a representative government should promote economic and social cohesion by ensuring equal opportunities for minorities, including equitable access to employment, education, healthcare, and social services, and by protecting them from hate crimes, violence, and persecution.[314]

The denial of internal self-determination is, however, a far less clear and intuitive category than 'gross and systematic violations' of human rights. Establishing a threshold for permitting secession in this case would require a thorough contextual analysis, accounting for factors such as the economic development and traditions of the state. Hannum aptly remarked that not every violation of internal self-determination would second secession.[315] For him, the government must be intransigent in forbidding the minority to speak its own language, excluding its members from participation in the parliament or denying any form of power-sharing.[316] It is thus not about fulfilling every wish of a minority as to the rights and their scope, but about the infringement of 'minimal' rights aimed to 'protect the existence' and assure participation in public life, as envisaged by the 1992 UN Declaration on Minority Rights.[317] Following this logic, the nonobservance of more 'ambitious' human rights associated with 'third and fourth generation' rights – often intertwined with a state's financial capacity – would hardly trigger secession.[318] On the other hand, a failure to fulfil distributive justice, which lies more directly within the remit of government responsibility, could tip the balance, particularly when financial

313 Raič (n 59) 284; J. Wright, 'Minority Groups, Autonomy, and Self-determination' 19(4) *Oxford Journal of Legal Studies* (1999) 621.

314 See Declaration on the Rights of Persons Belonging to National or Ethnic, Religious and Linguistic Minorities, UN Doc. 47/135 (18 Dec.1992) Articles 4, 5.

315 H. Hannum, 'The Right of Self-determination in the Twenty-First Century' 55 *Washington and Lee Law Review* (1998) 776–777.

316 *Ibid.*

317 Internal self-determination 'neither mandates the scope of that participation nor grants minorities a veto over all actions that might affect them'. H. Hannum, 'The Specter of Secession: Responding to Claims for Ethnic Self-determination' 77(2) *Foreign Affairs* (1998) 17.

318 Although positions on this matter may vary between more and less developed states, the represented axiological values and the perception of a state's general obligations – such as those related to the environment and stemming, among other things, from due diligence. See H. Krieger (ed.) *Due Diligence in the International Legal Order* (OUP 2020).

disparities disadvantage one group or entity.[319] Still, such imbalances may be deeply embedded in historical social contracts or ethno-historical contexts (e.g. Veneto in Italy, Bavaria in Germany, or Catalonia in Spain), making them difficult to reverse.

As a consequence, theorists have been keener on lumping two secession-permissive conditions together in a way that a violation of both is required. Alternatively, they 'borrow' and readjust the critical phrase 'gross and systematic' to underline the seriousness of the breach of internal self-determination and to justify secession.[320] For instance, Hannum talks about cultural *genocide*, which links elements of gross disrespect for human rights with violations of internal cultural self-determination.[321] Tomuschat notes that when a community suffers *structural* discrimination 'amounting to grave prejudice affecting their lives', it may seek secession.[322] Scharf speaks of an '*extremely* unrepresentative and oppressive' government, which may be ousted even at the cost of destabilization,[323] while judges Wildhaber and Ryssdal, in their concurring opinion, observe that if peoples are 'without representation *at all* or are *massively* underrepresented in an undemocratic and discriminatory way', a secession entitlement may arise.[324] Raič contends that discrimination should be so severe that it threatens the collective identity of the people.[325] From the foregoing, it is evident that the breach of internal self-determination must be of substantial gravity. Furthermore, even if the gravity condition is fulfilled, all the commentators simultaneously stress that secession is an 'exceptional situation' or a 'measure of last resort', to be invoked only after all other efforts to bring about change have failed.[326]

Legal doctrine as a justification for remedial secession usually cites the Friendly Relations Declaration, which provides a basis for liberation from oppression and domination. Sornarajah has noted that the Declaration safeguards a state's territorial integrity by making it immune to the application

319 Consult S. Tierney, 'The Search for a New Normativity: Thomas Franck, Post-Modern Neo-Tribalism and the Law of Self-determination' 13 *EJIL* (2002) 950.

320 See Tancredi, 'A Normative 'Due Process'' (n 93) 176–177; Van den Driest (n 113) 114.

321 Hannum, 'The Right of Self-determination' (n 315) 776.

322 Tomuschat, 'Secession and Self-determination' (n 302) 41.

323 M. Scharf, 'Earned Sovereignty: Juridical Underpinnings' 31(3) *Denver Journal of International Law & Policy* (2004) 384.

324 *Loizidou v. Turkey* (n 247) Concurring opinion of Judge Wildhaber, Joined by Judge Ryssdal.

325 Raič (n 59) 369.

326 Hannum, 'The Specter of Secession' (n 317) 16; Scharf (n 323) 384; Tomuschat, 'Secession and Self-determination' (n 302) 41.

of external self-determination, but only if the state ensures the protection of the rights of all its people. This relationship between the protection of human rights and the right to self-determination, represents, in effect, a 'sanction against the nonobservance of human rights'.[327] In other words, groups within the state may justifiably 'opt out' if the state no longer satisfies its obligation of conferring protection.[328] Buchheit argued that the potential for the right to remedial secession is implicit in the General Assembly's reluctance to uphold the territorial integrity of a state that fails to maintain a government representing the population within its territory, as stipulated in the Friendly Relations Declaration.[329]

Other scholars anchor their arguments in a broader conceptualization of colonialism, extending its logic to non-colonial contexts through the framework of 'internal colonialism'. According to Franck, if a minority that inhabits a clearly defined territory within a sovereign state 'persistently and egregiously is denied political and social equality and the opportunity to retain its cultural identity', international law could regard such practices as a form of colonialism.[330] Per Franck, the impossibility of labelling the oppressor state as a formal colonial power does not negate the applicability of decolonization principles. Judge Yusuf posited that 'the domination or oppression of one people by another within the boundaries of the state does not legally differ from oppression across the oceans (or saltwater domination) insofar as it constitutes an infringement of the equal rights of peoples'.[331] Arguing so, Yusuf *de facto* linked both potential secession entitlements outlined in paragraph 2 and paragraph 7 of the Friendly Relations Declaration. Crawford too advocated this point of view and stated that a central government may treat the population of a particular territory in such a way that it renders that territory essentially non-self-governing in relation to the rest of the state.[332] This suggests that there are no significant differences between these two doctrines, and the theory of internal colonialism can be understood as a variant of the qualified right to secession,

---

327 M. Sornarajah, 'Internal Colonialism and Humanitarian Intervention' 11(1) *Georgia Journal of International & Comparative Law* (1981) 54.

328 *Ibid.* 53.

329 Buchheit (n 119) 222.

330 T. Franck, 'Postmodern Tribalism and the Right to Secession' in C. Brölmann, R. Lefeber and M. Zieck (eds.) *Peoples and Minorities in International Law* (Martinus Nijhoff Publishers 1993) 13–14.

331 A. Yusuf, 'The Role that Equal Rights and Self-determination of Peoples can Play in the Current World Community' in A. Cassese (ed.) *Realizing Utopia: The Future of International Law* (OUP 2012) 381–382.

332 Crawford, *The Creation of States* (n 19) 126.

emphasizing the non-colonial nature of the situation in question. Finally, some scholars have endeavoured to demonstrate the customary law status of the right to secession in situations where a people are persistently denied the freedom to make a choice and are excluded from the life of the state, despite the lack of established state practice in this regard.[333]

Nevertheless, the legal underpinnings of the posited right to secede in response to breaches of internal self-determination, or remedial secession in general, remain fragile. They are neither grounded in treaty law nor in established custom, and in fact, primarily rely on the interpretations of a few soft law documents. This is underscored by the limited judicial commentary, such *obiter dicta* in *Quebec Secession Reference,* the concurring opinion of two judges in *Loizidou v. Turkey* and two separate opinions in the *Kosovo* Advisory Opinion,[334] as well as multiple circular references among commentators. *Nota bene,* these commentators remain very wary in pronouncing secession as a legal right due to its inherently qualified nature and scant state practice.[335]

The most alluded to 'safeguard clause' of the Friendly Relations Declaration is interpreted by proponents of remedial secession as protecting *peoples rather than governments.* But such *a contrario* interpretation is problematic. Arguably, it is inadequate to base such a significant change in the interpretation of a fundamental principle on an unclear clause, especially considering that the principle of territorial integrity remains a cornerstone of international law and precedes the 'safeguard clause' within the Declaration itself.[336] It is worth noting that although this clause was *mutatis mutandis* repeated in the 1993 Vienna Declaration and the 1995 UN Fiftieth Anniversary Declaration, it was omitted in the 1975 Helsinki Final Act, adopted just five years later, or the 2007 Declaration on the Rights of Indigenous Peoples, where territorial integrity

---

333 C. Ryngaert and C. Griffioen, 'The Relevance of the Right to Self - Determination in the Kosovo Matter: in Partial Response to Agora Papers' 8(3) *Chinese Journal of International Law* (2009) 579–580. For the lack of practice, they cite *Nicaragua* (n 169) paras 186–188. Cf. ICJ, *North Sea Continental Shelf (Federal Republic of Germany/Denmark and Federal Republic of Germany/Netherlands),* ICJ Rep. 1969, para 74, 'State practice (…) should have been both extensive and virtually uniform'.

334 *Reference re Secession of Quebec* (n 195) para 126; *Loizidou v. Turkey* (n 247); *Kosovo Advisory Opinion* (n 77) Judge Yusuf, para 11; Judge Trindade paras 180–181, 184, 205. More in 5.3.1.7. and 5.2.7.1.

335 See J. Vidmar, 'Remedial Secession in International Law: Theory and (Lack of) Practice' 6 *St Antony's International Review* (2010) 40; J. Summers, *Peoples and International Law: How Nationalism and Self-determination Shape a Contemporary Law of Nations* (Martinus Nijhoff 2007) 347.

336 M. Shaw, 'Peoples, Territorialism and Boundaries' 8(3) *EJIL* (1997) 483; Orakhelashvili (n 80) 13–14.

has to be adhered to 'unconditionally'.[337] Furthermore, there is no established mechanism to determine whether a state has failed to meet the conditions of the safeguard clause in a manner that would justify secession.[338] This absence precludes the development of a non-arbitrary procedure for determining when remedial secession might be invoked. As Xanthaki highlights, the practical dilemma remains 'who is the interpreter of the right to self-determination' and, by extension, who determines which nation may secede, and under what circumstances?[339] Finally, the historical and political context of the safeguard clause warrants attention. It was enacted during the era of apartheid in South Africa and may have been intended to address 'pariah states'.[340]

Equating self-determination with representative government, as proposed by the U.S. delegation during *travaux preparatoires* of the Friendly Relations Declaration was rejected.[341] Nevertheless, efforts to corroborate secession by virtue of governmental representativeness resurfaced during the proceedings before the ICJ in the *Kosovo* Advisory Opinion. Certain states explicitly referred to the Friendly Relations Declaration's 'safeguard clause',[342] yet did so in conjunction with 'gross' violations of other human rights and the exhaustion of all means to find a suitable solution. Conversely, other states strongly opposed an *a contrario* interpretation, viewing the Declaration as a reaffirmation of territorial integrity.[343] However, the *Kosovo* case, which accrued selective support cannot be construed as a rule-changer, especially because states underlined its

337 The Western States apparently favoured the inclusion of the 'representative government' clause to Article 46(1) of the Declaration. See (13 Sep. 2007) UN Doc. A/61/PV/107 (Australia) 11; (6 Feb. 2001) UN Doc. E/CN.4/2001/85 (Spain) para 83; (6 Dec. 1999) UN Doc. E/CN.4/2000/84 (Norway) 14, para 81. On the other hand, African States were against. See African Group, Draft Aide Memoire, UN Declaration on the Rights of Indigenous Peoples (9 Nov. 2006) para 3.3.

338 M. Shaw, 'The Role of Recognition and Non-Recognition with Respect to Secession: Notes on Some Relevant Issues' in J. Dahlitz (ed.) *Secession and International Law* (T.M.C. Asser Press 2003) 248.

339 A. Xanthaki, *Indigenous Rights and United Nations Standards. Self-determination, Culture and Land* (CUP 2007) 14.

340 P. Thornberry, 'Self-determination, Minorities, Human Rights: A Review of International Instruments' 38 *International and Comparative Law Quarterly* (1989) 877.

341 M. Halperin and D. Scheffer, *Self-determination in the New World Order* (Carnegie Endowment for Int'l Peace 1992) 24.

342 Written comments of Albania (17 Jul. 2009) paras 56–60; Written statement of Switzerland (15 Apr. 2009) paras 60–68; Written statement of Poland (14 Apr. 2009) paras 6.8–6.9; Written statement of Estonia (13 Apr. 2009) 5.

343 Written statement of Spain (14 Apr. 2009) para 24; Written statement of Argentina (17 Apr. 2009) para 97; Written statement of Cyprus (17 Apr. 2009) para 142; Oral submission of China (7 Dec. 2009) CR 2009/29 paras 22–26.

sui generis character. As Hilpold aptly noted, something designated as specific or exceptional and explicitly precluded from serving as a precedent cannot, by principle, influence the general understanding of a given rule.[344] Indeed, an examination of United Nations practice reveals that no formal support has been granted for the independent statehood of approximately thirty claimants in the post-WWII era, even following Kosovo. Anti-secession sentiments – exemplified by the UN's mission to Congo to suppress the secessionist attempt of Katanga and the institution's consistent insistence on territorial integrity – underscore the entrenched opposition to secession.[345] So far, only Bangladesh has managed to secede and gain UN membership following violations of internal self-determination. In contrast, numerous groups, such as the Kurds in Turkey or Iraq and the Tibetans in China, continue their struggles, illustrating states' clear aversion to secession.[346] The lack of practice, in turn, is steered by deeper political and legal considerations. On the one hand, states are reluctant to recognize ineffective entities or those created illegally, given their commitment to the stability doctrine. On the other, they are equally hesitant to intervene militarily to support and recognize secessionist movements, aware of the legal constraints and the potential repercussions of such actions – often the only viable means of effectuating new statehood.

To conclude, the asserted right to remedial secession continues to rely far more on compelling moral arguments than on established legal principles, although this dynamic may evolve over time. Presently, there are neither international nor, in most cases, effective domestic legal mechanisms to enforce the right to internal self-determination.[347] Should a government remain adamant in self-determination denial, cling rigidly to the notion of state sovereignty,

---

344 P. Hilpold, 'The Kosovo Case and International Law: Looking for Applicable Theories' *Chinese Journal of International Law* (2009) 54–56; P. Hilpold, *Autonomy and Self-determination* (Edgar 2018) 41–42. See also B. Jia, 'The Independence of Kosovo: A Unique Case of Secession?' 8 *Chinese Journal of International Law* (2009) 29–31; G. Zyberi, 'Self-determination through the Lens of the ICJ' 56 *Netherlands International Law Review* (2009) 443.

345 According to Fox, the UN mission in Congo almost brought the organization to the brink of constitutional breakdown and bankruptcy. Fox, 'Self-determination in the Post-Cold War Era' (n 83) 740.

346 Raič (n 59) 369; Hannum, 'The Right of Self-determination' (n 315) 777; R. McCorquodale, 'A Human Rights Approach' 43(4) *International and Comparative Law Quarterly* (1994) 880; J. Castellino, *International Law & Self-determination: The Interplay of the Politics of Territorial Possession with Formulations of 'National' Identity* (Martinus Nijhoff 2000) 43–44.

347 Raič (n 59) 313. See also T. Marauhn, 'Anspruch auf Sezession?' in H. J. Heintze (ed.) *Selbstbestimmungsrecht der Völker – Herausforderung der Staatenwelt* (Dietz 1997) 112, 119–120.

and disregard international recommendations for legislative reforms,[348] such a scenario may indeed resemble internal colonialism or alien occupation – sufficient to substantiate a moral claim to secession. International law should not remain silent in this regard.

Furthermore, while there is merit in acknowledging secession claims of those subjected to blatant and continuous abuses of basic human rights – such as the right to life and health – rights associated with internal self-determination (political, cultural, economic, and social) may also, if significantly and persistently violated, warrant similar considerations. Thus, the critical factors are the gravity and persistence of violations. Discrimination must be intentional, systematic, and continuous, excluding any possibility of achieving a peaceful resolution within the framework of the existing state structure.[349]

3.3.3 Compromisory Processes and Constitutional Arrangements

Independence achieved through constitutional provisions or negotiated settlements falls within the broader definition of secession, although some authors do not classify it as such due to the element of consent.[350]

Consensual secession occurs when a region or group seeks independence, and the parent state agrees to the separation through a negotiated process. This type of secession is marked by mutual agreement and typically involves a legal and political framework to ensure a peaceful and orderly transition.[351]

Under this framework, the secessionist region and the parent state engage in negotiations to determine the terms and conditions of secession. These agreements often address critical issues such as borders, citizenship, the division of assets and debts, and future relations between the two entities. The secession process is usually guided by constitutional provisions or laws of the parent state, which may outline specific procedures for achieving independence.[352] Treaties or agreements formalizing the secession process are often drafted and ratified by both parties. Additionally, referendums may be held to allow the population of the seceding region to express their will, as seen in Quebec (1995), Scotland (2014), and New Caledonia (2018). Parent states may also

348 See Human Rights Committee, *Anatoly Poplavny v. Belarus*, Communication No. 2019/2010 (2015); *Leonid Sudalenko v. Belarus*, Communication No. 2016/2010 (2015), Individual opinion of Committee member Sarah Cleveland (concurring).

349 Cassese (n 68) 119–120.

350 See 3.2.1.

351 D. Lefkowitz, *Philosophy and International Law: A Critical Introduction* (CUP 2020) 203.

352 See Constitution of the Federal Democratic Republic of Ethiopia (1995) Article 47; Constitution of Saint Kitts and Nevis (1983) Article 113; Constitution of the Republic of Uzbekistan (1992) Article 74.

conduct referendums or legislative votes to approve the secession agreement. Consensual secession generally facilitates smoother international recognition of the new state, as the process is viewed as legitimate and peaceful.

Examples of consensual secession include the dissolution of the union between Norway and Sweden in 1905. United under a single monarch, Norway sought independence, and after negotiations, a peaceful dissolution was agreed upon, leading to Norway's emergence as an independent state.[353] Another instance is the division of Czechoslovakia into the Czech Republic and Slovakia, commonly known as the 'Velvet Divorce'.[354] Both regions negotiated the terms of separation, leading to a peaceful and consensual secession. In Africa, after decades of civil war, Sudan and its southern region agreed to hold a referendum on independence. The 2011 referendum resulted in a vote for independence, and South Sudan emerged as a separate state with the consent of the Sudanese government.[355]

4 In Lieu of a Firm Conclusion: Reflections on Divided International Legal Perspectives on Secession in the 21st Century

A key challenge in determining the (non)existence of a right to secession lies in the inherent ambivalence of international law on this matter. However, this ostensibly agnostic stance is paradoxical, as legal scholars frequently depart from the presumed neutrality, actively engaging with the circumstances under which international law forbids, permits, or might permit secession.

The primary epistemological distinctions operate on two strata. The epicentre of the first variance revolves around the *apprehension* of the term secession *per se*, connoting such perplexities as whether secession constitutes a separate

353 Consult the Norwegian Storting Resolution (7 Jun. 1905) declaring the union with Sweden dissolved, adding that King Oscar II had ceased to act as King of Norway; and the Karlstad Agreement (23 Sept. 1905) where delegates from both countries negotiated terms for the dissolution, including the establishment of neutral zones and the demolition of certain fortifications. On 26 October 1905, King Oscar II recognized Norway as an independent state and renounced his claim to the Norwegian throne.

354 In the latter half of 1992, leaders Václav Klaus and Vladimír Mečiar reached an agreement for the two republics to separate by the end of the year. See J. Rychlík, 'The "Velvet Split" of Czechoslovakia (1989–1992)' 6(57) *Politeja* (2018) 169–187.

355 Consult the Comprehensive Peace Agreement (CPA) (2005) between the Sudanese government and the Sudan People's Liberation Movement, which ended decades of civil war and granted the southern region autonomy, with a provision for a future independence referendum. Referendum was held in January 2011, while in July South Sudan officially declared independence, and Sudan became the first country to recognize the new state.

institution of international law or it is subsumed within the right to self-determination, whether it can occur consensually, and whether colonies can legally 'secede' at all, among others.[356] The focal point of the second discord lies in the *applicability* of secession in sovereign states and raises questions about choosing, balancing, or accommodating two imperatives: the necessity of protecting human rights and democratic values versus the desideratum of maintaining the existing territorial order and, consequently, international stability.[357]

Traditionally, secession has been viewed as a para-legal instrument subordinate to the principle of territorial integrity, as evidenced by numerous international documents and the practices of states and international organizations. Conversely, modern perspectives challenge the sanctity of territorial integrity, arguing that passive state practice and inferential legal documents do not conclusively prohibit secession.[358] Proponents of the modern view even contend that international law should allow secession under specific circumstances.[359] Yet, aware of the limited weight of a few soft law documents, including the Friendly Relations Declaration, international legal scholarship remains extremely cautious in pronouncing a legal right to secession, and prefers to frame it as *de lege ferenda*.[360] The most pragmatic conciliatory stance emerges when a counterclaim to territorial integrity is circumvented by an agreed procedure potentially leading to secession, as exemplified by the 2014 Scottish independence referendum. Another felicitous vision presupposes that self-determination is a norm from which both the permissibility and prohibition of secession can be derived, with burgeoning practice lending credence to this duality – a point to be explored thoroughly in subsequent chapters.

---

356 See A. Zimmermann, 'Secession and the Law of State Succession' in M. Kohen (ed.) *Secession: International Law Perspectives* (CUP 2006) 210–211.

357 J. Vidmar, 'Territorial Integrity and the Law of Statehood' 44 *George Washington International Law Review* (2012) 707. Weller noted that a territorial integrity counterclaim loses validity when opposed by another 'grant of legal authority'. Such a grant 'might be made either by the predecessor states through their consent to secession or, perhaps, exceptionally, by collective international action of the U.N. Security Council or widespread recognition triggered by the opposed, but effective, unilateral creation of statehood'. M. Weller, 'Modesty Can Be a Virtue: Judicial Economy in the ICJ Kosovo Opinion' 24 *Leiden Journal of International Law* (2011) 129–130.

358 *See* Summers, 'The Principle of Territorial Integrity' (n 106) 42–58; J. Vidmar, *Democratic Statehood in International Law* (Hart 2013) 161.

359 On the changing perception of the right to secession see 'Introduction' in C. Walter, A. von Ungern- Sternberg and K. Abushov (eds.) *Self-determination and Secession in International Law* (OUP 2014) 3.

360 See Vidmar, 'Remedial Secession in International Law' (n 335) 39.

Without further ado, it is readily deducible that the widespread *non-liquet* orientation by necessity invites personal views, resulting in abundant polysemy even within like-minded camps. To avoid reiterating the arguments outlined earlier, it suffices to recap that the pro-secession faction is divided into those who indiscriminately favour secession (a minority) and those who allow it on the basis of the existence of particular conditions (the majority). Within the latter group, the most prevalent conditions are grave breaches of human rights and/or internal self-determination, which scholars are inclined to interpretate according to individually-set standards, and which can be accompanied by additional requirements, such as the existence of 'a people' or nation, territorial demarcation, or historical claims.[361] This can lead to paradoxes where, depending on the author's optics, one group may have a right to secede, while the other has it only to a certain extent or not at all. On the opposite spectrum, the anti-secession faction is similarly divided: those who oppose secession unconditionally (a significant percentage) and those who reject it only when achieved in violation of peremptory norms of international law, such as through the use of force or under apartheid (the majority).

As a result, there are scarcely any advocates of pure neutrality on this issue. Views on secession diverge not only due to the vagueness of legal precepts but also because of political predispositions and personal perspectives shaped by the details of specific cases and affinities with the parties involved. The field of secession is certainly not academically static, but the shortage of state practice inhibits more rapid normative development.[362]

---

361 For instance, Ryngaert and Griffioen only attribute the remedial right to secession to 'the "people" who have a distinct identity and represent a clear majority within a given territory'. See Ryngaert and Griffioen (n 333) 575–576.

362 See 'A Normative 'Due Process'' (n 93) 184.

CHAPTER 4

Internal Self-determination as a Method of Preventing Secession in International Law: Theoretical Approach

> In the middle of difficulty lies opportunity.
>
> ALBERT EINSTEIN

1 General Observations (Hypothesis)

Secession poses significant challenges in international politics and relations. When a region within a country seeks to break away and form its own independent state, it often leads to complex legal, political, and socio-economic issues, both domestically and internationally. Secession challenges the principles of sovereignty and territorial integrity, which are fundamental tenets of the international system. Furthermore, many secessionist movements, fuelled by grievances related to ethnic or national identity, result in violence, displacement of populations, and humanitarian crises. These movements can destabilize not only the state from which they seek to secede but also the wider region and exert an impact on the economy and diplomatic relations.

Well-informed of these repercussions, international leaders have long ago embarked on a journey in pursuit of solutions to mitigate the instability exacerbated by a growing number of secessionist movements. A broad range of political strategies have been tried over the years, with lesser and greater rates of success, whereas a magic bullet, which could operate on a global scale, still has not been found. Political dialogue and negotiation remain the most common approaches, requiring genuine engagement and goodwill from all stakeholders to succeed.

Strategies to address secessionist pressures include: (a) devolving power to grant greater autonomy and competencies to regions, thereby reducing feelings of marginalization; (b) promoting inclusive governance to ensure diverse populations are represented and have a voice in decision-making; (c) addressing economic disparities and ensuring fair resource distribution to maintain regional equity; (d) implementing policies of reconciliation and conflict

 | DOI:10.1163/9789004737501_005

resolution to rebuild trust, restore societal cohesion, and enhance security in post-conflict settings; and (e) providing international mediation and support, along with establishing legal and constitutional safeguards to protect minority rights and uphold the rule of law.[1]

The initiatives mentioned above are primarily aimed at appeasing rebellious factions, however, their scope and implementation can vary significantly. They are political, generally non-binding, and constructive measures, contrasting with coercive methods, which focus on forcibly suppressing secessionist movements. It should not be forgotten that states usually take an anti-secessionist stance and have at their disposal a wide diapason of actions, including legal remedies, such as injunctions or court orders, to prevent or dampen secessionist activities. Legal enforcement actions can be taken against individuals or groups engaged in activities deemed to be promoting secession in light of the domestic law. This raises a question: what measures could be taken from an international legal perspective to both placate pro-independence movements and encourage states to adopt and implement positive initiatives? Here is where the concept of internal self-determination comes to the fore. As the next chapter explores, ISD has gained significant traction in international practice and appears to be evolving into a preferred standard for resolving self-determination disputes – potentially even a customary legal rule. This chapter conducts a theoretical examination of ISD, addressing its definition and its value in preventing secession. The underlying hypothesis is that ISD represents a conciliatory approach between two extremes: the outright suppression of the rights-claiming entity by the parent state, which is increasingly viewed as illegitimate and contrary to international human rights norms, and the unilateral acquisition of independence by the entity concerned, which remains an undesirable outcome. ISD, in consequence, seeks to eliminate both extremes, which often exacerbate tensions and perpetuate conflict – frequently due to the failure to implement ISD at earlier stages. However, questions regarding the legitimacy and fairness of ISD surface, particularly concerning its seeming rigidity. Should secession be legally prohibited, and who has the authority to determine whether ISD is being upheld? These and other dilemmas are explored in Section 4.7.

2 Various Meanings of Internal Self-determination

Internal self-determination (ISD) remains a somewhat imprecise concept. States, when confronted with claims to secession, have used ISD both to

1 More in 4.4.–4.6.

support and to refute such claims, and referenced it in reports submitted to the Human Rights Committee on their implementation of Article 1 of the ICCPR, frequently in conjunction with the principle of territorial integrity. By doing so, states have framed ISD both as a right of peoples and as a counter-secession prerogative of states.[2]

On one occasion, ISD was equated with the free will of the people residing within a state and the principle prohibiting external intervention in their affairs.[3] Some commentators argue that this is the primary meaning of ISD, coined by the USSR and later included in the International Covenants on Human Rights at their insistence.[4] This interpretation stands in stark contrast to the efforts of the U.S. and UK, which sought to frame the concept as a mechanism for promoting representative democracy. During the International Experts Meeting on Further Study of the Concept of the Rights of Peoples, organized by UNESCO in 1989, it was observed that dynamic changes within the international community required UNESCO to reflect on peoples' rights in new contexts, including democratic governance.[5] Nevertheless, the primary interpretation, which corresponds to the texts in the Covenants and the Friendly Relations Declaration, is that peoples should have a free choice to shape their destiny as they please and to enjoy that freedom without external hindrance. In practice, the principles of free will and non-intervention have predominantly been interpreted politically as the right of all peoples to choose a representative government and exert control over it, including the power to amend it. However, this interpretation excludes hypothetical personal freedoms realizable by smaller collectives, such as the right of a subgroup within a population to secede or engage in other actions constrained by the state's

2 The counter-secession interpretation of ISD is discussed separately in Section 4.3.

3 R. Emerson, 'Self-determination' 65 *AJIL* (1971) 465–466; M. Koskenniemi, 'National Self-determination Today: Problems of Legal Theory and Practice' 43(2) *International and Comparative Law Quarterly* (1994) 248.

4 The USSR conceptualized self-determination as the emancipation of peoples from the yoke of the capitalist bourgeoisie. See A. Miaja de la Muela, *La Emancipación de los Pueblos Coloniales y el Derecho Internacional* (Tecnos 1968) 98–112; H. T. Mateu, 'Self-determination and Access to Independence under Current International Law: From Language to Concept' 23 *Spanish Yearbook of International Law* (2023) 55. Cf. P. Thornberry, 'The Democratic or Internal Aspect of Self-determination with Some Remarks on Federalism' in C. Tomuschat (ed.) *Modern Law of Self-determination* (Martinus Nijhoff 1993) 101 (who argues that external self-determination constitutes a 'continuous defense against external subversion or intervention'.) It is safe to say that self-determination, in general, prohibits any form of intervention.

5 UNESCO International Meeting of Experts, 'Further Study of the Concept of the Rights of Peoples' Final Report and Recommendations (22 Feb. 1990) UNESCO Doc. SHS-89/CONF.602/7, para 27.

legal framework.[6] According to the Kantian understanding of freedom, it must comply with 'universal law'. Therefore, any unreasonable or immoral claims, which interfere with others' freedoms, will not be considered legitimate and could be restricted by the state.[7]

In addition to external forces, free will may be endangered by authoritarian regimes or the 'reasonable' majority within a state. For that reason, ISD has also been conceived as a mechanism for protecting minority freedoms, encompassing principles of inclusiveness, non-discrimination, and autonomous self-governance.[8] Lastly, given that ISD must contribute to political, social, economic and cultural development, it by necessity connotes a plethora of human rights and freedoms. How can one shape a government without the right to vote? How can traditional culture be cultivated without securing land rights? How can development occur without the right to utilise natural resources? Without these guaranteed rights, one cannot speak of free and true self-determination.

There is general agreement that ISD, as opposed to ESD, is realised *within* the political and legal framework of a given state. Its aim is not territorial change, but rather to foster a relationship between a state's population and its government – one that reflects the will of the people and protects their rights and interests.[9] However, this does not preclude the possibility that a people, as a collective, may amend the political status of their state, nor does it rule out the potential for ISD, as exercised by a particular group, to evolve into ESD through mutual agreement.[10]

---

6 Cf. A. E. Eckert, 'Free Determination or the Determination to be Free? Self-determination and the Democratic Entitlement' 4(1) *UCLA Journal of International Law and Foreign Affairs* (1999) 60, 66–67.

7 A. Stilz, 'The Value of Self-determination' in A. D. Sobel, P. Vallentyne and S. Wall (eds.) *Oxford Studies in Political Philosophy* (2016 OUP) 118–121 (referring to groups like anarchists, fascists, and theocrats).

8 P. Bossacoma Busquets, 'Catalonia: Self-determination, Secession, and Integration' in B. C. Harzl and R. Petrov (eds.) *Unrecognized Entities: Perspectives in International, European and Constitutional Law* (Law in Eastern Europe, Brill 2022) 152–153; N. Shikova, *Self-determination and Secession In Between the Law, Theory and Practice* (Springer 2023) 197–211.

9 Thornberry (n 4) 127–128.

10 The Liechtenstein Draft Convention on Self-determination Through Self-Administration envisages such a transition. More in 5.2.5. See also K. Bobrowski, 'Prawo do Samostanowienia Narodów w Prawie Międzynarodowym – Aktualna Wykładnia' 7 *Krytyka Prawa* (2015) 31. Cf. V. P. Nanda, 'Self-determination Under International Law: Validity of Claims to Secede' 13 *Case Western Reserve Journal of International Law* (1981) 275 (where the author claims that ISD connotes the right to secession).

2.1 *ISD as a Free Will and Non-intervention*

Internal self-determination presupposes the freedom to determine one's collective destiny within a state.[11] The Friendly Relations Declaration, the International Covenants on Human Rights, the Helsinki Final Act, among many, stress the phrase 'freedom of determination'.[12] In the case of the entire population of a state, this freedom pertains to the territorially demarcated state; while in the case of a minority, this freedom encompasses both state affairs and community affairs, possibly within separately demarcated boundaries. Individuals self-determine freely within both areas.

The concept of internal self-determination is grounded in the idea of the sovereignty of the people, who must be free to determine their own destiny both within their parent state and on the international stage. The legitimacy of central authorities, as well as a state's international standing, rests fundamentally on the free will of the people, a notion central to the idea of democracy.[13] As the ICJ stated in its advisory opinion on Western Sahara, the essence of the principle of self-determination lies in 'the need to pay regard to the freely expressed will of peoples',[14] serving as a safeguard against oppression. This principle is further reflected in Articles 73 and 76 of the UN Charter, which underscore the importance of respecting the political aspirations and freely expressed will of the people.

What sort of internal self-determination freedom is at stake when the whole population of a state is concerned? A broad spectrum of matters might be put forward, since ISD entitles a people to choose their political affiliation, preserve their cultural, ethnic, historical or territorial identity, establish economic

11 As noted by Judge Higgins in her separate opinion: '"Peoples" necessarily exercise their right to self-determination within their own territory'. ICJ, *Legal Consequences of the Construction of a Wall in the Occupied Palestinian Territory*, Advisory Opinion, ICJ Rep. 2004, 215.

12 Helsinki Final Act in Part VIII pronounces 'By virtue of the principle of equal rights and self-determination of peoples, all peoples always have the right, in *full freedom*, to determine (...)' (emphasis added).

13 See Universal Declaration of Human Rights (UDHR), UNGA Res 217(III) (10 Dec. 1948) Article 1 (All human beings are born free and equal in dignity and rights). See Articles 13, 16–23 (on all other guaranteed freedoms). See also UN Commission on Human Rights, Sub-Commission on the Prevention of Discrimination and Protection of Minorities, 'The Right to Self-determination: Historical and Current Development on the Basis of United Nations Instruments'. Study Prepared by A. Cristescu (1981) UN Doc. E/CN.4/Sub.2/404/Rev.1, paras 228, 692.

14 ICJ, *Western Sahara*, Advisory Opinion, ICJ Rep. 1975, para 59.

and social institutions, and enact laws, including the constitution.[15] The ultimate significance lies less in whether a constitutional amendment is eventually passed and more in the possession of the ability – and thus the freedom – to initiate and participate in constitutional debates.[16] The sovereign people, either directly or through their representatives, can decide on matters such as joining or leaving international organizations, determining the political system, establishing political parties, setting emigration quotas, constructing nuclear facilities, or disallowing specific architectural elements like minarets on mosques, among others.[17] Legal doctrine, however, simplifies this extensive catalogue by encapsulating the free will of the people in their ability to elect and amend a government as their direct representative. Bobrowski equates ISD with the election of a government that represents the people,[18] while Cassese frames it as the right to 'elect and keep the government of its choice'.[19] As a consequence, ISD can be summarized as the right to a democratic form of government,[20] since it inherently implies a democratic process.[21]

Article 21 of the UDHR, which stipulates that 'everyone has the right to take part in the government of his country, directly or through freely chosen representatives' and that 'the will of the people shall be the basis of the authority of government', expressed through 'periodic and genuine elections', delineates rights now associated with ISD, though it does not explicitly label them as such.[22] This provision concretizes how free will should be exercised, disfavouring other methods of government change, such as violent protests, *coups d'état*,

15 G. Fox, 'Self-determination in the Post-Cold War Era: A New Internal Focus?' 16 *Michigan Journal of International Law* (1995) 752; A. Rosas, 'Internal Self-determination' in C. Tomuschat (ed.) *Modern Law of Self-determination* (Martinus Nijhoff Publishers 1993) 232; Bobrowski (n 8) 31.

16 M. Seymour, 'Internal Self-determination and Secession' in A. Pavković and P. Radan (eds.) *The Ashgate Research Companion to Secession* (Routledge 2011) 391.

17 In the 2009 Swiss minaret referendum, a constitutional amendment banning the construction of new minarets was approved by 57.5% of the participating voters. In 2023, Kazakh President Kassym-Jomart Tokayev announced a referendum in response to the nation's need to develop nuclear power.

18 Bobrowski (n 8) 31.

19 A. Cassese, 'Political Self-determination – Old Concepts and New Developments' in A. Cassese (ed.) *UN Law/Fundamental Rights: Two Topics in International Law* (Sijthoff & Noordhoff 1979) 137.

20 F. Kirgis, 'Editorial Comment: The Degrees of Self-determination in the United Nations Era' 88(2) *AJIL* (1994) 307.

21 Y. Beigbeder, *International Monitoring of Plebiscites, Referenda and National Elections: Self-determination and Transitions to Democracy* (International Studies in Human Rights, Brill Nijhoff 1994) 18.

22 UNGA Res 217A (n 13).

or, at worst, civil wars. State practice broadly aligns with this understanding,[23] as do the practices of international organizations, peace missions, and multilateral conferences. The Final Act of the Conference on Cambodia, for instance, emphasized the intent to 'ensure the exercise of the right to self-determination of the Cambodian people through free and fair elections'.[24] Similarly, the Human Rights Committee called on Congo to organise general elections as soon as possible to enable its citizens to exercise their rights under Articles 1 and 25 of the ICCPR.[25]

Although it is impossible to implement electoral patterns universally in all circumstances – such as removing a British monarch by vote or electing a Chinese President or Iranian Supreme Leader – election fraud, refusal to accept election results, or the removal of duly elected representatives are widely regarded as direct breaches of the right to internal self-determination. One example of such a breach could be the first elections to the Legislative Sejm in post-war Poland, which were rigged by the communists to formalize Soviet power.[26] Another example includes the 2000 Serbian presidential election, marred by widespread fraud and manipulation, which sparked mass protests and ultimately led to the ousting of President Slobodan Milošević. In Lesotho's report under Article 40 of the ICCPR, the annulment of an election result by the governing party – following its defeat – and the subsequent declaration of a state of emergency were identified as infringements of the people's internal self-determination.[27] The African Commission on Human and Peoples' Rights, despite the lack of provisions to safeguard governmental representation specifically through elections in the Banjul Charter, issued a few unequivocal

23 See Human Rights Committee, 'Third periodic report submitted by Armenia under article 40 of the Covenant' (30 Sep. 2019) UN Doc. CCPR/C/ARM/3; 'Fifth periodic report submitted by Jordan' (4 Dec. 2017) UN Doc. CCPR/C/JOR/5.

24 Final Act of the Paris Conference on Cambodia, Annex, UN Doc. A/46/608 & S/23177, reprinted in 31 *ILM* (1992) 180, 181. This phrase was reiterated by the Security Council in its resolution establishing the United Nations Transitional Authority in Cambodia. See UNSC Res 745 (28 Feb. 1992).

25 Human Rights Committee, 'Concluding Observations on the Second Periodic Report of the Congo' (27 Mar. 2000) UN Doc. CCPR/C/79/Add.118, para 20.

26 Between 4–11 February 1945, a conference of three allied powers – Great Britain, the United States and the Soviet Union – was held in Yalta. As a result, the Polish authorities were obliged to hold 'free and unrestricted elections as soon as possible'. Preparations for the elections began in March 1946 and took some time, including a popular referendum in June 1946 and the adoption of electoral law in September 1946.

27 Human Rights Committee, 'Initial report of States parties due in 1993: Addendum, Lesotho' (28 May 1998) UN Doc. CCPR/C/81/Add.14, paras 4, 8.

statements in support of electoral democracy.[28] In its resolution on Nigeria, the Commission demanded the 'handover of government to duly elected representatives of the people without unnecessary delay', while in its resolution on The Gambia, it characterized a coup as 'a flagrant and grave violation of the right of the Gambian people to freely choose their government'.[29] Clinging to power against the popular will violates internal self-determination and so does forcibly removing a democratically elected government.[30] The United States intervened multiple times to restore elected leadership. Examples include Grenada in 1983, where it sought to reinstate the government of Prime Minister Maurice Bishop, and Haiti in 1994, where a multinational intervention led to the restoration of President Jean-Bertrand Aristide.[31]

Respecting the popular will as expressed through elections that are not blatantly manipulated may not be sufficient to ensure that the popular will is truly fulfilled. If a population lacks an adequate choice of candidates – such as in the case of one-party systems, which are common in some Middle Eastern and former communist states – or if elections fail to produce meaningful change due to political narratives shaped by external forces (as in Eastern Europe under the Soviet Union or the European Union today), or if the margin of victory is arbitrarily manipulated to disadvantage the opposition, the legitimacy of the elections is compromised.[32] General Comment 25 of the UN Human Rights Committee, the Venice Commission's Code of Good Practice on Electoral

28 Article 13 of the African Charter on Human and Peoples' Rights (Banjul Charter) states: 'Every citizen shall have the right to participate freely in the government of his country, either directly or through freely chosen representatives in accordance with the provisions of the law'.

29 More in G. Fox, 'The Right to Political Participation in International Law' in G. Fox and B. Roth (eds.) *Democratic Governance and International Law* (2000) 67–68.

30 Community of Democracies Ministerial Meeting, 'Warsaw Declaration: Towards a Community of Democracies', reprinted in 39(6) *ILM* (2000) 1306.

31 Other states and organizations did too intervene to either establish the new leadership or to protect the old one, should it be democratically elected. For example, France intervened in Côte d'Ivoire in 2011 as part of Operation Licorne to support the internationally recognized government of President Alassane Ouattara against Laurent Gbagbo, who refused to cede power after losing the presidential election. The Economic Community of West African States (ECOWAS) intervened in The Gambia in 2017 to uphold the results of democratic elections ensuring the transfer of power to the democratically elected president, Adama Barrow, after former President Yahya Jammeh initially refused to step down. Intervention to impose a democratic system of government, however, appears to contradict the principle of non-intervention, which is a cornerstone of the right to self-determination. Eckert (n 6) 57–59.

32 'If voting changed anything, they'd make it illegal' is a famous quote by Emma Goldman, a Russian-born US political activist, anarchist and writer (1869–1940). A similar quote – 'If

Matters, and the Inter-Parliamentary Union's Declaration on Criteria for Free and Fair Elections outline a set of standards for elections to be considered free and genuine, and thus in line with the right to self-determination.[33] These standards include a legal framework that guarantees the right to vote, regular intervals for elections, stability in election-related laws, equal suffrage, accurate voter registration, a fair campaign process, and access to media and election observers.[34] For voters, to freely express their will, at least four key freedoms are vital: the freedom of thought, without which the prospective voters will feel compelled to adopt positions that they in good conscience do not support; the freedom of speech, without which the voters will not be able to articulate the views they actually hold; the freedom of the press, through which the voters circulate and acquire information; and the unrestricted access to information, which helps to critically assess policy proposals.[35]

Finalizing this thread, it should be noted that elections are not the only method of expressing free will (there can be referenda, plebiscites, consultations etc.) and it cannot be automatically assumed that a long-term delegation of authority to a leader, for example, a king constitutes a negation of representative government.[36]

Malevolent outside intervention in domestic affairs amounts to a breach of ISD since it seeks to distort the will of the people concerned and impose the will of others. Such intervention can take various forms, with election interference being one example. Allegedly, Russian troll farms distorted the social media landscape prior to the 2016 US presidential elections by authoring thousands of posts that deceived readers about their true origins. In addition, the hacking of Hillary Clinton's emails and those of other DNC officials, followed by their release to the media through the DCLeaks and Wikileaks, despite being true, created asymmetry and perverted the voters' deliberation.[37] Tsagourias,

---

voting made a difference, they wouldn't let us do it' – is attributed to American humourist Mark Twain (1835–1910).

33 See Council of Europe, *Using International Election Standards: Council of Europe Handbook for Civil Society Organisations* (Council of Europe Publishing 2016) 13–21.

34 Franck saw the root of democracy in the right to self-determination, as well as, to some extent, in the right to free and open elections and the freedom of expression. T. M. Franck, 'The Emerging Right to Democratic Governance' 86 *AJIL* (1992) 52, 77. Similarly, UK Representative to the General Assembly's Third Committee, R. Fursland. cited in 'United Kingdom Materials on International Law 1984' 55 *BYIL* (1984) 434.

35 J. D. Ohlin, *Election Interference International Law and the Future of Democracy* (CUP 2020) 99–100.

36 Rousseau conceded that a legitimate government based upon consent might include monarchy. J. J. Rousseau, *The Social Contract* (G. D. H. Cole trans., 1972) 29 n. 10.

37 Ohlin (n 35) 101–103.

in his deliberation on the right to self-determination, observed that 'external interference through disinformation combined with identity falsification, for example, distorts, undermines or inverses this process and nullifies the genuine expression and authority and will by the people'.[38] Another example of a ISD's violation through external intervention could be the establishment of ties between a state's government and an external subject (such as another state or organization) via security arrangements, incentives (such as investments or corruption), or coercive measures including threats and blackmail, causing the government to act against the wishes of the population. In such a case, the government ceases to be authentic and representative. This may indicate that ISD can be fragile in unstable democracies and that there is a void in-between electing and amending a government. A perplexing scenario arises when the international community dictates the external policies of a weaker state, potentially restricting the self-determination of its population in pursuit of higher aims, such as maintaining independence and peace. Yet, in the long term, this could be interpreted as being in compliance with the principle of self-determination, as seen in the Treaty of Saint-Germain and the Geneva Protocols, which prevented Austria from entering into any economic or financial negotiations that would jeopardize its independence.[39] Lastly, ISD might be violated through external military intervention, which is probably the best-known example of the correlation between the RSD and the principle of non-intervention. Any territorial acquisition against the will of the people concerned – whether the region or the entire state territory – violates ISD. Notable instances include China's invasion and annexation of Tibet in 1950, Israel's occupation of Palestinian territories since 1967, and Indonesia's annexation of East Timor in 1975. Authorized military interventions and externally introduced systems, intended to promote ISD, fall outside the scope of the prohibition on non-intervention, even though they may be imposed without

38 N. Tsagourias, 'Electoral Cyber Interference, Self-determination and the Principle of Non-Intervention in Cyberspace' in D. Broeders and B. van Den Berg (eds.) *Governing Cyberspace: Behaviour, Power and Diplomacy* (Rowman & Littlefield 2020) 51.

39 Article 88 of the Treaty of Saint-Germain provided that Austria's independence is inalienable except with the consent of the League of Nations. 226 CTS 8, 36. In Geneva's Protocol No. 1, Austria undertook not to grant 'to any state whatsoever a special regime or exclusive advantages calculated to threaten this independence.' 116 BFSP 85. See PCIJ, *Customs Régime between Germany and Austria (Protocol of March 19th, 1931)*, Advisory Opinion, PCIJ Ser. A/B No 41, ICGJ 287.

the consent of those directly affected, as exemplified by certain UN Security Council resolutions.[40]

2.2 *ISD as Inclusiveness and Non-discrimination*

Inclusiveness and non-discrimination, as embodiments of ISD, can be understood as part of the broader concept of governmental representation, which aims to reflect the free will of the people, unimpeded by external influence. While it is agreed that a government should mirror popular interests, this general principle requires some caveats. First of all, the realisation of the broader will of the people is restricted by the ruling party's programme and its commitment to implementing it. Furthermore, this will is typically that of the majority. In countries with two-party systems (the UK, the U.S., Australia) or where multiple parties unite to oppose the ruling party (as in Poland's 2023 parliamentary elections, where the Civic Coalition, the Left, and the Third Way formed a coalition government to secure a parliamentary majority against the incumbent Law and Justice Party, which won the highest number of votes in absolute terms), the government represents the will of slightly more than half of the electorate. Going further, Macron's victory over Le Pen in France's 2022 presidential elections, where he won 58.5% of the vote with a 72% turnout, indicates that the current president represents the will of only about 42% of eligible voters. Inclusiveness and non-discrimination in such cases are thus to be construed primarily through the procedural aspect of ISD (voting), provided that no irregularities are identified.[41]

Having established that a government formed through the free choice of the population may not fully reflect the political aspirations of the entire population, inclusiveness must be understood as transcending electoral outcomes. It encompasses the government's commitment to the foundational tenets of democracy – political equality, the rule of law, and the protection of individual rights and liberties. Thus, in addition to post-electoral passive inclusiveness, realised through governmental actions and policies, ISD presupposes active inclusiveness, reflected in equality and meaningful popular political

40 UNSC Res 1244 (10. Jun. 1999) established the UNMIK mission in Kosovo. Von Carlowitz argued that external assistance could further ISD in failed states and those embroiled in military conflict. See L. von Carlowitz, 'UNMIK Lawmaking between Effective Peace Support and Internal Self-determination' 41 *Archiv des Völkerrechts* (2003) 366–367. The presence of U.S. forces in Iraq and Afghanistan has evolved over time and has been subject to various agreements and negotiations.

41 Beigbeder, *International Monitoring of Plebiscites* (n 21) 41 (maintains that monitoring is a crucial aspect of the procedural right to self-determination).

participation of all groups.[42] In its written statement to the ICJ regarding Israel's occupation of Palestine, the League of Arab States described internal self-determination as a right to 'be treated equally, when it comes to group-identity, as citizens in States where they have citizenship (e.g. Palestinian citizens of Israel), and to have their distinct group-based identity respected and protected in such States'.[43] Article 5(c) of the International Convention on the Elimination of All Forms of Racial Discrimination (ICERD) specifies that individuals must not be discriminated against in their enjoyment of

> political rights, in particular the right to participate in elections-to vote and to stand for election-on the basis of universal and equal suffrage, to take part in the Government as well as in the conduct of public affairs at any level and to have equal access to public service.[44]

The UN Human Rights Committee in its General Comment No. 25 laid down the specificity of the conduct of public affairs, noting that it concerns 'the exercise of political power, in particular the exercise of legislative, executive and administrative powers' and 'the formulation and implementation of policy'.[45] Citizens are deemed to participate directly in the conduct of public affairs when they exercise power as members of legislative bodies, hold executive office, decide public issues through referendums or other electoral processes, and take part in formal consultative mechanisms established by the government.[46] On several occasions, it has been underscored that political participation has to take place on every level of state organization.[47]

Although it is common to construe inclusiveness through the prism of political engagement, due to its paramount significance, it should be remembered

---

42 UN Commission on Human Rights, Sub-Commission on Prevention of Discrimination and Protection of Minorities. 2nd Progress Report prepared by A. Eide (1 Jul. 1992) UN Doc. E/CN.4/Sub.2/1992/37, para 165; S. Joseph, J. Schultz and M. Castan, *The International Covenant on Civil and Political Rights: Cases, Materials, and Commentary* (OUP 2000) 103.

43 ICJ, *Legal Consequences arising from the Policies and Practices of Israel in the Occupied Palestinian Territory, including East Jerusalem*, Advisory Opinion, ICJ Rep. 2024, Written Submission of the League of Arab States (20 Jul. 2023) 4.d.

44 International Convention on the Elimination of All Forms of Racial Discrimination (1965) 660 UNTS 195, Article 5(c).

45 Human Rights Committee, General Comment No. 25: The right to participate in public affairs, voting rights and the right of equal access to public service (12 Jul. 1996) para 5.

46 *Ibid.* para 6.

47 See, among many, Human Rights Committee, 'Consideration of reports submitted by States parties under article 40 of the Covenant. Concluding observations: Ethiopia' (2011) UN Doc. CCPR/C/ETH/CO/1, para 26.

that ISD is also about social, economic and cultural participation. In one of its general comments, the Committee on Economic, Social and Cultural Rights noted: 'the right to take part in cultural life is also interdependent on other rights enshrined in the Covenant, including the right of all peoples to self-determination (art. 1) and the right to an adequate standard of living (art. 11)'.[48]

Therefore, it has been correctly observed that granting electoral rights to minorities is not sufficient, particularly if a state does not follow a proportional representation electoral system, which may leave them in an unfavourable position.[49] In the event of a potential conflict between the majority and the minority, the latter is at a disadvantage. In the absence of evidence of discrimination prohibited by regional (e.g., the ECHR) or international acts (e.g., the ICERD), the extent of participation in political life and the implementation of desired programs remains conditioned by the standard tenets of democracy.[50] Minorities involved in the conduct of public affairs may have to accept the outcomes of decision-making processes, which can lead to cultural insecurity.

So, even if a country, for instance Serbia, applies positive discrimination measures in the election process (such as the 'natural threshold'), by waiving the obligation for a minority to collect 10,000 votes to register a party and allowing minority parties to secure parliamentary membership with less than 3% of the votes (a rule applicable to other parties), it may be sufficient for established minority parties – like the Alliance of Vojvodina Hungarians (which gained 1.74% of the vote and secured six mandates in the 2023 Serbian parliamentary election) or the Party of Democratic Action of Sandžak (which gained 0.59% and secured two mandates) – but not enough for the Roma community due to its spatial dispersion and political heterogeneity, even though it accounts for 2.5% of the population, with some projections estimating that their number could be 3 to 4 times higher.[51]

For this reason, fully implementing ISD requires distinct constitutional and other legal guarantees that minimize the impact of the majority on minority affairs. These should be accompanied by a multifaceted political, social,

48 Committee on Economic, Social and Cultural Rights, General Comment No. 21, 'Right of everyone to take part in cultural life (art. 15, para 1(a), of the International Covenant on Economic, Social and Cultural Rights)' para 2.

49 H. Moris, 'Self-determination: An Affirmative Right or Mere Rhetoric?' 4 *ILSA Journal of International & Comparative Law* (1997) 211–212.

50 S. Wheatley, *Democracy, Minorities and International Law* (CUP 2009) 188–189.

51 CoE, Framework Convention for the Protection of National Minorities, Fourth Opinion on Serbia (26 Jun. 2019), Doc. CM(2020)6, para 5. See Minority Rights Group, 'Roma in Serbia' <https://minorityrights.org/communities/roma-14/>.

and economic inclusiveness agenda.[52] According to the Human Rights Committee's General Comment on Article 27 of the ICCPR, the rights of persons belonging to minorities 'may require (…) measures to ensure the effective participation of members of minority communities in decisions which affect them'.[53] A good example of a meaningful pluralistic society is the consociational democracy model, where cultural security is substantially guaranteed. In this model, minorities are recognized as having a share of power and a right of veto on issues vital to their interests. In addition, states should engage in reasoned political debate, seek consensus, and avoid regulating cultural practices that are opposed by representatives of national, ethnic, religious, or linguistic minorities.

During the wave of decolonization in the 1950s and 1960s, many newly independent African and Asian states violated democratic self-determination, yet the overall enthusiasm and focus on ESD often overshadowed these internal shortcomings. In many cases, the majority population was disenfranchised, with one elite class simply replacing another of a similar kind, while minorities often faced discrimination by their own states (e.g. East Pakistan, Biafra, Eritrea).[54] Nowadays, large-scale violations of ISD affecting the majority population – such as those seen under apartheid in South Africa – are rare, but milder forms of oppression are not infrequent (e.g. China, Turkey). These issues have been mitigated to some extent by the advancement of democratic systems, which enable the peaceful transition of power and the removal of oppressive governments.[55]

Consequently, in this outlook, ISD encompasses both a positive dimension, that is, inclusivity and a negative one, that is, the prohibition of discrimination. These dual aspects parallel the principles of free will and the prohibition of external interference. The relationship between inclusiveness and its

52 See, Government of Serbia, 'The Strategy of Social Inclusion of Roma for the Period From 2016 To 2025' <https://www.rcc.int/romaintegration2020/docs/5/strategy-for-inclusion-of-roma-in-north-macedonia-2022-2030>. See also Article 2 of the Act on National Councils of National Minorities of 2009 allowing all fifteen minorities of Serbia to set up their national councils (the application of non-territorial autonomy).

53 Human Rights Committee, General Comment No. 23: Article 27 (Rights of Minorities) (8 Apr. 1994) para 7.

54 M. Pomerance, *Self-determination in Law and Practice: The New Doctrine in the United Nations* (Martinus Nijhoff Publishers 1982) 37–42; G. J. Simpson, 'The Diffusion of Sovereignty: Self-determination in the Post-Colonial Age' 32 *Stanford Journal of International Law* (1996) 271–274.

55 During the era of apartheid in South Africa, elections were held, but they were highly manipulated to maintain the system of racial segregation and white minority rule.

antithesis, discrimination, was underscored in General Recommendation XXI of the Committee on the Elimination of Racial Discrimination, which guarantees

> (…) the right of every citizen to take part in the conduct of public affairs at any level (…). In consequence, governments are to represent the whole population without distinction as to race, colour, descent, national and ethnic origins.[56]

Critically, states cannot derogate from the implementation of ISD if it is to involve discrimination based solely on race, colour, sex, language, religion, or social origin.[57]

2.3 *ISD as Self-Government and Territorial Autonomy*

In conventional wisdom, the right to self-determination is understood as the right to self-rule or self-government, encompassing the determination of external status and the management of internal affairs, free from outside interference and in accordance with the people's will.[58] Self-government, as noted, can be endangered both from outside the state and from within, particularly in the case of minorities. Since the latter aspect is less protected by traditional international law (the prohibition of aggression and intervention in the internal affairs of other states being inter-state rules) and, ironically, by the very right to self-determination itself,[59] it deserves more academic and institutional attention. This attention should aim at compelling states to comply with ISD of minorities, in line with the evolving international human rights framework.[60] It has been suggested that autonomy is the most optimal vehicle for securing

56 CERD, General Recommendation 21: The right to self-determination (8 Mar. 1996) para 4.

57 See, ICCPR, Article 4(1). It seems that states would in any case hardly derogate from applying Article 1 of the ICCPR, given that such derogation would likely be inconsistent with their other obligations under international law, hence inadmissible.

58 Article 7 of the Agreement on the path to normalisation between Kosovo and Serbia mentions 'an appropriate level of self-management for the Serbian community in Kosovo' <https://www.eeas.europa.eu/eeas/belgrade-pristina-dialogue-agreement-path-normalisation-between-kosovo-and-serbia_en>.

59 'It is plausible to see the external side of self-determination as parasitic on the internal one. We have a duty not to interfere with a foreign political order because that order reflects the will of the people subject to it'. Stilz, 'The Value of Self-determination' (n 7) 99.

60 'The 'neutral state' is a creature of myth and, therefore, in the absence of special arrangements, a minority group may find itself effectively disenfranchised'. J. Wright, 'Minority Groups, Autonomy, and Self Determination' 19(4) *Oxford Journal of Legal Studies* (1999) 620.

minorities' self-government, with some even calling it the 'queen of minority protection instruments'.[61] In a similar vein, Wright contended:

> In order for the whole people to be represented in government without 'distinction as to race, creed or colour', minority groups should have some measure of autonomy over the matters of particular relevance to their ethnic, cultural, religious or linguistic identity, thus achieving de facto parity with the dominant group who, by the fact of numerical domination, control those matters (relating to ethnic, cultural, religious, and linguistic identity) affecting them.[62]

The rationale behind this control is rooted in the principle of equality among peoples. Without meaningful political participation or representation, minority groups may face oppression from the majority, particularly concerning the cultural aspects of their lives. Stilz, another proponent of autonomous arrangements within multicultural states, argues that 'the value of self-determination requires states to move away from a unitary legal order, toward a more pluralistic constitution that can accommodate internal autonomy for their minorities'.[63] For her, the persistent alienation of these subgroups deserves an institutional response. In some cases, it may be morally required to redraw political boundaries to afford internal minorities greater self-determination.[64] Fox, while discussing ISD, singled out three categories: free elections, the protection of minority rights and the construction of autonomy regimes within states by international organizations, as in the case of Bosnia.[65] Rosas identified 'an autonomous status within the confines of a bigger State' as one of ISD's distinctive features.[66] It is also not uncommon to find references to autonomy within the ISD framework in state practice. Germany, for instance, maintained that 'internal self-determination means enjoying a degree of autonomy inside a larger entity, not leaving it altogether but, as a rule, deciding issues of local relevance on a local level'.[67]

---

61 P. Hilpold, *Autonomy and Self-determination: Between Legal Assertions and Utopian Aspirations* (Elgar 2018) 45, citing M. Brems, *Die Politische Integration Ethnischer Minderheiten* (Peter Lang 1997) 142.

62 Wright (n 60) 621.

63 A. Stilz, *Territorial Sovereignty: A Philosophical Exploration* (OUP 2019) 134.

64 Stilz, 'The Value of Self-determination' (n 7) 118–119.

65 Fox (n 15) 752–756.

66 Rosas (n 15) 232.

67 More in R. Kolb and T. Gazzini, 'The Autonomous Community of Catalonia and International Law' 31 *Swiss Review of International and European Law* (2021) 14.

Autonomy should not be misunderstood, as it often is, either as the first step toward independence or as an alternative to self-determination. The main purpose of autonomy is to fulfil self-determination within the borders of a state, so it should be read both as the alternative to *and* an expression of self-determination. This interpretation can also be deduced from its etymology: in Greek, *auto* and *nomos* together mean self-rule or self-determination.[68]

There is not a singular definition of autonomy; instead, autonomy systems can manifest in various forms (cultural, educational, personal, religious, territorial/non-territorial and the like.) Each autonomous entity tends to have its own distinct characteristics. Typically, territorial control is a defining feature of most autonomous entities. Cultural autonomy distinguishes itself from territorial autonomy in several ways: governance is entrusted to a culturally defined group rather than one defined by territory; self-management is confined to cultural matters exclusively; and cultural authority extends only to individuals identified as part of that cultural group.[69]

At first glance, one might consider an autonomous entity to be situated functionally between a mere system for protecting minorities and the implementation of self-determination leading to territorial alterations. In reality, while minority rights primarily aim to safeguard individual liberties, they can also protect collective rights and exhibit a collective dimension, as demonstrated in matters like place naming and political representation.[70]

The concept of (regional) autonomy lacks recognition in general international law, and states are not obligated to grant such autonomy to distinct groups within their territories, with a notable exception of indigenous peoples.[71]

68 Hilpold (n 61) 44–45.

69 A. Eide, 'Cultural Autonomy: Concept, Content, History and Role in the World Order' in M. Suksi (ed.) *Autonomy: Applications and Implications* (Brill 1998) 525. See also M. Suksi, 'Non-Territorial Autonomy: The Meaning of '(Non-)Territoriality" in T. H. Malloy and F. Palermo (ed.) *Minority Accommodation through Territorial and Non-Territorial Autonomy* (OUP 2015) (noting that NTA comprises personal autonomy, functional autonomy, and national cultural autonomy and that territorial autonomy implements Articles 1 and 25 of the ICCPR as well as Article 3 of the Optional Protocol of the ECHR, thus realising ISD) 85–93, 112–113.

70 Hilpold (n 61) 45.

71 P. Thornberry, 'Images of Autonomy and Individual and Collective Rights in International Instruments on the Rights of Minorities' in M. Suksi (ed.) *Autonomy: Applications and Implications* (Brill 1998) 111–124. See also IIFFMCG, The Report, vol. II (2009) 139–140. Article 4 of the Declaration on the Rights of Indigenous Peoples (UNDRIP) provides 'Indigenous peoples, in exercising their right to self-determination, have the right to autonomy or self-government in matters relating to their internal and local affairs, as well as ways and means for financing their autonomous functions'. UN Doc. A/Res/61/295 (13 Sep. 2007).

Despite the growing interest in decentralization and autonomy during the 1990s, and the diminishing importance of the principles of non-interference and domestic jurisdiction in contemporary international law, the principles articulated in the Friendly Relations Declaration remain relevant to discussions of autonomy. It seems that unless a state has undertaken specific international commitments to endorse autonomous arrangements, the decision to grant autonomy ultimately rests within the discretion of that state.[72]

States may also deliberately misinterpret or revoke previously granted autonomy provisions, a move that would almost inevitably trigger grassroots resistance and potentially ignite secessionist claims. Thus, it is essential to grant a meaningful form of autonomy – whether territorial or non-territorial – to minorities to fulfil the requirements of ISD and to minimize secessionist pressures and animosities, particularly in post-conflict societies.[73] According to the updated Local Autonomy Index (LAI), the Nordic countries and Switzerland rank highest as positive examples, whereas Kosovo, Turkey, and Hungary stand out as cases warranting concern or scrutiny.[74] In Saudi Arabia, the Hijaz region could significantly benefit from enhanced autonomy, particularly in managing critical aspects such as pilgrimage administration and the safeguarding of Holy Sites. By granting Hijaz greater authority in these areas, Riyadh could promote more inclusive and financially efficient governance, ensuring the effective fulfilment of pilgrims' needs and the preservation of these sacred locations.[75]

2.4 *ISD as a Conglomerate of Human Rights*

To secure the principles of democratic governance, non-discrimination, and autonomous arrangements, ISD must be systematically correlated with broader human rights. It has been noted that human rights are interdependent and the RSD both relies upon and reinforces other human rights, all the more so given its dual nature as a collective and individual right.[76] During the meeting of the UN Third Committee (Social, Humanitarian and Cultural) on the elimination of racism, racial discrimination, xenophobia and related intolerance, the RSD

72 H. Heintze, 'On the Legal Understanding of Autonomy' in M. Suksi (ed.) *Autonomy: Applications and Implications* (Brill 1998) 7–32; L. Hannikainen, 'Self-determination and Autonomy in International Law' in *Ibid.* 86–87.

73 S. Wolff and M. Weller, 'Self-determination and Autonomy: A Conceptual Introduction' in *Autonomy, Self-governance and Conflict Resolution* (Routledge 2008) 2.

74 A. Ladner, N. Keuffer, and A. Bastianen, 'Local autonomy around the world: the updated and extended Local Autonomy Index (LAI 2.0)' *Regional and Federal Studies* (2023) 15–16.

75 M. Dahlan, *The Hijaz: The First Islamic State* (OUP 2018) 339–374.

76 See 2.1. and 2.7.

was seen as an integral element of basic human rights and fundamental freedoms.[77] The representative of Maldives stated that 'it is only through the realization of this very basic right of people to determine, with no compulsion or coercion, their own future, political status and independence that we can begin to address others such as dignity, justice, progress and equity'. The representatives of Bolivia and Jordan echoed that sentiment, underscoring that respect for the principle of self-determination is 'a precondition for the enjoyment of other human rights, and no other right could be fully enjoyed without it'.[78]

The number of rights and freedoms associated with internal self-determination is large and can be divided into thematic components: political, economic, social and cultural.[79] Political rights were discussed in the preceding subsections and, broadly speaking, denote the right of peoples to choose and develop their internal political system through the exercise of civil and political rights. Notable rights include participation in government, protection from discrimination based on characteristics such as race, religion, or political opinion, and freedoms of thought, conscience, religion, expression, peaceful assembly, and association – all crucial to the exercise of self-determination.[80] Political ISD also entails legal frameworks that support these rights. For instance, the Human Rights Committee has acknowledged Ethiopia's legal recognition of ethnic and linguistic communities' self-determination at the regional state level under its 'ethnic federalism' system. However, the Committee expressed concern about the exclusion of ethnic and linguistic minorities residing outside designated regions and recommended broader recognition and political representation at both regional and federal levels.[81] Legal guarantees, therefore, are vital to facilitating ISD within a state.[82]

Political ISD likewise involves cooperation between central governments and minorities institutions. The Human Rights Committee, in its observations on Guatemala, commended initiatives such as the 2009–2012 Programme for

77 UN Third Committee, 'Self-determination Integral to Basic Human Rights, Fundamental Freedoms' (2013) UN Doc. GA/SHC/4085.

78 *Ibid.*

79 The catalogue of illustrated rights is by no means exhaustive. The ICJ recently correlated the RSD with climate change and all rights that stem therefrom. ICJ, *Obligations of States in respect of Climate Change*, Advisory Opinion, ICJ Rep. 2025, para 357.

80 Study Prepared by A. Cristescu (n 13) paras 319–324. See also Article 2 of the UDHR.

81 Human Rights Committee, 'Consideration of reports submitted by States parties under article 40 of the Covenant. Concluding observations of the Human Rights Committee: Ethiopia' (2011) UN Doc. CCPR/C/ETH/CO/1, para 26. See also UN Doc. CCPR/E/ETH/1, paras 4–14.

82 See Human Rights Committee, General Comment No. 12: Article 1 (Right to Self-determination), The Right to Self-determination of Peoples (13 Mar. 1984) para 3.

the Development of Indigenous Peoples and constitutional reforms aimed at upholding indigenous rights. However, the Committee expressed regret over inadequate consultation with indigenous peoples regarding decisions affecting their rights and urged Guatemala to comply with international obligations for prior, informed consultations. Furthermore, the Committee emphasized the importance of recognizing and duly considering all decisions made by indigenous peoples during such consultations.[83] Last but not least, political ISD may also connote the right to choose one's nationality, as established in Opinion No. 2 of the Badinter Commission.[84]

Within the purview of economic ISD, peoples have the right to determine their economic systems and pursue their development goals. This implies control over natural resources and economic assets within their territory, including the right to manage and benefit from resources such as land, minerals, water, and forests. For instance, the 1993 Nunavut Agreement granted Canada's indigenous Inuit population a large territory with significant control over their land and resources,[85] whereas Bolivia's 2009 Constitution recognizes the rights of indigenous peoples to self-determination, including economic sovereignty over their ancestral lands and resources.[86]

The European Court of Justice reaffirmed this principle in its 2018 decision on Western Sahara, ruling that the waters adjacent to Western Sahara, according to public international law, fall outside Morocco's sovereign jurisdiction. Therefore, these waters cannot be included within the term 'Moroccan fishing zone' mentioned in the Fisheries Partnership Agreement between the EU and Morocco, as it would be a breach of economic self-determination of the people of Western Sahara.[87]

Economic ISD also entails the ability to determine economic policies, trade relations, and development strategies free from external interference. This concept includes economic sovereignty – the capacity to make independent

83 Human Rights Committee, 'Consideration of reports submitted by States parties under article 40 of the Covenant. Concluding observations: Guatemala' (2012) Doc. CCPR/C/GTM/CO3, para 27.

84 Badinter Commission, Opinion No. 2 (11 Jan. 1992), reprinted in 3 *EJIL* (1992) 184.

85 Nunavut Land Claims Agreement Act. S.C. 1993, c. 29. The NLCA encompasses 42 chapters that cover a wide array of political and environmental rights and concerns. These include wildlife management and harvesting rights, land, water, and environmental management regimes, heritage resources, parks and conservation areas, and public sector employment and contracting.

86 The Constitution of Bolivia (2009) Articles 30, 403.

87 ECJ, *Western Sahara Campaign UK v Commissioners for Her Majesty's Revenue and Customs and Secretary of State for Environment, Food and Rural Affairs* (2018), C-266/16. See also ECJ, *Council v Front Polisario* (2016) C-104/16.

decisions regarding economic affairs without coercion or domination. Finally, peoples exercising economic ISD have the right to participate in decision-making processes affecting their lives, such as shaping economic policies, budget allocation, and resource management. In its concluding observations on Argentina, the Committee on Economic, Social and Cultural Rights expressed apprehension regarding the incomplete implementation of Act No. 26160 (extended by Act No. 26554) concerning the possession and ownership of lands traditionally inhabited by indigenous peoples. It highlighted procedural delays in issuing ownership titles to these lands and expressed alarm over persistent threats, displacements, and violent evictions of indigenous peoples from their traditional lands in numerous provinces. Additionally, the Committee noted deficiencies in consultation processes with affected indigenous communities, which in some cases led to the exploitation of natural resources in territories traditionally occupied by these peoples.[88]

Economic and social rights are directly linked with the broader goal of social development. These rights include the right to work, just and favourable working conditions, social security, the freedom of trade union activities, protection and assistance for families, mothers, and children, the right to the highest attainable standard of physical and mental health, adequate living standards, the continuous improvement of living conditions, and the right to education.[89] Historical experience shows that positive social development enhances the fulfilment of these rights by creating institutional, economic, and infrastructural conditions conducive to their realization. Conversely, progressive implementation and protection of economic and social rights actively contribute to social development, generating more equitable and stable societies.

Within the scope of cultural ISD, both the procedural and substantive rights warrant a mention. Article 22 of the UDHR guarantees everyone the right to realize, through national efforts and international cooperation, 'the economic, social and cultural rights indispensable for his dignity and the free development of his personality', whereas Article 27 stipulates that 'everyone has the right freely to participate in the cultural life of the community'.[90] The ICERD, in Article 7, obliges states to adopt 'immediate and effective measures, particularly in the fields of teaching, education, culture (…) to combating prejudices

88 CESCR, 'Consideration of reports submitted by States parties under articles 16 and 17 of the Covenant. Concluding Observations: Argentina' (2011) Doc. E/C.12/ARG/CO/3, paras 8–9.

89 Study Prepared by A. Cristescu (n 13) para 581.

90 Similarly, Article 15 of ICESCR, which, in addition, provides for the right to 'enjoy the benefits of scientific progress and its applications'.

which lead to racial discrimination and to promoting understanding, tolerance and friendship'.[91] In more specific terms, Article 4 of the UNESCO Convention against Discrimination in Education obliges states to ensure equality of opportunity and treatment in education, in particular by making primary education free and compulsory, and ensuring that higher education is equally accessible to all based on individual capacity.[92]

With regard to indigenous peoples, the 2007 Declaration on the Rights of Indigenous Peoples sets out their right to maintain and strengthen their cultural institutions and to participate fully in the cultural life of the state.[93] It further affirms that indigenous peoples and individuals 'have the right not to be subjected to forced assimilation or destruction of their culture'.[94] The Declaration also mentions the revitalization of cultural traditions and customs granting rights to 'maintain, protect and develop the past, present and future manifestations of their cultures, such as archaeological and historical sites, artefacts, designs, ceremonies, technologies and visual and performing arts and literature'.[95]

Cultural expression, therefore, encompasses the freedom to participate in cultural events, celebrate festivals, and access cultural materials and institutions.[96] Religion and language, as forms of cultural expression, play a crucial role in preserving national identity. In its 2019 opinion on Serbia, issued within the Framework Convention for the Protection of National Minorities, the Advisory Committee noted that some representatives of Vlach communities reported 'attempts from the Romanian Orthodox Church to publicly deny the right of Vlachs to self-determine their national minority and religious affiliation'. It made a similar observation with regard to persons belonging to the Egyptian minority, seeing it as a violation of ISD.[97] The linguistic rights

91 ICERD, Article 7.

92 Convention against Discrimination in Education (1960) 429 UNTS 93.

93 UNDRIP, Article 5.

94 *Ibid.* Article 8.

95 *Ibid*, Article 11.

96 Consult the European Charter for Regional or Minority Languages (1992) ETS 148, Article 12 – Cultural activities and facilities. The right of indigenous peoples to establish and use their own media based on the content and scope of the right to freedom of expression and in view of the right to self-determination was recognized by the IACtHR in its October 6, 2021, judgement in the *Case of the Maya Kaqchikel Indigenous Peoples of Sumpango et al. v. Guatemala*, para 95. See Separate Opinion of Judge Eduardo Ferrer Mac-Gregor Poisot, paras 21–24.

97 Council of Europe Advisory Committee on the Framework Convention for the Protection of National Minorities, 'Fourth Opinion on Serbia' (2019) Doc. ACFC/OP/IV(2019)001, para 69.

of minorities incorporate the right to use their language in education, public administration, and media, as well as the right to receive education in their mother tongue. According to the Framework Convention, in areas inhabited traditionally by national minorities, communication between the persons and administration should, as far as possible, be conducted in their national language.[98] Similarly, such communities should have the ability to display names, such as town names, in their minority language.[99]

3 Internal Self-determination as a Secession Prevention Method

It is generally agreed that ISD is realised within the confines of existing states. Unlike ESD, it does not purport to seek independence from an 'alien' ruler, *ergo* does not exhibit offensive international characteristics, but operates as a defensive right against a state's own government. Moreover, both ESD and ISD have been interpreted as rights of the whole population, where minorities generally defer to the will of the majority.[100] Stated differently, minorities do not possess a distinct right that could undermine or otherwise jeopardize the position or preferences of the majority.

While ISD affords certain privileges to minorities, such as self-governance and autonomy (e.g. as outlined in Article 4 of the UN Declaration on the Rights of Indigenous Peoples), the denial of their right to secession (per Article 46 of the same Declaration and the Badinter Commission's Opinion No. 2) underscores another key purpose of ISD: to preclude secession.[101] Secession, as elaborated upon in the previous chapter, is generally discouraged both internationally and nationally. States and international organizations prefer to handle the issue of secession discreetly, wary of the potential Pandora's Box effect it may unleash. They tend to engage with secessionist aspirations or conflicts

98 Framework Convention for the Protection of National Minorities (1995) ETS 157, Article 10(2). See also European Charter for Regional or Minority Languages (n 96) Article 7.

99 Framework Convention (n 98) Article 11(3).

100 Mateu, 'Self-determination and Access to Independence' (n 4) 56–57.

101 Article 46 of UNDRIP sets forth that 'Nothing in this Declaration may be interpreted as implying for any State, people, group or person any right to engage in any activity or to perform any act contrary to the Charter of the United Nations or construed as authorizing or encouraging any action which would dismember or impair, totally or in part, the territorial integrity or political unity of sovereign and independent States'. In Opinion No.2, the Badinter Commission explicitly rejected the right of the Serbian population in Croatia and Bosnia to (external) self-determination, but affirmed their other human rights connected to ISD, in particular, the right to recognition of their identity under international law.

only when they serve their strategic interests or when these issues have already gained significant international spotlight. As a result, only a limited number of secessionist movements and conflicts have been formally addressed on the international stage.

As the next chapter will demonstrate, this discouragement is even more pronounced when states aacord ISD. A growing number of states and international organizations interpret the RSD primarily through the lens of ISD, as reflected in their reports and official statements. This prioritization of ISD, as Oetter argues, 'makes an argument for a right to secession even more difficult'.[102]

3.1 *Orthodox and Qualified Counter-Secession Visions of ISD*

ISD's counter-secession incarnation can be viewed from a two-fold perspective: as a legal doctrine or as a political instrument. The first, more extreme interpretation assumes that, from a legal standpoint, ISD prohibits secession, either outright or conditionally. The outright approach asserts that internal self-determination stands in opposition to external self-determination, constituting a post-colonial norm that governs all populations within a state's territory, including minorities. Under this framework, ESD is confined to reclaiming sovereignty and territorial integrity for colonies or occupied territories or serves as a prerogative of all peoples to alter their international status. Meanwhile, ISD – often now equated with the RSD – safeguards the collective entitlement of the entire population against both external compromises and internal threats posed by unrepresentative or oppressive governments. Unilateral secession, whether internally or externally induced, constitutes a violation of this collective right, as it undermines the territorial integrity and unity of the state, which represents all its peoples. As such, ISD complements the principle of territorial integrity, bridging the gap in its perceived inter-state application.[103] There exists no level of implementation of ISD in the outright model, either quantitative or qualitative, which could relativize the ISD's validity in secession prevention. That is why, it could be termed as the orthodox ISD counter-secession conception. In another view of ISD as a legal method or a rule, there is a precondition that if a central government pleases secession-oriented population with political, economic, social, and

102 S. Oeter, 'The Kosovo Case – An Unfortunate Precedent' 75 *ZaöRV* (2015) 62.

103 'In fact, it is difficult to think of a situation where a secessionist self-determination claim would not be disputed by the argument that it violates the self-determination rights – the territorial integrity – [of] the larger community'. Koskenniemi (n 3) 260. For criticism of the *ad intra* applicability of the principle of territorial integrity see 3.3.1.

cultural rights, then secession should not be permitted. Stated differently, the fulfilment of ISD renders secession illegal under international law. According to this view, internal self-determination *prima facie* excludes nationalistic and democratic secession, which are part of the primary secession theories, but its stance towards remedial secession based on violations of internal self-determination remains ambivalent. In this scenario, ISD is a qualified right of states, and could be termed as such.

Since the rule approach assumes the operation within a legal framework, it requires recourse to ISD's status under international law and scrutiny of its legal bindingness. Regrettably, there is still substantial shortage of state and international organizations practice in articulating the existence of a separate right to internal self-determination, and all the more so within the context of its counter-secession value.[104] Among the very scarce practice, the German oral statement in the *Kosovo* case could be brought up, as it alluded to the 'denial of the democratic *right* to internal self-determination',[105] which could befit the qualified counter-secession vision of ISD.[106] A similar conclusion could be inferred from the Supreme Court of Canada's ruling in the *Quebec* case, where the Court suggested that 'when a people is blocked from the meaningful exercise of its *right* to self-determination internally, it is entitled, as a last resort, to exercise it by secession'.[107] However, it is an inverted proposition, indicating when secession could be allowed, not prohibited. The inverted reading of the safeguard clause outlined in the Friendly Relations Declaration, which lays down *principles*, has, as already discussed, been contested.[108]

104 In the *Kosovo AO*, Cyprus stated: 'The Article (1 of the Human Rights Covenants) as a whole, however, impliedly recognises the right of access to political systems, and economic and cultural rights. This is termed internal self-determination'. Written Statement of Cyprus (2009) para 132.

105 Oral Statement of Germany (2 Dec. 2009) para 39. See also Oral statement of Belarus: 'The internal right of self-determination usually means (…)' (3 Dec. 2009) CR 2009/27, 29. Similarly Albania: the 'right to internal self-determination [of the Kosovar Albanians] was continuously denied by the Serb authorities'. Written Statement of the Republic of Albania (14 Apr. 2009) 40, para 75; the Netherlands: '(…) the absence of a government which represents the whole people belonging to a territory as a violation of the right to internal self-determination'. Written Statement of the Kingdom of The Netherlands (17 Apr. 2009) 9, para 3.10.

106 Germany indeed in its written statement claimed that 'while self-determination should, for the sake of the stability of the international system, normally be enjoyed and exercised inside the existing framework of States, it may exceptionally legitimize secession if this can be shown to be the only remedy against a prolonged and rigorous refusal of internal self-determination'. Statement of the Federal Republic of Germany (2009) 34.

107 *Reference re Secession of Quebec*, para 134.

108 See 3.3.3.2.

International legal scholarship has characterized ISD varyingly, both as a principle and as a right, but mainly within a defensive frame, framing it as a right of peoples against their own government. Hannum talks about a 'new principle of international law (…) which recognises the right of minority and indigenous communities to exercise meaningful internal self-determination and control over their own affairs'.[109] Wright in 1999 expressed hesitance writing that 'even if the argument that a minority is a people is accepted, and the view taken that internal self-determination is a right in international law (…)',[110] while Hilpold in 2018 was considerably bolder in his expression that 'ever broader recognition finds, however, the right to 'internal self-determination'.[111] Given these diverging perspectives, it seems prudent to share Shikova's observation that ISD is a right *in statu nascendi*, as this best mirrors its present-day standing in the international legal order.[112]

It should be borne in mind that the RSD has travelled a thorny way to achieve legal recognition, evolving from a political principle into a legal norm, and ultimately a right, despite persistent ambiguities.[113] ISD as a stand-alone concept, clearly lacks corresponding institutional and treaty-based recognition.[114] However, a question may be asked if it really needs one. After all, it forms part of the already acknowledged right (the RSD), which is nowadays clearly associated with it. Some modern authors, like Mateu, entirely assimilate ISD with the RSD.[115] The ICJ in the 2019 *Chagos Advisory Opinion* confirmed that the RSD has more than one (colonial) variant, implicitly alluding to ISD.[116] Moreover, ISD, due to its less invasive connotations, does not face the addressees conundrum, while the contours of its content can crystallize in the course of state

109 H. Hannum, *Autonomy, Sovereignty, and Self-determination; The Accommodation of Conflicting Rights* (University of Pennsylvania Press 1990) 473.
110 Wright (n 60) 628.
111 Hilpold (n 61) 42.
112 Shikova, *Self-determination and Secession* (n 8) 222.
113 Crawford supported a compromisory terminology of the 'legal principle'. J. Crawford, 'Book Review: Self-determination of Peoples. A Legal Reappraisal' 90 *AJIL* (1996) 331. Thierry still denies a status of a right to the RSD against the backdrop of its lack of clarity and non-uniform application. S. Tierney, 'The Search for a New Normativity: Thomas Franck, Post-modern Neo-tribalism and the Law of Self-determination' 13(4) *EJIL* (2002) 941.
114 See 2.2. (history of the right to self-determination).
115 Generally, Mateu, 'Self-determination and Access to Independence' (n 4).
116 ICJ, *Legal Consequences of the Separation of the Chagos Archipelago from Mauritius in 1965*, Advisory Opinion, ICJ Rep. 2019, para 144.

practice.[117] Nevertheless, the key question remains: does ISD operate merely as an obligation incumbent upon states or also as a right enabling states to maintain territorial integrity?[118] In this context, it is necessary to assess which legal approach – whether orthodox or qualified – finds more robust foundation in *opinio juris* and state practice.[119] Such an assessment is crucial for determining whether ISD can effectively challenge international law's traditional paradigm of neutrality toward secession and the enduring primacy of sovereignty and territorial integrity as the guiding principles opposing secession.[120]

One could indeed question the added value of the orthodox counter-secession vision of internal self-determination and the extent to which it truly differs from the principle of territorial integrity and the secession negation theories. From this perspective, ISD risks being reduced to a rhetorical device – a hollow slogan lacking substantive legal content. However, this critique should not overshadow the fact that ISD in its orthodox form, however theoretically vacuous, is often invoked in contemporary discussions on the application of the right to self-determination. A more nuanced and legally compelling explanation of ISD as a norm preventing secession emerges when examining its conditional nature. Unlike the orthodox approach which employs rigid, utilitarian interpretations of the RSD or relies on a superficial reading of state/institutional practices to categorically reject secession – the qualified conception of ISD demonstrates greater normative sophistication. This more nuanced framework, explicitly and elaborately referenced in state practice, domestic jurisprudence, and international institutional decisions, operates as a context-dependent mechanism that may either legitimate or preclude secession based

117 N. Shikova, 'Practicing Internal Self-determination Vis-a-Vis Vital Quests for Secession' 17(2) *German Law Journal* (2019) 251–261 (discussing also the divergencies of motives leading to secession).

118 Cf. J. Crawford, 'The Rights of Peoples: Peoples or Governments?' 9 *Bulletin of the Australian Society of Legal Philosophy* (1985) 136.

119 *Opinio juris* is, 'a belief that this practice is rendered obligatory by the existence of a rule requiring it. (…) The States concerned must feel that they are conforming to what amounts to a legal obligation'. ICJ, *North Sea Continental Shelf*, Judgment, ICJ Rep. 1969, 44. Greenwood criticized this definition for not reflecting the fact that *opinio juris* may pertain also to permissive rules and was not content with the word 'belief'. He proposed the following phrasing instead, seeing *opinio juris* 'as the assertion of a legal right or the acknowledgment of a legal obligation'. C. Greenwood, 'Sources of International Law: An Introduction' <https://legal.un.org/avl/pdf/ls/greenwood_outline.pdf>.

120 Note that the majority of states in the proceedings before the ICJ in the Kosovo case either referred to the principle of territorial integrity or to remedial secession, which, *nota bene*, predicates on ISD's breach as an argument for secession. More on the status of ISD in contemporary international law in 5.4.

on specific factual circumstances. The conditionality leitmotif finds its origins in the *Åland* case and the safeguard clause of the Friendly Relations Declaration, holding that secession should be prohibited as long as a government is deemed representative of the entire population. States argue both in favour of maintaining territorial integrity, citing the Friendly Relations Declaration, and against it, pointing to the same document. Proponents of remedial secession base their thesis on breaches of ISD, yet this is at best a *de lege ferenda* interpretation, since it is unclear whether this could be read *a contrario* and whether independence should be the ultimate outcome. On the other hand, the fundamental interpretation of the safeguard clause remains established law (*de lege lata*). States which acknowledge the possibility of remedial secession based on the Friendly Relations Declaration *a fortiori* affirm the validity of the primary interpretation of the safeguard clause.

Although the *Åland* case was a bilateral dispute between Sweden and Finland, adjudicated by bodies appointed by the League of Nations, its impact is universal and long-lasting. As O'Brien, the UN Under-Secretary-General for Legal Affairs, observed, the *Åland* case contributed to the 'formation of the general rule of international law about the peaceful settlement of international disputes' and the conclusions of the Committee of Jurists and the Commission of Rapporteurs regarding the principle of self-determination and the protection of minorities remain relevant today.[121] As O'Brien further submitted, 'if the rights of minorities are being respected and its cultural identity is fully protected in situations such as the one in question, a demand for secession does not seem to be justified'.[122] Similarly, while adopted as a General Assembly resolution, the Friendly Relations Declaration cannot be dismissed as merely non-binding. Its substantial normative weight is evidenced by three compelling factors: (1) extensive incorporation into state practice; (2) repeated invocation by international institutions; and (3) authoritative judicial recognition through multiple ICJ advisory opinions and judgments – most notably in the *Western Sahara* (1975), *Legal Consequences of the Wall* (2004), and *Chagos Archipelago* (2019) cases.[123] Even though, as the UK noted in its submission in the *Kosovo*

121 P. O'Brien, 'The Åland Islands Solution: A Precedent for Successful International Disputes Settlement' (17 Jan. 2012) <https://legal.un.org/ola/media/info_from_lc/POB%20Alands%20Islands%20Exhibition%20opening.pdf>.

122 *Ibid.* 2–3.

123 Á. Trujillo del Arco, 'El 50° aniversario de la Declaración sobre las Relaciones de amistad y su papel en la Jurisprudencia de la Corte Internacional de Justicia' 37 *Anuario Español De Derecho Internacional* (2021) 251–277.

case,[124] the qualified ISD framework arguably constitutes the closest legal approximation to secession prohibition, effectively superseding territorial integrity as a countervailing principle in contemporary practice.

The second, more moderate approach conceptualizes ISD not merely as a legal method or normative rule, but also, or concurrently, as a political instrument for preventing secession. This terminological and substantive distinction circumvents the burden of a narrow perception of ISD's counter-secession value solely through the lens of positive law. Framing ISD as a political method renders it more inclusive, flexible and solution-oriented. Accordingly, ISD's validity is not measured exclusively by its existence as a legal rule but as a broader political tool. When seen as a political tool, internal self-determination can be tailored to meet the unique circumstances and evolving needs of different groups and regions. Political solutions, achieved through negotiation, compromise, and dialogue, provide a dynamic approach to conflict resolution. In contrast, legal frameworks tend to be rigid, requiring precise procedures, institutions, and standards – including the threshold for ISD to maintain territorial integrity and a 'self-determination court'.[125] Legalistic approaches may also result in prolonged, adversarial processes, which could exacerbate tensions. In its political framing, ISD allows for the resolution of grievances through political reforms, autonomy arrangements, or decentralization – solutions not explicitly required by international law – thus reducing the motivation for secession. By contrast, legal interpretations often focus narrowly on rights and entitlements without necessarily promoting inclusive governance or addressing the underlying political and social issues driving secessionist movements.

Only the qualified counter-secession method of ISD, whether legal or political, can be considered truly pragmatic. Within the orthodox ambit, ISD appears as a static argumentative tool utilized by the ruling cadre. In other words, it serves as a method of secession prevention, based merely on references to domestic law and counter-secession inclinations in the international arena. In contrast, the qualified vision of ISD is underpinned by practical, methodical actions, where it takes the form of a systematic and structured approach aimed at maintaining territorial integrity.[126] This approach necessitates proactive efforts from the parent state and predicates upon a well-informed strategy

124 'It is the United Kingdom's position that international law contains neither a right of unilateral secession nor the denial *per se* of such a right' (emphasis is original). Written Statement of the United Kingdom (17 Apr. 2009) para 1.14.

125 See 4.7.

126 Authors who view ISD as a method of preventing secession often employ alternative, and at times quaint, terminology. Shikova, for instance, refers to ISD as 'a magic cure' for secession. Shikova, 'Practicing Internal Self-determination' (n 117) 263. More in 4.3.

that incorporates the implementation of policies and frameworks promoting autonomy and self-governance among groups within the state. In line with this reasoning, ISD exists as a set of rights, privileges and freedoms that should be afforded to groups living within a state's territory. These entitlements span four critical dimensions: (1) political representation, (2) economic participation, (3) social inclusion, and (4) cultural preservation. However, if ISD is not viewed as a legal method imposing direct obligations on the state but rather as a political strategy for addressing groups with secessionist demands, questions of consequences inevitably arise. Without a legal obligation, secession would not be entirely excluded as a remedy under the political model if the state fails to implement ISD effectively or respond adequately to secessionist demands. Nonetheless, it is assumed that nearly all secessionist demands arise from issues related to the improper or insufficient implementation of ISD. Consequently, by correctly and comprehensively implementing ISD, the aspirations of these groups would be satisfied, potentially eliminating their motive to assert secessionist demands.

Therefore, ISD ought to be seen as an empirical method for preventing secession, substantiated in law and politics, whereas the law can in and of itself be likewise used as an argument in counter secession discourse.

Concluding, it is important to note that ISD is not the only available method used to prevent secession. Secession can also be averted through international mediation or support, which ensures security and stability, or by addressing other motives for secession that are not directly related to the implementation of ISD.[127] Relatedly, the protection of fundamental human rights could also prevent secession, but contrary to the argument for remedial secession, such a protection could hardly be disentangled from the implementation of ISD.[128] Also, it is not to say that ISD is only a counter-secession method. It can similarly play a role in peacebuilding processes, democratization, political reforms and environmental governance.[129]

127 See 3.1. and 4.6.

128 When ISD is respected, it is highly unlikely that fundamental human rights are breached. On the other hand, when a state violates ISD, it may or may not resort to egregious crimes, such as killings. This is an additional argument that supports the case for remedial secession.

129 See, *inter alia,* E. Demir, 'The Right to Internal Self-determination in Peacebuilding Processes: A Reinterpretation of the Concept of Local Ownership from a Legal Perspective (2017) 8 *The Age of Human Rights Journal* 18–48; C. Carletti, 'Sustaining Peace and Internal Self-determination in the UN Perspective' in J. R. Avgustin (ed.) *The United Nations: Friend or Foe of Self-determination?* (E-International Relations Publishing 2020) 47–69.

4 Secession Prevention Tools of ISD

ISD embraces a range of instruments that can be utilized to prevent secession. Paradoxically, these mechanisms are concurrently the defining features of ISD. Naturally, only positive mechanisms – those conforming with principles of inclusivity and good governance – are considered integral to ISD. Actions such as the forceful alteration of ethnic composition, including population transfers, while falling within the broader spectrum of anti-secession measures, are explicitly excluded, as they contradict the *raison d'être* of ISD. The effectiveness of such *positive* secession-prevention tools depends critically on their substantive implementation. Their mere theoretical availability is insufficient to advance credible counter-secession objectives. Fundamentally, ISD mechanisms aim to foster the creation of a well-governed state, with the underlying assumption that a well-functioning state is inherently more resilient against dismemberment.

Among the various aspects of ISD that constitute anti-secession tools available to states, three widely acknowledged and interrelated mechanisms stand out: democratic governance, federalism, and autonomism. Federalism and autonomism share a critical and intuitive feature that is particularly significant for minorities: they foster a psychological sense of separateness.[130]

4.1 *Democratic Governance*

Democratic governance refers to the processes and structures that enable effective citizen participation in decision-making, ensure the accountability of leaders, uphold the rule of law, and safeguard human rights. It emphasizes the importance of political inclusiveness and responsiveness to the needs and aspirations of all societal groups. As one of the UNESCO's statements pronounces, internal self-determination is 'a reminder of the ultimate accountability of every State and every political system to the peoples who live under its legal jurisdiction'.[131] This section expands on the brief presentation of democratic governance introduced in Chapter II, exploring its multifaceted connections with ISD,[132] and demonstrates how democratic governance can act as a deterrent to secession, thereby fortifying national unity.[133]

130 M. Shaw, 'Territory in International Law' (1982) 13 *Netherlands Yearbook of International Law* 61.

131 UN Doc. E/CN.4/Sub.2/1992/6 (24 Jul. 1992) para 3(d).

132 See 2.3.2.

133 A. Buchanan, 'Democracy and Secession' in M. Moore (ed.) *National Self-determination and Secession* (OUP 1998) 14–33.

Unaddressed grievances count as one of the primary drivers of secessionist movements, often arising from perceived or real injustices such as economic marginalization, political exclusion, cultural suppression, or human rights violations. Democratic governance can address these issues by providing mechanisms for redress and inclusion. By ensuring fair and free elections, representation in legislative bodies, and participation in decision-making processes, democratic governance offers all groups an opportunity to engage politically. Proportional representation systems guarantee that political representation reflects the population's diversity, enabling minority groups to gain representation in parliament proportionate to their size, ensuring their voices are heard in the national policy-making process. In deeply divided societies, power-sharing arrangements – such as coalition governments, consociationalism, and veto powers for minority groups – can prevent secessionist movements by requiring the consent of representatives from all significant groups for major political decisions. These arrangements promote political stability and inclusivity, thereby reducing disenfranchisement. Affirmative action policies in political representation, as well as in public employment, and education can rectify historical injustices, ensuring fair representation of marginalized groups and fostering trust and loyalty among all societal segments.

Democratic institutions promote accountability and transparency, which are crucial for addressing corruption and abuse of power – common grievances for many secessionist groups. Mechanisms such as independent judiciary, a free press, and civil society oversight help hold leaders accountable, diminishing perceptions of injustice. Furthermore, democratic governance is closely linked with the protection of human rights. Ensuring that the rights of all citizens are respected, regardless of their ethnic, religious, or cultural background, helps to alleviate grievances that could otherwise fuel secessionist tendencies.[134] Institutions like human rights commissions and ombudsman offices play crucial roles in safeguarding these rights.

Another important facet of preventing secession through democratic governance is promoting cultural recognition and integration. Policies that celebrate cultural diversity, such as multilingual education, cultural festivals, and legal recognition of minority languages, foster an inclusive national identity. By integrating diverse cultural identities into the national narrative, democratic states can prevent cultural alienation and the desire for secession.

Finally, economic inequality and underdevelopment are significant drivers of secessionist movements. Democratic governance promotes economic

134 S. Dion, 'Why is Secession Difficult in Well-Established Democracies? Lessons from Quebec' 26(2) *British Journal of Political Science* (1996) 269–283.

inclusivity through equitable development policies, social safety nets, and inclusive economic planning. Ensuring that all regions and communities benefit from national development reduces economic disparities that could otherwise lead to secessionist movements.

As noted earlier, linking the realization of ISD with a democratic system of governance is quite common in doctrine.[135] However, while the argument for establishing a democratic system of governance to implement the right to internal self-determination holds merit, it does not mean that such a system should automatically conform to the Western conception of democracy. This approach risks imposing a specific political model on the people, which contradicts the essence of self-determination – the free choice of the people. It is important to note that there is no universally accepted model of democracy. Indeed, democracy exists in various forms, encompassing different degrees of political participation and representation. As one author has pointed out, many global regimes, though not resembling Western parliamentary systems, can still be considered true representatives of their people, in alignment with their own social and historical traditions.[136]

Certain authors contend that ISD cannot be reduced to the rights outlined in Article 25 of the ICCPR and the Western model of democracy, due to the distinct nature of these rights and the right to self-determination enshrined in Article 1. Rosas maintains that Article 1, affirming the self-determination of all peoples, reflects customary international law and possesses a peremptory character. However, as he asserts, Article 25 does not exhibit the same customary nature or imperative character. The very necessity of supplementing Article 25 with Articles 19, 21, and 22 of the ICCPR underscores that electoral mechanisms alone cannot define ISD.[137] Raič further develops this critique,[138] proposing that ISD's representativeness requirement should be measured not

135 2.3.2.; S. Whitley, 'Democracy in International Law: A European Perspective' 51 *International and Comparative Law Quarterly* (2002) 232; F. Jankov and V. Ćorić, 'Uti Possidetis i Pravo na Samoopredeljenje' 13 *Pravni život* (2007) 97; V. Dimitrijević, M. Paunović and V. Đerić, *Ljudska Prava: Udžbenik* (Belgrade Center for Human Rights 1997) 397.

136 J. Salmon, 'Internal Aspects of the Right to Self-determination: Towards a Democratic Legitimacy Principle?' in C. Tomuschat (ed.) *Modern Law of Self-determination* (Martinus Nijhoff 1993) 280.

137 Rosas (n 15) 247.

138 D. Raič, *Statehood and the Law of Self-determination* (Martinus Nijhoff Publishers 2002) 272–273.

by institutional mimicry of Western systems,[139] but by substantive popular consent – however culturally or historically expressed.[140]

4.2 *Federalism*

Before delving into the crux of the matter, it is essential to clarify key concepts, specifically the terms 'federalism', 'federation', and 'federal political system'. In contemporary theoretical discourse, federalism is seen as a normative and philosophical concept, while 'federation' refers to its institutional manifestation, particularly in the form of a federal state.[141] Federalism advocates for a division of powers between central and regional governments, while federation is the actual political entity organized under federal principles.

King was among the first scholars to distinguish between federalism and federation, defining federalism as an ideological response to the centralization or decentralization of power, particularly on a territorial basis. This conceptual distinction allows for the identification of centralist, decentralist, and balanced forms of federalism. According to King's definition, a federation is a specific

> institutional arrangement that takes the form of a sovereign state and differs from other such states solely because its central government incorporates regional units into its decision-making processes on a constitutionally established basis.[142]

In the words of another author, a federation is the 'most complete institutional expression of federalism'.[143] The etymological roots of federalism can be traced back to the Latin word 'foedus', which means 'alliances' or 'leagues' formed by states for defensive purposes. Federalists advocate for the establishment of 'federal political systems' that incorporate elements of both 'shared rule' and 'self-rule',[144] often to address self-determination disputes.[145]

---

139 *Ibid.* 275–276.

140 *Ibid.* 278–279.

141 R. Podolnjak, 'Mi, Narod Federacije! Ustavotvorna Vlast u Klasičnim i Suverenim Federacijama' 37(2) *Pravni Vjesnik: Časopis za Pravne i Društvene Znanosti Pravnog Fakulteta Sveučilišta J.J. Strossmayera u Osijeku* (2021) 9.

142 P. King, *Federalism and Federation* (Croom Helm 1982) 77.

143 A. Bačić, 'Politička Gramatika Federalizma i Hrvatsko Iskustvo' in B. Smerdel (ed.) *Primena Federalnog Načela i Pouke Ustavne Reforme 1971* (Centar za Demokraciju i Pravo Miko Tripalo i Pravni fakultet u Zagrebu 2007) 46.

144 D.J. Elazar, *Exploring Federalism* (University of Alabama Press 1987) 5–8, 84–85, 233.

145 B. O'Leary, 'Federalism and Federation' <https://pesd.princeton.edu/node/431>.

The right to self-determination holds a significant place in the theory of federalism. Yet, one of the key issues concerning the RSD in federations is determining who possesses this right and how it can be exercised. In federal theory, any territorial entity with the right to self-determination – that is, the right of its inhabitants to decide their political status – has the potential to either join an existing federal political system or form its own. This choice allows the entity to be part of a larger political structure while maintaining a degree of autonomy. Certain theoretical models extend this logic to include a potential right of secession, though such provisions remain exceptional in practice, typically requiring explicit constitutional entrenchment. While the ultimate bearers of the right to self-determination are undeniably the people, federal systems, like decolonization processes, privilege geographically-defined units, *ergo* states, over ethno-cultural groups as legitimate ESD claimants.[146] Federations are known for their reluctance towards secession, with only a few federal constitutions contemplating its possibility. This resilience stems from the foundational principles of unity and perpetuity that underpin federal systems.[147]

Consequently, a central focus of federalism scholarship lies in understanding how federal institutional designs can accommodate and satisfy the self-determination aspirations of minority groups. Stefanović, for instance, believes that the constitutional structure of a multinational state should be based on the federal principle, because only such an arrangement can ensure the freedom and autonomy of the nations that make up the state.[148] Kymlicka argues that it is entirely natural for multinational countries to adopt federal systems, given that states formed as federations of peoples are inherently suited to political arrangements based on federal principles.[149] Burgess reinforces this perspective, asserting that federalism represents 'the most successful institutional response to national demands for recognition in multinational democracies'.[150] Norman takes this argument further by highlighting that multinational federalism involves recognizing and accommodating the aspirations of national minorities for self-government, mainly by establishing provinces (or equivalent subunits) where one or more minority groups constitute a clear

146 See 2.6.

147 See 3.3.3.3 and 5.2.6.

148 Cited after M. Stanković, *Preobražaji Federalne Države: Deset Rasprava o Promenjenoj Prirodi i Suštini Federalizma* (Pravni Fakultet Univerziteta u Beogradu 2020) 93.

149 W. Kymlicka, *Politics in the Vernacular: Nationalism, Multiculturalism and Citizenship* (OUP 2001) 96.

150 M. Burgess, *Comparative Federalism: Theory and Practice* (Routledge 2006) 129.

majority, enabling them to exercise a range of sovereign powers.[151] Karmis and Norman, in their study on federalism, observe that a major concern for theories of multinational federalism is determining the just or appropriate degree and type of self-determination for national minorities in federal states.[152] They argue that each federal system is largely shaped by its approach to specific issues,[153] with the division of powers being a critical starting point.[154] This revolves around the allocation of legislative and administrative powers between central and subunit governments. Some powers are exclusively vested in the central government (such as defence and immigration), while others are the sole domain of subunit governments (often related to social services). Many powers are shared between the two levels, including areas like transportation and education. Representation in central institutions is another significant issue.[155] How citizens, minority groups, and subunits are represented in key institutions of the federal state, such as the parliament, executive branch, supreme or constitutional court, central bank, civil service, and military, is crucial. Some constitutions guarantee minimum representation thresholds for minorities, while others rely on conventions or affirmative action programs to ensure adequate representation. In some multinational federations, national minorities may be underrepresented in federal institutions.

Another crucial issue in multinational federations involves reconciling subunit legal pluralism with national judicial coherence.[156] This is particularly salient in federations where constituent units have distinct legal systems and traditions (e.g. Louisiana and Quebec with their French-based civil law, or some Indian states using Muslim family law). The effective integration of these diverse legal frameworks into a unified judicial hierarchy, particularly at the appellate level, represents an essential mechanism for ensuring legal predictability while respecting regional diversity. Parallel to this legal challenge, federations must balance economic governance. While subunit governments often have significant powers to regulate commerce and trade, federal governments usually hold authority to maintain a relatively free market across the country. Finally, of particular importance to minorities within federations are the provisions governing constitutional amendments and secession. The role

151 W. Norman, *Negotiating Nationalism: Nation-Building, Federalism, and Secession in the Multinational State* (OUP 2006) 87–88.

152 D. Karmis and W. Norman, 'The Revival of Federalism in Normative Political Theory' in *Theories of Federalism: A Reader* (Palgrave Macmillan 2005) 13.

153 *Ibid.* 14.

154 *Ibid.*

155 *Ibid.*

156 *Ibid.*

of subunits, and by extension peoples, in these processes is a cornerstone of federal theory. Many argue that a system cannot be considered truly federal if it can be legally altered without the consent of subunits. Conversely, if subunits could amend the constitution without central government approval, the system would resemble a confederation rather than a federation.[157]

Federal systems can further address – or diffuse – claims for external self-determination by granting autonomy within the state.[158] They ensure self-rule in crucial domains like culture, language, religion, education, and sometimes development, while allowing communities to influence central governance, thereby promoting unity in diversity. The division of power, the extent of autonomy granted, and the influence subnational units have on joint decisions are key determinants of whether a population remains part of the state or seeks full independence.[159]

Moreover, the institutional design of federations, tailored to the specific historical and social contexts of the countries, plays a critical role in mitigating secessionist pressures.[160] Cases such as India and Malaysia demonstrate how carefully calibrated power distributions can simultaneously address diverse population needs while preserving national unity.[161] These systems grant regional governments sufficient autonomy to manage local affairs while maintaining central authority over matters essential to state cohesion. Anderson and Keil point out that the self-rule and shared rule structures, inherent in a federal system, highlight its ability to accommodate minority groups by granting them autonomous control over their economic, political, and social affairs.[162] Additionally, federalism enhances these groups' investment in the state by enabling them to influence central government decision-making processes. While federalism may not completely eliminate secessionist claims, it provides protection for minority groups and also benefits the majority. A properly functioning federal system should make the pursuit of independent

---

157 W. Norman, 'A Federalist Theory of Secession' in *Negotiating Nationalism: Nation-Building, Federalism, and Secession in the Multinational State* (OUP 2006) 170–215. See also K. A. Scott, 'Macrolevel Consent: A Defense of Federalism' 42(4) *Publius* (2012) 592–612.

158 E. M. Belser and R. Beglinger, 'Secession in Federal Systems: Voice Versus Exit' in J. Kincaid et al. (eds.) *Teaching Federalism* (Edward Elgar Publishing 2023) 179.

159 *Ibid.* 180.

160 More in 6.2.

161 Burgess (n 150) 138.

162 P. Anderson and S. Keil, 'Territorial Autonomy, Ethnic Conflict, and Secession: Between a Rock and a Hard Place?' in I. Lago (ed.) *Handbook on Decentralization, Devolution and the State* (Edward Elgar Publishing 2021) 239.

statehood unnecessary, thereby preserving the stability and territorial integrity of the state.[163]

Bermeo observes that historically, when central leaders granted increased autonomy to dissatisfied regions, they were typically rewarded with peace rather than instability.[164] She cites several examples to support this observation: In the early 1950s, when Tamil nationalists in India mobilized, many in New Delhi feared separatism and advocated for repression. However, when Jawaharlal Nehru granted the Tamils a separate state, the drive for separatism subsided.[165] Conversely, in the Punjab, a Sikh separatist rebellion persisted for years as Indira Gandhi refused concessions and attempted to suppress it through armed force. It was only after a new central government allowed a series of elections, bringing the major Sikh political party to power, that Sikh separatism was effectively quelled.[166] Bermeo concludes that it is often the refusal to federalize, rather than federalism itself, that stimulates secession.[167] For example, Tamils in Sri Lanka began to support a violent separatist movement only in 1976, after federalization was denied. Similarly, the southern Sudanese turned to separatism only after their demands for federalization were rejected.[168]

However, although the intention to fulfil the aspirations of national minorities through federalism is commendable, one must be mindful of the challenges it entails. As Kymlicka puts it, 'federalism is no panacea for the stresses and conflicts of multination states'.[169] He points out that the appropriateness of federal arrangements as a mechanism for safeguarding minority groups is primarily influenced by two elements – the distribution or allocation of powers and the manner in which boundaries are drawn.[170] According to Kymlicka, these two elements indicate that federal arrangements are not as flexible as many believe.[171] One constraint on federalism's capacity to accommodate national minorities is the difficulty in achieving the desired distribution of powers. However, in addition to power-sharing, there's also the need to

163 *Ibid.*

164 N. Bermeo, 'A New Look at Federalism: The Import of Institutions' 13(2) *Journal of Democracy* (2002) 105.

165 *Ibid.*

166 *Ibid.*

167 *Ibid.*

168 *Ibid.* 105–107.

169 W. Kymlicka, 'Federalism, Nationalism, and Multiculturalism' in D. Karmis and W. Norman (eds.) *Theories of Federalism: A Reader* (Palgrave Macmillan 2005) 272.

170 *Ibid.* 276–277.

171 *Ibid.* 283.

establish boundaries, an often-overlooked limitation on the adaptability of federal systems. For federalism to function as a genuine mechanism of self-governance, its territorial architecture must enable national minorities to form demographic majorities within defined subunits, as is the case with the Québécois in Quebec. This, unfortunately, is not feasible for certain national minorities, including many indigenous peoples in the United States or Canada, due to their smaller numbers and historical land dispossession, resulting in their communities often being dispersed, even crossing state or provincial lines. Even if we hypothetically assume these structural challenges have been overcome – that is, that powers are equitably allocated between central authorities and territorial units to preserve identity and enhance the political, economic, and social development of minority groups, and that territorial boundaries are appropriately drawn – there remains a constant threat that looms over even the most well-established federal arrangement: the possibility that a minority group that has developed self-governance may begin to seek secession.[172]

Federal arrangements make it easier for federal units to secede if they wish to do so.[173] Granting a territory in the form of a federal unit to a specific minority facilitates that minority's ability to organize referendums for secession. As McGarry and O'Leary point out, it is significantly more likely, as confirmed by the Badinter Commission's findings on the former Yugoslavia, that the international community will acknowledge a bid for independence coming from a federal unit rather than from a group lacking such a unit.[174]

Still, Belser and Beglinger note that secessionist movements tend to be more violent in unitary states that do not grant autonomy.[175] Federalism is seen as a peaceful response to secessionism by allowing regions to self-govern while remaining part of a larger state, thus ensuring fair access to power and resources. If groups are recognized as having the right to external self-determination in cases of severe oppression and serious violations of ISD, then, by contrast, the granting of self-rule and participation in shared governance serves to weaken secessionist claims and lowers the likelihood that new such states will be recognized by the international community.[176]

---

172 *Ibid.* 285–286.

173 J. McGarry and B. O'Leary, 'Federation and Managing Nations' in M. Burgess and J. Pinder (eds.) *Multinational Federations* (2007) 192.

174 *Ibid.*

175 Belser and Beglinger (n 158) 180.

176 *Ibid.*

4.3 *Autonomism*

Autonomism is a political and social theory that advocates for greater autonomy or self-governance for a specific region or community within a larger political entity, typically a nation-state.[177] Autonomists contend that certain regions or groups should possess the right to significant self-governance, enabling them to independently manage matters such as culture, language, education, and aspects of local governance, while remaining within the larger political entity. In numerous multinational democracies, federalism is often regarded as the most effective institutional framework for addressing the complexities of multinationalism, a view widely supported by academic scholarship.[178] However, there are instances where sub-state national communities, represented by autonomist nationalist parties, oppose the idea of federation as a suitable institutional framework accommodating their demands. Instead, many of these stateless nationalists advocate for autonomism.[179]

Autonomist proposals typically renounce outright independence, which sets them apart from independentist movements advocating full sovereignty. On the other hand, autonomism and federalism are linked as frameworks for managing diversity within multinational states, yet they are distinct in their scope and structure. Federalism is characterized by a constitutionally enshrined division of powers between central and constituent governments, where all subunits typically possess equal powers within a unified legal and institutional framework.[180] Autonomism diverges from this model in several ways. It often arises in regions with distinct ethnic or national identities and prioritizes localized self-governance without necessarily integrating these regions into the central decision-making structures of the state. Moreover, autonomism tends to offer fragmented and asymmetrical arrangements, in contrast to the uniform and homogenizing tendencies of classic federal systems.[181]

---

177 The terms 'self-government' and 'autonomy' are often used interchangeably, as self-government is considered a form of autonomy. K. Abushov, 'Autonomy as a Possible Solution to Self-determination Disputes: Does It Really Work?' 22(2) *International Journal on Minority and Group Rights* (2015) 191.

178 See J. G. Lluch, 'Towards a Theory of Autonomism' APSA *2009 Toronto Meeting Paper* (2009) 2.

179 *Ibid.*

180 'Autonomy is always a fragmented order, whereas a constituent [unit of a federation] is always part of a whole (…) The ties in a federal State are always stronger than those in an autonomy'. Heintze, 'On the Legal Understanding of Autonomy' (n 72) 25.

181 In some cases, autonomism may overlap with federal systems, particularly in proposals for asymmetric federalism, where certain subunits seek a degree of autonomy that exceeds traditional federal norms. Examples include nationalist movements within federations like Canada, where parties such as the Action Démocratique du Québec have advanced

The relationship between autonomism and self-determination warrants additional mention, as autonomism can be 'both an alternative to self-determination as well as an expression of it'.[182] Indeed, autonomism and self-determination go hand in hand, with both concepts aimed at preserving the identity of minority groups. However, autonomism is not the same as guaranteeing minority rights – the minority rights protection system is focused on safeguarding individuals, whereas autonomism is geared towards protecting and enhancing the collective identity of a group, although guaranteeing minority rights also contributes to this goal.

Finaly, for the sake of clarity, it is also important to distinguish between autonomy and autonomism, as well as between different forms of autonomy. Autonomy refers to the condition or quality of self-governance, allowing a region, group, or individual to make decisions independently while remaining under the broader authority of a larger state or organization. In contrast, autonomism is a political ideology or movement that actively advocates for the attainment or expansion of such autonomy.[183] Autonomy, in geopolitical contexts, typically refers to territorial autonomy, which involves entities tied to a specific territory and possessing certain legislative or administrative powers. This focus differs from personal or group autonomy, which applies to

---

proposals for significant political autonomy that challenge the traditional boundaries of federalism.

182 Hilpold (n 61) 44.

183 There are various concepts of autonomism, including: Marxist autonomism (political theory and movement that emphasizes the importance of worker self-management and direct action, operating independently of traditional political parties and unions); Anarchist Autonomism (this theory is based on the anarchist idea of rejecting state authority and centralization. Anarchist autonomism seeks to create self-managed communities that operate on principles of direct democracy, solidarity, and horizontal organization); Cultural Autonomism (cultural autonomism focuses on the right of ethnic, linguistic, or cultural communities to preserve and develop their own identity); Pragmatic Autonomism (it is based on practical reasons for granting autonomy, often as a means to reduce conflict or stabilize multi-ethnic states); Ecological Autonomism (this theory combines autonomist ideas with ecological philosophy. Proponents of ecological autonomism advocate for the creation of local communities that are economically and ecologically sustainable, self-sufficient, and resilient to global economic fluctuations). See W. Kymlicka, *Multicultural Citizenship: A Liberal Theory of Minority Rights* (OUP 1996); G. Katsiaficas, *The Subversion of Politics: European Autonomous Social Movements and the Decolonization of Everyday Life* (AK Press 2006); M. Hechter, *Containing nationalism* (OUP 2000); R. Lapidoth, *Autonomy: Flexible Solutions to Ethnic Conflicts* (United States Institute of Peace Press 1997); B. Latour, *Politics of Nature: How to Bring the Sciences into Democracy* (HUP 2004).

non-territorially organized groups exercising self-governance over particular aspects of their lives, such as religion or cultural practices.

Territorial autonomy can range from administrative autonomy, where the autonomous region only has executive powers, to full self-government, which includes legislative, judicial, and significant executive powers, excluding defence. In some cases, the central government may need to consider the autonomous region's concerns in foreign policy. Yet, as noted above, unlike federalism or confederation, the degree of autonomy does not alter the state's constitutional order.[184]

In geopolitics, autonomy can take various forms, depending on its depth and territoriality:

1. territorially delineated entities with legislative power, such as Catalonia, Euskadi, Galicia, Scotland, Gagauzia, the Åland Islands, Greenland, or South Tyrol;
2. non-territorially delineated entities with legislative power, resembling the Ottoman Millet – type systems found in Jordan, Lebanon, Syria, Israel, and Egypt;
3. territorially delineated entities holding regulatory and administrative power, such as Corsica, Crimea, Wales, Nunavut, or the Karbi Anglong District in Assam; and
4. non-territorially delineated entities with regulatory and administrative power, like the cultural self-governmental institutions in Estonia and certain regions of Sápmi.

Territorial autonomy thus refers specifically to entities tied to a defined geographic region and endowed with specific powers, encompassing cases under categories (i) and (iii).[185] It can be defined as 'an arrangement aimed at granting a certain degree of self-determination to a group that differs from the majority of the population in the State, and yet constitutes the majority in a specific region'.[186]

Autonomous arrangements, alongside federal systems, are often proposed as effective solutions for preventing and mitigating ethnic conflicts rooted in the people's right to self-determination. Both decentralization and special autonomy can serve as valuable tools for conflict resolution.[187] Decentralization, in

---

184 Abushov (n 177) 191.

185 A. Légaré and M. Suksi, 'Introduction: Rethinking the Forms of Autonomy at the Dawn of the 21st Century' 15 *International Journal on Minority and Group Rights* (2008) 143–147.

186 Lapidoth (n 183) 174.

187 Peace Mediation Essentials, 'Decentralization, Special Territorial Autonomy, and Peace Negotiations' <https://files.ethz.ch/isn/164697/PME_Mediation-and-Decentralization.pdf>.

particular, plays a crucial role in transforming conflicts, especially those with ethnopolitical dimensions or involving geographically concentrated minority groups. It facilitates the establishment of legitimate governing bodies at local and regional levels. By adhering to the principle of self-rule, issues central to group identity – often potentially divisive – can be addressed through democratic processes at lower levels of government or within autonomous regions. This approach allows homogenous groups to resolve sensitive matters and implement solutions they find suitable. Moreover, decentralization helps to reduce the risk of high-level conflicts that result in clear winners and losers.[188]

Autonomous arrangements are particularly well-suited as a strategy for conflict prevention in the case of territorially concentrated minorities. They provide specific ethnic or national groups with the means to secure cultural recognition and obtain tailored guarantees, laws, or advantages that address their needs.[189] The fundamental goal of any autonomy framework should centre on strengthening the enforcement of human and minority rights, with the ultimate aim of preventing conflicts both within and between states. However, it is essential to recognize that autonomy arrangements must be customized to fit unique circumstances. There is no universal principle in international law that mandates the automatic provision of autonomy to any particular group, except perhaps in the context of indigenous peoples.[190]

Autonomy often serves as a compromise between the demand for separate statehood and the desire to maintain a unitary state. It provides a potential long-term solution by mitigating the contentious issue of sovereignty.[191] Ghai observes that territorial autonomy can enhance the political integration of ethnic groups within a country by highlighting differences within those groups, leading to the fragmentation of previously unified ethnic parties.[192] This fragmentation allows for the formation of coalitions among similar ethnic parties across the state, as seen in Nigeria and India. As a result, local issues that might have escalated into national crises are instead managed at the local level.

However, although autonomy has proven to be an effective solution for secessionist conflicts in many cases, it should not be viewed as a panacea that unreservedly resolves such conflicts. Ghai notes that, despite the theoretical and practical advantages of autonomy, governments have repeatedly and strongly

188 *Ibid.* 3.

189 J. Bertrand, *Nationalism and Ethnic Conflict in Indonesia* (CUP 2004) 186.

190 H. J. Heintze, 'Territorial Autonomy: A possible Solution of Self-determination Conflicts?' <https://www.watchindonesia.de/1038/autonomy-solution-conflict-papua?lang=en>.

191 Y. Ghai, 'Autonomy as a Strategy for Diffusing Conflict' in P. Stern and D. Druckman, *International Conflict Resolution After the Cold War* (The National Academies 2000) 496.

192 *Ibid.* 497.

resisted it. This resistance is usually grounded in a fear that autonomy might strengthen ethnic solidarity and divisiveness, or entrench temporary trends in an era marked by identity politics.[193] Clearly, the idea of autonomy challenges in a way traditional notions of territorial integrity and national unity. Additionally, from the perspective of an ethnic majority seeking to maintain dominance, the reorganization of the state and redistribution of resources that autonomy entails might be deemed unacceptable.

Certain theorists believe that the basis for secession in multinational states can be the disregard for autonomous and federal arrangements, essentially the failure to uphold multinationalism. Bauböck, who advocates for a general right to federal autonomy, points out that there is a right to secession if such rights are 'persistently violated'.[194] He believes that a multinational state that respects and protects the rights of its minorities has a legitimate claim to unity. Buchanan cites 'serious and persistent violations of intra-State autonomy agreements by the State' as grounds for remedial secession.[195] However, he clarifies that he does not recognize a unilateral right to secession simply in response to violations of autonomous arrangements; rather, secession is justified only under two conditions: (1) the state is responsible for the breakdown of the autonomy arrangement, and (2) secession is the remedy of last resort.[196]

The literature presents an argument that Catalonia could leverage in favour of secession, based on Spain's persistent refusal to negotiate the terms of adequate, tailored autonomy.[197] While Buchanan makes the invocation of the right to remedial secession dependent on the prior violation of the autonomous arrangement by the parent state, Seymour believes that such a violation is not necessary but rather emphasizes the non-recognition or misrecognition of the primary right of sub-State nations to internal self-determination.[198] Yet, Busquets argues, if the violation of existing autonomous arrangements were the sole basis for secession, it could deter states from adopting such agreements

193 *Ibid.* 499.

194 R. Bauböck, 'Why Stay together? A Pluralist Approach to Secession and Federation' *Social Science Open Access Repository* <https://www.ssoar.info/ssoar/handle/document/26383>.

195 A. Buchanan, *Justice, Legitimacy, and Self-determination. Moral Foundations for International law* (OUP 2003) 222.

196 *Ibid.*

197 M. Sanjaume-Calvet, 'The Morality of Secession: Secessionist and Antisecessionist Arguments in the Catalan case' in X. Cuadras-Morató (ed.) *Catalonia: A New Independent State in Europe? A Debate on Secession within the European Union* (Routledge 2016) 82–106.

198 M. Seymour, 'Secession as a Remedial Right' 50(4) *Inquiry: An Interdisciplinary Journal of Philosophy* (2007) 395–423.

in the first place.[199] To address this concern, Patten introduces an additional basis for secession, which he refers to as the 'failure of recognition'. According to this proposal, the right to secession would arise if the state 'has failed to establish arrangements that extended recognition to a national minority'.[200] Patten asserts that national identity is recognized to the extent that its holders enjoy the right to self-governance. Therefore, the state's constitutional arrangement must provide a democratic forum in which holders of that identity, as a majority, can make collective decisions together as a group. This forum enables citizens with different national identities within the same political community to express their identities through collective decision-making. On the other hand, if constitutional arrangements do not provide a forum for self-governance for some national identities within the community, there is a 'failure of recognition'.[201]

In the academic discourse on autonomy, scholars have endeavoured to identify the conditions essential for the successful implementation of autonomous regimes for minorities in mitigating conflicts related to self-determination. It has been observed that the manner in which an autonomous regime is established affects its success. Autonomous regimes are more likely to endure and succeed in conflict prevention when negotiations occur through a democratic and participatory process, rather than when the terms of the regime are imposed unilaterally.[202] This democratic approach should extend beyond the initial establishment of autonomy; the ongoing success of autonomy is more probable in a democratic environment where the central authority is representative and has inclusive institutions. Another significant precondition for the success of an autonomous regime is the clear delineation of powers vested in autonomous units.[203] The allocation of powers is fundamental to the effective operation of autonomy, as it can serve as an early trigger for conflict, particularly when the autonomous entity seeks to pursue secession. This issue becomes even more pronounced when an entity, having achieved *de facto* secession, attempts to reintegrate into the parent state. Nevertheless, regardless of how well-defined the allocation of powers is between the central government and the autonomous entity, disputes often arise over which authority

199 P. Bossacoma Busquets, *Morality and Legality of Secession: A Theory of National Self-determination* (Palgrave Macmillan 2020) 180. See 5.2.7.3.

200 A. Patten, *Equal Recognition: The Moral Foundations of Minority Rights* (Princeton University Press 2014) 240.

201 *Ibid.* 242.

202 Bertrand (n 189) 187; F. Schulte, 'Ethnic Conflict Regulation Through Territorial Autonomy-A Configurational Analysis of Success and Failure' *SocArXiv* (2018) 19.

203 Schulte (n 202) 19; Ghai (n 191) 517.

is responsible for specific issues. Such disputes, especially in contentious areas, can escalate into conflicts, undermining the stability of the autonomous arrangement.[204]

For Abushov, the success of an autonomy system depends on the nature of the self-determination dispute. If the demand for self-determination seeks a stronger expression of identity, then autonomy can be a viable solution. Typically, this scenario applies to situations where a minority group feels threatened by specific policies of the central state, or in instances of state collapse. In these cases, granting greater self-governance often suffices to address secessionist aspirations of the minority. However, autonomy as a solution is less likely to succeed when the self-determination claim revolves around rectifying historical injustices related to contested sovereignty or irreconcilable territorial disputes.[205]

Dimitrijević notes that autonomy has struggled to establish itself as the dominant approach for addressing the protection of minority rights and the realization of the right to self-determination.[206] In this context, Dimitrijević mentions a paradox that is particularly noticeable in Central and Eastern Europe. Namely, due to the fear of external self-determination, i.e. the separation of part of the state, most states either do not guarantee internal self-determination sincerely and sufficiently or, more notably, deny any form of autonomy to minorities within their borders. This reluctance is driven by the belief that accommodating minority demands could set off erosive processes that would inevitably lead to secession. The paradox, however, lies in the fact that this states' stance – opposing any agreement with minority groups – actually stimulates the very processes they feverishly try to prevent. In other words, refusing even partial acceptance of the autonomy demands of minority groups can, in the long run, lead to the alienation of the entire minority community from crucial societal processes, the radicalization of their demands, and precipitate secession.[207]

It can be concluded that there are two important groups of factors that underpin the effectiveness of autonomous arrangements in preventing secessionist movements. The first group relates to eliminating the motives for secession. Given that many secessionist movements arise from a desire to establish an independent state due to perceived disrespect for national

204 Abushov (n 177) 190.

205 *Ibid.* 193–194.

206 V. Dimitrijević, *Savremeno Shvatanje Prava Naroda Na Samoopredeljenje* (Belgrade Centre for Human Rights 2011) 50.

207 *Ibid.* 51.

identity, autonomous arrangements can help foster and develop those identities within the parent state, thereby curbing secessionist tendencies. Thus, if the core of a self-determination dispute is the desire for greater expression of ethnic identity, autonomy may be the appropriate solution. In such cases, the secessionist aspirations of a minority feeling threatened within a given state will generally be diminished or eradicated with expanded autonomy.

The second group of factors pertains to the removal of the basis for secession linked to the denial of internal self-determination. When a parent state adequately grants autonomy to ethnic groups within its territory, it becomes more difficult for those groups to justify or pursue demands for independence, as the default position will favour territorial unity. Conversely, if the parent state denies or withdraws autonomy once it has been granted, the state hands them a weapon that they can use against it. The denial of autonomy can be seen as a violation of internal self-determination, thus serving as a basis for remedial secession.

5 Internal Self-determination and Other Legal Means of Secession Prevention

While internal self-determination remains a comparatively underdeveloped legal concept, states have long relied on more established doctrines to prevent secession. Foundational principles like territorial integrity, *uti possidetis juris*, non-intervention, the prohibition on the use of force, and anti-domination principles serve as primary safeguards of state unity. This section illustrates how these principles have evolved and become embedded in international law, explores their relationship to internal self-determination, and analyzes the key distinctions between them in the context of maintaining territorial integrity.

5.1 *Territorial Integrity*

The relationship between self-determination and the principle of territorial integrity has long been a focal point of international law theory.[208] Much has already been said about territorial integrity in chapter III, hence only key

208 See, among many, Koskenniemi (n 3) 260; L. Killen, 'Self-determination vs. Territorial Integrity' 10(1) *Nationalities Papers* (1982) 65–78; J. Trinidad, *Self-determination in Disputed Colonial Territories* (CUP 2018) 21–69; M. Sterio, *Secession in International Law: A New Framework* (Elgar 2018) 47–66.

points will be restated here for the sake of completeness and clarity.[209] Most importantly, although territorial integrity generally constrains the exercise of self-determination to preserve state unity, its normative force is not absolute.

The principle of territorial integrity, while conceptually rooted in the Westphalian state system, only attained robust legal protection in the twentieth century.[210] Prior to the general prohibition on the use of force, international law provided limited safeguards – merely restricting 'pacific' coercion and, under the League of Nations Covenant, imposing procedural constraints.[211] The 1928 Kellogg-Briand Pact marked a turning point by formally renouncing war as a tool of state policy.[212]

The principle of territorial integrity, enshrined in UN Charter Article 2(4) as a prohibition against forcible violation of states' territorial sovereignty, constitutes a foundational norm of international order. Its codification extends through regional frameworks (the OAS Charter – Articles 1, 12, and 20; the AU Charter Preamble; and the Helsinki Final Act – Principles I, II, IV, and VIII), post-Charter instruments (1970 Friendly Relations Resolution; 1974 Definition of Aggression); and post-Cold War developments (1990 Charter of Paris).[213]

The interpretation of self-determination through the lens of territorial integrity reveals two fundamental legal consequences: (1) the categorical exclusion of a generalized right to unilateral secession, and (2) the conditional nature of territorial integrity itself.[214] While the former preserves state unity as the normative baseline, the latter acknowledges that territorial sovereignty yields when confronted with peremptory norms of humanitarian law, fundamental human rights violations, or recognized cases of remedial secession.

This inherent tension between the two principles reflects what Peters identifies as the 'public law paradigm' – where competing norms are reconciled

---

209 See 3.3.2.1.

210 The Peace of Westphalia (1648), which ended the Thirty Years' War in Europe, is often cited as the origin of the modern concept of state sovereignty. B. Fassbender, 'Westphalia, Peace of (1648)' *Max Planck Encyclopedias of International Law* (2018).

211 According to Article 10 of the League of Nations Covenant, member states are obliged to 'protect and preserve' the territorial integrity and political independence of other members – an obligation consistent with President Wilson's Fourteenth Point, which proposed the creation of an association of nations for precisely this purpose. Covenant of the League of Nations (1919) 108 LNTS 18.

212 The signatory states promised not to use war to resolve 'disputes or conflicts of whatever nature or of whatever origin they may be, which may arise among them'. General Treaty for Renunciation of War as an Instrument of National Policy (Kellogg–Briand Pact) (1928) 94 LNTS 57.

213 See 3.3.2.1.

214 See 2.6.

through proportional balancing rather than absolute prioritization.[215] Under this approach, neither principle operates as an 'all-or-nothing' rule, but rather as variable interests whose weight depends on contextual factors,[216] including the severity of rights violations, the availability of effective internal remedies, and the historical and political specificities of each case.[217] Such balancing mirrors the methodology applied in the *Quebec Secession Reference*, where the Canadian Supreme Court recognized territorial integrity as presumptive but conditional upon the state's continued democratic legitimacy.

Absent remedial secession conditions, territorial integrity maintains normative primacy for three compelling reasons. First, historical imperfection – all borders reflect some degree of historical contingency or injustice, making their revision inherently problematic. Second, practical unworkability – the creation of new boundaries risks destabilizing effects that outweigh potential justice claims. Third, presumption of continuity – the *uti possidetis* principle favors existing arrangements to promote stability. Consequently, self-determination operates primarily as an internal right – one that transforms into an external claim only when the state fundamentally breaches its sovereign compact through sustained oppression or constitutional exclusion of minority groups.

5.2 *Uti Possidetis Juris*

Uti possidetis is a principle governing the succession of borders that were previously administrative. According to Shaw, the doctrine of *uti possidetis juris* ensures that a newly independent state inherits the same borders it had as an administrative unit within the territory of the colonial power. Thus, the principle operates within the context of sovereignty transfer and the creation of a new independent state, shaping and conditioning that process.[218]

The principle of *uti possidetis* has its origins in Roman law, where it referred to an order issued by a praetor (a judicial magistrate) to prevent disturbances in the possession of property that had been acquired lawfully, openly, and permanently (*lege, nec vi, nec clam, nec precario*).[219] Otherwise, preference was

215 A. Peters, 'Does Kosovo Lie in the Lotus-Land of Freedom?' 24 *Leiden Journal of International Law* (2011) 102.

216 *Ibid.*

217 S. F. Van den Driest, *Remedial Secession: A Right to External Self-determination as a Remedy to Serious Injustice* (Intersentia 2013) 166–167.

218 M. Shaw, 'The Heritage of States: The Principle of Uti Possidetis Juris Today' 67 *BYIL* (1996) 97–98.

219 G. Nesi, 'Uti possidetis Doctrine' *Max Planck Encyclopedias of International Law* (2018) para 1.

given to the party in actual occupation. This shifted the burden of proof of ownership to the party not in possession, significantly favouring the possessor. The concept of *uti possidetis* thus aimed at preserving the status quo of ownership, at least while the dispute was ongoing.

The doctrine of *uti possidetis* was later employed during the decolonization of Latin America, in a context quite different from that envisioned by Roman law.[220] The application had a dual purpose: first, to prevent the resurgence of European colonialism based on the argument that certain parts of the former colonial territory were *terra nullius* (land belonging to no one) and therefore open for occupation; and second, to avert boundary disputes between newly formed states.[221] *Uti possidetis* pertained to the continuity of colonial administrative borders after a change of sovereignty and the transformation of those borders into international boundaries. As such, *uti possidetis* became a method of demarcating international borders.[222] In instances where the precise location of administrative boundaries under colonial law was uncertain, international tribunals supplemented the principle with the application of *uti possidetis de facto* (concerning the effectiveness of the borders).[223] With respect to Latin American states, the principle of *uti possidetis juris* undoubtedly evolved into customary international law in the region.[224] However, in the *Frontier Dispute* case, the ICJ noted that

> the principle (*uti possidetis juris*) is not a special rule which pertains solely to one specific system of international law. It is a *general principle*, which is logically connected with the phenomenon of obtaining independence, wherever it occurs.[225]

The quoted passage suggests that *uti possidetis* may possess a universal character, meaning it can be invoked in post-colonial settings and is not limited

---

220 Raič (n 138) 298.

221 *Ibid.*; ICJ, *Land, Island and Maritime Frontier Dispute (El Salvador/Honduras)*, Judgment, ICJ Rep. 1992, 387.

222 Raič (n 138) 298.

223 F. de Paula Borda, 'Uti possidetis de facto – El principio brasileño' in *Límites de Colombia con Costa Rica* (Ulan Press 2002) 135–140.

224 Raič (n 138) 298–299. S. Torres Bernárdez, "Uti possidetis Juris Principle" in Historical Perspective' in K. Ginther (ed.) *Völkerrecht zwischen normativem Anspruch und politischer Realität: Festschrift für Karl Zemanek zum 65. Geburtstag* (Dunckler & Humboldt 1994) 417, 345–436.

225 ICJ, *Frontier Dispute (Burkina Faso/Republic of Mali)*, Judgment, ICJ Rep. 1986, 554, para 20 (emphasis added).

to cases of colonial independence. It could also be applied in contemporary cases of secession, for example. A few years after the ICJ's ruling, the Badinter Commission, which delivered legal opinions on the dissolution of Yugoslavia, confirmed the standing of *uti possidetis* as a general principle. However, it was willing to consider only the boundaries of Yugoslav republics as those that could be transformed into international ones,[226] rejecting its applicability to the Republic of Serbian Krajina, for instance. This raises the argument that *uti possidetis* was intended to support the creation of larger political units while preventing further fragmentation – a stance that remains ambiguous from both a legal and policy perspective.[227]

Since *uti possidetis* was used to both justify and obstruct secession, depending on the politically advantageous divisions, the Commission's reference to *uti possidetis* has been met with great caution in legal doctrine. Scholars have questioned not only the alleged universality of the principle and its selective application, but also its classification as a general principle under Article 38(1)(c) of the ICJ Statute.[228] This is because *uti possidetis* was not transferred from domestic law to international law; rather, it is a genuine international law concept. It has also been noted that a closer examination of the *Frontier Dispute* case, considering its context, reveals that neither the universality of *uti possidetis* nor its potential role in the creation of new states beyond decolonization can be clearly established. Indeed, in the paragraphs following the quoted passage, the Chamber observed that *uti possidetis* is 'a principle of a general kind which is logically connected with *this form of decolonization* wherever it occurs'[229] and that the principle is applicable only if the parties agree to implement it, highlighting the importance of consent.[230]

In Africa, states agreed in advance to inherit colonial borders, thus treating the principle as binding and not subject to subsequent challenge. Accordingly, *uti possidetis* represents a modality of applying self-determination for

226 Badinter Commission, Opinion No. 3 (11 Jan. 1992) para 2(3).

227 A. Peters, 'The Principle of *Uti Possidetis Juris*: How Relevant it is for Issues of Secession' in C. Walter et al. (eds.) *Self-determination and Secession in International Law* (OUP 2014) 95 (noting that the subsequent establishment of Kosovo in 2008 did not respect the boundary of Serbia).

228 *Ibid.* 99–100, 106. See also F. Fernandez Jankov and V. Ćorić, 'The Legality of Uti Possidetis in the Definition of Kosovo's Legal Status' in J. Ćorić (ed.) *Космет – Гордијев чвор* (Institut za Uporedno Pravo 2008) 81–87; O. Corten, 'Droit des peuples à disposer d'eux-mêmes et uti possidetis: deux faces d'une même medaille?' in O. Corten et al. (eds.) *Démembrements d'Etats et délimitations territoriales: l'uti possidetis en question(s)* (Bruylant 1999) 403, 432.

229 *Frontier Dispute* (n 225) para 23 (emphasis added).

230 *Ibid.* para 25.

entities that possess the right to external self-determination, such as Non-Self-Governing Territories,[231] whereas it is less likely to support groups within an already independent state in pursuing ESD and transforming administrative lines into international borders against the will of the central government.[232]

Admittedly, international law does not mandate to which level of frontiers *uti possidetis* pertains (so far it has only been utilized for the first-level state divisions, out of five in the USSR and out of three in Yugoslavia), who the beneficiaries of the principle are (states or nations fighting for independence) or whether it is a transient principle that only applies at the moment of gaining independence.[233] Therefore, in theory, secessionist movements, like those in Abkhazia and Nagorno Karabakh can rely on this principle to demarcate their boundaries. According to Ratner, the role of *uti possidetis*, consistent with its Roman law precursor, could be to maintain the status quo until the parties resolve their conflicting claims.[234] The application of this principle would also imply a certain form of consultation with the people of the disputed territory regarding their future. According to Ratner's proposal, this could be achieved through holding plebiscites as a mechanism of direct democracy. Plebiscites represent a logical solution in line with modern trends in self-determination but, at the same time, they pose challenges and frustrations. These difficulties arise from issues such as determining the location and size of the referendum area, defining the voting units, and demarcating borders as a result of the vote. However, solutions could be found by minimizing dissatisfaction among affected populations, or by balancing the number of opponents on both sides.[235] In the case of canton Jura in Switzerland, for example, the cascading referendums in disputed areas led to an outcome considered legitimate by all parties involved. In this way, by applying the principle of *uti possidetis* and consulting the people through referendums, ethnic and cultural heterogeneity could be preserved while respecting the self-determination of all communities within the disputed territory to the greatest extent possible.

---

231 Raič (n 138) 303–304.

232 See C. Walters, 'South Ossetia' in C. Walter et al. (eds.) *Self-determination and Secession in International Law* (OUP 2014) 182; F. Mirzayev, 'Abkhazia' in C. Walter et al. (eds.) *Self-determination and Secession in International Law* (OUP 2014) 203; H. Krüger, 'Nagorno-Karabakh' in C. Walter et al. (eds.) *Self-determination and Secession in International Law* (OUP 2014) 225–227.

233 Peters, 'The Principle of *Uti Possidetis Juris*' (n 227) 119–125.

234 S. R. Ratner, 'Drawing a Better Line: Uti Possidetis and Borders of New States' 90(4) *AJIL* (1996) 617–621.

235 *Ibid.* 622–623.

On the other hand, it should be borne in mind that the paramount purpose *of uti possidetis* is to maintain stability and order. In places like Africa, where leaders decided to adhere to it, *uti possidetis* remains a primary principle that protects the territorial integrity of states both in relations between neighbouring states and between states and groups within states. In other parts of the world, where there is no implicit or explicit consent to this principle, its application remains doubtful. Regardless of one's stance on the presumed universality of the principle, it should be interpreted in good faith for the benefit of both states and their populations. Therefore, it would be incongruous to assert its validity at the creation of one state today and then to reapply it for that state's further fragmentation tomorrow. Additionally, applying it to lower-range administrative boundaries in post-colonial settings could be perilous, potentially leading to anarchy. If we accept that Kosovo had a more or less clearly defined territory and could rely on *uti possidetis* at the time of its independence, then territorially concentrated Serbs in the northern part of that province could also invoke the same principle.[236]

Uti possidetis, interpreted as the presumption of maintaining the territorial integrity of new states (which over time become old states), appears to restrict the RSD in an external fashion. However, it does not inherently restrict the RSD in an internal fashion. Moreover, by genuinely implementing internal self-determination, states tend to bolster both the principle of territorial integrity and *uti possidetis*. On the other hand, *uti possidetis* is not a *jus cogens* norm, which permits no derogation. Therefore, peoples could 'deviate' from this principle, for instance, if their ISD is not respected, either by seeking an agreement to change their territorial configuration with the central government or by taking unilateral measures that may lead to independence.

5.3 *Non-intervention, Non-use of Force and Non-domination*

The principle of non-intervention, encompassing both the non-use of force and the prohibition of domination, constitutes a cornerstone of international law. It has evolved into a customary legal norm, particularly in its patently coercive manifestations.[237] It is unequivocally established that territorial alterations cannot be effected through intervention involving the threat or

236 M. A. Jovanović, *Kosovo i Metohija: Četiri Pravno-Politička Eseja* (Pravni Fakultet Univerziteta u Beogradu 2013) 21–22.

237 D. Lefkowitz, 'On the Foundation of Rights to Political Self-determination: Secession, Non-intervention, and Democratic Governance' 39(4) *Journal of Social Philosophy* (2008) 493. See UN Charter, Article 2. See also *Military and Paramilitary Activities (Nicaragua/United States of America)*, Judgement, Merits. ICJ Rep. 1986, paras 202–205.

use of military force, as such actions would usually result in domination and undermine the territorial integrity of a state. Furthermore, territorial changes cannot occur in contravention of the free and genuine consent of the affected populations.[238] On numerous occasions, states and international organizations have condemned the occupation of sovereign territories, which violated the will and rights of the people.[239] The continuous calls for the respect of the Palestinian people's right to self-determination, including the withdrawal of Israeli forces from the Occupied Territories, testify to the nonacceptance of conquest and domination by one nation over another.[240] Any forceful intervention and occupation suppresses the internal right to self-determination.[241] In consequence, states are prohibited from infringing upon other peoples' self-determination through conquest or domination, and are obligated not to recognize such violations.[242]

Importantly, the concept of domination should not be equated with the pursuit of political or economic control as framed in realist theories of international relations, which primarily focus on power dynamics and state interests, nor should it be conflated with hierarchical structures, such as those of the Great Powers or supranational entities like the European Union. Rather, it should be understood as the acute and enduring forceful subjugation of both territory and its people, akin to the forms of domination witnessed under colonialism or apartheid regimes, such as that in South Africa.[243] The UN General Assembly Resolution 31/6A explicitly condemned 'the establishment of

---

238 *Chagos Archipelago* (n 116) para 157.

239 Note that changes conducted to effectuate people's wishes, whether implicit or expressed in a referendum, which occur on recognized foreign territory, are also illegal (e.g. Crimea). Consult S. Janković, 'Prawo Międzynarodowe a Zmiany Terytorialne. Kazus Krymu' 14 *Problemy Współczesnego Prawa Międzynarodowego, Europejskiego i Porównawczego* (2016) 62–89.

240 See, among many, UN Doc. A/C.3/68/SR.40 (20 Nov. 2013) 2 (Bolivia), 3 (Maldives), 4 (United Arab Emirates); UN Doc. A/ES-10/L.30/Rev.1 (9 May 2024) preamble.

241 See UNGA Res 68/153 (15 Jan. 2014) para 2.

242 The Stimson Doctrine, articulated in response to the Japanese invasion of Manchuria in 1931, asserted that states should not recognize territorial changes or treaties brought about by aggression. UNSC Res 242 (1967) called for the withdrawal of Israeli armed forces from territories occupied in the Six-Day War and emphasized the inadmissibility of acquiring territory by war. Similarly, UNSC Res 497 (1981) declared Israel's annexation of the Golan Heights as 'null and void' and without international legal effect. The 1970 UN Friendly Relations Declaration set forth a general obligation on states not to recognize territorial acquisition resulting from the threat or use of force. UNGA Res 2625(XXV) (24 Oct. 1970) principle 1.

243 See A. Anghie, 'Domination' in J. d'Aspremont and S. Singh (eds.) *Concepts for International Law: Contributions to Disciplinary Thought* (CUP 2019) 222–236.

Bantustans as designed to consolidate the inhuman policies of apartheid, to destroy the territorial integrity of the country, to perpetuate white minority domination and to dispossess the African people of South Africa of their inalienable rights', rejected the declaration of independence of the Transkei, declaring it invalid, as well as called upon all states to deny any form of recognition to Transkei or other Bantustans.[244]

The recognition of secessionist claims constitutes further, 'non-forceful' manifestation of external intervention, which could be deemed illegal under certain circumstances. This is particularly true in cases when the parent state is still struggling to reestablish control and order (which often implies the lack of effectiveness of the putative entity), and if the establishment of 'new statehood' is connected to the violation of *jus cogens* norms.[245] Generally, however, the principle of non-intervention pertains to areas where a state retains the right to make autonomous decisions, grounded in the principle of territorial sovereignty. This encompasses choices related to the political, economic, social, and cultural systems, as well as the formulation of foreign policy.[246] The core significance of the principle of non-intervention lies in safeguarding the fundamental right to internal self-determination, ensuring that external actors or circumstances do not infringe upon a people's freedom to exercise their will or determine their own future.[247]

The definition of 'intervention' is not straightforward. It must be distinguished from mere interference, as Oppenheim observes: 'Interference must be forcible or dictatorial, or otherwise coercive, in effect depriving the state intervened against of control over the matter in question. Interference pure and simple is not intervention'.[248] Thus, the key distinguishing feature of intervention is coercion.[249] The ICJ also emphasized the element of coercion in the *Nicaragua* case, where it affirmed that coercion lies at the essence of prohibited intervention. This is particularly evident in instances where

---

244 UNGA Res 31/6 (26 Oct. 1976).

245 The archetypical example of premature recognition, reiterated by the authors, was the French recognition of the United States in 1778 at the time when Great Britain still treated it as a *casus belli*. See M. Fabry, *Recognizing States: International Society and the Establishment of New States Since 1776* (OUP 2010) 27. See also 3.3.2.3.

246 S. Janković and V. Roeben, 'Russia's Threat of Force in Ukraine' 11 *Journal on the Use of Force in International Law* (2024) 87–107.

247 See 4.2.1.

248 R. Y. Jennings and A. D. Watts, *Oppenheim's International Law* (OUP 1996) 428.

249 G. Nolte, 'Secession and External Intervention' in M. Kohen (ed.) *Secession: International Law Perspectives* (CUP 2006) 70–71. See also M. Milanović, 'Revisiting Coercion as an Element of Prohibited Intervention in International Law' 117(4) *AJIL* (2023) 601–650.

intervention involves the use of force, either through direct military action or indirectly through support for subversive or terrorist activities within the territory of another state.[250]

Intervention, often defined as the use of force, is prohibited in the context of international armed conflicts under international law. However, its applicability to internal armed conflicts remains a subject of debate among scholars and practitioners.[251] According to Pustorino, the principle of neutrality, or external non-intervention in civil wars, 'has never actually taken hold in international law except for the part concerning a ban on supporting insurrectionary movements'.[252] For Roscini, a government's actions to suppress an insurgency are generally regarded as falling within its domestic jurisdiction. However, the principle of external self-determination dictates that, in scenarios of colonial domination and foreign occupation, subjugated populations must be afforded the right to determine their international status.[253] In such cases, a state breaching this *erga omnes* obligation forfeits the ability to invoke the principle of non-intervention. ESD of subjugated peoples thus prohibits any form of assistance to colonial or occupying powers, irrespective of whether unrest has escalated into a civil war. To the contrary, providing military or non-military support to populations under colonial rule or foreign occupation is permissible when aimed at ending the unlawful situation. As Eze and Okeke have observed, 'the right of self-determination is not complete without political independence. And without full political independence of a people, the doctrine of non-intervention is meaningless to them'.[254]

However, the principle of non-intervention continues to apply to secessionist armed struggles outside the contexts of colonialism and foreign occupation as such cases do not confer a right to external self-determination.[255] Nonetheless, some commentators adopt a less restrictive perspective, advocating for limited forms of intervention to safeguard both internal and external self-determination in the post-colonial context. Cassese, for instance, asserts that

---

250 *Nicaragua* (n 237) para 205.

251 See ICJ, *Legality of the Threat or Use of Nuclear Weapons*, Advisory Opinion, ICJ Rep. 1996, para 89.

252 P. Pustorino, 'The Principle of Non-Intervention in Recent Non-International Armed Conflicts' 53 *Questions of International Law* (2018) 18. More broadly, P. Pustorino, *Movimenti insurrezionali e diritto internazionale* (Cacucci Editore 2018).

253 M. Roscini, *International Law and the Principle of Non-Intervention: History, Theory, and Interactions with Other Principles* (OUP 2024) 309.

254 K. U. Eze and G. N. Okeke, 'The Right of People to Self-determination and the Principle of Non-Interference in the Domestic Affairs of States' 7(1) *NALSAR Law Review* (2013) 148.

255 Roscini (n 253) 309.

every state has the authority to aid and assist peoples living in other states in their efforts to achieve self-determination, preferably through countermeasures.[256] For Cassese, states are no longer bound to remain silent in the face of governmental misconduct toward its population. Instead, they may challenge repressive actions and openly criticize the treatment of individuals within a government's jurisdiction.[257] This 'softer' form of intervention, short of deploying troops, aligns with the Human Rights Committee's General Comment No. 12, which states that

> all States parties to the Covenant should take positive action to facilitate realization of and respect for the right of peoples to self-determination. Such positive action must be consistent with the States' obligations under the Charter of the United Nations and under international law: in particular, States must refrain from interfering in the internal affairs of other States and thereby adversely affecting the exercise of the right to self-determination.[258]

Even though the Committee interpreted assistance in the realization of self-determination by the Non-Self-Governing and Trust Territories, it could be argued that the principle of non-intervention must yield to the right of states to support the legitimate aspirations of peoples for self-determination. Pustorino was more forthright in challenging the role of non-intervention in secession prevention and the maintenance of territorial integrity, positing that there might be good grounds for (military) intervention in favour of insurgents fighting against brutal and dictatorial governments, be them insurgents seeking to overthrow the government or to form an independent state.[259] In truth, Pustorino remained cautious in his statements, noting that it might be too early to establish 'a gradual equivalence between this specific category of insurgents and national liberation movements' as well as that the practice of external support for insurgencies has not yet consolidated.[260] Relatedly, it remains debatable to what extent Article 2(7) of the UN Charter, which

256 A. Cassese, *Self-determination of Peoples: A Legal Reappraisal* (CUP 1995) 155–158. Note that countermeasures must not be forcible. ILC, Responsibility of States for Internationally Wrongful Acts 'ARSIWA' in 'Report of the International Law Commission on the work of its fifty-third session, 23 April 1 June and 2 July – 10 August 2001', UN Doc. A/56/10 II (2) YILC, Article 50, para 1(a).

257 *Ibid.* 175–176.

258 Human Rights Committee, General Comment No. 12 (n 82) para 6.

259 Pustorino, 'The Principle of Non-Intervention' (n 252) 23–28.

260 *Ibid.* 28, 31.

prohibits the UN from intervening in matters inherently within domestic jurisdiction of member states, constrains the UN from intervening in secessionist conflicts that may lead to changes in territorial boundaries.[261]

In essence, however, there exists a strong connection between the principle of non-intervention and the prohibition of the use of force, particularly in relation to their role in safeguarding territorial integrity. Nolte has observed a fundamental overlap between these two principles, which becomes evident in the analysis of the first and third principles of the Friendly Relations Declaration.[262] The first principle, among others, underlines the duty to refrain from threatening or using force to alter existing international boundaries or lines of demarcation, as well as prohibits 'organizing or encouraging the organization of irregular forces or armed bands (…) for incursion into the territory of another state', whereas the third principle establishes that 'armed intervention and all other forms of interference or attempted threats against the personality of the state (…) is in violation of international law'.[263] These rules, which prohibit the use of force, are a specific application of the broader principle of non-intervention, representing its most critical manifestation in relation to sovereignty and territorial integrity.[264] The connection between non-intervention and the prohibition of the use of force is underscored by the resolutions of the United Nations General Assembly[265] and the judgments of the International Court of Justice, notably in the *Nicaragua* and *Armed Activities* cases.[266]

The prohibition of the threat or use of force is outlined in Article 2(4) of the United Nations Charter, which states: 'All Members shall refrain in their international relations from the threat or use of force against the territorial integrity or political independence of any state, or in any other manner inconsistent with the Purposes of the United Nations'.[267] The term 'use of force' refers specifically to armed force, whether applied directly or indirectly (e.g. through assisting another state in using armed force), and excludes political

261 Arguably, the determination of a boundary could fall within the competence of the UN Security Council to maintain peace and security.

262 Nolte (n 249) 71.

263 Friendly Relations Declaration (n 242) principles 1 and 3.

264 See The Responsibility to Protect, 'Report of the International Commission on Intervention and State Sovereignty' (2001) 6.14 (arguments that the military intervention should be decided by the UNSC).

265 See UNGA Res 3314 (XXIX) 'Definition of Aggression' (14 Dec. 1974) Article 3, subparagraph g.

266 *Nicaragua* (n 237) para 187; ICJ, *Case Concerning the Armed Activities on the Territory of the Congo (Democratic Republic of the Congo v Uganda)*, Judgment, ICJ Rep. 2005, para 148.

267 UN Charter, Article 2(4).

or economic coercion.[268] This prohibition of the threat or the use of force shall be considered a peremptory norm (*jus cogens*), meaning it is a fundamental principle that does not permit derogation.[269] According to Article 52 of the Vienna Convention on the Law of Treaties, treaties concluded under duress are not valid, including those involving territorial transfers or the erosion of sovereignty. This principle was notably salient in the case of Serbia, which was compelled to sign the Kumanovo Agreement in 1999 to halt NATO's bombing campaign.[270] Similarly, the use of military duress to acquire territory is regarded as illegal.[271] For example, the international community has not recognized the Turkish Republic of Northern Cyprus, calling for the withdrawal of Turkish force.[272] Likewise, Armenia's military support to consolidate the secession of Nagorno-Karabakh has been rejected, with international community calling for the withdrawal of Armenian forces.[273]

It is important to acknowledge that the prohibition on the threat and use of force is not absolute. The Charter provides three exceptions to this prohibition: collective measures taken by the Security Council in accordance with Chapter VII,[274] individual and collective self-defence,[275] and measures against former hostile states, which are now considered to have fallen into desuetude.[276] In

268 The same is accepted with reference to Articles 1(1) and 39 of the UN Charter that expressly refer to aggression. See C. Kreß, 'Aggression' in R. Geiß and N. Melzer (eds.) *The Oxford Handbook of the International Law of Global Security* (OUP 2021) 236. See also Y. Dinstein, 'Aggression' *Max Planck Encyclopedias of International Law* (September 2015) para 16.

269 Cf. A. Green, 'Questioning the Peremptory Status of the Prohibition of the Use of Force' 32 *Michigan Journal of International Law* (2011) 225–227 (arguing that only the use of force qualifies as *jus cogens* due to ongoing practices of threats).

270 E. Milano, 'Security Council Action in the Balkans: Reviewing the Legality of Kosovo's Territorial Status' 14 *EJIL* (2003) 1001–1005; A. Kleczkowska, 'Prohibition of Threats of Force: A Silently Contested Norm?' 83 *ZaöRV* (2023) 163.

271 *Legality of the Threat or Use of Nuclear Weapons* (n 251) para 47; Friendly Relations Declaration (n 242) principle 1.

272 UNSC Res 353 (20 Jul. 1974).

273 See UNGA Res 62/243 (14 Mar. 2008). Yet, UNSC Res 822 (30 Apr. 1993); 853 (29 Jul. 1993); 874 (14 Oct. 1993) and 884 (12 Nov.1993) demanded immediate withdrawal of 'local Armenian forces' from the specific regions beside NK, that later become known as 'Armenian-occupied territories surrounding Nagorno-Karabakh'.

274 UN Charter, Article 42.

275 *Ibid.* Article 51.

276 *Ibid.* Article 107 (Nothing in the present Charter shall invalidate or preclude action, in relation to any state which during the Second World War has been an enemy of any signatory to the present Charter, taken or authorized as a result of that war by the Governments having responsibility for such action).

its *Nuclear Weapons* advisory opinion, the ICJ observed that the legality of military threats hinges on whether the force used or intended to be used is or would be lawful.[277] This symmetry in the prohibition can be contested, particularly given the differing magnitudes of the prohibited actions and the practical challenges in applying this symmetry to the allowed exceptions.[278]

Overall, the principle of non-intervention has thus far contributed to maintaining stability and upholding the sovereignty and territorial integrity of existing states. The UN supported interventions in the Congo to suppress the secession of its Katanga province, while generally adhering to Article 2(7) of the UN Charter in secession conflicts. Thus, foreign assistance in combating irredentism is recognized, yet may be lawful only with the consent of the territorial state (intervention by invitation) or with the UN authorization.[279]

5.4 *Domestic Law*

Secession is also prohibited by domestic law in many states. Many constitutions contain explicit provisions against secession, often providing for autonomy or self-governance in the same paragraphs. In states that declare themselves 'indivisible', any attempt at secession is deemed unconstitutional. In federal states, constitutions typically delineate the powers of both federal and regional governments, explicitly prohibiting unilateral secession by constituent regions. Additionally, rulings by constitutional courts, statutes adopted by state parliaments, and executive measures further reinforce the prohibition of secession.

For instance, the preamble of the Chinese Constitution declares that China is a 'unified multiethnic state founded by the Chinese people of all ethnic groups', while Article 4 emphasizes the equality of all nationalities, adding that 'all areas inhabited by ethnic minorities shall practice regional autonomy, establish autonomous organs, and exercise the power to self-govern' yet 'all ethnic autonomous areas are inseparable parts of the People's Republic of China'.[280] Additionally, Article 52 stipulates that it is the duty of citizens of the People's Republic of China to safeguard the unity of the country and the solidarity of all its nationalities. China has enacted coercive domestic laws and issued

277 *Legality of the Threat or Use of Nuclear Weapons* (n 251) para 47.

278 Consult. S. Janković and V. Roeben, 'Mind the gap: The Determination, Legality and Consequences of Implicit Threats of Force' 38 *Leiden Journal of International Law* (2025).

279 Cf. Declaration on Inadmissibility of Intervention provides that 'no State shall (…) interfere in civil strife of another State', which appears to express a duty of third States to remain neutral towards any party to an internal conflict, including the government. UNGA Res 2131 (XX) (21 Dec. 1965).

280 Constitution of the People's Republic of China (1982) Article 4.

policy 'guidelines' to enforce these constitutional provisions, which apply both to the region of Taiwan as a whole and to individuals. The Anti-Secession Law, enacted in 2005, explicitly aims to prevent the secession of Taiwan from China.[281] It authorizes the use of non-peaceful means to prevent secession if all peaceful o are exhausted.[282] The guidelines issued jointly by the Supreme People's Court, the Supreme People's Procuratorate, the Ministry of Public Security, the Ministry of State Security and the Ministry of Justice in May 2024 state that, under Chinese law, acts of secession committed by Taiwanese 'separatists' are punishable crimes. These guidelines also permit trials in absentia and authorize the death penalty for those advocating Taiwan's independence.[283] In Spain, Article 2 of the 1978 Constitution affirms the 'indissoluble unity of the Spanish Nation, the common and indivisible homeland of all Spaniards', while also recognizing and guaranteeing 'the right to self-government of the nationalities and regions of which it is composed' and promoting solidarity among them.[284] The Spanish Constitutional Court has consistently ruled against any attempts at secession, including the 2017 Catalan independence referendum, declaring such attempts unconstitutional.[285] In the United States, while the Constitution does not expressly address the issue of secession, it was effectively settled through the Civil War and the Supreme Court's ruling in *Texas v. White*, in which the Court ruled that states do not possess the right to unilaterally secede, describing the United States as 'an indestructible Union' from which no state may withdraw on its own accord.[286]

Internal self-determination complements domestic laws prohibiting secession by providing a legal and political framework that addresses demands for autonomy and self-governance without undermining the state's territorial integrity. Courts play a crucial role in maintaining this balance, interpreting

281 Anti-Secession Law, adopted at the Third Session of the Tenth National People's Congress on 14 March 2005.

282 *Ibid.* Article 8. See also India's Unlawful Activities (Prevention) Act, 1967. The Constitution (Application to Jammu and Kashmir) Amendment Order, 1969 established that, under Article 248 of the Indian Constitution (residuary powers of legislation), Parliament has exclusive power to make any law with respect to 'prevention of activities directed towards disclaiming, questioning or disrupting the sovereignty and territorial integrity of India (...) or secession of a part of the territory of India from the Union or causing insult to the Indian National Flag, the Indian National Anthem and the Constitution of India'.

283 J. Cohen, 'Chinese Government Expands Criminalization of Taiwanese Identity' *Human Rights Watch* (4 Jul. 2024) <https://www.hrw.org/news/2024/07/04/chinese-government-expands-criminalization-taiwanese-identity>.

284 Spanish Constitution (1978) Article 2.

285 More in 5.2.7.2.

286 *Texas v. White*, 74 U.S. 700 (1868).

constitutional provisions, and resolving disputes between central and regional governments. In Canada, the Constitution Act (1982) along with subsequent legal interpretations, provides a framework for Quebec's autonomy. The *Reference re Secession of Quebec* (1998) clarified the legal principles governing secession, leading Parliament to enact the Clarity Act (2000), which outlines the conditions for any future secession attempt, emphasizing negotiation and adherence to constitutional procedures.[287] Similarly, Jammu and Kashmir historically enjoyed significant autonomy under Article 370 of the Indian Constitution (1950-2019).[288] This illustrates how autonomy in domestic law can be used to address secessionist tendencies.

6 Non-legal Methods of Secession Prevention

In addition to legal methods, non-legal strategies also play a significant role in mitigating secessionist conflicts, though they often operate within a broader legal frameworks. While conflicts arising from the exercise of the right to self-determination have long been a focus in international relations theory, Krause notes that counter-secession – the strategies states employ to prevent secession – is more common than secession itself yet remains understudied in academic literature. This gap suggests that preventive measures against secession warrant further scholarly attention. However, as Krause observes, the number of studies dedicated to counter-secession is gradually increasing.[289]

Proposed non-legal approaches include demobilization strategies (e.g., disarming insurgent groups), internal engagement (e.g., political concessions or autonomy arrangements), and external engagement (e.g., diplomatic efforts to deter foreign support for secessionists). The following sections will examine these methods in detail, assessing their effectiveness and limitations.

6.1 *Demobilization (Generally)*

Demobilization can be considered as part of a broader strategy known as disarmament, demobilization, and reintegration, often abbreviated as DDR. DDR programs are primarily designed to address post-conflict situations by helping

287 An Act to give effect to the requirement for clarity as set out in the opinion of the Supreme Court of Canada in the Quebec Secession Reference, S.C. 2000, c. 26.

288 In December 2023, the Indian Supreme Court upheld the Union Government's 2019 decision to repeal the special status accorded to the state of Jammu & Kashmir under Article 370, 2023 INSC 1058.

289 P. Krause, 'The Strategies of Counter-Secession: How States Prevent Independence' 28(3) *Nations and Nationalism* (2022) 788.

ex-combatants transition to civilian life.[290] In addition to their primary focus, these programs serve as significant tools for preventing the escalation of conflicts and can also contribute to preventing secession. The tools developed by DDR practitioners have the potential to assist in managing non-state armed groups throughout the entire conflict cycle. These tools are applicable regardless of the conflict's narrative and during all phases of armed group formation and existence. They encompass a wide range of functions, including early warning systems for conflict prevention, a deeper understanding of the factors driving armed group activities (such as typologies of armed actors), efforts to prevent recruitment, enhancing the resilience of communities vulnerable to recruitment, and the effective implementation of DDR programs, among other aspects.[291]

Disarmament involves the collection, documentation, regulation, and disposal of small arms, ammunition, explosives, and both light and heavy combat weapons from combatants, and frequently from the civilian population as well. It also encompasses the establishment of responsible arms management initiatives.[292] Demobilization is the structured and regulated process of releasing of active combatants from armed forces or other armed groups. The initial phase of demobilization can vary from processing individuals at temporary facilities to gathering troops at designated camps, which are referred to as cantonment sites, encampments, assembly areas, or barracks.[293] Reintegration refers to the process through which former combatants transition to civilian life, obtaining civilian status and gaining access to employment and income sources. This process is fundamentally social and economic, with a flexible duration. Reintegration includes various forms of support, such as financial aid or in-kind compensation, vocational training, and opportunities for income-generating activities.[294]

---

290 InterAgency Working Group on DDR (IAWG – DDR), *Operational Guide to the Integrated Disarmament, Demobilization and Reintegration Standards* (*IDDRS*) (UN 2010) 24.

291 Preventive role of DDR/CVR; <https://www.un.org/peacebuilding/sites/www.un.org.peacebuilding/files/pb_review_thematic_paper_orolsi_ddrs_-_preventative_role_of_ddr_and_cvr-final.pdf>. See also UNGA Res 70/262 (27 Apr. 2016) and UNSC Res 2282(2016) (27 Apr. 2016) reviewing the United Nations peacebuilding architecture. Both texts emphasize that 'a comprehensive approach to (…) inclusive and effective disarmament, demobilization and reintegration programmes (…) is critical to (..) preventing countries from lapsing or relapsing into conflict'.

292 InterAgency Working Group on DDR (n 290) 121–134.

293 *Ibid.* 143–156.

294 *Ibid.* 157–169.

In what way can DDR programs and processes help suppress secessionist conflicts? Firstly, they can assist in disarming armed groups that oppose central authority or seek independence, thereby reducing their capacity to pursue secessionist aims. By removing weapons and demobilizing fighters, DDR programs diminish the operational capabilities of these groups and mitigate the threat of violent secession. However, disarmament is not the central goal of a DDR process. Rather, DDR views combatants as individuals and community members, aiming to create a political, economic, and social environment that discourages armed violence. While disarmament is a step towards this goal, it can be postponed, altered, or skipped if deemed counterproductive.[295] DDR also focuses on reintegrating former combatants into society by providing training and opportunities for civilian life, helping build trust and reduce motivations for secession. Furthermore, DDR promotes inclusive political processes and dialogue between conflicting parties, creating opportunities for peacefully resolving political differences. Finally, DDR programs can foster economic prosperity in post-conflict regions through training and employment opportunities, reducing the appeal of secessionist movements.

The success of a DDR program depends on several prerequisites that must be ensured. DDR should be viewed as part of the political process of peace consolidation and stability assurance, rather than merely a technical activity. Therefore, it must be tailored to the local political context and the economic and social conditions of the country undergoing the DDR process.[296] To ensure the success of the DDR process, several guidelines should be considered.

1. Commitment to Peace: Has the commitment to achieving peace, including that of regional actors, been evaluated?
2. Inclusion in Peace Agreement: Is the DDR process included in the peace agreement, and is there a sufficient agreement on the general framework for DDR policy?
3. Oversight Organization: Does the peace agreement establish an organization responsible for overseeing the implementation of DDR? If not, how will consensus on these matters be reached?
4. International Support: Are major international stakeholders willing to contribute to the development and support of mediation mechanisms and to exert coordinated political, economic, and security pressure to

295 Preventive role of DDR/CVR (n 291).
296 N. Ball, *Disarmament, Demobilization and Reintegration: Mapping Issues, Dilemmas and Guiding Principles*. (Clingendael Institute 2006) 1.

ensure DDR is carried out within the broader peace process? If not, how will these roles be fulfilled?[297]

Demobilization, as a strategy aimed at dismantling secessionist movements, necessitates a clear understanding of their underlying dynamics. Basta identifies three key characteristics that define every secessionist situation.[298]

The first relates to the purpose of secession, which is not always constant. If the goal of achieving independence is to address instrumental issues, such as ensuring the security of the population, resolving this threat could neutralize the secessionist agenda. However, de-escalation becomes more complicated when the goal shifts towards symbolic recognition, especially after creating a public impression that such recognition is unattainable within the existing state's borders. Therefore, the purpose of secession informs the gravity of the secessionist claim and how easy or difficult it is for secessionist organizations to change their course.[299]

The second characteristic pertains to the organizational structure of the independence movement. A unified and well-organized movement is more likely to pivot from pursuing secession to engaging in political dialogue with fewer political costs compared to a movement with multiple factions competing for the same constituency. At the same time, fragmented movements are easier to manipulate and can collapse due to internal clashes.

Finally, Basta points out the post-secession dynamics between secessionist parties and the central government as critical to preventing the recurrence of secessionist claims. He argues that demobilization can be achieved through different constellations of the 'voice' and 'exit' strategy: offering concessions with a potential path to secession, offering concessions while foreclosing the way out of the union, or disregarding both 'voice' and 'exit' options.[300] It is hard to conclusively determine which strategy would yield the most optimal results.

Nevertheless, Basta makes an interesting observation that cognitive and social processes underpin secessionist movements and may be difficult for the opposing party to control. Therefore, demobilization efforts would need to focus on shifting people's conviction that secession is needed or desirable,

297 *Ibid.* 4.

298 K. Basta, 'Secessionist De-Mobilization: From 'Exit' Back to 'Voice'' in R. D. Griffiths, A. Pavković and P. Radan (eds.) *The Routledge Handbook of Self-determination and Secession* (Routledge 2023) 407.

299 *Ibid.* 407–408.

300 *Ibid.*

which is very challenging.[301] If support for secession crosses the 'hegemonic' threshold, any individual or organization dissuaded from secession will face substantial countervailing pressure.[302]

6.2 *Internal and External Engagement*

Internal engagement refers to the involvement of various domestic actor, particularly state institutions and local communities, in preventing and managing conflicts within a state's territory. This approach targets the underlying causes of conflict and aims to build consensus and mutual understanding among those directly affected. Internal engagement typically involves the national government, which implements policies, enforces laws, and undertakes initiatives such as negotiation, peacebuilding, and governance reform to address grievances and maintain stability.

Krause has identified four phases in the process of secession – identity formation, group mobilization, (un)armed struggle, and international recognition. According to Krause, the most advantages undertaking for a state facing potential secession is to prevent the onset of the first phase (identity formation) by obstructing the development of a distinct group identity and instead fostering a cohesive national identity.[303] He emphasizes that cultural assimilation is the earliest and most proactive strategy to prevent secession, working to ensure that religious, ethnic, ideological, and regional identities are not mobilized along separatist lines.[304] In this context, he highlights the example of the United States, which successfully built a unified national identity that superseded multiple regional ones, thereby reducing the likelihood of regional secession.

Another tactic employed by states in the early stages, preceding organized armed secessionist mobilization, is the manipulation of a region's demographic geography to prevent the emergence of a coherent population that might seek autonomy or secession.[305] For ethnic groups, settlement patterns, including where they reside and whether they constitute a majority or minority,

301 Even if the government is correct in some of its arguments, they might still be insufficient. On the other hand, as Mark Twain once said, 'it's easier to fool people than to convince them that they have been fooled'.

302 On the regime threshold and the ideological threshold viewed through the prism of the hegemonic theory of Antonio Gramsci see I. Lustick, 'Thresholds of Opportunity and Barriers to Change in the Right-Sizing of States' in B. O'Leary, I. Lustick, and T. Callaghy (eds.) *Right-sizing the State: The Politics of Moving Borders* (OUP 2001) 74–101.

303 Krause (n 289) 418.

304 *Ibid.*

305 *Ibid.*

play a significant role in shaping both the potential and credibility of a group's efforts to seek independence.[306] When an ethnic group is heavily concentrated in a particular region, particularly if it is their ancestral homeland, the likelihood increases that they will view control over the territory as non-negotiable and pursue independence. In such contexts, civilian displacement becomes a strategic tool for the parent state to disrupt demographic cohesion. This can be done by physically dispersing or detaining members of the national group, separating them from one another and/or restricting their movement. Additionally, the state may move non-separatist civilians into the area to alter regional demographics.[307] Krause also illustrates other methods practiced by states, including administrative organization, banning secessionist political activity, fragmenting secessionist movements, engaging in violent repression, and applying economic pressure.[308]

Internal political, economic and cultural coercion is widely applied against secessionists, with its intensity varying based on the resources and strategic position of the parent state. For instance, China, as powerful state, exerts substantial influence over Taiwan and Tibet. As a major trade partner and investor in Taiwan, China leverages this economic interdependence to apply pressure, using economic benefits or sanctions to influence Taiwan's political decisions. China also controls the flow of tourists to Taiwan, affecting its economy, especially the tourism sector, and thus constituting a pressure mechanism against Taiwanese subversive actions. Additionally, China uses media and information campaigns to promote the narrative of a single Chinese nation and to undermine Taiwanese identity and independence sentiment.[309] In Tibet, China controls the flow of information by restricting access to foreign media and the internet while promoting the Chinese language and culture. It seeks to co-opt local Tibetan leaders into the Chinese Communist Party by offering them positions of power and economic benefits to ensure their loyalty. Furthermore, China maintains significant presence of military and paramilitary forces to maintain order and suppress any uprisings.[310] In cases of the already

306 M. Toft, 'Indivisible Territory, Geographic Concentration, and Ethnic War' 12(2) *Security Studies* (2002) 84–85.

307 Krause (n 289) 419.

308 *Ibid.*

309 However, recent data indicates that Chinese interference is contributing to a growing number of people in Taiwan identifying as 'Taiwanese' rather than 'Chinese'. See Z. Li, 'The Evolution of Identity in Taiwan' *The Diplomat* (25 Dec. 2023) <https://thediplomat.com/2023/12/the-evolution-of-identity-in-taiwan/>.

310 W. W. Smith, *China's Tibet?: Autonomy or Assimilation* (Rowman & Littlefield Publishers 2008) 165–213.

completed secessions that are permanently denied by the central government, states could resort to military force to reestablish control over the lost territory, as Azerbaijan did with Nagorno Karabakh. However, disagreement in the doctrine persists on whether territorial titles and associated rights are permanent and whether aggressive actions taken before or during the conflict can affect the recognized titleholder's claim.[311]

States may also employ less coercive methods, focusing on formal approaches to maintain their claim to the territory. This can involve using legal and judicial avenues to challenge the claim to independent statehood, as well as limiting interactions with breakaway territories to prevent informal legitimization. This strategy has been used by Serbia and Cyprus, both of which continue to assert sovereignty over territories they do not currently control.[312]

Finally, governments may choose to engage constructively with statehood claimants, especially if their demands stem from legitimate grievances. In such cases, the state may attempt to address root causes or mitigate the drivers of secession, even when some factors lie beyond its direct control. This can involve offering financial incentives to the region and its people, providing increased territorial or non-territorial autonomy, implementing consociational arrangements, and allowing political organization based on identity lines. More broadly, these efforts often revolve around the substantive realization of internal self-determination. However, this strategy does not always guarantee success. Recent practices show that while decentralization can contain or prevent self-determination conflicts, it can also, in some cases, exacerbate state disintegration.[313]

Secession prevention methods can also manifest externally through efforts to gather diplomatic support against a region's secession. This involves mobilizing the entire diplomatic apparatus, starting with the Ministry of Foreign Affairs and extending to embassies abroad. Such diplomatic efforts are often costly and challenging for many states A more efficient and cost-effective approach is to leverage a permanent mission at the UN, which can act as a central hub for diplomatic activities. Additionally, annual sessions of the General

---

311 See V. Roeben and S. Janković, 'Validity of Contested Title to Territory in Frozen Conflict Zones: The Case of Nagorno Karabakh with Particular Reference to the 2020 War' 39 *Chinese (Taiwan) Yearbook of International Law and Affairs* (2022) 73–110.

312 See J. Ker-Lindsay, 'Countering Secession' in R. D. Griffiths, A. Pavković and P. Radan (eds.) *The Routledge Handbook of Self-determination and Secession* (Routledge 2023) 389–399.

313 Consult A. Juon and K. M. Bakke, 'Managing Self-determination Struggles Through Decentralization' in R. D. Griffiths, A. Pavković and P. Radan (eds.) *The Routledge Handbook of Self-determination and Secession* (Routledge 2023). See also D. Siroky and J. Cuffe, 'Lost Autonomy, Nationalism and Separatism' 48(1) *Comparative Political Studies* (2015) 4.

Assembly provide a valuable platform for diplomatic engagement, facilitating direct bilateral meetings with other heads of state and government.

States can likewise rely on major international and regional powers to represent their interests in global forums. This is particularly conspicuous with Serbia, which benefits from the support of China and Russia, and Kosovo, which has the backing of the United States and its allies.[314] Enlisting the support of one or more permanent members of the Security Council is particularly advantageous when attempting to block a secessionist entity from gaining full UN membership. Klich defines *de facto* states as those lacking sufficient recognition to gain entry into the United Nations.[315] Pegg, however, notes that this definition excludes borderline cases like Kosovo and Taiwan from the debate.[316] Despite Kosovo being recognized by around a hundred states and Taiwan by twelve, neither entity meets Klich's criteria for statehood, as they do not possess the requisite recognition for UN membership. According to Article 4(2) of the UN Charter, the General Assembly and the Security Council are involved in admitting states to UN, with the General Assembly voting based on the Security Council's recommendation. Therefore, any permanent member of the Security Council can veto the admission of a disputed entity, as exemplified by Russia's stance on Kosovo and China's position on Taiwan.[317]

Secession prevention predominantly concerns thwarting international recognition of the claimant. This can involve various strategies such as leveraging traditional alliances, reciprocity, coercion, financial incentives, and persona inducements. For instance, Guatemalan president Alfonso Portillo pleaded guilty in federal court in New York to accepting $2.5 million in bribes from Taiwanese officials in exchange for assurances of continued diplomatic recognition. Similarly, Vasil Tupurkovski, a prominent Macedonian politician and former member of the Presidency of Yugoslavia, was accused of accepting financial incentives in exchange for Macedonia's diplomatic recognition of Taiwan in 1999.[318] Despite such anomalous cases of states acting in pursuit

314 Consult J. Ker-Lindsay, *The Foreign Policy of Counter Secession: Preventing the Recognition of Contested States* (OUP 2012) 109–117.

315 S. T. Klich, *Normative Standing: De Facto State Identity and International Legitimation* (PhD thesis, Australian National University 2018) 37. See also *The Importance of Recognition for a State: A Critical Appraisal of the Declaratory Theory of Recognition and the Concept of Statehood* (PhD thesis, University of Dundee 2020) 62, 159.

316 S. Pegg, 'How Parent States Prevent Recognition' in R. D. Griffiths, A. Pavković and P. Radan (eds.) *The Routledge Handbook of Self-determination and Secession* (Routledge 2023) 436.

317 *Ibid.*

318 See A. G. Jain, 'Recognition of States in International Law: For Sale' *EJIL:Talk!* (21 Apr. 2014).

of narrow interests, the broader pattern has been one of relative success in denying international recognition to secessionist movements. However, outright defeating these movements has proven more challenging. This duality is likely to persist.

A corollary to the non-recognition strategy in secession prevention is the effort to ostracize would-be states from the international stage. The parent state, often in coordination with its allies, strive to prevent any official interactions with the contested entity, such as establishing economic and diplomatic relations. They also endeavor to block these entities from joining international organizations, which could bolster their status and weaken the parent state's position. Despite these efforts, unofficial engagements often persist. For instance, the EU maintains relations with Abkhazia and Ossetia under its Non-Recognition and Engagement Policy, providing humanitarian assistance to these regions. Greece recognizes Kosovo's passports for humanitarian reasons, while Palestine holds non-member observer state status at the UN. Taiwan is a member of the World Trade Organization under the name 'Separate Customs Territory of Taiwan, Penghu, Kinmen, and Matsu', and the Holy See has had observer status at the Council of Europe since 1970.[319] As Pegg aptly noted, 'parent states can largely run the table on preventing recognition, but they struggle with limited success to deny secessionists some degree of legitimization'.[320]

Allegiance to the parent state in terms of non-recognition or isolating the contested entity (at least formally) depends on several factors. Chief among these are adherence to international legal norms – especially the principle of territorial integrity, specific geopolitical interests, the economic position of the state opposing secession, and its overall reputation. This includes considerations of whether the state has been implicated in systematic and egregious human rights abuses.[321]

It is important to note that the strategy used to counter secession, whether short-term or long-term, coercive or peaceful, is influenced by the intensity of the secessionist movement, its international legitimacy, and the geopolitical posture of the affected state. Consequently, a state might choose not to

---

319 Consult B. Coppieters, 'Engagement Without Recognition' in G. Visoka, J. Doyle and E. Newman (eds.) *Routledge Handbook of State Recognition* (Routledge 2019) 241–252.

320 Pegg (n 316) 429.

321 L. Rohrbach, 'Patterns of Strategic Interaction in Self-determination Disputes: A Comparative Analysis of East Timor, Aceh and West Papua' in R. D. Griffiths and D. Muro (eds.) *Strategies of Secession and Counter-Secession* (ECPR Press 2020) 200–221 (arguing that the international community not only ultimately determines the outcome of self-determination disputes, but also influences the strategies and tactics employed by key actors – particularly in cases where the government is uncompromising).

engage extensively in international lobbying and instead focus on domestic measures to varying degrees, as seen as Spain's differentiated responses to Basque and Catalan separatism, or China's contrasting strategies toward Tibet and Taiwan.[322]

7 Challenges in Utilizing ISD as a Tool to Prevent Secession

This section examines potential obstacles to the hypothesis that secession should be ruled out on the basis of the principle of internal self-determination, particularly in cases when a state complies with this principle.

At first glance, ISD might seem too narrow to satisfy various demands of secessionist entities, rendering it an insufficient or even ill-suited mechanism. For instance, ISD has little to say about past grievances and the subjective sense of belonging to the state, which might have resulted from historical territorial divisions between rulers and states. Groups with a legacy of grievances against the state might find it difficult to trust that their rights will be consistently upheld. Therefore, past injustices or enduring tensions can make them skeptical of remaining within the state, regardless of current accommodations. Furthermore, some groups may feel that their distinct cultural, historical, or national identities are not *adequately* respected or represented. These perceptions may lead to demands for disproportionate political autonomy, enhanced self-governance, or expanded competencies to manage their economic affairs and improve their prosperity. Finally, the desire for international recognition and the benefits that come with being a sovereign state, such as participation in international organizations and the capacity to enter bilateral agreements, can drive groups to pursue independence notwithstanding existing internal self-determination arrangements. Security concerns can also play a role. Most of these motivations coincide with the reasons for secession elaborated in Chapter III.[323]

Although proposing internal self-determination as a method of preventing secession may seem challenging in polarized societies or among groups whose primary aim is independence, it is important to recognize that ISD represents a compromise solution, designed to address a wide range of political, social, economic, and cultural needs. Consequently, the critique of its 'inherent

322 Consult A. Butt, 'State Strategies Against Secessionists' in R. D. Griffiths and D. Muro (eds.) *Strategies of Secession and Counter-Secession* (ECPR Press 2020) 69–83.

323 See 3.1.

insufficiency', intended solely to justify a push toward independence, should not undermine its legitimacy or applicability.

This section will therefore only partially address human desires related to independence. Instead, it will focus on the legal, technical, and theoretical aspects surrounding the concept of ISD. First, its general validity in terms of international law will be considered, followed by an analysis of its precision and universality. The final two subsections will delve into the broader question of ISD's fairness, considering its historical absence and its ostensible tensions with liberal and democratic theories.

7.1 *The Neutrality of Secession Paradigm in International Law*

International law has traditionally regarded the creation or dissolution of states as socio-political phenomena, rather than matters governed by legal rules. From Jelinek onwards, secession has been considered neither explicitly permitted nor prohibited by international law, but as a factual occurrence.[324] Thus, international law does not recognize a right for ethnic, religious, or linguistic groups to secede, nor does it impose specific criteria for secessionist statehood beyond the quadripartite factual framework articulated in the Montevideo Convention. However, these criteria must be more distinctly demonstrated in cases of secession than in instances of state dissolution or devolution (separation with consent). Secession, as a unilateral act carried out without the consent of the parent state, requires the seceding entity to convincingly demonstrate that it has overcome the presumption of the parent state's effectiveness and its claim to territorial integrity.[325]

324 Jellinek expressed it patently: 'Unhaltbarkeit aller Versuche (...) die Entstehung der Staaten juristisch zu konstruieren'. G. Jellinek, *Allgemeine Staatslehre* (first published 1900, O Häring 1966) 263–264, 266. Klafkowski noted: 'State practice generally views the creation of a State as the result of a historical process that is not governed by international law' (own translation). A. Klafkowski, *Prawo Międzynarodowe Publiczne* (PWN 1966) 145–146. Consult also K. Czubocha, *Pojęcie Państwa i Procesy Państwowotwórcze we Współczesnym Prawie Międzynarodowym* (Adam Marszałek 2012) 61–72.

325 J. Crawford, *The Creation of States in International Law* (OUP 2006) 55–70, 97 (seeing effectiveness as a prime statehood criterion) 59–60, 383–384, 443 (arguing for a higher level of independence in the event of secession). See also F. Finck, 'The State between Fact and Law: The Role of Recognition and the Conditions under which It Is Granted in the Creation of New State' XXXVI *Polish Yearbook of International Law* (2016) 51, 53, 59, 74–77 (contending that effectiveness without recognition does not lead to proper statehood and that non-recognized entities are not States – they lack a legal status and ensuing attributes of international legal personality). Similarly, J. d'Aspremont, 'The International Law of Statehood: Craftsmanship for the Elucidation and Regulation of Births and Deaths in the International Society' 29 *Connecticut Journal of International Law* (2014) 207 (suggest-

The perspective of legal ambivalence regarding secession stems from international law being primarily a framework for state-to-state relations, emphasizing territorial integrity and other rules that do not directly govern the actions of non-state actors. As such, groups challenging the territorial integrity of their parent state are not necessarily violating international law. Secession, in this context, has been treated a 'legal fact' rather than a 'legal act', with statehood contingent upon effective control and recognition.[326]

This 'legal vacuum' or 'silence' of international law on secession is in great part conspicuous in the ICJ's conclusion in the *Kosovo* case, where it determined that the 2008 declaration of independence by the 'peoples of Kosovo' did not violate international law.[327] This conclusion led some to infer that the Court applied the *Lotus* principle, which holds that what is not explicitly prohibited is permitted. Judge Simma, however, critiqued the Court for not recognizing the outdated nature of this view,[328] while others, like Peters, suggested that the Court's choice of the term 'non-violation' hinted at a nuanced middle ground, reflecting the broader spectrum of international law, which includes not only prohibitions and permissions but also recommendations and guidelines.[329]

In truth, the Court did not make a definitive ruling on whether Kosovo had a right to secede or met traditional statehood criteria, acknowledging that there was no consensus on the legality of secession. Yet, it indicated that the secession *process* could be illegal if it involved 'egregious violations of norms of general international law', such as those recognized by the UN Security Council in the cases of Rhodesia, Northern Cyprus, and the Republika Srpska.[330] This

ing that a State as a factual situation should not be determined solely by internal, but also by external effectiveness, which, in turn, depends on international recognition).

326 G. Abi-Saab, 'Conclusions' in M. Kohen (ed.) *Secession: International Law Perspectives* (CUP 2006) 471.

327 ICJ, *Accordance with International Law of the Unilateral Declaration of Independence in Respect of Kosovo*, Advisory Opinion, ICJ Rep. 2010, paras 81, 84, 109, 123 (the Court arrived at the conclusion that (…) the authors of the declaration of independence of 17 February 2008 did not act as one of the Provisional Institutions of Self-Government within the Constitutional Framework, but rather as persons who acted together in their capacity as representatives of the people of Kosovo outside the framework of the interim administration).

328 Declaration of Judge Bruno Simma, 79 para 2. See *S.S. 'Lotus*, Judgment No. 9, 1927, PCIJ, Series A, No. 10, 18.

329 Peters, 'Does Kosovo Lie in the Lotus-Land of Freedom?' (n 215) 99 (noting that while 'being in accordance with' the law carries a positive connotation, the assertion that an act does not violate the law maintains a more neutral connotation).

330 *Kosovo Advisory Opinion* (n 327) para 81. See 3.3.2.3.

dictum is in line with earlier state submissions emphasizing that the process of state formation should be evaluated not only on the facts but also on the legality of the methods through which statehood is pursued. The United States, for example, posited that while declarations of independence generally do not violate international law, they could become unlawful if associated with actions like the establishment of an apartheid regime.[331] Thus, international law might intervene earlier in the secession process, regulating the procedural legitimacy of secession.[332]

The challenge to the paradigm of international law's neutrality regarding secession and, more broadly, state creation, has, however, a deeper historical context. The era of decolonization significantly altered this understanding. During this period, the principle of self-determination provided a legal foundation for the creation of new states, affirming the right of peoples under foreign domination to assert independence without needing to meet strict statehood criteria. This represented a shift from perceiving state creation as purely a factual matter to recognizing it as a legal issue rooted in the principles of equality and self-determination.[333]

Contemporary state practice and institutional developments reveal a procedural and normative evolution that has gradually supplemented – though not wholly displaced – the traditionally factual dimensions of secession. While effective control remains a cornerstone of statehood, its application is increasingly mediated by norms favoring negotiated solutions and democratic processes, such as referenda or constitutional pathways to independence. This 'proceduralization' of statehood is exemplified by the consensual dissolutions of the Soviet Union and Czechoslovakia as well as the negotiated separations of Eritrea from Ethiopia, Montenegro from the State Union of Serbia and Montenegro, and South Sudan from Sudan.[334] Further reinforcing this shift, instruments like the 1991 EC Declaration on Recognition explicitly tied statehood legitimacy to human rights, democracy, and the rule of law,

---

331 *Ibid.* Written Statement of the United States of America (17 Apr. 2009) 56. In the similar vein, Written Statement of the Government of Japan (17 Apr. 2009) 3.

332 *Ibid.* Separate Opinion of Judge Jusuf, 220. See also G. Landi, 'Neutrality of International Law Towards Secession: An Old-Fashioned Story or the Beginning of a New Chapter?' 9(7) *ESIL Conference Paper Series* (2017) 6.

333 A. Tancredi, 'A Normative 'Due Process' in the Creation of States Through Secession' in M. Kohen (ed.) *Secession: International Law Perspectives* (CUP 2006) 175. Consult 2.2.2.

334 See J. Vidmar, *Democratic Statehood in International Law: The Emergence of New States in Post-Cold War Practice* (Hart 2013) 235–242. See also J. Vidmar, 'The Scottish Independence Referendum in an International Context' 51 *Canadian Yearbook of International Law* (2014) 259, 262, 272.

signaling a departure from a purely effectiveness-based doctrine.[335] The contested but influential concept of remedial secession adds another layer of normative complexity, requiring evaluative criteria beyond mere factual control (e.g., grave human rights violations) as a justification. Collectively, these developments demonstrate international law's growing engagement with the political, humanitarian, and procedural dimensions of secession, even as it retains its formal neutrality on unilateral claims.[336]

International legal scholarship has likewise acknowledged the influence of international law over the secession process and its outcome.[337] Scholars such as Crawford underline that statehood is not simply a factual matter but a legal status that depends on the application of certain rules and practices. The very act of state creation, therefore, cannot be entirely detached from international law, as it requires conformity with prevailing norms – from human rights to territorial integrity.[338] Tancredi, goes further and proposes a model for 'procedural legitimacy' in secession, stressing that lawful secession must satisfy specific criteria: non-reliance on unlawful foreign intervention; democratic validation, such as through referenda; and respect for *uti possidetis*, ensuring the stability of inherited borders.[339] However, as Landi observes, the practical application of these conditions remains fraught with challenges. For instance, even in cases like *Quebec*, where a referendum was held, opposition from minority groups (e.g., Indigenous peoples and anglophones) complicated claims to democratic legitimacy.[340] Thus, while referenda may enhance

---

335 European Community, 'Declaration of Guidelines on the Recognition of New States in Eastern Europe and in the Former Soviet Union' (16 Dec. 1991), reprinted in 4 *EJIL* 72. See also Independent International Fact-Finding Mission on the Conflict in Georgia (IIFFMCG), The Report, vol. II (2009) 136–137.

336 O. C. Okafor, 'The International Law of Secession and the Protection of the Human Rights of Oppressed Substate Groups: Yesterday, Today and Tomorrow' *Nigerian Yearbook of International Law* (2017) 151–152.

337 Findi and Basir distinguish between the factual occurrence of secession and the legal question of the 'right to secede'. If secession is seen as a domestic issue affecting the survival of a state, they contend, international law may remain neutral. However, according to them the 'right to secede' is considered a legal issue, hence international law could address its legality. P. A. Findi and S. M. Basir, 'Legality of Secession under International Law' 24(5) *International Journal of Psychosocial Rehabilitation* (2020) 2370.

338 Crawford, *The Creation of States* (n 325) 5 (note his infamous saying that 'A State is not a fact in the sense that a chair is a fact; it is a fact in the sense in which it may be said a treaty is a fact: that is, a legal status attaching to a certain state of affairs by virtue of certain rules or practices').

339 Tancredi (n 333) 190–191.

340 Landi (n 332) 8

the perceived legitimacy of secessionist projects, they do not – and cannot – automatically confer a right to secede under international law.[341]

The purported neutrality of international law on secession inevitably touches upon the question of territorial integrity. The ICJ and the Supreme Court of Canada both held that secessionist groups are not bound by the principle of territorial integrity, as this principle governs state-to-state relations.[342] However, the increasing role of non-state actors in international law raises questions about the applicability of territorial integrity to secessionist entities. Shaw, for instance, contends that territorial integrity may now extend to protecting peoples, not just states, reflecting an evolution in the classical Westphalian order.[343]

In conclusion, although secession remains a legally contested and politically fraught issue, international law's traditional stance of neutrality is demonstrably eroding. Today, it regulates both the process and consequences of secession, increasingly incorporating human rights norms, democratic principles, and territorial stability concerns into statehood assessments. Crucially, international law now navigates a dual reality: acknowledging the factual power dynamics of secession while demanding legal legitimacy – a balance that increasingly bridges the gap between effectiveness and justice.

As already observed in Chapter III, the notion of international law's pure neutrality toward secession is both theoretically and empirically untenable. State practice and jurisprudence increasingly categorize secessionist claims along a spectrum – from permitted or justified to disfavored or prohibited.[344]

---

341 A. Peters, 'Sense and Nonsense of Territorial Referendums in Ukraine, and Why the 16 March Referendum in Crimea Does Not Justify Crimea's Alteration of Territorial Status under International Law' *EJIL:Talk!* (16 Apr. 2014).

342 *Kosovo Advisory Opinion* (n 327) para 80. See J. Crawford, 'Response to Experts Reports of the *Amicus Curiae*' in A. Bayefsky (ed.) *Self-determination in International Law: Quebec and Lessons Learned: Legal Opinions* (Kluwer Law International 2000) 157. See also G. Abi-Saab, 'The Effectivity Required of an Entity that Declares its Independence in Order for it to be Considered a State in International Law' in *ibid.* 72–73; A. Pellet, 'Legal Opinion on Certain Questions of International Law Raised by the Reference' in *ibid.* para 19; M. Shaw, 'Re: Order in Council P.C. 1996–1497 of 30 September 1996' in *ibid.* paras 39–41.

343 CR 2009/24, 66. Similarly, Van den Driest (n 217) 162; I. Cismas, 'Secession in Theory and Practice: The Case of Kosovo and Beyond' 2(2) *Goettingen Journal of International Law* (2010) 549–550 fn. 81. Still, only 6 out of 43 states participating in the proceedings argued that territorial integrity actually created such a prohibition for non-state actors. M. Milanović, 'Arguing the Kosovo Case' in M. Woods and M. Milanović (eds.) *The Law and Politics of the Kosovo Advisory Opinion* (OUP 2015) 44.

344 See 3.3. See also M. Milanovic, 'A Footnote on Secession' *EJIL:Talk!* (26 Oct. 2017). Consult Written Statement of the United Kingdom (17 Apr. 2009) para 5.11 ('This is not to say that international law favours the dismemberment of a State's territory, nor, in particular, that

Within this framework, the hypothesis of ISD as a secession-regulation mechanism emerges as less antagonistic than it might initially appear.

7.2 *Threshold for Disallowing Secession and Competent Authority*

ISD has been said to have two secession-prevention incarnations: one tantamount to the blanket denial of secession, and another that guarantees territorial integrity contingent upon the fulfillment of ISD's defining features (free will, inclusiveness, autonomy, and the protection of human rights as outlined in the International Covenants on Human Rights).[345] This raises critical questions: What threshold fulfills ISD to block secession, and can its non-fulfillment justify secession? More specifically, how should the adequacy of inclusiveness, autonomy, and other ISD components be determined, and who is competent to adjudicate such issues? Given these questions have not yet been answered by the doctrine, it is apt to consult institutional practice and scholarly opinions to identify a suitable balance and to suggest competent authorities for evaluating such claims.

Institutions such as the UN Human Rights Committee, the European Court of Human Rights, and the African Commission on Human and Peoples' Rights play a role in enforcing human rights but tend to avoid explicitly linking breaches of ISD to a right of secession. For example, in a number of communications to the African Commission, non-governmental organizations accused Mauritania of persecuting and marginalizing its black population – acts that were framed as discriminatory and as constituting a denial of the principle of equality of peoples enshrined in Article 19 of the African Charter.[346] The Commission concluded that the information made available to it did not allow it to establish with certainty the violation of Article 19 of the Charter in the forms alleged. However, it identified and condemned the existence of discriminatory practices against certain groups of the Mauritanian population.[347] Despite this, the Commission was reluctant to elaborate on potential far-reaching consequences of the breach Article 19. The preponderance of the territorial integrity principle is also evident in the Commission's decision in the *Katanga* case, where the Commission was unwilling to establish a breach of Article 13(1) – the right to participate in government – yet it did elaborate

it favours secessionist claims. Rather, international law favours the territorial integrity of States in the interests of stability and the peaceful settlement of disputes, including disputes arising within a State'.) *Favoritism* in itself deviates from the neutrality thesis.

345 See 4.2.

346 ACHPR, *Malawi African Association and Others v. Mauritania,* Communication Nos. 54/91-61/91-96/93-98/93-164/97_196/97-210/98 (2000).

347 *Ibid.* para 142.

on the potential consequences of such a breach. The statement that 'in the absence of *concrete* evidence of violations of human rights *to the point* that the territorial integrity of Zaire should be called to question' implies that a violation must be substantial to warrant considerations of secession.[348] In this context, it can be concluded that, like other international bodies, the African Commission generally confines itself to identifying rights violations and urging the concerned state to take necessary legislative and regulatory measures to address the violations.[349] On the other hand, when allegations are framed in conjunction with the right to self-determination, a breach, even if identified, is deemed insufficient to trigger secession. The high threshold for secession – or conversely, the relatively low threshold for maintaining territorial integrity – has also been emphasized by proponents of the theory of remedial secession.[350] Beyond the currently undefined substantive threshold for violations of fundamental rights, which must be 'gross and systematic,[351] there exists a further barrier in the form of a procedural threshold. This requires the exhaustion of all alternative measures that would preserve the territorial integrity of the state before secession can be considered. Finally, while the international human rights framework promotes non-discrimination and the protection of fundamental rights, it stops short of endorsing secession in cases of ISD failures.[352] Moreover, it remains doubtful whether autonomy arrangements can be scrutinized for this purpose, given the absence of an international legal obligation to establish such arrangements.

Remedies for the denial of ISD should thus primarily be sought within the framework of ISD itself, through actions towards the cessation of persisting

---

348 ACHPR, *Katangese Peoples' Congress v. Zaïre*, Communication No. 75/92 (1995) para 6. See also ACHPR, *Kevin Ngwanga Gumne et al. v. Cameroon* Comm. Communication No. 266/2003 (2009) paras 194–198.

349 F. Ouguergouz and D. L. Tehindrazanarivelo, 'The Question of Secession in Africa' in M. Kohen (ed.) *Secession: International Law Perspectives* (CUP 2006) 275.

350 Dimitrijević, *Savremeno Shvatanje* (n 206) 36; B. Simma (ed.) *The Charter of the United Nations: A Commentary* (OUP 1995) 58; M. Weller, *Escaping the Self-determination Trap* (Martinus Nijhoff Publishers 2008) 59. Tomuschat equated the conditions for the permissibility of humanitarian intervention with the conditions under which a group suffering grave discrimination may invoke a right to self-determination and secession. C. Tomuschat, 'Secession and Self-determination' in M. Kohen (ed.) *Secession: International Law Perspectives* (CUP 2006) 44.

351 See 3.3.3.1.

352 R. C. A. White, 'Self-determination: Time for a Re-Assessment?' 28(2) *Netherlands International Law Review* (1981) 164 (notes that a high degree of discrimination reflects the status of secession as a last, remedial resort, while lesser degrees of discrimination should be processed through the international human rights protection system).

violations. Ideally, such efforts would be supplemented by the implementation of positive measures to compensate for the prior denial of rights. Alternatively, or concurrently solutions within another interrelated segment of ISD might be proposed. For example, the introduction of an autonomy regime in cases involving racial discrimination. Negotiations are also highlighted as a means to realize ISD.[353] Raič pointed to the example of the former Yugoslav republics, where the international community, particularly the European Community and its member states, initially deemed the declarations of independence by Slovenia and Croatia premature. The Brioni Agreement established that their aspirations should have been addressed within the framework of Yugoslavia, emphasizing negotiations as the preferred course of action.[354] In the same vein, Kosovo's independence has been criticized for failing to exhaust negotiation processes and for not implementing alternative territorial arrangements that could have upheld ISD. These shortcomings, among other factors, have contributed to Kosovo's standing as a controversial precedent in international law.[355]

Beyond the challenge of qualitatively and quantitatively identifying provisional ISD counter-secession conditions and establishing the threshold necessary to safeguard territorial integrity, an equally pressing issue concerns the authority competent to adjudicate the legitimacy of secession claims and assess a state's compliance with ISD? This presents a profoundly intricate question that exposes the limitations of international law.

Proposals often suggest that the International Court of Justice could serve as an impartial arbiter.[356] However, the ICJ's procedural mechanisms pose significant barriers for secessionist groups. The Court operates under two primary frameworks: contentious jurisdiction, where one state files a claim against another, and advisory jurisdiction, where the Court issues legal opinions at the request of a competent UN body. Neither mechanism permits a secessionist group to bring a claim directly before the ICJ, as such groups lack statehood status and thus cannot initiate proceedings. In academic discourse,

353 Raič (n 138) 371.

354 *Ibid.*

355 See S. Oeter, 'The Kosovo Case' (n 102) 65–67; S. Trifunovska, 'The Impact of the 'Kosovo Precedent' on Self-determination Struggles' in J. Summers (ed.) *Kosovo: A Precedent?* (Brill 2011) 384.

356 See, for example, A. Coleman, 'Determining the Legitimacy of Claims for Self-determination: A Role for the International Court of Justice and the Use of Preconditions' 6(1) *St Antony's International Review* (2010); D. Sloss, 'Using International Court of Justice Advisory Opinions to Adjudicate Secessionist Claims' 42(2) *Santa Clara Law Review* (2002).

the potential utility of advisory opinions has been highlighted as an indirect means of addressing disputes between parent states and secessionist entities.[357] For instance, a UN body sympathetic to the group's cause (e.g., the General Assembly) could request an opinion on the legality of the state's conduct under ISD norms. Yet, this introduces a political dimension, as the likelihood of such a request depends on the geopolitical alignment of the secessionist group's supporters.

Sloss proposes the creation of an 'International Court of Self-determination' to address claims of self-determination violations.[358] While this idea holds potential as a long-term solution, it is currently unrealistic due to political and institutional hurdles. The General Assembly seems more suited to establish rules for self-determination claims, though Ablan highlights its limitations, such as geopolitical interests and the non-binding nature of its resolutions, which hinder effective implementation. Ablan's alternative 'signal and affirm' method proposes that the GA outlines principles in resolutions, enabling the International Court of Justice to adjudicate disputes based on these principles.[359] This method could balance institutional strengths and weaknesses of the UN system.

Under this approach, the GA could adopt a declaration on the criteria for ISD. In cases where a minority claims denial of ISD, the ICJ could assess secession requests by applying GA-established criteria, supplemented by reports from international bodies or human rights organizations.

Notwithstanding these theoretical proposals, the practical consequences of ISD denial remain poorly defined. Current doctrine and practice have only identified tentative conditions for a state to fulfill on its territory. While it is generally accepted that states must realize ISD in good faith and cooperate with international organizations, neither legal scholarship nor state practice has established a clear threshold for safeguarding territorial integrity. This threshold cannot be readily inferred, even by analogy, from the remedial secession theory. Logically, such a threshold would be relatively low, especially given that not all components of ISD are regarded as mandatory under international law and that a breach of ISD should, in essence, be accompanied by other 'gross and systematic' human rights violations to trigger for secession. Additionally, all non-secessionist remedies must first be exhausted. However, if ISD violations are systemic, persistent, and irremediable, one could argue for

357 Sloss (n 356) 357.

358 *Ibid.* 369.

359 R. Ablan, 'Signal and Affirm: How the United Nations Should Articulate the Right to Remedial Secession' 45(1) *Vanderbilt Journal of International Law* (2012) 236.

secession.[360] Still, the academic and institutional inertia in indicating a tentative required threshold of ISD, which would suffice to prevent secession, could be translated as lending support to the orthodox version of ISD.

7.3 *The Universality of the Rule*

Another significant challenge to the validity of the counter-secessionist hypothesis of internal self-determination lies in its universality. While the breadth of the right to self-determination has generally been assessed in terms of its recipients, the universality of ISD concerns its global reception and interpretation. This raises questions such as: Can we distinguish between Western and non-Western perspectives on ISD and does ISD carry anti-secession connotations everywhere? Additionally, to what extent does differential state compliance with ISD obligations undermine the purported equilibrium between territorial integrity and self-determination claims?

Attending to the first of these interconnected dilemmas, it can be argued that a residual distinction persists in how Western and Global South states perceive self-determination. Western states have traditionally placed greater emphasis on the internal aspect of self-determination, while Third World countries considered the application of self-determination in its external aspect to be of greater significance. Cassese once observed, 'to socialist countries, self-determination means only 'external' self-determination and only for peoples subject to colonial or racist rule or to foreign occupation'.[361] Accordingly, the fact that there might be states that do not recognize the concept of ISD at all can be problematic for the validity of the posed hypothesis, especially in its qualified variant.

Nonetheless, it is very important to highlight that attitudes towards ISD are evolving. As shown in other parts of this Chapter and will be demonstrated in Chapter V, the normative weight of ISD is increasingly accentuated. Even where not explicitly named, it is often implicit in institutional arrangements and emerging norms. The historical context explains early resistance to ISD in the Global South. For post-colonial states, self-determination was initially synonymous with liberation from colonial rule – a strictly external conception focused on sovereignty and non-intervention. This aligned with both the

360 Raič observed that according to contemporary international law, there are no legal remedies for the implementation of the right to self-determination at the international level, and such legal remedies are very rare at the national level as well. What remains are primarily means outside the sphere of law. Raič (n 138) 371.

361 A. Cassese, *UN Law, Fundamental Rights: Two Topics in International Law* (Martinus Nijhoff Publishers 1979) 140.

decolonization imperative and the prevailing Cold War-era legal framework.[362] Given the slow and contested process of decolonization – often resisted by Western powers, many of which were themselves under authoritarian regimes at the time – broader interpretations of self-determination (e.g., as ISD) were understandably marginal in the early post-WWII period.[363] In fact, Western states only tentatively began to engage with ISD during this era, and even then, merely as a complement to the dominant independence paradigm.[364]

The roots of ISD can actually be traced back to a 1950 initiative by Saudi Arabia and Afghanistan before the Third Committee of the General Assembly. Saudi Arabia proposed that the Human Rights Committee study how self-determination could apply universally – ensuring freedom for all peoples, not only those under colonial rule.[365] This reveals an early Global South perspective that viewed external and internal self-determination as interconnected: political independence from colonial rule was seen as a necessary but *insufficient* condition for genuine self-determination; and that both newly independent states and established sovereign powers bore obligations to uphold self-determination internally.[366]

In any case, the former emphasis laid on ESD by the Third World and socialist states, as once stressed by Cassese, should be re-evaluated. First of all, many former socialist states (e.g. Poland, Czechia, Romania) have since integrated into the Western political order, adopting its broader interpretations of self-determination. Second, and more critically, a paradigm shift in understanding the right to self-determination has emerged globally, including among traditionally ESD-focused states. For instance, India's 1979 reservation to Article 1 of the Covenants on Human Rights stipulated that the right to self-determination applied only to peoples under foreign domination, not to sovereign states or groups within them. However, in 1995, India formally acknowledged that the RSD encompasses both external and internal aspects, though it emphasized

362 *Ibid.* 314–315.

363 E.g. Portugal held onto its African colonies, including Angola, Mozambique, and Guinea-Bissau, until the mid-1970s. The Carnation Revolution in Portugal in 1974 led to the rapid decolonization of its overseas territories.

364 10 GAOR, 1955, 3rd Cmttee 643rd mtg., UN Doc. A/C.3/SR.643 (Belgium) paras 8–14; 10 GAOR, 1955, 3rd Cmttee 652nd mtg., UN Doc. A/C.3/SR.652 (United Kingdom) paras 16–24; 10 GAOR, 1955, 3rd Cmttee 674th mtg., UN Doc. A/C.3/SR.674 (Canada) paras 13–16.

365 Draft 1st International Covenant on Human Rights and measures of implementation: Afghanistan and Saudi Arabia: Revised amendment to the joint draft resolution submitted by Brazil, Turkey and the United States of America, UN Doc. A/C.3/L.88/ReV.l (7 Nov. 1950). See also UN Doc. A/C.3/SR.309 (9 Nov. 1950) paras 51–57.

366 K. Senaratne, 'Internal Self-determination in International Law: A Critical Third-World Perspective' 3 *Asian Journal of International Law* 319, 323.

that the internal dimension (ISD) must operate within the framework of territorial integrity.[367] In the 2004 Geneva discussions, India framed the RSD as the right to participate in national life through democratic institutions, but explicitly divorced it from any secessionist implications.[368] India's trajectory reflects a broader trend: while states now accept ISD's relevance, they deliberately frame it as a territorial integrity-preserving mechanism.

In the proceedings before the ICJ regarding Israel's occupation of Palestine, Egypt argued that the right to self-determination confers the entitlement to determine both external and internal political status, and that it 'can only be exercised by peoples within specific territorial units'.[369] The League of Arab States explicitly mentioned internal self-determination as applicable law in this case, which entitles Palestinians to equal treatment, prohibits discrimination (including apartheid), and grants various political and minority rights to protect and preserve their distinct group identity.[370] China, on the other hand, belongs to a group that staunchly insists on limiting the application of the RSD to 'peoples under colonial rule or foreign occupation', likely to exclude any right to remedial secession through this phrasing.[371] Although this narrow, one-off interpretation of the RSD could, in theory, be sufficient to refute ISD's counter-secession implications (by virtue of its non-recognition), the situation is not entirely one-dimensional. China's official stance on the 'pluralistic unity of the Chinese nation' and the exercise of the RSD 'by the *whole* Chinese people' points to the orthodox version of ISD, which is historically grounded,[372] while the acknowledgement before the CESCR that minorities inside China may exercise the RSD through autonomy (without such an obligation on the

---

367 Human Rights Committee, 'Addendum to the Third Periodic Reports of States Parties Due in 1992 India', UN Doc. CCPR/C/76/Add.6 (17 Jun. 1995) 12–13.

368 Statements Made by Mr. Hardeep Singh Puri, Ambassador and Permanent Representative of India at the 60th Session of the Commission on Human Rights (15 Mar. 2004) <https://www.mea.gov.in/Speeches-Statements.htm?dtl/3124/Statements+Made+by+Mr+Hardeep+Singh+Puri+Ambassador+and+Permanent+Representative+of+India+at+the+60th+Session+of+the+Commission+on+Human+Rights+Geneva>.

369 ICJ, *Legal Consequences arising from the Policies and Practices of Israel in the Occupied Palestinian Territory, including East Jerusalem,* Advisory Opinion, ICJ Rep. 2024, Written submission of the Arab Republic of Egypt (25 Jul. 2023) para 216.

370 *Ibid.* Written Submission of the League of Arab States (20 Jul. 2023) 4.d.

371 *Ibid.* Written Statement of the People's Republic of China (25 Jul. 2023) paras 37–38. In the same vein, *Kosovo Advisory Opinion* (n 327) Written Statement of the People's Republic of China (16 Apr. 2009) 3–7.

372 The Common Program of the Chinese People's Political Consultative Conference, Preamble; the 1954 Constitution of the People's Republic of China, Preamble, Articles 2, 3, 6, 7. See L. Wang, 'The Right to Self-determination in the Chinese Context' in *Self-determination and Minority Rights in China* (Brill 2019) 108–109.

state) alludes to an imperfect version of a qualified vision of ISD.[373] Consequently, the apprehension of the RSD as ISD is gaining momentum and the RSD cannot be seen solely through the prism of the decolonization process.

Of higher relevance are the divergences transpiring in connection with the interpretation of ISD, with some viewing it exclusively as a state's obligation toward its population, while others interpret it as a right protecting territorial integrity, either in its orthodox or qualified form. In the instance of a broader applicability, a challenge arises in establishing ISD as a clear and narrow principle, given that its position is usually inferred from other norms or that states concurrently use a plethora of principles to oppose secession. Sri Lanka, for instance, in its report to the Human Rights Committee recognized ISD as enshrined in the 1992 United Nations Declaration on the Rights of the Minorities and the 1993 Vienna Declaration and Programme of Action, yet stipulated that 'this does not imply that Sri Lanka countenance it as a universal norm that provides a basis for unilateral secession leading to the fragmentation of existing nation states'.[374] Iran in the *Kosovo* case stated that 'the right to self-determination for minorities is an internal one and means their entitlement to democracy and human rights and does not involve any right to secession. This means that the right of self-determination is not a principle of exclusion or separation but a principle of inclusion'.[375]

Such stances, although underpinned by the qualified version ideal, do not go as far to uncritically link territorial integrity with respect for ISD. On the African Continent, the OAU Charter emphasizes the territorial integrity of states and essentially denies the right to secession, whereas the African Charter gives a certain potential to that right. In recent years, however, the emphasis on the

373 China was once prompted by the Committee on Economic, Social and Cultural Rights to clarify the extent to which advocacy for self-determination by officially recognized ethnic minorities – such as Tibetans, Mongols, and Uygurs – is considered lawful under its domestic legal regime. In response, China asserted that it respects freedom of speech and emphasized that 'regional self-rule is practiced where ethnic minorities live in compact communities with the establishment of autonomous organs and the exercise of the right to self-rule'. See Replies by the Government of the People's Republic of China to the list of issues (E/C.12/Q/CHN/1) to be taken up in connection with the consideration of the initial report of the People's Republic of China concerning the rights referred to in articles 1–15 of the International Covenant on Economic, Social and Cultural Rights, UN Doc. E/1990/5/Add.59 (4 Mar. 2004) 5–6.

374 Human Rights Committee, 'Consideration of reports submitted by States parties under article 40 of the Covenant, Fourth periodic report of Sri Lanka' (2002) Doc. CCPR/C/LKA/2002/4, para 2.

375 *Kosovo Advisory Opinion* (n 327) Written Statement of the Islamic Republic of Iran (17 Apr. 2009) para 4.1.

internal aspect of self-determination seems to bring these two positions closer together.[376] Still, it remains to be seen whether the still ill-defined scope and content of internal self-determination will be seen as an alternative to secession or whether the protection of territorial integrity will come to depend on the articulation of a more precisely defined threshold for the implementation of ISD.[377]

Finally, the discrepancies can likewise occur in the way a particular state sees components of ISD and how it implements them to prevent secession. While generalized rules, principles, and ideals can be identified through doctrinal understanding of ISD and state practice – such as the adoption and ratification of human rights treaties – states implement more specific mechanisms with varying intensity, shaped by unique social, political, and economic conditions.[378] This leads to a conclusion that the implementation of ISD, also as a secession-prevention method, is more individualistic than universal and should be assessed on a case-by-case basis.[379] Mongolia, for instance, in one of its reports mentioned the registration of 692 religious organizations and noted that the State Great Hural, the highest organ of state power, 'shall consist of 76 members and the members of the State Great Hural shall be elected by citizens of Mongolia entitled to vote, on the basis of universal, free, direct suffrage by secret ballot for a term of four years'.[380] Brazil highlighted policies to improve conditions for vulnerable groups, such as indigenous peoples and Roma communities, and introduced the Bolsa Família program for income transfer.[381] Although these countries do not themselves exhibit secessionist tendencies, they illustrate that ISD can be seen as a 'toolbox' offering various arrangements, embracing autonomy or federalism, to meet the aspirations of minorities while preserving state boundaries and thereby reducing the risk of violent conflicts.[382]

---

376 Ouguergouz and Tehindrazanarivelo (n 349) 261.

377 Cf. 5.3.2.2.1.

378 See 5.5.

379 Shikova, 'Practicing Internal Self-determination' (n 117) 251–263. See also N. Skikova, 'Analysis of the Systems for Representation of Minorities in Public Administration: The Case of the Republic of North Macedonia' 22(1) *Journal on Ethnopolitics and Minority Issues in Europe* (2023) 94–125.

380 Human Rights Committee, 'Consideration of reports submitted by States parties under article 40 of the Covenant, Sixth periodic report of Mongolia' (2016) Doc. CCPR/C/MNG/6, paras 5, 9.

381 Human Rights Committee, 'Consideration of reports submitted by States parties under article 40 of the Covenant, Third periodic report of Brazil' (2021) Doc. CCPR/C/BRA/3, 9.

382 M. Weller, 'Self-determination and Peace-Making' in M. Weller, M. Retter and A. Varga (eds.) *International Law and Peace Settlements* (CUP 2021) 408–424. Weller, however, does

However, the implementation of ISD in practice is not universal. Many human rights associated with ISD, such as freedom of expression, religious equality, and women's rights, continue to be violated globally. In some states, like China (in relation to Uyghurs and Tibetans), ISD is disregarded, and secession is opposed outright.[383] In conflict-affected regions, such as Yemen or Cameroon, the lack of respect for ISD exacerbates secessionist tensions.[384]

In conclusion, while the principle of internal self-determination is broadly recognized across diverse regions, its interpretation and implementation are shaped by distinct economic, political, and cultural contexts. These contextual nuances permeate all components of ISD – from participatory governance and inclusivity to autonomy and the protection of fundamental human rights. In many Third World countries, the legacy of colonialism complicates the full realization of ISD, often reinforcing a prioritization of territorial integrity. Nonetheless, these countries increasingly acknowledge the importance of internal self-determination, particularly the rights of communities to participate in decision-making processes and preserve their cultural heritage. As such, the scope of ISD's universal relevance is gradually expanding, including in its counter-secession manifestation, with each state tailoring its approach to fit its specific national context.

7.4 *Applicability in Existing v. Aspiring States: Exploring Incommensurability*

This subchapter questions the fairness of applying modern internal self-determination norms to prohibit secession today, given that most existing states achieved sovereignty without facing comparable legal barriers. While remedial secession theorists tie historical injustices to present claims, the counter-secessionist application of ISD risks entrenching inequity by holding contemporary minorities to standards their rulers never faced.

Owing to its novelty, ISD in its counter-secession incarnation was rarely considered in the past as a right of states. It might have been seen as a right of the people, but only within the imperfect and piecemeal ambit of human rights protection. Though early modern thinkers like de las Casas, de Vitoria, and Diderot voiced concerns about human rights in colonial contexts, advocating

---

not exclude other variants allowing for secession, should the continued unity of a state become unviable. 431.

383 OHCHR, 'Assessment of Human Rights Concerns in the Xinjiang Uyghur Autonomous Region, People's Republic of China' (31 Aug. 2022).

384 C. Buchanan, 'Pioneering Peace Pathways: Making Connections to End Violent Conflict' 29 *Accord* (2020) 54, 56.

for the protection of indigenous peoples,[385] ISD as a more comprehensive concept emerged only in the 20th century. Besides, early states did not have a general legal obligation to respect territorial integrity, and territorial configurations were often determined by wars or agreements rather than legal norms.[386]

Even during the Renaissance, European rulers occasionally invoked the protection of religious minorities to legitimize territorial claims, but the explicit defence of territorial integrity based on the rights of subjects or populations was not common.[387] Rulers more often justified territorial integrity through dynastic claims or legal agreements, rather than by appealing to the protection of individual or collective rights. The Holy Roman Empire and the Spanish Empire, for instance, enforced unity through religious conformity, while

385 See B. de las Casas, *A Short Account of the Destruction of the Indies* (1552), reprinted in (Penguin Books Ltd. 1992); F. de Vitoria, 'Relectiones' (lecture) (1538–1539) elaborated by A. Anghie, 'Francisco De Vitoria and the Colonial Origins of International Law' 5(3) *Social & Legal Studies* 321–335; D. Diderot, *Encyclopédie ou Dictionnaire raisonné des sciences, des arts et des métiers* (1751–1772).

386 Marxsen contends that the concept of territorial integrity emerged as a general principle of international law during the course of the 19th century. He refers to Heffter's 1844 treatise on European public international law, who spoke of the territorial principle (*ius territorii*) that grants a 'right to integrity or inviolability of states'. Marxsen also refers to the 1856 'General Treaty for the Re-Establishment of Peace between Austria, France, Great Britain, Prussia, Sardinia and Turkey, and Russia' in which the signatories committed themselves to 'respect the independence and territorial integrity of the Ottoman Empire'. C. Marxsen, 'Territorial Integrity in International Law – Its Concept and Implications for Crimea' (2015) 75 *ZaöRV* 7–8. Note that almost all 20th century legal instruments link territorial integrity with non-use of force. Article 10 of the Covenant of the League of Nations declared that 'the Members of the League undertake to respect and preserve as against external aggression the territorial integrity and existing political independence of all the Members of the League'. Article 11 of the 1933 Montevideo Convention on Rights and Duties of States set forth that 'the territory of a State is inviolate and may not be the object of military occupation nor of other measures of force imposed by another State directly or indirectly or for any motive whatever even temporary'. Article 2(4) of the United Nations Charter underlined that 'all Members shall refrain in their international relations from the threat or use of force against the territorial integrity or political independence of any State'.

387 For instance, the Edict of Nantes issued by King Henry IV of France in 1598 granted religious tolerance and certain rights to Protestant Huguenots. See G. Campbell (ed.) *The Oxford Dictionary of the Renaissance* (OUP 2003). In India, the Mughal Empire, especially under Emperor Akbar (1556–1605), was known for its policy of religious tolerance and inclusiveness. Akbar abolished the jizya tax on non-Muslims and included Hindus in his administration. See C. B. Asher and C. Talbot, *India Before Europe* (CUP 2006) 115, 152.

economic and military factors often proved decisive in maintaining territorial control.[388]

The decolonization process, which granted independence to former colonies based on the *uti possidetis juris* principle, did not consider ethnic divisions or whether new states would respect internal self-determination of their peoples. However, where state boundaries were arbitrarily or forcefully imposed, a critical dilemma arises: would it not be fair to allow the possibility of correcting current borders *without* recourse to ISD?

This tension over historical justice extends to theories advocating a primary right to secession. Although these theories encounter resistance nowadays due to the prevailing legal emphasis on territorial integrity and ISD, it is worth interrogating whether the legal tools used to prevent secession align with demands for retrospective justice, especially considering that these principles were not universally endorsed when many modern states were created.

Historically, the absence of international organizations, like the United Nations, meant that secessionist entities often lacked formal mechanisms for recognition, and relied on military power and de facto governance. This raises a question of why new state-candidates should face a more difficult – political or legal – obstacle than those created under different historical circumstances?

UN independent expert de Zayas, in his report, emphasized the imperative of timely delineation of borders to preempt future conflicts. He noted that borders sometimes result from unsaintly means and should not be seen as immutable.[389] While protecting territorial integrity is a core principle, it does not imply that borders cannot change, especially in post-colonial contexts where boundaries frequently fail to correspond with ethnic, cultural, or linguistic divisions. Such misalignments, according to de Zayas, may necessitate revisions in line with Article 2(3) of the UN Charter, which obligates states to resolve disputes peacefully.[390] In his view, the principle of territorial integrity should likewise not be a pretext for neglecting the responsibility to protect human rights.[391] Equality and non-discrimination are vital to the internal stability of states; however, these principles alone may not suffice to preserve unity in cases where populations no longer wish to remain part of the same political community. A *fortiori* rigid adherence to *uti possidetis juris*, designed

388 M. Herrero Sánchez, 'Spanish Theories of Empire: A Catholic and Polycentric Monarchy' in J. Tellkamp (ed.) *A Companion to Early Modern Spanish Imperial Political and Social Thought* (Brill's Companions to European History, vol. 21, 2020) 17–52.

389 A. De Zayas, 'Promotion of a democratic and equitable international order: note / by the Secretary-General', UN Doc. A/69/272 (7 Aug. 2014) para 51.

390 *Ibid.* para 72.

391 *Ibid.* para 70.

to 'freeze' borders, risks exacerbating claims of secession, especially if based on current violations of ISD.[392]

Busquets, referring to multinational contracts and drawing on Locke and Rawls' social contract theories, contrasts historical and contemporary state formation in terms of legal-political entitlements and obstacles. He suggests that in the past, political communities were often formed by force, such as through colonization or conquest,[393] but some states were formed voluntarily (e.g. the Polish-Lithuanian Commonwealth or Czechoslovakia). In such cases, ISD did not impede separation, as it did not exist at the time. Busquets highlights that secession only began to attract significant attention in political theory in the late 20th century, with thinkers such as Rawls and Dworkin typically conceptualizing states as uninational entities, sidelining the complexities of multinational societies.[394]

To address this gap, Busquets proposes that the idea of sovereignty be reconsidered, emphasizing the role of the people (*demos*) over the state power (*krates*).[395] This would potentially open the door to secession referenda, a position increasingly debated in contemporary political and legal scholarship. Nevertheless, the mainstream international law remains resistant: it broadly rejects secession rooted in historical grievances, and it does not offer mechanisms to correct borders of existing states. As such, ISD fits within the mainstream argument – it advocates for *demotic pluralism,* which confers substantial sovereign powers on other ethnic groups within the state, albeit short of independence.[396]

Ultimately, the potential historical bias inherent in introducing new norms to prohibit secession must be interrogated through the dual lenses of legal evolution and the foundational values of the contemporary international order.

---

392 A. Stilz, 'Decolonization and Self-determination' (2015) 32(1) *Social Philosophy and Policy* 1–18. See also Peters, 'The Principle of *Uti Possidetis Juris*' (n 227) 95–137.

393 Busquets, *Morality and Legality of Secession* (n 199) 12–13.

394 Note that contractual unions often specified indissolubility. The Polish Lithuanian Commonwealth was created with the aim of forming a lasting and stable political union between the Kingdom of Poland and the Grand Duchy of Lithuania. See Act of the Union of Lublin (1569). See also the Treaty of Versailles (1871) on the unification of Germany.

395 Busquets, *Morality and Legality of Secession* (n 199) 10–11. Note that seeing states through the lens of the idea of constitutionalism and vesting popular sovereignty in constituent people established by arbitrary *faits accomplis,* in fact, constitutes a tacit approval of the previous territorial configurations. See W. Kymlicka, *Multicultural Citizenship* (n 183) 28; W. Kymlicka, *Politics in the Vernacular* (n 149) 221.

396 In contrast, *demotic monism* is the term which identifies a single demos or sovereign people within the State, hence, is closely related to the idea of nation-State. S. Tierney, *Constitutional Referendums. The Theory and Practice of Republican Deliberation* (OPU 2012) 138.

While acknowledging the inherent tensions between self-determination and territorial integrity, which have thus far been addressed through a suboptimal balancing approach, the progressive development of international legal should also be considered, especially if it aims to foster positive social change and enhance the coherence of the scientific discipline. Historically, ISD was not recognized as a codified right in its modern form. Yet the gradual entrenchment of human rights and participatory governance norms has elevated ISD into a broadly accepted principle – one that now anchors critical debates on secession, even as it exposes the paradox of applying present-day standards to redress historical inequities.

7.5 *In Contradiction with Liberal Democracy?*

This section deliberates whether the counter-secession ramifications of ISD accord with liberal and democratic theories. At first glance, ISD appears to conflict with liberal theory, which prioritizes individual interests, whereas ISD seeks to protect collective identities and states, particularly in its orthodox counter-secession form.[397] As a fundamentally collective right, self-determination can hardly be squared with liberal theories grounded in 'methodological individualism', a paradigm which ascribes ontological primacy only to individuals.[398] At the centre of liberal theory is the individual as the 'supreme entity of any political unit', whose rights and freedoms must be respected and protected by the state.[399]

Liberal theorist Buchanan has attempted to bridge this divide by extending his conception of justificatory individualism, where groups do not directly hold rights, but rather their interests are a shorthand for the interests of individuals within the group.[400] In this view, the 'group agent' is merely an extrinsic representation of the collective interests of its members. Buchanan, though, rejects using cultural integrity as a rationale for collective self-determination, arguing

397 The orthodox version of ISD is de facto tantamount to the protection of territorial integrity since it is not contingent on the meaningful implementation of ISD. See 4.3.1.

398 The fundamental moral principle of 'justificatory individualism' lies in the 'moral equality principle', which relies on the Kantian premise that 'all persons are entitled to equal respect and concern' and that 'each is to be treated as an end'. See A. Preda, 'Group Rights and Group Agency' (2012) 9(2) *Journal of Moral Philosophy* 230; R. Tuomela, *Social Ontology* (OUP 2013) 10.

399 K. Senaratne, *Internal Self-determination in International Law History, Theory, and Practice* (CUP 2021) 14.

400 For Buchanan, groups are in principle devoid of moral rights, so the right to self-determination of indigenous people is a 'legal right'. Buchanan, *Justice, Legitimacy, and Self-determination* (n 195) 255–256.

that it creates an irresolvable conflict between respect for individual rights and cultural preservation.[401]

Liberal theory generally advocates for a political order derived from the consent of the governed, conceptualized through a social contract where individuals agree to form a society that protects their rights and promotes the common good. Under this framework, the state's legitimacy stems from respecting individual rights, including life, liberty, and property. Since liberal democracy is based on the consent of free and equal citizens, the counter-secession narrative of ISD appears to contradict this by limiting individuals' ability to secede from a state even when certain standards are met.[402]

However, liberal and democratic theories, while championing individual liberty, also recognize the need to balance this with considerations of political stability, the rights of other groups, and international law. Thus, liberalism's seeming endorsement of external self-determination is not necessarily a negation of ISD, but requires careful, context-sensitive application. The generic understanding of liberal and democratic theories often overlooks the diversity of approaches within these categories and the complexities they entail.[403] For example, democratic processes can result in the election of non-democratic leaders, and liberals may not prioritize collective interests.[404] Therefore, a purely libertarian or majoritarian system may fail to respect the rights of minorities, potentially conflicting with ISD.[405]

The European Commission of Human Rights has emphasized that democracy's legitimacy hinges on fostering participatory inclusivity – a system where majority rule incorporates minority voices. This vision aligns with two distinct democratic paradigms: consensual (deliberative) democracy and majoritarian (competitive) democracy.[406] In consensual democracies, legitimacy arises from negotiation and compromise, whereas in majoritarian systems, decisions

401 *Ibid.* 207.

402 Busquets, *Morality and Legality of Secession* (n 199) 11; A. Buchanan, *Secession. The Morality of Political Divorce from Fort Sumter to Lithuania and Quebec* (Boulder Westview 1991) 4, 30.

403 See 4.4.2.–4.4.3.

404 M. Freeman, 'The Right to Self-determination in International Politics: Six Theories in Search of a Policy' 25(3) *Review of International Studies* (1999) 362; G. Graham, 'Liberalism and Democracy' 9(2) *Journal of Applied Philosophy* (1992) 151. See also F. Martinez Cruz, 'The Right to self-determination of Peoples: Notes on its Compatibility with Three Models of Global Order' 11(1) *Mexican Law Review* (2018) 85–101.

405 Heintze, 'Territorial Autonomy' (n 190).

406 '(…) not democracy but a *democratic society*', where the majority considers the interests of all groups and peoples in the State, not merely those of its supporters and respects the individual freedoms' 12 *Yearbook of the European Convention on Human Rights* (1969) 179.

are based on the majority's will. Both systems present arguments for and against the right to secede.[407] Consensual democracies assume the status quo is fair, whereas majoritarian systems can lead to minority oppression without protections like the right to secede.[408] Persistent minorities, unable to change their status, may undermine the legitimacy of a democratic order. A democratic system that perpetuates inequality between groups is no longer justifiable. Therefore, reconciling ISD's counter-secession stance with democratic and liberal theories requires a nuanced approach.

Theories limiting the right to secede generally hold that secession is only valid under remedial circumstances, when internal self-determination is denied or violated. This theory to a great extent aligns with the principle of protecting territorial integrity, but it raises questions about the fairness of this presumption, particularly when a group expresses a clear desire to secede. Some argue that territorial integrity should not be an inviolable principle, especially when there is a clear demand for secession from a group.

Busquets and Buchanan compare the multinational state union to marriage, observing that civil law typically allows untroubled unilateral divorce, whereas public law prevents secession even when the relationship has deteriorated.[409] For minority nations, the freedom to choose whether to remain in a state is not guaranteed, as seen in the failure of Kosovo to unite with Albania or of Republika Srpska to merge with Serbia.[410] This discrepancy between civil and public law highlights the limitations of ISD's reliance on constitutionalism and federalism, which restrict the ability of individuals and groups to determine their status within and beyond the state.[411]

There are also critiques of the remedial right to secession, particularly its potential for misuse. Critics like Keating argue that it may encourage violent confrontations or provoke repressive reactions from the parent state, as secessionists might attempt to depict themselves as oppressed peoples to legitimize their claims.[412] In some cases, such as Kosovo, the international community

---

407 M. Ferrín and E. Hernández, 'Preferences for Consensus and Majoritarian Democracy: Long- and Short-Term Influences' 13(2) *European Political Science Review* (2021) 209.

408 Busquets, *Morality and Legality of Secession* (n 199) 256.

409 *Ibid.* 336–337; A. Buchanan, *Secession. The Morality of Political Divorce* (n 402) 7.

410 See W. Norman, *Negotiating Nationalism: Nation-Building, Federalism, and Secession in the Multinational State* (OUP 2006) 171.

411 Generally, the processes of joining and leaving are fundamentally different from the terms of participation within the state. See J. Ruiz Soroa, 'El Derecho a Decidir Como Idea Borrosa', *El País* (29 Oct. 2012).

412 M. Keating, 'Rethinking sovereignty. Independence-lite, Devolution-max and National Accommodation' 16 *Revista d'Estudis Autonomics i Federals* (2012) 14–15.

supported secession despite evidence that it might not have been a sustainable solution.

The alternative to the concept of a remedial right to secession includes various primary rights theories, such as choice theories and democratic theories, discussed in Chapter III.[413] These theories assert that every community inherently has the right to secede if it so desires, irrespective of past human rights violations. Advocates of the primary right to secession reject the notion that this right will inevitably lead to chaos or a proliferation of micro-states. On the contrary, they argue that guaranteeing the primary right to secession would promote stability and enhance political representation.[414] By embedding the right to secession within constitutional or international law, states would become more responsive to the desires of their constituent units. Nevertheless, primary rights theories face significant challenges within democratic and liberal frameworks. For example, ascriptive theories, which focus on shared collective traits such as nationality or culture, risk excluding or discriminating against minority groups within the seceding entity. In contrast, plebiscitary theories, grounded in an individual's right to decide, including the choice to separate, avoid this issue. However, they risk perpetuating cycles of self-determination claims from new minorities within the newly formed state, potentially creating a precarious and unstable order.[415] Consequently, some critics contend that such countenance of the plebiscitary theory resembles much more libertarianism than liberalism.[416]

To address these perplexities, Busquets, in his study, presents a theory of secession based on a hypothetical multinational contract.[417] Such a contract between national communities elucidates principles of justice within the

413 See 3.2.3.

414 See C. H. Wellman, *A Theory of Secession. The Case for Political Self–Determination* (CUP 2005) 34–64, 97–127.

415 C. Huang, 'Situating the Moral Basis for Secession in Territorial Rights: A Dualist and Non-alienation Account' 11(2) *Moral Philosophy and Politics* (2024) 351. According to Beran, secession should be prohibited if, among other things, the group seeking to secede is too small to assume the essential responsibilities of an independent state; if it aims to exploit or oppress a subgroup that cannot secede in return due to territorial dispersion and other reasons; if that group is located in an area that is culturally, economically, or militarily significant for the interests of the existing state, and other reasons. H. Beran 'A Liberal Theory of Secession' 32(1) *Political Studies* (1984) 30–31.

416 D. Mladić and S. Buzar, 'Kritika Plebiscitarne Teorije Secesije' 70(2) *Obnovljeni Život* (2015) 236–237, 241.

417 Busquets, *Morality and Legality of Secession* (n 199) 9–70.

multinational state, also through the prism of external self-determination.[418] Namely, this contract theory supports a moral entitlement to secede, but not without limits. Secession must be pursued through democratic processes, with good faith negotiations, and must respect human and minority rights. The prospective state formed through secession must ensure, among others, that the parent state's wealth is not substantially altered, and no serious harm is caused to third parties.[419]

All things considered, it is challenging to definitively establish that the liberal or democratic right to secession directly derives from or is inherently contained within the liberal-democratic rights of individuals. Theories of secession are ostensibly rooted in liberal and democratic ideals; however, given the comprehensiveness of these notions – spanning variations such as neo-liberalism, cultural liberalism, and deliberative democracy – their consequentiality is not obvious, not least because secession itself may, in certain contexts, be illiberal or undemocratic. On the other hand, democratic theory is compatible with the qualified vision of ISD and its anti-secession value, as it praises the unity and stability of democratic states. The proper construction of the democratic theory is that it strives to resolve conflicts and grievances through democratic processes by ensuring that all groups are represented, and their rights protected within the existing state structure. Therefore, the democratic theory rather supports than opposes ISD as a way to ensure inclusive governance and protect minority rights. While it may be cautious about external self-determination or secession, democratic theory still acknowledges its legitimacy in cases of severe injustice or when democratic mechanisms within the state fail to provide adequate redress.

Liberal theory, similarly to democratic theory, does not inherently stand in opposition to internal self-determination and its counter-secession value. Instead, in its proper reading, liberal theory generally supports the principle of self-determination, emphasizing individual rights, autonomy, and the protection of minority groups within a state. Overall, it seeks to uphold solutions that respect both the unity of the state and the individual rights of its diverse populations.

418 Since nations (and their members) are the best judges of their group interests, they should be both entitled to form a union, and upon evolution or a change of circumstances, also to leave it. Busquets, *Morality and Legality of Secession* (n 199) 30. See also A. Margalit and J. Raz, 'National self-determination' (1990) 87 *Journal of Philosophy* 457.

419 Busquets, *Morality and Legality of Secession* (n 199) 32.

8 The Added Value of Internal Self-determination

The principial aim of this oeuvre is to show that ISD can be a viable mechanism for preventing secession. Various meanings of ISD, which can be also construed as its anti-secession tools, were discussed in this chapter with varying degrees of detail. However, apart from stating the main aim of ISD and its tools, it is worth devoting some time to the broader benefits that the implementation of ISD brings to the international community, primarily in terms of preserving border stability, preventing self-determination-related conflicts, and safeguarding human rights.

8.1 *Stability of Borders and Conflict Avoidance*

Internal self-determination is essential for preserving border stability. By granting autonomy and self-governance to various groups within existing borders, respecting their basic human rights, and complying with the policy of inclusiveness, states can substantially reduce the pressure for secession and subsequent border changes. This approach is particularly relevant in multi-ethnic, multi-linguistic, and multi-religious societies where different groups may seek greater control over their affairs. For example, the federal structure of Switzerland, which accommodates its diverse linguistic and cultural groups, has contributed to the stability of its borders. Similarly, Spain's autonomous communities, such as Galicia and the Basque Country, though not without tensions, have provided a framework for these regions to express their distinct identities while remaining part of the Spanish state.

Internal self-determination also serves as a preventive mechanism against conflicts. By addressing the root causes of dissatisfaction and alienation among different groups, it reduces the likelihood of violent uprisings and insurgencies. When people feel that their cultural, social, and economic rights are respected and protected, they are less likely to resort to violence to achieve their goals. This principle is exemplified in the case of Belgium, where the federal system accommodates the Flemish and Walloon regions, thus diffusing potential conflicts arising from linguistic and cultural differences. Similarly, in Canada, the recognition of Quebec's distinct society and the establishment of a federal system have helped to manage the aspirations of the Francophone population within the larger Canadian federation.

As such, ISD poses a direct challenge to the legitimacy of regimes that disregard the will and needs of their people. A regime that treats its population in this manner effectively delegitimizes itself. Therefore, as Fox concludes, an internal right becomes almost as confrontational to the interests of states as a right to secession, potentially leading to fragmentation.[420] Fox points out the continued significance of ISD even in the post-colonial era by comparing Security Council resolutions that have, on several occasions, determined that acts of domestic oppression constitute a 'threat to peace' and, in this sense, activated the collective security system reminiscent to Resolution 1514 and its progeny that supported oppressed colonial peoples in their quest for liberation.[421] The international community have thus stood alongside the oppressed population against their parent states, much as it did with colonized peoples. Therefore, although ISD primarily serves the preservation of existing state structures, it also constitutes a warning.

The territorial integrity of a state is at risk when ethnic minorities within its territory are dissatisfied with their status, and their economic, cultural, and political development. From a political perspective, groups that engage in conflict or seek independence may do so because they believe they have insufficient political influence relative to what they deserve. Socially or culturally, they might engage in conflict because they perceive their language as undervalued or their religion as unprotected. Economically, conflict may arise when they feel burdened by an unfair share of taxes within their countries.[422] Therefore, it can be said that the grievances of these groups relate to what we have identified as the content of ISD. The central argument is that by ensuring ISD for minorities within the state's territory, their demands will be addressed, leading to the preservation of the stability of state borders and the prevention of self-determination-related conflicts. The international community must, therefore, attempt to resolve conflicts within the framework of internal self-determination principles before supporting the right of a nation to external self-determination with its potentially burdensome consequences. Although this strategy has not been explicitly formulated on the international stage, it derives from principles promoting friendly relations. The pursuit of external self-determination is less justified when people live within a democratic system, that is, when they can effectively exercise their right to internal self-determination.[423]

Having said that, it is worth recalling the benefits of the stability of borders and conflict avoidance, to which ISD is said to contribute.

The stability of borders ensures predictability, fosters peace, and facilitates cooperation among nations. Stable borders reduce the likelihood of conflicts,

---

420 Fox (n 15) 758.

421 *Ibid.* 759.

422 More broadly in 3.1.

423 Bobrowski (n 8) 30.

support economic development, and promote the well-being of people. In an interconnected world, where national boundaries define the scope of sovereignty and influence, maintaining stable borders is crucial for global stability and security. Disputed borders can lead to tensions and armed confrontations, as seen in numerous historical and contemporary examples.[424] Clear and recognized borders help in delineating territorial limits and prevent encroachments that might provoke hostilities. When borders are stable, states can allocate fewer resources to military defense and focus on other areas such as development, healthcare, and education. This reallocation of resources promotes overall national well-being and reduces the arms race, contributing to global peace.

International law is built on the principle of sovereignty, where each state has supreme authority within its territory. Stable borders help in clearly defining the scope of this authority. It ensures that states can govern without external interference, thus upholding the principle of non-intervention enshrined in the UN Charter.[425] Stable borders provide a basis for international agreements and treaties. When borders are recognized and uncontested, states can enter into agreements regarding trade, environmental protection, and other areas of mutual interest with greater confidence. Conversely, contested borders hinder such agreements. In its latest advisory opinion regarding legal consequences arising from the policies and practices of Israel in the Occupied Palestinian Territory, the ICJ underlined that states are under an obligation to abstain from treaty relations with Israel or entering into economic or trade dealings with Israel in all cases in which it purports to act on behalf of the Occupied Palestinian Territory.[426]

The stability of borders is also crucial for political integration and economic activities. Persistent instability hinders accession to geopolitical and military alliances, such as the EU or NATO, as illustrated by examples of Serbia, Bosnia, Georgia and Ukraine, which face challenges from entrenched secessionist entities. Volatile borders can disrupt trade routes and supply chains, leading to economic losses. To the contrary, stable borders facilitate smooth cross-border

---

424 See M. Kohen and M. Hébié, *Research Handbook on Territorial Disputes in International Law* (Elgar 2018).

425 As Simmons argues 'borders define neighbors that are governed by the international law of neighborliness. In turn, the law of neighborliness forbids states from using sovereignty and security justifications to exempt border regions from obligations under international human rights law'. B. Simmons, 'International Borders: Yours, Mine, and Ours International Borders: Yours, Mine, and Ours' *University of Chicago Legal Forum* (2023) 243.

426 *Legal Consequences arising from the Policies and Practices of Israel in the Occupied Palestinian Territory, including East Jerusalem*, Advisory Opinion, ICJ Rep. 2024, para 278.

trade and attract foreign investment, as investors prefer predictable and peaceful environments. Many resources such as rivers, minerals, and forests span across borders. Stable borders allow for joint management and sustainable utilization of these resources.[427] Disputed borders, on the other hand, can lead to conflicts over resource control, undermining economic stability.

Finally, secure and well-defined borders contribute to the protection of populations by providing a secure environment. Border disputes can lead to displacement of people, human rights abuses, and humanitarian crises. A notable example is the conflict between Ethiopia and Eritrea over the border, which lasted from 1998 to 2000. The war resulted in tens of thousands of deaths and the displacement of hundreds of thousands of people.[428] Ensuring border stability helps in safeguarding the rights and lives of those living near borders. Stable borders facilitate the management of migration and refugee flows. It allows states to implement effective border controls and policies that protect the rights of migrants and refugees while ensuring security and order.[429]

When it comes to conflict avoidance, a long list of matters can be mentioned. To start with the most obvious one: the preservation of human life and reduction of suffering. Avoiding conflicts prevents the loss of lives and reduces physical and psychological suffering. Civilians often bear the brunt of conflicts. By avoiding conflict, the safety and well-being of non-combatants, including vulnerable groups like women, children, and the elderly, are protected.[430]

Within the purview of economic stability and growth, economic continuity and foreign investment come to the fore. Conflicts disrupt economic activities,

---

427 For example, the Nile River, which flows through multiple countries in Northeast Africa, is a vital water resource shared by Egypt, Sudan, Ethiopia, and several other nations. Stable borders and cooperative agreements, such as the Nile Basin Initiative, enable these countries to manage and utilize the river's resources sustainably.

428 The war officially came to an end with the signing of the Algiers Agreement on 12 December 2000. However, the border dispute's aftermath continued to affect the lives of those in the conflict zones long after active hostilities ceased. On Apr. 13, 2002, the Eritrea-Ethiopia Boundary Commission, in collaboration with the Permanent Court of Arbitration in The Hague, delivered a 'final and binding' verdict. The ruling allocated some territory to each country, awarding Badme, the flashpoint of the conflict, to Eritrea.

429 Frontex, the European Border and Coast Guard Agency, plays a pivotal role in ensuring the security and management of the European Union's external borders. Frontex's mandate includes a wide range of activities aimed at enhancing border security, facilitating legal migration, combating illegal immigration, and contributing to the overall security of the Schengen Area.

430 See Declaration on the Protection of Women and Children in Emergency and Armed Conflict (14 Dec. 1974) UN Doc. A/RES/3318(XXIX). See also ICRC, 'The Principle of Distinction between Civilians and Combatants' <https://ihl-databases.icrc.org/en/customary-ihl/v2/rule1>.

leading to loss of income, destruction of infrastructure, and economic instability. One notable example of how conflicts disrupt economic activities is the Syrian Civil War. The war, which began in 2011, has had devastating impacts on Syria's economy.[431] Avoiding conflict ensures that businesses can operate normally, trade flows are uninterrupted, and economies can grow. On the other hand, stability attracts foreign investment. Investors are more likely to invest in regions where the risk of conflict is low, leading to job creation and economic development.

Conflicts likewise impact on social cohesion and community well-being. Conflict-avoidance fosters social cohesion and harmony. It helps in building trust among different community groups, reducing ethnic, religious, and cultural tensions. Continuous conflict or the threat of conflict can lead to widespread mental health issues, including trauma, anxiety, and depression.[432] Avoiding conflict helps maintain the mental well-being of the population.

Conflicts often result in the destruction of cultural and historical sites. Avoiding conflict helps preserve the cultural heritage and history of a region. Stability encourages cultural exchanges and tourism, fostering mutual understanding and respect among different cultures.[433]

Last but not least, political stability is essential for effective governance. Conflict-avoidance ensures that governments can function without interruption, implementing policies and maintaining law and order. Stable environments are conducive to democratic processes. Elections and other democratic practices can occur smoothly without the disruptions caused by conflict.

To sum up, internal self-determination can be instrumental in conflict avoidance and stability of borders. By addressing the needs and grievances of diverse groups through various means, ISD reduces pressures for secession and border changes. It fosters inclusive governance, social cohesion, and balanced economic development, mitigating potential sources of conflict. In doing so, ISD not only preserves territorial integrity but also promotes a more stable and peaceful society.

---

431 The conflict has resulted in widespread loss of income for millions of Syrians. Many businesses, factories, and farms have been destroyed or abandoned, leaving people without jobs and sources of income. The tourism industry, once a significant contributor to Syria's GDP, has been decimated due to the ongoing violence. Consult, World Bank Group, *The Toll of War: The Economic and Social Consequences of the Conflict in Syria* (2017).

432 R. S. Murthy and R. Lakshminarayana, 'Mental Health Consequences of War: A Brief Review of Research Findings' 5(1) *World Psychiatry* (2006) 25–30. UN News, 'One-in-Five Suffers Mental Health Condition in Conflict Zones, New UN Figures Reveal' (12 Jun. 2019) <https://news.un.org/en/story/2019/06/1040281>.

433 Consult R. O'Keefe, *The Protection of Cultural Property in Armed Conflict* (CUP 2009).

8.2 *Protection and Advancement of Human Rights*

McCorquodale's human rights approach to self-determination asserts that the right cannot be interpreted in isolation but must be harmonized with other rights within the framework of international human rights law. This methodology prioritizes safeguarding all rights collectively rather than elevating self-determination above competing entitlements. By seeking equilibrium between conflicting claims, it aims to preserve the maximum possible protection for each right within contextual constraints. Crucially, this approach expands the repertoire of self-determination beyond secession, offering alternative mechanisms such as: federal or devolved political structures to empower group agency; legal guarantees for minority rights (e.g. language protections, cultural autonomy); formal recognition of distinct group status within the state and; consociational democracy models that institutionalize power-sharing.[434] The impact of implementing of ISD on other human rights is clearly discernible: by ensuring that regions can develop policies tailored to their specific economic needs or allowing local control over resources, ISD activates and strengthens the right to economic development and right to fair resource management, respectively. In the same vein, providing education that reflects the cultural and linguistic identities of minority groups augments the right to culturally relevant education, while ensuring that legal systems respect the customs and traditions of minority groups evidences the existence of civil rights, such as the right to a fair trial.

Accordingly, the right to self-determination is an essential condition the effective guarantee of individual human rights, as emphasized multiple times by the UN General Assembly,[435] the Human Rights Committee,[436] the Commission on Human Rights,[437] the Arbitration Commission of the International

434 R. McCorquodale, 'Self-determination: A Human Rights Approach' 43(4) *International and Comparative Law Quarterly* (1994) 882.

435 E.g. UNGA Res 43/105 (8 Dec. 1988) para 1 ('universal realization of the right of all peoples (…) to self-determination is a fundamental condition for the effective guarantee and observance of human rights and for the preservation and promotion of such rights').

436 Human Rights Committee, General Comment No. 12 (n 82) para 1 ('the right of self-determination is of particular importance because its realization is an essential condition for the effective guarantee and observance of individual human rights and for the promotion and strengthening of those rights').

437 UN Commission on Human Rights, 'The Right of Peoples to Self-determination and its Application to Peoples Under Colonial or Alien Domination or Foreign Occupation', UN Doc. E/CN.4/RES/1983/4 (15 Feb. 1983) preamble ('Reiterating its affirmation the importance of the effective realization of the right of peoples to self-determination (…) as imperative for the enjoyment of human rights').

Conference on the Former Yugoslavia,[438] numerous states,[439] and doctrine.[440] This relationship is not confined to colonial situations. Dominance over a people or their subjugation by a state constitutes a systematic denial of the fundamental rights of individuals within that group. Self-determination emerges as a natural extension of the principle of individual freedom, as the development of personal identity is inextricably tied to the preservation of collective identity. Thus, the fulfilment of individual freedom and protection of individual identity assume and require the freedom of a people organized in the form of a state to govern themselves.

ISD is also important for the protection of minority rights. It is a more comprehensive right than the minority rights guaranteed by Article 27 of the ICCPR. As Thornberry highlights, there is a qualitative difference between the right to self-determination and minority rights.[441] The right to self-determination implies overarching entitlements in cultural, economic, and political realms, essentially translating to political control and other associated forms of authority. In contrast, minority rights are finite, enumerated, and exclude political control. Thornberry further observes that the current norms governing minority rights are restricted and insufficient to counter forced assimilation or integration.[442] Senaratne further critiques the limitations of the individual human rights framework in protecting minorities.[443] While minority individuals retain equal political rights under the ICCPR, these guarantees fail to prevent the 'tyranny of the majority'.[444] For instance, the ICCPR does not mandate minority participation in constitution-making processes, nor does it require states to prioritize minority interests in policymaking. A majority-elected government could thus legitimately enact laws that marginalize minorities, even inadvertently, under the guise of democratic legitimacy.[445]

Political participation is crucial for minority groups. In Article 2(2) of the Declaration on the Rights of Persons belonging to National or Ethnic, Religious

---

438 Badinter Commission, Opinion No. 2 (n 84) para 3 (the principle of the right to self-determination serves to safeguard human rights).

439 UN Doc. A/C.3/SR.309 (9 Nov. 1950) paras 52–53 (Afghanistan) para 60 (Soviet Union). See also UN Doc. A/C.3/SR. 647 (28 Oct. 1955) para 1 (Greece) para 38 (Yugoslavia).

440 H. Gros-Espiell, *The Right to Self-determination: Implementation of United Nations Resolutions: Study* (United Nations 1980) 10.

441 P. Thornberry, 'Self-determination, Minorities, Human Rights: A Review of International Instruments' 38(4) *International and Comparative Law Quarterly* (1989) 880–881.

442 *Ibid.* 881.

443 Senaratne, *Internal Self-determination* (n 399) 78.

444 Wheatley (n 50) 153.

445 *Ibid.*

and Linguistic Minorities, it is stated that 'persons belonging to minorities have the right to participate effectively in (...) public life'.[446] Public life encompasses various rights, including those related to participation in elections, candidacy, holding public office, and other political and administrative domains.[447] Based on these rights, members of minorities can protect their interests and values, as well as 'contribute to political change in the larger society'.[448] Therefore, minorities require protection of their collective rights, which is something that the ICCPR, as an instrument designed to protect individual rights, does not provide.

In conclusion, the paramount function of self-determination lies in its role in guaranteeing and respecting individual human rights, which represents an evolution from its original goal – the preservation and development of the collective identity of a group. This shift became evident following World War II, paralleling the processes of decolonization and the growing recognition of individual human rights in international law.[449] The integration of self-determination into legal frameworks highlighted its dual role in protecting both collective identities and individual rights. Moreover, just as self-determination is crucial for the respect of human rights, the reverse also holds true. The right to internal self-determination cannot be considered respected if there are widespread violations of basic human rights by the parent state. This reciprocal relationship underscores that a state's respect for self-determination inherently requires the protection of individual human rights, ensuring that all groups within the state can participate freely and fairly in their governance and cultural expression. Consequently, internal self-determination becomes a benchmark for evaluating a state's commitment to upholding both the collective rights of groups and the fundamental rights of individuals.

9 Opinion of Commentators

This chapter will end with a synthesis of scholarly opinions on the application of internal self-determination as a mechanism to prevent secession. As will be shown, there is substantial support for this hypothesis in the doctrine, and

446 UNGA Res 47/135 'Declaration on the Rights of Persons Belonging to National or Ethnic, Religious and Linguistic Minorities' (18 Dec. 1992).

447 A. Eide, 'Commentary to the Declaration on the Rights of Persons Belonging to National or Ethnic, Religious and Linguistic Minorities', UN Doc. E/CN.4/Sub.2/AC.5/2001/2 (2 Apr. 2001) para 36.

448 *Ibid.* para 35.

449 Raič (n 138) 242.

it is considered the most optimal solution for resolving the apparent conflict between the state's and (minority) people's territorial sovereignty.

Professor Crawford, a public international law icon with vast expertise in the law of statehood, was favourable to the idea that respect for human rights and citizen participation are prerequisites of good statehood. For him, self-determination for peoples within a state should be achieved on the basis of respect for its territorial integrity. A state whose government complies with the principle of internal self-determination, meaning it 'represents the whole people of its territory without distinction of any kind, that is to say, on a basis of equality, and in particular without discrimination on grounds of race, creed or colour', is entitled to the protection of its territorial integrity.[450] Stated differently, the people of such a state exercise their right to self-determination by participating in the government on an equal basis. Despite Crawford's insistence on the effectiveness of new states and the continuity of existing ones, he appeared to acknowledge self-determination as both a criterion for statehood and a measure of continuity for states that conduct themselves in accordance with ISD.[451]

Oeter, a German professor of international law, addressed the issue of internal self-determination in his article on the Kosovo precedent.[452] He noted that the construction of self-determination should be based on 'a clear pre-eminence of "internal self-determination"', understood as 'various models of effective participation in internal political decision-making'.[453] Oeter believes that the provisions and the spirit of the Friendly Relations Declaration clearly prioritize territorial integrity over any right to separate statehood. In his view, the principle of territorial integrity protects not only unitary states but also federations and other quasi-federal state models which were formed for historical reasons based on agreements between the parties. As long as no 'exceptional grounds' exist, self-determination should be exercised internally, maintains the German authority.[454] Citing Eide, Oeter concludes that internal self-determination serves as a 'productive alternative' to boundless claims for

450 J. Crawford, 'State Practice in International Law in Relation to Secession' 69 *British Yearbook of International Law* (1998) 113–114; Crawford, *The Creation of States* (n 325) 118–119, 417.

451 On independence as a statehood criterion see Crawford, *The Creation of States* (n 325) 62–63. On self-determination as a statehood criterion see J. Crawford, 'The Creation of the State of Palestine: Too Much Too Soon?' 1 *EJIL* (1990) 307, 309.

452 S. Oeter, 'The Kosovo Case' (n 102) 51–74.

453 *Ibid.* 59.

454 *Ibid.*

independent statehood by ever smaller political entities, helping to avoid *circulus vitiosus* of continuous secessionist demands.[455]

Franck, a distinguished U.S. international law scholar, is renowned for his influential article *The Emerging Right to Democratic Governance*, published in the American Journal of International Law, where he articulated the notion of democratic governance – now widely seen as foundational to internal self-determination. Over the course of his career, Franck's views on secession evolved. In his final major work, *Fairness in International Law and Institutions*, he appeared to sympathize with the concept of remedial secession but refrained from explicitly endorsing it, likely due to its implications for the international community and the competing interests of various groups. Franck sought to deconstruct the colonial order by suggesting that fairness discourse could mediate the tension between self-determination and *uti possidetis juris*. He referred to the plight of minorities within sovereign states who are 'persistently and egregiously denied political and social equality and the opportunity to retain their cultural identity', and advocated for an extension of the principle of self-determination, without explicitly naming secession as the sole remedy.[456] Some scholars have aligned Franck's perspective with liberal theories of secession, identifying traces of a distributive justice approach, wherein secession might be permissible if wealth distribution within a state is discriminatory.[457] Nonetheless, Franck's core assertion – that 'self-determination postulates the right of a people organized in an established territory to determine its collective political destiny in a democratic fashion' – underscores his preference for a qualified vision of ISD.[458] He argued that the right to self-determination has transitioned from being a principle of exclusion (secession) to one of inclusion, emphasizing the right to participate in democratic governance. This perspective reinforces the primacy of ISD over external self-determination in most contexts.

Shikova, who conducted in-depth research in internal self-determination, observed that while it is not a guaranteed solution against secession, internal self-determination tends to reduce the drive for external self-determination and lessens secessionist tendencies. Self-governance, as a crucial embodiment of ISD, enables sociocultural groups to preserve their distinctive characteristics.

---

455 *Ibid.* 60. See A. Eide, 'In Search of Constructive Alternatives to Secession' in C. Tomuschat (ed.) *Modern Law of Self-determination* (Martinus Nijhoff 1993) 139.

456 T. M. Franck, *Fairness in International Law and Institutions* (Clarendon Press 1995) 144–145, 160.

457 Tierney, 'The Search for a New Normativity' (113) 950.

458 Franck, 'The Emerging Right to Democratic Governance' (n 34) 52, 59.

For instance, Scotland and the Basque Country, the cases she scrutinized, have maintained their unique features over the centuries thanks to internal self-government.[459]

Saul, in his article, explains that framing self-determination as a human right integrates it into the established legal framework of human rights. Following McCorquodale's approach, he argues that as a non-absolute right, the exercise of self-determination must be limited by conditions such as those outlined in Article 5(1) of the Covenants on Human Rights, which state that 'nothing in the present Covenant may be interpreted as implying for any State, group or person any right to engage in any activity or perform any act aimed at the destruction of any of the rights and freedoms recognized herein'.[460] Therefore, the right to self-determination must be balanced with other human rights, including freedom of expression and freedom of religion. The resulting solutions from this balancing do not necessarily include secession for a group within a state claiming the right to self-determination. Instead, other options, such as the creation of a federation, might be considered more appropriate, given the need to accommodate the individual rights of inhabitants within a territory. In this context, framing self-determination as an individual human right helps to explain the development of the concept of internal self-determination as an alternative to external self-determination.

Stilz in her works argues that self-determination is a significant moral claim that must be considered with respect to specific circumstances: it does not inherently grant a right to secede and can sometimes be justifiably overridden.[461] She asserts that self-determination is not always best achieved through the formation of an independent state; other arrangements such as confederal institutions, internal autonomy, or devolution can often be more suitable alternatives.[462] When a persistent minority lacks alignment, it may have a strong claim to greater self-determination, but this claim must be weighed against various competing concerns. This assessment is crucial to determine (i) whether the group holds an all-things-considered right and (ii) which institutional arrangement is most appropriate for fulfilling that right. In some instances, the claim to self-determination is outweighed by urgent competing reasons, such as the risk of civil or international war, ethnic violence, a high probability of human

459 Shikova, 'Practicing Internal Self-determination' (n 117) 263.

460 M. Saul, 'The Normative Status of Self-determination in International Law: A Formula for Uncertainty in the Scope and Content of the Right?' 11(4) *Human Rights Law Review* (2011) 627. See also McCorquodale, 'Self-determination: A Human Rights Approach' (n 434) 877.

461 Stilz, 'The Value of Self-determination' (n 7) 118–119.

462 Stilz, *Territorial Sovereignty* (n 63) 136.

rights violations, or when the costs of institutional reform are so substantial that they jeopardize the performance of essential state functions.[463] In consequence, the moral reasons supporting self-determination are not absolute and must be carefully balanced against a range of countervailing concerns in each specific case.

Summers, an acknowledged specialist in modern self-determination law, refers to the value and role of internal self-determination in preventing secession in his opus *Peoples and International Law*. As the author observes, one of the functions of the distinction between internal and external self-determination is to weaken claims for independence.[464] This distinction, as Summers argues, is rooted in state sovereignty and gains importance when sovereignty and territorial integrity impose limits on the exercise of self-determination. Citing the *Quebec* case, Summers underscores that self-determination is predominantly exercised internally. Summers extrapolates from this ruling that the ISD/ESD dichotomy inherently restricts secessionist demands to preserve territorial cohesion. Crucially, he clarifies that this distinction does not erect a rigid hierarchy of rights. Instead, ISD and ESD can coexist dynamically within stable states, even if the terminology framing these concepts remains imperfect. This coexistence, according to Summers, avoids prompting secession or undermining territorial integrity.[465]

This concise summary of influential authors' viewpoints underscores that internal self-determination is a valuable mechanism for preventing secession. Most scholars posit that ISD achieves its intended purpose of deterring secession when it is meaningfully exercised i.e. guaranteed and effectively implemented by states – thereby endorsing a qualified interpretation of ISD. However, this assumption often lacks detailed substantiation regarding what ISD precisely entails, the specific measures states must take to secure it, and the scope of its implementation. These questions are more frequently explored to justify secession in particular cases rather than to oppose it under ordinary circumstances.[466] A recurring concern among authors is that governments, including authoritarian regimes, may declare themselves democratic without meeting the requisite standards in practice.[467] As Thornberry notes, states can readily claim compliance with ISD requirements on the international stage,

---

463 *Ibid.*

464 J. Summers, *Peoples and International Law* (Brill 2014) 66.

465 *Ibid.* See also J. Summers, 'The Internal and External Aspects of Self-determination Reconsidered' in D. French (ed.) *Statehood and Self-determination Reconciling Tradition and Modernity in International Law* (CUP 2013) 239–241, 247–249.

466 More in 5.6. and 6.1.

467 Thornberry, 'The Democratic or Internal Aspect of Self-determination' (n 4) 101.

yet such claims are neither easily verifiable nor subject to effective sanctions. In this regard, he cites a spokesman of an indigenous Inuit tribe who argued that proponents of an independent Quebec may not genuinely represent the entire population of the territory, despite official declarations of democratic governance.[468]

The degree of acceptance – whether direct or indirect – of the hypothesis advanced in this book also depends on the epistemological frameworks embraced by scholars from related disciplines. Political scientists and philosophers aligned with realist theory tend to be more state-centric, and their beliefs may be even more rigid than those expressed herein. Conversely, those influenced by liberalism and ethical theory are likely to support the rights of peoples, often referring to their moral entitlements, identity elements, and the autonomy to choose the system most conducive to their development, including the possibility of an independent state. Still, certain scholars argue that secession should not be granted solely on the basis of identity, even though an independent state might be the most optimal solution for protecting national culture.[469] For example, Bousquet acknowledges the legitimacy of secession based on a multinational contract but concedes that this view is far from being embraced under current international law. Instead, he advocates for milder, compromise-based solutions that prioritize dialogue and emphasize internal self-determination as a pragmatic approach to addressing such disputes.[470]

468 *Ibid.* 117.

469 H. Lee, 'The Identity Argument for National Self-determination' 26(2) *Public Affairs Quarterly* (2012) 136.

470 Busquets, *Morality and Legality of Secession* (n 199) 175–176.

CHAPTER 5

Internal Self-determination as a Method of Preventing Secession in International Law: State and International Organizations Practice

> When it is obvious that the goals cannot be reached,
> don't adjust the goals, adjust the action steps.
>
> CONFUCIUS

∵

1 Prolegomenon

Internal self-determination (ISD) is said to have originated in Western legal and political thought in order both to maintain the relevance of the right to self-determination in the wake of the almost completed decolonization process and to augment the protection of peoples in existing states.[1] The 1975 Conference on Security and Co-operation in Europe (CSCE) Helsinki Final Act, signed by all then-existing European countries, along with the US and Canada, clearly distinguished between the internal and external aspects of the right to self-determination and corroborated its continuity. It states:

> By virtue of the principle of equal rights and self-determination of peoples, all peoples *always* have the right, in full freedom, to determine, when and as they wish, their *internal* and external political status, without external interference, and to pursue as they wish their political, economic, social and cultural development.[2]

The Western concept of internal self-determination is fundamentally value-driven, with various authors and politicians increasingly linking it to

1 F. Kirgis, 'Editorial Comment: The Degrees of Self-determination in the United Nations Era' 88(2) *AJIL* (1994) 305; G. Fox, 'Self-determination in the Post-Cold War Era: A New Internal Focus?' 16(3) *Michigan Journal of International Law* (1995) 733–735. See 4.8.2., fn. 435–440.

2 The 1975 Helsinki Final Act, Principle VIII (emphasis added).

 | DOI:10.1163/9789004737501_006

democratic governance, political freedom, and human rights.[3] On some occasions, prospective compliance with the said standards was a decisive factor in obtaining recognition for a state, as evidenced in the 1991 EC Guidelines on the Recognition of New States, where internal self-determination was a political precondition for accepting external self-determination.[4] Such an ideological inclination made the established division of self-determination divisive itself. During the Cold War, socialist and Third World states interpreted governmental representativeness – the foundation of internal self-determination – according to their own paradigms, with some explicitly rejecting the Western democratic model.[5] This, in turn, reinforced their adherence to the classical notion of 'independence-entitlement'.[6] India and China still predominantly apprehend the right to self-determination as applicable solely to the people under foreign domination, asserting that this right cannot be used to undermine the sovereignty and territorial integrity of the already existing states.[7] Burma once argued that 'to understand it [self-determination] as covering peoples who constituted a sovereign State would have the effect of re-writing history to suit a political concept'.[8] Accordingly, the following questions may arise: whether internal self-determination and its concomitant secession-prevention value is a universal concept and whether the Western conceptualization does not in reality serve a (different) purpose of promoting equality, representatives and accountability of the ruling cadre? Yet, as will be shown,

3 See K. Senaratne, 'Internal Self-determination in International Law: A Critical Third-World Perspective' 3 *Asian Journal of International Law* (2013) 307–308.

4 European Community, 'Declaration of Guidelines on the Recognition of New States in Eastern Europe and in the Former Soviet Union' (16 Dec. 1991), reprinted in 4 *EJIL* 72. See also P. Pazartzis, 'Secession and International Law: The European Dimension' in M. Kohen (ed.) *Secession: International Law Perspectives* (CUP 2006) 372. Notably, the breach of ISD by the regime in Rhodesia led to its non-recognition by the international community, despite the fact that it met the standard criteria for statehood. See G. Anderson, 'Unilateral Non-Colonial Secession and Internal Self-determination: A Right of Newly Seceded Peoples to Democracy?' 34(1) *Arizona Journal of International and Comparative Law* (2017) 37–41.

5 For over seventy years, the Russians have argued that true representative government is best embodied in a Communist form. In contrast, East Asian countries have maintained that Western-style democracy is not applicable to East Asia. See H. Moris, 'Self-determination: An Affirmative Right or Mere Rhetoric?' 4 *ILSA Journal of International and Comparative Law* (1997) 211–212.

6 A. Cassese, 'Political Self-determination – Old Concepts and New Developments' in A. Cassese (ed.) *UN Law, Fundamental Rights: Two Topics in International Law* (Sijthoff & Noordhoff 1979) 140; P. Thornberry, *International Law and the Rights of Minorities* (Clarendon Press 1991) 217.

7 Senaratne (n 3) 316–317.

8 UN Doc. A/AC.125/SR.68 (4 Dec. 1967) 8. See also UN Doc. A/C.3/51/SR.28 (19 Sep. 1997) 16.

ISD is gaining ever broader acceptance, while its manifold understanding does not compete with its anti-secessionist value. In the end, the very wording 'internal' implies that all rights and privileges associated with this concept are to be realized within the borders of existing states, as opposed to external self-determination. This was underlined by the Netherlands as early as 1952:

> The idea of self-determination was a complex of ideas rather than a single concept. Thus the principle of internal self-determination, or self-determination on the national level, should be distinguished from that of external self-determination, or self-determination on the international level. The former was the right of a nation, already constituted as a State, to choose its form of government and to determine the policy it meant to pursue. The latter was the right of a group which considered itself a nation to form a State of its own.[9]

Regardless of the variations in the understanding of internal self-determination outlined in chapter IV (as the unimpeded entitlement to choose a political and economic system, to enjoy autonomy, or not to be discriminated against etc.),[10] the most vexed issue in international practice is whether ISD is construed as being conterminous with a blanket denial of secession or whether only its full realization secures territorial cohesion. Western states and authors generally support the view that ISD should not be reduced to a plain slogan or *de facto* equated with the principle of territorial integrity. Instead, they argue that only genuine respect for ISD constitutes a fair compromise between state sovereignty and territorial wholeness on the one hand and morality and good governance on the other. Arguing to the contrary would be detrimental to minorities and the whole idea of internal self-determination would lose its significance as a tool to compel governments to uphold the principle of equal rights. Given the lack of robust international legal remedies (sanctions can occur but not in the form of a separation entitlement), the argument for the

9 7 GAOR, 1952, 3rd Cmttee., 447th mtg., UN Doc. A/C.3/SR.447, para 4. Arguably, the internal/external dichotomy was coined by the Netherlands during the negotiations preceding Indonesian independence in 1949. The Netherlands argued that different populations of Indonesia had the (internal) right to determine their position within the federation (the United States of Indonesia) and the (external) right to dissociate their respective territories from the United States of Indonesia and perhaps form new associations with the Dutch. UN Commission for Indonesia: Special Report to the Security Council on the Round Table Conference UN Doc. S/1417 (10 Nov. 1949) para 52.

10 See 4.2.

fulfilment of ISD is all the more cogent.[11] Scarce and deficient international legal instruments to enforce internal self-determination leave populations within a state reliant on foreign recognition of their circumstances, including the potential recognition of their independence.[12]

The so-called 'state and international organizations approach' is designed to illustrate the practice of international organizations and states, including their courts and quasi-judicial bodies, regarding internal self-determination as an obstacle to secession. To this end, a wide array of state actions – such as official pronouncements during the *travaux preparatoires* of agreements or submissions to courts and other bodies – as well as actions by international organizations, including their resolutions and declarations, and judicial decisions (e.g. judgments and advisory opinions) are scrutinized with the aim of extrapolating either direct or indirect support for territorial integrity in the context of ISD. Given the increased and informed institutional practice in invoking internal self-determination when addressing the issue of secession, the possible emergence of a customary international law rule to this end will also be discussed. Although institutional practice in this regard is largely contextual and depends on country-specific factors, such as legal traditions, historical narratives, and societal customs, its scope and repeated methodology may testify to solidifying the rule of internal self-determination as prohibiting secession through inductive reasoning.[13] It is a separate question whether such an inference of a rule, essentially regarding non-state actors, can be considered equitable; much like the prevailing counter-secession attitude of national courts (*quis custodiet ipsos custodes*).[14]

2 State Practice

The prohibition of secession by virtue of the existence or fulfilment of internal self-determination can be inferred from the practice of states from multiple angles. Firstly, through the scrutiny of opinions expressed by states in the process of drafting international documents, such as proposals submitted during the preparation of the Friendly Relations Declaration. Secondly, it

11 'A claim of a right to secede from a repressive dictatorship may be regarded as *legitimate*'. Kirgis (n 1) 304 (emphasis added).

12 P. Bossacoma Busquets, 'Catalonia: Self-determination, Secession, and Integration' in B. C. Harzl and R. Petrov (eds.) *Unrecognized Entities: Perspectives in International, European and Constitutional Law* (Brill 2022) 151.

13 S. Talmon, 'Determining Customary International Law: The ICJ's Methodology between Induction, Deduction and Assertion' 26(2) *EJIL* (2015) 421.

14 Consult R. M. Hanna, 'Right to Self-determination in In Re Secession of Quebec' 23(1) *Maryland Journal of International Law* (1999) 242–245.

is possible to deduce the viewpoint of states on this issue by analysing their submissions to international bodies or courts. In this regard, special attention should be paid to state reports submitted to the UN Human Rights Committee under Article 40 on their realization of Article 1 of the ICCPR (the right to self-determination), submissions to the Third Committee of the UN General Assembly (Social, Humanitarian & Cultural Issues), as well as pleadings before the International Court of Justice during the *Kosovo* Advisory Opinion, where states articulated their views on unilateral declarations of independence, remedial secession, and the relationship between self-determination and territorial integrity. In addition, domestic laws, especially constitutional provisions, can be indicative of states' perceptions of ISD. Finally, domestic judicial practices, especially those of constitutional or supreme courts, are significant for understanding the correlation between internal self-determination and secession.[15]

2.1 *Travaux Préparatoires: Friendly Relations Declaration*

The problem of the scope and validity of the right to self-determination resurfaced during the preparation of the text of the Friendly Relations Declaration.[16] It comes as no surprise if one takes into account the provision of paragraph 4 of the Principle of Equal Rights and Self-determination of Peoples, which stipulates that self-determination is to be realised through 'the establishment of a sovereign and independent State, the free association or integration with an independent State or the emergence into any other political status freely determined by a people'.[17] Despite a few views (expressed by Burma, India, Nigeria and Ghana) on confining self-determination to the people under colonial domination,[18] withholding it to racial and religious minorities in already existing states (Cyprus),[19] granting the right to the people constitutionally entitled

15 The stance of states could also be extracted from public officials' statements and general policies, taking into account the historical context. Alternatively, a shorthand approach could be to reference the list of states that adopted the UN Friendly Relations Declaration or the Vienna Declaration and Programme of Action. Yet, due to the amplitude and diversity of state statements on the one hand and their potential simplicity on the other, such stances will not be elaborated.

16 From 1963 until the last session in 1970, this task was led by the UN Special Committee. See UNGA Res 1966(XVIII) (16 Dec. 1963).

17 UNGA Res 2625(XXV) 'Declaration on Principles of International Law concerning Friendly Relations and Cooperation among States in accordance with the Charter of the United Nations' (24 Oct. 1970) (Friendly Relations Declaration) Principle V, paragraph 4.

18 UN Doc. A/AC.125/SR.68 (4 Dec. 1967) (Burma) 8, (India) 10. UN Doc. A/AC.125/SR.91 (1968) (Nigeria) 111, (Ghana) 115.

19 UN Doc. A/5725 (22 Jul. 1964) 28.

to it,[20] or even creating a list of eligible territories (the United States and the United Kingdom),[21] the ultimate consensus was reached to maintain the *universality* of the right's addresses – 'all people' have the said right.[22] The alleged universality, in turn, provoked a problem of greater significance, namely the need for striking a balance between territorial integrity and the right to self-determination. To address this, the overwhelming majority of states opined that self-determination should not impair territorial integrity. Among them were Australia, Kenya, Canada, Senegal, Spain, Guatemala, Argentina, Nigeria, and Greece, to mention just a few.[23] Paragraph 8 of the Principle makes it clear that states should 'refrain from any action aimed at the partial or total disruption of the national unity or territorial integrity of another state or country'. This effectively means that states fulfil their obligation to promote the right to external self-determination by doing so with reference to entities where the right has not yet been realised (colonies),[24] but they must not misuse this right in already independent states, for example, by supporting armed secessionist movements or extending recognition to them.[25] On the other hand, states should respect and promote the equal rights of peoples and their right to cultural, social and economic self-determination exercised internally, as well as any other internal political status consented by the people living within a multinational state.

The most vexing issue of the Declaration relates to the formulation of paragraph 7, which protects territorial integrity if governments are representative. This clause contains an element of conditionality and strengthens the

20 Report of the Special Committee on Principles of International Law concerning Friendly Relations and Cooperation among States (hereinafter: Report of the Special Committee) 24 GAOR, 1969, Supp. No. 4, UN Doc. A/7619, para 156.

21 Report of the Special Committee (1966) para 459; Report of the Special Committee (1967) para 176.

22 25 GAOR, 1970, Supp. No.18, 41. Note the UK's hesitance in using the term 'right', which was deemed to engender the secession entitlement, but this view was expressed in 1964, prior to the adoption of the Covenants. Consideration of Principles of International Law Concerning Friendly Relations and Co-Operation Among States in Accordance with the Charter of the United Nations: Comments Received from Governments, UN Doc. A/5725/Add.4 (22 Sep. 1964) (UK) 5–6.

23 21 GAOR, 1966, 6th Cmttee. 935th mtg., UN Doc. A/C.6/SR.935 (Australia) para 8; 22 GAOR, 1967, 6th Cmttee., 997th mtg., UN Doc. A/C.6/SR.997 (Kenya) para 6; *Ibid.* 999th mtg., UN. Doc. A/C.6/SR.999 (Canada) para 30; *Ibid.* 1002nd mtg., UN. Doc. A/C.6/SR.1002 (Senegal) para 3; *Ibid.* (Spain) para 49; 23 GAOR, 1968, 6th Cmttee, 1086th mtg., UN Doc. A/C.6/SR.1086 (Guatemala) para 53; 24 GAOR, 1969, 6th Cmttee. 1161st mtg., UN Doc. A/C.6/SR.1161 (Argentina) para 18; *Ibid.* 1162nd mtg., UN Doc. A/C.6/SR.1162 (Nigeria) para 90; *Ibid.* 1181st mtg., UN Doc. A/C.6/SR.1181 (Greece) para 33.

24 Principle 5, paragraph 2.

25 UN Doc. A/AC.125/SR.107 (1969) (Yugoslavia) 78–79.

necessity of the realisation of internal self-determination by dint of a sanction. This stands in stark contrast to other documents providing for the unconditional superiority of territorial integrity in already established states. Still, one could wonder whether the concluding paragraph 8 does not in reality trump the conditional formulation of paragraph 7.

The *travaux préparatoires* suggest that states were reluctant to read paragraph 7 in negative terms, preferring instead to amplify the secession prohibition in democratic states.[26] Thus, it could be argued that paragraph 7, on the one hand, concretized the meaning of internal self-determination by demanding representativeness, while on the other, augmented the prohibition of secession. The initial drafts were quite intuitive. The U.S. proposition stipulated:

> The existence of a sovereign and independent State possessing representative Government, effectively functioning as such to all distinct peoples within its territory is presumed to satisfy the principle of equal rights and self-determination as regards those peoples.[27]

The UK furnished a very similar idea – if states possess 'a representative government, effectively functioning as such with respect to all distinct peoples within their territory', those states 'shall be considered to be conducting themselves in conformity with this principle as regards those peoples'.[28] This would mean that self-determination is fulfilled in states representing the whole population and, by implication, any further claims to this right would be excluded. The U.S. and the UK underlined that their proposals were not intended to condone secessionist movements.[29] Australia endorsed those suggestions arguing that 'the principle of equal rights and self-determination of peoples, should not be used internationally to disrupt the unity and dismember the territory of existing states', maintaining however that states should protect minorities by implementing the RSD through effective representative institutions.[30] Yet, in view of the various interpretation possibilities of the phrase 'representative

26 J. Summers, *Peoples and International Law* (Brill 2014) 225–227.

27 Report of the Special Committee (1966) para 459.

28 UN Doc. A/AC.125/L.44 (19 Jul. 1967) 8–9.

29 UN Doc. A/AC.125/SR.69 (4 Dec. 1967) (UK) 19; UN Doc. A/AC.125/SR.105 (1969) (UK) 55. See also the comment by the UK Foreign Minister that 'it is widely accepted at the United Nations that the right of self-determination does not give every distinct group or territorial sub-division within a state the right to secede from it and thereby dismember the territorial integrity or political unity of sovereign independents' 54 *British Yearbook of International Law* (1983) 409. Cited in the Written statement of Serbia (17 Apr. 2009) para 563, fn. 538. UN Doc. A/AC.125/SR.92 (1968) (U.S.) 133.

30 UN Doc. A/AC.125/SR.107 (4 Sep. 1969) (Australia) 75.

government', stronger written assurances were sought. Italian representative declared that the incorporation of the saving clause ensured 'that the principle would not be interpreted in such a way as to undermine the territorial integrity of independent States, which was safeguarded as fundamental by the Charter'.[31] As a result, Italy went a step further and in 1970 proposed an informal draft stipulating that

> states enjoying full sovereignty and independence, and possessed of a government representing the whole of their population, shall be considered to be conducting themselves in conformity with the principle of equal rights and self-determination of peoples as regards that population. Nothing in the foregoing paragraphs shall be construed as authorizing any action which would impair, totally or in part, the territorial integrity, or political unity, of such States.[32]

The draft was seconded by Canada and Poland, arguing that such language cannot be understood to justify territorial changes of states. For Canada, any reading of the text as giving a right to a dislocation of a state within which various communities had been 'co-habiting successfully and peacefully' was inconceivable.[33] Poland, on the other hand, cautioned about the potential territorial pretensions by neighbouring states, which should be categorically excluded.[34] The final adopted version was quite similar and provides:

> Nothing in the foregoing paragraphs shall be construed as authorizing or encouraging any action which would dismember or impair, totally or in part, the territorial integrity or political unity of sovereign and independent States conducting themselves in compliance with the principle of equal rights and self-determination of peoples as described above and thus possessed of a government representing the whole people belonging to the territory without distinction as to race, creed or colour.

Although some present-day commentaries interpret the safeguard clause as both preventing and authorising secession, the opinions expressed by states at the time of the adoption of the Declaration were clearly against the possibility of secession. As observed by France in 1970,

---

31 Report of the Special Committee (1969) para 187.
32 Report of the Special Committee (1970) para 63.
33 UN Doc. A/AC.125/SR.114 (1970) (Canada) 57.
34 *Ibid.* (Poland) 58.

> it was no less obvious that the exercise of that right must not result in the destruction of what already existed and met the requirements of that principle: that was indeed the effect of the safeguard clause in the seventh and eighth paragraphs.[35]

Kohen posits that the right to self-determination was originally conceived by states as applicable not to specific national, ethnic, tribal, racial, or religious minority groups, but rather to entire populations.[36] Thornbury and Quane, representing a similar view, earlier concluded that self-determination should be achieved and externally supported if a *whole* population is discriminated by an oppressive, imposed government.[37] Notably, South Africa in defence of its apartheid misdeeds, was the only state who argued that paragraph 7 may be seen as applicable to minorities within states.[38] Hilpold, in consequence, construed the whole Principle of Equal Rights and Self-determination, including paragraph 7, as primarily relevant to colonial situations, which he likened to South Africa's apartheid regime.[39] Fox, by reviewing previous state and institutional responses to secessionist crises in Katanga and Biafra, ruled out the presumption of an *a contrario* reading of the safeguard clause in reference to already independent states.[40]

Summing up, in the preparation of the Friendly Relations Declaration states struck a balance between the principles of self-determination and territorial integrity. External self-determination was envisaged for peoples under colonial or alien domination and racially oppressed majorities represented by national liberation movements, whereas internal self-determination was primarily intended for established states, with its fulfilment through representative governance serving as an additional guarantee against subversive motives. There is nothing in the *travaux préparatoires* that would suggest that unrepresentative governments could be liable to territorial dismemberment.[41]

---

35 *Ibid.* (France) 48.

36 M. Kohen, 'Self-determination' in J. E. Viñuales (ed.) *The Principles of the Friendly Relations Declaration* (CUP 2020) 143–147.

37 P. Thomberry, 'Self-determination, Minorities, Human Rights: A Review of International Instruments' 38 *International and Comparative Law Quarterly* (1989) 877; H. Quane, 'The United Nations and the Evolving Right to Self Determination' 47 *International and Comparative Law Quarterly* (1998) 563.

38 UN Doc. A/C.6/SR.1184 (28 Sep. 1970) (South Africa) para 15.

39 P. Hilpold, *Autonomy and Self-determination: Between Legal Assertions and Utopian Aspirations* (Elgar 2018) 38.

40 Fox (n 1) 740–747.

41 Arguably, only the Netherlands viewed Paragraph 7 as potentially authorizing secession. See UN Doc. A/AC.125/SR.107 (1969) 85. This position has changed in the *Kosovo Advisory*

2.2 *Debates in the United Nations General Assembly Third Committee (Social, Humanitarian and Cultural Issues)*

During the debates in the UN General Assembly, state representatives advanced arguments reflecting divergent interpretations of the RSD. In 1952, Mrs. Roosevelt of the US pronounced in the Third Committee that 'the right of self-determination did not mean the right of secession' and that it should not be interpreted rigidly, either as independence or slavery. A more nuanced version, which accommodates the needs of the people and interests of the states, is preferred. As a good example of such cohabitation, befitting the notion of ISD, she referred to the continued French legal system in Louisiana, Spanish as one of the official languages in Arizona and New Mexico's legislature, the ability to worship in the language of people's choice throughout the US as well as the possibility to choose the teacher and programme in every US state and town.[42] Accordingly, in the United States 'every group of the population enjoyed the right to self-determination', while to 'grant the automatic exercise of the absolute right of political self-determination to every section of the population would be detrimental to the interests of the population as a whole'.[43] In 1996, Myanmar's delegate speaking to the UN Third Committee invoked the Vienna Declaration stipulating that self-determination does not authorize any sort of territorial dismemberment of independent states; it applies only to the people under colonial or alien occupation. Yet, he added that 'Myanmar was engaged in a broad-based national dialogue aimed at meeting the aspirations of the numerous national ethnic groups in order to create a pluralist, multi-party democracy in a modern and developed State', alluding *de facto* to internal self-determination.[44] Since the agenda item was titled 'the right of peoples to self-determination', Myanmar implicitly tried to show that respect for ISD augments territorial integrity, despite its traditionally rigid stance on the matter. The Indian delegate argued similarly, mentioning the Vienna Declaration and the UN Secretary-General's warning about the dangers of limitless fragmentation if every ethnic, religious or linguistic minority could invoke self-determination as a separation entitlement. This interpretation was accompanied by the observation that 'democratic societies provided adequate scope for the self-determination of peoples' and that self-determination 'could not be used to encourage the division or disintegration

---

Opinion where a dozen of states advocated for remedial secession on the basis of Paragraph 7. See Summers (n 26) 237–238.

42 UN Doc. A/C.3/SR.447 (18 Nov. 1952) 174.

43 *Ibid.* 174–175.

44 UN Doc. A/C.3/51/SR.28 (19 Sep. 1997) 16.

of pluralist, sovereign, democratic States'.[45] Here, a clear indication of ISD being a method of preventing secession could be seen. The representative of Ukraine at the same session pointed out that 'the right to self-determination could not be equated with separatism' but could be granted only 'to an ethnic *entity* within the general framework of the right to national self-determination', particularly when such an entity constitutes a compact community or a majority in a specific territory.[46] At the same time, the representative mentioned that Ukraine had granted broad administrative and territorial autonomy to Crimea as well as adopted non-discriminatory measures, consistent with internationally recognized principles of human rights, to solve the social and economic problems of the region. With this sentence, the Ukrainian representative endorsed the correlation between ISD and anti-secession. The Iraqi envoy underlined that the Iraqi Constitution protects the rights of Kurds and the other two minorities in Iraq - Syrians and Turks, who are permitted to have political parties and associations through which they express their aspirations and opinions. In addition, the constitution provides for equality among all linguistic, religious and national groups, and, against that background, those minorities do not possess the right to independence and must respect the territorial integrity of the state.[47] Again, the presumption of adherence to ISD as bolstering territorial wholeness is perceptible. At the 26th session of the Third Committee of the General Assembly, a Sudanese diplomat submitted that self-determination should not be used 'as an excuse for seeking to bring about the disintegration of States, interfering in their internal affairs or undermining their political unity and territorial integrity', which is in line with the viewpoint of the Organization of African Unity. With regard to the value of ISD, he added that Sudan regards the presence of different languages, ethnic groups and creeds within its territory as a source of enrichment for the country, as a 'factor tending to foster its unity, not its disintegration'.[48] The Brazilian representative at the same session stated that self-determination should not be misinterpreted as leading to 'acts of fragmentation or separatism based exclusively on ethnic considerations', and, all the more, should not be used against states with 'legitimate governments which fully respect democratic principles and protect the rights of minorities'.[49] The Russian delegate, after denying the right to secede to extremist groups that were 'increasingly using

45 *Ibid.* 4.

46 *Ibid.* See also UN Doc. E/CN.4/1996/SR.7 (2 May 1996) para 31.

47 *Ibid.* 11.

48 UN Doc. A/C.3/51/SR.26 (18 Sep. 1997) 7.

49 *Ibid.* 13.

the slogan of self-determination', laid down the real contemporary purpose of the RSD, which, in his view, lies in its internal character. According to him, the 1996 Cultural and National Autonomy Act envisaged the exercise of self-determination by the peoples of the Russian Federation through

> various forms of national and cultural self-determination which encompassed the principles of the right of citizens to associate themselves freely with a particular ethnic group, organization and autonomy, diversity in methods of internal organization, a combination of social initiatives with State support, respect for the language, culture, traditions and customs of citizens of different ethnicities and respect for law and order.[50]

Consequently, it is 'federalism and national and cultural self-determination', not 'violence, separatism and extremism', which reaffirms a people's 'political status in addition to ensuring their economic, social and cultural development and well-being'.[51]

2.3 *Reports to the Human Rights Committee*

According to Article 40 of the ICCPR, state parties are obliged to submit periodic reports on the implementation of the provisions incorporated in the Covenant. Judging by the reports, the overwhelming majority of states understand self-determination in its internal fashion and furnish information as to how they comply with their obligations.[52] This could be translated as corroboration of the thesis that self-determination in sovereign states should be respected and that states see it as their obligation towards their inhabitants rather than as an entitlement of a group to secede.[53] Albania in its report noted that the Albanian people exercise their self-determination on the strength of the Constitution of the Republic of Albania and the international agreements to which

50 *Ibid.* 15.

51 *Ibid.*

52 Taylor remarks, however, that states do so inadequately or confuse Article 1 with other provisions, particularly Article 25 (e.g. by responding to Article 1 through reference to election laws) or Article 27 (e.g. by addressing only minority issues). P. M. Taylor, *A Commentary on the International Covenant on Civil and Political Rights: The UN Human Rights Committee's Monitoring of ICCPR Rights* (CUP 2020) 55.

53 Out of the 97 state reports analysed by Quane, 69 (or 79%) directly or indirectly comment on internal self-determination. H. Quane, 'A Right to Self-determination for the Kosovo Albanians?' 13 *Leiden Journal of International Law* (2000) 221, fn.17.

Albania is a party.[54] Referring to the economic aspect of the RSD, Albania mentioned the Law on the Restitution and Compensation of Property, which provides for the restitution or compensation for the confiscated, expropriated or nationalized property under the communist regime from 1944 onwards. As shown in the previous chapter, ISD is often conceived as a conglomerate of human rights, and, arguably, their provision and respect bolsters state's territorial integrity.[55] Angola too linked self-determination to its constitution, in particular Article 2, which addresses the democratic nature of the state and the sovereignty of the people, and Article 3, which stipulates how this popular sovereignty is exercised – through universal, free, equal, direct, secret and periodic suffrage in referendums and various forms established in the constitution.[56] The report also proffers that Angola protects the land rights of rural communities, including those based on use and custom as well as fosters 'friendly and cooperative relations with all States and peoples on the basis of the principles enshrined in the Constitution and respect for national sovereignty and independence and equality between States and the rights of peoples to self-determination'.[57] Germany, in its fourth periodic report, observed that the Cold War prevented the German people for a long time from freely determining their own political status and that while the free determination of a political status is very important, in the established states the internal aspect is crucial. In Germany, the Basic Law of the Federal Republic of Germany secures the free democratic basic order and lays the foundations for the economic, social and cultural development, over which individuals exert political influence through elections and public participation.[58] Denmark, on the other hand, presented very lengthy information on its compliance with Article 1 of the ICCPR in its fifth periodic report, in which it outlined the relationship between Denmark proper on the one hand and Greenland and the Faroe Islands on the other. Denmark referred to the Home Rule Arrangements with Greenland and the Faroe Islands, which recognize self-governance of both communities, envisage assembly and governmental bodies, allow two members of each community to sit in the Danish Parliament and recognize both Faroe and Greenlandic

54 Consideration of reports submitted by States parties under article 40 of the Covenant, Second Periodic Report by Albania, UN Doc. CCPR/C/ALB/2 (2011) 8.

55 See 4.2.4.

56 Consideration of reports submitted by States parties under article 40 of the Covenant, Second Periodic Report by Angola, UN Doc. CCPR/C/AGO/2 (2017) 5–6. As illustrated in 4.2.1., free will is the cornerstone of ISD.

57 *Ibid.* 6.

58 Consideration of reports submitted by States parties under article 40 of the Covenant, Fourth Periodic Report by Germany, UN Doc. CCPR/C/84/Add.5 (1996) 5–6.

languages as principal languages, along with their separate flags.[59] The report delineates further possibilities of the transfer of power to the public authorities of Greenland and the Faroe Islands, which is in line with advocating ISD, but, interestingly, does not oppose the independence of the communities should they choose to separate.[60] An equally interesting example is that of New Zealand, which in its report expressed its commitment to furthering self-determination of Tokelau, an island distanced from its shores by almost 4,000 km, which it currently administers. New Zealand, apart from devolving powers to local institutions, expressed readiness to enter into a free association with the island inhabited by 1,500 people, should Tokelauans decide to change their status from a Non-Self-Governing Territory (curiously enough, no reference to the independence option is made).[61] The fifth Peruvian periodic report at its very beginning remarks that 'self-determination means the political participation of peoples'. In light of this, Peru struggles to provide national identity document (NID) to every citizen (at the moment of the report, 2011, 85.1 per cent of members of Amazonian native communities had a NID), which will enable the exercise of political rights: 'to take part in referendums, put forward legislative proposals, remove or recall authorities and demand accountability'.[62] The report further states that Peru recognizes and protects the rights of indigenous peoples to the lands that they traditionally occupy and use as a means of subsistence. Additionally, Peru acknowledges and safeguards the nation's ethnic and cultural pluralism, aims to ensure a healthy environment for all, and shares the wealth from hydrocarbon exploitation.[63] In its previous report, Peru presented a more explicit correlation between ISD and the prohibition of secession, stating first that the Peruvian State is 'one and indivisible', noting later that it adheres to the principles of decentralization and representatives.[64] India, in its third report, opined against external self-determination in post-colonial settings while acknowledging the existence of internal self-determination,

---

59 Consideration of reports submitted by States parties under article 40 of the Covenant, Fifth Periodic Report by Denmark, UN Doc. CCPR/C/DNK/5 (2007) 3–9.

60 *Ibid.* 6, 10–11.

61 Consideration of reports submitted by States parties under article 40 of the Covenant, Fifth Periodic Report by New Zealand, UN Doc. CCPR/C/NZL/5 (2008) 18. In February 2006, and again in October 2007, Tokelau held referenda on its political status, in which the population voted to remain a colony, as the required two-thirds majority for a change in status was not achieved.

62 Consideration of reports submitted by States parties under article 40 of the Covenant, Fifth Periodic Report by Peru, UN Doc. CCPR/C/PER/5 (2011) 8.

63 *Ibid.* 8–9.

64 Consideration of reports submitted by States parties under article 40 of the Covenant, Fourth Periodic Report by Peru, UN Doc. CCPR/C/PER/98/4 (1998) 3.

which includes the right of the people to choose their government and the broader right to democratic governance. India's stance is augmented by its reference to the slightly amended safeguard clause in the Vienna Declaration and Programme of Action and the UN 50th Anniversary Declaration.[65] The United States of America in its report noted that self-determination remains a core principle of American governance, as reflected in Articles I and II of the Constitution, and proceeded to debate the situation of the Insular Areas (Puerto Rico, Guan, American Samoa, the U.S. Virgin Islands, the Northern Mariana Islands, the Marshall Islands, the Federated States of Micronesia, and Palau) as well as the status of American Indians and Alaska Natives. It noted that the Insular Areas constitute an 'integral part of the U.S. political family', while the latter population spans over 100 million acres of U.S. territory.[66] The United States expressed its commitment to enhancing tribal autonomy, underscoring that tribal leaders must be an integral part of every solution that pertains to them. To this end, many consultations and conferences are held, and huge financial resources are allocated to tribes, either as compensation for land use or to support future development.[67] Russia's seventh periodic report makes clear that 'the right to self-determination in the Russian Federation is exercised through various autonomous ethnic territories and autonomous ethnic and cultural organizations'.[68] Russia maintains that ethnic identity, geographical considerations, and other distinctive features of each constituent entity are duly considered and that the role of local self-government within the system of elected bodies in the Russian Federation has been considerably enhanced. The dual principles of self-determination and federalism are enshrined in the Russian Constitution.[69]

Accordingly, states very rarely comment on the right to external self-determination, either domestically or internationally, and mainly interpret the RSD as a lasting cultural, economic and social development obligation towards the people of a state. Politically, self-determination is generally restricted to autonomy, participation, and non-discrimination, which are safeguarded by the appropriate legal framework.

---

65 Consideration of reports submitted by States parties under article 40 of the Covenant, Third Periodic Report by India, UN Doc. CCPR/C/76/Add.6 (1996) 13.

66 Consideration of reports submitted by States parties under article 40 of the Covenant, Fourth Periodic Report by the United States of America, UN Doc. CCPR/C/USA/4 (2012) 7–8.

67 *Ibid.* 8–9.

68 Consideration of reports submitted by States parties under article 40 of the Covenant, Seventh Periodic Report by Russian Federation, UN Doc. CCPR/C/RUS/7 (2013) 3.

69 *Ibid.*

2.4 *Submissions in the ICJ's Kosovo Case*

The Kosovo case has attracted considerable attention of states. In total, 43 states plus Kosovo made submissions before the Court, either in writing or orally.[70] Among those participating in the proceedings were five permanent members of the UN Security Council, hence the Kosovo case is considered as a valuable source of *opinio juris* on important issues of general international law, including self-determination and territorial integrity.[71]

The stances of states on ISD as a method of preventing secession are best extrapolated from their broader views on secession. In truth, not all states broached the subject, restricting themselves to the posed question, while some others stuck to the traditional view that secession is not regulated by international law.[72] Among those that pronounced remedial secession (and, by extension, the failure of internal self-determination as a justification for secession) were Albania, Germany, the Netherlands, Finland, Switzerland, Estonia, Slovenia, Ireland, Latvia, Poland, Jordan, and Russia. Albania in its Written Comments contended that Kosovar Albanians had established parallel institutions because of their unfair treatment in Serbia (then the FRY), evidenced in their exclusion from public life, dismissal from jobs, or the denial of education to Albanian pupils in their native language, which was tantamount to the breach of internal self-determination.[73] Albania endorsed secession beyond decolonization upon meeting specific requirements, such as discrimination and other human rights abuses (which it argued Kosovo had experienced) and derived the entitlement for secession from the 'safeguard clause' of the Friendly Relations Declaration.[74] As was observed,

> It is incorrect that a reading of the safeguard clause can in any way be used as an argument against secession in a situation as Kosovo. This is exactly what the paragraph wanted to avoid by limiting its applicability to situations where States conduct themselves in compliance with the principle of equal rights and self-determination of peoples and are possessed of a government representing the whole people without distinction as to race, creed and colour.[75]

---

70 There were two written and one oral round. M. Milanović, 'Arguing the Kosovo Case' in M. Woods and M. Milanović (eds.) *The Law and Politics of the Kosovo Advisory Opinion* (OUP 2015) 23.

71 *Ibid.*

72 See, *inter alia*, Written Statement of Sierra Leone (15 Apr. 2009) 1–2; Written Statement of the Czech Republic (14 Apr. 2009) 7; Written Statement of France (7 Apr. 2009) 25–28.

73 Written Comments of Albania (Jul. 2009) 13–14.

74 *Ibid.* 32–35.

75 *Ibid.* 34.

In December 2009, Jordan addressed the issue of territorial integrity in a public sitting, suggesting that this principle is not absolute. Jordan referenced both the Friendly Relations Declaration and the Vienna Declaration to support this view. Moreover, Jordan acknowledged the historical injustices faced by native Albanians, highlighting persecution, police brutality, arbitrary imprisonment, and the revocation of Kosovo's autonomy. In Jordan's assessment, these circumstances satisfied the high threshold necessary for the transition from ISD to ESD in the specific context of Kosovo.[76] Jordan made a noteworthy observation, asserting that any attempt to revert to the status *quo ante* – prior to Kosovo's unilateral declaration of independence – would amount to a violation of the population's right to self-determination.[77] Germany in its Verbal Note concurred with the differentiation between internal and external self-determination, whereby internal self-determination denotes a level of autonomy inside a larger entity, in which relevant local matters can be decided, and is a preferred modality for the realization of self-determination in the contemporary international order.[78] Nonetheless, it acknowledged that secession may occur in post-colonial times, but *only* if it is meant to contribute to the realization of ISD. To this end, Germany referred to the *Quebec* case and posited:

> For this condition to be met, it is required that the authorities of the State in which a certain, distinct group is living consistently and over a considerable period of time deny to this group any right to have a say in matters directly concerning it, by denying it any decisional autonomy as well as any meaningful participation in the deliberations on the central level. (...) it is really the denial of internal self-determination which counts for this argument.[79]

The Written Statement of the Netherlands neatly demonstrates the correlation between ISD and territorial integrity. After distinguishing between internal and external self-determination, the Netherlands submitted that

> outside the context of non-self-governing territories, foreign occupation and consensual agreement – a people must, *in principle*, seek to exercise the right to political self-determination with respect for the principle of

76 Public sitting (9 Dec. 2009) CR 2009/31, 29, 32–33.

77 *Ibid.* 35–36.

78 Public sitting (2 Dec. 2009) CR 2009/26, 30.

79 Written Statement of Germany (Verbalnote No. 54) (15 Apr. 2009) 35.

territorial integrity and thus exercise its right within existing international boundaries.[80]

According to the Netherlands, the right to political self-determination may evolve into a right to external self-determination in exceptional circumstances, i.e. in unique cases, or cases *sui generis*, yet this is an exception to the *rule*, and therefore should be construed narrowly.[81] During the public sitting in December in The Hague, Azerbaijan noted the existence of internal and external aspects of self-determination. Referring to the works of acclaimed scholars, like Higgins and Cassese, and drawing on the practice of states and international organizations, particularly the Human Rights Committee, Azerbaijan concluded that minorities cannot secede under present-day international law, but should exercise their RSD internally, where it confers multiple rights.[82] Belarus, in the same sitting, distinguished ESD and ISD, noting that 'internal right of self-determination usually means the right of ethnic minorities for self-determination' (...) which 'is implemented within the borders of the existing States and may involve such modes as national-cultural autonomy, territorial autonomy, federation, active participation in the single State's governance'.[83] After assessing the concept to remedial secession and, in consequence rejecting it, Belarus underlined the validity of the central thesis that 'if central authorities respect the right to self-determination without any discrimination and the territory, notwithstanding this, demands for secession, such secession would be a *manifest* violation of the principles of self-determination territorial integrity and inviolability of frontiers'.[84] Stated differently, honouring ISD strengthens territorial integrity, whereas its disrespect is rather inconsequential. The Russian Federation in its Written Statement maintained that self-determination in Russia is exercised through constituent entities, such as republics and autonomous regions, as well as through local national/cultural autonomous entities and that it believed that 'that the same principles may and should be applied (and indeed are often applied) in other countries', an approach that is 'well-founded in the applicable

80 Written Statement of the Kingdom of the Netherlands (17 Apr. 2009) 8.

81 *Ibid.*

82 Public sitting (3 Dec. 2009) CR 2009/27, 21–24. See also Human Rights Committee, General Comment No. 23 (8 Apr. 1994) paras 3.1 and 3.2 (Article 27 of the Covenant cannot prejudice the sovereignty and territorial integrity of States). To the same effect, the commentary to the Declaration on the Rights of Persons Belonging to National or Ethnic, Religious and Linguistic Minorities, UN Doc. E/CN.4/Sub.2/AC.5/2001/2, para 15.

83 *Ibid.* 29.

84 *Ibid.* 30 (emphasis added).

principles and rules of international law'.[85] Referring to the correlation between self-determination and territorial integrity, Russia maintained that the basis for this relationship is to be found in the so-called 'safeguard clause'. Accordingly, it pointed out that

> this passage suggests that a State that respects the rights of peoples living in its territory, is protected by the principle of territorial integrity from the implementation of the right to self-determination in the form of secession ("external self-determination").[86]

Russia, alluding to the ruling in the *Quebec* case, which found no inherent incompatibility between maintaining the territorial integrity of existing states and the right of a people to achieve a full measure of self-determination, concluded that 'internal self-determination is in fact preferred in the postcolonial world', whereas secession is allowed only as a last resort.[87]

The coexistence of territorial integrity and the RSD is also evident in the pleadings of other states opposed to Kosovo's independence.[88] Cyprus, for example, maintained that the RSD 'applies between the State and all its population, giving people the right to choose the form of government and have access to constitutional rights. This is internal self-determination'.[89] Thus, Serbia bears a duty to secure ISD for Albanians as a minority group,[90] while no right to secession exists. Such a right, Cyprus concluded, is neither recognized under customary international law nor supported by the UN or state practice.[91] Especially, it cannot be inferred from the inverted reading of the Friendly Relations Declaration's safeguard clause – any such right would require a positive legal basis. By so arguing, Cyprus reaffirmed its restrictive reading of the clause. In the same vein, Serbia submitted that

> international law recognises the right of self-determination with regard to peoples within independent States as meaning the right of such peoples to participate in the governance of such States and generally to benefit

85 Written Statement by the Russian Federation (16 Apr. 2009) 2.

86 *Ibid.* 29–30.

87 *Ibid.* 30, 32.

88 Serbia, Argentina, Cyprus, Spain, China, Iran and Slovakia. Azerbaijan, Romania, Venezuela and Bolivia. Vietnam and Belarus. Libya remained the only pro–Serbian country that did not comment on remedial secession or the issue of territorial integrity.

89 Written Statement of Cyprus (17 Apr. 2009) para 135.

90 *Ibid.* para 139.

91 *Ibid.* para 143.

> from the collective expression of relevant human rights but strictly and solely within the territorial framework of the State in question.

Consequently, purely anti-secession views, including those rejecting remedial secession, can hardly corroborate the cause-and-effect relationship between the ISD and the prohibition of secession. However, pleadings such as those by Cyprus and Serbia, which allude to ISD and the incumbent obligations of the state, testify to their particular viewpoint of the RSD. Conversely, the pro-remedial–secession argument befits more convincingly the said relationship, for there internal self-determination prohibits secession as long as it is complied with. Lastly, one must admit that the neutrality of international law on secession further complicates this relationship. If international law is silent on secession, states may dispense ISD at their discretion, but such discretion would not necessarily safeguard their territorial integrity. However, if international law indeed obliges states to secure the enjoyment of the RSD to peoples (as it arguably does), then it is not fair to say that the same law remains neutral on the prospective secession. Why would states bear the duty to provide for the RSD internally, only for those same peoples to secede without any legal consequence under international law? This inconsistency is indeed perplexing.

If we agree that states participating in the Kosovo proceedings constitute a representative sample of the international community, then it follows that the international community is in a state of conflict over the relationship between territorial integrity and the right to secession, arguably emanating from the RSD (14 states denied the existence of the right to remedial secession, 14 endorsed it, while 25 remained neutral).[92] This division marks a notable departure from the more uniform state practice observed during the drafting of the Friendly Relations Declaration. On the other hand, it highlights the enduring relevance of ISD in existing states, also as a method to forestall secession. Nevertheless, it must be acknowledged that the Kosovo proceedings were among the most complex in the history of the Court, and the advisory opinion itself was significantly shaped by political considerations.[93]

92 For instance, Jordan argued that 'a right to external self-determination which in the case takes the form of the assertion of a right to unilateral secession'. Public sitting (9 Dec. 2009) CR 2009/31, 36.

93 Private conversation with Professor Crawford and Judge Simma at the Lauterpacht Centre for International Law, Michaelmas Term 2013.

2.5 *The Liechtenstein Initiative on Self-determination*

It is useful to more broadly reflect on 'the Liechtenstein Initiative on Self-determination', which has focused on applying self-determination within states, with an aim to prevent and resolve conflicts without resorting to secession. Lichtenstein indeed has been a champion in advocating internal self-determination.

Shortly after its admission to the United Nations in 1990, it drafted a Convention on Self-determination Through Self-Administration, which was debated in the General Assembly. However, due to politically sensitive issues – particularly those concerning the establishment of a regime that is not only precise but also practical and effective in implementation – the Convention was not enacted.[94] However, the Draft Convention serves as a vital foundation for further discussions and refinement with the goal of developing a framework that is both operational and acceptable to all stakeholders involved. The essence of the Draft Convention lies in prioritizing self-administration over complete independence. As Watts, the co-author of the Convention, has observed, in many circumstances 'self-administration by itself may be a sufficient exercise of the right of self-determination, without the need to move on to full independence' and added that:

> there is no advantage to be gained by insisting on independence and thus excluding other kinds of status if, in particular circumstances, they would grant a community all it wants in order to be able to acknowledge its distinctive characteristics without forcing it to assume the additional burdens of a wholly independent existence.[95]

In Article 2 of the proposed Convention, the concept of self-administration is elaborated within the broader framework of self-determination. According to this provision, states are obliged to 'respect the aspiration' of all communities within their territory for an 'appropriate degree' of self-administration and ensure that such self-administration is granted to them. This commitment is flexible because the level of self-administration deemed 'appropriate' will vary based on the specific circumstances of each community. Article 4 of the Draft Convention delineates the responsibilities of each State Party regarding

---

94 The text of the Draft Convention can be found in A. Watts, 'The Liechtenstein Draft Convention on Self-determination through Self-Administration: A Commentary' in W. Danspeckgruber and A. Watts (eds.) *Self-determination and Self-Administration A Sourcebook* (Lynne Rienner Publishers 1997) 36–45.

95 *Ibid.* 22–23.

communities within its territory. These responsibilities include granting community members the right to preserve their culture, religion, and language (subparagraph a), allowing participation in public affairs and elections at various levels (subparagraph b), permitting the establishment of a community organization for the purposes of representation (subparagraph c), enabling the election of representatives for this organization (subparagraph d), establishing governmental organs primarily concerned with the community's interests (subparagraph e), involving elected representatives in decisions related to state funds and other matters affecting the community (subparagraph f), and refraining from discrimination based on the community's distinctive characteristics (subparagraph g). As Watts notes, none of these rights is fundamentally novel or onerous for states to accord; to a considerable extent, they reflect obligations that states have already assumed under various human rights instruments and correspond to practices already adopted in many jurisdictions.[96] The Draft becomes more intricate in its subsequent articles, which employ a gradational system that progressively endows communities with additional competencies, but only upon the declaration of the State Party and the community's demonstrated capacity to fulfill its roles under the preceding provisions. For instance, Article 5 stipulates that a community may be granted the right to establish its own police forces or to nominate judges for lower courts within the community's area, provided it has effectively implemented Article 4. Additionally, the State Party may wish to confer upon the community the right to raise taxes payable by its members to cover communal expenses, or the right to enact laws on matters of local concern, as outlined in Article 6.[97] Finally, under Article 7 (which does not demand a declaration but merely a 'discussion' with the State Party), the community may be granted the right to pursue independence, provided it has exercised its broad-ranging competencies set out in the preceding articles for a reasonable period of time. Such a gradational model of self-administration, while structured and conditional, may appear overambitious, or even destabilizing, for some states, given its eventual reference to independence, despite the Draft Convention's overall anti-secessionist orientation.[98]

---

96 *Ibid.* 27.

97 Note that Articles 5 and 6 reserve the right to the State Party to grant these additional competencies to the community, allowing it to exercise such rights within the limits of the Constitution and laws of the State, and in accordance with agreements and arrangements made between the State and the community in connection with these rights.

98 E. Cárdenas and M. Fernanda Cañás, 'The Limits of Self-determination' in W. Danspeckgruber (ed.) *The Self-determination of Peoples: Community, Nation, and State in an Interdependent World* (Lynne Rienner Publishers 2002) 116.

In 2000, the Liechtenstein Institute on Self-determination at Princeton University was founded to further develop the Initiative. In 2016, in collaboration with the Permanent Mission of Liechtenstein to the United Nations, the Institute organized a colloquium in Triesenberg, Liechtenstein, on the theme 'Reconciling Self-determination and Territorial Integrity: Models of Self-Governance as Tools to Promote Peace and Stability in Europe', which issued political and academic recommendations aimed at creating better guidelines on how to evaluate future self-determination claims, implement the Draft Convention in troubled places and secure the reconciliation of territorial integrity and self-determination in the OSCE region.[99] In 2018, a conference on the theme 'Self-determination in Conflict Prevention and Resolution' was held in New York, which concluded that self-determination should be understood to 'encompass expressions of self-governance, autonomy and self-government, as it is used, for example, in the area of indigenous peoples' rights' and that 'an appropriate level of self-governance consulted and agreed between the state and a community is the most promising option for resolving self-determination conflicts'.[100] In 2021, the two institutions issued the 'Handbook on the Prevention and Resolution of Self-determination Conflicts', which right at the beginning of its 'guidelines' underlines that the Liechtenstein Initiative on Self-determination is convinced that 'self-determination can be expressed "internally," i.e. without the formation of an independent state, as has previously been made clear with respect to Indigenous peoples'.[101] At the same time, it was stressed that it 'prioritizes solutions that include forms of self-governance', so that relevant communities may exercise authority and influence over matters affecting them.[102]

From the foregoing, it is clear that the Liechtenstein Initiative supports the thesis of ISD being a secession-prevention mode.

2.6 *National Legislation*

It is well known that a constitution defines the basis of the state's system, delineates the competencies of its most significant authorities, and establishes their mutual relationships. It typically also includes a catalogue of

---

99 Letter dated 15 June 2016 from the Permanent Representative of Liechtenstein to the United Nations addressed to the Secretary-General, UN Doc. A/70/955–S/2016/547 (23 Jun. 2016).

100 Letter dated 10 July 2019 from the Permanent Representative of Liechtenstein to the United Nations addressed to the Secretary-General, UN Doc. A/73/945 (15 Jul. 2019) 3.

101 Liechtenstein Institute on Self-determination & Liechtenstein Ministry of Foreign Affairs, *Handbook on the Prevention and Resolution of Self-determination Conflicts* (Trustees of Princeton University 2021) 5.

102 *Ibid.*

individual freedoms and rights. Constitutional references to popular sovereignty, democratic governance, the rule of law, institutions of self-government, representative bodies, and human rights have much in common with internal self-determination. Constitutions, in fact, provide the paramount framework for ISD, as the territorial, political and legal organization of state affairs must accord with these foundational legal documents.

Not without reason, state reports to the Human Rights Committee in relation to compliance with Article 1 of the ICCPR increasingly provide detailed descriptions of state's system of government or its constitution, indicating that states attach greater importance to the internal aspect of self-determination.[103]

State constitutions or national laws of a lower rank generally do not explicitly correlate the maintenance of territorial integrity with respect for internal self-determination. However, such a correlation is implicitly embedded in constitutional ideas or theories, such as federalism, constitutional pluralism, and integrative constitutionalism, which emphasize principles like subsidiarity and the accommodation of diversity within a unified state framework. Philosophical theories like communitarianism, liberal nationalism, and democratic theory align well with constitutionalism, as they uphold individual rights while safeguarding social and political unity for the benefit of all.[104] Furthermore, constitutional provisions on civil, political and territorial rights are sometimes articulated jointly with the 'territorial wholeness' of a state. For instance, Article 2 of the Spanish Constitution, stipulates that 'the Constitution is based on the indissoluble unity of the Spanish nation, the (…) indivisible homeland of all Spaniards, and recognises and guarantees the right to autonomy of the nationalities and regions of which make it is composed',[105] while Article 5 of the Italian Constitution sets out that 'the Republic, which is one and indivisible, recognises and promotes local autonomy; it applies the fullest measure of administrative decentralisation in services dependent on the state and adjusts the principles and methods of its legislation to the requirements of autonomy and decentralisation'.[106] These examples point to the balance between protecting minority rights and upholding the existing constitutional and

103 Quane, 'A Right to Self-determination for the Kosovo Albanians?' (n 53) 221.

104 Consult section 4.4. See also M. Kumm, 'The Cosmopolitan Turn in Constitutionalism: An Integrated Conception of Public Law' 20 *Indiana Journal of Global Legal Studies* (2013) 629 (who argues that national constitutional legitimacy depends, in part, on how the national constitution is integrated into and relates to the wider legal and political world. Only 'a state that incorporates and reflects the global legitimacy conditions for claims to sovereignty in its constitutional structure and foreign policy - is a legitimate state').

105 The Spanish Constitution (1978) Article 2.

106 The Constitution of the Italian Republic (1947) Article 5.

territorial framework. Some constitutions make direct references to the RSD. For instance, Article 235 of the South African Constitution provides that

> the right of the South African people as a whole to self-determination, as manifested in this Constitution, does not preclude (…) recognition of the notion of the right of self-determination of any community sharing a common cultural and language heritage, within a territorial entity in the Republic or in any other way, determined by national legislation.[107]

The South African Constitutional Court seconded the state unity indicating that the Constitution provides no options for separatism or independence of a group within the State, thereby making clear that its self-determination provisions pertain exclusively to ISD.[108] Similarly, the Russian Constitution highlights ISD by setting forth that the 'federal structure of the Russian Federation is based on its state integrity (…) the equality and self-determination of peoples in the Russian Federation'.[109] This suggests that the RSD can only be exercised within the framework of the Russian Federation. Other national laws are in line with the constitutional provisions (framework) regarding territorial integrity and either implicitly or explicitly provide for ISD, especially concerning regions or minorities. The 1998 Scotland Act, among others, established the Scottish Parliament and granted it legislative powers over specific areas such as education, health, and justice, all within the framework of the United Kingdom.[110] The 2014 Statute of the Autonomous Province of Vojvodina defines the province as a territorial community of the Republic of Serbia in Article 1, while subsequent provisions outline human and minority rights (Part II) and the province's competences (Part III).[111] The 2018 Principles Respecting the Government of Canada's Relationship with Indigenous Peoples expressly recognize that 'all relations with Indigenous peoples need to be based on the recognition and implementation of their right to self-determination, including the inherent right of self-government' (Principle 1).[112] The Attorney-General's Department of the Australian Government has interpreted Section 3 of the

107 The Constitution of the Republic of South Africa (1997) Article 235.

108 Venice Commission, Bulletin on Constitutional Case-Law, 1996–3-020.

109 The Constitution of the Russian Federation (1993) Article 5.3.

110 The Scotland Act 1998 (c. 46).

111 The Statute of the Autonomous Province of Vojvodina, Official Gazette of AP Vojvodina, No. 20/2014.

112 Department of Justice of Canada, 'Principles respecting the Government of Canada's relationship with Indigenous peoples' (2018) <https://www.justice.gc.ca/eng/csj-sjc/principles-principes.html>.

Aboriginal and Torres Strait Islander Act 2005 (which mandates maximum participation of Aboriginal persons and Torres Strait Islanders in the formulation and implementation of government policies that affect them) as tantamount to recognizing self-determination for these communities.[113] Internal self-determination is particularly relevant for minorities, hence the existence of separate territorial structures conforms to the idea of ISD.

Constitutionalism is not, in principle, compatible with secessionism. For figures such as Madison and later Lincoln, constitutionalism implied perpetuity. As argued, 'no government proper ever had a provision in its organic law for its own termination'.[114] Secession stands in contradiction to the nature and purpose of the federal state,[115] which is not merely 'a mechanical assembly of atomized parts, but rather a unified state that transcends the individual interests and wills of its federal units'.[116] In contrast, secession is more characteristic of confederations, where the consensual relationship among confederated states inherently allows for such a possibility. As argued, the right to secession 'immanent to the confederation, as a consensual relationship of confederated states, is not a trait of federal units; federation presupposes a federal state, therefore undoubtedly a state, a single authentic state'.[117] Freeman a long time ago noticed that a federation is 'essentially a permanent union' and that the constitution of a federation cannot 'contain rules on its own dissolution'.[118] Similarly, King posited that every federation strives to 'preserve some form of unity', so the existence of formal rules on secession would be 'contrary to that'.[119]

Although it is very uncommon to identify constitutional provisions on secession in federal states, they do occur sometimes.[120] In view of that, the following categorization may be suggested: (a) federal constitutions that explicitly forbid

113 Australian Attorney General's Department, 'Right to self-determination Public Sector Guidance Sheet' <https://www.ag.gov.au/rights-and-protections/human-rights-and-anti-discrimination/human-rights-scrutiny/public-sector-guidance-sheets/right-self-determination>.

114 First Inaugural Address (4 Mar. 1861), reprinted in T. Harry Williams (ed.) *Selected Writings and Speeches of Abraham Lincoln* (Hendricks 1943) 17.

115 M. Stanković, 'Secesija u Ustavnoj Praksi Federalnih Država' in K. Čavoški (ed.) *Secesija Sa Stanovišta Unutrašnjeg i Međunarodnog Prava i Njene Političke Posledice* (Serbian Academy of Sciences and Arts 2020) 342.

116 R. Marković, *Ustavno Pravo i Političke Institucije* (IP Justinijan 2003) 464.

117 M. Jovičić, *Državnost Federalnih Jedinica* (Izdavačka Zadruga Politika i Društvo 1992) 57.

118 E. Freeman, *History of Federal Government in Greece and Italy* (J. E. Bury ed., Macmillan and Co 1972) 90.

119 P. King, *Federalism and Federation* (Beckenham 1982) 112.

120 See F. Palermo and K. Kössler, *Comparative Federalism – Constitutional Arrangements and Case Law* (OUP 2017) 105.

secession (e.g. the United States,[121] Australia,[122] Brazil[123] or India[124]); (b) federal constitutions which allow secession, yet only declaratory (e.g. the USSR, where starting from 1924, legal procedures of vindicating secessions were absent and the necessary political context was missing);[125] (c) federal constitutions that provide for the right to secession and the way to realize that right (e.g. the Constitution of the Union of Burma from 1947, which devoted an entire chapter to the right to secession: Chapter X, Articles 201–206); and (d) federal constitutions which permit secession through negotiations (e.g. Canada, where following an advisory opinion from the Supreme Court of Canada on Quebec's right to secession, Canada passed the Clarity Act, which transferred elements of the decision into the constitutional framework).[126]

Considering the proposed categorisation, it should be noted that out of the twenty current federal constitutions, only two allow secession in an outright manner (Saint Kitts and Nevis and Ethiopia), albeit with stringent procedures and thresholds for success. In Saint Kitts and Nevis, a two-thirds majority in Parliament is required, while in Ethiopia, a resolution by a local council must be followed by a federal referendum within three years, where a simple majority suffices.[127] Canada represents a unique case where secession is permitted through a negotiated process. Accordingly, the majority of the federal constitutions either categorically proscribe secession (and assume sanctions for the

121 Consult *Texas v. White*, 74 U.S. 700 (1868).

122 In the preamble it defines the federation as 'indissoluble'.

123 Article 1 reads 'The Federative Republic of Brazil, formed by the indissoluble union of the states and municipalities (...)'.

124 Indian constitution is likewise believed to belong to that group. It uses the expression 'Union' because it is a federation that is not the result of an agreement, and in its absence of agreement 'no country has the right to secede'. See Parliament of India, Constituent Assembly Debates, vol. VII (4 Nov. 1948) 43.

125 Palermo and Kössler (n 120) 50, 107. Those constitutional norms aimed to create the fiction of voluntary alliance and 'free exit', that is, to serve as a means of integrating minority groups into the federation. See Stankovic (n 115) 345.

126 Stanković (n 115) 349.

127 According to the 1983 Constitution of St. Kitts and Nevis, Nevis, as a smaller entity, has the right to withdraw from the federation. The procedure of unilateral secession was even put into practice in 1998, but in the referendum on the independence of Nevis, slightly less than 62% of the voters voted for secession, which was insufficient. Article 39(4) of the Constitution of Ethiopia of 1994 regulates secession. However, it is interesting that in Ethiopia not federal units, but 'nations, nationalities, and people' are holders of the right to secession. Ethiopian secession process is very complex and unclear'. See M. Stanković, 'Federalism in Africa: The Case of Ethiopia' 56(2) *Annals of the Faculty of Law in Belgrade* (2008) 256–259.

seceding attempts)[128] or effectively disallow secession by failing to establish any procedures for its realization.

Finally, one might debate whether leaving virtually no room for secession in unitary states and federations alike is just, given the possibility of non-realization or even restriction of ISD. It is conceivable that those state constitutions that provide for secession of its constituent parts envisioned it as a remedy for the failure to internal self-determination. In truth, this is not explicitly mentioned but can be extrapolated from the freedom left to the people to decide on their future. Such a decision may be taken in the wake of a prolonged disagreement with central authorities over substantial issues, but also persistent disrespect or marginalization. In such cases, however, we can speak of a hybrid form of secession, which is unilateral in practice (most likely undertaken against the will of the central government), yet consensual in principle (since permission was granted beforehand and retains normative validity).[129] Otherwise, the spirit of constitutionalism is designed to protect the state's perpetuity, and constitutions are (still) not a place to look for a moral and legal basis of secession, which, might be resolved by a political agreement, special amendments, or, as a last resort, through rebellion.[130]

2.7 *Domestic Judicial Practice*

Although the valid principle is that international law treats internal, national law as a fact, the analysis of state constitutions and subordinate legal acts could serve as a valuable source in establishing ISD as a norm that prevents secession in international law, pursuant to Article 38 of the ICJ Statute, which refers to the general principles of law recognized by civilized nations. In a similar way, decisions of domestic courts represent a way of creating practice as an element of customary rule. Therefore, this section, will focus on significant decisions of domestic courts regarding issues of self-determination and secession.

128 'If the consequences of punishment are sufficiently unappealing to potential defectors, then the threat of secession as part of a bargaining strategy would not itself credible and therefore would not be used'. M. Filippov, P. Ordeshook and O. Shvetsova, *Designing Federalism: A Theory of Self-Sustainable Federal Institutions* (CUP 2004) 106.

129 Similar discussions are led in the context of the dismemberment of Yugoslavia.

130 C. R. Sunstein, 'Constitutionalism and Secession' 58(2) *The University of Chicago Law Review* (1991) 635. The Russian Constitutional Court responded to the attempts of certain sub-federal entities to secede from the Russian Federation in the early 1990s, stating that the only fair and legal way to solve that problem was through negotiations between the federation and all interested Russian federal units. Resolution of the Constitutional Court of the Russian Federation of 13 March 1992 N 3-P, VKS RF No.1 (1993).

2.7.1 Canada

Probably the most influential domestic court decision on the RSD and its value is that of the Supreme Court of Canada in the *Reference re Secession of Quebec*.[131] The case arose in the context of growing tensions and the possibility of Quebec holding another referendum on sovereignty.[132] The Federal Government sought clarification from the Supreme Court on the following questions:

1. Under the Constitution of Canada, can the National Assembly, legislature or government of Quebec effect the secession of Quebec from Canada unilaterally?
2. Does international law give the National Assembly, legislature or government of Quebec the right to effect the secession of Quebec from Canada unilaterally? In this regard, is there a right to self-determination under international law that would give the National Assembly, legislature or government of Quebec the right to effect the secession of Quebec from Canada unilaterally?
3. In the event of a conflict between domestic and international law on the right of the National Assembly, legislature or government of Quebec to effect the secession of Quebec from Canada unilaterally, which would take precedence in Canada?

The Court answered the first two questions in the negative, rendering the third question moot. Regarding domestic law, the Court's response was grounded in four constitutional principles: democracy, federalism, the rule of law, and the protection of minorities. The Court rejected the frequently advanced argument by secessionists that a positive result in a referendum on secession would suffice to effect Quebec's independence. Secessionists claimed that following such a result, Quebec would automatically exit the Canadian legal order and come under the jurisdiction of international law. However, the Court held that while the democratic principle – one of the four core constitutional principles – requires that significant weight be accorded to a clear expression of the will of the people of Quebec to secede, a referendum result, in itself, has no direct legal effect within Canada's constitutional order and cannot unilaterally bring about secession.[133] Yet, a clear expression of the will of the people of Quebec to secede, free from ambiguity both in the referendum question and in the level of support achieved, would confer legitimacy on Quebec's efforts to initiate

131 *Reference re Secession of Quebec* (1998) 2 SCR 217.

132 The first referendum was held in 1980, however Quebec voters rejected the proposal, with approximately 60% voting against sovereignty-association and around 40% voting in favor.

133 *Reference re Secession of Quebec* (n 131) para 87.

constitutional amendments for secession through lawful means. Additionally, the federalism principle, in conjunction with democracy, establishes a reciprocal obligation for all parties to Confederation to negotiate constitutional changes in good faith.[134] Accordingly, if a referendum result were clearly in favour of secession, the Court held that there would be an obligation to negotiate, involving Quebec, other provinces, and the federal government. Quebec would have the right to initiate a debate and secession process within Canadian institutions, reflecting the need to balance the will of Quebec's population with that of the entire country.[135]

The Court also addressed the argument of effectiveness, commonly invoked in international law, which suggests that a group achieving *de facto* independence enhances its chances of legal recognition. The Court unanimously rejected this argument under the Canadian constitution, stating: 'the law may be broken as long as it can be broken successfully' is a notion contrary to the rule of law and must be dismissed.[136]

Turning to a more tuned international law analysis, the Court assessed secession and the RSD in light of various international instruments, including the Friendly Relations Declaration and the Helsinki Final Act. It reaffirmed that the international law principle of self-determination operates within a framework of respect for the territorial integrity of existing states. Crucially, the Court argued that RSD is 'normally fulfilled through internal self-determination – a people's pursuit of its political, economic, social, and cultural development within the framework of an existing state'.[137] It recognized external self-determination as permissible only in three circumstances: during decolonization, when a people is under foreign domination, or when a people is denied internal self-determination. Conversely,

> a state whose government represents the whole of the people or peoples resident within its territory, on a basis of equality and without discrimination, and respects the principles of self-determination in its own internal arrangements, is entitled to the protection under international law of its territorial integrity.[138]

134 *Ibid.* para 88.

135 *Ibid.* paras 149–153 (it will be for the *political actors* to determine what constitutes 'a clear majority on a clear question' in the circumstances under which a future referendum vote may be taken. Equally, in the event of demonstrated majority support for Quebec secession, the content and process of the negotiations will be for the political actors to settle).

136 *Ibid.* para 108.

137 *Ibid.* para 126.

138 *Ibid.* paras 130, 138.

Pursuing this logic, the Court established that Canada had not been in breach of ISD of Québécois, and that the continuing failure to reach agreement on amendments to the Constitution did not amount to a denial of self-determination, hence Canada is entitled to enjoy the international legal protection of its borders.

Speaking of the effectiveness principle, the Court stated that its role was to assess whether a right to secession exists, not to evaluate *de facto* situations. While *de facto* secession might attract legal recognition in some cases, it does not retroactively create a legal right to secession.[139]

In sum, the Supreme Court of Canada relied heavily on the principle of territorial integrity, implicitly assuming that peoples, as non-state entities, are bound by this principle.

2.7.2 Spain

After the end of Franco's regime and the advent of democratic reforms in Spain, the Catalan self-determination movement began to gain momentum.[140] The last two decades have been particularly dynamic for Catalonia's pursuit of its RSD, shaped both by Catalan initiatives and the responses of the Spanish state, especially its Constitutional Tribunal.[141]

In 2010, the Constitutional Tribunal declared several provisions of the 2006 Statute of Autonomy of Catalonia (SAC) unconstitutional, claiming that national sovereignty belongs exclusively to the 'Spanish people', while the 'people of Catalonia' only hold powers provided by the SAC and the Spanish Constitution.[142] Two years later, the Catalan authorities passed a resolution proclaiming Catalonia as 'a new State of Europe' on the basis of their 'right to decide', which, they argued, stemmed from the inalienable right to self-determination.[143] In early 2013, the Catalan Parliament adopted Resolution 5/X containing a declaration of sovereignty and claiming the right of the

139 *Ibid.* paras 140–146.

140 K. Guruparan, *Internal Self-determination in Public International Law* (PhD thesis, UCL 2019) 209–228; D. Turp, et al. *The Catalan Independence Referendum: An Assessment of the Process of Self-determination* (2017 IRAI); A. Peters, 'Populist International Law? The Suspended Independence and the Normative Value of the Referendum on Catalonia' *EJIL:Talk!* (12 Oct. 2017); M. Weller, 'Secession and Self-determination in Western Europe: The Case of Catalonia' *EJIL: Talk!* (18 Oct. 2017).

141 See G. Galán, 'Del derecho a decidir a la independencia: la peculiaridad del proceso secesionista en Cataluña' 4 *Istituzioni del Federalismo* (2014) 885–907; E. R. Molés, 'The Catalan Sovereignty Process and the Spanish Constitutional Court. An Analysis of Reciprocal Impacts' 54 *Revista Catalana de Derecho Público* (2017) 24–61.

142 Constitutional Tribunal, Judgment 31/2010 (28 Jun. 2010) BOE-A-2010-11409.

143 Res. 742/IX (27 Sep. 2012) <https://www.parlament.cat/document/intrade/6026>.

people of Catalonia to decide their political future in accordance with nine principles.[144] However, the Constitutional Tribunal swiftly invalidated this and similar resolutions, reaffirming the indivisibility of Spanish sovereignty. While acknowledging that the 'right to decide' might be viewed as a political aspiration consistent with the Constitution's principles of democratic legitimacy, pluralism, and legality, the Tribunal held that it could not be interpreted as a manifestation of the right to self-determination.[145]

In November 2014, the Catalan authorities organized a non-binding referendum on independence, which was likewise declared unconstitutional.[146] The leaders of the initiative faced political repercussions.[147] The Catalan authorities did not surrender and adopted a few more resolutions promulgating, among others, 'the start of the process to create an independent Catalan State in the form of a republic' and the 'disconnection' from the Spanish law.[148] In return, the Spanish Parliament passed the law on the effective enforcement of the Constitutional Tribunal judgments.[149] The saga continued and culminated in the organisation of a referendum on self-determination in 2017 and the subsequent declaration of independence endorsed by the Catalan Parliament. The Constitutional Tribunal stuck down the Self-determination Referendum Act and the Juridical Transition and founding of the Republic Act adopted earlier by the Catalan Parliament, while the Spanish government, with the authorization of the Senate, dismissed the Catalan government and called for new elections in Catalonia. Concurrently, nine secessionist leaders were imprisoned.[150]

The Constitutional Tribunal's reasoning has been primarily based on the domestic legal framework, with international law playing a secondary role. The justices have been reluctant to rule that Catalonia or Catalan peoples hold any right to independence. Notably, the Tribunal refers to the Catalan RSD as merely 'an alleged right to self-determination',[151] explicitly noting that 'this 'right' [to

144 Res. 5/X (23 Jan. 2013) <https://www.parlament.cat/document/intrade/7176>.

145 Constitutional Tribunal, Judgment 42/2014 (25 Mar. 2014) BOE-A-2014-3885; Judgment 46/2015 (5 Mar. 2015) BOE-A-2015-3824.

146 Constitutional Tribunal, Judgment 31/2015 (25 Feb. 2015) BOE-A-2015-2832.

147 R. Kolb and T. Gazzini, 'The Autonomous Community of Catalonia and International Law' 31 *Swiss Review of International and European Law* (2021) 6.

148 See Res 1/XI (9 Nov. 2015) <https://www.parlament.cat/document/intrade/153127>; Res. 263/XI (27 Jul. 2016) <https://www.parlament.cat/document/intrade/175266>.

149 Law 15/2015 (16 Oct. 2015) BOE-A-2015-11160.

150 Busquets (n 12) 150.

151 Constitutional Tribunal, Judgment 114/2017 (17 Oct. 2017) – Unconstitutionality of the Law on the Referendum – <https://www.tribunalconstitucional.es/ResolucionesTraducidas/Ley%20referendum%20ENGLISH.pdf> 8.

self-determination] is obviously not recognized by the Constitution'.[152] The Tribunal appeared to confine its interpretation of self-determination to its external dimension, while implicitly – though not explicitly – recognizing the existence of internal self-determination within the constitutional framework. The Tribunal's found that the 'unilateral access to the independence' existed only in cases of 'alien subjugation, domination and exploitation'.[153] It invoked the ICCPR, the Declaration on the Granting of Independence to Colonial Countries and Peoples and the Declaration on the Occasion of the Fiftieth Anniversary of the United Nations to support its conclusion that territorial integrity takes precedence over the ESD in the absence of alien domination, foreign occupation or discrimination.[154] As with the case of the Canada's Supreme Court, the Tribunal emphasized that the Spanish Government is representative of the whole population and that, under the Spanish Constitution and other relevant laws, 'such participation (…) is enjoyed by every Spaniard who benefits from the political status of being Catalan'.[155]

In sum, the Tribunal does not recognize Catalans' external right to self-determination. Its reasoning, though containing some ambiguities, acknowledges that ISD is a legally recognized right, but one that must be interpreted in strict compliance with the principle of territorial integrity. Compared to Canada's Court, which allows negotiable solutions, the Spanish Tribunal is more strict and more inclined towards the orthodox version ISD as a method of preventing secession, though this stems mainly from its reliance on domestic law and limited engagement with the human rights situation of Catalans.

152 *Ibid.* 9.

153 *Ibid.* 10. Though, it acknowledged that the constitutional order is amendable, including provisions concerning the identity and unity of the sovereign. Constitutional Tribunal, Judgment 124/2017 (8 Nov. 2017) – the Law of Juridical Transition – <https://www.tribunalconstitucional.es/ResolucionesTraducidas/Ley%20transitoriedad%20ENGLISH.pdf> 12. See also Judgments 48/2003, 103/2008, 42/2014, 259/2015.

154 Judgment 114/2017 (n 151) 10.

155 *Ibid.* See Organic Act 6/2006 of the 19th of July, on the Reform of the Statute of Autonomy of Catalonia, Article 7. See also Kolb and Gazzini (n 147) 14–15 (arguing that the Autonomous Community of Catalonia has one of the most developed self-government, comparable to that of regions within major federal states in Europe). Cf. Busquets (n 12) 153 (contending that while the autonomous community of Catalonia apparently has broad self-government powers (self-rule dimension), it possesses narrow formal powers to influence the central institutions (shared-rule dimension).

2.7.3 United Kingdom

On 23 November 2022, the Supreme Court of the United Kingdom delivered a unanimous ruling addressing a reference made by the Lord Advocate, the chief legal officer of the Scottish Government.[156] The reference sought clarity on whether the proposed Scottish Independence Referendum Bill, which asks, 'Should Scotland be an independent country?', falls outside the legislative competence of the Scottish Parliament under the Scotland Act of 1998. Specifically, it questioned whether the bill concerned matters reserved to the UK Parliament, such as those pertaining to the Union of Scotland and England or the sovereignty of the UK Parliament.[157] The Lord Advocate, invoked paragraph 34 of Schedule 6 of the Scotland Act 1998 to submit the reference. Separately, the Advocate General for Scotland, representing the UK Government, also challenged the bill's competency, arguing it 'relates to reserved matters', particularly the constitutional integrity of the Union and the authority of the UK Parliament.

The Court concluded that the draft Bill indeed related to reserved matters, rendering it outside the legislative authority of the Scottish Parliament. Following this determination, the Court addressed arguments from the Scottish National Party (SNP), which had intervened in the case.[158] The SNP contended that the right to self-determination is a fundamental principle of international law and argued for a presumption favoring domestic legislation's compatibility with international law. According to the SNP, interpreting the phrase 'relates to' narrowly would permit the Scottish Parliament to legislate for a 'non-self-executing referendum' consistent with the right to self-determination, while a broader interpretation would preclude such legislation. To support their stance, the SNP cited Article 1 of the UN Charter, General Assembly Resolution 1514 of 1960, and provisions in the ICCPR and ICESCR that affirm the right to self-determination.[159]

The Court, while recognizing the presumption in favor of interpreting domestic law in conformity with international obligations, clarified that this principle applies only when the statutory language is ambiguous.[160] The Court further held that 'the principle of self-determination is simply not in play here'.[161] Drawing on precedents, including case law on Quebec's status

156 *Reference by the Lord Advocate of devolution issues under paragraph 34 of Schedule 6 to the Scotland Act 1998*, [2022] UKSC 31.

157 The Scotland Act (n 110).

158 Written Submissions on Behalf of the Scottish National Party <https://www.snp.org/the-snps-supreme-court-submission-on-the-independence-referendum/>.

159 *Ibid.* 3.2–3.3.

160 Reference by the Lord Advocate (n 156) para 87.

161 *Ibid.* para 88.

in Canada and the UK's submission to the International Court of Justice in the *Kosovo* advisory opinion (2009), the Court emphasized that international law generally supports the territorial integrity of states and does not confer a unilateral right to secession outside specific contexts. The UK court reiterated Canada's Supreme Court reasoning that 'Canada was a sovereign and independent state conducting itself in compliance with the principle of equal rights and self-determination of peoples and thus possessed of a government representing the whole people belonging to the territory without distinction' and 'the then current constitutional arrangements within Canada did not place Quebecers in a disadvantaged position within the scope of the international law rule'.[162] In the following paragraph, the UK court concurred with the reasoning that, in the absence of circumstances of colonialism, foreign occupation, and the breach of ISD, peoples are expected to achieve self-determination within the framework of their existing state. As it stated, 'these observations apply with equal force to the position of Scotland and the people of Scotland within the United Kingdom'. The Court concluded that 'nothing in the allocation of powers, however widely or narrowly interpreted, infringes any principle of self-determination' *a fortiori* 'the legislation establishes and promotes a system of devolution founded on principles of subsidiarity', *ergo* in and of itself enhances ISD.[163] The Court reiterated that devolution legislation, including the Scotland Act, must be interpreted as any other statute, adhering to the interpretative rules set forth by the Act itself. Applying a presumption to either increase or decrease devolved powers would be inappropriate.

Even though the Court acknowledged that respect for internal self-determination obviates secession, it is regrettable that it did not provide a more detailed analysis, especially considering the recency of the case.[164] This omission is compounded by the SNP submission, which failed to more explicitly articulate ISD and frame its argument for a non-binding referendum squarely on this concept. Instead, the submission merely noted the distinction between ISD and ESD within the territorially applicable context.[165]

162 *Ibid.* para 89.

163 *Ibid.* para 90.

164 Consult L. Raible, 'Self-determination at the UK Supreme Court and the Failure of International Law' 27(2) *Edinburgh Law Review* (2023) 219–225; K. Istrefi, 'The UK Supreme Court in the Scottish Case: Revitalising the Doctrine of Remedial Secession' *EJIL:Talk!* (14 Dec. 2022). See also M. Weller, 'The UK Supreme Court Reference on a Referendum for Scotland and the Right to Constitutional Self-determination: Part II' *EJIL:Talk!* (13 Dec. 2022) (noting that the ruling overlooks the doctrine of constitutional self-determination).

165 Written Submissions on Behalf of the Scottish National Party (n 158) 4.1–4.2.

2.7.4 Russia

Parallel to the declarations of sovereignty by the Soviet Union republics (Estonia in November 1988, Lithuania, Latvia, Azerbaijan in the course of 1989, and Russia itself in June 1990), which instantiated the collapse of the Soviet Union, a number autonomous republics within the Russian Soviet Federative Socialist Republic (RSFSR) followed suit and declared sovereignty.[166] Among various independence movements inside the Russian SFSR, Tatarstan and Chechnya should be singled out. Namely, they have long histories of resistance to Russian rule, originating in events predating the demise of the Soviet Union, and both were subject to Russian Constitutional Court decisions in the 1990s, where the right of peoples to self-determination under international law was discussed.[167]

2.7.4.1 *Tatarstan*

Shortly after the declaration of sovereignty, demonstrations and political strikes spread throughout the 4 million Tatarstan region, where slightly more than 50% are Volga Tatars, a Turkic ethnic group practising Sunni Islam religion.[168] On 21 February 1992, the Supreme Soviet of the Tatar ASSR, responding to the nationalist movement, decided to hold a referendum to decide upon the future status of the republic.[169] The population was asked:

> Do you agree that the Tatarstan Republic is a sovereign state, a subject of international law that constructs its relations with the Russian Federation and other republics and states on the basis of treaties between equal parties? Yes, or No?[170]

Approximately 61% of those who went to the referendum voted 'yes' to the sovereignty of Tatarstan. This was seen as a first step towards the independence of this Russian federal unit. But before the referendum actually took place, the former Constitutional Court of Russia found that Tatarstan and its inhabitants

166 J. Socher, *Russia and the Right to Self-Determination in the Post-Soviet Space* (OUP 2021) 57.

167 *Ibid.* 59.

168 M. Bennigsen-Broxup, 'Tatarstan and the Tatars' in G. Smith (ed.) *The Nationalities Question in the Post- Soviet States* (Longman 1996) 75– 77. On the referendum see also A. Peters, *Das Gebietsreferendum im Völkerrecht: seine Bedeutung im Licht der Staatenpraxis nach 1989* (Nomos 1995) 203–208.

169 See more in D. Raič, *Statehood and the Law of Self-determination* (Kluwer Law International 2002) 256, fn. 130; Summers (n 26) 49, 396, 402–403.

170 Quotation from the English translation of the Russian Constitutional Court's Tatarstan Decision (1992) in *Statutes & Decisions: The Laws of the USSR and its Successor States* (M.E. Sharpe Incorporated 1994) 39.

enjoy the RSD, but it must be consistent with two key principles: (i) the territorial integrity of the Russian Federation and (ii) respect for human rights.[171] The Court mentioned common Article 1 of the Covenants on Human Rights (ratified by the Presidium of the Supreme Soviet of the Soviet Union on 18 September 1973) as well the General Assembly Friendly Relations Declaration of 1970 as relevant international law documents which outline the content and modes of the implementation of the RSD. The Court was of the opinion that the exercise of the right to self-determination in the form of unilateral independence from an existing state constitutes an 'abuse of the right and not the exercise of the right'.[172] It also raised objections towards the referendum question for its lack of precision, arguing that this ambiguity denied citizens both 'the right to the free expression of their will' and 'the right to participate in the discussion and adoption of laws and decisions of national importance', as protected under the constitutions of Tatarstan and the Russian Federation.[173] Nevertheless, the Court noted that the Republic of Tatarstan has 'the right to raise the issue of its state and legal status, inasmuch as this right is derivative from the right of the People to self-determination', which is 'guaranteed in the Russian Federation (Article 3)' and 'may be exercised in various national-state and national-cultural forms'.[174]

As mentioned before, regardless of the Court's decision, the referendum took place. However, Tatarstan lacked the factual power to implement its sovereignty. Eventually, in 1994, Tatarstan and Russia reached an agreement granting the republic extensive autonomy and internal self-determination.[175] This could serve as an example of how to reconcile the RSD with the preservation of state territorial integrity.

2.7.4.2 *Chechnya*

A similar approach to that in the Tatarstan case was adopted by the Russian Constitutional Court in 1995 in a case concerning Chechnya.[176] The Court reasoned that the RSD 'must not be interpreted as sanctioning or encouraging any actions that would lead to the division or the complete violation of the

171 *Ibid.* 40.

172 *Ibid.*

173 Summers (n 26) 403.

174 Russian Constitutional Court's Tatarstan Decision (n 170) 39.

175 M. Weller, 'Settling Self-determination Conflicts: Recent Developments'20(1) *EJIL* (2009) 135.

176 On the case of Chechnya and its relevance to the discourse on remedial secession and the right to self-determination, see generally M. Sterio, *The Right to Self-determination Under International Law: "Selfistans," Secession, and the Rule of the Great Powers* (Routledge 2015) 131–141; Raič (n 169) 373–378.

territorial integrity or political unity of sovereign and independent states acting in accordance with the principle of the equal rights and self-determination of nations'.[177] The case is interesting since the Court admitted historical injustices towards the Chechen people, in particular deportations faced under the Stalin regime.[178] Despite these violations, which remained unremedied by the Soviet Union or Russia, the Court held that the Chechen secessionists were not legitimate representatives of the Chechen people but rather illegal armed forces, as there was no freely elected parliament in Chechnya at the time, and the region was in the midst of a non-international armed conflict.[179]

After the war and the crush of the rebel forces, a new Chechen Constitution was enacted in 2003, which accepted that Chechnya is an integral part of the Russian Federation.[180] The Constitution of the Chechen Republic clearly states that 'the territory of the Chechen Republic is one and indivisible and forms an inalienable part of the territory of the Russian Federation'.[181] The Constitutional Court of Russia has repeatedly asserted that the 1993 Russian Constitution does not recognize a right to secession for any federal subject. Alluding to Article 66(5), which permits changes to a region's status only through 'mutual agreement' between the federal government and the constituent entity, the Court has drawn parallels to the 1978 RSFSR Constitution to claim historical continuity in upholding territorial integrity.[182] However, this analogy is legally and historically misleading. While the 1978 RSFSR Constitution included Article 69 – a provision mirroring Article 72 of the 1977 USSR Constitution – this granted *Union Republics* like the RSFSR a nominal right to secede from *the Soviet Union*. Crucially, this right did not extend to internal regions such as Chechnya, which were always defined as inseparable parts of the RSFSR. The Court's conflation of these distinct frameworks – Soviet-era federalism (which permitted Union Republics to leave the USSR) and post-1993 Russian constitutional law (which denies secession outright) – ignores the hierarchical nature of Soviet governance and the RSFSR's own denial of secession rights to

177 Summers (n 26) 72, fn. 151.

178 Accused by Stalin of welcoming the Germans in World War II, the entire Chechen nation of 489,000 people was deported to Soviet Central Asia in 1944; an estimated 200,000 died there of hunger and disease. See L. Aron, 'Chechnya' Report by American Enterprise Institute (2003) <https://www.aei.org/research-products/report/chechnya/>.

179 Summers (n 26) 403–404.

180 Weller (n 175) 136.

181 Constitution of the Chechen Republic (2003) Article 1(2). Critics argue that the Constitution (although adopted via a referendum) was drafted under Russian oversight and reflected Moscow's political goals rather than genuine Chechen self-determination.

182 Constitution of the Russian Federation (1993) Article 66(5).

its sub-republics.[183] In addition, faults were found in the Constitutional Court's reference to international law, especially the saving clause of the Friendly Relations Declaration. The Court selectively cited the clause (without the latter part referring to governmental representativeness) and opined that it unreservedly protects the unity of a state. Socher observed that such a reading turned its 'potential meaning into its exact opposite',[184] while Gaeta commented that the Court 'misinterpreted the very meaning of the saving clause embodied in the Declaration', and rightly concluded that without a proper examination of the representativeness of the Russian government, the Court's contention that the preservation of territorial integrity of Russia is in accordance with international law, is not tenable.[185]

2.7.5 Italy

The Italian Constitutional Court has ruled on the constitutionality of two proposed referenda in the Veneto region. Specifically, it reviewed the validity of two Regional Laws adopted in 2014 that aimed to initiate referenda on greater autonomy and potential independence.[186] The court upheld the application of the Italian federal Government, declaring such laws void.

In 2014, Veneto made a fourth attempt to address autonomy and independence through two Regional Laws. Law No. 15 proposed a consultative referendum on regional autonomy, seeking public input on five questions, including whether Veneto should become a special-status region and retain 80% of the taxes collected within its territory. The law also authorized negotiations with the central government to define the referendum's framework and to pursue further autonomy for Veneto. If negotiations failed, the Regional President could initiate the referendum. Law No. 16, on the other hand, sought a referendum asking voters if Veneto should become an independent and sovereign republic. It also tasked regional authorities with defending Veneto's right to

183 Socher (n 166) 85. Cf. A. Cassese, *Self-determination of Peoples: A Legal Reappraisal* (CUP 1995) 264 (stating that Article 72 remained a dead letter).

184 Socher (n 166) 86.

185 P. Gaeta, 'The Armed Conflict in Chechnya before the Russian Constitutional Court' 7 *EJIL* (1996) 565–566.

186 *Sentenze* No. 470/1992, 496/2000 and 118/2015. In 2001–2002, the Veneto Regional Council approved a law for an advisory referendum on transferring state functions in health, education, and local police to the region. The central government under Giuliano Amato challenged it in the Constitutional Court, but the challenge was withdrawn by the subsequent Silvio Berlusconi government.

self-determination at national and international levels.[187] The Italian government challenged both laws before the Constitutional Court. Law No. 15 was declared unconstitutional in part – four of its five referendum questions were struck down, while Law No. 16 was annulled in its entirety in Judgment No. 118/2015.[188] The Court emphasized that referendums must align with constitutional principles, serve as instruments for democratic participation, and respect the framework established by the constitution and regional statutes. It ruled that regional referendums cannot involve matters of constitutional-level significance, such as territorial integrity or tax sovereignty.[189] The Court further clarified that while regions may regulate referendums within their competencies, such initiatives must comply with constitutional limits, ensuring harmony between regional autonomy and national unity. In Veneto's case, Articles 26 and 27 of the Regional Statute exclude referendums on taxation, budgetary issues, and constitutionally mandated matters, reinforcing the consistent position of the Constitutional Court.

The judges emphasized that Italy is a unified state that guarantees local autonomy, which does not equate to sovereignty nor does it place local authorities on par with federal institutions. Thereby, local autonomy, although capable of extension (contrary to Spain),[190] 'cannot be taken to extremes so as to result in the fragmentation of the legal order and cannot be invoked as justification for initiatives involving the consultation of the electorate – albeit only for consultative purposes – concerning prospective secession with a view to the creation of a new sovereign body'.[191] The Court accordingly stated that 'a referendum initiative, as also that under examination, at odds with the unity of the Republic could never involve the legitimate exercise of power by regional institutions and is therefore *extra ordinem*'. As a result, such a referendum 'seeks to subvert the institutions in a manner that is inherently incompatible with the founding principles of the unity and indivisibility of the Republic laid down in Article 5 of the Constitution'.[192] The Court thus clearly opined against secession, implying that 'social and institutional pluralism and territorial autonomy, in addition to an openness to supranational integration' are

187 I. Spigno, 'Constitutional Judges and Secession. Lessons from Canada ... Twenty Years Later' 9(3) *Perspectives on Federalism* (2017) 118–119.

188 Constitutional Court of Italy, Judgement No. 118/2015.

189 See A. Savanović, '"VENEXIT" – Venice Secession Movement' 8(15) *Politeia* (2018) 43.

190 J. CastellàAndreu, 'Referendums on Secession' in S. Granata-Menghini and Z. Caga Tanyar (eds.) *Venice Commission Thirty-Year Quest for Democracy through Law 1990–2020* (Juristförlaget i Lund 2020) 157.

191 *Sentenza* No. 118/2015 (n 188) para 7.2.

192 *Ibid.*

adequate expressions of ISD and, as such, should not open the gate to 'extreme' movements.

In any case, the secessionist movement in Veneto represents an interesting case reflecting political, legal, and philosophical perspectives on secession and the right to self-determination. Further cases before the Court, particularly those pertaining to ISD, are to be expected given the strong sentiment for separateness and autonomy in this Italian region.[193]

2.7.6 Sri Lanka

The Supreme Court of Sri Lanka considered the RSD in 2008 as a result of the Presidential Reference seeking an opinion on Sri Lanka's constitutional compliance with the ICCPR provisions, and in 2017 when it ruled in the case *Chandrasoma v. Senathirajah*.

In its first pronouncement, the Court under its 'consultative jurisdiction' regarded the RSD in an anachronistic and attenuated way, as exclusively and conveniently grounded in the UNGA Resolution 2625 (XXV), noting that the 'concept [of self-determination of peoples] applies only in a decolonization context and cannot be applied or be interpreted in a manner prejudicial to the sovereignty and territorial integrity of an Independent State'.[194] Evaluating the submission made by the Counsel for the 1st and 2nd intervenient petitioners imploring for the statutory recognition of internal self-determination, the Court observed that in accordance with Article 3 of the Constitution, 'in the Republic of Sri Lanka sovereignty is in the People and is inalienable'. Thus, 'sovereignty is reposed in the People as a whole and it cannot be contended that any group or part of the totality of People should have a separate right of self-determination'.[195] By restricting the application of self-determination to colonialism, the Court rejected its continuity. Furthermore, the Court's opinion rebuffs the plurality inherent in the concept of 'peoples' and instead

---

193 According to Plebiscito.eu's staff, 2.36 million Venetians (63.2% of all eligible voters) participated in the online referendum and 89.1% of them (that is to say 56.6% of all eligible voters) voted 'yes' to independence. Based on that the Declaration of Independence of the Venetian Republic was adopted on 21 March 2014 <https://plebiscito.eu/news/dichiarazione-di-indipendenza-della-repubblica-veneta/>. In 2017, the Venetian autonomy referendum took place. With the turnout of 57.2%, 98.1% of participants voted 'yes' for further forms and special conditions of autonomy to be attributed to the Region of Veneto – one of five questions which were not struck down by the Constitutional Court in *Sentenza* No. 118/2015.

194 *Centre for Policy Alternative (Guarantee) Ltd and Three Others (In the matter of a Reference under Article 129(1) of the Constitution)* [2009] 2 SLR 389, 404.

195 *Ibid.* 402.

perceives the people of Sri Lanka as one totality intertwined with the notion of 'sovereignty', thereby impliedly repudiating internal self-determination of any minority.[196]

A much less controversial and conservative approach was taken by the Supreme Court in its 2017 *Chandrasoma v. Senathirajah* judgement.[197] In this ruling, the Court recognised the right of peoples to self-determination and affirmed its compatibility with the constitution. The Court was inclined to accept the Respondent's submission that 'it is "peoples" who are repositories under international law of the right to self-determination' and that the Tamil people are a 'people', thereby entitled to the right.[198] The judgement thus departs from the Court's previous stance in that it accepts the continuous validity of the RSD, particularly in relation to minorities. However, the Court was evidently on the side that the RSD operates internally in established states, stating that 'invocation of self-determination does not amount to a demand for a separate State, as the right is sometimes to be used internally within the territory of an existing State'.[199] It is nevertheless possible that the Court also considered the RSD's external variant as *ultima ratio* by citing the following passage from the *Reference re Secession of Quebec*

> A state whose government represent the whole of the people or peoples resident within its territory, on the basis of equality and without discrimination and respects the principle of self-determination in its internal arrangements, is entitled to maintain its territorial integrity under international law and to have that territorial integrity recognized by other states.[200]

and quoting the separate opinion of Judge Cançado Trindade in the *Kosovo* Advisory Opinion, who pointed out that

> recent developments in contemporary international law were to disclose both the external and internal dimensions of the right of self-determination of peoples: the former meant the right of every people to be free from any form of foreign domination, and the latter referred to

196 See N. K. Ashokbharan, 'The Right to Self Determination in Sri Lankan Constitutional Law: An Appraisal of the Sri Lankan Supreme Court Judgement in Chandrasoma v Senathirajah' (2019) <https://papers.ssrn.com/sol3/papers.cfm?abstract_id=3486097> 7.

197 *Chandrasoma v. Senathirajah*, SC Spl. 03/2014, SCM 04.08.2017.

198 *Ibid.* 15.

199 *Ibid.* 17.

200 *Ibid.* 15–16.

> the right of every people to choose their destiny in accordance with their own will, if necessary – in case of systematic oppression and subjugation – against their own government.[201]

The Sri Lankan Supreme Court believed that these judicial pronouncements form nowadays the benchmark in conceptualizing self-determination, which prioritizes the internal dimension that stands in harmony with the principle of territorial integrity. This is reflected in the final finding of the judgement that ISD of the ITAK (former Federal Party representing the Sri Lankan Tamil ethnic minority) may include 'advocating for a federalist form of government by devolving more powers to the provinces within the framework of a unitary state', which could not be considered as advocating separatism contrary to Article 157A of the Constitution.[202]

3 International Organizations Practice

International organizations can likewise be credited with advancing the concept of internal self-determination as a means of secession prevention. In this regard, international organizations, like states, generally appear to agree. However, it remains unclear whether international organizations and states equate the maintenance of a state's territorial integrity with the fulfillment of ISD or if ISD is merely used as an empty slogan (perhaps as a goal yet to be achieved) that opposes external self-determination in modern times. Differences may also be evident in the interpretation of ISD itself, particularly in the breadth and scope of entitlements accorded to populations, which would constitute explicit or implicit grounds for opposing secession.

This section first outlines the practices of international, followed by regional, organizations, bearing in mind that these bodies are influenced by states. The emphasis here is on uncovering these organizations' stance on ISD and the prohibition of secession by exploring their practices, including the actions of their political agents, such as the OSCE High Commissioner or the UN Secretary-General, as well as the salient documents enacted under their aegis.

International adjudicative practice incorporated in this section encompasses the work of human rights courts and bodies operating at both universal

201 *Ibid.* 16.

202 *Ibid.* 18. See also J. Wickramaratne, 'Assuring Equality, Autonomy and Territorial Integrity in Sri Lanka' in E. M. Belser and T. Bächler et al. (eds.) *The Principle of Equality in Diverse States Reconciling Autonomy with Equal Rights and Opportunities* (Brill 2021) 181 ff.

and regional levels. Attention is given to the ICJ's advisory opinion on Kosovo's unilateral declaration of independence, illustrating the Court's approach and the individual opinions of judges on self-determination and secession, in contrast to the positions of states outlined earlier in this chapter. Equally important is the practice of various human rights committees and commissions established by conventions or formed *ad hoc,* such as the Venice Commission/CoE, the Badinter Commission/EC, the Inter-American Commission on Human Rights/OAS or the African Commission on Human and Peoples' Rights/AU.

3.1 *The United Nations*

Within the United Nations, three main declarations deserve particular attention: the Vienna Declaration and Programme of Action adopted at the World Conference on Human Rights in 1993 as well as the Friendly Relations Declaration and the UN Fiftieth Anniversary Declaration adopted by the General Assembly in 1970 and 1995 respectively. They directly corroborate the relationship between the respect for ISD and territorial integrity. A fourth, more specific yet equally relevant, declaration is the UN Declaration on the Rights of Indigenous People (UNDRIP), which implicitly acknowledges this correlation by indicating that self-determination should be exercised within existing states. Although these declarations are non-binding, they represent a political commitment made by the participating states to uphold and promote the principles and objectives outlined within them, carrying considerable moral and political weight. They reflect the consensus of the international community on key human rights issues and provide a roadmap for action. As such, they serve as reference points for states, international organizations, civil society groups, and other stakeholders in their efforts to advance general and specific human rights agendas. Moreover, although non-binding, elements of the declarations have been incorporated into subsequent international agreements and instruments.[203]

This section also analyzes two additional bodies of the United Nations: the UN Secretary-General (UNSG) and the Human Rights Council (HRC). Even though the analysed statements from the UNSG are more indicative of its

203 For example, countries like Bolivia, Ecuador, and Mexico have incorporated indigenous rights into their constitutions, often citing UNDRIP as a source of inspiration. In 2016, the Organization of American States (OAS) adopted the American Declaration on the Rights of Indigenous Peoples, which heavily draws from UNDRIP. Viñuales labelled the Friendly Relations Declaration as the 'constitution' of international law, emphasizing its foundational significance. See J. Viñuales, 'The Forgotten Constitution: The UN Friendly Relations Declaration at 50' *EJIL:Talk!* (23 Arp. 2020).

anti-secession inclination, and the elaborated actions of the HRC focus on ISD and hardly ever mention secession, certain traits allow us to deduce a tighter correlation between the two precepts.

3.1.1 World Conference on Human Rights

The World Conference on Human Rights was a significant international event dedicated to the promotion and protection of human rights globally. Held in Vienna in 1993, is often referred to as the Vienna World Conference on Human Rights.[204] This conference marked a crucial moment in the advancement of human rights, as it reaffirmed the universality, indivisibility, and interdependence of human rights. Key outcomes of the Vienna World Conference on Human Rights included the adoption of the Vienna Declaration and Programme of Action, the recognition of women's rights, an emphasis on human rights education, and the recommendation for the establishment of the Office of the United Nations High Commissioner for Human Rights (OHCHR).[205]

3.1.1.1 *Vienna Declaration and Programme of Action*

The Vienna Declaration and Programme of Action, which contains the most significant passage on ISD and the prohibition of secession, was adopted by consensus by representatives of 171 States.[206] The Declaration, in its second point, underlines that 'all peoples have the right of self-determination' which provides them with the opportunity to 'freely determine their political status' and notes that this right is inalienable and its denial constitutes a violation of human rights. However, the Declaration stresses that, in accordance with the Friendly Relations Declaration's safeguard clause, self-determination

> shall not be construed as authorizing or encouraging any action which would dismember or impair, totally or in part, the territorial integrity or political unity of sovereign and independent States conducting themselves in compliance with the principle of equal rights and self-determination of peoples and thus possessed of a Government representing the whole people belonging to the territory without distinction of any kind.[207]

---

204 The conference was envisaged by the General Assembly in 1990. See UNGA Res 45/155 (18 Dec. 1990).

205 Half a year later, the General Assembly decided that the Office shall be located at Geneva and shall have a liaison office in New York. See UNGA Res 48/141 (7 Jan. 1994) para 6.

206 Vienna Declaration and Programme of Action, adopted by The World Conference on Human Rights, UN Doc. A/Conf. 157/23 (25 Jun. 1993).

207 *Ibid.* Point 2, paragraph 3.

This formulation restricts the RSD by conditioning it on the territorial integrity of states, but only of those that are representative. Although the RSD exception resembles the one enshrined in the Friendly Relations Declaration, the Vienna Declaration brings a novelty – unlike the Friendly Relations Declaration it does not enumerate particular grounds for discrimination, but uses a general clause – 'without distinction of *any kind*'. This can be considered as a pro-RSD achievement; in order to preserve territory, discrimination based on any ground must be eliminated. As a result, the Declaration strikes a balance between the aspirations of peoples on the one side, and state interests on the other, by tethering territorial integrity to governmental representativeness – a core tenet of ISD.

3.1.2 UN General Assembly resolutions

In opposition to the Vienna Declaration and Programme of Action, three other Declarations were adopted in the form of resolutions at the General Assembly forum in New York. The 1970 Friendly Relations Declaration is the foundational document underscoring the connection between the respect for ISD and the prohibition of secession, upon which subsequent instruments rely, including the above-described 1993 Vienna Declaration, and the 1995 UN Fiftieth Anniversary Declaration. The 2007 Declaration on the Rights of Indigenous Peoples, while not making territorial integrity explicitly dependent on the respect for ISD, is undoubtedly a document focused on ISD that simultaneously prohibits secession.

3.1.2.1 *Friendly Relations Declaration*

The Declaration on Principles of International Law concerning Friendly Relations and Co-operation among States in accordance with the Charter of the United Nations, known in its abbreviated form as the Friendly Relations Declaration, was adopted without a vote in 1970 by the General Assembly with the intention 'to act as an elucidation of certain important Charter provisions', including the issue of self-determination.[208] The Declaration was termed by the chairman of the Sixth Committee as the greatest document since the UN Charter,[209] the ICJ observed that it reflects customary international law,[210]

208 M. Shaw, *International Law* (CUP 2017) 200.

209 25 GAOR, 1970, 6th Cmttee. 1860th mtg., UN Doc. A/PV.1860 (6 Oct. 1970) para 32.

210 ICJ, *Accordance with International Law of the Unilateral Declaration of Independence in Respect of Kosovo,* Advisory Opinion, ICJ Rep. 2010, para 80.

while the scholarship agrees that it contains seven 'fundamental principles of international law'.[211]

According to Principle V of the Declaration (the principle of equal rights and self-determination of peoples), 'all peoples have the right freely to determine, without external interference, their political status and to pursue their economic, social and cultural development, and every State has the duty to respect this right in accordance with the provisions of the Charter'.[212] The right to self-determination, as presented here, is to be executed by peoples themselves; hence, it is not merely a privilege dependent upon a state's good faith in fulfilling its duty to respect this principle. In fact, according to paragraph 2 of Principle V, states 'have a duty to promote (…) the realization of the principle'. Paragraphs 5 and 6, alongside the *travaux préparatoires*, indicate that self-determination is rather not directed to groups within independent states.[213] Rendering foreign assistance, as envisaged by paragraph 5, for independence claims is recognized solely with regard to liberation movements; such assistance would otherwise contradict the principle of non-intervention in domestic affairs. Paragraph 6 notes that colonies and NSGT have a distinct status from their administrating powers, which allows for their factual independence or the association or integration with the independent state, but is conceptually hardly compatible with secession.[214] Be that as it may, the Declaration confronts the matter of post-colonial secession in paragraph 7 by adding a disclaimer, which substantially limits the RSD by explicitly securing territorial integrity. Paragraph 7 spells out:

> Nothing in the foregoing paragraphs shall be construed as authorizing or encouraging any action which would dismember or impair, totally or in part, the territorial integrity or political unity of sovereign and independent States conducting themselves in compliance with the principle of equal rights and self-determination of peoples as described above and thus possessed of a government representing the whole people belonging to the territory without distinction as to race, creed or colour.

---

211 The others are the protection of human rights; the duty to co-operate in the economic, social and cultural fields; the non-appropriation of Outer Space, the prevention of environmental harm, and the principles of international humanitarian law. See J. E. Viñuales, 'The Fundamental Principles of International Law-An Enduring Ideal?' in J. E. Viñuales (ed.) *The UN Friendly Relations Declaration at 50* (CUP 2020) 3–4.

212 Friendly Relations Declaration, Principle V, paragraph 1.

213 See section 5.2.1.

214 See 3.2.1.-3.2.2.

Still, a literal reading of the passage suggests that the preservation of territorial unity is not expressed in absolute terms. Only if states' governments are *representative* (if they represent the people of the entire territory), secession is off the table. Such a clause has been known in legal parlance as a 'safeguard clause' or 'limiting clause'.[215] The requirement of representativeness must be understood as the expression of ISD of all peoples residing within the state.[216] A government shall not be deemed representative if it curbs fundamental human rights, encompassing the right to self-determination. But whether unrepresentativeness provides grounds for secession remains controversial. Some authors support such *a contario* reading of the safeguard clause, but add that for a remedial secession right to occur, mass and grave human rights violations must also be present.[217] In any case, both readings of the safeguard clause corroborate the thesis that ESD should be rejected when ISD is observed by the parent state.[218]

In addition, this conclusion is supported by paragraph 4 of the Principle, which states 'the establishment of a sovereign and independent State, the free association or integration with an independent State or *the emergence into any other political status* freely determined by a people constitute modes of implementing the right of self-determination by that people'. The emphasized part can be interpreted as creating a method of exercising the RSD even within the existing country.[219]

In sum, the Friendly Relations Declaration might be read as broadening the scope of the RSD beyond a purely colonial context, while still safeguarding existing states through the principle of territorial integrity. This implies that the RSD can be exercised in both internal and external forms. Yet, ISD remains

---

215 Cassese, *Self-determination of Peoples* (n 183) 115–118; B. Roth, 'The Relevance of Democratic Principles to the Self-determination Norm' in P. Hilpold (ed.) *Autonomy and Self-determination* (Elgar 2018) 63–64.

216 J. Crawford, *The Creation of States in International Law* (OUP 2006) 118–119.

217 See J. Vidmar, 'Remedial Secession in International Law: Theory and (Lack of) Practice' 6 *St Antony's International Review* (2010) 40; V. Dimitrijević, *Savremeno Shvatanje Prava Naroda na Samoopredeljenje* (Belgrade Centre for Human Rights 2011) 31–34.

218 F. Capotorti, 'Cours General de Droit International Public' 248 *Recueil des Cours* IV (1994) 36; J. Dugard and D. Raič, 'The Role of Recognition in the Law and Practice of Secession' in M. Kohen (ed.) *Secession: International Law Perspectives* (CUP 2006) 104–106.

219 One could identify the third reading of the safeguard clause inferred from the fact that the Declaration speaks only about the relations between States. Thus, internal groups are not bound by the clause, but they enjoy the right to secession if the representativeness condition is not met. See Dugard and Raič, 'The Role of Recognition in the Law and Practice of Secession' (n 218) 103–105 (emphasis added).

the exclusive method if the state is representative of all peoples within its territory.

3.1.2.2 *UN Fiftieth Anniversary Declaration*

The Declaration on the Occasion of the Fiftieth Anniversary of the United Nations (UN Fiftieth Anniversary Declaration) was adopted by the General Assembly on 24 October 1995 to commemorate the 50th anniversary of the founding of the United Nations.[220] This declaration marked a significant milestone in the history of the organization and provided an opportunity for member states to reflect on the achievements and challenges faced by the UN over the preceding five decades.

This Declaration first recognized the impact of self-determination on the attainment of freedom by colonized people and those living under apartheid and reaffirmed the right to self-determination for all currently subjugated or occupied people, who are entitled 'to take legitimate action in accordance with the Charter of the United Nations to realize their inalienable right of self-determination'.[221] However, this

> shall not be construed as authorizing or encouraging any action that would dismember or impair, totally or in part, the territorial integrity or political unity of sovereign and independent States conducting themselves in compliance with the principle of equal rights and self-determination of peoples and thus possessed of a Government representing the whole people belonging to the territory without distinction of any kind.[222]

This excerpt directly reproduces wording from the Vienna Declaration and Programme of Action, adopted two years earlier. The UN Fiftieth Anniversary Declaration is the last document of such a profile that confirms the territorial unity of a state that adheres to internal self-determination,[223] yet it continues to be cited by national and international bodies and institutions for this

220 UNGA Res 50/6 'The Declaration on the Occasion of the Fiftieth Anniversary of the United Nations' (9 Nov. 1995).

221 *Ibid.* (Peace) point 1.

222 *Ibid.*

223 UNGA Res 75/1 'The Declaration on the commemoration of the seventy-fifth anniversary of the United Nations' (21 Sep. 2020) only mentions self-determination as the UN Charter's provision, alongside the principle of sovereign equality of all States, respect of their territorial integrity and political independence.

purpose.[224] Notably, considering that all three aforementioned declarations were adopted without a vote – by acclamation – the elaborated passage, *mutatis mutandis*, significantly reflects the current position of states on the application of self-determination.

3.1.2.3 *Declaration on the Rights of Indigenous Peoples*

In 2007, the UN General Assembly adopted the Declaration on the Rights of Indigenous Peoples (UNDRIP), alas not unanimously. 144 states were in favour, 4 voted against, while 11 abstained.[225] The document elaborates on various rights of the indigenous peoples, many of which can be linked to the concept of internal self-determination. In particular, indigenous people are granted 'the right to autonomy or self-government in matters relating to their internal and local affairs, as well as ways and means for financing their autonomous functions' (Article 4) and 'the right to maintain and strengthen their distinct political, legal, economic, social and cultural institutions, while retaining their right to participate fully, if they so choose, in the political, economic, social and cultural life of the State' (Article 5).[226] The Declaration also introduces the concept of 'free, prior and informed consent' requiring that states obtain consent before undertaking measures that could potentially undermine the rights and identity of an indigenous community (Article 19). This procedural right ensures that affected peoples are meaningfully engaged in the decision-making process. Notably, the right 'to be consulted' and the obligation 'to receive permission' originate from the right to self-determination and serve as safeguards over lands, resources and other spheres of life, extending beyond the context of indigenous peoples.[227]

In positioning the UNDRIP as an essentially internal aspect of the RSD, it is important to reflect on the debates that preceded the adoption of the Declaration. These discussions reveal state attitudes toward the self-determination of indigenous populations – a particularly vulnerable group – and provide insights into the general application of RSD and the counter-secession value of ISD. The Commission on Human Rights established a working group in 1995 tasked with drafting a declaration on the rights of indigenous peoples.

224 Among many examples, India cited it in its state report to the Human Rights Committee and the Constitutional Court of Spain referred to it in its judgment on Catalonia's independence.

225 UNGA Res 61/295 'The Declaration on the Rights of Indigenous Peoples' (13 Sep. 2007).

226 See also International Labour Organization's Convention Concerning Indigenous and Tribal Peoples in Independent Countries (No. 169) (27 Jun. 1989) 28 *ILM* 1382.

227 UN FAO, 'Free Prior and Informed Consent: An Indigenous Peoples' Right and a Good Practice for Local Communities' (2016) 12.

According to the report of this body, the majority of states emphasized that self-determination for indigenous peoples should encompass the right to autonomy and cultural rights.[228] A representative of Mexico highlighted that self-determination of indigenous peoples should always be interpreted in accordance with national legislation and with full respect for the principles of sovereignty and territorial integrity.[229] The representative of Japan stated that Japan does not recognize collective rights,[230] while several representatives of states believed that the concepts of 'self-determination' and 'peoples' are not clearly defined in international law.[231] The representative of Pakistan openly endorsed the qualified version of ISD, stating that sovereign states 'in order to be entitled to respect for territorial integrity, should conduct themselves in compliance with the principles of equal rights and self-determination and should be possessed of a government representing the whole people'.[232] On the other hand, the representatives of indigenous communities have warned that the concept of self-determination in the Declaration must be expressed in the same manner as in the Covenants, as any attempt to diminish the qualify the right to self-determination of indigenous peoples would constitute racial discrimination. They also stated that the division between external and internal self-determination is not helpful as it associates self-determination with secession, and emphasized that, although the majority of indigenous peoples will exercise self-determination through autonomy and self-governing arrangements, it is unacceptable and discriminatory to reduce self-determination to an internal form alone.[233]

The representative of Guatemala affirmed that it is not necessary to redefine or limit the concept of self-determination. While self-determination was associated with movements for independence during the colonial period, peoples and national groups in modern independent states are able to achieve their political, economic, social, and cultural development through various forms of decentralization and autonomy.[234] The majority of representatives agreed that the participation of indigenous peoples in decision-making processes, rights to lands they traditionally inhabit, and access to natural resources, as well as

228 Commission on Human Rights, 'Report of the Working Group on a draft United Nations declaration on the rights of indigenous peoples established in accordance with Commission resolution 1995/32' (6 Feb. 2001) UN Doc. E/CN.4/2001/85, paras 69, 82, 83.

229 *Ibid.* para 64.

230 *Ibid.* para 65.

231 *Ibid.* para 68.

232 *Ibid.* para 77.

233 *Ibid.* para 79.

234 *Ibid.* para 88.

various forms of autonomy, are essential ways to implement the right to self-determination for indigenous peoples. On the other hand, the application of external self-determination leading to the disruption of territorial integrity was rejected, considering that 'indigenous peoples form part of the nation-state and thus should respect its territorial integrity and national sovereignty'.[235] The U.S. delegation, in line with this general stance, was directed to support the use of the term 'internal self-determination' in both the UN and OAS declarations on Indigenous rights, and to acknowledge that although self-determination is an evolving concept, it is 'limited by the principle of territorial integrity and, therefore, must be exercised within the existing States'.[236] In consequence, a safeguard clause protecting sovereign states was incorporated into the UNDRIP. Article 46 stipulates that the Declaration cannot

> be interpreted as implying for any State, *people, group or person* any right to engage in any activity or to perform any act contrary to the Charter of the United Nations or construed as authorizing or encouraging any action which would dismember or impair, totally or in part, the territorial integrity or political unity of sovereign and independent States.

Remarkably, the Declaration explicitly mentions that the principle of territorial integrity applies to both states and non–state entities. However, there is no condition of representativeness, namely territorial integrity is not qualified by the requirement that a government represents the whole population, a clause which can be traced to previous three declarations. Hence, the rights envisaged by the Declaration can be invoked only *internally* within existing states[237] due to the limits imposed by the principle of territorial unity.[238] The Declaration makes crystal clear that the RSD cannot be interpreted as *allowing* or *not prohibiting* secession, thus, there is no neutral zone.

---

235 *Ibid.* para 110.

236 Letter and cable from Robert A. Bradtke, Executive Secretary, U.S. Nat'l Sec. Council, to Kristie A. Kinney, Executive Secretary, U.S. Dep't of State (18 Jan. 2001). Cited from R. Coulter, 'The Law of Self-determination and the United Nations Declaration on the Rights of Indigenous Peoples' 15(1) UCLA *Journal of International Law and Foreign Affairs* (2010) 21, fn. 52 (emphasis added).

237 T. Koivurova, 'Sovereign States and Self-Determining Peoples: Carving Out a Place for Transnational Indigenous Peoples in a World of Sovereign States' 12 *International Community Law Review* (2010) 203.

238 Summers (n 26) 262–270.

The UNDRIP is the most recent prominent attempt to deal with the issue of self-determination. Although it concerns particular recipients – the indigenous peoples – it illustrates two trends: (a) that self-determination is becoming a very broad and meaningful right, and (b) that it is intended to be exercised internally, ideally by all minorities.[239] This is what the US delegation might have had in mind by indicating the right's evolutionary character.[240] Yet, by eschewing the reference to the *respect* of ISD, which, *nota bene*, is hardly measurable, states effectively gained *carte blanche* as far as their territory is at stake. In the absence of an 'endogenous' sanction, the implementation of vital provisions should be sought through alternative channels. The global adherence to UNDRIP still leaves much to be desired.[241]

3.1.3 UN Secretary-General

The United Nations Secretary-General (UNSG) has dealt with internal self-determination and secession sporadically. Nevertheless, several statements and reports merit observation and they could be beneficial for establishing a correlation between the two aspects.

Regarding secession, in 1970, UNSG U Thant emphatically denounced it as an option of engendering territorial changes,[242] while in the 1990s, UNSG Boutros-Ghali took a milder view, which incorporated the recourse to human rights and the necessity of responding to the interests of both the state and its population – by and large befitting the idea of ISD and its concomitant counter-secession value. The following quote illustrates this point well:

> The United Nations has not closed its door. Yet if every ethnic, religious or linguistic group claimed statehood, there would be no limit to fragmentation, and peace, security and economic well-being for all would become ever more difficult to achieve (...)

239 The Special Rapporteur on the rights of indigenous people noted in her report to the General Assembly that the content of Article 4, that is, self-determination through autonomy and self-government has both internal and external aspects. See UN Doc. A/74/149 (17 Jul. 2019).

240 See Coulter, 'The Law of Self-determination' (n 236) 17–22.

241 ILA Res 5/2012 'Rights of Indigenous Peoples' (2012) (noting that UNDRIP as a whole cannot yet be considered as a statement of existing customary international law, and recommending ways to implement the document by states). See also D. Mamo (ed.) *The Indigenous World 2024* (Eks-Skolens Grafisk Design & Tryk 2024).

242 See 3.3.2.1.2.3.

> The sovereignty, territorial integrity and independence of States within the established international system, and the principle of self-determination for peoples, both of great value and importance, must not be permitted to work against each other in the period ahead. Respect for democratic principles at all levels of social existence is crucial: in communities, within States and within the community of States. Our constant duty should be to maintain the integrity of each while finding a balanced design for all.[243]

Boutros-Ghali reiterated his views in his seminal work *Agenda for Peace,* where he observed that many modern conflicts arise, not from military threats between states, but from claims of nationalism and sovereignty, as well as from ethnic, religious, social, cultural, and linguistic despair. He opted for a balance between good internal governance and the demands of an ever more interdependent world. As such, this view largely subscribes to the thesis that secession should generally be deemed prohibited, though it may be considered permissible (a possibility he does not explicitly state) in light of the evolving understanding of state sovereignty as less absolute and exclusive.[244]

Conflict prevention and settlement have remained the preoccupation of subsequent UNSGs. Kofi Annan in his 2004 Cyprus reunification plan (the Annan Plan) strived to resolve the longstanding Cyprus dispute by proposing a comprehensive, constitution-like arrangement, which favoured the unity of the island on the basis of a bicommunal, bizonal federation.[245] Ban Ki-moon and his successor António Guterres have maintained the policy of 'neutrality' with regard to the unilateral declarations of independence, particularly in situations where the UN Security Council has not provided clear guidance.[246] Both have favoured the spirit of dialogue and peacebuilding approaches that they believe will ultimately benefit the populations involved.

---

243 B. Boutros-Ghali, 'An Agenda for Peace Preventive Diplomacy, Peacemaking and Peacekeeping' Report of the Secretary-General pursuant to the statement adopted by the Summit Meeting of the Security Council on 31 January 1992, UN Doc. A/47/217 (17 Jan. 1992) paras 17, 19.

244 B. Boutros-Ghali, *Agenda for Peace* (United Nations 1995) 6.

245 The Comprehensive Settlement of the Cyprus Problem (31 Mar. 2004) <https://peacemaker.un.org/sites/default/files/document/files/2024/05/annanplanmarch302004.pdf>.

246 See Report of the Secretary-General on the United Nations Interim Administration Mission in Kosovo (24 Nov. 2008) UN Doc. S/2008/692 (hereinafter: Report of the SG on Kosovo) paras 26, 46, 49–50. Cf. Report of the SG on Kosovo (29 Jun. 2007) UN Doc. S /2007/395, para 2. ('I conveyed both his [SG' Special Envoy on Kosovo, Mr. M. Ahtisaari] future status report and his settlement proposal to the Security Council, with my full support').

A notable example of this ongoing approach is the United Nations Interim Administration Mission in Kosovo (UNMIK), which continues to operate under UNSC Resolution 1244.[247] The mission's primary goals include promoting peace, security, stability, and respect for human rights in Kosovo and the region. Despite Kosovo's declaration of independence in 2008, its cooperation with the OSCE and EULEX, UNMIK remains active, which underscores the UN and the UNSG's preference for supporting internal self-determination over engaging in debates about secession.[248]

Besides, the Secretary-General is obliged, based on cyclic General Assembly resolutions titled 'Universal realization of the right of peoples to self-determination', to submit reports to this body regarding the universal application of the right of peoples to self-determination.[249] In these reports, the UNSG provides an overview of the activities of various organs and specialized UN bodies concerning the implementation of the right to self-determination during the reporting period. These reports typically address the well-known issues within the self-determination discourse, reaffirming the right to self-determination for the Palestinian people,[250] including the establishment of an independent state, the right to self-determination for Non-Self-Governing Territories, also encompassing the right to independent statehood,[251] the need for a referendum in Western Sahara as a means of the realisation of the right to self-determination by the people of Western Sahara,[252] and finally, the negative impact of foreign occupation, alien domination and the use of mercenaries on the exercise of the right to self-determination.[253]

---

247 UN Doc. S/RES/1244 (10 Jun. 1999) point 20.

248 Report of the SG on Kosovo (2 Apr. 2024) UN Doc. S/2024/282 ('In pursuit of its goals, UNMIK continues its constructive engagement with Pristina and Belgrade, all communities in Kosovo, and regional and international actors'). See, in particular, sections IV (Rule of law and human rights), VI (Returns, reconciliations, cultural heritage and community relations) and VII (Trust-building, partnership and cooperation).

249 The most recent request was through Resolution 78/193. See UN Doc. A/RES/78/193 (22 Dec. 2023) point 6.

250 Reports of the Secretary-General, 'Right of peoples to self-determination' UN Doc. A/54/327 (7 Sep. 1999) and UN Doc. A/78/261 (31 Jul. 2023).

251 Reports of the Secretary-General, 'Right of peoples to self-determination' UN Doc. A/73/329 (20 Aug. 2018) and UN Doc. A/76/276 (9 Aug. 2021).

252 Reports of the Secretary-General, 'Right of peoples to self-determination' UN Doc. A/54/327 (7 Sep. 1999); UN Doc. A/57/312 (15 Aug. 2002) and UN Doc. A/66/172 (22 Jul. 2011).

253 Reports of the Secretary-General, 'Right of peoples to self-determination' UN Doc. A/64/360 (18 Sep. 2009) and UN Doc. A/77/265 (3 Aug. 2022).

Although these formulations indicate mostly the external aspect of self-determination, the reports include references to the internal dimension of the right as well, predominantly through summaries of the activities of the UN Human Rights Council and human rights treaty bodies. The 2023 report, for instance, states that the HRC noted the adverse effects of climate change on the effective enjoyment of the RSD, and reaffirmed the interrelatedness of this right with a democratic and equitable international order.[254] The report further observed that the Special Rapporteur on the human rights of internally displaced persons warned that development-induced displacement affects indigenous peoples, infringing their right to self-determination. The report also stressed that 'inadequate disclosure and consultation with affected populations regarding the acquisition of their lands, as well as a lack of consent, could have also infringed on the right of self-determination'.[255] Additionally, the report referenced General Comment No. 39 (2022) of the Committee on the Elimination of Discrimination against Women regarding the rights of Indigenous women and girls. It was noted that the environmental degradation as well as dispossession, lack of legal recognition and unauthorized use of Indigenous territories, lands and natural resources were direct threats to self-determination, cultural integrity and survival of Indigenous women and girls, as was 'the unauthorized use and appropriation of their technical knowledge, spiritual practice and cultural heritage by State actors and third parties'.[256] From the foregoing, it is possible not only to deduce different meanings of ISD but also to observe that UNSG places significant importance on this issue, as evidenced by the increasingly detailed and comprehensive nature of recent reports.

In sum, it seems that UNSGs have been reluctant to accept the creation of new states outside the colonial or similar context, particularly in conflict situations where a parent state opposes secession. On the other hand, they have consistently demanded respect for internal self-determination, *inter alia*, through the promotion of democratization and the rule of law. This commitment is evidenced by their support for the establishment of institutional

---

254 Report of the Secretary-General, 'Right of peoples to self-determination' (31 Jul. 2023) UN Doc. A/78/261, 10. See also HRC Res 50/9 'Human rights and climate change' (14 Jul. 2022); HRC Res 51/11 'Promotion of a democratic and equitable international order' (12 Oct. 2022).

255 *Ibid.* 11. See also Report of the Special Rapporteur on the human rights of internally displaced persons. Prepared by C. Jimenez-Damary (18 Jul. 2022) UN Doc. A/77/182.

256 *Ibid.* 15. See also Committee on the Elimination of Discrimination against Women (CEDAW), General recommendation No. 39 (2022) on the rights of Indigenous women and Girls (26 Oct. 2022) UN Doc. CEDAW/C/GC/39, para 54.

structures, such as the Provisional Institutions of Self-Government in 2002 or EULEX in 2008 in Kosovo,[257] and by offering their good offices in efforts to resolve the Cyprus issue, all aimed at enhancing the enjoyment of internal self-determination.[258]

3.1.4 Human Rights Council

The Human Rights Council (HRC) is a UN body that replaced the UN Commission on Human Rights in 2006 by the decision of the UN General Assembly.[259] The Council's mission is to promote and protect human rights around the world, and its activities focus, broadly speaking, on furthering internal self-determination. In general, the Council addresses current and progressive obligations of states towards their populations by pronouncing on such issues as freedom of expression, freedom of association and assembly, freedom of belief and religion, racial and ethnic minorities rights, women's rights, and the rights of the LGBT community.

With regard to the juxtaposition of the RSD and secession, the UN Human Rights Council and its predecessor have not been particularly prolific. However, in 1992, the Commission on Human Rights' Special Rapporteur on Possible Ways and Means of Facilitating the Peaceful and Constructive Solution of Problems Involving Minorities noted in the 2nd progress report that:

> the question of a unilateral right to self-determination is extremely doubtful. It is overridden by the basic principle of territorial integrity, provided, however, that the State conducts itself in accordance with the principle of equal rights and self-determination of peoples and is possessed of a government representing the whole people of the territory without distinction as to race, creed or colour. It must be kept in mind that the most basic principle of self-determination is that of the right of popular participation in the government of the State as an entity. When the Government does not allow all segments and all peoples to

257 Provisional Institutions existed effectively until Kosovo's declaration of independence (DOI) in 2008. Note the insistence of UNSG on 'standards before status' until the DOI. See Reports of the SG on Kosovo UN Doc. S/2004/348 (30 Apr. 2004) para 60; UN Doc. S/2005/335 (23 May 2005) para 13.

258 See, among others, Report of the Secretary-General on his mission of good offices in Cyprus (3 Jan. 2024) UN Doc. S/2024/13.

259 UNGA Res 60/251 (3 Apr. 2006).

> participate, the question of the right to self-determination of the different components becomes more pertinent.[260]

The Rapporteur added that national or ethnic groups, living compactly together on a territory inside a sovereign State, will therefore have the onus of proof that they have a right to secede under international law. If that cannot be convincingly demonstrated to the international community, other States are not entitled to encourage secessionist efforts.[261] As a result, the Rapporteur followed the Friendly Relations Declaration's safeguard clause, and anticipated its reiteration, *mutatis mutandis*, in the 1993 Vienna Declaration and Programme of Action. The UN Human Rights Council, for its part, in 2011 adopted Resolution 18/6 on the promotion of a democratic and equitable international order, establishing the mandate of an Independent Expert tasked with submitting thematic reports to both the Council and the General Assembly.[262] In his 2014 report on self-determination, the Independent Expert stressed 'the advantages of the internal dimension of self-determination' and added that 'when human rights are enjoyed by all peoples without discrimination and populations have the feeling that they are in control of their destinies, they will be less disposed to seek external self-determination'.[263] Nevertheless, as he admitted, his report focused mostly on external self-determination, thus he also, in specific circumstances, endorsed secession.[264] The 2021 draft report of the Expert Mechanism on the Rights of Indigenous Peoples considered the history of the right to self-determination and noted that the adoption of the Friendly Relations Declaration was a 'pivotal moment' in the development of the RSD beyond the decolonization context, signalling a shift of self-determination 'beyond concerns about State sovereignty and involved a deeper examination of the term "peoples" and the meaning of self-determination for peoples internally within a State'.[265] The report, apart from favouring the implementation of the RSD

260 UN Commission on Human Rights, Sub-Commission on Prevention of Discrimination and Protection of Minorities, 'Possible ways and means of facilitating the peaceful and constructive solution of problems involving minorities'. Second Progress Report submitted by A. Eide (1 Jul. 1992) UN Doc. E/CN 4/Sub 2/1992/37, para 165.

261 *Ibid.* para 166.

262 HRC Res 18/6 'Promotion of a democratic and equitable international order '(13 Oct. 2011). See also HRC Res 68/175 (18 Dec. 2013).

263 UNGA, 'Interim report of the Independent Expert on the promotion of a democratic and equitable international order' submitted by A. de Zayas (7 Aug. 2014) UN Doc. A/69/272, paras 11, 13.

264 *Ibid.* paras 3, 28, 29, 52.

265 HRC Draft report 'Efforts to implement the United Nations Declaration on the Rights of Indigenous Peoples: indigenous peoples and the right to self-determination' (3 May 2021) 3. UN Doc. A/HRC/EMRIP/2021/2, para 5.

internally, makes an interesting observation regarding the external dimension of the RSD as applied to indigenous peoples, viewing it as the right of those divided by international borders to maintain and develop contacts, relations and cooperation. It also sees the external dimension as the indigenous peoples' 'right to determine their place in the international community based upon the principle of equal rights'—not as a right to separate statehood, but as a right to participate in international forums and decision-making processes.[266]

The Council's activities testify that it strives to protect the existing right to self-determination from external menaces or to further its external application by peoples who have been specifically designated as its holders. This is evident from the scrutiny of its most recent sessions. At its forty-sixth session, the Human Rights Council, in Resolution 45/5, affirmed the negative impact of unilateral coercive measures on the enjoyment of self-determination, referring to the final document and declaration adopted at the eighteenth summit of Heads of State and Government of the Movement of Non-Aligned Countries.[267] In its Resolution 46/25, the Council reaffirmed the inalienable, permanent and unqualified right of the Palestinian people to self-determination, including their right to live in freedom, justice and dignity, and their right to an independent State of Palestine.[268] The maintenance of territorial integrity on account of providing ISD is therefore presumed from its silence on secession in established states and its consistent focus on urging states to abide by aspects of which ISD is comprised. It would be incongruous to assume that the HRC could support the dismemberment of states that comply with ISD, knowing that the such fragmentation would likely lead to a situation that clashes with its overarching objectives.[269]

3.1.5 Human Rights Committee

The UN Human Rights Committee is an international (quasi-judicial) body vested with the authority to monitor the implementation of the ICCPR by its State parties. It does so in three ways: issuing views on individual complaints (i), general comments (ii), and observations on state reports on human rights (iii).

---

266 *Ibid.* paras 16–17, 31.

267 HRC Res 45/5 'Human rights and unilateral coercive measures' (6 Oct. 2020).

268 HRC Res 46/25 'Right of the Palestinian people to self-determination' (24 Mar. 2021).

269 During the dissolution of the former Yugoslavia, for example, the Commission on Human Rights focused on human rights abuses but did not endorse any territorial changes. See UN Commission on Human Rights, 'Situation of human rights in the territory of the former Yugoslavia' (23 Feb. 1993) UN Doc. E/CN.4/RES/1993/7, para 2.

Individual complaints are enabled by virtue of the Optional Protocol (OP) to the ICCPR, which allows individuals to lodge complaints ('communications') with the Committee that their rights under the Covenant are violated by a State Party. The Committee has repeatedly stressed that the RSD is a *collective right*, and, as such, it cannot be the subject of a communication under the OP. In *Lubicon Lake Band v. Canada*, the Committee argued that the OP permits only *individuals* to file complaints to protect their rights, hence the RSD, as a collective right, cannot be invoked.[270] This stance was later reaffirmed in subsequent jurisprudence, where the Committee held that 'no claim for self-determination may be brought under the Optional Protocol' and that it 'can receive and consider communications only if they emanate from individuals'.[271]

In terms of the second method, in 1984, the Committee issued General Comment No. 12 on Article 1 of the ICCPR.[272] The Comment is of a general nature, without particularities which could help us understand the precise meaning and scope of Article 1. The RSD is, according to the Comment, 'of particular importance because its realization is an essential condition for the effective guarantee and observance of individual human rights and for the promotion and strengthening of those rights'.[273] Thus, the RSD is presented as a *sine qua non* for the enjoyment of all other rights under the Covenant. Although the Human Rights Committee did not mention ISD, it still said that State parties should not confine themselves to providing information on election laws (paragraph 3) but 'describe the constitutional and political processes which in practice allow the exercise of this right' (paragraph 4). This can be interpreted as imposing a *positive obligation* on States to facilitate ISD for groups qualifying as 'peoples'.

The Committee also linked Article 1 to other international instruments concerning the right of all peoples to self-determination, in particular the Friendly Relations Declaration (paragraph 7). If one bears in mind that the

---

270 Human Rights Committee, *Chief Bernard Ominayak and Lubicon Lake Band v. Canada*, Communication No. 167/1984 (26 Mar. 1990) paras 13.3. and 32.1.

271 See also the following cases on the RSD and Article 1 of the ICCPR: *Mikmaq v. Canada*, Communication No. 78/1980 (29 Jul. 1984); *Kitok v. Sweden*, Communication No. 197/1985 (27 Jul. 1988); *Marshall et al. v. Canada*, Communication No. 205/1986 (4 Nov. 1991); *EP et al. v. Colombia*, Communication No. 318/1988 (25 Jul. 1990); *AB et al. v. Italy*, Communication No. 413/1990 (1991); *RL et al. v. Canada*, Communication No. 358/1989 (5 Nov. 1991); *Apirana Mahuika et al. v. New Zealand*, Communication No. 547/1993 (27 Oct. 2000); *JGA Diergaardt et al. v. Namibia*, Communication No. 760/1997 (25 Jul. 2000); *Gillot et al. v. France*, Communication No. 932/2000 (15 Jul. 2002). Further, M. Nowak, *U.N. Covenant on Civil and Political Rights: CCPR commentary* (N.P. Engel 2005) 18–19 (emphasis added).

272 Human Rights Committee, General Comment No. 12: Article 1 (Right to Self-determination), The Right to Self-determination of Peoples (13 Mar. 1984).

273 *Ibid.* para 1.

Declaration calls for the protection of state territory and the fulfilment of the RSD within states, then it could be inferred that the Committee likewise supports the premise that the RSD should be exercised in accordance with the principle of territorial integrity.

Generally speaking, the Committee appears reluctant to deal with the RSD outside of the colonial or indigenous peoples' context, which suggests that it does not aim to promote its external application in established states.[274] On the other hand, the Committee regularly comments on internal self-determination in states, directly or indirectly, but usually in conjunction with alleged violations of individual rights. For instance, in one observation on Finland concerning the rights of indigenous Sami people, the Committee called on the authorities to review section 3 of the Act on the Sami Parliament. The goal was to ensure that 'the criteria for eligibility to vote in Sami Parliament elections are defined and applied in a manner that respects the right of the Sami people to exercise their internal self-determination in accordance with articles 25 and 27 of the Covenant'.[275] Similarly, in concluding observations on Morocco's report, the Committee noted that, notwithstanding the obligation to determine the status of Western Sahara in good faith, Morocco must respect the freedom of movement of the people in Western Sahara and conduct meaningful consultations concerning development projects and resource extraction.[276] In that sense, the Committee embraced the concept of ISD – in the former case, Finland was called to enable the political participation of the Sami people through amending domestic legislation, while in the latter, ISD played an equally important role as ESD, irrespective of colonial ramifications of Western Sahara.

The Committee on Economic, Social and Cultural Rights (CESCR) monitors the implementation of the ICESCR in a manner devoid of political bias. Still, the Committee frequently underscores the importance of meaningful

---

274 Guruparan (n 140) 47. Higgins, a member of the Committee between 1985–1995, noted that 'external self-determination requires a state to take action in its foreign policy consistent with the attainment of self-determination in the remaining areas of colonial or racist occupation. But internal self-determination is directed to their own peoples'. R. Higgins, 'Postmodern Tribalism and the Right to Secession, Comments' in C. Brölmann, R. Lefeber and M. Zieck (eds.) *Peoples and Minorities in International Law* (Martinus Nijhoff Publishers 1993) 31. Shaw *de facto* equated self-determination with ISD and saw the Human Rights Committee as the body entrusted with the implementation of the RSD in the post-colonial context. M. Shaw, *International Law* (CUP 2021) 261.

275 Human Rights Committee, *Klemetti Käkkäläjärvi et al. v. Finland*, Communication No. 2950/2017 (2018) paras 9.10–9.11.

276 Human Rights Committee, 'Concluding observations on the sixth periodic report of Morocco' (2016) Doc. CCPR/C/MAR/CO/6, para 10.

participation in decision-making processes, particularly for marginalized or disadvantaged groups, as a cornerstone for the effective realization of economic, social, and cultural rights. Moreover, the CESCR acknowledges that the principle of self-determination is pivotal in empowering communities to shape their own development agendas and address systemic inequalities.[277]

3.1.6 Committee on the Elimination of All Forms of Racial Discrimination

The Committee on the Elimination of all Forms of Racial Discrimination (CERD) is a body similar to the Human Rights Committee, yet with a distinct mandate: to monitor the implementation of the International Convention on the Elimination of All Forms of Racial Discrimination (ICERD) by the State parties. Like the Human Rights Committee, it issues observations on periodic state reports, general recommendations and views about individual complaints for alleged violations of the Convention. In General Recommendation No. 21,[278] the CERD dealt with the RSD and explicitly divided this right into two parts: external and internal. In the Committee's opinion, ISD represents

> the rights of all peoples to pursue freely their economic, social and cultural development without outside interference. In that respect there exists a link with the right of every citizen to take part in the conduct of public affairs at any level as referred to in article 5(c) of the International Convention on the Elimination of All Forms of Racial Discrimination. In consequence, governments are to represent the whole population without distinction as to race, colour, decent, national, or ethnic origins. The external aspect of self-determination implies that all peoples have the right to determine freely their political status and their place in the international community based upon the principle of equal rights and exemplified by the liberation of peoples from colonialism and by the prohibition to subject peoples to alien subjugation, domination, and exploitation.[279]

---

277 See CESCR, 'Concluding observations on the fourth periodic report of Ecuador' (2019) Doc. E/C.12/ECU/CO/4; CESCR, 'Concluding observations on the fourth periodic report of Israel' (2019) Doc. E/C.12/ISR/CO/4.

278 CERD, General Recommendation XXI(48) (8 Mar. 1996).

279 *Ibid.* para 4. Such a position is not without criticism, as the CERD omits the political dimension of ISD. It is illogical to confine the political aspect of the RSD solely to its external form, given that the political aspirations of peoples can be accommodated within existing states through various means (e.g., local autonomy). While it is encouraging that a body such as the CERD has formally acknowledged the dichotomy of the RSD,

In the following paragraphs, the CERD clearly restricts the applicability of the RSD in established states to the internal sphere. It argues that, to 'fully respect the rights of all peoples *within* a State, Governments are once again called upon to adhere to and fully implement international human rights instruments'.[280] It is recommended that governments, paying due regard to Article 2 of the ICERD, protect the rights of ethnic groups to live with dignity, preserve their culture, share equitably in the benefits of national development, and participate meaningfully in the governance of their countries.

In paragraph 6, the CERD relied on the Friendly Relations Declaration safeguard clause and expressly stated that this Recommendation cannot be interpreted

> as authorizing or encouraging any action which would dismember or impair, totally or in part, the territorial integrity or political unity of sovereign and independent States conducting themselves in compliance with the principle of equal rights and self-determination of peoples and possessing a Government representing the whole people belonging to the territory, without distinction as to race, creed or colour.[281]

In consequence, the CERD found that 'international law has not recognized a general right of peoples to unilaterally declare secession from a state', but acknowledged that territorial divisions can occur as a result of a free agreement among the parties involved.

Such CERD's stance appears somewhat ambivalent. On one hand, it categorically denies a right to unilateral secession, but on the other, it seems to leave room for acknowledgment in certain extreme situations, which could be interpreted as a sign of progress. Valencia Rodríguez observed that the Committee members were not keen on encouraging secession,[282] as evidenced by their support for consensual outcomes. Nonetheless, participants in a seminar on ICERD implementation – focused on Articles 4 and 6, including Valencia Rodríguez – argued that the Convention should not categorically prohibit secession. Instead, they suggested that it could be allowed in three exceptional

---

the Recommendation lacks persuasive force because it excludes the political rights of 'peoples' from the scope of ISD.

280 *Ibid.* para 5 (emphasis added).

281 *Ibid.* para 6.

282 CERD, 'Summary record of the 1147th meeting' (13 Mar. 1996) UN Doc. CERD/C/SR.1147, para 25, (Mr. Wolfrum: 'the Committee should make plain its opposition to secession') para 23, (Mr. Rechetov) para 24, (Mr. van Boven) para 27, (Mr. Garvalov) para 29, (Mr. Ferrero Costa) para 31.

situations: (1) when the RSD is explicitly recognized in a country's constitution, (2) when all interested parties agree to secession, or (3) when a segment of the population is denied the right to participate freely in public affairs or is deprived of civil, political, economic, social, or cultural rights.[283] Whatever the Committee's stance on the denial of ISD as grounds for secession, it unequivocally excluded the possibility of secession when a state is in full compliance with its human rights obligations.

3.1.7 International Court of Justice

The ICJ has dealt with the RSD in various contentious cases and advisory opinions, most of which pertained to decolonization.[284] A few relevant observations stemming from the Court's jurisprudence are worthy of note. First and foremost, the Court has not explicitly stated that there is a right to ESD outside the colonial context.[285] In the second place, the Court has not addressed ISD *par excellence*, as ISD concerns the vertical relationship between the state and its population, rather than the horizontal relationship among states, which fall within the ICJ's primary mandate.[286] However, it managed to identify several material aspects of both external and internal self-determination. In its *Western Sahara* advisory opinion, the ICJ said that 'the application of the right of self-determination require[d] a free and genuine expression of the will of the peoples concerned'.[287] Therefore, the people *themselves* must be *freely* oriented towards exercising the RSD. In the *East Timor* case, the Court

283 UN Commission on Human Rights, 'Report of the United Nations seminar to access the implementation of the International Convention on the Elimination of All Forms of Racial Discrimination with particular reference to articles 4 and 6' (5 Dec. 1996) UN Doc. E/CN.4/1997/68/Add.1, para 27.

284 ICJ, *International Status of South-West Africa*, Advisory Opinion, ICJ Rep. 1950; ICJ, *South West Africa Cases (Ethiopia v. South Africa; Liberia v. South Africa) (Second Phase)*, Judgment, ICJ Rep. 1966; ICJ, *Legal Consequences for States of the Continued Presence of South Africa in Namibia (South West Africa) notwithstanding Security Council Resolution 276* (1970), Advisory Opinion, ICJ Rep. 1971; ICJ, *Western Sahara*, Advisory Opinion, ICJ Rep. 1975; ICJ, *Case Concerning East Timor (Portugal v. Australia)*, Judgment, ICJ Rep. 1995; ICJ, *Legal Consequences of the Construction of a Wall in the Occupied Palestinian Territory*, Advisory Opinion, ICJ Rep. 2004; ICJ, *Kosovo Advisory Opinion* (n 210); ICJ, *Legal Consequences of the Separation of the Chagos Archipelago from Mauritius in 1965*, Advisory Opinion, ICJ Rep. 2019.

285 *Kosovo Advisory Opinion* (n 210) para 82. See also G. Zyberi 'Self-determination Through the Lens of the International Court of Justice' 56 *Netherlands International Law Review* (2009) 435.

286 K. Senaratne, *Internal Self-determination in International Law* (CUP 2021) chapter 8 'Internal Self-determination in the Courts of Law', 214.

287 *Western Sahara* (n 284) para 55.

accepted Portugal's claim that the RSD has an *erga omnes* character, further noting that it is a fundamental principle of contemporary international law.[288] The *erga omnes* nature of this right was later confirmed in the advisory opinion on Israel's construction of a wall in the Occupied Palestinian Territory (OPT).[289] In that opinion, the ICJ referred to the 1970 Friendly Relations Declaration, underlining that states bear the duty to refrain from any forcible action which deprives peoples of their right to self-determination, a duty specifically directed at Israel to protect the Palestinian RSD.[290] The Court found that the 'construction, along with measures taken previously, thus severely impede[d] the exercise by the Palestinian people of its right to self-determination, and [was] therefore a breach of Israel's obligation to respect that right'.[291] The Court noted that the construction of the wall would bring about alterations to the demographic composition in the OPT, thereby infringing the Palestinian RSD, However, this should be understood in broader terms – as a physical barrier for Palestinians to enjoy rights normally exercised by peoples within states (civil, political, economic, social and cultural rights).[292] It might be implied that the discriminatory and anti-Palestinian actions, including violations of humanitarian law, further substantiated the Court's conclusion on the breach of the RSD.[293] On the other hand, the RSD, as an *erga omnes* right, can be achieved not only through ESD, but also by 'the emergence into any other political status', potentially within existing states.

The *Kosovo* case was one of the most debated in relation to the RSD. As outlined before, numerous states contributed statements on this case.[294] Although many expected, even hoped for the Court's detailed opinion on the RSD, secession and territorial integrity (especially since Kosovo did not fit into a colonial or any similar context), the majority decided to issue a narrow interpretation

288 *East Timor* (n 284) para 29.

289 *Construction of a Wall* (n 284) paras 155–156.

290 *Ibid.* paras 86–88.

291 *Ibid.* para 122.

292 See HRC, 'Report of the independent international fact-finding mission to investigate the implications of the Israeli settlements on the civil, political, economic, social and cultural rights of the Palestinian people throughout the Occupied Palestinian Territory, including East Jerusalem' (7 Feb. 2023) UN Doc. A/HRC/22/63.

293 According to Article 1(4) of Additional Protocol I to the Geneva Conventions, the rules of IHL of international armed conflicts apply to 'armed conflicts in which peoples are fighting against colonial domination and alien occupation and against racist régimes in the exercise of their right of self-determination' 1125 UNTS 17512.

294 See 5.2.4.

of the question.[295] It focused solely on the legality of Kosovo's declaration of independence, ruling that the declaration itself did not violate international law.[296]

The advisory opinion itself is silent on the question of IDS' value. However, the separate opinions of Judge Cançado Trindade and Judge Yusuf are useful in shedding light on ISD and its counter-secession implications. These two judges considered that there is a basis to recognize the right to ESD in certain remedial circumstances. Judge Yusuf's observation that the RSD can be realized within the state without jeopardizing the sovereignty of the state precedes his discussion on remedial secession and should be treated as foundational. Accordingly,

> In this post-colonial conception, the right of self-determination chiefly operates inside the boundaries of existing States in various forms and guises, particularly as a right of the entire population of the State to determine its own political, economic and social destiny and to choose a representative government; and, equally, as a right of a defined part of the population, which has distinctive characteristics on the basis of race or ethnicity, to participate in the political life of the State, to be represented in its government and not to be discriminated against.[297]

In Judge Cançado Trindade's opinion, respect for ISD and territorial integrity in contemporary international law go hand in hand. As a result, 'no State can (…) commit atrocities and then rely on a claim of territorial integrity notwithstanding the sentiments and ineluctable resentments of the "people" or "population" victimized'.[298] For the judge, peoples 'under permanent adversity or systematic repression' are the bearers of ESD.[299] Consequently, the guarantee of a state's territorial integrity is rooted in the guarantee and non-violation of ISD.[300]

295 Such a narrow interpretation was criticized. See Separate Opinions of Judge Bruno Simma and Judge Abdul G. Koroma.

296 *Kosovo Advisory Opinion* (n 210) para 84.

297 Separate Opinion of Judge Yusuf (2010) para 9.

298 Separate Opinion of Judge Cançado Trindade (2010) para 176.

299 *Ibid.* para 184.

300 *Ibid.* paras 178–180 (quoting the 'celebrated' resolution 2625 (XXV) of 1970); paras 145, 150 (referring to the denial of ISD by states). Judge Trindade at one point seemed to conflate the entitlements stemming from ISD and ESD by stating that 'the emancipation of peoples came to be inspired by the principle of self-determination, more precisely internal self-determination, so as to oppose tyranny', para 174.

All in all, the ICJ has been criticized for adhering to a traditional, colonial-era approach to self-determination, denoting solely the determination of a new political status, at the expense of a broader recourse to human rights. For Hilpold, this omission in the *Chagos* Advisory Opinion of 2019 should be a 'wake-up call' since self-determination is a fundamental human right and such a juridical intersection could not only help to close the gap between Article 1 of the Covenants and the remaining articles, but also establish the concept of remedial secession. This would impact on the realisation of the RSD, including independence, and would create a legal basis for continuing involvement in internal affairs of the newly independent colonies.[301] 'Humanizing' self-determination would in consequence develop the concept of ISD and would be consistent with an emphasis laid on human rights protection by other UN bodies.[302]

3.2 *Regional Organizations Approach*

In this part, regional approaches to internal self-determination as a mechanism for preventing secession will be elaborated, drawing on the practices and instruments of regional organizations. This part will show the similarities and differences between regional standpoints and illustrate the evolution of viewpoints on the RSD from purely external self-determination to internal self-determination, in particular in the Global South. Regional approaches represent a middle ground between universal frameworks and individual state-level interpretations of ISD, making this dynamic both analytically significant and methodologically challenging.

3.2.1 Europe (OSCE/EU/CoE)

In Europe, three major regional organizations come to mind as far as internal self-determination is concerned – the Organization for Security and Co-operation in Europe (OSCE), the European Union (EU) and the Council of Europe (CoE). The documents adopted by these organizations alongside the practice of their organs demonstrate that ISD forms the bedrock of their agenda, which has been invoked both to denounce secession and to accept new statehood claims, let alone its clear entrenchment in membership criteria.[303]

---

301 P. Hilpold, 'Humanizing' the Law of Self-determination – the Chagos Island Case' 91 *Nordic Journal of International Law* (2022) 189–215.

302 See D. M. Amann, 'Chagos AO' 113 *AJIL* (2019) 790 (assertions of human rights prototypically stand at odds with assertions of state sovereignty). See also C. Tomuschat, 'The Security Council and Jus Cogens' in E. Canizzaro (ed.) *The Present and Future of Jus Cogens* (Sapienza Università Editrice 2015) 82–85.

303 The EU accession criteria, known as the Copenhagen criteria, require the stability of institutions that guarantee democracy, the rule of law, human rights, and the respect for and

3.2.1.1 *Organization for Security and Co-operation in Europe* (OSCE)

The Organization for Security and Co-operation in Europe (OSCE) is an intergovernmental organization focused on promoting security, stability, and cooperation in the Euro-Atlantic region. The OSCE's approach to internal self-determination is rooted in its srong commitment to human rights, democracy, and the rule of law, as outlined in its foundational documents, including the Helsinki Final Act of 1975.[304]

Regarding internal self-determination, the OSCE recognizes the importance of allowing individuals and communities within its participating States to freely determine their political, economic, social, and cultural development within existing state boundaries. This includes respecting the rights of national, ethnic, linguistic, and religious minorities and ensuring their full participation in public life. The OSCE supports internal self-determination through various means, including:

1. Protection of Minority Rights: The OSCE monitors and promotes the protection of minority rights within its participating States, advocating for measures to prevent discrimination, promote equal opportunities, and preserve the cultural identity and linguistic heritage of minority communities.[305]
2. Democratic Governance: The OSCE works to strengthen democratic institutions, electoral processes, and the rule of law in its participating States, ensuring that all citizens have the opportunity to participate in decision-making processes and hold their governments accountable.[306]
3. Conflict Prevention and Resolution: The OSCE engages in conflict prevention and resolution efforts to address tensions and disputes within its participating States, facilitating dialogue, negotiation, and confidence-building measures to resolve conflicts peacefully and promote reconciliation among different communities.[307]

---

protection of minorities. Additionally, Article 4 of the Council of Europe Statute stipulates that states applying for membership must accept and uphold democratic values.

304 Conference on Security and Co-operation in Europe (CSCE): Final Act of Helsinki (1 Aug. 1975), reprinted in 14 *ILM* (1975) 1293–1325.

305 The OSCE High Commissioner on National Minorities (HCNM) works to address ethnic tensions and to prevent hostilities over national minority issues.

306 The OSCE Office for Democratic Institutions and Human Rights (ODIHR) supports the efforts of participating States to improve democratic governance by developing multiparty political landscapes, increasing the level of women's participation in politics, strengthening parliaments, preventing the abuse of state resources, and following up on the recommendations made by election observation missions.

307 The Organization's main tools to address this cycle include its network of field operations and the Conflict Prevention Centre (CPC).

4. Human Dimension Activities: The OSCE conducts human dimension activities, including monitoring missions, election observation missions, and capacity-building programs, to promote respect for human rights, fundamental freedoms, and the principles of non-discrimination and tolerance.[308]

Overall, the OSCE's approach to ISD is guided by its commitments to democracy, human rights, and the peaceful resolution of conflicts, with a focus on promoting inclusive governance, respect for diversity, and the protection of minority rights within its participating States. The OSCE High Commissioner on National Minorities, Max van der Stoel, on one occasion emphasized that the RSD should be exercised within the framework of the state to 'ensure national minorities their full identity and to enable them to live free and achieve their aims, especially in the cultural and educational fields', while on another noted that 'internal self-determination can balance the seemingly antithetical concepts of self-determination and the maintenance of frontiers'.[309] Lamberto Zannier, High Commissioner from 2017 to 2020, observed in his reflections that striking a balance between the principle of state sovereignty and the right of self-determination – two pillars of the CSCE Helsinki Final Act – 'appears increasingly difficult', however, 'promoting the sustainable integration of diverse and multi-ethnic societies is one of the most effective tools to prevent modern conflicts (...) and to counter trends towards separatism and secessionism'.[310]

A perusal of the Helsinki Final Act, which is not legally binding but regarded at the time of drafting as 'consistent' with international law indicates a strong proclivity against nonconsensual secession.[311] Even though Principle VIII of the Act unambiguously speaks of the invariable determination of both internal and external political status, it also clarifies that states' respect

308 More in OSCE, *Human Dimension Commitments* (Volume 1, Thematic Compilation 2005) <https://www.osce.org/files/f/documents/f/d/16363.pdf>.

309 OSCE HCNM, Speech by Max van der Stoel at a Seminar, Prague (13 May 1994); and Speech by Max van der Stoel at the Royal Institute of International Affairs in London, 'Preventing Inter-Ethnic Conflict' (9 Jul. 1999). See also Address to an international seminar on Legal Aspects of Minority Rights 'Participation in Decision-Making Processes and Bilateral Agreements on Minority Rights' held in Zagreb (4 Dec. 2000) ('self-administration or self-governance can allow minorities to have greater say and control over decisions that affect them' yet 'territorial self-governance should not be equated with secession').

310 OSCE HCNM/Institute for Peace Research and Security Policy of the University of Hamburg, *HCNM at 25: Personal Reflections of the High Commissioners* (OSCE HCNM 2018) 38–39.

311 J. Paust, 'Transnational Freedom of Speech: Legal Aspects of the Helsinki Final Act' 45 *Law and Contemporary Problems* (1982) 55–57. See also ILA, 'Report of the Fifty-Eight Conference' (1980) 130 ('The result of the Conference should ... be a common declaration but not a legal instrument').

for the RSD should conform to the UN Charter and 'the relevant norms of international law, including those relating to territorial integrity of States'.[312] These restrictive formulations were repeated in the 1989 Vienna Document,[313] the 1990 Charter of Paris for a New Europe (which emphasizes the Copenhagen Document on democratization adopted earlier that year);[314] and the 1991 Moscow Document (which gives effect to the Copenhagen Document's reinforcement of full respect for human rights, pluralistic democracy, and the rule of law).[315] Furthermore, the principles of territorial integrity and inviolability of frontiers, enshrined in Principles III and IV of the Helsinki Final Act, stand in opposition to the realization of the RSD externally. They forbid states to conduct 'any action inconsistent with the purposes and principles of the Charter of the United Nations against the territorial integrity, political independence or the unity of any participating State', which translates to an obligation not to provide military support or extend recognition to secessionist movements.

This led Summers to conclude that the 'intent in the reference to territorial integrity was to prevent self-determination being used to legitimise secession',[316] while Guruparan argued that OSCE states conceived the RSD as applicable internally, within established states, with that right to be exercised by the whole population.[317] As such, it seems that the OSCE has given precedence to ISD over ESD, possibly viewing ISD as a viable alternative to secession. Such an inference aligns particularly well with the subsequently developed conviction that a profound system change, grounded in Western ideals, would bring about 'a lasting order of peace, security, justice, and

---

312 Principe VIII, paragraph 1.

313 Concluding Document of the Vienna Meeting 1986 of representatives of the participating States of the Conference on Security and Co-operation in Europe, held on the basis of the provisions of the Final Act relating to the follow-up to the conference (1989) Principle 4.

314 Charter of Paris for a New Europe (1990) 5. The Document of the Copenhagen Meeting of the Conference on the Human Dimension of the CSCE (1990) contained very convoluted wording on autonomy for minorities, which did not appear in the Final Act due to states' worry that it may be a 'first step in the direction of secession'. See H. Hazewinkel, 'Self-determination, Territorial Integrity and the OSCE' *Helsinki Monitor* (2007) 297.

315 Document of the Moscow Meeting of the Conference on the Human Dimension of the CSCE (1991) 29.

316 Summers (n 26) 278. Russel, the principal U.S. negotiator in Helsinki, argued that the Soviets had long sought an inter-bloc meeting, which made the Conference indeed historic. However, he contended that their primary goal was to solidify their territorial gains in Europe, including the German Democratic Republic, and to legitimize these with the principle of inviolability of frontiers. See H. S. Russel, 'The Helsinki Declaration: Brobdingnag or Lilliput?' 70(2) *AJIL* (1976) 244.

317 Guruparan (n 140) 50.

cooperation in Europe', thereby logically superseding secessionist pretensions.[318] The 1999 General Principles of the Lund Recommendations on the Effective Participation of National Minorities in Public Life appear to corroborate this, noting that the inclusion of minorities serves 'the objective of good governance by responding to the interests of the whole population (...) ultimately strengthening the integrity of the State'.[319]

Inasmuch as the Helsinki Final Act, in principle, supports a qualified counter-secession version of internal self-determination, the OSCE's practices from the early 1990s onward have more firmly solidified this stance.

3.2.1.2 *European Union*

The EU is undoubtedly the most powerful and recognizable Western organization. Its core principles – freedom, democracy, equality, and the rule of law – along with its promotion of peace and stability and its comprehensive body of secondary legislation, truly embody the integrative and inclusive nature of internal self-determination.[320] The European Union's stance on the relationship between ISD and secession can be inferred from its historical and contemporary state recognition practice. The EU's recognition policy is rooted in the acknowledgment of a people's entitlement to self-governance (*demos kratos*), which can be further substantiated by legal, moral, and political considerations, such as adherence to democratic governance standards.[321]

This latter strand became particularly evident during the early 1990s in the context of the dissolution of the Soviet Union and the transformations in Eastern Europe. In 1991, the European Communities (the predecessors of the EU)

---

318 Moscow Document (n 315) 29. See H. Heintze, 'Contradictory Principles in the Helsinki Final Act?' in *OSCE Yearbook 2004* (Baden-Baden 2005) 289–299. See also the proposal by the Netherlands in Geneva (3 Oct. 1973) quoted in *Conferentie over Veiligheid en Samenwerking in Europa* (Netherlands Ministry of Foreign Affairs 1976) 244.

319 Note that the word 'territorial' is omitted. OSCE High Commissioner on National Minorities, 'The Lund Recommendations on the Effective Participation of National Minorities in Public Life'(1 Sep. 1999) 16.

320 Note, however, that neither the EU, nor the discussed below Council of Europe, specifically recognize the right to self-determination. N. Leverat, 'The Right to National Self-determination within the EU: a Legal Investigation' 8 *Euborders Working Paper Series* (2017) 4.

321 The recognition of Palestine by Norway, Ireland, Spain and Slovenia in the spring 2024 fits within the moral 'stream' of democracy. See S. Janković, 'Four Streams of Democracy and the Recognition of States: The EU Perspective' 22 *Spanish Yearbook of International Law* (2018) 55–76. See also J. M. Ruda, 'Recognition of States and Governments' in M. Bedjaoui (ed.) *International Law: Achievements and Prospects* (Martinus Nijhoff 1991) 449–465.

adopted the Declaration on the Guidelines on the Recognition of New States in Eastern Europe and the Soviet Union. The Guidelines' relevant part reads:

> The Community and its Member States confirm their attachment to the principles of the Helsinki Final Act and the Charter of Paris, in particular the principle of self-determination (...)
>
> Therefore, they adopt a common position on the process of recognition of these new States, which requires: (...)
>
> 1. guarantees for the rights of ethnic and national groups and minorities in accordance with the commitments subscribed to in the framework of the CSCE:
> 2. respect for the inviolability of all frontiers which can only be changed by peaceful means and by common agreement.[322]

The European Community was thus prepared to recognize federal units seeking independence, but such recognition was contingent upon meeting certain conditions. Chief among these was the protection of minorities: if newly formed states provided adequate protection for minority rights, recognition could be conferred. In some instances, recognition was granted or withheld at the expense of the traditional criterion of effectiveness.[323] In general, however, the EC's recognition policy implies two key points. First, nations (or peoples) within the newly established states should enjoy minority rights and benefit from democratic principles enshrined in the Charter of Paris. For example, Russians living throughout Soviet republics, not only in Russia, would be entitled to ISD. Second, the borders of newly created states are deemed inviolable and can only be altered through peaceful means, such as mutual agreement. Consequently, it could be inferred that the EC (now the EU) endorses representative and democratic states and governments, and regards their territorial integrity as intact, so long as democratic norms continue to be upheld.

---

322 Reprinted in 4 *EJIL* (1993) 72.

323 Procrastination in receiving assurances from Kyrgyzstan, Tajikistan and Georgia on their readiness to conform with the requirements enunciated in the 'Guidelines' postponed their recognition by the EC Member States until 16 January 1992 (Kyrgyzstan and Tajikistan) and 23 March 1992 (Georgia). See also D. Turk, 'Recognition of States: A Comment' 4 *EJIL* (1993) 68. Note that the recognition of 'new' states indicates that the EC *a priori* accepted their *legal* existence as states, subscribing to the declaratory theory of recognition. This stance aligns with Badinter Opinion No. 1, which emphasized that 'the existence or disappearance of the state is a question of fact; that the effects of recognition by other states are purely declaratory'. Badinter Commission, Opinion No. 1 (29 Nov. 1991), reprinted in 3 *EJIL* (1992) 182.

This reasoning was confirmed in the Declaration on Yugoslavia adopted at the extraordinary ministerial meeting in Brussels in 1991, which made the accrual of recognition *expressis verbis* dependent on the acceptance of commitments contained in the Guidelines.[324] However, at the onset of the crisis, Yugoslavia was seen as a country to be preserved. In October 1990, the foreign ministers of the EC adopted a declaration, without discussion, highlighting their 'wish that the present process of democratic evolution in Yugoslavia will succeed in the framework of a development of respect for human rights and the preservation of the unity and the territorial integrity of that country'.[325] This demonstrates that ISD was a more preferred solution than secession, and indeed a solution that can stop the process of secession. However, by August 1991, with the disintegration of Yugoslavia underway, the EC established the Arbitration Commission (the Badinter Commission) to provide legal advice on issues arising from the fragmentation of Yugoslavia, in particular the recognition of emerging Yugoslav republics. The Commission considered the republics to have ESD within the framework of *uti possidetis*, while the people within those new states were entitled to ISD. In Opinion No. 2, the Commission required the new states to recognize the identity of ethnic, religious, or linguistic communities, such as the significant Serb minority in Croatia.[326] However, no right to secession from the republics was recognized, implying that entities like Kosovo in Serbia, the Republic of Serbian Krajina in Croatia (created in 1991), Gagauzia in Moldova and Chechnya in Russia were to benefit from ISD rather than ESD.[327] Thus, while the Soviet and Yugoslav republics were granted the right to independence under certain conditions, groups within these new states had to be content with minority rights, which largely correspond to the internal dimension of the RSD. According to Pellet, the Commission's rapporteur, the main intent of Badinter principles was to combine the avoidance of territorial disputes with the protection of minority communities' rights within the newly formed states. As stated, 'such arrangements [separating ethnicity from citizenship] would have the immense merit of guaranteeing the rights

---

324 European Political Cooperation, 'Guidelines on the Recognition of New States in Eastern Europe and in the Soviet Union', adopted at an Extraordinary EPC Ministerial Meeting at Brussels (16 Dec. 1991), reprinted in 31 *ILM* (1992) 1485.

325 Conclusions of the EC Presidency (Italy) regarding the European Council in Rome (28–29 Oct. 1990) Doc. SN 304/90 llEV 2.

326 Badinter Commission, Opinion No. 2 (11 Jan. 1992), reprinted in 3 *EJIL* (1992) 183–184.

327 C. Navari, 'Territoriality, Self-determination and Crimea after Badinter' 90(6) *International Affairs* (2014) 1305.

of peoples – and the individuals of whom they are composed – while avoiding the fragmentation and weakening of States'.[328]

A few years later, a similar stance was taken by the Spanish representative in the Third Committee of the General Assembly, speaking on behalf of the European Union. Mr. Laclaustra maintained that the tension between self-determination and territorial integrity, which often leads to bloody crises, could be mitigated through democratic and representative political structures.[329] This argument strongly supports the ISD's counter-secession role.

More recent EU practice is also notable. In 2008, the Council of the European Union established an independent mission to investigate the origins and course of the conflict in Georgia, including with regard to international law, humanitarian law and human rights. According to the mission's report, 'the 'internal' aspect of the right to self-determination, to be realized within the framework of a state, does not infringe on the territorial integrity of the state concerned. However, if the right to self-determination is interpreted as granting the right to secession (external right to self-determination), the two principles are incompatible'.[330] The mission furthered this argument by claiming that the external aspect of the RSD 'in form of a secession is not accepted in state practice', while 'outside the colonial context, self-determination is basically limited to internal self-determination.'[331] Hence, the report supported the view that non-state entities are bound by the principle of territorial integrity and rejected ESD claims of South Ossetia and Abkhazia.[332] Nonetheless, the report does not provide a conclusive stance on the mission's view of ISD as a secession prevention method. It seems to reject the theory of remedial secession and interprets the safeguard clause as reinforcing territorial integrity, aligning more closely with the orthodox interpretation of ISD.[333] All in all, the mission, reflecting the broader position of the EU, condemned irredentism in Georgia. If one looks at the EU's inertia towards the Catalan protests in 2017 or the ongoing Scottish independence movement, it becomes clear that the EU, as a union, supports integration rather than disintegration.

---

328 A. Pellet, 'The Opinions of the Badinter Arbitration Committee: A Second Breath for the Self-determination of Peoples' 3(1) *EJIL* (1992) 183.

329 UN Doc. A/C.3/50/SR.4 (16 Oct. 1995) para 5.

330 Independent International Fact-Finding Mission on the Conflict in Georgia (IIFFMCG), The Report, vol. II (2009) 136.

331 *Ibid.* 141.

332 *Ibid.* 144–147.

333 *Ibid.* 137–141 (arguing that Kosovo was a precedent).

3.2.1.3 *Council of Europe (CoE)*

The Council of Europe, founded in 1949, promotes the rights of individuals and communities to participate in decision-making processes and to freely determine their political, economic, social, and cultural development within the framework of existing state boundaries. This includes respecting the rights of national, ethnic, linguistic, and religious minorities and ensuring their full participation in public life, with a particular emphasis recently placed on the Roma, Europe's largest minority.[334]

In 2011, the Parliamentary Assembly of the Council of Europe (PACE) adopted a resolution 'National Sovereignty and Statehood in Contemporary International Law: The Need for Clarification',[335] which deals with the problem of minority rights, the RSD and the protection of state sovereignty and territorial integrity. The resolution emphasizes that 'even if international law were to recognise a right of national or ethnic minorities or even, in some cases, national majorities, to self-determination, such a right would *not give rise to an automatic right to secession*'.[336] In addition, the Assembly recalled that the RSD 'should first and foremost be implemented by way of the protection of minority rights as foreseen in the (...) Framework Convention for the Protection of National Minorities (...) and Assembly Resolution 1334 (2003) on positive experiences of autonomous regions as a source of inspiration for conflict resolution in Europe'.[337] Self-determination crises should be addressed through reconciliation and dialogue, with the Assembly committed to supporting national parliaments to prevent recourse to violence and secession.[338] This evidently suggests that ISD can and should be used to thwart secession.

The Framework Convention for the Protection of National Minorities, referenced in the resolution, seeks to provide a framework for safeguarding minority rights while preserving territorial integrity.[339] Article 21 stipulates that 'nothing in the present framework Convention shall be interpreted as implying any right to engage in any activity or perform any act contrary to the fundamental

334 See Council of Europe, *Strategic Action Plan for Roma and Traveller Inclusion (2020–2025)* (Council of Europe 2020). The CoE also advocates freedom of expression and of the media, freedom of assembly and equality. It has launched campaigns on issues such as child protection and online hate speech. In addition, the CoE helps member states fight corruption and terrorism and undertake necessary judicial reforms.

335 PACE Res 1832 'National Sovereignty and Statehood in Contemporary International Law: The Need for Clarification' (4 Nov. 2011).

336 *Ibid.* Article 7 (emphasis added).

337 *Ibid.*

338 *Ibid.* Article 8.2.

339 Framework Convention for the Protection of National Minorities (1 Feb. 1995) ETS No. 157.

principles of international law and in particular of the sovereign equality, *territorial integrity* and political independence of States'.[340] The preamble reinforces this focus on territorial integrity, asserting that minority rights protection must be ensured by 'respecting the territorial integrity and national sovereignty of States'. The second document, Resolution 1334, adopts a similar approach regarding minority rights and the territorial coherence of states.[341] It emphasizes that territorial autonomy must 'be based on the territorial integrity and sovereignty of states', and clarifies that autonomy should not be regarded as a precursor to secession.[342] Quite the opposite, autonomy 'allows a minority group within a state to exercise its rights and preserve its cultural identity, while providing certain guarantees of the state's unity, sovereignty and territorial integrity'.[343]

Additionally, the European Charter for Regional or Minority Languages, another Council of Europe convention addressing minority rights,[344] similarly upholds the preservation of state territorial integrity. Article 5 of the Charter requires that 'nothing in this Charter may be interpreted as implying any right to engage in any activity or perform any action in contravention of the purposes of the Charter of the United Nations or other obligations under international law, including the principle of the sovereignty and territorial integrity of States'.[345] The Charter's preamble underscores that 'the aim of the Council of Europe is to achieve a greater unity *between its members*', and implies that this goal can be achieved by safeguarding the historical regional or minority languages of Europe, thereby supporting the qualified version of ISD as a method of secession prevention. As the penultimate preambular paragraph notes,

> realising that the protection and promotion of regional or minority languages in the different countries and regions of Europe represent an important contribution to the building of a Europe based on the principles of democracy and cultural diversity within the framework of national sovereignty and territorial integrity.[346]

---

340 *Ibid.* Article 21 (emphasis added).

341 PACE Res 1334 'Positive Experiences of Autonomous Regions as a Source of Inspiration for Conflict Resolution in Europe' (24 Jun. 2003) Article 17.

342 *Ibid.* Article 9.

343 *Ibid.* Article 10.

344 European Charter for Regional or Minority Languages (5 Nov. 1992) ETS. 148.

345 *Ibid.* Article 5.

346 *Ibid.* Preamble.

The European Commission for Democracy through Law (Venice Commission), a consultative entity within the Council of Europe, has also dealt with issues related to ISD and secession. Comprising impartial specialists in constitutional law, the Venice Commission's primary objective is to provide legal guidance to member states through 'legal opinions' on proposed or existing legislation undergoing scrutiny. Additionally, it conducts research and publishes studies on relevant topics.[347]

The Venice Commission in one of its reports concluded that constitutions generally oppose secession and instead emphasise principles such as territorial integrity, the indivisibility of the state, and national unity.[348] It furthered this point by saying that 'there is no general recognition in constitutional law of the right to self-determination, nor any common definition of those who are entitled to it and its content'.[349] Finally, the Commission indicated that:

> Internal self-determination may be exercised by the assertion of specific fundamental rights, with a collective character, in particular in the cultural sphere, or even by federalism, regionalism or other forms of local self-government within the state with all due regard to territorial integrity. Apart from the aforementioned cultural autonomy, federalism, regionalism, and possibly local self-government, may be mentioned. In particular, the establishment of public authorities – federated entities especially – and the alteration of their boundaries may constitute a form of self-determination. This broad interpretation of the internal aspect of self-determination is intended to avert conflicts which might carry a risk of secession. On balance, while in very general terms secession is alien to constitutional law, self-determination, primarily construed as internal, is an element frequently incorporated in constitutional law but needing to be dissociated from secession.[350]

From the foregoing, it is clear that the Commission not only summarized the general stance of constitutional law on secession but also highlighted the anti-secessionist value of internal self-determination and the prevailing

347 Venice Commission Res (2002) 3 'Adopting the Revised Statute of the European Commission for Democracy through Law' (21 Feb. 2002) Articles 2–3.

348 Venice Commission, 'Self-determination and Secession in Constitutional Law', Doc. CDL-INF (2000) 2, 3.

349 *Ibid.* 13.

350 *Ibid.*

predisposition of states in this regard.[351] The Commission opined that internal self-determination, as enshrined in national constitutions, stems from general international law, while commentators view the ICCPR as a concrete example of cross-fertilization between constitutional and international law regarding ISD.[352]

3.2.2 Africa and the Middle East

3.2.2.1 Africa

Africa's approach to internal self-determination as a safeguard against secession is evolving: it treats internal self-determination as a tool for granting autonomy and redressing grievances within existing state borders, not as a licence for secession.

Many Africa's states to mitigate the reality of disgruntled societies and often intractable armed conflicts have been pushed to restructure their governance systems and reintroduce subnational autonomy into their political agendas. Following the collapse of early federative experiments after colonial independence (e.g. the short-lived Mali federation formed by Sudan and Senegal in 1959, the Federation of Rhodesia and Nyasaland formed by present-day Malawi and Zambia in 1953) and the prioritization of national unity over decentralization from the 1960s through the early 1990s, autonomous or semi-autonomous subnational units have recently reemerged. This resurgence, seen in federal or semi-federal structures like South African provinces, Kenyan counties, Nigerian states, and Ethiopian regions, aims to address ethnic diversity and curb secessionist movements.[353]

---

351 Consult: Venice Commission, 'Compilation of Venice Commission Opinions Concerning Constitutional and Legal Provisions for the Protection of Local Self-Government', Doc. CDL-PI(2016)002.

352 Guruparan (n 140) 163. Cf. European Charter for Regional or Minority Languages (n 344) which in the preamble refers to the ICCPR, the Helsinki Final Act of 1975 and the document of the Copenhagen Meeting of 1990.

353 While territorial autonomy has helped manage ethnic diversity and prevent large-scale ethnic conflicts, calls for secession persist in some federations, notably in Ethiopia, Nigeria, and the DRC. In Ethiopia, groups like the Oromo Liberation Front (OLF) and the Ogaden National Liberation Front (ONLF) continue armed movements for independent states for the Oromo and Somali ethnic groups, respectively. In Nigeria, non-militant movements like MASSOB seek to revive the Biafra secession of 1967–70, while militant groups like MEND advocate for an independent Ijaw state. Meanwhile, secessionist ambitions in the DRC occasionally resurface, as seen in a 2012 secession plot in the mineral-rich Katanga province, echoing its attempt in the 1960s. See Y. T. Fessha, 'Federalism, Territorial Autonomy and the Management of Ethnic Diversity in Africa: Reading the Balance Sheet' 363 *L' Europe en Formation* (2012) 273, 282. Lewis and Widmeier claim that African civil conflicts are in the main 'centre-seeking', as opposed to independence seeking, despite high levels of ethnic diversity and the presence of economic and anti-government

Across the African continent, administrative and political decentralization has been pursued in parallel with the growing recognition of diversity and minority rights, as well as efforts to strengthen democratic institutions, ensure free and fair elections, and protect civil liberties. Together, these measures contribute to fostering a sense of ownership and empowerment among citizens. Additionally, many countries and organizations have implemented policies to safeguard cultural heritage, languages, and traditional practices,[354] while emphasizing the importance of democratic governance, inclusive political participation, and respect for human rights as integral components of internal self-determination.[355] Collectively, these initiatives can be rightly perceived as effective mechanisms to prevent disintegration.

The opportunity for citizens of African states to exercise ISD is not the only political strategy employed to prevent secession. The anti-secessionist manifestation is evident on at least three additional fronts: regional integration processes, reverence for the colonial independence struggles, and the underlying legal framework. First, regional economic communities, such as the Economic Community of West African States (ECOWAS), the East African Community (EAC), the Economic Community of Central African States (ECCAS), and the Southern African Development Community (SADC) promote integration, cooperation, and solidarity *among member states*.[356] Second, African leaders and

---

grievances. J. S. Lewis and M. Widmeier, 'Territorial Origins of Center-Seeking and Self-determination Claims in Africa' 94 *Political Geography* (2022) 2–4.

354 'It is estimated that between 6,000 and 7,000 languages are currently spoken worldwide, of which approximately half, if not more, will disappear by the end of this century (…) This is especially relevant in the context of Africa, where around a third of the world's languages are based.' See S. Quattrini, 'A Rights-Based Framework for Minority and Indigenous Languages in Africa: From Endangerment to Revitalization' *Minority Rights Group International* (2019) 4. See also UNGA Res 71/178 (16 Dec. 2016).

355 See Treaty for the Establishment of the East African Community (as amended on 14 December 2006 and 20 August 2007) Article 6 (emphasizing mutual trust, political will and sovereign equality; (…) good governance including adherence to the principles of democracy, the rule of law, accountability, transparency, social justice, equal opportunities, gender equality, as well as the recognition, promotion and protection of human and peoples rights in accordance with the provisions of the African Charter on Human and Peoples' Rights).

356 Consult ECOWAS, 'Declaration of Political Principles of the Economic Community of West African States' (1991), Doc. A/DCL.1/7/91 (advancing economic cooperation and *integration* in a political environment of peace, security and stability by declaring, among others, respect for human rights and fundamental freedoms and reaffirming the determination to refrain from any threat or use of forces against the territorial integrity or political independence of any Member State). See also ECOWAS Commission, Revised Treaty of ECOWAS (2010), Preamble ('conscious of the over-riding need to encourage, foster and

institutions deeply value the mid-20th century struggles for self-determination, which involved the assertion of national identity and the establishment of sovereign nation-states. As a result, unity and cohesion remain central objectives; the RSD in its external form, is viewed as applicable primarily to former colonial territories, whereas its internal dimension is understood as the right of a state's population to pursue its development free from external interference.[357]

As regards the legal framework, the Charter of the Organization of African Unity (OAU), done in 1963 in the city of Addis Ababa, speaks of 'the unity and solidarity' of the African States and the respect for the sovereignty and territorial integrity of each State.[358] In 1964, the OAU's Assembly of Heads of State and Government, at its first ordinary session in Cairo, adopted a resolution affirming the principle of *uti possidetis* to uphold colonial borders.[359] This principle has consistently been invoked to reject internal claims to independence,[360] with notable examples including Somaliland (Somalia), the island of Anjouan (Comoros), and Biafra (Nigeria).[361] Article 3 of the Constitutive Act of the African Union (successor of the OAU) sets out the objectives of the organization as follows: the unity and solidarity between the countries and peoples of Africa; the *defence* of sovereignty, territorial integrity and independence of its Member States (...) the promotion of peace, security and stability, the promotion of democratic principles and institutions and the sustainable development at economic, social and cultural levels as well as the adherence to the African Charter of Human and Peoples' Rights.[362] While the Constitutive Act does not explicitly mention the right to self-determination, it reflects a synthesis of internal self-determination principles and a firm anti-secessionist stance.

accelerate the economic and social development of our *States* in order to improve the living standards of our people).

357 S. Dersso, 'International Law and the Self-determination of South Sudan' *Institute for Security Studies: Paper 231* (2012) 3, 8.

358 Charter of the Organization of African Unity (25 May 1963) 479 UNTS 39, Articles II 1(a) and III (3).

359 OAU/AHG Res 16(I) 'Border Disputes Among African States' (Jul. 1964). In the same vein, 'Algiers Declaration' (Jul. 1999) Doc. AHG/Decl.1 (XXXV) 3.

360 S. Blay, 'Changing African Perspectives on the Right of Self-determination in the Wake of the Banjul Charter on Human and Peoples' Rights' 29 *Journal of African Law* (1985) 152–153.

361 R. Murray, *Human Rights in Africa: From the OAU to the African Union* (CUP 2005) 14.

362 Constitutive Act of the African Union (11 Jul. 2000) 2158 UNTS 3, Article 3 (emphasis added).

The African Charter of Human and Peoples' Rights (Banjul Charter) introduces the RSD by virtue of Article 20, a provision that gives a binding legal nature to the RSD. The Article states:

1. All peoples shall have the right to existence. They shall have the unquestionable and inalienable right to self-determination. They shall freely determine their political status and shall pursue their economic and social development according to the policy they have freely chosen.
2. Colonized or oppressed peoples shall have the right to free themselves from the bonds of domination by resorting to any means recognized by the international community.
3. All peoples shall have the right to the assistance of the State Parties to the present Charter in their liberation struggle against foreign domination, be it political, economic or cultural.[363]

No concrete definition of the RSD, including its content and holders, was given making it a 'chameleon-like concept', just as was the case with other treaties and non-binding acts. But, the Charter still differentiates between two groups: (1) 'all peoples' and (2) 'colonized or oppressed peoples'. The term 'colonized peoples' is reserved for those people who were under colonial administration at the time the Charter was being drafted,[364] while the category 'oppressed peoples' could also be associated with a neo-colonial context and concern the relation between the people of a country and its government.[365] Both categories are vested with the right to independence. On the other hand, peoples who are neither colonized nor oppressed are not presumed to hold a right to secession, but are expected to exercise self-determination internally.[366] This interpretation is shared by the majority of commentators, does justice to the founding documents of the OAU and AU and, most importantly, has been endorsed by the African Commission on Human and Peoples' Rights (ACHPR), the body tasked with interpreting the Charter and promoting human rights across the continent.

In 1992, the Katangese Peoples' Congress (KPC) petitioned the ACHPR to recognize the KPC as a liberation movement and, on the basis of the denial

363 The African Charter of Human and Peoples' Rights (27 Jun. 1981) 1520 UNTS 217, Article 20. It is worth saying that the Charter has no provisions on territorial integrity.

364 ACHPR, *Front for the Liberation of the State of Cabinda v. Republic of Angola*, Communication No. 328/06 (2013) para 124.

365 S. Salomon, 'Self-determination in the Case Law of the African Commission: Lessons for Europe' 50(3) *Verfassung und Recht in Übersee / Law and Politics in Africa, Asia and Latin America* (2017) 231.

366 D. Shelton, 'Self-determination in Regional Human Rights Law: From Kosovo to Cameroon' 105 *AJIL* (2011) 64.

of self-determination, recognize Katanga as an independent state and secure support for the evacuation of Zaire (now known as the Democratic Republic of the Congo) from the region.[367] The ACHPR observed that

> self-determination may be exercised in any of the following ways independence, self-government, local government, federalism, confederalism, unitarism or any other form of relations that accords with the wishes of the people but fully cognisant of other recognised principles such as sovereignty and territorial integrity.[368]

Basically, the Commission offered a variety of ways to consume the RSD. Independence could fit ESD, while others are the ISD's emanations. Nonetheless, the Commission could not establish any violation of the Charter's human rights, in particular the right to participate in government as guaranteed by Article 13(1) of the African Charter. Hence, the group was obliged to 'exercise a variant of self-determination that is compatible with the sovereignty and territorial integrity of Zaire'.[369]

The findings from the *Katangese Peoples* case were reaffirmed in *Kevin Mgwanga Gunme et al. v. Cameroon*.[370] The Commission noted that it cannot establish a right that would impair the territorial unity of Cameroon, despite the fact that violations of Articles 2, 4, 5, 6, 7, 11, and 19 of the Charter occurred.[371] These violations were simply not deemed 'sufficient', and the Southern Cameroonians (represented by Gunme) were able to participate in the work of the government, so Article 13 of the Charter was not violated.[372] In the decision, the Commission ruled that secession should not be 'the sole avenue open to the Southern Cameroonians' (mentioning self-government, confederacy, or federation) and that remaining grievances should be resolved through a 'comprehensive national dialogue'.[373] Thus, the state must reform and change

367 ACHPR, *Katangese Peoples' Congress v. Zaire*, Communication No. 75/92 (1995).

368 *Ibid.* para 4.

369 *Ibid.* paras 6–7.

370 ACHPR, *Mgwanga Gunme et al. v. Cameroon*, Communication No. 266/2003 (2009).

371 *Ibid.* para 194 (The Commission found violations of the following rights: right to freedom from discrimination, right to life, prohibition of torture and cruel, inhuman and degrading treatment, right to personal liberty and protection from arbitrary arrest, right to fair trial, right to freedom of assembly, right of all peoples to equality and rights).

372 *Ibid.* para 197 ('The Commission holds the view that when a Complainant seeks to invoke Article 20 of the African Charter, it must satisfy the Commission that the two conditions under Article 20.2 namely oppression and domination have been met').

373 *Ibid.* paras 191, 203.

enabling peoples to enjoy various rights under the RSD, but secession is not allowed. Accordingly, the Commission only ostensibly envisages ESD and it would be surprising to see it cross – what remains for now an imaginary threshold – permitting secession, especially given the references in both cases to the Banjul Charter and the ensuing 'obligation' to 'respect sovereignty and territorial integrity'.[374] Be that as it may, the ACHPR confirmed that ISD should be exercised primarily within existing state structures, and that respect for ISD can, in turn, reinforce the stability and legitimacy of state institutions.[375] As noted, despite the reluctance to recognize the right to secession in practice, its theoretical elaboration may actually contribute to strengthening human rights, and lead to more democratic, decentralized governments in Africa.[376] In many cases, the ACHPR referred to the RSD in conjunction with other Charter rights, thereby equating it with domestically exercised ISD. In the *Cabinda* case, for instance, the ACHPR opined that Article 21 of the Charter obliges a state to ensure the participation of representatives of sub-state groups – such as the Cabindan people in decisions concerning the management of national wealth and natural resources.[377]

Overall, while Africa's approach to internal self-determination is diverse and context-specific, it is generally characterized by a commitment to sovereignty, territorial integrity, unity, diversity, democracy, and respect for human rights.[378]

374 *Ibid.* paras 189–190. See also ICJ, *Frontier Dispute (Burkina Faso/Republic of Mali)*, Judgment, ICJ Rep. 1986, para 20 (*uti possidetis*). Consult Summers (n 26) 381–383; Shelton (n 366) 67–70.

375 'In post-colonial Africa, the right to self-determination can be enjoyed within the existing territories and with full respect for the sovereignty and territorial integrity of State Parties to the Charter'. *Front for the Liberation of the State of Cabinda v. Republic of Angola* (n 364) para 126.

376 Salomon, 'Self-determination in the Case Law of the African Commission' (n 365) 236.

377 *Front for the Liberation of the State of Cabinda v. Republic of Angola* (n 364) para 131.

378 Consult C. Mojekwu, 'Self-determination: The African Perspective' in Y. Alexander and R. A. Friedlander (eds.) *Self-determination: National, Regional and Global Dimensions* (Rutledge 1980) 221-235; B. Neuberger, *National Self-determination in Postcolonial Africa* (Lynne Rienner Publications 1986); P. Aka, *Navigating the Tension Between Sovereignty and Self-determination in Postcolonial Africa* (Palgrave Macmillan 2023) 51–96. Judge Ouguergouz observed that problems surrounding the right of African peoples to self-determination cannot be stated in terms other than those of 'official' decolonization. F. Ouguergouz, *The African Charter of Human and Peoples' Rights: A Comprehensive Agenda for Human Rights and Substantive Democracy in Africa* (Kluwer Law Intrenational 2003) 251. The ICJ held that the external RSD existed in the 1960s in terms of decoloniali-zation. *Chagos Archipelago* (n 284) para 150.

3.2.2.2 *Middle East*

The Arab Charter on Human Rights, enacted in 2004 within the Arab League and ratified by 16 states, is perhaps the most unfamiliar and the least influential regional human rights treaty.[379] Therefore, there has not been much debate about the Charter's contribution to international human rights law and the RSD.

Article 2 (1) stipulates that 'all peoples have the right of self-determination and to control over their natural wealth and resources, and the right to freely choose their political system and to freely pursue their economic, social and cultural development'.[380] According to paragraph 2, 'all peoples have the right to national sovereignty and territorial integrity', while paragraphs 3 and 4 set out that Zionism, racism, and foreign occupation constitute major barriers to the exercise of fundamental human rights (including self-determination) and that such practices may be resisted by the people.

Notably, the Charter frames territorial integrity differently – almost inversely – compared to more influential international instruments, such as the Friendly Relations Declaration. Rather than viewing territorial integrity as a limitation on the RSD in favor of states, the Charter aligns it with a people's right. Although the Charter does not sanction secession directly, it would be contrary to others' rights and does not arise from paragraph 1 of Article 2, which speaks of a determination of a political system, not *status*.

Some scholars argue that the Charter's reference to territorial integrity reflects the parties' intent to support Palestinian independence and the broader statehood movement.[381] This interpretation is supported by reports to the Arab Human Rights Committee under Article 48, where states often reference Palestine and highlight their international activities relevant to Article 2.[382] However, others, like Iraq and Kuwait, likewise address issues of political participation and democracy, touching on the internal dimensions of self-determination.[383]

379 Syria, one of the 22 Member States of the League of Arab States, has been suspended from the organization since 2011. The International Justice Resource Center, 'Middle East and North Africa' <https://ijrcenter.org/regional/middle-east-and-north-africa/>.

380 Arab Charter on Human Rights (2004) Doc. CHR/NONE/2004/40/Rev.1.

381 Summers (n 26) 390–392. See also the Organisation of Islamic Cooperation (OIC) Charter which supports and empowers the Palestinian people to exercise their right to self-determination and establish their sovereign State with Al-Quds Al-Sharif as its capital. OIC Charter (1972) OXIO 662, para 8.

382 The first report submitted by the Hashemite Kingdom of Jordan (2010) 12; The first report submitted by the People's Democratic Republic of Algeria (2011) 13.

383 The first report submitted by Iraq (2014) 19; The first report submitted by Kuwait (2016) 18.

3.2.3 South and North America

Even though the Americas have experienced some secessionist movements in the past (e.g. Gran Colombia and the Republic of Rio Grande), most countries in the region prioritize national unity and territorial integrity while also recognizing the importance of autonomy, decentralization, and respect for minority rights within the framework of the nation-state.[384] Efforts toward regional integration and cooperation further underscore the commitment to collective identity and solidarity among both South and North American nations.

After their emancipation struggles, Latin American states tended to regard self-determination through a much narrower lens, either as support for liberation movements *elsewhere*, or as a principle of non-intervention in domestic affairs, mainly aimed at countering U.S. influence.[385] This perspective is evident in the fact that neither the Charter of the Organization of American States (OAS) nor other significant instruments under the OAS: the American Declaration on the Rights and Duties of Man (1948) and the American Convention on Human Rights (1969) explicitly mention self-determination.[386] Furthermore, the OAS has shown a marked reluctance to address the theoretical issues surrounding self-determination, including the definition of 'peoples'.[387] It was therefore unsurprising that, in its 1983 report on the Miskito people of Nicaragua, the Inter-American Commission on Human Rights (IACHR) concluded that

> the current status of international law does not allow the view that the ethnic groups of the Atlantic zone of Nicaragua have a right to political autonomy and self-determination, special legal protection is recognized for the use of their language, the observance of their religion, and

384 Separatist sentiments have been expressed in the islands of Nevis, Barbuda and Tobago, and these resulted in special constitutional measures for the devolution of power in those islands. In 1969, an unsuccessful violent secessionist rebellion broke out in the Rupununi region of Guyana. The 1967 Anguilla secession was described as 'one of the earliest and most serious threats to the territorial integrity of a Caribbean state'. See the statement of the Permanent Representative of Guyana to the Committee on Hemispheric Security at its meeting held on 29 October 2002. Doc. CP/CSH/INF.14/02 add. 2.

385 N. Lerner, 'Self-determination: The Latin American Perspective' in Y. Alexander and R. Friedlander (eds.) *Self-determination: National, Regional, And Global Dimensions* (Routledge 1980) 63–67.

386 *Ibid.* See also OAS, Inter-American Democratic Charter (2001) OAS Doc. OEA/SerP/AG/Res.l.

387 The General Secretariat of the OAS refused to comment 'either on behalf of the Organization or its own behalf' on the study prepared by the UN Special Rapporteur Hector Gros Espiell 'Implementation of the United Nations resolutions relating to the right of people under colonial and alien domination to self-determination'. UN Doc. E/CN.4/Sub.2/390 (1977) 60.

> in general, all those aspects related to the preservation of their cultural identity.[388]

One can, however, qualify the view that the IACHR was aware of ISD, but given the absence of any mention of the RSD in OAS documents at the time of the report, it was indeed difficult to refer to ISD.[389]

A shift in the perception of the RSD across the Americas emerged in the 1990s, when states began to acknowledge the internal aspect of the RSD for minorities, particularly Indigenous peoples. This shift, like in the case of Africa, was prompted by an 'inward' turn toward reconstituting community-based forms of self-governance and a defence strategy for the preservation of indigenous habitats, but also as a political agenda of states aimed at addressing conflicts and protecting territorial unity.[390] Various legal acts in American states address ISD of minorities, underlining at the same time territorial integrity of a state. For instance, Article 2 of the Constitution of Bolivia provides:

> Given the pre-colonial existence of nations and rural native indigenous peoples and their ancestral control over their territories, their free determination, consisting of the right to autonomy, self-government, their culture, recognition of their institutions and the consolidation of their territorial entities, is guaranteed within the framework of the unity of the State, in accordance with this Constitution and the law.[391]

Article 169 of the Venezuelan constitution reads:

> Legislation enacted to implement constitutional principles relating to Municipalities and other local entities shall establish various structures for the organization, governance and administration of the same, including as regards the determination of their powers and resources, taking into account conditions relating to population, economic development,

388 IACHR, 'Report on the Situation of a Segment of the Nicaraguan Population of Miskito Origin' (1983) Part II, para 15 <https://www.cidh.org/countryrep/Miskitoeng/part2.htm>.

389 Note, however, that the ouright rejection of the RSD and political autonomy could have been reinforced by Mr. Wiggins' argument that the Indigenous Indian population of Nicaragua possessed a defined territory, a permanent population, and a government capable of external relations (resembling the 1933 Montevideo Convention's definition of a State). *Ibid.* para 8.

390 M. Gonzalez, 'Indigenous Territorial Autonomy in Latin America: An Overview' 10(1) *Latin American and Caribbean Ethnic Studies* (2015) 13.

391 Constitution of Bolivia (2009) Article 2. See also Article 30.

> ability to generate their own tax revenues, geographical location, historical and cultural elements and other relevant factors. In particular, such legislation shall establish the options for organizing the system of local administration and government that shall be adopted by Municipalities with native populations. In all cases, the municipal structure shall be democratic and consistent with the inherent nature of local government.[392]

The constitution notably situates indigenous territorial autonomy within the framework of existing municipalities. Consequently, legal scholars have observed that constitutional provisions render indigenous territorial autonomy ambiguously defined, effectively reaffirming the municipality as the preferred mechanism for achieving indigenous self-determination.[393]

In parallel with state actions, regional organizations have recently commenced to bring ISD into focus. This is evidenced by the adoption of the Inter-American Democratic Charter in 2001 and the 2005 Declaration of Florida: The Benefits of Democracy, which stresses the need to promote and defend the representative democracy, including a pluralistic system of political parties, political participation, and periodic elections.[394] In 2021, the IACHR rejected the Nicaraguan Act to Defend the Rights of the People to Independence, Sovereignty, and Self-determination for Peace approved by the National Assembly. The IACHR opined that the Act gives unfettered discretion to the state authorities to exclude the political participation of peoples accused of 'leading or financing a *coup d'état*', 'promoting terrorist acts', or 'inciting foreign interference in internal affairs', which would be contrary to Article 23 of the American Convention on Human Rights guaranteeing all citizens the right to partake in

---

392 Constitution of Venezuela (1999) Article 169. See also *Mesa* (table) agreements between the Zapatista Army of National Liberation (ZANL) and the Mexican government 'Derechos y Cultura Indígena' and 'Democracia y Justicia del Diálogo'(the San Andrés Accords, 1996) on autonomy, recognition, and rights to the indigenous population of Mexico <https://ucdpged.uu.se/peaceagreements/fulltext/Mex%2019960216.pdf>. In Columbia, Decree 2164 defines the *resguardo* as a legal and socio-political institution of a special nature, consisting of one or more indigenous communities, which possess its territory through a title of communal property, and it rules itself and organizes its internal life through an autonomous organization. Ministerio de Agricultura de Colombia, Decree 2164 (1995) Article 21.

393 Gonzalez (n 390) 21–22. See also R. Colmenares, 'El Derecho a La Autonomia De Los Pueblos Indigenas De Venezuela' 21 *Revista del Centro de Investigaciones Penales y Criminológicas* (2002) 185–217.

394 Declaration of Florida: Delivering the Benefits of Democracy (2005) OAS Doc. AG/DEC. 41 (XXXV-O/05).

the conduct of public affairs.[395] Besides, a plenitude of activities within the OAS regarding the recognition of ISD of indigenous peoples can be identified, ranging from OAS General Assembly resolutions,[396] through the adoption in 2016 of the American Declaration on the Rights of Indigenous Peoples[397] and finishing with the publication of reports.[398] Notably, the 2021 IACHR's report titled 'Right to Self-determination of Indigenous and Tribal Peoples' gives ample suggestions on how to understand and implement self-determination (naturally in the context of indigenous peoples), but could serve as a good example of how to conceive it in a *general* context. It notes first, that ISD is a contextualized right, which must be aimed at a particular community in order to appropriately acknowledge and harmonize its aspirations.[399] In addition, the RSD must be understood as 'the basis for dialogue for the construction of a new relationship *between these peoples and States* that can lead to specific arrangements for indigenous and tribal peoples to determine their economic, social and cultural development and other aspects of self-determination'.[400] The RSD is also seen there through a two-fold approach. Firstly, interculturally, which demands the recognition of cultural differences on the basis of non-discrimination and power sharing in decision-making on development priorities. Secondly, as reparative justice, which aims to redress historical injustices through various means and guarantees of non-repetition in the existing political union.[401] As such, the IACHR explicitly rejected secession as an option for indigenous peoples, affirming that it is not a valid remedy for past injustices.

This tendency to understand the right to self-determination in its internal fashion and, as a result, rejecting its application externally in modern times is also seen in the jurisprudence of the Inter-American Court of Human Rights (IACtHR), which in *Saramaka People v. Suriname* first invoked the right to self-determination in the context of the right to land and resources under Article

395 IACHR Press Release, 'IACHR Rejects Passing of Law Restricting Political Rights in Nicaragua' (6 Jan. 2021) No. 003/21.

396 OAS General Assembly Res 'Promotion of the Rights of Indigenous Peoples' (2009) OAS Doc. AG/RES. 2448 (XXXIX-O/09) and OAS General Assembly Res 'Promotion and Protection of Human Rights: Declaration on the Rights of Indigenous Peoples in the Americas' (2019) OAS Doc. AG/RES. 2941 (XLIX-O/19).

397 American Declaration on the Rights of Indigenous Peoples (2016) OAS Doc. AG/RES.2888 (XLVI-O/16).

398 IACHR/IWGIA, 'Right to Self-determination of Indigenous and Tribal Peoples' (2021) <https://www.oas.org/en/iachr/reports/pdfs/self-determination-EN.pdf>.

399 *Ibid.* para 5.

400 *Ibid.* (emphasis added).

401 *Ibid.* paras 8–9.

21 of the American Convention on Human Rights.[402] The Court noted that the Committee on Economic, Social, and Cultural Rights had interpreted that common Article 1 of the 1966 Covenants is also applicable to indigenous peoples.[403] Accordingly, based on the right to self-determination (of indigenous peoples) under the mentioned Article 1 of the Covenants, they can 'freely determine their economic, social, and cultural development' and 'freely dispose of their natural wealth and resources' so that they are not deprived of their means of subsistence (there is no reference to political status). The Court considered that the interpretative rules contained in Article 29(b) of the American Convention prevent it from interpreting Article 21 of the Convention in a way that would limit the enjoyment and application of the rights in that article to a lesser extent than guaranteed by the Covenants.[404] In line with this, the Court concluded that Article 21 of the Convention indicates the right of members of indigenous and tribal communities to freely determine and implement their economic, social, and cultural development, including the right to enjoy their special spiritual connection to the territory they have traditionally used and inhabited.[405] Based on this, the state must adopt special measures to recognize, respect, protect, and guarantee the communal property rights of these communities over their ancestral territories.[406]

In discussions on the RSD and territorial integrity, both North and South American states generally prioritize the latter, though North American states tend to do so more uncritically regarding their own territories. The Kosovo case underscores this, as all four participating Latin American states expressed unfavourable views on secession. For example, Argentina asserted that the principle of territorial integrity binds both states and non-state entities[407] and that this principle supersedes the RSD. This stance was further evidenced in Argentina's support for the territorial unity of Croatia, Bosnia and Herzegovina, and Georgia. Regarding Georgia, Argentina called upon 'the concerned Parties to find a negotiated and mutually acceptable solution to the currently existing conflict that respects the principles universally accepted by International Law, such as the territorial integrity of States'.[408] It seems that Argentina is generally

402 IACtHR, *Saramaka People. v. Suriname*, Preliminary Objections, Merits, Reparations, and Costs (ser. C) No. 172 (28 Nov. 2007).

403 *Ibid.* para 93.

404 *Ibid.*

405 *Ibid.* para 95.

406 *Ibid.* para 96.

407 Written statement of Argentina (Apr. 2009) para 150.

408 *Ibid.* 32, fn. 73.

devoted to securing territories of existing states,[409] most probably due to its stance on the Falkland Islands. Similarly, Bolivia, Brazil, and Venezuela oppose Kosovo's statehood,[410] albeit without detailed justification. Canada, though not directly involved in the Kosovo case, likely maintains a negative view of secession, as indicated by its Supreme Court's stance on Quebec's secession. The United States, on the other hand, explicitly supported Kosovo's independence, arguing that the principle of territorial integrity applies only between states and emphasizing the neutrality of international law on secession.[411] Yet, the U.S. had denied the independence of Chechnya, supporting 'the sovereignty and territorial integrity of the Russian Federation' and opposing boundary changes 'whether in the form of aggression by one state against another or in the form of armed secessionist movements'.[412] This reveals an ambiguity regarding the U.S. position on whether territorial integrity can be invoked against internal secessionist claims. What remains clear, however, is that both the U.S. and Canada endorse ISD for minorities on their territories, viewing this as an adequate means of preserving territorial unity.[413]

3.2.4 Asia and Australia

A closer look at the Asia-Pacific region reveals the absence of a cohesive regional human rights regime, though gradual progress has been made, reflected in the establishment of the ASEAN Intergovernmental Commission on Human Rights in 2009 and the adoption of the ASEAN Human Rights Declaration in 2012. Notably, however, neither addresses the right to self-determination.[414]

---

409 E.g. during the adoption of the UNSC Res 1244 (10 Jun. 1999) Argentina called for a solution that will 'respect the sovereignty and territorial integrity of the Federal Republic of Yugoslavia'. See Mr. Petrella (Argentina), UN Doc. S/PV.4011 (1999) 18–19. See also Mr. Argüello (Argentina), UN Doc. A/63/PV.22 (2008) 12. Cited by Argentina (n 407) 4–5, fn. 1 and 2.

410 Written statement of Bolivia (17 Jul. 2009); Written statement of Brazil (17 Apr. 2009); Written statement of Venezuela (24 Apr. 2009); Venezuela, OS, CR 2009/33 (11 Dec. 2009) 12–13.

411 Written statement of the United States of America (17 Jul. 2009) 50–51, 69.

412 Deputy Secretary of State Strobe Talbott, 'Supporting Democracy and Economic Reform in the New Independent States' 6 *U.S. State Dept. Dispatch* (1995) 119, 120.

413 Consult Principles respecting the Government of Canada's relationship with Indigenous peoples, <https://www.justice.gc.ca/eng/csj-sjc/principles-principes.html>; Indian Self-determination and Education Assistance Act Public Law No: 93–638 (01/04/1975); The US Tribal Self-Governance Act of 1994 5 USC 565.

414 See ASEAN (Association of Southeast Asian Nations) Intergovernmental Commission on Human Rights (AICHR) <https://aichr.org/about-aichr-2/>; ASEAN Human Rights Declaration (2012) <https://asean.org/asean-human-rights-declaration/>. See also OHCHR Statement, 'Looking to a New Human Rights System for Asia and the Pacific' (11 Oct. 2023)

The Bangkok Declaration, adopted in 1993 at the Asia regional preparatory meeting for the World Conference on Human Rights, stressed that the RSD 'is applicable to peoples under alien or colonial domination and foreign occupation and should not be used to undermine the territorial integrity, national sovereignty and political independence of States'.[415] This indicates that Asian states were reluctant to recognize any secession entitlement stemming from the RSD, even in cases involving violations of ISD. Such a stance contrasts with the Vienna Declaration adopted the same year which reiterated the qualified version of ISD as the secession prevention mechanism. Independence movements, often facing systemic oppression, have received very limited support across the region, as illustrated by cases like Chechnya (Russia),[416] Tibet (China),[417] Aceh (Indonesia),[418] Papua (Indonesia),[419] Karen (Myanmar),[420] Naga (India/Myanmar),[421] Kashmir (India)[422] and Bougainville (Papua New Guinea).[423] Bangladesh serves as an exception; around 60 states recognized its independence, partly in response to Pakistan's denial of its internal RSD. However, Bangladesh was admitted to the UN in 1974 only after it was recognized by Pakistan, its former parent state.[424] Documents such as the ASEAN Charter, the Declaration of the East Asia Summit on the Principles for Mutually Beneficial Relations and the ASEAN Outlook on the Indo-Pacific (AOIP) all reaffirm

---

<https://www.ohchr.org/en/statements/2023/10/looking-new-human-rights-system-asia-and-pacific>.

415 Report of the Regional Meeting for Asia of the World Conference on Human Rights, Bangkok, 29 March-2 Apr. 1993. Doc. A/CONF.157/ASRM/8, para 13.

416 Raič (n 169) 375–378; Crawford (n 216) 408–410.

417 Written statement of Cyprus (3 Apr. 2009) para 153.

418 Guruparan (n 140) 169–180; J. Bertrand, 'Aceh: From Violent Insurgency to Broad-Based Autonomy' in *Democracy and Nationalism in Southeast Asia: From Secessionist Mobilization to Conflict Resolution* (CUP 2021) 72.

419 Written statement of Cyprus (n 417) para 153.

420 S. Loonga, A. Manbyband and F. McConnell, 'Rethinking Self-determination: Colonial and Relational Geographies in Asia' *Territory, Politics, Governance* (2022) 7–8.

421 *Ibid.* See R. Vashum, *Naga's Right to Self-determination: An Anthropological-historical Perspective* (Mittal Publications 2005) 111–145.

422 Crawford (n 216) 403.

423 H. A. Amankwah, 'Self-determination Asia-Pacific Style: Alien Domination and Freedom's Tortuous Path Revisited' 5 *James Cook University Law Review* (1998) 148–157. In July 2021, the governments of Papua New Guinea and Bougainville reached an agreement that would grant Bougainville independence by 2027, contingent on ratification by Papua New Guinea's parliament. As of June 2024, the parliament has yet to ratify the agreement.

424 Raič (n 169) 335–342; Li–ann Thio, 'International law and Secession in the Asia and Pacific Regions' in M. Kohen (ed.) *Secession: International Law Perspectives* (CUP 2006) 306; Crawford (n 216) 140–143, 393.

ASEAN's commitment to sovereignty and non-interference. These principles strongly influence the region's approach to self-determination, prioritizing regional stability, peace, and adherence to international law, while underscoring ASEAN's 'centrality' in fostering cooperation. Importantly, these documents stop short of endorsing external self-determination or independence movements.[425] Instead, they focus on peaceful dispute resolution, non-intervention in each other's affairs (including non-recognition of secessionist claims), respect for diversity, and the promotion of human rights for the welfare of all populations – encouraging an internal implementation of self-determination.

As Thio observes, only a few constitutions in the Asia-Pacific region, and indeed globally, provide for secession. Rather, many emphasize decentralization within a framework of national unity, stressing territorial integrity and the indivisibility of the state.[426] Those that enshrine self-determination as a guiding principle for international relations often align it with territorial cohesion. For instance, Timor-Leste's 2002 Constitution states that in international relations, 'the Democratic Republic of East Timor governs itself according to the principles of national independence, the right of the Peoples to self-determination and independence' (Part I, Article 8). Similarly, the 1987 Constitution of the Philippines asserts, 'in its relations with other states the paramount consideration shall be national sovereignty, territorial integrity, national interest, and the right to self-determination' (Article 2, section 7).

The way Asian countries perceive the right to self-determination is also evident in their reports to human rights bodies, such as the Human Rights Committee. Secession issues within their territories are mostly framed within the context of Article 27 of the International Covenant on Civil and Political Rights (ICCPR) rather than within the framework of Article 1, which relates to the right to self-determination.[427]

However, although most Asia-Pacific states have diverse populations, this diversity does not necessarily translate into secessionist claims. Often, minority groups focus their demands on greater autonomy and political participation

---

425 Charter of the Association of Southeast Asian Nations (2007) Preamble, Chapter 1; the East Asia Summit on the Principles tor Mutually Beneficial Relations (2011); the ASEAN Outlook on the Indo-Pacific (2019) Point IV. ASEAN never addressed the East Timor problem as one of self-determination, to avoid offending Indonesian sensitivities, and therefore characterised the issue as the need to promote 'reconciliation, rehabilitation and reconstruction' to stabilise East Timor: Joint Communique, 33rd ASEAN Ministerial Meeting (Jul. 2000) <http://www.aseansec.org/13413.htm>.

426 Li-ann Thio (n 424) 308–309.

427 *Ibid.* 310.

rather than outright independence.[428] This trend is visible in conflict cases, such as Sri Lanka, where the Liberation Tigers of Tamil Eelam (LTTE) shifted from a strict independence stance to negotiating self-governance with the government following the 2002 ceasefire agreement.[429] LTTE leader Prabhakaran stated they ware 'prepared to consider favourably a political framework that offers substantial regional autonomy and self-government in our homeland on the basis of our right to internal self-determination'.[430] Cats-Baril observes that the constitutional acknowledgment of autonomy and self-determination can function as a preventative measure against secessionism, postponing the necessity for direct talks concerning territorial delineations and the transfer of authority, all the while redressing historical grievances or demands.[431] This dynamic is evident in the cases of Bangladesh and the Philippines, where constitutional recognition of autonomy has been utilized. Nonetheless, it is essential to highlight that both instances underscore the significance of substantial and well-funded decentralization in attaining a lasting peace.

In the Philippines, the region of Muslim Mindanao has been fighting for greater autonomy since the colonial era. Previously, Muslim Mindanao-based groups equated self-determination with secession, but peace negotiations have shifted the discourse towards autonomy arrangements within the framework of the Philippine state. The 1976 Tripoli Agreement marked a turning point towards a negotiated resolution focused on enhanced autonomy for the Muslim Mindanao populace while upholding the territorial integrity of the Philippine state.[432] The Constitution of 1987 recognized the need for autonomous regions in Muslim Mindanao and the Cordilleras, taking into account their common historical, cultural, and social characteristics.[433] The intention was to grant these regions internal self-determination through autonomy and devolution of powers, in an effort to address secessionist claims put forward by the Mindanao movement. However, the implementation of autonomy fell short, with local communities feeling

428 Li–ann Thio (n 424) 312.

429 Agreement on a Ceasefire between the Government of the Democratic Socialist Republic of Sri Lanka and the LTTE (22 Feb. 2002) <https://peacemaker.un.org/sites/peacemaker.un.org/files/LK_020222_CeasefireAgreementGovernment-LiberationTigersTamilEelam.pdf>.

430 A. Balasingham, *War and Peace: Armed Struggle and Peace Efforts of Liberation Tigers* (Fairmax 2004) 401. More in K. Senaratne, *Internal Self-determination in International Law: History, Theory and Practice* (CUP 2021) chapter 6 'Sri Lanka'.

431 A. Cats-Baril, 'Self-determination' *Constitution Brief of IDEA* (2018) 5–6 <https://www.idea.int/sites/default/files/publications/self-determination-constitution-brief.pdf>.

432 *Ibid.* 6.

433 The Constitution of the Republic of the Philippines (1987) Article X, Sections 1, 15.

frustrated by limited development and an insufficient devolution of power. Nevertheless, subsequent efforts, including the 1996 Final Agreement on Mindanao[434] the 2001 Law on Mindanao's autonomy,[435] and the 2018 Bangsamoro Organic Law,[436] have continued to address the issue and show that negotiated agreements can pave the way for a peaceful resolution of religious conflicts.

Similarly, the Chittagong Hill Tracts (CHT) in Bangladesh had a history of autonomy, even during British colonial rule. However, after Bangladesh gained independence, the special status of the region was not recognized by the state, leading to violent conflicts over self-determination for two decades.[437] The eventual CHT Peace Accord brought about positive change by acknowledging the distinct ethnicity and status of the people of the CHT.[438] The establishment of a Regional Council with tribal representation and obligations for the Government of Bangladesh to consult the Council on CHT-related matters were significant steps toward greater self-determination. The commitment to institutional reform, including the creation of a Commission and a Ministry to address CHT's concerns, further solidified the accord's impact. While the CHT Peace Accord was not constitutionalized, many of its principles were legislated and institutionalized, indicating a practical implementation of the agreement. These examples highlight the value of negotiated agreements in addressing secessionist movements and resolving protracted conflicts through peaceful and inclusive means.[439]

Australia implements internal self-determination primarily through policies and programs aimed at empowering indigenous peoples and recognizing their rights to self-governance, cultural preservation, and decision-making within their communities. Some key mechanisms through which Australia supports internal self-determination for indigenous peoples include the 1993 Native Title Act, recognizing and protecting the land rights and interests of

434 Mindanao Final Agreement (1996) <https://peaceaccords.nd.edu/accord/mindanao-final-agreement>.

435 Republic Act No. 9054 (2001) <https://lawphil.net/statutes/repacts/ra2001/ra_9054_2001.html>.

436 Republic Act No. 11054 (2018) <https://lawphil.net/statutes/repacts/ra2018/ra_11054_2018.html>. As an organic act, it provided for the basic structure of government for Bangsamoro, following the agreements set forth in the Comprehensive Agreement on the Bangsamoro peace agreement signed between the government of the Philippines and the Moro Islamic Liberation Front in 2014.

437 P. Chakrabotry, 'Ethnic Conflict in the Chittagong Hill Tracts (CHT) of Bangladesh: Politics of Homogenization' 75(2) *The Indian Journal of Political Science* (2014) 297–304.

438 Chittagong Hill Tracts Accord (1997) <https://peacemaker.un.org/sites/default/files/document/files/2024/05/bd971202chittagong20hill20tracts20peace20accord.pdf>.

439 Cats-Baril (n 431) 6.

Aboriginal and Torres Strait Islander peoples based on traditional laws and customs or the establishment of indigenous representative bodies, land councils, and community-controlled organizations providing for self-governance.[440] In Aotearoa New Zealand, the founding constitutional document, the Treaty of Waitangi, sets out the values to be applied in advancing Indigenous rights within the country. The values of *kaitiakitanga* (guardianship), *manaakitanga* (generosity and care), and *whanaungatanga* (connectedness) emphasize that Māori should be at the forefront of decision-making on issues of significance to the community.[441]

4 Internal Self-determination as Customary International Law?

The 20th-century state and international organizations practice indicates that internal self-determination has become a popular reference, clearly distinguishable from external self-determination. In consequence, a question appears as to whether ISD could be treated as customary international law (CIL). To what extent was Cassese right in claiming in 1995 that 'there are grounds for holding the view that a customary rule of internal self-determination as a right of the whole population of a sovereign State is currently taking shape in the international community'?[442] To answer this question one first needs to clarify the scope and objective of ISD, in particular, if it is taken generally as an obligation towards the population or, in addition, as a norm which prohibits secession. Cassese's further assertion that 'under this customary norm, the whole people of every State would have the right freely to choose its rulers, through a democratic and pluralistic process and in particular by means of free and genuine elections' referred to the state-obligation aspect, leaving broader implications

440 Native Title Act 1993 (Cth). See also Australian High Court's landmark decision in *Mabo v Queensland* (No. 2), which rejected the doctrine *terra nullius* in Australia and recognised pre-existing native title rights. (1992) HCA 23. Australia has engaged in reconciliation efforts and treaty negotiations with Indigenous peoples in some states and territories, aiming to address historical injustices.

441 New Zeeland Foreign Affairs & Trade, 'Expert Mechanism on the Rights of Indigenous Peoples: New Zealand National Statement', *Ministry Statements & Speeches* (21 Jul. 2023) <https://www.mfat.govt.nz/en/media-and-resources/expert-mechanism-on-the-rights-of-indigenous-peoples-new-zealand-national-statement>. See Treaty of Waitangi Act 1975, Public Act 1975 No. 114.

442 Cassese, *Self-determination of Peoples* (n 183) 347.

of such an obligation untouched.[443] That could imply differences in rules of self-determination and their status.[444]

In both cases, however, the encumbrance of the content surfaces. In the obligation-centred scenario, ISD transpires as an omnibus of individual and collective human rights, including those to self-government, territorial autonomy, and democratic governance, yet without a clear indication of how ISD is to be operationalized (e.g. through devolution, consensus-based decision-making or community-oriented governance).[445] Such a broad perception of ISD not only draws accusations questioning the need for and efficacy of an overarching approach – comparable to dabates around the right to a healthy environment (comprising clean air, a safe climate, healthy ecosystems, biodiversity and access to safe water),[446] but also cast doubts on the legal status of its constituent parts. If not even all rights enshrined in the Universal Declaration of Human Rights are considered CIL,[447] a corresponding status of the still unrecognized right to autonomy in international law[448] – or the divisive notions of representativeness and democratic governance – is surely out of the question. Both, in obligation- and right-cantered incarnations, it remains unclear what counts as a meaningful observance of ISD. In the counter-secession option specifically, a question of a (universal?) threshold arises, which would, on the one hand, allow and, on the other, disallow secession, and, furthermore, what institution would be competent to monitor this process? Still, the clarity of a norm, though desirable, is not generally taken as a precondition for its CIL status, as evidenced by ongoing debates regarding the legality of self-defence (pre-emptive v. preventive), Article 2(4) of the UN Charter (use of force v. use of threats), the late definition and criminalization of

443 *Ibid.*

444 M. Saul, 'The Normative Status of Self-determination in International Law: A Formula for Uncertainty in the Scope and Content of the Right?' 11(4) *Human Rights Law Review* (2011) 625.

445 L. Hannikainen, 'Self-determination and Autonomy in International Law' in M. Suksi (ed.) *Autonomy: Applications and Implications* (Brill 1998) 85–88.

446 See S. Janković, 'Conceptual Problems of the Right to Breathe Clean Air' 22 *German Law Journal* (2021) 174. Consult UNGA Res 'The human right to a clean, healthy and sustainable environment', UN Doc. A/RES/76/300 (28 Jul. 2022).

447 See W. A. Schabas, *The Customary International Law of Human Rights* (OUP 2021) 4. Consult Human Rights Committee, General Comment No. 24: Issues relating to reservations made upon ratification or accession to the Covenant or the Optional Protocols thereto, or in relation to declarations under art. 41 of the Covenant (4 Nov. 1994) para 10.

448 See G. Gilbert, 'Autonomy and Minority Groups: A Right in International Law' 35 *Cornell International Law Journal* (2002) 309–314.

aggression (in 1974 and 2010, respectively) and the concept of the right to self-determination itself, which still has 'undefined' addressees.[449]

In reference to *opinio juris* and practice of states, two constituent elements of CIL, it might be mentioned that ISD, in contrast to a number of human rights and humanitarian law principles, is neither codified nor extensively debated in international fora for such purpose.[450] Instead, it is largely implied or juxtaposed with other rights and principles, which likewise is not a favourable occurrence for its standalone CIL status. As noted, in the secession-prohibition scenario, ISD can be viewed from a twofold perspective: as a blanket denial of secession or as a qualified denial of secession. State and institutional practice varies largely in that regard; hence it is impossible to establish a uniform interpretation custom. On the other hand, ISD is the common denominator for almost all multiethnic states facing secessionist pressures. The manner in which states interpret ISD appears thus less relevant, as its main rationale is certainly to counterbalance or outweigh secessionist claims. Moreover, if one considers the overall consensus at the adoption of the Friendly Relations Declaration containing the safeguard clause, then the attitude of states towards the application of self-determination in post-colonial settings becomes unmistakably clear.[451] The International Law Commission's observation that the relevant practice 'must be general, meaning that it must be sufficiently widespread and representative, as well as consistent' does not mean that it must be permanent or time-bound.[452] Rather, it depends on the context, that is, when the

---

449 On self-defence see A. S. Deeks, 'Taming the Doctrine of Pre-Emption' in M. Weller (ed.) *The Oxford Handbook of the Use of Force in International Law* (OUP 2015) 661- 678. On Article 2(4) see S. Janković and V. Roeben, 'Mind the Gap: The Determination, Legality and Consequences of Implicit Threats of Force' 38 *Leiden Journal of International Law* (2025). On aggression see J. Crawford, 'The International Law Commission's Work on Aggression' in C. Kreß and S. Barriga (eds.) *The Crime of Aggression: A Commentary* (CUP 2017) 233–243. On the RSD see 2.6.

450 In case of the right to a healthy environment, the process and engagement is visible. See 'Framework Principles on Human Rights and the Environment (UN Report, 2018) UN Doc. A/HRC/37/59; Report of the Special Rapporteur on the issue of human rights obligations relating to the enjoyment of a safe, clean, healthy and sustainable environment, (19 Jul. 2018) UN Doc. A/73/188; and the HRC Res 48/13 'The human right to a clean, healthy and sustainable environment' (18 Oct. 2021).

451 'The effect of consent to the text of such resolutions (...) may be understood as an acceptance of the validity of the rule or set of rules declared by the resolution by themselves'. ICJ, *Military and Paramilitary Activities in and against Nicaragua (Nicaragua v. United States of America)* Judgment, ICJ Rep. 1986, para 188.

452 ILC, 'Draft Conclusions on the Identification of Customary Law' (2018), Commentary on Conclusion 8. II (2) YILC 100–102.

respective practice is triggered by particular circumstances.[453] These circumstances include, among others, the discussed obligation to report on Article 1 of the ICCPR to the Human Rights Committee or pleadings in the *Kosovo* case, where states reconfirmed the validity of the principle of territorial integrity, especially when ISD is respected.

Considering the above, there are two possibilities. First, the substantial lack of practice involving explicit discussions and references to ISD as a CIL norm by institutions and states – combined with its overarching and indeterminate content – *a fortiori* suggests that its status as a CIL mechanism for preventing secession cannot be established. Conversely, if one bears in mind the ICJ's attribution of the CIL status to the right to self-determination (in its entirety), despite its its general reference to 'all peoples', along with the adoption without a vote of the Friendly Relations Declaration and the subsequent consistent and purposive practice of states and courts (e.g. supreme courts of Canada and Sri Lanka), then this points to ISD being on a promising trajectory to becoming a custom which averts secession.[454]

5 Towards the Definition of ISD's Content: What Does a State Need to Do?

The multiplicity of possible definitions of ISD, shaped by varied and context-dependent understandings of its objectives, affects not only ISD's status as a legal norm and its potential recognition as CIL, but also complicates the identification of specific state obligations – whether in fulfilling ISD as a general duty or in operationalizing it within counter-secession scenarios. Nevertheless, an examination of state and institutional practice, expressed either individually or collectively, provides certain indicators that may assist in delineating the substantive requirements of ISD.

In collective, hence rather general terms, i.e. those agreed in treaties or decided by an international organ for a bigger number of addressees, the obligations arising from ISD may be illustrated from two different points of view. First, it could be said what states should not do (*a negative perspective*). States and their agents are prohibited from engaging in human rights

453 *Ibid.* 94–95. Commentary on Conclusion 3. See also Conclusion 7.

454 See N. Jones, 'Self-determination and the Right of Peoples to Participate in International Law-Making' *British Yearbook of International Law* (2021) 4. Note, however, that in the *Chagos* AO, the Court determined its CIL status with reference to UNGA Res 1515(XV) (decolonization). See *Chagos Archipelago* (n 284) paras 149–154.

violations and discriminatory practices, and must refrain from breaches of international criminal law and international humanitarian law. Conduct such as war crimes, mass atrocities against civilians, torture, or forced population displacements inherently fails to satisfy ISD standards.[455] Additionally, states should not deny the exercise of ISD, regardless of its precise content. By way of example, according to Article 27 of the ICCPR, ethnic, religious or linguistic minorities shall not be denied the right 'to enjoy their own culture, to profess and practise their own religion, or to use their own language'. The other view revolves around affirmative obligations of a state (*a positive perspective*). In most common terms, these obligations boil down to ensuring equal rights and genuinely representing the whole people of the territory without distinction as to race, creed or colour. They have been enshrined, *inter alia*, in the safeguard clause of the Friendly Relations Declaration, the Vienna Declaration and Programme of Action and the UN Fiftieth Anniversary Declaration. A government is deemed representative if it conducts its affairs on the basis of equality before the law, ensures core democratic freedoms, such as freedom of expression (Article 19 ICCPR), freedom of association (Article 22 ICCPR), and protects civil and political rights, including the rights to political participation, voting, peaceful assembly, and to be heard through an independent judicial mechanism – an essential feature of democratic governance based on the separation of powers.[456] What comes under government representation is also the procedural aspect of ISD, namely the obligation to consult minorities, in particular Indigenous peoples, on matters vital for their communities (Articles 15, 17, 19, 30, 32 of UNDRIP).[457] UN bodies, when dealing with states' obligations towards minorities within their territories, again with particular emphasis on Indigenous peoples, underlined various cultural, religious and linguistic rights, which could be regarded as ISD-protected rights.[458]

455 The prohibition to attack civilians and those hors de combat are core fundamental principles of IHL. Consult also UDHR: Article 4 (prohibition of slavery or servitude); Article 5 (prohibition of torture, cruel, inhuman or degrading treatment or punishment); Article 9 (prohibition of arbitrary arrest, detention or exile); Article 12 (prohibition of arbitrary interference with one's privacy, family, home or correspondence, nor to attacks upon his honour and reputation); Article 17 (prohibition of arbitrarily deprivation of property) etc.

456 E. Mora, 'Los Elementos Centrales de la Democracia Representativa en el Derecho Interamericano' 21 *Anuario Mexicano de Derecho Internacional* (2021) 93–123.

457 In South Africa, for example, the Parliament, when voting a law related to the customs or traditions of a community, must refer the draft legislation to the National House of Tradition Leaders. See also OSCE HCNM, 'Recommendations on the Effective Participation of National Minorities in Social and Economic Life & Explanatory Note' (2023).

458 Although Article 27 is to be distinguished from Article 1 of the ICCPR based on the collectiveness of addressees in line with General Comment 23, the Human Rights Committee's jurisprudence has linked self-determination with Articles 25, 26 and 27 of the ICCPR. See *Apirana Mahuika et al. v. New Zealand*, Communication No. 547/1993 (2000) para 9.2; *JGA*

They include the right to fishing,[459] the right to practice reindeer herding,[460] the protection of pastures and livestock against threats such as artificially induced droughts,[461] the publication of minority–language press,[462] the use of minority languages in education and and broader linguistic preservation, among others. In cases examined under the ICCPR, the Human Rights Committee decisions were based on the proportionality test, i.e. whether a due balance has been established between the rights of minorities and the the legitimate aims pursued by the state (e.g. economic development). This boosts the idea that the RSD as a human right is qualified and may be subject to justified limitations where other significant public interests are at stake.

Beyond the protection of fundamental rights and freedoms, as well as respecting some particular human rights resulting from the protection of culture, there is a burgeoning tendency to incorporate autonomy under ISD. This would circumvent the generally recognized proviso of the non-existence of the separate right to autonomy under international law. Given that autonomy implies self-regulation or self-governance,[463] it is not difficult to assimilate it with self-determination. Autonomy encompasses a structural arrangement that ensures a group's meaningful participation in decision-making processes on matters essential to the preservation of its identity.[464] Many states in their statements before international organizations underlined the importance of autonomy in their states (e.g. Russia) and elsewhere (the U.S. and Germany in reference to Kosovo), reported that they ensure autonomy in their constitutions (Italy and Spain) and confirmed that it could be a solution to ethnic conflicts (Philippines, Pakistan), which included the enactment of new laws on self-governance, the establishment of

Diergaardt et al v. Namibia, Communication No. 760/1997 (2000) para 10.3; *Gillot et al. v. France*, Communication No. 932/2000 (2002) paras 13.4 and 13.16. See also A. Verstichel, 'Recent Developments in the UN Human Rights Committee's Approach to Minorities, with a Focus on Effective Participation' 12(1) *International Journal on Minority and Group Rights* (2005) 27–28; S. Joseph and M. Castan, *The International Covenant on Civil and Political rights: Cases, Materials, and Commentary* (OUP 2013) 841–866.

459 Human Rights Committee, *Howard v. Canada*, Communication No. 879/1999 (2005) para 12.4.

460 Human Rights Committee, *Kitok v. Sweden*, Communication No. 197/85 (1988) paras 9.1–9.3.

461 Human Rights Committee, *Poma Poma v. Peru*, Communication No. 1457/06 (2009) para 7.7.

462 Human Rights Committee, *Mavlonov and Sa'di v. Uzbekistan*, Communication No. 1334/04 (2009) para 8.7.

463 The ancient Greek word autonomy is derived from two words: auto ('self') and nomos ('law' or 'rule').

464 V. Dimitrijević, *Savremeno Shvatanje Prava Naroda Na Samoopredeljenje* (Belgrade Centre for Human Rights 2011) 50–52.

new decentralized institutions and the cooperation with them. The Liechtenstein Draft Convention on Self-determination Through Self-Administration is all about autonomy, despite not mentioning it (e.g. by demanding an appropriate form of organization where it could represent the community's interests and establishing organs of self-government), while UNDRIP in Article 4 explicitly mentions the right to autonomy. It is important to add that autonomy does not necessarily need to be territorial: non-territorial autonomy provides a more viable solution for minorities spread around the state.[465]

As far as individual, hence more specific, state practice regarding ISD is concerned, various patterns transpire. These patterns, shaped by self-imposed or externally induced historical circumstances, continue to be applied. They include, among others, vesting certain regions with their own parliaments or regional governments, reserved seats for the peoples' representatives in all or some of the governmental branches, reserved seats for such representatives in central parliaments (often in an upper house), and special political mechanisms for safeguarding the identity of distinct groups. If constituted, local parliaments may regulate a wide range of issues – from political to economic, social, and cultural issues, such as pensions, particular kinds of taxes, housing and real estate, and education. In some cases, regions may have their own judiciary, either independent or loosely connected to the national judicial system.

A few examples illustrating the potential content of ISD, particularly where such measures have helped resolve or alleviate conflicts and secessionist claims, include the following:

a In Canada, the provinces that make up the federal state possess certain rights that afford them special status and protection from the effects of simple majority rule. Each province is represented in the federal parliament, with Quebec distinguished by a range of unique rights and privileges. For example, Quebec is allocated a guaranteed and fixed number of seats in the House of Commons, and specific rules govern the selection of its senators to the Senate. French is officially recognized as the province's official language, and three of the nine judges on the Supreme Court must be appointed from Quebec. Quebec operates under a distinct civil law system, in contrast to the common law system used in the rest of Canada; the province

465 Such type of autonomy is recognized in Hungary, Latvia, and the Russian Federation, as well as Serbia, Estonia, and Finland. Paragraph 17 of the so-called Lund Recommendations points out that '[n]on-territorial forms of governance are useful for the maintenance and development of the identity and culture of national minorities'. Generally, B. Kuzmany, *Vom Umgang mit nationaler Vielfalt Eine Geschichte der nicht-territorialen Autonomie in Europa* (De Gruyter 2024).

has its own courts, with judges drawn exclusively from members of the local bar. It also bears authority in certain social and economic areas, such as pensions, housing, family policy, and financial assistance.[466]

b The United Kingdom as the world's oldest democracy has introduced constitutional amendments aimed at decentralizing power. These changes have particularly strengthened the position of Scotland and Northern Ireland, while Wales's ties with the central government remain tight. Scottish autonomy is greater than Northern Ireland's due to the broader scope of powers held by Scottish institutions – especially the Scottish Parliament. These include control over local government and finance, housing, transport, sport, education and training, the legal system (including law and order), agriculture, forestry, fisheries, the arts, the countryside, and economic development. The Scottish Parliament, uniquely among the devolved institutions, possesses a limited authority to vary taxes, and it must sanction the Scottish budget. It also retains the ability to discuss issues of both national and international significance, regardless of whether they fall under devolved or reserved powers.[467]

c In Bosnia and Herzegovina, the three main ethnic groups (Croats, Bosniaks, and Serbs) are recognized as 'constituent peoples' and granted significant powers to preserve interethnic balance and sustain peace after the war. The country is divided into two federal entities (Republika Srpska and the Federation of Bosnia and Herzegovina) and the Brčko District, which is a condominium shared by the two entities. Serbs form the majority in Republika Srpska, while Croats and Bosniaks mainly live in the Federation of BiH, with Bosniaks being the majority there. The political system includes features of internal self-determination: a tripartite presidency with one member from each constituent group, and a 15-member House of Peoples, with equal representation (five each) from the three groups. The constitution provides for an entity veto mechanism, which allows decisions unfavorable to any group to be blocked through institutional processes, ultimately requiring a national vote. In addition, entities have a broad range of powers when it comes to

466 See more C. Bélanger, *Quebec, the Constitution and Special Status* (2020) <http://faculty.marianopolis.edu/c.belanger/quebechistory/readings/special.htm>.

467 P. Leopold, 'National and Regional Experiments with Autonomous Arrangements' in Z. Skurbaty (ed.) *Beyond a One-Dimensional State: An Emerging Right to Autonomy?* (The Raoul Wallenberg Institute Human Rights Library 2004) 511.

legislative regulation since there is a presumption that all spheres where a central government is not explicitly in charge, shall be regulated by entities.[468]

d In Indonesia, the 2005 Memorandum of Understanding (MoU) between the Acehnese people and the central government marked a significant milestone toward resolving conflict. Regardless of the fact that the MoU was not incorporated into the constitution and that the Indonesian parliament enacted a law that reduced the scope of the RSD of the Acehnese people to a certain point, the agreement is still a valuable example of how granting the internal dimension of the RSD can mitigate secessionist aspirations. The pivotal MoU's clause reads that 'Aceh will exercise authority within all sectors of public affairs (…) except in the fields of foreign affairs, external defence, national security, monetary and fiscal matters, justice and freedom of religion'.[469]

From the described examples, one can conclude that: (i) states ought to grant peoples of specific regions a degree of autonomy to manage their own institutions, (ii) certain areas that are not critical to the functioning of the state as a whole should be left for regions and peoples to regulate, and (iii) effective mechanisms should exist to prevent central authorities from unilaterally undermining the status of these peoples within the country.[470]

In conclusion, in order to preserve territorial unity, a state struggling with the RSD demands should act *cumulatively* in two directions: (i) protect the individual rights of members of the group, (ii) establish a dedicated framework that safeguards the group's collective identity.

---

468 The Constitution prescribes that ten areas fall under the scope of the federal regulation. Constitution of the Federation of Bosnia and Herzegovina (1994) Article III 1. Over time, the powers and institutions of the federal state enlarged to the detriment of entities' authorities.

469 Memorandum of Understanding between the Government of the Republic of Indonesia and the Free Aceh Movement (2005) <https://web.archive.org/web/20130418023930/http://www.aceh-mm.org/download/english/Helsinki%20MoU.pdf>.

470 For instance, Kosovo lost its autonomy in 1992 as a result of the newly adopted Serbian Constitution. The autonomy existed previously under the SFRY, and this course of events was one of the reasons for the subsequent armed conflict in Kosovo.

CHAPTER 6

Internal Self-determination in European States

> Better to illuminate than merely to shine,
> to deliver to others contemplated truths
> than merely to contemplate.
>
> THOMAS AQUINAS

1 Preface

Internal self-determination can play a crucial role in addressing secessionist tendencies in various regions by granting greater political autonomy, economic self-management, and cultural rights according to the specific needs of the populations. In Belgium, ISD can mitigate moderate secessionist pressures by addressing regional disparities. In Kosovo, ISD could stabilize the region by protecting the rights and cultural heritage of the Serbian minority. Historically, in Republika Srpska Krajina, ISD measures might have prevented conflict by offering meaningful territorial autonomy arrangements. Bavaria's low secessionist tendencies are well managed through existing Germany's federal system, which grants substantial autonomy to the Länder in areas such as education, culture, policing, and local government, as well as through the influence that Bavaria and the Christian Social Union exert over national policies. For the Sámi indigenous people in Finland, ISD measures such as self-governance and cultural preservation are crucial in addressing their aspirations, though these do not include secessionist aims given their low numbers and scattered presence throughout the Arctic states. In general, however, the implementation or absence of ISD has significant implications. Failure to apply it appropriately can fuel secessionist movements, whereas successful application can serve as a model for other states facing similar demands.

Chapter IV outlined various meanings of ISD, noting that its genuine implementation reflects a positive relationship between the government and the governed, where the former provides a framework for the free expression of the will of the people. People's sovereignty should be overarching and embrace all segments of a given society, making the governance framework inclusive

 | DOI:10.1163/9789004737501_007

and, where necessary, providing additional protection and privileges to minorities under its jurisdiction to truly represent their interests.

This chapter will examine past and present examples of European states and regions where ISD has been particularly relevant due to their multiethnic composition and the role it plays in maintaining social cohesion and traditions. It will explore various interpretations of ISD and show how they operate in specific contexts, such as federal arrangements and cultural rights in Germany (Bavaria), linguistic political divisions in Belgium, the preservation and protection of the traditional rights of indigenous peoples in Finland, and the discussion over the safeguarding of Serbian cultural heritage and the formation of the Association of Serb-majority Municipalities in Kosovo. These examples illustrate that there is no one-size-fits-all understanding and implementation of ISD, as different states and communities prioritize different aspects. Consequently, these variations, reflect, to varying degrees, past, present, and future autonomy and secession motives, as well as states' counter-secession strategies.

In contrast to the previous chapter, which explored state and institutional interpretations of ISD, including its scope, and application as an anti-secession mechanism, this chapter will adopt a grassroots perspective. It will focus on the needs of affected groups and individuals concerning self-determination, illustrating how these needs inform the content of ISD – from fishing permits for the Sámi people to the establishment of vehicle license plates in Kosovo. The chapter will also explore various ways these needs are expressed and addressed, including protests, the formation of national movements, legislative initiatives, negotiations, and more. While some of these aspirations have been realized and are evident in long-term state policies or legal acts, others remain unfulfilled, reflected in piecemeal state actions, symbolic declarations, or ongoing pleas for self-governance and political arrangements aligned with people's aspirations. In a broader context, this chapter will present state models in which peoples have desired and continue to desire to live, thereby influencing the reconceptualization of sovereignty and state organization itself.

2 Internal Self-determination in Federal European States

2.1 *Belgium (Flanders, Wallonia and Brussels)*

Belgium is marked by two dominant language communities: the Flemish-speaking population in the north (Flanders) and the French-speaking population in the south (Wallonia).[1] Thus, Flemish (Dutch) is the official language

1 Pursuant to Article 4 of the Belgian Constitution, 'Belgium has four linguistic areas: The French-speaking area, the Dutch-speaking area, the bilingual area of Brussels Capital, and

in the north, while French is the official language in the south. Belgium represents an area where Romance and Germanic cultures meet, as 'the dividing line between the southern, Latin, and northern, Germanic part of Europe passes precisely through Belgian territory'.[2]

Since its formation, Belgium has experienced persistent conflict among its linguistic communities, though these tensions have remained peaceful. Over time, various forms of dissatisfaction emerged on both sides, rooted fundamentally in the language issue. The majority of the population has always spoken Dutch, while French was the sole language of the state, law, and elite culture in the 19th century. The Flemish-Walloon dispute dates back to the secession of the Kingdom of Belgium from the Netherlands in 1831 when the dominance of the minority Walloon group in the administrative and managerial apparatus was established.[3] Walloons, who speak one of the French dialects, comprised about 31% of the country's population and held sway in the administration and political life over the 58% of the population of Flemish origin, who speak Dutch. The privileged status of Walloons, due to their proximity to French culture, has made them, in terms of national or ethnic sentiments, closer to the identity of Belgians. On the other hand, Flemings, who belonged to lower social strata and held few managerial positions in the division of labor, had to pursue personal advancement in the French language and within a value system outside their own cultural matrix.[4]

Due to the linguistic subjugation of the Flemings, the so-called Flemish Movement emerged in the 19th century.[5] On the other hand, the economic inequality between the northern (Flemish) and southern (Walloon) parts of Belgium, which became particularly pronounced after World War II, also spurred the creation of a national movement on the Walloon side.[6] The Flemish nationalist

---

the German-speaking area'. Only around 1% of the population uses German as the first language. Flemish is a West Germanic language most closely related to Dutch and generally regarded as the Belgian variant of Dutch.

2 K. Deschouwer, 'Kingdom of Belgium' in J. Kincaid and A. Tarr (eds.) *Constitutional Origins, Structure, and Change in Federal Countries* (McGill-Queen's University Press 2005) 49.

3 C. Driessen, *Geschichte Belgiens: Die Gespaltene Nation* (Friedrich Pustet 2023) 93–102.

4 G. Bašić. *Multikulturalizam i Etnicitet (Institut Društvenih Nauka 2018) 111.*

5 The Flemish Movement was a significant and influential nationalist movement. It was primarily composed of intellectuals, writers, academics, priests, and activists. After a petition (*petitionnement*) to parliament (1840) had led to the establishment of a *Grievencommissie* (Commission of Grievances, 1856–59), bilingualism was recognized in the northern provinces of Belgium. J. Rock, 'The Flemish Movement' *Encyclopaedia of Romantic Nationalism in Europe* <https://ernie.uva.nl/viewer.p/21/56/object/122-159663>.

6 M. Stanković, *Preobražaji Federalne Države* (Pravni Fakultet Univerziteta u Beogradu 2020) 141.

movement gained strength when, in 2010, the separatist Flemish nationalist party, the New Flemish Alliance (N-VA), became the dominant party in Flanders and the largest party in Belgium. Despite this, the complex nature of Belgian politics and the requirement for coalition governments meant that the N-VA was not able to unilaterally implement its full self-determination agenda and fundamentally change the Belgian institutional structure.[7]

Regardless of the undeniable fact that Flemish nationalism, articulated and advocated by the Flemish Movement, has been a persistent and major cause of political and social tensions, the conflict between the country's national groups cannot be reduced solely to the Flemish struggle for linguistic parity with Francophones. Particularly in the second half of the last century, the evolving social crisis ceased to resemble a typical conflict between two disputing parties. Instead of merely focusing on Flemish efforts for equality based on cultural identity and directed against the Francophone population, two additional problems emerged, each involving different actors.

Firstly, Walloon nationalism arose as a consequence of socio-economic dissatisfaction aimed at Flanders and Brussels. Secondly, Brussels (Francophone) nationalism emerged as a response to the developed center versus the less developed periphery, directed towards the rest of the state. Although each of these struggles is nominally led by different factions of the Belgian population, their main characteristic is mutual interweaving and intertwining, making it difficult to assert that they unfold independently of each other at any given moment.[8]

2.1.1 The Specifics of Belgian Federalism

Until 1970, Belgium was a unitary centralized state, but during the seventies and eighties, it transformed into a federal state. Determining the exact moment of this transition is challenging, but most analysts place this transformation

7 The sixth state reform of Belgium, finalized in October 2011, introduced changes to the country's federal structure to create a more efficient federal state with more autonomous entities. The Brussels-Halle-Vilvoorde (BHV) electoral district was split into separate districts for Flemish Brabant and Brussels-Capital. In addition, the Brussels judicial district was reformed to include separate Dutch-speaking and French-speaking courts, each with its own president and judges. The N-VA was not part of the agreement due to the staunch stance on Flemish nationalism and their demands for extensive regional autonomy, which clashed with the positions of the Walloon parties and other coalition partners. In consequence, the N-VA was also not part of the future government. See Institutioneel Akkoord Voor de Zesde Staatshervorming (11 Oct. 2011) <https://www.lachambre.be/kvvcr/pdf_sections/home/FRtexte%20dirrupo.pdf>.

8 More in M. Stanković, *Belgijski Federalizam* (Pravni Fakultet Univerziteta u Beogradu 2009) 44–105.

between 1980 and 1989, before the official constitutionalization of its federal status in 1993.[9]

Drawing from the lessons learned during the first 140 years of their 1831 Constitution – characterized by a well-constructed legal text but inadequate solutions for societal needs – the Belgians, through various stages of federalization, sought to develop a constitutional framework that would satisfy all citizens and ensure the peaceful coexistence of different ethnic groups within a unified state.[10] They aimed to create a 'living constitution', one that could be continuously adapted to reflect social changes, thereby ensuring that the constitution remains relevant and responsive to the state of society.

Based on Article 1 of the 1993 Constitution, Belgium is 'a federal state composed of Communities and Regions'. There are three constitutionally recognized Communities: the Flemish Community, the French Community, and the German-speaking Community. Correspondingly, there are three Regions: the Flemish Region, the Walloon Region, and the Brussels-Capital Region.[11] Communities, defined by language, have governments and parliaments with exclusive powers over culture, healthcare, education, and family policy, while Regions are responsible for employment, public works, and the environment.[12] Subnational governments also enjoy substantial spending autonomy, managing 46 percent of total spending, while generating only 16 percent of total tax revenues.[13] This intricate institutional framework represents a compromise between the Flemish perspective, which sees Belgium primarily as a bicultural nation comprising Dutch and French-speaking regions, and the Francophone viewpoint, which regards Belgium as

9 J. Poirier, 'Who is Afraid of (Con) Federalism?' in K. Deschouwer and J. Poirier (eds.) *(Con) federalism: Cure or Curse?* (Re-Bel initiative 2015) 32.

10 Stanković, *Belgijski Federalizam* (n 8) 57.

11 Articles 2–3 of the Belgian Constitution. See also M. Adams, 'Disabling Constitutionalism. Can the Politics of the Belgian Constitution be Explained?' *12(2) International Journal of Constitutional Law (2014) 283.*

12 Chapter IV (On Communities and Regions) of the Belgian Constitution. Note there is a Flemish Government, but there is no separate Flemish Community Parliament because the Flemish Parliament and Government handle both regional and community matters, and that the situation in Brussels is an exception to the territorial rule. See B. Maddens, 'Flanders' in D. Turp and M. Sanjaume-Calvet (eds.) *The Emergence of a Democratic Right to Self-determination in Europe* (Centre Maurits Coppieters 2016) 236.

13 Y. C. Wong, 'Fiscal Federalism in Belgium: Challenges in Restoring Fiscal Sustainability' IMF Selected Issues Papers (2023) 2 (with the combined effect of strong revenue centralization and decentralization of spending to subnational governments, Belgium's vertical fiscal imbalance – the share of sub-national own spending not financed through own revenues – was high at 50 percent in 2019).

consisting of three distinct socio-economic regions, with Brussels being recognized as a separate and equal entity.[14]

According to the Belgian Constitution, all powers 'emanate from the Nation' and are 'exercised in the manner laid down by the Constitution'.[15] This provision corroborates the importance of sovereign will as a cornerstone of democratic governance and a foundational principle of ISD.[16] Article 4 of the Belgian Constitution stipulates that changes to the linguistic political divisions can only be made by the linguistic communities themselves, requiring a substantial (2/3 majority) approval during the enactment of any law to this end.[17] Any amendment without this approval would breach ISD of the affected community.

The monarch, federal government, and the judiciary play key roles in the horizontal organization of power at the federal level.[18] While Regions and Communities in Belgium possess significant competencies, federal authority extends throughout the country and regulates issues that are not exclusively entrusted to subnational entities. Core areas such as policing, immigration, national security, and fiscal policy are managed by the federal government and parliament.[19] This distribution of powers ensures that both regional autonomy and federal cohesion are maintained, balancing the interests of the Communities and Regions with the need for unified governance across the state.

In the theory of federalism, Belgium represents an unusual model. According to Stanković, the Belgian federal political system is characterized by four peculiarities: dualism, bipolarity, asymmetry, and its deviation from many principles defining a federation.[20]

---

14 W. Swenden and M. T. Jans, ''Will it Stay or Will it Go?' Federalism and the Sustainability of Belgium' in M. Brans et al. (eds.) *The Politics of Belgium. Institutions and Policy under Bipolar and Centrifugal Federalism* (Routledge 2009) 15–32.

15 Article 33 of the Belgian Constitution.

16 Note that the 1831 Constitution conceived people's sovereignty in an equal manner (Article 25). The Belgian 1831 Constitution was widely praised. Dicey once remarked, it was 'very near to a written reproduction of the English constitution'. V. Dicey, *Introduction to the Study of the Law of the Constitution* (Macmillan and Co 1889) 85.

17 Article 4, paragraph 3 of the Belgian Constitution.

18 L. Despotović and Đ. Stojanović, 'Belgijska Konsocijativna Demokratija, Skica za Portret 'Neuspešnog' Federalizma' 8(2) *Megatrend Revija* (2011) 94.

19 *Ibid.* 94–97. Consult Article 37 of the Constitution (federal executive power belongs to the King, but it is exercised by the federal government. This includes implementing laws, ensuring internal and external security, and managing public administration.); Article 77 of the Constitution (outlines the areas where the House of Representatives and the Senate have equal power, such as revising the Constitution, laws concerning the organization of the judiciary, and laws relating to the State's administrative boundaries).

20 Stanković, *Preobražaji Federalne Države* (n 6) 142.

Firstly, the most distinctive feature of the Belgian federal model lies in its complex composition, *ergo*, the coexistence of two qualitatively and quantitatively different categories of federal constituents: three Communities and three Regions. These entities have significant overlap but are not completely territorially congruent, making Belgium's arrangement much more complex than that of other federations, which are simply divided into territorially defined member states.[21] Secondly, although defined by the constitution as a dual-layer federation consisting of six political entities, Belgium operates more simply in practice, with socio-political life primarily unfolding between two opposing poles: the Dutch-speaking Flemish and the French-speaking Walloons. Bilingual Brussels, which is predominantly French-speaking, occasionally appears as a distinct political actor. The small German-speaking Community, comprising less than one percent of the population, remains politically marginal.[22] So, although conceived as a multiparty federal state, established primarily to secure equilibrium between ethnic groups, Belgium in practice remains split into two halves. This division is best illustrated by its development as a *sui generis* two-party federation. This phenomenon is described in theory as 'bipolarity' (*bipolarité*) and 'confrontation federalism' (*le fédéralisme de confrontation*).[23] Thirdly, the Belgian federation is asymmetric.[24] This asymmetry occurs in two ways: institutionally, through the merger of the Flemish Community and regional institutions into unified Flemish bodies without a similar process on the French-speaking side; and in terms of competencies, with federated units not being fully equal in their powers. The Brussels-Capital Region has narrower jurisdiction compared to the Walloon and Flemish Regions, and the German-speaking Community is significantly less empowered than its French- and Dutch-speaking counterparts. Fourthly, Belgium diverges from almost all commonly accepted federal standards. Some aspects bring it closer to a decentralized unitary state, while others place it among the

21 *Ibid.* According to Lecours, such an intriguing feature can only be understood in the context of the historical struggle of the Flemish movement for cultural-linguistic equality, as well as the later upheavals of the Walloon movement for economic autonomy. A Lecours, 'Belgium (Kingdom of Belgium)' in A. Griffiths (ed.) *Handbook of Federal Countries* (McGill-Queen's University Press 2005) 62.

22 *Ibid.* 142–143.

23 A. Alen, *La Belgique: Un Fédéralisme Bipolaire et Centrifuge* (Ministère des affaires étrangères du commerce extérieur et de la coopération au développement 1990) 8; F. Delpérée, *Le droit Constitutionnel de la Belgique* (Bruylant 2000) 390.

24 Stanković, *Preobražaji Federalne Države* (n 6) 143.

weakest federations.[25] For instance, the Belgian federation exhibits distinctly unitary characteristics in the absence of separate judicial organs for federal units, the lack of constitutions for those units, and the retention of residual competencies by the federal level.

It can be said that Belgium somewhat represents an amalgamation of federal and confederal elements. From a formal standpoint, Belgium operates as a federation rather than a confederation. However, certain institutional features reflect confederal or consociational elements, particularly in their emphasis on consensus-based decision-making between linguistic groups.[26]

The Belgian model exemplifies a federation shaped by binationalism, designed as a shared political framework for its two principal communities. This unique arrangement, while seeking its own answers, points to remnants of a unitary past and significantly softens the application of federal principles. Examples include a centralized monarchy, predominantly federal control over core social security, residual competencies held by the federation, and a unitary procedure for revising the federal constitution. On the other hand, institutional mechanisms reflect a distinctly confederal logic, such as the right of federated units to conclude international agreements, the division of parliamentarians into language groups in both houses of parliament, the 'alarm bell' procedure, parity in the composition of federal executive, and constitutional conventions stipulating unanimous decision-making within the federal government.[27]

2.1.1.1 *The Changing Institutional Structure*

As previously noted, one of the main goals of the Belgian constitutional arrangement is its adaptability to societal changes. Despite considerable difficulties and the continued need for compromises, the constitutional framework established in 1993 functions reasonably well in practice, which serves as a testament to its validity.[28] More importantly, Belgian constitutionalists succeeded in ensuring the flexibility of their constitution despite its considerable formal rigidity. The necessity for ongoing amendments is entirely anticipated

25 *Ibid.* 144.

26 Poirier (n 9) 31–33.

27 Z. Miljko, 'Belgijski Primjer Federalizacije' 22(1) *Mostariensia: Časopis za Društvene Humanističke Znanosti* (2018) 342.

28 Stanković, *Belgijski Federalizam* (n 8) 93.

and aligns with the evolutionary nature of Belgian federalism, particularly in light of the persistent centrifugal forces within the state.[29]

To date, Belgium has undergone a total of six state reforms. The devolution process in Belgium is characterized by two key principles: gradualism and pragmatism. The objective of these reforms has not been a constitutional revolution – building anew on the ruins of the old – but rather constitutional reform, building upon the foundations of the existing. This is most evident in the incremental nature of the constitutional changes. In crafting new constitutional solutions, Belgian constitution-makers did not strictly adhere to existing theoretical and comparative models; instead, they sought to tailor the norms to the specificities of Belgian society. This approach often led to the creation of entirely new legal institutions unique to the Belgian constitutional system. The ingenuity of Belgian constitution-makers lies in their pragmatic approach to federalism, with some solutions displaying a level of originality reminiscent of the genius of the American Founding Fathers.[30]

The first state reform in Belgium took place in 1970, following an extensive political debate that ultimately entered the constitutional arena. The objectives of this reform were twofold: to preserve unity in the conduct of general state policy and to introduce new features of cultural and territorial autonomy into the constitutional framework, thereby adapting the existing organization of power to newly created institutions. The primary task of the constitution-makers was to reflect the heterogeneity of Belgian society within the Constitution, lay the foundations for its future institutional development, and construct a new model of state organization. Notably, this reform introduced two previously non-existent constitutional categories – the cultural community (*communauté culturelle*) and the region (*région*). These categories served as precursors to today's federal entities.[31]

Following the parliamentary elections in 2007, Belgium entered a deep political crisis, one of the most severe in its history, which persisted until the end of 2011. The crisis was exacerbated by the absence of mechanisms to enforce timely government formation. Specifically, there were no constitutional provisions mandating the formation of a government within a set period, with

29 *Ibid.*

30 Stanković, *Preobražaji Federalne Države* (n 6) 141–142. See also M. Jovičić, *Savremeni Federalizam: Uporednopravna Studija* (Institut za Uporedno Pravo 1973) 16 (contending that American federalism developed in a pragmatic way by searching for solutions for particular situations).

31 M. Stanković, 'Šesta Državna Reforma U Belgiji – Novi, ali ne i Poslednji Stadijum Devolucije' 62(2) *Anali Pravnog fakulteta u Beogradu* (2014) 118.

the consequence that the parliament's mandate would expire if it failed to do so. As a result, Belgium experienced unprecedented delays in forming the Council of Ministers, exceeding six months on one occasion and lasting over a year on another. The political crisis in Belgium was marked by constant tension among the national communities, rooted in differing perspectives on the direction of further state reforms and conflicting views on the electoral and judicial district of Brussels-Halle-Vilvoorde (BHV).[32] The situation in Brussels remained a central point of contention in the Flemish-French-speaking conflict. Flemish political parties persistently advocated for further devolution of powers from the federation to the Communities and Regions, as well as the division of the BHV district, which they deemed unconstitutional. Conversely, French-speaking political parties favored preserving the status quo. After the 2010 elections, debates on other significant economic issues, including public debt, deficit reduction, and social system reform, intensified. On these matters, Flemish and French-speaking political parties held diametrically opposed views: the former supported reducing expenditure as a solution, while the latter proposed increasing revenue through significant tax hikes. The political crisis lasted until December 2011, when a new federal government was formed, whose program included the division of the BHV district, and policies aimed at resolving the economic crisis.[33]

The immediate trigger of the crisis was the victory of the Flemish Christian Democrats (*Christen-Democratisch en Vlaams*) and the New Flemish Alliance (*Nieuw-Vlaamse Alliantie,* N-VA) in the 2007 parliamentary elections, given that these two parties supported comprehensive state reform and the division of the BHV district. New elections were held in June 2010, and immediately after the announcement of the results and seat distribution, it was clear that the political crisis was not resolved but would likely deepen. In Flanders, the separatist and conservative N-VA emerged as the largest party, while among the French-speaking electorate, the Socialist Party (*Parti Socialiste*) – which advocated for preserving unity within the Belgian kingdom – received the most support. Thus, the Flemish electorate predominantly backed a right-wing separatist platform, while the Francophone electorate placed their trust in the unionist left.[34]

Constitutional scholars generally concur that the system has become even more intricate due to the sixth reform, raising concerns about its sustainability. Many anticipate that, in the coming years, the constitutional court will face

32 *Ibid.* 124.

33 *Ibid.* 125.

34 *Ibid.* 125–126.

an overwhelming caseload and will need to impose order on the chaotic distribution of powers. Additionally, some constitutional experts highlight a democratic deficit at the federal level. Despite substantial federal competences, the cohesive pan-Belgian political sphere necessary to justify federal policymaking is no longer present. Consequently, there are calls either to revive a shared Belgian political identity or to further decentralize the federal level.[35]

2.1.2 Manifesto for an Independent Flanders within Europe

In 2005, the 'Reflection Group', composed of sixteen Flemish businessmen and academics, prepared a report analyzing Belgium's structural issues. This group convened at the 'Warande', an exclusive Flemish men's club in Brussels located near the American ambassador's residence. The resulting document, became known as the 'Manifesto for an Independent Flanders within Europe'.[36] According to Mnookin and Verbeke, the arguments of the Manifesto can be summarized as follows: (a) the independence of Flanders is the only durable solution to a range of problems facing Flanders, among which are the divergent needs and goals of Flanders and Wallonia caused by their profound cultural and economic differences; (b) proponents of Flanders' independence believe that the two regions (Flanders and Wallonia) are artificially held together by a 'maladjusted and inefficient' federal governmental structure with antimajoritarian restrictions and a 'chaotic distribution of powers'; (c) the economic development of Flanders is jeopardized by the inability to implement effective policymaking, particularly considering challenges such as an aging population, ever-growing globalization, and increasing international competition; (d) given that Flanders possesses a distinct identity and sufficient institutional capacity, it is seen as meeting the criteria of a national community capable of functioning as an independent European state.[37]

Mnookin and Verbeke note that the Manifesto was primarily supported by Flemish business and academic communities rather than by Flemish nationalists.[38] Nonetheless, the Manifesto reignited the debate between the Flemish and Walloon regions, fostering a growing sentiment for Flemish independence among many Flemish citizens. Political parties began to capitalize on this sentiment, with leaders like Bart de Wever of the New

35 Maddens (n 12) 239.

36 I. de Warande, 'Manifesto for an Independent Flanders within Europe', Brussels, Belgium (Nov. 2005).

37 R. Mnookin and A. Verbeke, 'Persistent Nonviolent Conflict with no Reconciliation: The Flemish and Walloons in Belgium' 72 *Law and Contemporary Problems* (2009) 152–153.

38 *Ibid.* 153.

Flemish Alliance emphasizing Flemish autonomy during the 2010 Belgian parliamentary elections.[39] De Wever argued that post-election governance would depend on the Francophones' willingness to enable Belgium to function effectively. He criticized Francophone Wallonia for its poor governance, which, he claimed, resulted in higher unemployment in Flanders.[40] De Wever highlighted the long-standing division within Belgium, stating that the country effectively operates as two separate democracies, each with its own political, social, economic, and cultural systems, and this division continues to deepen.[41] In the 2024 elections, the N-VA maintained its position as the largest party in Belgium's parliament, narrowly beating the far-right *Vlaams Belang* (VB). One month after the elections, Flemish leader Bart De Wever was appointed *formateur* (creator) of the federal government by the head of state, King Philippe.[42] Despite its electoral success, the N-VA's long-term goal of Flemish independence has been tempered to a push for confederalism, a less radical stance that avoids the immediate dissolution of Belgium. According to the majority of commentators, the dissolution of Belgium is far from inevitable. The political and economic importance of Brussels, which includes hosting the EU and NATO headquarters, remains crucial for both Flanders and Wallonia. Additionally, Belgium's significant role in the international arena has, up to now, provided strong incentives for continued cooperation among its federated entities.[43]

2.1.3 Minority Protection v. Majority Rule in Belgian Consociational Federalism

The Belgian federal system, as demonstrated, is not based on majority rule but rather exemplifies a 'consociational democracy'. Consociationalism is deeply embedded in Belgian politics, having been institutionalized well before the emergence of federalism. It captures how Belgium's constitutional system,

---

39 J. Demessemaeker, 'The Intricate National Identity of Belgians' (2018) <https://www.linkedin.com/pulse/intricate-national-identity-belgians-john-demessemaeker>.

40 Deutsche Welle, 'Belgija – „Dve Demokratije"' (14 Jun. 2010) <https://www.dw.com/sr/belgija-dve-demokratije/a-5681687>.

41 *Ibid.*

42 J. P. Stroobants. 'Flemish Nationalist Bart De Wever Called to Form a Government in Belgium' (11 Jul. 2024) *LeMonde* <https://www.lemonde.fr/en/international/article/2024/07/11/flemish-nationalist-bart-de-wever-called-to-form-a-government-in-belgium_6681366_4.html>.

43 Stanković, Preobražaji Federalne Države (n 6) 146; R. L. Watts, *Comparing Federal Systems in the 1990s* (Queen's University 1996) 27; J. Wouters and A. Andrione-Moylan, 'Federalism: A Lifeline for Belgium?' 57 *Jura Falconis* (2021) 768.

which is fundamentally indirect, non-majoritarian, and representative, has historically managed ethno-linguistic conflicts at the elite level. The development of devolution as a means to diffuse and resolve conflicts can be viewed as a result of these consociational dynamics. Lijphart notably defined consociationalism as 'government by elite cartel to turn a democracy with a fragmented political culture into a stable democracy'.[44] Consociational mechanisms in Belgium are established through explicit constitutional and legal norms. At the federal level, Belgium ensures that public services, the diplomatic corps, and the military are composed in a manner that accurately reflects the linguistic or national structure of the Belgian population.[45] Significant constitutional mechanisms for protecting the French-speaking minority include the parity composition of the federal government, the 'alarm bell' procedure (group veto), and the requirement of special laws, which elevate linguistic groups to central actors in federal legislative processes.[46] Characteristics of the Belgian federal system that point to a consociational model include:

1. Unique Negotiating Model: The negotiation process in Belgium is often considered more important than its outcomes. The focus is on the form of negotiation, which assumes that all parties seek fair negotiations where each party achieves some of its political goals. This model emphasizes process over substance;
2. Lack of a Central Power Base: The Belgian federal system lacks a clearly defined autonomous and institutionalized center that would protect the national interest at the federal level. This role is not fulfilled by the king, except symbolically. The absence of such a political center implies a lack of formal political hierarchy and partnership among political competitors;
3. Climate of Looseness and Confusion: The absence of a clear federal center results in a system characterized by looseness and confusion. This contradictory system leads to two main outcomes: it strengthens the

44 A. Lijphart, 'Consociational Democracy' 21(2) *World Politics* (1969) 2016.

45 Stanković, Preobražaji Federalne Države (n 6) 112. The so-called 'alarm bell' procedure allows for 25% of the MPs of any language group to interrupt parliamentary proceedings if a proposal is deemed to impinge upon the interests of their community. Then, the Federal Council of Ministers must present an amended version of the proposal within thirty days. Although theoretically, the new proposal can be approved with a simple majority, in practice, this is politically unfeasible, particularly because each of the language communities is represented by half of the senior ministers. See D. Sinardet, 'Le Fédéralisme Consociatif Belge: Vecteur d'instabilité?'136(1) *Pouvoirs* (2011) 29–30.

46 *Ibid.*

power of negotiating elite leaders while simultaneously creating a centrifugal spiral that significantly bolsters the positions of regional elites.[47] The complex federal government formation in Belgium is heavily influenced by consociational dynamics, particularly the need for consensus and effective vetoes. Since 1954, all governments have been coalition-based, bridging both ethno-linguistic and socio-economic divides. Coalition agreements, especially regarding further devolution, are built on these consensual mechanisms. While consociationalism is seen as essential for maintaining Belgian unity, it also acts as a centrifugal force, by rewarding behaviors that exacerbate ethno-linguistic tensions. This creates few incentives to bridge these divides, particularly in the lead-up to elections, where adversarial positions have often proven electorally successful, especially since the fragmentation of nation-wide political parties. The protection of minority interests, particularly for the Francophone community, often deepens frustration within the Flemish majority.[48]

The competencies of the Communities indicate that the Framework Convention for the Protection of National Minorities and the European Charter for Regional or Minority Languages have been implemented to safeguard minority rights in many areas. Additionally, linguistic minorities in the Belgian federal context enjoy full autonomy. However, the French-speaking minority in Belgium continues to express a sense of disadvantage. Despite having jurisdiction over the French-speaking Region and certain institutions in the bilingual Brussels-Capital Region, they feel constrained. They seek to extend their influence under the 'personality interpretation' of minority rights, aiming to serve all French-speaking citizens across Belgium, including in Flanders. This would involve providing financial support, such as subsidies, to French-speaking cultural associations in Dutch-speaking regions. However, this approach conflicts with the territoriality principle, which prohibits such actions beyond designated territories.[49]

An exemplary case of the application of consociational mechanisms at the regional level in federal Belgium is the Brussels-Capital Region. In this region, well-established means exist to protect the Flemish minority, which serve as equivalents to the mechanisms for protecting the French-speaking minority at the federal level.[50]

47 Despotović and Stojanović (n 18) 97.

48 Wouters and Andrione-Moylan (n 43) 764–766.

49 L. Veny and B. Warnez, 'Techniques for Protecting Minority Languages under Belgian Federalism' 23(2) *International Journal on Minority and Group Rights* (2016) 218.

50 Stanković, *Preobražaji Federalne Države* (n 6) 112.

For example, the executive of the Brussels-Capital Region is composed of an equal number of members from both the Dutch and French linguistic communities, with the exception of the Minister-President, who is typically a representative of the Francophone majority. This arrangement mirrors the constitutional norm regarding the composition of the federal government (Council of Ministers), which also includes an equal number of ministers from both language communities. The Prime Minister at the federal level is considered linguistically neutral, although the office is typically held by a member of the Flemish majority. Additionally, the Brussels regional executive is elected through a complex procedure requiring a so-called double majority.[51]

Therefore, consociational mechanisms in Belgium, both at the level of the Brussels-Capital Region and at the federal level, serve as crucial safeguards against the disintegration of the Belgian state. However, as mentioned, these mechanisms are not without their weaknesses. They can gradually deepen divisions and further institutionalise segmentation. In elections to the Brussels Regional Parliament, parties from different linguistic groups are not permitted to form pre-election coalitions, even if they share the same ideology. Each voter must indicate to which linguistic community they belong and can only vote for parties representing that community.[52]

Still, as Swenden argues, the antagonism between the Dutch and French linguistic groups is not so severe as to preclude the formation of bilingual or bicommunal electoral lists, if parties were allowed to create them.[53] Evidence supporting this claim is found in the Brussels Region, where, in the municipal elections held every six years across all 19 municipalities, alliances between Flemish and Francophone parties are permitted and frequently formed by parties with common ideologies (social democrats, greens, liberals). At this level consociational power-sharing mechanisms are underdeveloped, while these sorts of coalitions constitute about one-third of the total number of lists participating in these elections.[54]

2.2 *Germany (Bavaria)*

Bavaria, the largest state in the Federal Republic of Germany, encompasses nearly one-fifth of the nation's total land area. Its culture stands apart from other regions of Germany, having cultivated a strong Bavarian identity since its

---

51 *Ibid.*

52 *Ibid.* 112–113.

53 W. Swenden, *Federalism and Regionalism in Western Europe: A Comparative and Thematic Analysis* (Springer 2006) 284.

54 *Ibid.*

establishment as a duchy in the sixth century. Politically, Bavarians lean more conservative and Catholic compared to voters in other German regions.[55] While traditional factors such as religion and the left-right political spectrum continue to shape Bavarian politics, there's also an ongoing discourse surrounding Bavaria's semi-autonomous status.[56]

Germany's emergence in the 19th century can be attributed to the determined struggle of the German people for national unification. Factors such as ethnic homogeneity, the timing and manner of its formation, its democratic evolution, and economic strength have positioned Germany as one of the most stable federations in the world.[57] Bavaria, however, has long harbored aspirations to preserve its distinct identity, which have deep historical roots.

The German Reich, established in 1871, was a unique instance of asymmetrical monarchical federalism, a model that has not been replicated since. The 1871 Constitution created a federation led by the German Emperor, who also served as the King of Prussia. While the majority of federal units within the German Empire were monarchies – kingdoms, duchies, and principalities – the Empire also included three republican city-states: Hamburg, Bremen, and Lübeck. These federal units were not equal in status. Prussia's dominant role, solidified through its political and military successes, was evident not only in the fact that the Prussian King held the title of German Emperor but also in Prussia's significant representation in imperial institutions, enabling it to influence decisions and prevent constitutional changes.[58]

Within this framework, the Kingdom of Bavaria held a particularly privileged position, reflecting the asymmetry of German monarchical federalism. Bavaria's unique status was marked by its right to conclude international agreements (*iura singularia*), specific exemptions from federal jurisdiction (such as

---

55 The expression 'grüß Gott' is a greeting in Southern Germany and Austria (more specifically the Upper German Sprachraum, especially in Bavaria, Franconia, Swabia, Austria, and South Tyrol). Article 131(2) of the Constitution of Bavaria stipulates that 'the paramount educational goals shall be the reverence of God, respect of religious beliefs and human dignity, self-composure (…)'. <https://www.bayern.landtag.de/fileadmin/Internet_Dokumente/Sonstiges_P/BV_Verfassung_Englisch_formatiert_14-12-16.pdf>.

56 D. Eichert, 'Separation amidst Integration: The Redefining Influence of the European Union on Secessionist Party Policy' 7(2) *Journal of International Organizations Studies* (2016) 72.

57 M. Stanković, 'Secesija u Ustavnoj Praksi Federalnih Država' in Z. Knežević and K. Čavoški (eds.) *Secesija sa Stanovišta Unutrašnjeg i Međunarodnog Prava i Njene Političke Posledice* (Serbian Academy of Sciences and Arts 2020) 351.

58 V. Đurić, 'Srpsko Viđenje Državnog Uređenja Posleratne Jugoslovenske Države i Uporedno Pravo' in J. Ćirić and M. Đorđević (eds.) *Sto Godina od Početka Prvog Svetskog Rata: Istorijske i Pravne Studije* (Institut za Uporedno Pravo Intermex 2014) 685.

in the areas of railways and postal services), and a guaranteed number of seats in the Imperial Diet.[59] This special status underscores Bavaria's longstanding desire to maintain its distinctiveness within the broader German federation.

One of the distinct characteristics of Bavaria is that, traditionally, the vast majority of its population has adhered to the Catholic faith, with Protestants being a clear minority. This contrasts with other parts of Germany, where Protestants are more prevalent. Despite its cultural and political affinities with Catholic Austria rather than Protestant Prussia, Bavaria became part of the German Empire during the period from 1866 to 1871. Like other states within the German Empire, Bavaria was subjected to the hegemonic rule of Prussia, which held a dominant position in the federation, although Bavaria itself supported the idea of 'one country, two systems.' Nonetheless, Bavaria retained certain special rights within the German Empire, including the ability to maintain its own diplomatic representations abroad.[60]

The collapse of the Second Reich after World War I reignited Bavarian aspirations to preserve their distinctiveness. This period saw the emergence of various factions with different visions for Bavaria's future. Some Bavarian monarchists and nationalists advocated for restoring an independent Wittelsbach monarchy. Others supported establishing a separate Bavarian republic. A third faction pushed for union (*Anschluss*) with Austria, particularly targeting neighboring regions like North Tyrol and Upper Austria. Simultaneously, a radical communist faction seized power in Munich, briefly establishing the Bavarian Soviet Republic. Although all these efforts ultimately failed, leading to Bavaria's integration into the German Weimar Republic in 1919, the movement for self-determination persisted. The Bavarian People's Party (*Bayerische Volkspartei* – BVP) emerged as the leading advocate of separatist ideas, becoming the dominant political force in Bavaria between the two world wars.

2.2.1 German Federal Model and Bavaria

From the perspective of state organization, the Federal Republic of Germany is a federation composed of 16 federal states, known as Länder. The foundation of German federalism lies in the functional distribution of competencies, often referred to as cooperative federalism.[61] Federalism serves as the essential

59 *Ibid.* See also H. Mohnhaupt, 'Die Edition von Privilegien als Rechtsquellen in Deutschland und in ihrer Europäischen Perspektive' 7(3) *Krakowskie Studia z Historii Państwa i Prawa* (2014) 419–432.

60 Stanković, 'Secesija u Ustavnoj Praksi Federalnih Država' (n 57) 351–352.

61 S. Orlović, 'Politički Sistem, Izbori i Formiranje Vlade u Nemačkoj' (15) *Politički Život* (2018) 11. See R. Sturm, 'Cooperative Federalism and the Dominant Role of Consensus in German Federalism' *50 Shades of Federalism* (2018) (arguing that the cooperative federal-

link between the Federal Republic and its Länder, ensuring a balance of power. Over centuries, a strong sense of political and cultural unity has developed within Germany, with the Free State of Bavaria particularly valuing its rich history. This sentiment is further reinforced by Bavaria's considerable size and population, which render it one of the most influential federal states and a firm proponent of federalism.[62] Cooperative federalism in Germany involves collaboration between the federal government (Bund) and the federal units (Länder) in the execution of state functions. There is a balanced division of power and political responsibility between the federal government and the state governments. Officials from the state governments play a role in electing the Federal President and appointing judges to the main federal courts. Germany's territorial organization comprises multiple levels of government: the federal authority (Bund), 16 federal states (Länder), 401 Kreise (counties at the intermediary level, including 107 'kreisfreie Städte' and 294 'Landkreise', and 11,054 Gemeinden (municipalities at the local level).[63] The Bund functions as the central authority endowed with the powers of a federal government, while Germany is structured as a relatively decentralized federation comprising both the Länder and federal institutions. In this structure, the Bund and the Länder operate as constitutionally distinct, but interdependent, levels of government.[64] The Bund and the Länder are almost equal partners, each subject to the broader, yet somewhat loosely defined, framework of the federation.[65]

Bavaria is home to three major dialects: Bavarian, Franconian, and Swabian. Although Bavaria does not possess a distinct language like the Basques, there are notable linguistic differences within the region. A speaker of Bavarian dialect, for instance, may use it in conversation with someone from northern Germany, who might struggle to understand the exchange. Additionally, it can be challenging for Bavarians, particularly those in rural areas, to speak standard German (*Hochdeutsch*), as it is not commonly used in their daily lives.[66] The Bavarian Constitution underscores the importance of education in fostering a sense of attachment to the homeland (*Heimat*), a sentiment closely linked

ism is becoming unitary for three main reasons: the lack of a culture of federalism, the development of the welfare state, whose central promise is the idea of equality, and the centralization of the political party system).

62 J. C. Karl, 'Bavaria is Germany, Isn't it? The Case of the German Land Bavaria. A Historical and Political Approach' 3 *Revista Internacional de los Estudios Vascos* (2008) 129.

63 European Committee of the Regions, 'Germany – Division of Powers' <https://portal.cor.europa.eu/divisionpowers/Pages/Germany-Introduction.aspx>.

64 A. Gunlicks, *The Länder and German Federalism* (Manchester University Press 2003) 55.

65 G. Kisker, 'The West German Federal Constitutional Court as Guardian of the Federal System' 19(4) *Publius: The Journal of Federalism* (1989) 47–49.

66 Karl (n 62) 129.

to the use of local dialects. For many Bavarian children, these dialects serve as their mother tongue (*Muttersprache*).[67] Hochholzer notes that dialects remain the primary mode of communication for many Bavarian children and play a crucial role in preserving their regional cultural identity.[68]

The legislative authority at the federal level in Germany is vested in the Bundestag, the lower house of Parliament, and the Bundesrat, which represents the federal states and functions as the second, upper house of Parliament. The Bundestag is the primary legislative body responsible for enacting federal laws. It is composed of a minimum of 598 members, who are elected every four years through a unique electoral system that combines elements of both majority voting and proportional representation.[69]

The Bundesrat serves as the representation of the federal states in Germany. It is composed of 69 members who are not directly elected but are instead delegated by the governments of each state. The number of representatives each state is entitled to is proportional to its population. The Bundesrat plays a crucial role in the legislative process, as it must approve laws passed by the Bundestag. If the Bundesrat does not approve a particular law, the Bundestag can only enact it with a larger majority, such as an absolute majority. If all members of the Bundesrat vote against a law, it cannot be enacted in its current form.

Currently, the first chamber of the Bavarian Parliament, the Landtag, is composed of 180 members who are elected every five years under an enhanced proportional representation system.[70] The State Government holds the highest executive authority in Bavaria and is also elected for a five-year term. It is composed of the Minister-President, the State Ministers, and the State Secretaries.[71] The Minister-President plays a central role in Bavarian governance by setting the political agenda, chairing the State Government, representing Bavaria on the international stage, conferring honors and medals of merit, and overseeing the administration's activities.

The Bavarian Constitution permits any individual or association who believes their rights have been infringed to lodge a complaint with the Bavarian Constitutional Court. The Constitution also grants extensive rights to

67 E. V. Koneva and S. K. Gural, 'The Role of Dialects in the German Society' 200 *Procedia-Social and Behavioral Sciences* (2015) 249.

68 Cited in *ibid.*

69 R. Manojlović, 'Javna Uprava i Politički Sustav Savezne Republike Njemačke: Modernizacija Kroz Očuvanje Tradicije' 15(1) *Hrvatska i Komparativna Javna Uprava: Časopis za Teoriju i Praksu Javne Uprave* (2015) 145.

70 Bavarian Constitution, Articles 13–16.

71 *Ibid.* Articles 43–44.

initiate popular initiatives and referendums, mechanisms that have been frequently utilized for issues related to the Bavarian Constitution or legislation.[72] A notable example is the 1998 abolition of the Bavarian Senate, which was achieved through a referendum.[73]

Notably, Article 1 of the Bavarian Constitution defines Bavaria as a 'Free State' (*Freistaat*). As Karl observes, the framers of the Constitution deliberately opted for the term *Freistaat* to avoid using the foreign, Latin-derived term Republic. Although several German states adopted this designation after World War I to signify their new republican status, Bavaria has uniquely retained and emphasized the title as a marker of its distinct identity within Germany. This can be viewed as an assertion of ISD, namely political and cultural autonomy within an existing state.[74]

2.2.2 Bavaria's Pursuit of Self-Governance and the Question of Secession

Due to its historical and economic peculiarities, Bavaria has consistently aspired to self-govern within the framework of the German federation. This aspiration has been expressed through the programs of political parties in Bavaria. In the post-war years, two regional parties emerged in competition: the Bavarian Party (BP) and the Christian Social Union (CSU). The BP, to this day, advocates for Bavaria's separate statehood, while the CSU, an autonomist party, is fully integrated into the federal framework of German politics. Both parties promote the distinctiveness of Bavaria. To safeguard its special interests and identity, Bavaria has consistently maintained an independent stance in national affairs, promoting a decentralized model of federalism as a solution to Germany's structural challenges.[75] This position has been steadfastly championed by Bavaria's 'state party' – the CSU.[76] The CSU, established in 1945, quickly became a representative of Bavarian Christian-conservative ideology. It plays a crucial role at the intersection of religion and politics within Bavaria's national identity, significantly shaping Bavarian nationalism. Operating exclusively in Bavaria, the CSU serves as the regional counterpart to the Christian Democratic

---

72 *Ibid.* Articles 60–69. Consult W. Reutter, *Constitutional Courts in the German States History, Structure, and Functions* (Springer 2024) 73–88.

73 K.J. Nagel and A. Holesch, 'Bavaria: Another Case of a Right to Decide?' 19 *Political Theory Working Paper* (2017) 5.

74 Karl (n 62) 133.

75 See D. Dorondo, *Bavaria and German Federalism: Reich to Republic, 1918–33, 1945–49* (Springer 1992).

76 E. Hepburn and D. Hough, 'Regionalist Parties and the Mobilization of Territorial Difference in Germany' 47(1) *Government and Opposition* (2012) 82.

Union (CDU), which is active in the other German states.[77] The CSU's primary goal has been to safeguard Bavaria's distinct interests, unique identity, cultural heritage, and political autonomy. To achieve this, the party has consistently advocated for a robust form of federalism, characterized by the decentralization of powers, greater autonomy in regional policies, and a strengthened role for the Bundesrat. The CSU has portrayed Bavaria as a nation (*Heimat*) in its own right, insisting that its uniqueness deserves recognition within Germany.[78] However, Sturm argues that there is a widespread misinterpretation of the party's intentions, which is often perceived as seeking greater autonomy for Bavaria or advocating for increased decentralization of state powers in Germany.[79] According to Sturm, this misconception is partly cultivated by the party itself, which promotes its image as a champion of federalism. In reality, while the CSU maintains a distinct regional identity, its primary objective is to exert substantial influence on national politics by capitalizing on its strong electoral base in Bavaria.[80]

In early 1946, while the CSU was allowed to operate as a political party, the BP did not receive full authorization until March 1948.[81] After the war, all Bavarian parties emphasized the necessity of a federal system in Germany that would grant maximum autonomy to Bavaria. However, the Bavarian Party's (BP) advocacy for separatism remained on the fringe of political discourse and emerged too late to have a significant impact. Crucially, the BP did not exist during the drafting of Bavaria's 1946 Constitution, and did not partake in the 1949 Basic Law negotiations, as it held no government role. Bavaria ultimately abstained from ratifying the Basic Law, protesting insufficient state autonomy, while pragmatically accepting its authority.[82] The Bavarian Party primarily represented the Catholic, conservative, and agrarian values of the rural communities in Old Bavaria.[83] Unlike other parties, the BP was less inclined to pursue reconciliation between the Catholic South and the Lutheran Protestant north in Bavaria. Instead, it advocated for significant constitutional reforms, evolving

77 P. Isacks, 'Fractured Europe' (2017) <https://repository.lsu.edu/cgi/viewcontent.cgi?article=1719&context=honors_etd> 62.

78 *Ibid.* 86.

79 R. Sturm, 'Counter-Secessionism and Autonomy in the Federal System of Germany: The Case of Bavaria' in D. Muro and E. Woertz (eds.) *Secession and Counter-Secession. An International Relations Perspective* (CIDOB 2018) 93.

80 *Ibid.*

81 *Ibid.* 92.

82 *Ibid.*

83 E. Hepburn, *The New Politics of Autonomy. Territorial Strategies and the Uses of European Integration by Political Parties in Scotland, Bavaria and Sardinia 1979–2005* (European University Institute 2007) 113.

from a stance of radical federalism to one of outright separatism. This position was motivated by a desire to prevent domination by the so-called 'Prussians', whose ideal scenario, in the BP's view, would have been the establishment of a centralized state favoring the development of the northern regions.[84] The narrative advanced by the Bavarian Party suggests that Bavaria had been misled into joining the German Reich in 1871 and had since been subjected to Prussian dominance. According to this interpretation, Prussian militarism was responsible for leading Germany into two world wars, causing disproportionate suffering to the Bavarian people.[85]

The CSU still managed to win the majority of the Bavaria's electorate. Since the 1960s, the BP, limited by its narrow focus on representing the Catholic rural population, has diminished to a micro-party, unable to capture more than 5% of the vote. Although the BP's goal of achieving independence within Europe has led to a slight increase in support, this growth remains too marginal to exert any significant influence on Bavarian politics. The CSU's vision of Bavaria within Europe, integrated with Germany, continues to resonate far more strongly with voters than the idea of separation from the Federal Republic.[86]

Nagel and Holesch observe that Bavarian independence is presently not a serious political concern in Germany.[87] However, many Bavarian politicians display considerable self-assurance, frequently asserting that 'Bavaria could go it alone'. The German media often capitalizes on these assertions, questioning whether a region the size of the Czech Republic, yet perceiving itself to be as significant as Russia, can be taken seriously as an independent entity.[88]

Eberhard Sinner, then Bavarian Minister of European and Federal Affairs, made a notable statement in an interview:

> Bavaria is one of the oldest states in Europe ... We are very different from the rest of Germany, we like to be independent. We fight for more competences and powers for the regions; we are leading the fight – other regions that are hyphenated have no tradition ... Bavaria is very similar to Scotland. We see ourselves as a nation.[89]

84 *Ibid.*
85 Sturm (n 79) 92.
86 Hepburn, *The New Politics of Autonomy* (n 83) 113.
87 Nagel and Holesch (n 73) 1.
88 *Ibid.*
89 E. Hepburn, 'The Neglected Nation: The CSU and the Territorial Cleavage in Bavarian Party Politics' 17(2) *German Politics* (2008) 184.

This assertion reflects the Bavarian view of themselves as a distinct nation with aspirations for greater autonomy. The sense of distinctiveness and the right to self-determination, both internal and external, is a sentiment shared by many groups that consider themselves separate nations. Hepburn notes that Sinner's use of the term 'nation' is unusual, given that in German political discourse, the term is generally avoided due to its association with the nationalism and expansionism of the Third Reich.[90] She argues that the use of this language by CSU politicians may be a deliberate effort to align Bavaria with the category of European 'stateless nations'. In doing so, the CSU seeks recognition for Bavaria as a unique political and cultural entity, 'on a par with the stateless nations of the developed world'.[91]

Leavitt believes that Bavaria's economic transformation in the years following the Second World War played a key role in strengthening its cultural and political regionalism, thereby reducing strong calls for Bavarian secession in two significant ways. Firstly, the division of fiscal responsibilities between the Federal Government and the various Länder allowed Bavaria to tailor policies and solutions to its specific challenges, thereby addressing regional needs more effectively. Additionally, the substantial degree of economic autonomy permitted the regional government to bolster local industries. Secondly, Bavaria greatly benefited from the timing of its industrialization, which further reinforced Bavarian regionalism by strengthening its economy. From the formation of the German state until the Second World War, Bavaria's economy was predominantly agricultural and less industrialized compared to most other German regions. As a result, Bavaria was well-positioned to profit significantly from the technology transfer it either inherited or adapted from German or foreign sources.[92] This late industrialization allowed Bavaria to modernize rapidly and integrate advanced technologies, giving it a competitive edge and contributing to its economic resilience.

Thus, Bavaria has strong motives for remaining within Germany. However, as Sturm notes, the Bavarian case highlights the contradictions inherent in unitary federalism. On the one hand, Bavarian political leaders actively pursue a significant role in national politics and are willing to accept a reduction in regional autonomy as a necessary compromise. On the other hand,

90 *Ibid.* 185.

91 *Ibid.*

92 J. F. Leavitt, *Regionalism and Secession* (Doctoral dissertation, Monterey, California: Naval Postgraduate School 2015) 34–35.

the Bavarian government asserts its right to act independently whenever it is politically advantageous.[93]

Bavarian self-determination is safeguarded within the framework of the Federal Constitution (*Grundgesetz*), which grants all Länder equal rights to self-governance and constitutionally protects their autonomy. The proponents of Bavarian secession argue that Article 1, paragraph 2 of the UN Charter applies to the Bavarian people, and potentially even to its distinct cultural regions. They also invoke the 1975 OSCE Helsinki Final Act, ratified by the Federal Republic, which recognizes the right of peoples to determine their political status without external interference. Citing Article 25 of the Basic Law, these advocates maintain that the right to self-determination may have precedence under German constitutional law.[94]

Nagel and Holesch submit that according to the predominant interpretation of German constitutional history, Bavaria voluntarily joined the Federal Republic.[95] However, proponents of Bavaria's implicit right to secession contend that the *Grundgesetz* does not explicitly prohibit secession: it simply omits any mention of it.[96] Public opinion in Bavaria shows the strongest inclination towards independence compared to other federal states. For example, in 2011, 40 percent of Bavarians opted for secession. Follow-up research from 2017 indicates that 32 percent of respondents favored an independent Bavaria, separate from both the rest of Germany and the European Union.[97]

93 R. Sturm, 'Unitary Federalism–Germany Ignores the Original Spirit of its Constitution' 28 *Revista d'estudis Autonòmics i Federals* (2018) 42.

94 Nagel and Holesch (n 73) 3. See Bayernpartei, 'Eigenstaatlichkeit' <https://bayernpartei.de/eigenstaatlichkeit/>. See also 'Weiß-blaue Grundsätze der Bayernpartei' (2023) 53 <https://bayernpartei.de/programm/>. Article 25 of the German Basic Law states that 'the general rules of international law shall be an integral part of federal law' and that these rules 'take precedence over the laws and directly create rights and duties for the inhabitants of the federal territory'. However, this does not mean that self-determination, as interpreted by Bavarian secessionists, would be recognized under German law. The German legal framework and the Basic Law strongly emphasize the territorial integrity of the federal state and do not support the right to secession for any of the Länder. See also 3.3.2.2.2 referring, among others, to the Decision 2 BvR 349/16.

95 Nagel and Holesch (n 73) 4. Consult J. F. Lindner, "Austritt' des Freistaates Bayern aus der Bundesrepublik Deutschland?' 4 *Bayrische Verwaltungsblätter* (2014) 97–102.

96 *Ibid.*

97 Daily Sabah, 'Almost 1 in 3 Bavarians for Independence from Germany and EU' (18 Jul. 2017) <https://www.dailysabah.com/europe/2017/07/18/almost-1-in-3-bavarians-for-independence-from-germany-and-eu>.

3 Internal Self-determination in Unitary European States

3.1 *Finland*

In ethnic terms, Finland is often considered one of the most homogeneous countries in Europe. However, this assessment primarily stems from Finland's categorization of its population by native language rather than ethnicity.[98] Finland does not explicitly affirm, neither through its parliament nor its constitution, multinationalism, and the Swedish-speaking Finns, who comprise approximately 5.3% of the total population, are officially described as a 'linguistic minority'.[99] This minority is not only notable for its size but also for its unique legal and cultural status within Finland. The highest concentration of Swedish-speaking Finns is found in the Åland Islands, where they constitute around 88% of the population. The Åland Islands are distinct in terms of their extensive autonomy and special rights to preserve the Swedish language and culture. However, it is important to note that Åland residents represent only about 5% of the entire Swedish-speaking minority in Finland, meaning their circumstances differ considerably from those of Swedish speakers in other parts of the country.

The issue of the right to self-determination in Finland is characterized by three main factors: official bilingualism, a three-tiered governance structure, and the distinct case of self-determination for the Sámi people. In the following paragraphs, these factors will be examined to illustrate how Finland interprets and implements the internal right of peoples to self-determination.

3.1.1 Bilingualism

For centuries, Finland was an integral part of the Kingdom of Sweden, during which the majority of the population spoke Finnish. However, Swedish was the language of administration, law, and higher education. Following Finland's separation from Sweden in 1808–1809, the country became a Grand Duchy within the Russian Empire. During this transition, Sweden's Constitution and laws were largely retained within Finnish jurisdiction, and the administrative

98 N. Raduški, 'Položaj Nacionalnih Manjina u Razvijenim Evropskim Zemljama' 3 *Migracijske i Etničke Teme* (2008) 245.

99 Minority Rights Group, 'Finland' <https://minorityrights.org/country/finland/>; Multiculturalism Policies in Contemporary Democracies, 'Finland' <https://www.queensu.ca/mcp/national-minorities/resultsbycountry-nm/finland-nm>. See Venice Commission, 'Comments on the Constitution of Finland' (13 Sep. 2007), CDL(2007)075, 5 (raising the question of the scope of Finland's ratification of the Framework Convention on National Minorities in light of the phrase 'other groups' mentioned in section 17(3), which does not let one to conclude who actually counts as a 'national minority').

and judicial systems continued to function much as they had before, with Swedish remaining the predominant language.[100]

During the initial two decades of Russian rule, Finland enjoyed significant autonomy, which laid the groundwork for the development of the Finnish state.[101] The Lutheran Church maintained its prominent position in Finnish society, and Swedish remained the official language. This period of autonomy coincided with a rise in national romanticism, which fostered a growing sense of Finnish identity and led to efforts to distance the country from both Russian and Swedish influences in social and cultural affairs. This national awakening (*Kansallinen herääminen*) gave rise to a strong movement advocating for the increased use of the Finnish language in education, research, and administration. From the mid-1860s onward, significant efforts were made to elevate Finnish to a functional language for education, administration, and judicial purposes.[102] In 1863, an imperial decree officially recognized both Swedish and Finnish as the official languages of autonomous Finland, for use in administration and courts. However, the establishment of these two official languages was not without challenges and can be seen as the beginning of a linguistic divide between the Finnish and Swedish-speaking populations.[103]

In December 1917, the Finnish Parliament declared Finland's independence. Following a brief and intense civil war in the first half of 1918, Finland was established as a republic in 1919. That same year, a Constitutional Act was enacted, officially declaring Finland a bilingual country. Section 14 of this Act stipulated that the national languages of Finland would be Finnish and Swedish.[104] Moreover, it granted individuals the right to use their native language – either Finnish or Swedish – when presenting cases before courts of law and administrative authorities. They were also entitled to receive judgments and decisions in their own language, ensuring linguistic equality in legal and administrative matters.

Finland's independence was soon recognized by several countries, including Sweden, which notably did not condition its recognition on guarantees for the Swedish-speaking population. Sweden showed limited interest in the

100 M. J. R. Suksi, 'Legal Implications of the Constitutional Principle of two National Languages in Finland: Symmetry with the Possibility of Asymmetry' (67) *Revista de Llengua i Dret* (2017) 10.

101 S. Latomaa and P. Nuolijärvi, 'The Language Situation in Finland' 3(2) *Current Issues in Language Planning* (2002) 97.

102 Suksi, 'Legal Implications of the Constitutional Principle' (n 100) 10–11.

103 *Ibid.*

104 Constitution Act of Finland (1919).

status of Swedish speakers beyond its borders, although there was significant interest in the Åland Islands, likely due to military considerations.[105]

In the aftermath of World War I, Finland sought to distance itself from the newly established states that formed its 'formal' reference group in global politics. Instead, Finland aimed to emphasize the continuity of its statehood, tracing its origins back to the 19th century. This strategic positioning was intended to assert Finland's identity as an established state when engaging with the international community, especially at a time when other, long-established states were reasserting their presence on the global stage.

Finland's diplomatic efforts were successful. In July 1921, the League of Nations did not require Finland to conclude a minority protection treaty, a demand routinely imposed on newly independent states. This decision distinguished Finland from its peers by acknowledging its claim to institutional continuity and established statehood rooted in the autonomous Grand Duchy period. The emphasis on historical continuity allowed Finland to navigate international relations effectively and to establish itself as a distinct entity in the post-World War I geopolitical landscape.[106]

According to Section 51 of the Constitution of Finland (731/1999), 'the Finnish or Swedish languages are used in parliamentary work'. As noted by Suksi, this provision allows for speeches in both Finnish and Swedish during plenary sessions and committee meetings of the Parliament.[107] However, additional language regulations are provided in the parliament's Rules of Procedure, specifically in Section 76, which establishes Finnish as the primary working language in plenary sessions.[108] In essence, this means that the Finnish text serves as the foundation for parliamentary proceedings, while the Swedish text is prepared thereafter by the parliament's translation services. Despite this, the final legislative documents – referred to as the Parliament's answer – along with other official documents such as committee opinions, statements, and written proposals from the Speaker's Council, are issued in both Finnish and Swedish. If any issues arise in the formulation of the Swedish version of the Parliament's answer to the government, it falls upon the Speaker's Council to resolve them.

In accordance with Section 17(1) of the Finnish Constitution, Finnish and Swedish are recognized as the national languages of Finland. Section 17(3) further acknowledges the Sámi, Roma, and sign languages, designating them as minority languages relative to the national languages, which function as

105 Suksi, 'Legal Implications of the Constitutional Principle' (n 100) 13.

106 *Ibid.*

107 *Ibid.* 16.

108 The Rules of Procedure of the Parliament <https://www.global-regulation.com/translation/finland/646351/the-rules-of-procedure-of-the-parliament.html>.

majority languages. Section 17(2) of the Constitution guarantees 'the right of everyone to use his or her own language, either Finnish or Swedish, before courts of law and other authorities, and to receive official documents in that language'. Furthermore, 'the public authorities shall provide for the cultural and societal needs of the Finnish-speaking and Swedish-speaking populations of the country on an equal basis'. The first sentence of this provision underscores the fundamental right of individuals to receive decisions regarding their rights, benefits, or obligations in their own language. However, this right is not directly applicable and enforceable at the constitutional level; instead, it is implemented through legislative acts passed by parliament.[109]

The second sentence of Section 17(2) permits positive discrimination in favor of one linguistic group, provided that legitimate and objective reasons exist for such preferential treatment. While there is no single comprehensive statute that ensures the linguistic rights outlined in Section 17(2), several legislative acts collectively contribute to this guarantee. Among these, the Language Act (423/2003) is the primary legislation that establishes the fundamental provisions for implementing the linguistic rights guaranteed by Section 17(2) of the Constitution.[110]

The Language Act incorporates a dual approach, combining the territorial principle with the principle of individual rights, which results in a nuanced application of constitutional linguistic rights across Finland. This approach allows for a tailored provision of linguistic services based on the linguistic composition of municipalities. Specifically, bilingual municipalities – where either the Finnish – or Swedish-speaking population exceeds 8 percent of the total inhabitants, or where the minority population numbers at least 3,000 persons – are required to provide equal services in the language of the minority.[111] This framework represents a slight departure from the universal application of linguistic rights throughout the entire country, reflecting the need to address the specific linguistic needs of different regions.[112] The Language Act of 2003 is largely based on the earlier Act of 1922, particularly in its approach to categorizing municipalities by language and defining the duties of authorities.

---

109 Suksi, 'Legal Implications of the Constitutional Principle' (n 100) 18.

110 P. Tallroth, 'Multilingualism in Finland: A Legal Perspective' 1 *International Journal of Language & Law* (2012) 37.

111 Section 5(2) provides that 'a municipality is designated bilingual if the population includes both Finnish and Swedish speakers and the minority comprises at least eight percent of the population or at least 3,000 persons. A bilingual municipality is designated unilingual if the minority comprises less than 3,000 persons and its proportion has decreased below six percent'. It remains pretty unclear how to treat the middle zone.

112 Suksi, 'Legal Implications of the Constitutional Principle' (n 100) 18–19.

According to the Language Act, both Swedish-speaking and Finnish-speaking citizens have the right to use their respective languages in interactions with central authorities and within bilingual municipalities.[113] Authorities are required to provide services in both national languages proactively, without waiting for a specific request. Moreover, they are obligated to ensure that signs, forms, brochures, and other written materials are accessible and prominently displayed in both languages. In practice, this means that individuals registered as Swedish speakers receive all state-level documents, such as tax declarations and information about presidential and parliamentary elections, in Swedish. However, at the municipal level, the availability of services in a particular language depends on whether the municipality is officially bilingual or not.[114]

Suksi observes that, since significant legal sources in the Finnish legal system are issued in both Finnish and Swedish, individuals working within public authorities and courts of law, regardless of the language used, can comprehend the legislator's intent concerning specific legal provisions.[115] However, it is important to highlight that decisions in legal proceedings are published in the language in which the proceedings were initiated. Consequently, jurisprudence, which constitutes another critical source of law, is typically available only in Finnish, rather than in both languages.[116]

3.1.2 Three Levels of Governance

Finland operates under a governmental system structured across three levels: the central government, 19 regions, and 310 municipalities.[117] Although Finland is a unitary state, it is characterized by a significant degree of decentralization, with substantial responsibilities and powers devolved to local governments, while the central government maintains a regulatory role. Like Sweden, Finland follows a model of 'centrally framed local autonomy', in which municipalities enjoy significant discretion in managing and financing local policies, whereas the state sets the overarching regulatory framework to mitigate regional

113 O. P. Salo, 'Finland's Official Bilingualism – a Bed of Roses or of Procrustes?' in J. Blommaert et al (eds.) *Dangerous multilingualism: Northern Perspectives on Order, Purity and Normality* (Palgrave Macmillan 2012) 28.

114 *Ibid.*

115 M. Suksi, 'Finnish and Swedish as National Languages of Finland: A Linguistic Human Rights Success Story – Why and How?' in T. Skutnabb-Kangas and R. Phillipson (eds.) *The Handbook of Linguistic Human Rights* (Wiley Blackwell 2022) 449.

116 *Ibid.*

117 European Committee of the Regions, 'Finland – Fiscal Powers' <https://portal.cor.europa.eu/divisionpowers/Pages/Finland-Fiscal-Powers.aspx>.

disparities.[118] With the key role of the central and local authorities, the role of the mid-level authorities (i.e. regional level) has remained minor.[119] While Finland has primarily implemented administrative decentralization, Sweden has also embraced political and fiscal decentralization. In Finland, the extent of decentralization has largely been confined to deconcentration and delegation, whereas Sweden has pursued devolution as well.[120]

Local self-government in Finland traces its origins to legislation from the 1860s, which continues to underpin the current system's core principles. Following Finland's independence from Russia in 1917, new legislation was enacted, introducing universal direct suffrage at the municipal level. Since then, local government has gradually evolved. A significant milestone occurred in 1995 with the adoption of the Local Government Act, which was later revised in 2015. Both the Constitution and the Act underline that local government administration must be founded on self-government by citizens.[121] Additionally, the Åland Islands have been granted special status as a self-governing, unilingual province since 1921, designed to preserve the Swedish language, culture, and traditional local institutions on the archipelago.[122]

In October 1991, Finland acceded to the European Charter of Local Self-Government reflecting the country's longstanding commitment to the

---

118 See V. Renko et al., 'Pursuing Decentralisation: Regional Cultural Policies in Finland and Sweden' 28(3) *International Journal of Cultural Policy* (2022) 344. See OECD, 'Making Decentralisation Work: A Handbook for Policy-Makers' (2019) 50 (showing Finland as a country with highly decentralised spending and high tax revenues).

119 Y. Kazepov, *Rescaling Social Policies towards Multilevel Governance in Europe* (Routledge 2010) 56.

120 Deconcentration involves the redistribution of authority only within the central government, where selected functions are taken over by the field offices of the central government on a regional level. See A. Bajo, I. Klemenčić and M. Primorac, 'Asimetrična Decentralizacija Na Primjeru Odabranih Država Članica Europske Unije' 16(1) *Hrvatska i Komparativna Javna Uprava: Časopis za Teoriju i Praksu Javne Uprave* (2016) 41. See also M. Rossi, 'Decentralization – Initial Experiences and Expectations of the SDC' in C. Vuffray et al. (eds.) *Décentralisation et Développement* (Swiss Development Cooperation 1999) 17. In Finland, the transfer of authority to the regional level has taken place as deconcentration where the state has redistributed authority only within the central government. The transfer of the authority to the regional government bodies has taken place administratively but it has not been based on regional policy or distinctions. Renko, 'Pursuing Decentralisation' (n 118) 351.

121 See Council of Europe, 'Structure and Operation of Local and Regional Democracy: Finland' (Council of Europe Publishing 1997) 5.

122 Self-Administration in Åland Act (1144/91).

principles of local self-governance.[123] The Charter defines local self-government as 'the right and the ability of local authorities, within the limits of the law, to regulate and manage a substantial share of public affairs under their own responsibility and in the interests of the local population'. This right is to be exercised by councils or assemblies composed of members freely elected by secret ballot, based on direct, equal, and universal suffrage, with the possibility of establishing executive organs or committees accountable to them.[124] Article 3 of the Charter acknowledges that, in certain instances, the legal authority to administer public affairs may require more specific definition through national legislation. Nevertheless, the article emphasizes the autonomy of local authorities, which are intended to operate under their own responsibility rather than merely as extensions of national authorities.[125] The Charter intentionally refrains from exhaustively defining the powers of local authorities, recognizing the complexity of interpreting what constitutes 'local affairs'. Restricting local authorities to matters of limited significance could marginalize their role and ISD of the people concerned while issues such as national defense are typically reserved for central authorities. The Charter's aim is for local authorities to possess a broad range of responsibilities that can be effectively managed at the local level.[126]

Finland has fully internalized this concept. The country can be described as a 'municipal state', where municipalities have traditionally played pivotal role in governance, being responsible for approximately two-thirds of all public services. As a result, the scope of local government in Finland is extensive.[127]

Today, the fundamental principles of local self-government in Finland include: (a) representative decision-making, (b) task and service responsibilities, (c) the power to plan and organize economic and administrative matters, and (d) the right to taxation.[128] The Local Government Act outlines the

123 European Charter of Local Self-Government (15 Oct. 1985) <https://rm.coe.int/european-charter-of-local-self-government-eng/1680a87cc3>.

124 *Ibid.* Article 3.

125 Explanatory Report to the European Charter of Local Self-Government (15 Oct. 1985) 4, <https://rm.coe.int/16800ca437>.

126 *Ibid.* 4–5.

127 H. Vakkala, L. M. Sinervo and A. Jäntti, 'Local Self-government in Finland' in B. Brezovnik et al. (eds.) *Local Self-Government in Europe* (Institute for Local Self-Government 2021) 180.

128 Municipalities have the authority to impose a flat percentage income tax, typically ranging from 16 to 22 percent, and are responsible for delivering two-thirds of public services. They manage various community services, including schools, healthcare, water supply, and local streets. See Sections 51(5) and 66 of the Act. However, the maintenance of highways, lawmaking, and policing fall under the jurisdiction of the central government. Local Government Act (365/1995; amendments up to 325/2012 included) <https://www.finlex.fi/en/laki/kaannokset/1995/en19950365_20120325.pdf>.

autonomy, organizational structure, decision-making authority, and responsibilities of municipalities, ensuring that these principles continue to guide local governance.

3.1.3 The Question of the Sámi People

The Sámi homelands (*Sápmi*) are situated in Lapland, the northernmost region of Europe, spanning the Norwegian provinces of Finnmark, Tromsø, and parts of Nordland, as well as the northernmost areas of Sweden and Finland. These territories also extend to the Kola Peninsula in Russia.[129]

The Sámi people have endured centuries of marginalization in Finland, both legally and socially. Legal marginalization has occurred through laws affecting traditional practices such as reindeer herding, fishing, and education. Socio-psychologically, the Sámi have been viewed by many Finns as less valuable and uncivilized, perpetuating their marginalized status.[130] The Finnish authorities, in favor of state interests, considered the Sámi to be a primitive people who had 'a similar relationship to land as to the air'.[131] This assumption was used to justify the confiscation of land from the Sámi people.[132] However, since the 1970s, all Nordic governments have advocated for the preservation of Sámi culture in the international arena.

The Sámi people's struggle for their rights has led to several significant milestones: the inclusion of a provision in the 1995 Constitution that recognizes the Sámi as the indigenous people of Finland, affirming their rights in accordance with Article 27 of the International Covenant on Civil and Political Rights, the adoption of the Sámi Parliament Act; and an increasing judicial recognition of Sámi rights, particularly concerning issues related to their traditional way of life. While these decisions have affirmed the importance of indigenous rights for the Sámi within the framework of Finnish law, they have rarely placed Sámi interests above competing state or private interests.[133] The Human Rights Committee has established a test to determine what constitutes a prohibited denial of cultural rights under Article 27 of the ICCPR. In the case of *Länsman*

129 R. Toivanen, 'The Saami People and Nordic Civil Societies' in N. Götz and J. Hackmann (eds.) *Civil Society in the Baltic Sea Region* (Routledge 2017) 235.

130 R. Toivanen, 'From Ignorance to Effective Inclusion: The Role of National Minorities within the Finnish Consensus Culture' in P. A. Kraus and P. Kivisto (eds.) *The Challenge of Minority Integration Politics and Policies in the Nordic Nations* (DeGruyter 2015) 122.

131 Toivanen, 'The Saami People and Nordic Civil Societies' (n 129) 282.

132 *Ibid.*

133 M. Scheinin, 'Indigenous Peoples' Right to Fish: Recent Recognition of Sámi Rights in Finland Through Civil Disobedience and Criminal Trial' in D. Cambou and Ø. Ravna (eds.) *The Significance of Sámi Rights* (Routledge 2023) 37.

v. Finland, the Committee determined that minorities or indigenous peoples have the right to protect their traditional activities, such as hunting, fishing, and, as in this specific case, reindeer herding.[134] The Committee concluded that state measures threatening these activities could amount to a denial of the right to enjoy minority culture.[135] This line of reasoning was further upheld in the case of *Äärelä and Näkkäläjärvi v. Finland*, where the petitioners, who were reindeer herders and members of the indigenous Sámi community, claimed a violation of Article 27.[136] They argued that permitting the construction of a road in an area used for reindeer herding constituted, among other things, a denial of their right to enjoy their own culture, *ergo* ISD, with reindeer herding being an integral part of that culture.[137]

In addressing the claim of a violation of Article 27 of the Covenant, the Committee first established that the petitioners were unquestionably members of a minority culture and that reindeer herding was an essential part of their cultural identity. The Committee then reiterated that the key question in such cases is whether the impact on reindeer herding is so significant that the state has failed to protect the petitioners' right to enjoy their culture. This standard is referred to as the 'sustainability criterion'.[138] In this specific case, based on the facts presented, the Committee was unable to determine whether the logging activities in question failed to meet this criterion.[139]

A significant aspect of this case, however, is the Finnish government's emphasis on the importance of effective participation by the individuals involved in decision-making processes affecting them, in line with the Committee's previous practice. The Finnish government referenced the *Länsman* case, noting that the Committee, in that instance, focused on whether the individuals involved had been able to participate meaningfully in decisions regarding their rights and interests.[140]

Despite positive developments, there have also been notable setbacks, such as the disregard for internal self-determination of the Sámi by the Supreme Administrative Court of Finland. When ruling on who is eligible to participate

---

134 Human Rights Committee, *Jouni E. Länsman et al. v. Finland*, Communication No. 671/1995 (30 Oct. 1996) para 10.2.

135 *Ibid.* paras 10.1, 10.4.

136 Human Rights Committee, *Äärelä and Näkkäläjärvi v. Finland*, Communication No. 779/1997 (24 Oct. 2001).

137 *Ibid.* para 3.1. See also Human Rights Committee, *Ailsa Roy v. Australia*, Communication No. 3585/2019 (15 Mar. 2023) para 3.13.

138 F. Viljoen, 'Fact-Finding by UN Human Rights Complaints Bodies – Analysis and Suggested Reforms' 8 *Max Planck Yearbook of United Nations Law* (2004) 70.

139 *Äärelä and Näkkäläjärvi v. Finland* (n 136) para 7.6.

140 *Ibid.* para 4.6.

in the elections for the Sámi Parliament, the Court diverged from the traditional interpretation of Section 3 of the Act on the Sámi Parliament and permitted applications from individuals who had been deemed ineligible to vote by the Sámi Parliament itself.[141]

As a result, a petition was submitted to the Human Rights Committee, alleging, among other things, a violation of Article 27 of the ICCPR. The petition underscored the critical role of the Sámi Parliament in protecting the Sámi people's right to enjoy their culture and language, noting that even the State party recognized the Sámi Parliament as 'the conduit for securing the free, prior, and informed consent of the Sámi people in matters that may affect their interests'.[142] The Committee criticized the Supreme Administrative Court for relying on 'overall consideration' based on a person's self-identification as Sámi rather than adhering to the formal criteria in Section 3. This approach undermined the Sámi Parliament's authority to determine Sámi identity, a vital aspect of Sámi self-determination. Consequently, Finland was urged to ensure that the criteria for voting eligibility in Sámi Parliament elections respect the Sámi people's right to internal self-determination, in line with Articles 25 and 27 of the Covenant.[143]

The *Vetsijoki* case before the Finnish Supreme Court is also significant, as it addresses the infringement of the traditional fishing rights of the Sámi people. In July 2017, three women and the teenage son of one of them were caught engaging in deliberate illegal salmon fishing on the banks of the Deatnu (Teno) River, which lies on the border between Finland and Norway and is renowned as one of the best rivers for salmon fishing in Europe. The women, all members of the Sámi community and active as Sámi politicians and activists, claimed ancestral fishing rights in the area, passed down through generations. Nevertheless, the Finnish authorities required them to obtain daily fishing licences sold by the state-owned enterprise responsible for forest and water management. The new regulations, which were enacted without the statutory requirement of negotiations with the Sámi, imposed

141 According to Section 3, a Sámi means a person who considers himself a Sámi, provided: (1) that he himself or at least one of his parents or grandparents has learnt Sámi as his first language; (2) that he is a descendent of a person who has been entered in a land, taxation or population register as a mountain, forest or fishing Lapp; or (3) that at least one of his parents has or could have been registered as an elector for an election to the Sámi Delegation or the Sámi Parliament.

142 Human Rights Committee, *Tiina Sanila-Aikio v. Finland*, Communication No. 2668/2015 (1 Nov. 2018) para 1.2.

143 *Ibid.* para 6.11. Note that the violation was established 'under article 25, read alone and in conjunction with article 27, as interpreted in the light of article 1 of the Covenant'.

strict restrictions on traditional and subsistence fishing by the Sámi, while simultaneously making allowances for tourist fishing.[144]

After these three women and a teenager (who was of the age of criminal responsibility) were prosecuted for illegal fishing, they were initially acquitted based on the constitutional and human rights they possess as members of the Sámi indigenous community. However, the prosecutor appealed the acquittal directly to the Supreme Court. In April 2022, the Supreme Court upheld the acquittal of all defendants. The Court recognized that Section 10 of the Fishing Act requires Sámi individuals to carry a valid fishing permit for the type of fishing the defendants engaged in.[145] Therefore, the Court had to determine whether applying this regulation as a basis for criminal conviction was in manifest conflict with the Constitution. Notably, it cited Section 17(3) of the Constitution, which grants the Sámi, as an indigenous people, the right to maintain and develop their own language and culture.[146] The Court acknowledged that salmon fishing in the Deatnu River is deeply intertwined with Sámi culture, and that the use of a fishing rod, as in this case, is integral to that cultural practice.[147] Drawing on case law from the Human Rights Committee, the Supreme Court concluded that the concept of 'culture' includes, particularly for indigenous peoples, their traditional forms of economic activity.[148]

The Court also determined that the constitutionally protected fishing rights of the local Sámi are not absolute, as they can be limited by the right to a healthy environment provided in Section 20 of the Constitution, particularly to protect stocks of migratory fish.[149] However, the Court ultimately found that Section 10 of the Fishing Act imposed significant limitations on the fishing rights integral to the Sámi people's culture, as it subjected members of this indigenous community to the same conditions as other individuals. The limited availability of fishing permits, which were often sold to tourists before Sámi individuals could obtain them, highlighted the lack of a specific quota for the Sámi, thereby disproportionately affecting their ability to practice their traditional fishing rights.[150]

The Court explicitly established that treating indigenous Sámi in the same manner as non-indigenous individuals can, in itself, constitute a violation of

144 Scheinin (n 133) 40.
145 KKO 2022:26, para 16.
146 *Ibid.* para 21.
147 *Ibid.* para 22.
148 *Ibid.* para 25.
149 *Ibid.* para 42.
150 *Ibid.* paras 43–44.

Sámi rights.[151] In doing so, the Supreme Court aligned with the approach of the European Court of Human Rights, which has held that treating individuals identically when they are in different situations may constitute prohibited discrimination. In addition to this ruling, the Supreme Court of Finland has issued two more judgments related to the protection of fishing rights for members of the Sámi people.[152] This represents a significant advancement in recognizing the rights of the Sámi as indigenous peoples, particularly in acknowledging that their traditional fishing practices are integral to their cultural self-determination, taking into account factors such as timing, location, and fishing methods.

However, as Scheinin has noted, these judgments also have certain shortcomings. For instance, the Supreme Court overlooked intergenerational cultural transmission as a core dimension of indigenous 'culture' under international law. Moreover, while acknowledging fishing as a traditional economic activity tied to self-determination, the Court failed to address its socio-cultural centrality – specifically, how salmon fishing sustains Sámi language preservation, kinship networks, and collective identity beyond mere subsistence.[153]

Other scholars, like Toivanen, regard Finland's failure to ratify the International Labour Organisation's (ILO) Convention 169 as a denial of internal self-determination for the indigenous Sámi population. Toivanen argues that ratification would compel Finland to more rigorously respect the land rights of the Sámi people, including their entitlement to use traditional lands for social and economic purposes.[154] Historically, these lands belonged to Sámi villages, but now about 90 percent of them are under state ownership. Despite repeated promises to ratify the Convention, Finland has yet to do so. The Committee on the Elimination of Racial Discrimination, among others, highlighted this need in its 2009 and 2017 concluding observations.[155] Land disputes persist, and in 2015, the United Nations Special Rapporteur on the rights of indigenous peoples criticized Finland's draft law on the management of state-owned

151 *Ibid.* para 40.

152 Supreme Court of Finland, KKO:2022:25; Lapland District Court (*Lapin käräjäoikeus*), Judgment No. 22/130234 of 12 August 2022.

153 Scheinin (n 133) 47.

154 Toivanen, 'From Ignorance to Effective Inclusion' (n 130) 123. See Article 7 of the ILO Convention. Note that Finland in 2007 voted for the adoption of the UN Declaration of the Rights of Indigenous Peoples.

155 CERD, 'Consideration of Reports Submitted by States Parties Under Article 9 of the Convention. Concluding observations: Finland' (13 Mar. 2009) UN Doc. CERD/C/FIN/CO/19; CERD, 'Concluding observations on the twenty-third periodic report of Finland' (8 Jun. 2017) UN Doc. CERD/C/FIN/CO/23.

lands. This draft law proposed transferring authority for logging activities on state-owned lands, including those in the Sámi Homeland region, to a state-owned enterprise. The Special Rapporteur specifically condemned the lack of consultation with the Sámi people regarding the draft law, viewing it as a violation of the Declaration on the Rights of Indigenous Peoples, which Finland has endorsed.[156]

4 Internal Self-determination in Former European States

4.1 *The Historical Case of Yugoslav Federalism and Its Implications Today*

The following analysis examines the application of internal self-determination in the context of the disintegration of Yugoslavia, focusing on how this right was interpreted by the inhabitants of the states and quasi-states that emerged from the former federation. To properly assess the application of self-determination in the Yugoslav case, it is essential first to establish a definition of the 'Yugoslav people'. However, this proves problematic, given that the legal definition of a 'people' for the purposes of self-determination often lacks precision, a point that has been previously demonstrated.

The 1974 Yugoslav Constitution provides some insight into this issue. In the introductory part, where the basic principles are outlined, it states:

> The nations of Yugoslavia, proceeding from the right of every nation to self-determination, including the right to secession (...) have, together with the nationalities with which they live, united in a federal republic of free and equal nations and nationalities and founded a socialist federal community of working people – the Socialist Federal Republic of Yugoslavia.[157]

This provision explicitly recognizes self-determination, including secession, as a foundational principle within the multi-ethnic structure of the Socialist Federal Republic of Yugoslavia (SFRY). Crucially, it establishes that only the

---

156 UN Press Release, 'Finland/Indigenous peoples: New Bill Threatens Sami's Rights to Their Traditional Lands and Livelihood' (17 Dec. 2015) <https://www.ohchr.org/en/press-releases/2015/12/finland-indigenous-peoples-new-bill-threatens-samis-rights-their-traditional?LangID=E&NewsID=16897>.

157 Constitution of Yugoslavia (1947), Basic Principles, pt. I, para 1.

designated 'nations' (*narodi*), not 'nationalities' (*narodnosti*), were bearers of the right to self-determination within the SFRY. The term 'nationality' began to be used in 1974 to refer to national minorities. However, in the Yugoslav context, nationality was a specific political designation denoting a status more significant than that of a minority, yet not on par with that of the constituent peoples.[158] Thus, rather than the concepts of 'nation and national minority', the terms 'people and nationality' (*narod i narodnost*) were employed to describe the various groups within Yugoslavia. The Constitution of the SFRY restricted the right to self-determination, including the right to secession, to the six constituent peoples: Slovenes, Croats, Muslims (Bosniaks), Serbs, Montenegrins, and Macedonians.[159] Yugoslav nationalities, such as the Albanians, who were the largest of these groups, did not enjoy the constitutional right to self-determination, including the right to secession. Furthermore, while the constitutional recognition of self-determination implicitly included secession, this right could not be exercised unilaterally. As Simović observes, the placement of this provision within the preamble's basic principles suggests its function was primarily symbolic rather than operational, serving to emphasize the state's voluntary foundation rather than establishing an actionable legal mechanism.[160]

The constitutional crisis in Yugoslavia arose from disputes over the future political relations between the federal republics and autonomous provinces. The process of the SFRY's disintegration is generally considered to have begun in 1990 and culminated in the signing of the Dayton Peace Agreement on 14 December 1995.

Yugoslav federalism underwent significant evolution from the late 1940s until the 1980s.[161] Following Tito's death in 1980, nationalist sentiments within Yugoslavia's ethnic communities began to intensify. For instance, in 1981, Albanian uprisings in Kosovo marked the first significant manifestation of nationalism since the Croatian nationalist movement of 1971.[162] The Albanians demanded recognition as a constituent nation and the elevation of Kosovo's status to

158 M. Marković, *Samoopredeljenje Između Autonomije i Otcepljenja* (Helsinki Committee for Human Rights 1998) 12.

159 Article 1 of the Constitution.

160 D. Simović, 'Raspad Jugoslavije i Pravo Na Secesiju u Svetlosti Uporednog Ustavnog Prava' in Z. Knežević and K. Čavoški (eds.) *Secesija sa Stanovišta Unutrašnjeg i Međunarodnog Prava i Njene Političke Posledice* (Serbian Academy of Sciences and Arts 2020) 409–410.

161 P. Radan, *The Break-up of Yugoslavia and International Law* (Routledge 2002) 153.

162 A. Pavković, *The Fragmentation of Yugoslavia: Nationalism and War in the Balkans* (Palgrave Macmillan 2000) 86–87.

that of a republic. The federal authorities, with the support of all republics, suppressed these uprisings. However, tensions continued to rise, particularly regarding the status of Kosovo. Serbia's push to reintegrate Kosovo met opposition from other republics, notably Slovenia. Serbia ultimately achieved this through amendments to the Serbian Constitution in February 1989 and July 1990, which effectively dismantled Kosovo's autonomy within Serbia. The dissolution of the Kosovar Parliament and the imposition of direct rule from Belgrade marked a significant shift in the region's political landscape.

As the political crisis deepened, differing visions for the future of Yugoslavia emerged among its republics. Serbia advocated for a more centralized federation, while other republics, particularly Croatia and Slovenia, favored transforming Yugoslavia into a confederation of sovereign states.[163] In the first half of 1991, a series of summits among the republic presidents yielded proposals for the constitutional restructuring of Yugoslavia, with some drafts effectively envisioning its division into independent states. The presidents of Bosnia and Herzegovina and Macedonia sought a middle ground between centralization and disintegration, proposing a flexible model of relations between the republics.[164]

During this period of heightened political tensions, the international community began to focus more intently on the fate of Yugoslavia. Although international leaders called for the preservation of Yugoslavia's integrity and condemned secessionist threats, such pronouncements were largely rhetorical. The United States, in particular, expressed support for maintaining Yugoslavia's territorial unity but made it clear that they would not engage militarily to enforce this objective. As it became increasingly apparent that the international community would refrain from active intervention in the Yugoslav crisis, leaders in Slovenia and Croatia interpreted this as tacit approval – or a 'green light' – to advance their secessionist agendas.[165]

Concurrently, Yugoslavia's dissolution refocused great-power attention on the unresolved 'Eastern Question', echoing historical patterns in Balkan conflicts. As Radan observes, 'the disintegration of Yugoslavia became a laboratory for these great powers to reformulate and enforce a new understanding of the

163 Radan, *The Break-up of Yugoslavia* (n 161) 154.
164 Pavković, *The Fragmentation of Yugoslavia* (n 162) 125–127.
165 Radan, *The Break-up of Yugoslavia* (n 161) 155–156.

right of peoples to self-determination'.[166] This recalibration was amplified by the post-1989 surge in self-determination claims across Eastern Europe, with the Yugoslav crisis epitomizing the region's destabilizing potential.

4.1.1 Internal Self-determination in Serbian Municipalities in Croatia

The 1990 Preamble to the Croatian Constitution reaffirmed the 'millenary statehood' of Croatia, emphasizing both the thousand-year identity of the Croatian nation and the continuity of its statehood.[167] It established the Republic of Croatia as the national state of the Croatian people, while also recognizing it as the state of members of autochthonous national minorities.[168]

For the Serbs, being classified as a national minority was unacceptable, especially considering that under the 1974 Yugoslav Constitution, they had the status of a constituent people.[169] As Jović notes, the peoples and nationalities of the former Yugoslavia were deeply concerned about the prospect of becoming minorities within the newly established states. This status was seen not only as a marker of subordination but also as a loss of previously acquired rights.[170] The political and legal implications of the change in the Serbs' status were significant. As Tuđman repeatedly emphasized, by being reclassified as a minority, the Serbs were effectively deprived of the right to self-determination.[171] This denial was further entrenched by Article 6 of the 1990 Constitution, which declared that any activities by 'any political party' that threatened Croatia's 'independence, unity, or territorial integrity' constituted a criminal offense.

In late 1991, under pressure from the international community, Croatia adopted the Constitutional Law on Human Rights and Freedoms and on the Rights of Ethnic and National Communities or Minorities in the Republic of Croatia. This law granted national minorities, exceeding eight percent of the total population, the right to proportional representation at all levels of

---

166 P. Radan, 'Republika Srpska Krajina and the Right of People to Self-determination' 36(1) *Istorija 20. Veka* (2018) 10.

167 Ustav Republike Hrvatske (the Constitution of the Republic of Croatia) 41 *Narodne Novine* (Official Gazette) (7 May 2001).

168 *Ibid.*

169 The Constitution, apart from Serbs, listed Czechs, Slovaks, Italians, Hungarians, Jews, Germans, Austrians, Ukrainians, Rusyns, Bosniaks, Slovenians, Montenegrins, Macedonians, Russians, Bulgarians, Poles, Roma, Romanians, Turks, Vlachs and Albanians as national minorities.

170 D. Jović, 'Strah od Postajanja Manjinom i Sukob u Prethodnoj Jugoslaviji' 65 *Reč* (2002) 113–130.

171 Radan, 'Republika Srpska Krajina' (n 166) 13.

government. It also conferred special self-governing status on municipalities where ethnic or national minorities formed a significant majority (Article 21). These provisions were specifically intended to address the status of Serbs in Croatia, who, according to the 1991 census, constituted more than eight percent of the population.

However, these legal protections were only effectively in place during the period of Serbian control over occupied territories in Croatia. After Operation Storm in 1995, which led to a mass exodus of Serbs from Croatia, the Croatian Parliament adopted the Constitutional Law on the Temporary Suspension of Certain Provisions of the Constitutional Law on Human Rights and Freedoms and on the Rights of Ethnic and National Communities or Minorities in the Republic of Croatia.[172] This law temporarily suspended the rights previously guaranteed to the Serbian minority. The suspension remained in effect until the 2001 population census.

During this period, the Croatian Parliament also amended the electoral law, introducing controversial measures regarding voting and special political representation for the diaspora. On one hand, Croatian authorities made significant efforts to encourage participation in national elections among Croats living abroad, while on the other hand, they did little to protect the rights of the Serbian minority members who had fled after Operation Storm.[173]

By the end of the 1990s, the return of Serbian refugees had become one of the most challenging topics in Croatian politics. Following Operation Storm, the Croatian government implemented various measures that hindered the return and reintegration of Serbian refugees. These included legal barriers to acquiring or confirming citizenship,[174] discrimination in access to resources for property reconstruction,[175] difficulties in reclaiming property and restoring tenancy rights,[176] and the suspension of legislative protections for human

172 Ustavni Zakon o Ljudskim Pravima i Slobodama i o Pravima Etničkih i Nacionalnih Zajednica ili Manjina u Republici Hrvatskoj (the Constitutional Law on Human Rights and Freedoms and the Rights of Ethnic and National Communities or Minorities in the Republic of Croatia) 34 *Narodne Novine* (Official Gazette) (17 Jun. 1992).

173 V. Koska, 'Slučaj Srpske Manjine u Hrvatskoj' 2(5) *Političke Analize: Tromjesečnik aa Hrvatsku i Međunarodnu Politiku* (2011) 52.

174 Human Rights Watch, 'Croatia, Impunity for Abuses Committed During Operation Storm and the Denial of the Right of Refugees to Return to the Krajina' (1996) <https://www.hrw.org/reports/1996/Croatia.htm>; Human Rights Watch, 'Croatia: Second Class Citizens: The Serbs of Croatia' (1999) <https://www.hrw.org/report/1999/03/01/second-class-citizens/serbs-croatia>.

175 HRW (1999).

176 HRW (1996).

and minority rights.[177] As a result, many international organizations, including the Human Rights Watch, labelled these practices by Croatian authorities as 'bureaucratic ethnic cleansing'.[178]

However, the late 1990s and early 2000s marked the beginning of gradual policy changes toward the Serbian minority. In 2000, a new centre-left government introduced significant legislation safeguarding minority rights, including the use of the Serbian language and Cyrillic script, as well as education in the minority language and in accordance with a distinct curriculum.[179] The 2002 Constitutional Law on the Rights of National Minorities further solidified these changes by affirming the right to cultural autonomy and legally mandating minority representation in all institutions and at all levels of government through a series of mechanisms.

The following section will consider internal self-determination of the Serbian population in municipalities in Croatia focusing on the development of national aspirations and the creation of the Serbian Autonomous Region.

4.1.1.1 Croatian Aspirations for Independent Statehood

In the aftermath of the Second World War, the first significant nationalist movement in Croatia emerged during the so-called 'Croatian Spring' of the late 1960s and early 1970s. However, after Tito suppressed the Croatian liberal leadership in December 1971, with purges lasting throughout 1972, Croatian nationalism remained largely dormant until the late 1980s.[180] With the victory of Franjo Tuđman and his Croatian Democratic Union (HDZ) in the 1990 elections, demands for secession based on the principle of self-determination resurfaced. The HDZ's political platform emphasized the establishment of an 'independent, sovereign, and democratic Croatia'.[181] To achieve this goal, it was necessary to amend the existing Constitution of the Socialist Republic of Croatia from 1974, which firmly entrenched Croatia as a part of the SFRY and provided for many common features, such as the use of Croatian literary language considered as the standard form of the national language used by both Croats and Serbs in Croatia, and referred to as Croatian or Serbian.[182]

---

177 *Ibid.*

178 Koska (n 173) 52.

179 Law on the Use of Language and Script of National Minorities in the Republic of Croatia and Law on Education in the Language and Script of National Minorities, 55 *Narodne Novine* (Official Gazette) (27 May 2000).

180 Radan, *The Break-up of Yugoslavia* (n 161) 174.

181 *Ibid.* 175, fn. 91.

182 Ustav Socijalističke Republike Hrvatske (the Constitution of the Socialist Republic of Croatia) 8 *Narodne Novine* (Official Gazette) (22 Feb. 1974) Article 138.

The new Constitution was adopted on 22 December 1990 (known as the 'Christmas Constitution') and it effectively served as a declaration of Croatia's independence.[183] Unlike the 1974 Croatian Constitution, which established that both Serbs and Croats were constituent nations, the new Constitution defined the Republic of Croatia as a national state composed of the Croatian nation and specific national minorities, including Serbs. A significant consequence of this redefinition was that Serbs, as a national minority, were no longer recognized as having the right to self-determination.[184] Article 2 of the Constitution further stipulated that the Croatian Parliament (*Sabor*) and the people would directly decide on any association with other states or alliances. Moreover, it affirmed that Croatia would retain full sovereignty in determining the scope of any delegated powers and the freedom to withdraw from such alliances.

According to the Constitution, Croatia would remain part of Yugoslavia 'until a new agreement of Yugoslav republics or until the Croatian Sabor decides otherwise'.[185] If the territorial integrity or interests of Croatia were threatened within Yugoslavia, Croatia reserved the right, based on the principle of self-determination, to take necessary measures to protect its interests.[186]

Significant decisions that paved the way for Croatia to establish itself as a subject of international law were made in 1991. In April of that year, the Croatian President called for a referendum, posing two questions to the voters: whether Croatia, as a sovereign and independent state, should enter into an association with other independent republics, or remain within a unified Yugoslavia.[187] A significant majority of the Croatian electorate opted for sovereignty and independence.[188]

On 25 June 1991, the Croatian Parliament adopted critical constitutional acts that proclaimed Croatia's independence and sovereignty: the Constitutional Decision on Sovereignty and Independence of the Republic of Croatia and the Declaration on the Establishment of the Sovereign and Independent Republic

183 Ustav Republike Hrvatske (the Constitution of the Republic of Croatia) 56 *Narodne Novine* (Official Gazette) (22 Dec. 1990). Article 11 established the Croatian coat of arms, Article 12 stipulated that the Croatian language and the Latin script are in official use in the Republic of Croatia, and Article 13 designated Zagreb as the capital of the Republic of Croatia.

184 Radan, *The Break-up of Yugoslavia* (n 161) 176.

185 Article 140 of the Constitution.

186 *Ibid.*

187 B. Vukas, 'The Process of the Establishment of the Independence of the Republic of Croatia from the Perspective of International Law' 7(1) *Review of Croatian History* (2011) 19.

188 *Ibid.*

of Croatia.[189] The Constitutional Decision asserted that Croatian independence was based on 'the inalienable, inexhaustible, indivisible, and non-transferable right of the Croatian people to self-determination'.[190] The Declaration stated that even under the previous constitutions of the SFRY, Croatia had the right to self-determination, including the right to secession.[191] Both instruments affirmed that Croatia's international borders would correspond to its existing republican borders and those parts of the Yugoslav international borders relevant to Croatia. The Declaration also underscored Croatia's long-standing statehood, tracing its origins back over thirteen centuries, and confirmed its intent to seek international recognition.[192] However, both the Constitutional Decision and the Declaration were declared unconstitutional and annulled by the Constitutional Court of the SFRY in October and November 1991.[193]

4.1.1.1.1 The Creation of the Serbian Autonomous Region

The opposition of Croatia's Serbs to the 1990 Constitution was mainly articulated through the Serbian Democratic Party (SDP), which was established on 17 February 1990 under the leadership of Dr. Jovan Rašković. The SDP garnered most of its support from rural areas, particularly those in and around Knin.[194]

---

189 Ustavna Odluka o Suverenosti i Samostalnosti Republike Hrvatske (Constitutional Decision on Sovereignty and Independence of the Republic of Croatia) 31 *Narodne Novine* 872 (Official Gazette) (25 Jun. 1991); Deklaracija o Proglašenju Suverene i Samostalne Republike Hrvatske (Declaration on the Establishment of the Sovereign and Independent Republic of Croatia) 31 *Narodne Novine* 875 (Official Gazette) (25 Jun. 1991).

190 Constitutional Decision on Sovereignty and Independence of the Republic of Croatia (n 189) Preamble.

191 Declaration on the Establishment of the Sovereign and Independent Republic of Croatia (n 189) Point IV.

192 While Croatia declared independence in June 1991, the international community did not immediately recognize it due to ongoing negotiations and the complex situation in Yugoslavia. Full international recognition came in early 1992. Of the universally recognized countries, Iceland was the first to recognize Croatia, on 19 December 1991, followed by Germany and the Vatican. In the Serbian public discourse, Germany and the Vatican are often considered key actors in the dissolution of Yugoslavia.

193 Odluka o ocenivanju ustavnosti Ustavne odluke o suverenosti i samostalnosti Republike Hrvatske (Decision on the Assessment of the Constitutionality of the Constitutional Decision on the Sovereignty and Independence of the Republic of Croatia) (16 Oct 1991); Odluka o ocenivanju ustavnosti Deklaracije o proglašenju suverene i samostalne Republike Hrvatske (Decision on the Assessment of the Constitutionality of the Declaration on the Proclamation of the Sovereign and Independent Republic of Croatia) (13 Nov. 1991) avaialble in M. Buzadžić, *Secesija Bivših Jugoslovenskih Republika U Svetlosti Odluka Ustavnog Suda Jugoslavije: Zbirka Dokumenata s Uvodnom Raspravom* (Novinsko-izdavačka Ustanova, Službeni List SRJ 1994) 156 and 159 respectively.

194 Radan, 'Republika Srpska Krajina' (n 166) 14.

On 18 May 1991, a smaller group of Serbs, mainly based in Zagreb, founded the Serbian People's Party (SPP). The SPP advocated for collaboration with the Croatian government, aiming to reduce nationalist tensions and promote a Croatian identity grounded in civic principles rather than ethnic nationalism.[195]

Initially, the SDP also adopted a more moderate stance, advocating for cultural autonomy for Serbs within Croatia. However, it struggled with internal organization, functioning more as a political movement than a well-structured party. In the first half of 1990, the moderate faction within the SDP remained dominant. Yet, the party's lack of cohesion and a clear organizational framework increasingly posed challenges for its leader, Jovan Rašković.[196]

At a June 1990 meeting between Franjo Tuđman and Jovan Rašković, the two leaders agreed that Serbs in Croatia would be granted cultural autonomy. It was decided that the next step toward establishing a 'democratically negotiated agreement' would be initiated by Rašković, who was to present Tuđman with a detailed proposal for this autonomy.[197] However, as the political climate intensified, radical positions on both sides began to gain traction, and the prospect for cultural autonomy as a viable solution gradually diminished. During its election campaign, the Croatian Democratic Union (HDZ) had highlighted the disproportionate representation of Serbs in official positions, and after winning the election, many Serbs were indeed dismissed from their jobs or coerced into signing loyalty pledges.[198]

On 25 July 1990, the SDP organized a rally of Croatia's Serbs in Srb (*Srpski Sabor*), where a Declaration on the Sovereignty and Autonomy of the Serbian People and a decision on the formation of the Serbian National Council were adopted. The Declaration asserted that within the borders of the SR Croatia, which is the state of the Serbian people living in the SR Croatia, the Serbian people are, based on their geographical, historical, social, and cultural characteristics, a sovereign people with all the rights that sovereignty entails. It further stated that the Serbian people in Croatia had the right to determine, either in cooperation with the Croatian people or independently, the federal or confederal organization of the state when establishing new relations in Yugoslavia. The Declaration emphasized that the future form of Yugoslav unity could not be

195 N. Barić, 'The Establishment and Public Activity of the Serbian People's Party in 1991' 7(1) *Review of Croatian History* (2011) 79–102.

196 N. Caspersen, 'The Thorny Issue of Ethnic Autonomy in Croatia: Serb Leaders and Proposals for Autonomy' 3 *Journal on Ethnopolitics and Minority Issues in Europe* (2003) 4.

197 R. Hislope, 'The Generosity Moment: Ethnic Politics, Democratic Consolidation and the State in Yugoslavia (Croatia), South Africa and Czechoslovakia' 5(1) *Democratization* (1998) 73.

198 Caspersen (n 196) 4.

decided without the participation of the Serbian people in Croatia, particularly in scenarios involving legitimate secession.[199] It underscored that 'peoples secede, not states', and that the Serbian people reserved the right to decide with whom they would live, under what regime, and how they would connect with other nations in Yugoslavia. The Declaration concluded that 'nobody else has the historical right to determine the fate of the Serbian nation, which has inhabited these areas for centuries, long before the Croatian state was created.'[200] Based on this claim to sovereignty, the Serbian people in Croatia asserted their right to autonomy, with the scope of that autonomy to be determined by the federal or confederal organization of Yugoslavia.

The Serbian National Council, as the executive body of the Serbian Sabor, was granted the authority to organize referendums and to represent the Serbian people in 'other issues relating to the establishment of Serbian sovereignty and autonomy'.[201] The Council was declared an independent body, tasked with implementing the decisions of the Serbian Sabor and the Declaration, as well as with formulating questions on which the Serbian Sabor and the Serbian people would express their views through a referendum. Additionally, the Serbian Sabor, through this Declaration, proclaimed 'null and void for the Serbian people in Croatia all constitutional and legal changes which deny its sovereignty as a nation and undermine its right to autonomy'.[202]

Based on the expressed will of the Serbian people during the plebiscite on Serbian autonomy, held from 19 August to 2 September 1990, the Serbian National Council, at its 4th session on 30 September 1990, in Srb, determined that the Serbian people had opted for Serbian autonomy in the ethnic and historical territories they inhabited within the current borders of the Republic of Croatia as a federal unit of the SFRY. Following the expressed will, the Serbian National Council formally proclaimed Serbian autonomy.[203]

On 19 December 1991, Milan Babić, the president of the Serbian Autonomous Oblast of Krajina (SAO Krajina) and Goran Hadžić, the leader of the SAO Eastern Slavonia, Baranja, and Western Srem, declared the establishment of a new state, called the Republika Srpska Krajina (RSK). They announced that these

199 Deklaracija o Suverenosti i Autonomiji Srpskog Naroda (Declaration on the Sovereignty and Autonomy of the Serbian People) (25 Jul. 1990) Point 1, available in S. Radulović, *Sudbina Krajine* (Dan Graf 1996) 123–4.

200 *Ibid.*

201 *Ibid.* Point 4.

202 M. Dakić, *Srpska Krajina, Istorijski Temelji i Nastanak* (Iskra 1994) 52.

203 A. Martinović, 'Državno-pravni Razvoj Republike Srpske Krajine' 44 *Baština* (2018) 377.

areas were uniting to form a single Serbian state within Croatia. By February 1992, both regions had officially declared their independence from Croatia.[204]

The Serbian population of the Republika Srpska Krajina and the Republika Srpska have traditionally expressed a strong desire for a permanent union and the formation of a shared state. However, the international community, due to its longstanding support for the idea of a single, unitary Bosnia, was not in favor of Serbian integration.[205] Despite these objections and the associated political risks, the assemblies of Republika Srpska Krajina and Republika Srpska adopted a joint Declaration in the autumn of 1992. This Declaration called for, among other things, the unification of their legal systems, the adoption of common state symbols, a joint educational framework, and the intensification of cooperation in the domains of foreign affairs, media, communication, transport, culture, social and health protection, trade, energy, and environmental policy. The Declaration also emphasized a commitment to national unification. Dakić notes that the aspiration toward Serbian unity between Republika Srpska Krajina and Republika Srpska was further affirmed by a referendum held on 20 June 1993. Although immediate political unification did not materialize, the referendum reflected a prevailing belief among the Serbian population of Republika Srpska Krajina that there was no longer a legitimate basis for maintaining what they viewed as artificial borders dividing a single people.[206]

Lord Carrington's plan for resolving the Yugoslav crisis (the Carrington Plan), unveiled on 17 October 1991, proposed that all six Yugoslav republics become independent, sovereign, and internationally recognized states, without altering their borders. The plan allowed for the possibility of a loose association or alliance among these states. In regions where Serbs constituted a majority, the plan provided for significant territorial and political autonomy outside of Serbia. This autonomy included the right to use national symbols and flags of their choice, the entitlement to a secondary nationality, an independent educational system, and the establishment of their own parliament and administrative institutions.[207]

Milošević rejected the Carrington Plan, arguing that it effectively 'abolished a state that had continuously existed for 70 years' within the European community. He criticized the plan for omitting the principle of self-determination

---

204 A. Petricusic, 'Nation-Building in Croatia and the Treatment of Minorities: Rights and Wrongs' 349 L' *Europe en Formation* (2008) 136.

205 Dakić (n 202) 60.

206 *Ibid.*

207 Caspersen (n 196) 10.

for peoples and emphasized the importance of all Serbs living in a single state, rather than being divided among multiple independent republics connected by only a loose framework of interstate relations.[208] Woodward observes that the Carrington Plan was also unacceptable to the Croatian government.[209] While Milošević was open to some earlier versions of the plan, the authorities in Krajina completely rejected it.

The Z-4 Plan, or the Agreement on Krajina, Slavonia, Southern Baranja, and Western Srem, unveiled in January 1995, proposed the peaceful reintegration of the Republic of Serbian Krajina into Croatia's constitutional order. It offered Serbs in Krajina broad political, economic, and cultural autonomy, and aimed to end ongoing military hostilities. However, the plan was never the subject of meaningful or sincere negotiations, and thus remained a dead letter.[210]

From 4 to 7 August 1995, in just four days, the Republic of Serbian Krajina was defeated (Operation Storm). This military operation effectively ended the war in Croatia, nullified the Z-4 Plan, abolished the UN-protected zones, and resulted in the killing of approximately 2,650 people and the expulsion of around 240,000 Serbs from their ancestral homes. The operation also led to the destruction of property valued at hundreds of millions of dollars.[211]

The Dayton Agreement established Bosnia and Herzegovina as a unified state comprising two entities: the Federation of Bosnia and Herzegovina (created by the Washington Agreement of 1994, with a predominantly Bosniak and Croatian population) and the Republika Srpska (with a predominantly Serbian population). These entities are separated by an inter-entity boundary line, which serves as an administrative border. The Republika Srpska controls 49% of the total territory of Bosnia and Herzegovina, though it lost control over Sarajevo and several other cities in eastern Bosnia. In parallel, the Erdut Agreement, officially known as the Basic Agreement on the Region of Eastern Slavonia, Baranja, and Western Sirmium, was signed on 12 November 1995 in the village of Erdut. This accord facilitated the peaceful reintegration of these regions into the Republic of Croatia, bringing them under Croatian sovereignty and constitutional order. The agreement was brokered with the assistance of the United Nations and provided for a transitional period during which the United Nations Transitional

208 D. Dašić, 'Neki Unutrašnji i Međunarodni Aspekti Krize i Raspada Jugoslavije' in B. Knežić and J. Ćirić (eds.) *20 Godina od Razbijanja SFRJ* (Institut za Uporedno Pravo 2011) 171.

209 S. Woodward, *Balkan Tragedy: Chaos and dissolution after the Cold War* (Brookings Institution 1995) 182.

210 Dašić (n 208) 178.

211 *Ibid.*

Administration for Eastern Slavonia, Baranja, and Western Sirmium (UNTAES) would oversee the region. Key provisions of the Erdut Agreement included the protection of minority rights, the return of refugees and displaced persons, demilitarization, and the eventual full reintegration of the region into Croatia by 1998.[212]

4.1.2 Internal Self-determination in Kosovo

Kosovo and Metohija hold significant importance in Serbian national history. Discussions about Kosovo typically begin with the Battle of Kosovo Polje in 1389, in which the Serbian forces suffered a defeat at the hands of the advancing Ottoman army. This region, located in the southwest of Serbia, is bordered by central Serbia, North Macedonia, Albania, and Montenegro.

As a distinct geopolitical entity, Kosovo and Metohija emerged in 1912, when, following decisions made during the Balkan Wars, this part of the former medieval Serbia – then under Ottoman rule – was reintegrated into the Kingdom of Serbia and the Kingdom of Montenegro.[213] Over time, the territory now known as Kosovo and Metohija was inhabited by various peoples and governed by different rulers. In ancient and Roman times, much of the northeastern Adriatic coast and its hinterland were inhabited by Illyrians, who were largely assimilated and/or displaced by Slavs. Today's Albanians, who inhabit the southwestern part of the Balkan Peninsula, including Kosovo and Metohija, are often regarded as descendants of the Illyrians.

For nearly nine centuries, Kosovo and Metohija have been home to two distinct ethnic communities – Serbs and Albanians – who differ in language, culture, and religion. Relations between these communities have rarely attained a state of genuine harmony or mutual understanding.[214] This longstanding discord culminated at the end of the 20th century, leading to NATO's military intervention against the Federal Republic of Yugoslavia (FRY) in 1999. This intervention played a key role in the subsequent separation of Kosovo and Metohija from the FRY and Serbia.

The following analysis will examine the status of Kosovo as an autonomous province within Serbia, embracing the dialogue between Belgrade and Pristina under the auspices of the European Union. This exploration aims to provide

212 Basic Agreement on the Region of Eastern Slavonia, Baranja and Western Sirmium (Erdut Agreement) (12 Nov. 1995) <https://peacemaker.un.org/croatia-erdutagreement95>. See J. P Klein, 'The Prospects for Eastern Croatia: The Significance of the UN's. Undiscovered Mission' 142(2) *RUSI Journal* (1997) 19–24.

213 T. Mirković, 'Kosovo and Metohija: Nine Centuries After' 66(2) *Vojno Delo* (2014) 187. See also the Treaty of London (1913).

214 *Ibid.* 186.

insights into the application of internal self-determination in this conflict-ridden territory.

4.1.2.1 *Kosovo as an Autonomous Province in Socialist Serbia*

Kosovo and Metohija, as an autonomous unit within Socialist Serbia, has its roots in the 1st session of the Regional People's Liberation Committee held between 31 December 1943 and 2 January 1944. This session, following the decisions of the Anti-Fascist Council for the National Liberation of Yugoslavia (AVNOJ), laid the groundwork for post-war Yugoslavia.[215] The formal status of autonomous units, including the Autonomous Kosovo-Metohija Region (AKMO), was legally established with the adoption of the first Constitution of the Federal People's Republic of Yugoslavia on 31 January 1946, and the first Constitution of the People's Republic of Serbia on 17 January 1947. While the authorities of the Kingdom of Yugoslavia created territorial units in Kosovo and Metohija in such a way that Serbs constituted the majority population in each, the Communist Party of Yugoslavia (CPY) pursued the opposite policy by consolidating majority-Albanian districts within Serbia into a single entity.[216]

Autonomous units in socialist Yugoslavia represented a unique form of governance that emerged in 1945, evolving alongside the socio-political system. The constitutional and legal status of these units was not rigidly defined but was established where necessary to address national issues in ethnically diverse territories. In the People's Republic of Serbia, two such units were formed: the Autonomous Province of Vojvodina and the Autonomous Kosovo-Metohija Region (AKMO).[217] The creation of AKMO was influenced by several factors, including its ethnic composition, economic underdevelopment, and historical context.[218] In exercising their competences, the autonomous authorities were responsible for taking care of 'the development and strengthening of brotherhood and unity among the nationalities living in their territory, as well as the realization of the rights of national minorities established by the constitution'.[219]

The AKMO Statute, adopted in 1948, although influenced by the 1945 law on the establishment of AKMO, is considered as the first legal document to

---

215 S. Aksić, 'Položaj Autonomne Pokrajine Kosova i Metohije u Ustavnom Sistemu Jugoslavije' 11(3) *Anali Pravnog Fakulteta u Beogradu* (1963) 362.

216 I. Vukadinović, *Autonomija Kosova i Metohije u Srbiji (1945–1969)* (PhD Thesis, University of Belgrade 2020) 137.

217 Zakon o Administrativnoj Podeli Srbije (Law on the Administrative Division of Serbia) 28 *Službeni Glasnik* (Official Gazette of Serbia) (1945) Article 1.

218 Aksić (n 215) 364.

219 Constitutional Law of Serbia (1953) Article 15.

articulate the reasons for its formation and the goals of its existence.[220] In its second article, the Statute states that 'the Kosovo-Metohija Region enjoys autonomous rights with the aim of realizing the rights of national minorities established by the Constitution of the Federal People's Republic of Yugoslavia and the Constitution of the People's Republic of Serbia, as well as promoting the principle of fraternal cooperation among peoples'. The third article specifies that 'the Serbian and Albanian languages are used equally in all state services in AKMO', and that 'proceedings before the courts are conducted in either Serbian or Albanian'.[221]

While Article 2 affirms that the region's autonomy was established to safeguard minority rights, Article 3 makes clear which minority was chiefly in view. The equal status granted exclusively to the Albanian language – rather than to the languages of other minorities such as the Roma or Turks – suggests that the Statute was designed primarily to address the position of the Albanian population in Serbia. As Vukadinović observes, Articles 2 and 3 of the Statute provide a level of clarity absent in earlier constitutional and legal acts, indicating that the formation of AKMO was specifically aimed at securing rights for Kosovo's Albanian community.[222]

The 'Second' Yugoslavia (1945–1992) adopted a federal structure influenced by the Soviet model of autonomies, as outlined in the 1936 Constitution of the USSR. In 1963, the constitutional status of Kosovo was elevated from an autonomous region (*autonomna oblast*) to an autonomous province (*autonomna pokrajina*), thereby placing it on an equal constitutional footing with Vojvodina. By the late 1960s – particularly following the promulgation of the 1974 Constitution – these provinces acquired enhanced legal standing, approximating that of the republics. In practice, they began to function with significant autonomy. Kosovo and Metohija, in particular, evolved into a state-national framework in which the Albanian population constituted a numerical majority. This structure enabled the Albanian national minority to address its status within the Yugoslav constitutional order through local institutions.

Within the Autonomous Province of Kosovo and Metohija, a bureaucratic ruling class emerged, predominantly composed of ethnic Albanians, who oversaw the allocation of funds from both the Yugoslav federation and the

---

220 Vukadinović (n 216) 260.

221 AJ, Fund 836, Office of the Marshal of Yugoslavia, II-5-a-2/16, Statute of the Autonomous Kosovo-Metohija Region in the People's Republic of Serbia. Cf. Zakon o Ustanovljenju i Ustrojstvu Autonomne Kosovsko-Metohijske Oblasti (Law on the Establishment and Organizational Set Up of the Autonomous Kosovo-Metohija Region) 48 *Službeni Glasnik* (Official Gazette of Serbia) (1945) (providing for the principle of equality of all nationalities (*narodnosti*) and citizens and the right to education in their own language in Articles 4–5).

222 Vukadinović (n 216) 261.

Republic of Serbia intended for the accelerated development of the province. However, instead of cultivating greater loyalty to the Yugoslav state, this process coincided with the growth of Albanian nationalism and separatism. The Albanian bureaucratic elite played a significant role in fostering this shift.[223]

Kosovo functioned in practice as a self-governing province within the Yugoslav federation. As noted by Poulton, during the 1980s, 'the Kosovo Albanians were not repressed culturally. Kosovo was, in effect, an Albanian polity with the Albanian language in official use, Albanian television, radio, and press, and with an ethnic Albanian government. Even the courts, which were used to prosecute those calling for a republic for Kosovo, were staffed by ethnic Albanian judges'.[224] During this decade, Kosovo Albanians were also represented at the highest levels of the Yugoslav state and party apparatus. For instance, in 1984–85, the presidency of the League of Yugoslav Communists was held by Ali Shukrija, and in 1986–87, the President of the Presidency of Yugoslavia was Sinan Hasani.

The 1990 Constitution of the Republic of Serbia marked a 'radical turn' in the status and powers of autonomous provinces. Under this new constitutional framework, autonomous provinces were no longer constitutive elements of the federation but were instead designated as 'political-territorial autonomies'.[225] Article 108 stated: 'Autonomous provinces are formed in accordance with the special national, historical, cultural, and other characteristics of their territories'.[226]

Špadijer emphasizes that the 1990 Constitution, like those of other republics, was based on the concept of citizenship. Within this framework, the rights and freedoms of national minorities were protected on an individual basis – implying that individuals were regarded primarily as citizens, with national affiliation (such as Albanian, Hungarian, or Bulgarian) considered secondary.[227]

223 M. Milosavljević, 'Teritorijalna Autonomija i Nacionalne Manjine u Srbiji' 24 *Politički Život* (2023) 86.

224 H. Poulton, 'Macedonians and Albanians as Yugoslavs' in D. Djokić (ed.) *Yugoslavism: Histories of a Failed Idea, 1918–1992* (C. Hurst & Co. Publishers 2003) 131.

225 Note that in March 1989, the Serbian parliament passed constitutional amendments that effectively revoked the autonomy granted to Kosovo (and Vojvodina) under the 1974 Constitution of the Socialist Federal Republic of Yugoslavia (SFRY). These amendments gave the central government in Serbia direct control over key aspects of governance in Kosovo, such as the police, judiciary, and economic policy, which previously were under the jurisdiction of the provincial authorities.

226 Ustav Republike Srbije (Constitution of the Republic of Serbia) 1 *Službeni Glasnik Republike Srbije* (Official Gazette of the Republic of Serbia) (1990).

227 B. Špadijer, 'Politički Sistem Jugoslavije i Manjinsko Pitanje' in M. Macura and V. Stanovčić (eds.) *Položaj Manjina u Saveznoj Republici Jugoslaviji* (Serbian Academy of Sciences and Arts 1996) 142.

Some theoretical interpretations suggest that, under the 1990 Constitution of the Republic of Serbia, Albanians had a status somewhat comparable to the German-speaking population in South Tyrol.[228] Purusant to the Autonomy Statute of 1972, South Tyrol possessed two types of legislative powers: primary (covering bilingualism, cultural institutions, and spatial planning) and secondary (including local policing, education at primary and secondary levels, commerce, and employment categorization).[229] However, under the 1974 SFRY Constitution, the Autonomous Province of Kosovo enjoyed a much higher degree of autonomy than South Tyrol. Nevertheless, this level of autonomy was ultimately deemed insufficient by the Albanian population, contributing to persistent political and ethnic tensions.[230]

4.1.2.1.1 UDI, UNMIK and the EU Belgrade-Pristina Dialogue

The international community, which had faced significant challenges during the wars in Croatia and especially in Bosnia and Herzegovina in the 1990s, was primarily focused on preventing further bloodshed during the conflict in Kosovo in the late 1990s, rather than delving deeply into its background. The primary objective was not only to achieve peace but also to restore the credibility of the United Nations, which had been questioned during previous conflicts.[231]

In 1998, the United Nations Security Council adopted Resolutions 1160, 1199, and 1203, which imposed an arms embargo on the Federal Republic of Yugoslavia, called for a cessation of hostilities, and mandated access for international monitors.[232] NATO, led by the United States, perceived a political opportunity in the situation and initiated military action against Yugoslavia in 1999, known as Operation Allied Force, without obtaining prior approval from the UN Security Council. This operation involved all NATO member states except Iceland.[233]

Subsequently, the UN Security Council adopted Resolution 1244 in 1999, which laid the foundation for establishing peace in Kosovo. The resolution

228 S. Orlović, *Politički Život Srbije- Između Partokratije i Demokratije* (Službeni Glasnik 2008) 226.

229 N. Drobnjaković, 'Iskustvo Južnog Tirola i Rešavanje Položaja Nacionalnih Manjina' in M. Macura and V. Stanovčić (eds.) *Položaj Manjina u Saveznoj Republici Jugoslaviji* (Serbian Academy of Sciences and Arts 1996) 479.

230 M. Milosavljević-Stević, 'Teritorijalna Autonomija i Nacionalne Manjine u Srbiji' 24 *Politički Život* (2023) 87. For a comprehensive review of the status of the Albanian minority under relevant Serbian legal acts, refer to Serbia's written submission in the Kosovo case before the International Court of Justice (17 Apr. 2009) 61–112.

231 I. Marijan, 'Kosovo i Abhazija-Pitanje Neovisnosti' 24 *Polemos* (2021) 67.

232 UNSC Res 1160 (31 Mar. 1998); 1199 (23 Sep. 1998); 1203 (24 Oct. 1998).

233 Note, yet, that Iceland maintains no standing army, the only NATO member for which this is the case. Island supported the operation by other non-forceful means.

appointed a Special Representative, accountable to the UN Secretary-General, and authorized the deployment of international military forces, while affirming Yugoslav sovereignty over Kosovo.[234] The international peacekeeping forces in Kosovo (Kosovo Force – KFOR) operate under NATO command rather than the United Nations.

The issue of Kosovo's independence gained strategic importance for NATO, particularly in the context of its eastward expansion and the consequent reduction of Russia's influence in the region. Critics argue that if NATO's primary concern had been the prevention of humanitarian crises, similar military interventions would have been conducted in other global conflict zones as well.[235]

In 1989, Serbia revoked Kosovo's autonomy, prompting the Albanian population to declare independence in 1991. However, this declaration was not recognized internationally, and the Kosovo authorities were unable to establish effective control over the entire territory. Following NATO's intervention in 1999, Kosovo was placed under international administration, effectively becoming an international protectorate, although it remained legally a part of the Federal Republic of Yugoslavia. Thus, while Kosovo was under international governance, Serbia retained formal sovereignty over the region.

In mid-March 2007, Martti Ahtisaari, the UN Special Envoy for the status of Kosovo and Metohija, presented his plan – comprising a 'Report' and a 'Comprehensive Proposal for the Kosovo Status Settlement' – to the UN Secretary-General. On 26 March, with full support, the Secretary-General forwarded the proposal to the Security Council.[236] This followed fourteen months of negotiations, as mandated by UN Security Council Resolution 1244, which had called for a political process to determine the future status of Kosovo. Despite these efforts, the negotiations failed to produce a compromise between Serbia and the Kosovo Albanian leadership.

In April 2007, the UN Security Council, prompted by Russia, decided to send a mission to Kosovo and Metohija to gather first-hand information on the progress in implementing agreed standards and other relevant matters.[237] During the visit, the Serbian government reiterated its proposal for 'supervised autonomy' for Kosovo. According to this proposal, Kosovo would be granted legislative, executive, and judicial powers, while Serbia would retain control over foreign policy, defense, border control, monetary and customs policy, as well

234 UNSC Res 1244 (10 Jun. 1999).

235 Marijan (n 231) 68.

236 Report of the Special Envoy of the Secretary-General on Kosovo's Future Status (26 Mar. 2007) UN Doc. S/2007/168.

237 M. Weller, 'Kosovo's Final Status' 84(6) *International Affairs* (2008) 1223.

as the protection of Serbian religious and cultural heritage and human rights. Additionally, Kosovo would continue to be represented in Serbian institutions. However, the Kosovar authorities persisted in their demand for full independence, leading the mission to conclude that the positions of the two sides on the Kosovo settlement proposal 'remain far apart'.[238]

A few days before Pristina's unilateral declaration of independence, discussions were held in Helsinki during which Martti Ahtisaari asserted that Kosovo possessed a compelling moral justification for secession and independence, given the oppression experienced by the Albanian majority in the territory under the authoritarian Serbian regime between 1989 and 1999.[239]

The declaration of independence of the Republic of Kosovo on 17 February 2008 was preceded by numerous disturbances and minor incidents involving both Albanians and Serbs. The most serious conflicts occurred in 2004, when attacks on Kosovo Serbs took place in several cities and villages, leading to the destruction of many sacred buildings and cultural monuments. These events prompted a large number of Serbs to leave Kosovo, reducing their presence to a majority only in the northern part of the region.[240] Shortly thereafter, the Albanian leadership moved towards the final step of severing all ties with Serbia, or what was then the state union of Serbia and Montenegro. Kosovo's declaration of independence dealt a significant blow to Serbia, marking yet another setback in a series of challenges the country faced since 1991.[241]

The dialogue between Belgrade and Pristina, facilitated and strongly encouraged by the European Union, began on 8 March 2011. The choice of the term 'dialogue' is significant, as it reflects the deliberate avoidance of the term 'negotiations', which would suggest an international status to the talks – an implication that was unacceptable to Belgrade. After the United Nations' efforts in this area proved unsuccessful, particularly with the rejection of the Ahtisaari Plan by both the Security Council and the Republic of Serbia, the European Union established a solid foundation and prerequisites for its mediation efforts.[242] Firstly, the European Union had already accumulated some mediation experience in the Western Balkans, although not always acting

238 Report of the Security Council Mission on the Kosovo Issue (4 May 2007) UN Doc. s/2007/256, para 59.

239 S. Bose, 'Kosovo to Kashmir: The Self-determination Dilemma' *Open Democracy* (22 May 2008) <https://www.opendemocracy.net/en/kosovo-to-kashmir-autonomy-secession-and-democracy/>.

240 HRW Report, 'Failure to Protect: Anti-minority Violence in Kosovo, March 2004' 16(6) *Human Rights Watch* (2004) 7–63.

241 Marijan (n 231) 68.

242 J. Perić, 'Evropska Unija Kao Posrednik u Dijalogu Beograda i Prištine–Kritički Osvrt' 68 *Međunarodna Politika* (2017) 24.

independently. Additionally, the advisory opinion of the International Court of Justice in 2010, which stated that Kosovo's declaration of independence was not contrary to international law, served as an important point of reference. However, the factor that likely had the most significant impact on the EU's authority as a mediator, alongside the agreement of the disputing parties, was the shared aspirations of both Belgrade and Pristina for EU membership. As Perić observes, this situation makes the Union the most effective mediator, as no other actor possesses such leverage over the parties in the dialogue, with the ability to use progress in EU integration as both a 'carrot' and a 'stick.' In deeply conflicted situations like that of Belgrade and Pristina, the potential for leverage is crucial, as the threat of sanctions or the promise of rewards can profoundly influence the parties' commitment to the dialogue.[243]

Mediation in the technical dialogue has yielded significant positive outcomes. These include agreements on freedom of movement, civil registries, customs stamps, cadastral records, mutual recognition of university diplomas, integrated border/administrative line management, and regional representation and cooperation.[244] Following the fifth round of political negotiations, on 20 February 2013 discussions between Belgrade and Pristina concerning the position of Serbs in northern Kosovo began, with a focus on the four municipalities with a Serbian majority.[245] At Serbia's insistence, NATO was involved in the negotiations during April 2013, serving as a guarantor of the agreement between Belgrade and Pristina, with the aim of preventing potential security threats in northern Kosovo.

In April 2013, the ninth round of negotiations culminated in the 'First Agreement of Principles Governing the Normalization of Relations'.[246] This Agreement outlined the formation of an Association/Community of Serb Majority Municipalities in Kosovo, which would include not only the four northern municipalities but also certain municipalities with significant Serbian populations in central Kosovo. These provisions were derived from the Ahtisaari Plan, which Serbia and Russia had rejected in 2007. The Agreement stipulated that this Community would function according to its statute, with a president, vice president, assembly, and council. It was also emphasized that the community

---

243 *Ibid.* 25.

244 D. Đukanović, 'Odnosi Između Beograda i Prištine: od Tehničkog do Političkog Dijaloga' 65(3) *Medunarodni Problemi* (2013) 367–371. Note that the first four rounds of dialogue did not produce concrete agreements, as they were focused on establishing the foundations and principles for the dialogue process.

245 *Ibid.* 373.

246 First Agreement of Principles Governing the Normalisation of Relations (Brussels Agreement) (19 Apr. 2013) <https://www.srbija.gov.rs/specijal/en/120394>.

would operate within the constitutional framework and existing legislation of Kosovo.[247]

The Association of Serb Majority Municipalities in Kosovo was not intended to establish a classical form of ethnic territorial autonomy. Instead, it aimed to enhance the collective rights of the Serbian community through strengthened local self-government. As such, the Agreement did not seek to transform Kosovo into a complex entity (e.g. a federation, confederation, or union) but rather to preserve its existing unitary structure while significantly decentralizing and empowering local governance.[248]

The Brussels Agreement, however, is often regarded as constituting *de facto* recognition of Kosovo's independence. Namely, Article 10 of the Agreement envisages the abolition of the Serbian judiciary, which had been legally operating in Kosovo and Metohija since 2008 under the Serbian law on the Seats and Territorial Jurisdictions of Courts, and the establishment of an Albanian judiciary.[249] As noted by Mirović, Article 10 grossly undermines not only the 2008 Law but also the constitutional principles of a unified judicial authority and legal system, which stipulate that the judicial system in the Republic of Serbia is singular and cannot have courts organized in any part of its territory that are separate from the central judicial system.[250] Mirović concludes that, according to the classical legal definition whereby every state possesses its judiciary, it is evident that by Article 10 of the Brussels Agreement, Belgrade has *de facto* recognized the secessionist entity.[251] There are, in fact, other provisions within the Brussels Agreement that could be interpreted as implicitly recognizing Kosovo, and these interpretations have been affirmed through subsequent legal and political developments. Notably, these include the disbandment of the Serbian Ministry of Internal Affairs (MUP) in Kosovo and Metohija, which had 1,200 employees until 2013, the abolition of Civil Protection, the electoral system and local self-government, as well as the transfer of control over the energy and telecommunications sectors.[252] Crucially, the Brussels Agreement

247 *Ibid.* Articles 1–5.

248 Đukanović (n 244) 374.

249 Law on the Seats and Territorial Jurisdictions of Courts and Public Prosecutor's Offices, 116 Official Gazette of the Republic of Serbia (2008).

250 D. Mirović, 'Sedam Godina Briselskog Sporazuma' in Z. Knežević and K. Čavoški (eds.) *Secesija sa Stanovišta Unutrašnjeg i Međunarodnog Prava i Njene Političke Posledice* (Serbian Academy of Sciences and Arts 2020) 303.

251 *Ibid.*

252 Up until 2013, there were offices of the MUP in the suburbs of Pristina. These offices issued documents to both Serbs and Albanians who needed them for international travel. The Brussels Agreement and supplementary agreements on the judiciary signed between

makes no mention of UN Security Council Resolution 1244 or the Serbian Constitution, which serve as 'guardians' of Serbian territorial integrity on the domestic and international plane.

Following a prolonged stalemate in the dialogue, a diplomatic initiative by the United States led to the so-called 'Washington Agreement' between Belgrade and Pristina in 2020. The parties signed separate but coordinated documents, one of the key provisions being a one-year moratorium on Kosovo's applications for membership in international organizations. In parallel, Serbia committed to suspending its de-recognition campaign by refraining from formal and informal requests to any state or international organization to withhold or withdraw recognition of Kosovo as an independent state.[253]

In September 2021, a political crisis erupted in northern Kosovo following the Kosovo government's decision to ban Serbian license plates. Kosovo Serbs protested after vehicles with Serbian plates in Kosovo were required to pay a tax of 5 euros to exchange them for temporary Kosovo license plates, valid for 60 days. This led to local ethnic Serbs blockading roads leading to

---

2013 and 2017 resulted in the dissolution of the Serbian judiciary that had been functioning in the territory of Kosovo and Metohija since 1999. With the 2017 Regulation on the Exercise of Special Rights of Judicial Officials, Serbia incentivized the employment of Serbian judges and prosecutors within the secessionist Albanian system. Specifically, a special Kosovo allowance (special pension) was introduced for those employed who accepted the Albanian system. Civil Protection was established in May 2006 based on the Law on Defense and the Law on Local Self-Government. It consisted of around 500 people, mostly former soldiers residing in northern Kosovo and Metohija. In practice, this fulfilled Article 4 of UN Security Council Resolution 1244, which grants the right for the return of the Serbian military to Kosovo and Metohija. Civil Protection was officially disbanded by the Vučić–Mustafa agreement in 2015. At the time of its disbandment, it had around 1,000 members, 800 in northern Kosovo and Metohija, and the rest south of the Ibar River. The agreement stipulated that the equipment of Civil Protection be handed over urgently to the secessionists in Pristina. Following the Brussels Agreement, the then Serbian Prime Minister concluded two agreements with Kosovo's Prime Minister Thaçi on energy and telecommunications in 2013. After these agreements, Serbian telecommunications and the energy system began operating according to Albanian secessionist laws and within their legal system. Based on these agreements, the International Telecommunication Union (ITU) assigned the country code 383 to Kosovo with the assistance of Serbia and Austria in 2016. 'Telenor' and 'VIP' ceased operations in Kosovo and Metohija. More in D. Mirović, 'Čas Anatomije za Briselski Sporazum' *Novi Standard* (23 Nov. 2019) <https://standard.rs/2019/11/23/d-mirovic-cas-anatomije-za-briselski-sporazum/>. See Brussels Agreement (n 246) Articles 7–15.

253 R. Muharremi, 'The "Washington Agreement" Between Kosovo and Serbia' 25(4) *ASIL Insights* (2021). A. Lazarević and S. Surlić, 'Princip Teritorijalnog Integriteta: Političke Posledice Traganja za Finalnim Statusom Kosova i Metohije' 80(2) *Srpska Politička Misao* (2023) 123.

two border crossings with Serbia in northern Kosovo. In response, the Serbian Armed Forces raised the combat readiness of their troops along the border with Kosovo and began transporting military equipment, including combat aircraft and helicopters, to the border area. Similar crises occurred in July and August 2022, as well as in November and December of the same year, again revolving around issues related to ID cards and car license plates.[254] In late 2023, the government of Serbia, citing 'practical reasons' (to ease the situation of individuals and enable their freedom of movement), decided to allow cars with Kosovo registration plates to enter central Serbia. In return, Kosovo abolished the requirement for Serbian cars crossing the administrative line/border to place stickers covering Serbian national emblems on their plates.[255]

The tensions in 2021 and 2022 prompted the EU to seek a more concrete solution to the issues between Pristina and Belgrade. In autumn 2022, a Franco-German proposal for the normalization of relations was introduced, which soon gained the approval of the whole EU, and as such become a new 'European' proposal.[256] This proposal reaffirms the separate paths toward European Union membership for both parties, without mutual obstruction, a principle initially defined in Article 14 of the Brussels Agreement. A potentially significant shift in Serbia's policy regarding the recognition of Kosovo's self-proclaimed independence is highlighted in Article 4, which states that neither party can represent the other in the international sphere or act on its behalf, which also connotes that 'Serbia will not object to Kosovo's membership in any international organization'.[257] A particularly important and sensitive issue concerns local self-government for Kosovo Serbs. On this question, the agreement asks the parties to commit to guaranteeing 'an appropriate level of self-management for the Serbian community in Kosovo' and stipulates the formalization of the status of the Serbian Orthodox Church in Kosovo.[258] Without

254 M. Engjelllushe, 'The Politics of Dialogue: How the EU Can Change the Conservation in Kosovo and Serbia' *European Council on Foreign Relations* (15 Mar. 2023) <https://ecfr.eu/publication/the-politics-of-dialogue-how-the-eu-can-change-the-conversation-in-kosovo-and-serbia/>.

255 N1, 'Kosovske Tablice od Nove Godine Mogu u Centralnu Srbiju – Bez Nalepnica' (25 Dec. 2023) <https://n1info.rs/vesti/kosovske-tablice-od-nove-godine-mogu-u-centralnu-srbiju-bez-nalepnica/>.

256 H. Kreft, 'The Franco-German Proposal to Normalise Relations between Serbia and Kosovo: A Historic Opportunity to Unblock the EU Accession Perspective for the Entire Western Balkans' 16(1) *Foreign Policy Review* (2023) 175.

257 Belgrade-Pristina Dialogue: EU Proposal – Agreement on the path to normalisation between Kosovo and Serbia (2023) <https://www.eeas.europa.eu/eeas/belgrade-pristina-dialogue-agreement-path-normalisation-between-kosovo-and-serbia_en > Article 4.

258 *Ibid.* Article 7.

explicitly mentioning formal recognition of independence, the Agreement's text certainly requires Belgrade to accept Kosovo as a separate political entity that operates independently of the state of Serbia, including within international frameworks.[259]

Serbia has committed to accepting mutual recognition of all documents and not opposing further international confirmation of Kosovo's independence in exchange for the formation of the Association of Serb-Majority Municipalities (ZSO) by Pristina. The Constitutional Court of Kosovo has established that the formation of the ZSO is a requirement arising from the 2013 Brussels Agreement.[260] However, the political leadership in Kosovo has been reluctant to implement this provision, leading to a stalemate in mediated negotiations. The ZSO remains a major point of contention, significantly hindering progress toward normalization. This impasse also contributed to the Committee of Ministers' refusal to consider Kosovo's membership in the Council of Europe in early 2024, despite a prior recommendation by the Parliamentary Assembly.[261]

The long-term consequences of the dialogue between Serbia and Kosovo remain highly unpredictable, and it is uncertain whether any positive outcomes beyond those already achieved will emerge. Serbia's foreign policy stance is characterized by two 'nos': no formal recognition of Kosovo's independence and no support for Kosovo's membership in the UN.[262] Kosovo, meanwhile, continues to struggle to establish itself as a state and seeks further international recognition.[263]

Although the Kosovo issue is likely to continue being viewed through a territorial lens due to competing sovereignty claims, it is recommended that future

259 Lazarević and Surlić (n 253) 124; Kreft (n 256) 176.

260 Judgement of 23 December 2015 No. K0130/15.

261 France, Italy and Germany insisted on the establishment of the Association of Serb-majority Municipalities prior to the consideration of the admission. See S. Janković, 'Serbia's Lobbying to Oppose the Srebrenica Genocide Resolution in the UN General Assembly and the Admission of Kosovo to the Council of Europe' 22 *Review of International, European and Comparative Law* (2024). See also PACE, Application by Kosovo for membership of the Council of Europe, Vote on Opinion – Doc. 15958 <https://pace.coe.int/en/votes/39707>; PACE Committee on Political Affairs and Democracy, Report of Dora Bakoyannis on the Application by Kosovo for membership of the Council of Europe, Doc. 15958 (28 Mar. 2024).

262 Politika, 'Vučić: Nikada Neću Pristati na Priznanje i Ulazak Kosova u UN, o Svemu Ostalom Možemo da Pregovaramo' (28 Feb. 2023) <https://www.politika.rs/scc/clanak/540193/vucic-sastanak-brisel-kosovo>.

263 Consult G. Visoka, *Acting Like a State: Kosovo and the Everyday Making of Statehood* (Routledge 2018).

negotiations incorporate non-territorial autonomy (NTA) approaches, which are particularly relevant for the protection of Serbian cultural and historical heritage. The Serbian population in central Kosovo, especially south of the Ibar River, where many medieval monasteries and churches are located, resides in small municipalities or enclaves surrounded by majority-Albanian communities. In this context, the traditional Westphalian nation-state discourse, which views autonomy as something belonging to groups competing for territorial ownership, is insufficient. It should be supplemented, at a minimum, by NTA approaches.[264] Furthermore, the existing legal framework in Kosovo, combined with the limited mandate and operational capacity of Serb national councils (both within Kosovo and regionally, as seen in Croatia and Montenegro), has proven insufficient in scope and efficacy. Consequently, these structures have failed to ensure the comprehensive safeguarding of Serbian cultural and religious heritage across Kosovo.[265]

---

264 F. Palermo, 'Owned or Shared? Territorial Autonomy in the Minority Discourse' in T. H. Malloy and F. Palermo (eds.) *Minority Accommodation through Territorial and Non–territorial Autonomy* (OUP 2015) 29.

265 J. Ćeriman and A. Pavlović, 'Beyond the Territory Principle: Non-Territorial Approach to the Kosovo Question(s)' 31(3) *Philosophy and Society* (2020) 340–358.

CHAPTER 7

Conclusions

> If I would be fortunate to achieve some of my ideals,
> it would be on the behalf of the whole humanity.
> If those hopes would become fulfilled,
> the most exciting thought would be that it is a deed of a Serb.
>
> NIKOLA TESLA

This book has embarked on a comprehensive exploration of the principle of self-determination, specifically its internal aspect, and its capacity to serve as a mechanism for preventing secession. Through meticulous analysis of legal instruments, the practices of states and international organizations, and theoretical frameworks, the study has sought to clarify the contours of internal self-determination (ISD) and establish its significance in contemporary international law.

The posed hypothesis that ISD can effectively avert secession retains its validity despite potential challenges, such as its universal applicability and its ostensible contradiction with democratic and liberal theories. This hypothesis finds its particular strength in the nuanced understanding and practical application of ISD (a qualified vision), as opposed to an uncritical, orthodox interpretation that merely positions ISD as the antithesis of external self-determination (ESD) – a view that risks reducing ISD to a linguistic argument aligned with the principle of territorial integrity. Accordingly, the study has illustrated that ISD, when genuinely implemented, reconciles territorial integrity with peoples' self-determination, offering a balanced solution that respects state sovereignty without destabilizing established norms of territorial unity.

Curiously enough, the solution to the tension between territorial integrity and self-determination has been found within the self-determination norm itself, more precisely in its internal variant. This approach is reminiscent of doctrinal observations suggesting that autonomy is not merely an alternative to self-determination but an expression of it. By ensuring that peoples within a state can exercise their political, social, and cultural rights, ISD addresses the root causes of secessionist movements. This proactive approach mitigates the need for external self-determination and the consequent risks of conflict and fragmentation.

 | DOI:10.1163/9789004737501_008

The ideas presented in this book contribute to the maintenance of international peace and stability as envisaged by states, particularly through the reinforcement of territorial integrity. At the same time, they promote the improvement of self-government and the respect for human rights as envisaged by the peoples concerned. ISD, thus, emerges as a principle that not only harmonizes these seemingly conflicting objectives but also enhances the legitimacy and responsiveness of governments to their diverse populations. ISD, in this construction, serves both as a primary right of peoples, and a consequential right of states.

In contrast to the binary and often antagonistic dynamic of territorial integrity and secession, ISD provides a de-escalating framework. By placing a significant obligation on states to uphold the internal aspects of self-determination, the norm shifts the focus from irreconcilable rights claims to practical governance solutions. This approach reduces the likelihood of secessionist conflicts by addressing grievances before they escalate into demands for independence.

One of the key contributions of this book is its detailed analysis of relevant clauses from the Friendly Relations Declaration (1970), the Vienna Declaration and Programme of Action (1993), and the UN Fiftieth Anniversary Declaration (1995). These declarations, while considered soft law, were adopted by acclamation by the international community and provide critical insights into the relationship between ISD and territorial integrity. By examining these documents, the book elucidates how international law, even in its non-binding forms, can shape state behavior and influence the resolution of secessionist disputes.

Structurally, the Friendly Relations Declaration establishes the foundational framework. The Vienna and Fiftieth Anniversary Declarations reaffirm *mutatis mutandis* its core prohibition: self-determination cannot authorize actions impairing the territorial integrity or political unity of sovereign states that:

(i) uphold equal rights and self-determination of peoples, and
(ii) possess governments representing their entire population without distinction.

Notably, the Vienna Declaration most explicitly articulates ISD's constituent principles – democratic governance, inclusive participation, and human rights respect – thereby crystallizing the modern understanding of this norm. These provisions anchor contemporary debates on remedial secession, wherein the safeguard clause undergoes inverse interpretation (*de lege ferenda*), contrasting with its primary textual meaning (*de lege lata*).

Discussions on secession, still considered taboo among states and international organizations due to their sensitivity, typically arise when specific situations escalate and attract political attention. Such was the case in the proceedings before the ICJ in the *Kosovo* case, where the prohibition of secession was either uncritically pronounced or grounded in principles of representativeness and inclusiveness – core tenets of ISD. The latter, as posited, provides a more accurate interpretation. For instance, in 1995, the African Commission on Human and Peoples' Rights, responding to Katanga's peoples petition, established that the territorial integrity of Zaire could not be compromised as long as the state guaranteed the right to participation in government and upheld other human rights. The Commission advocated for local government, federalism, or confederalism – forms of governance consistent with ISD – because they align with state sovereignty and territorial integrity. Similarly, in 1998, the Canadian Supreme Court, in its landmark judgment on the *Quebec* case, emphasized that the right to self-determination should primarily be exercised internally. The Court highlighted that this is particularly true when a state conducts itself on the basis of equality, non-discrimination, and other principles embodied in ISD. This judgment has since served as a benchmark, influencing decisions such as the Sri Lankan Supreme Court's 2017 judgment in *Chandrasoma v. Senathirajah* and the UK Supreme Court's 2022 *Reference on a Referendum for Scotland*, both of which referenced the *Quebec* judgment in conceptualizing contemporary self-determination, prioritizing its functional internal dimension as compatible with territorial integrity.

This book has sought to emphasize the validity of ISD as a tool for secession prevention, advocating for its broader incorporation into legal discourse. It underscores the holistic significance of ISD, rather than isolating its components – such as governmental representativeness, as outlined in the aforementioned UNGA Declarations – and demonstrates its strength, particularly when contrasted with the principle of territorial integrity. While territorial integrity is adversarial in nature and often interpreted in the inter-state sphere, ISD focuses on the most critical trigger of secession: endogenous movements. By doing so, it identifies these movements as direct recipients of the norm, providing a more effective framework for addressing secessionist pressures.

The book's methodological approach, grounded in international legal positivism, emphasizes the analysis of existing legal norms and their practical application. This approach involves scrutinizing both hard law, such as treaties and conventions, and soft law, such as declarations and resolutions, to clarify the contours of ISD and its role in preventing secession. By engaging with these legal instruments in light of their implementation, the book aims to provide a comprehensive understanding of ISD and its potential as a counter-secession mechanism as well as its position within international law.

Chapter 4 of the book examines the theoretical underpinnings of internal self-determination, unpacking its multifaceted character – encompassing free will, inclusiveness, self-governance, and a broad array of human rights – which often function as counter-secession modalities. The chapter outlines two conceptualizations of ISD as a counter-secession mechanism: the orthodox and the qualified. It endorses the latter, which upholds the territorial integrity of states that comply with ISD, while refraining from rigidly interpreting non-compliance as a ground for secession. Beyond this typological distinction, the chapter interrogates whether the counter-secessionary role of ISD ought to be understood as a political or a legal method. It also identifies specific instruments inherent in ISD's definition – namely, democratic governance, federalism, and autonomism – and situates them alongside both legal and non-legal principles of counter-secession, such as non-intervention, territorial integrity, *uti possidetis juris*, demobilization, and external engagement. Furthermore, the chapter critically engages with several obstacles that hinder the conceptualization of ISD as a legal counter-secession framework. One key challenge stems from the divergent global interpretations and valuations of ISD, which complicate the establishment of a tentative universal threshold of implementation capable of disqualifying secessionist claims. A related concern is the absence of a recognized authority to monitor ISD compliance, particularly given states' longstanding resistance to external scrutiny in matters of sovereignty. Another obstacle arises from the potential dissonance between the legal codification of ISD and the ethno-historical identities of secessionist communities, which may perceive such codification as an affront to dignity and historical justice – especially given that the formation of many existing states was not subject to comparable legal constraints. The final and strictly legal impediment concerns the enduring doctrine of secession's legal neutrality. Nonetheless, the emergence of new normative frameworks suggests a growing responsiveness to evolving geopolitical realities. These developments are particularly defensible when they serve a broader normative purpose, as arguably exemplified by the concept of ISD.

Chapter 5 expands on this analysis by examining the application of ISD by states and international organizations across all continents. It demonstrates the direct or indirect alignment of states and organizations with the proposed hypothesis, drawing on: (a) domestic legislation, judicial decisions, and initiatives, including the noteworthy Liechtenstein Initiative on Self-determination; (b) regional perspectives, such as those found in the Personal Reflections of the OSCE High Commissioners, the Bangkok Declaration, and the Banjul Charter; and (c) global approaches, as exemplified by the ICJ, the UN Human Rights Council, and the Human Rights Committee as well as key statements from prominent authorities, including O'Brien, the UN Under-Secretary-General for Legal Affairs, who stressed that, 'if the rights of minorities are being respected and their cultural identity is fully protected in situations such as the one in question, a demand for secession does not seem to be justified'.[1] This chapter therefore not only provides a platform for establishing the content, meaning, and position of ISD within the broader framework of international law, but also offers a detailed account of how ISD can be implemented to prevent secession and promote stability.

In parallel, the research underscores the need to address the legal lacuna surrounding secession by advancing a regulatory framework that clarifies when secession ought to be prohibited. In doing so, it substantiates a tripartite model within international law – distinguishing between prohibited, permissible, and ambivalent cases of secession – and specifically expands the scope of the prohibition category.[2] This contribution enhances the normative coherence of international law in a domain long marked by doctrinal uncertainty.

By engaging legal doctrine, state practice, and theoretical insights, the book demonstrates that ISD holds significant promise for addressing systemic gaps in the law of statehood. It may evolve into a meaningful instrument within the international legal architecture, contributing to the field's adaptability and normative refinement.

Central to this framework is the qualified conception of ISD, advanced not merely as a counter-secession mechanism but as a rights-based approach capable of reconciling state authority with the legitimate aspirations of peoples. Rather than framing ISD solely as a constraint or a remedy, the analysis positions it as a constructive normative principle embedded in democratic governance, federal arrangements, and inclusive participation.

In conclusion, the book advocates for the recognition and operationalization of ISD as a core component of the international legal order. Institutions such as the International Law Association and the International Law Commission have a key role to play in advancing its conceptual development and practical applicability. The proposed framework reconfigures the relationship between self-determination and territorial integrity, offering a more principled and inclusive approach to governance within existing state boundaries. Embracing ISD proactively creates environments where all peoples can thrive, thereby preventing the emergence of secessionist movements and ensuring sustainable long-term peace.

---

1 P. O'Brien, 'The Åland Islands Solution: A Precedent for Successful International Disputes Settlement' (17 Jan. 2012) <https://legal.un.org/ola/media/info_from_lc/POB%20Aalands%20Islands%20Exhibition%20opening.pdf>.

2 M. Milanovic, 'A Footnote on Secession' *EJIL:Talk!* (26 Oct. 2017).

Index